# READINGS FOR
# SOCIOLOGY

# RECENT SOCIOLOGY TITLES FROM W. W. NORTON

*Code of the Street* by Elijah Anderson

*The Cosmopolitan Canopy* by Elijah Anderson

*Social Problems*, Second Edition, by Joel Best

*You May Ask Yourself: An Introduction to Thinking like a Sociologist*, Third Edition, by Dalton Conley

*The Real World: An Introduction to Sociology*, Fourth Edition, by Kerry Ferris and Jill Stein

*Introduction to Sociology*, Ninth Edition, by Anthony Giddens, Mitchell Duneier, Richard P. Appelbaum, and Deborah Carr

*Essentials of Sociology*, Fifth Edition, by Anthony Giddens, Mitchell Duneier, Richard P. Appelbaum, and Deborah Carr

*Mix It Up: Popular Culture, Mass Media, and Society* by David Grazian

*The Contexts Reader*, Second Edition, edited by Douglas Hartmann and Christopher Uggen

*The Society Pages: Color Lines and Racial Angles* edited by Douglas Hartmann and Christopher Uggen

*The Society Pages: Crime and the Punished* edited by Douglas Hartmann and Christopher Uggen

*The Society Pages: The Social Side of Politics* edited by Douglas Hartmann and Christopher Uggen

*Doing Race* edited by Hazel Rose Markus and Paula M. L. Moya

*Families as They Really Are*, Second Edition, edited by Barbara J. Risman and Virginia Rutter

*The Sociology of News*, Second Edition, by Michael Schudson

*The Social Construction of Sexuality*, Second Edition, by Steven Seidman

*Sex Matters: The Sexuality and Society Reader*, Fourth Edition, edited by Mindy Stombler, Dawn M. Baunach, Wendy O. Simonds, Elroi J. Windsor, and Elisabeth O. Burgess

*Gender: Ideas, Interactions, Institutions* by Lisa Wade and Myra Marx Ferree

*More than Just Race* by William Julius Wilson

*Cultural Sociology: An Introductory Reader* edited by Matt Wray

*American Society: How It Really Works* by Erik Olin Wright and Joel Rogers

**To learn more about Norton Sociology, please visit wwnorton.com/soc.**

EIGHTH EDITION

# READINGS FOR
# SOCIOLOGY

EDITED BY

## Garth Massey

W. W. Norton & Company ■ New York ■ London

W. W. Norton & Company has been independent since its founding in 1923, when William Warder Norton and Mary D. Herter Norton first published lectures delivered at the People's Institute, the adult education division of New York City's Cooper Union. The firm soon expanded its program beyond the Institute, publishing books by celebrated academics from America and abroad. By midcentury, the two major pillars of Norton's publishing program—trade books and college texts—were firmly established. In the 1950s, the Norton family transferred control of the company to its employees, and today—with a staff of four hundred and a comparable number of trade, college, and professional titles published each year—W. W. Norton & Company stands as the largest and oldest publishing house owned wholly by its employees.

Editor: Sasha Levitt
Assistant Editors: Thea Goodrich and Mary Williams
Project Editor: Sujin Hong
Production Manager: Vanessa Nuttry
Design Director: Hope Miller Goodell
Permissions Manager: Elizabeth Trammell
Composition: Westchester Book Group
Manufacturing: Quad/Graphics-Fairfield

Library of Congress Cataloging-in-Publication Data.

Readings for sociology / edited by Garth Massey.—Eighth edition.
   pages cm
Includes bibliographical references.
ISBN 978-0-393-93884-5 (pbk.)
1. Sociology. I. Massey, Garth.
HM585.R427 2015
301—dc23

2014047581

W. W. Norton & Company, Inc., 500 Fifth Avenue, New York, NY 10110
www.wwnorton.com

W. W. Norton & Company Ltd., Castle House, 75/76 Wells Street, London W1T 3QT

3   4   5   6   7   8   9   0

# CONTENTS

# PART 4: SOCIAL INTERACTION AND IDENTITY

# PART 5: SOCIAL INEQUALITY AND ORGANIZATIONS

## PART 6: SOCIAL CONTROL AND ORGANIZATIONAL POWER

## PART 7: SOCIAL INSTITUTIONS

## PART 8: SOCIAL CHANGE

# PREFACE

Most students reading this book will not take another sociology course. Those who do are unlikely to major in sociology, and only a few sociology majors will pursue a career of sociological research and teaching. In a society that increasingly puts a premium on education for employment, sociology may seem like a luxury few can afford. That would be a big mistake. The sociological perspective has great value to both students today and those for whom their introductory sociology course is a distant memory.

The sociological perspective is fundamental to living in a complex, diverse society. A glimpse through sociology's lens helps make the events of the day comprehensible, as well as helps us successfully navigate through life and become a positive contributor to a better world. Perhaps you value innovation and progress or you hope to find more personal freedom in a just society, or perhaps you want to challenge authority or encourage mutual awareness and respect. If you are looking for solutions to social problems, or you simply refuse to live what Socrates called "the unexamined life," sociology has much to offer.

*Readings for Sociology* is not a comprehensive guide to the discipline of sociology. Its essays say little about quantitative data and statistical techniques that many practitioners of sociology consider fundamental to their research. Rather, most of the readings are descriptive accounts that approach their subject in ways you may never have encountered. Many of them are case studies. Others offer illuminating historical background. And others draw comparisons across different societies. All the authors look at some aspect of the social world in a new way.

One criterion in selecting these readings is that each provides insights into what might not otherwise be revealed. This is what Peter Berger describes in the first essay, "Sociology as an Individual Pastime," as a challenge to what everybody thinks they already know. Many of them transport you into entirely new social worlds, offering unexpected and perhaps unpleasant, problematic, even disquieting portraits of how people live, cope, and challenge their situation and acquire some measure of security and dignity. Elijah Anderson's "The Code of the Streets" accomplishes this, and so do the essays about waitresses, men in battle, families visiting Disneyland, brides-to-be, Latina high schoolers, toy store employees, and members of isolated religious communities.

After decades of reading, researching, and thinking about why people do what they do, I remain fascinated by the intersection of the personal and the public. C. Wright Mills's idea of the "sociological imagination," which is discussed in the second reading, remains a touchstone and is infused in the readings offered here. As Mills shows us, we learn to be the bearers of our cultures, molding our activities, personalities, and perspectives to the situational features we take for granted. Human beings, however, are not merely cultural repositories or reactive creatures. We are creative, and we exercise human agency in novel, unpredictable ways. We reconfigure, resist, ignore, and turn the tables on what society gives or expects of us. Among other readings that emphasize this, I have included in this Eighth Edition an excerpt from James C. Scott's latest book *Two Cheers for Anarchism* that recommends we all start doing "anarchist calisthenics."

In a recent survey conducted by the American Sociological Association, sociology majors were most likely to attribute their interest in sociology to the new concepts they learned in their courses. The concepts of social class, socialization, and race/ethnicity remain central to this book, but the readings will also introduce many other concepts, from those of Erving Goffman and Michel Foucault to Annette Lareau's "concerted cultivation," Michael Kimmel's "construction of masculinity," Jen'nan Ghazal Read and John P. Bartkowski's "identity negotiation," George Ritzer's "McDonalization," Arlie Russell Hochschild's "emotional geography," Christine L. Williams's "interpellation," and Beth Montemurro's "liminality."

Professors and instructors who have assigned *Readings for Sociology* in the past will see that it continues to focus on topics at the core of sociology, especially work and social inequality (race, class, and gender). The thirteen new readings maintain this emphasis while strengthening other areas and taking new directions.

Most students reading this book will go on to have—or already have—long-term intimate relationships and children of their own. Because this is the only sociology course many students will take, *Readings for Sociology* emphasizes interpersonal relations, families, and social interaction, topics I consider fundamental to making sense of everyday life. In addition to several readings from the earlier edition, including Julia Twigg's account of intimate care for the elderly in "The Body and Bathing," new readings by Donna L. Franklin ("African Americans and the Birth of the Modern Marriage") and Kathleen Gerson ("Falling Back on Plan B") look at interpersonal relations within the context of the family and the family-to-be, respectively.

One thing apparent in this edition of *Readings for Sociology* is its attention to morality. I believe students need to think about the questions raised in Kelman and Hamilton's analysis of the My Lai massacre. I have added new readings that provide sociological frames for questions of morality. Garrett Hardin's "The Tragedy of the Commons" is a classic essay that raises uncomfortable questions about the personal and the public. In "Employing Parents

Who Can't Make a Living," Lisa Dodson brings to light "subtle acts of resistance" required by those supervising people who are "working hard but living poor" in the wake of the Great Recession. Rhys H. Williams examines the importance of moral superiority claims among evangelical Christians in "Politicized Evangelicalism and Secular Elites," while James C. Scott asks readers: If a time comes when you have to defend justice, will you be ready?

Three current, critically important issues—information technology and its challenge to personal privacy, social tumult throughout the Middle East, and the use of personal computer technology to effect social change—are addressed in newly added readings by Michel Foucault from his classic *Discipline and Punish*, Hussein Agha and Robert Malley in their prophetic examination of revolution in the Middle East, and George Packer's encounter with young Silicon Valley entrepreneurs.

In addition to Agha and Malley's essay on the Arab uprising, two other new readings examine contemporary social movements. In his essay "Occupy's Predicament," Todd Gitlin—one of sociology's finest observers of contemporary society and social movements—analyzes the short-lived Occupy Movement, created by young people fed up with the growing gap between the ultra-rich and the rest of us. Rhys Williams examines "framing" by the more conventional social movement of politicized evangelical Protestants who are successfully linking religion and politics.

The growth of the low-wage economy, especially in the aftermath of the Great Recession of 2008–2010, commended inclusion of both Lisa Dodson's chapter from *The Moral Underground* and an essay by Christine L. Williams, author of *Inside Toyland*, which is also an outstanding introduction to how sociologists study organizational behavior. Andrew Cherlin's "One Thousand and Forty-Nine Reasons Why It's Hard to Know When a Fact Is a Fact" focuses on critical reading in an age of instant information via the Internet. While working on another project, I read Stuart and Elizabeth Ewen's *Channels of Desire* and, though written several years ago, was struck by its relevance today in understanding celebrity culture in democratic societies.

I am excited by the new readings and wish I could join in on your discussions of them. The sociological insights and the peculiar ways of seeing that sociology offers can make you uncomfortable, but they can also be liberating. That's what drew me to sociology and—many decades later—keeps me intrigued by what the discipline has to offer. It is a pleasure and a privilege to share some of this with you.

# TO THE INSTRUCTOR

| Sociological Principles | Corresponding Readings |
|---|---|
| 1. Introduction to Theory | 1, 2, 3, 4, 5, 7, 24, 30, 31, 37, 43 |
| 2. Methods | 1, 6, 8, 9 |
| 3. Culture and Society | 10, 11, 12, 13, 14, 19, 33, 38, 39, 40 |
| 4. Socialization and the Life Cycle | 11, 14, 15, 16, 17, 20, 21, 27 |
| 5. Social Interaction and Everyday Life | 4, 11, 12, 18, 21, 28, 32 |
| 6. Groups and Large Organizations | 5, 11, 21, 25, 26, 31, 32, 33, 34, 35, 36, 42, 44, 45 |
| 7. Deviance and Crime | 5, 12, 16, 23, 25, 31, 37 |
| 8. Stratification and Inequality | 12, 15, 21, 23, 24, 25, 29, 30, 32, 34, 48 |
| 9. Globalization and Global Inequality | 11, 24, 46, 49 |
| 10. Gender and Gender Inequality | 14, 16, 17, 21, 23, 29, 34, 38, 47 |
| 11. Ethnicity and Race | 8, 12, 21, 22, 25, 29, 34, 40, 41, 47 |
| 12. Aging | 20, 38, 40, 44 |
| 13. Government, Power, and Social Movements | 3, 5, 10, 24, 31, 35, 41, 45, 47, 48, 50, 51 |
| 14. Work and Political Economy | 13, 24, 25, 26, 30, 34, 35, 42, 43, 46 |
| 15. Family and Intimate Relationships | 4, 14, 15, 17, 38, 39, 40, 41, 42 |
| 16. Education and the Mass Media | 10, 13, 21, 23, 29, 31, 51 |
| 17. Religion | 43, 44, 45 |
| 18. Health and the Body | 8, 13, 20, 49 |
| 21. Population and the Environment | 3, 35, 36, 47, 49 |
| 21. Conflict, War, and Revolution | 5, 24, 50 |

# PART ONE

# THE STUDY
# OF SOCIOLOGY

# 1

## Sociology as an Individual Pastime

FROM *Invitation to Sociology*

PETER L. BERGER

*What does it mean to "think sociologically"? In this selection from his book* Invitation to Sociology, *Peter Berger explains why sociologists are so annoying to the powers that be, the purveyors of conventional wisdom, advertisers, politicians, and others with a vested interest in your going along with their view of things. Sociologists have a reputation for stirring up the waters and occasionally making trouble. For Berger, this is just part of the way sociologists see the world.*

It is gratifying from certain value positions (including some of this writer's) that sociological insights have served in a number of instances to improve the lot of groups of human beings by uncovering morally shocking conditions or by clearing away collective illusions or by showing that socially desired results could be obtained in more humane fashion. One might point, for example, to some applications of sociological knowledge in the penological practice of Western countries. Or one might cite the use made of sociological studies in the Supreme Court decision of 1954 on racial segregation in the public schools. Or one could look at the applications of other sociological studies to the humane planning of urban redevelopment. Certainly the sociologist who is morally and politically sensitive will derive gratification from such instances. But, once more, it will be well to keep in mind that what is at issue here is not sociological understanding as such but certain applications of this understanding. It is not difficult to see how the same understanding could be applied with opposite intentions. Thus the sociological understanding of the dynamics of racial prejudice can be applied effectively by those promoting intragroup hatred as well as by those wanting to spread tolerance. And the sociological understanding of the nature of human solidarity can be employed in the service of both totalitarian and democratic regimes.

\* \* \*

One [more recent] image [of the sociologist is that of] a gatherer of statistics about human behavior. The sociologist is here seen essentially as an aide-de-camp to an IBM machine. He\* goes out with a questionnaire, interviews

---

\*Berger wrote this in 1963 using gendered language (preferring *he* to the now-standard *he/she*). Today more than half of all sociology students are women. [*Editor's note*]

people selected at random, then goes home, enters his tabulations onto innumerable punch cards, which are then fed into a machine. In all of this, of course, he is supported by a large staff and a very large budget. Included in this image is the implication that the results of all this effort are picayune, a pedantic restatement of what everybody knows anyway. As one observer remarked pithily, a sociologist is a fellow who spends $100,000 to find his way to a house of ill repute.

This image of the sociologist has been strengthened in the public mind by the activities of many agencies that might well be called parasociological, mainly agencies concerned with public opinion and market trends. The pollster has become a well-known figure in American life, importuning people about their views from foreign policy to toilet paper. Since the methods used in the pollster business bear close resemblance to sociological research, the growth of this image of the sociologist is understandable. The Kinsey studies of American sexual behavior have probably greatly augmented the impact of this image. The fundamental sociological question, whether concerned with premarital petting or with Republican votes or with the incidence of gang knifings, is always presumed to be "how often?" or "how many?"

\* \* \*

Now it must be admitted, albeit regretfully, that this image of the sociologist and his trade is not altogether a product of fantasy. Beginning shortly after World War I, American sociology turned rather resolutely away from theory to an intensive preoccupation with narrowly circumscribed empirical studies. In connection with this turn, sociologists increasingly refined their research techniques. Among these, very naturally, statistical techniques figured prominently. Since about the mid 1940s there has been a revival of interest in sociological theory, and there are good indications that this tendency away from a narrow empiricism is continuing to gather momentum. It remains true, however, that a goodly part of the sociological enterprise in this country continues to consist of little studies of obscure fragments of social life, irrelevant to any broader theoretical concern. One glance at the table of contents of the major sociological journals or at the list of papers read at sociological conventions will confirm this statement.

\* \* \*

Statistical data by themselves do not make sociology. They become sociology only when they are sociologically interpreted, put within a theoretical frame of reference that is sociological. Simple counting, or even correlating different items that one counts, is not sociology. There is almost no sociology in the Kinsey reports. This does not mean that the data in these studies are not true or that they cannot be relevant to sociological understanding. They are, taken by themselves, raw materials that can be used in sociological interpretation. The interpretation, however, must be broader than the data themselves. So the sociologist cannot arrest himself at the frequency tables of premarital petting or extramarital pederasty. These enumerations are meaningful to him only in terms of their much broader implications for an understanding of institutions and values in our society. To arrive at such understanding the sociologist will often have to apply statistical techniques, especially when he is dealing with the mass phenomena of modern social life. But sociology consists of statistics as little as philology consists of conjugating irregular verbs or chemistry of making nasty smells in test tubes.

Sociology has, from its beginnings, understood itself as a science. There has been much controversy about the precise meaning of this self-definition. * * * But the allegiance of sociologists to the scientific ethos has meant everywhere a willingness to be bound by certain scientific canons of procedure. If the sociologist remains faithful to his calling, his statements must be arrived at through the observation of certain rules of evidence that allow others to check on or to repeat or to develop his findings further. It is this scientific discipline that often supplies the motive for reading a sociological work as against, say, a novel on the same topic that might describe matters in much more impressive and convincing language. As sociologists tried to develop their scientific rules of evidence, they were compelled to reflect upon methodological problems. This is why methodology is a necessary and valid part of the sociological enterprise.

At the same time it is quite true that some sociologists, especially in America, have become so preoccupied with methodological questions that they have ceased to be interested in society at all. As a result, they have found out nothing of significance about any aspect of social life, since in science as in love a concentration on technique is quite likely to lead to impotence. Much of this fixation on methodology can be explained in terms of the urge of a relatively new discipline to find acceptance on the academic scene. Since science is an almost sacred entity among Americans in general and American academicians in particular, the desire to emulate the procedures of the older natural sciences is very strong among the newcomers in the marketplace of erudition.

* * *

As they become more secure in their academic status, it may be expected that this methodological inferiority complex will diminish even further.

The charge that many sociologists write in a barbaric dialect must also be admitted with similar reservations. Any scientific discipline must develop a terminology. This is self-evident for a discipline such as, say, nuclear physics that deals with matters unknown to most people and for which no words exist in common speech. However, terminology is possibly even more important for the social sciences, just because their subject matter *is* familiar and just because words *do* exist to denote it. Because we are well acquainted with the social institutions that surround us, our perception of them is imprecise and often erroneous. In very much the same way most of us will have considerable difficulty giving an accurate description of our parents, husbands or wives, children or close friends. Also, our language is often (and perhaps bless-edly) vague and confusing in its references to social reality. Take for an example the concept of *class*, a very important one in sociology. There must be dozens of meanings that this term may have in common speech—income brackets, races, ethnic groups, power cliques, intelligence ratings, and many others. It is obvious that the sociologist must have a precise, unambiguous definition of the concept if his work is to proceed with any degree of scientific rigor. In view of these facts, one can understand that some sociologists have been tempted to invent altogether new words to avoid the semantic traps of the vernacular usage.

Finally, we would look at an image of the sociologist not so much in his pro-fessional role as in his being, supposedly, a certain kind of person. This is the image of the sociologist as a detached, sardonic observer, and a cold manipu-lator of men. Where this image prevails, it may represent an ironic triumph of the sociologist's own efforts to be accepted as a genuine scientist. The sociolo-gist here becomes the self-appointed superior man, standing off from the warm vitality of common existence, finding his satisfactions not in living but in coolly appraising the lives of others, filing them away in little categories, and thus presumably missing the real significance of what he is observing. Further, there is the notion that, when he involves himself in social processes at all, the soci-ologist does so as an uncommitted technician, putting his manipulative skills at the disposal of the powers that be.

This last image is probably not very widely held. * * * As a general portrait of the contemporary sociologist it is certainly a gross distortion. It fits very few individuals that anyone is likely to meet in this country today. The prob-lem of the political role of the social scientist is, nevertheless, a very genuine one. For instance, the employment of sociologists by certain branches of indus-try and government raises moral questions that ought to be faced more widely than they have been so far. These are, however, moral questions that concern all men in positions of responsibility in modern society. The image of the sociologist as an observer without compassion and a manipulator without conscience need not detain us further here. * * * As for contemporary sociolo-gists, most of them would lack the emotional equipment for such a role, even if they should aspire to it in moments of feverish fantasy.

How then are we to conceive of the sociologist? In discussing the various images of him that abound in the popular mind we have already brought out certain elements that would have to go into our conception.

* * *

The sociologist, then, is someone concerned with understanding society in a disciplined way. The nature of this discipline is scientific. This means that what the sociologist finds and says about the social phenomena he studies occurs within a certain rather strictly defined frame of reference. One of the main char-acteristics of this scientific frame of reference is that operations are bound by certain rules of evidence. As a scientist, the sociologist tries to be objective, to control his personal preferences and prejudices, to perceive clearly rather than to judge normatively. This restraint, of course, does not embrace the totality of the sociologist's existence as a human being, but is limited to his operations *qua* sociologist. Nor does the sociologist claim that his frame of reference is the only one within which society can be looked at. For that matter, very few scientists in any field would claim today that one should look at the world only scientifically. The botanist looking at a daffodil has no reason to dispute the right of the poet to look at the same object in a very different manner. There are many ways of playing. The point is not that one denies other people's games but that one is clear about the rules of one's own. The game of the sociologist, then, uses scientific rules. As a result, the sociologist must be clear in his own mind as to the meaning of these rules. That is, he must concern himself with methodological questions. Methodology does not constitute his goal. The latter, let us recall once more, is the attempt to understand society. Methodology helps in reaching this goal. In order to understand society, or that segment of it that he is studying at the moment, the sociologist will use a variety of means. Among these are statistical techniques. Statistics can be very useful in answering certain sociological questions. But statistics does not constitute sociology. As a scientist, the sociologist will have to be concerned with the exact significance of the terms he is using. That is, he will have to be careful about terminology. This does not have to mean that he must invent a new language of his own, but it does mean that he cannot naively use the language of everyday discourse. Finally, the interest of the sociologist is primarily theoretical. That is, he is interested in understanding for its own sake. He may be aware of or even concerned with the practical applicability and consequences of his findings, but at that point he leaves the sociological frame of reference as such and moves into realms of values, beliefs and ideas that he shares with other men who are not sociologists.

\* \* \*

## [THE MOTIVATION TO DO SOCIOLOGY]

[W]e would like to go a little bit further here and ask a somewhat more personal (and therefore, no doubt, more controversial) question. We would like to ask not only what it is that the sociologist is doing but also what it is that drives him to it. Or, to use the phrase Max Weber used in a similar connection, we want to inquire a little into the nature of the sociologist's demon. In doing so, we shall evoke an image that is not so much ideal-typical in the above sense but more confessional in the sense of personal commitment. Again, we are not interested in excommunicating anyone. The game of sociology goes on in a spacious playground. We are just describing a little more closely those we would like to tempt to join our game.

We would say then that the sociologist (that is, the one we would really like to invite to our game) is a person intensively, endlessly, shamelessly interested in the doings of men. His natural habitat is all the human gathering places of the world, wherever men come together. The sociologist may be interested in many other things. But his consuming interest remains in the world of men, their institutions, their history, their passions. And since he is interested in men, nothing that men do can be altogether tedious for him. He will naturally be interested in the events that engage men's ultimate beliefs, their moments of tragedy and grandeur and ecstasy. But he will also be fascinated by the common place, the everyday. He will know reverence, but this reverence will not prevent him from wanting to see and to understand. He may sometimes feel revulsion or contempt. But this also will not deter him from wanting to have his questions answered. The sociologist, in his quest for understanding, moves through the world of men without respect for the usual lines of demarcation. Nobility and degradation, power and obscurity, intelligence and folly—these are equally *interesting* to him, however unequal they maybe in his personal values or tastes. Thus his questions may lead him to all possible levels of society, the best and the least known places, the most respected and the most despised. And, if he is a good sociologist, he will find himself in all these places because his own questions have so taken possession of him that he has little choice but to seek for answers.

It would be possible to say the same things in a lower key. We could say that the sociologist, but for the grace of his academic title, is the man who must listen to gossip despite himself, who is tempted to look through keyholes, to read other peoples mail, to open closed cabinets. Before some otherwise unoccupied psychologist sets out now to construct an aptitude test for sociologists on the basis of sublimated voyeurism, let us quickly say that we are speaking merely by way of analogy. Perhaps some little boys consumed with curiosity to watch their maiden aunts in the bathroom later become inveterate sociologists. This is quite uninteresting. What interests us is the curiosity that grips any sociologist in front of a closed door behind which there are human voices. If he is a good sociologist, he will want to open that door, to understand these voices. Behind each closed door he will anticipate some new facet of human life not yet perceived and understood.

The sociologist will occupy himself with matters that others regard as too sacred or as too distasteful for dispassionate investigation. He will find rewarding the company of priests or of prostitutes, depending not on his personal preferences but on the questions he happens to be asking at the moment. He will also concern himself with matters that others may find much too boring. He will be interested in the human interaction that goes with warfare or with great intellectual discoveries, but also in the relations between people employed in a restaurant or between a group of little girls playing with their dolls. His main focus of attention is not the ultimate significance of what men do, but the action in itself, as another example of the infinite richness of human conduct. So much for the image of our playmate.

In these journeys through the world of men the sociologist will inevitably encounter other professional Peeping Toms. Sometimes these will resent his presence, feeling that he is poaching on their preserves. In some places the sociologist will meet up with the economist, in others with the political scientist, in yet others with the psychologist or the ethnologist. Yet chances are that the questions that have brought him to these same places are different from the ones that propelled his fellow-trespassers. The sociologist's questions always remain essentially the same: "What are people doing with each other here?" "What are their relationships to each other?" "How are these relationships organized in institutions?" "What are the collective ideas that move men and institutions?" In trying to answer these questions in specific instances, the sociologist will, of course, have to deal with economic or political matters, but he will do so in a way rather different from that of the economist or the political scientist. The scene that he contemplates is the same human scene that these other scientists concern themselves with. But the sociologist's angle of vision is different. When this is understood, it becomes clear that it makes little sense to try to stake out a special enclave within which the sociologist will carry on business in his own right. * * * There is, however, one traveler whose path the sociologist will cross more often than anyone else's on his journeys. This is the historian. Indeed, as soon as the sociologist turns from the present to the past, his preoccupations are very hard indeed to distinguish from those of the historian. However, we shall leave this relationship to a later part of our considerations. Suffice it to say here that the sociological journey will be much impoverished unless it is punctuated frequently by conversation with that other particular traveler.

Any intellectual activity derives excitement from the moment it becomes a trail of discovery. In some fields of learning this is the discovery of worlds previously unthought and unthinkable. This is the excitement of the astronomer or of the nuclear physicist on the antipodal boundaries of the realities that man is capable of conceiving. But it can also be the excitement of bacteriology or geology. In a different way it can be the excitement of the linguist discovering new realms of human expression or of the anthropologist exploring human customs in faraway countries. In such discovery, when undertaken with passion, a widening of awareness, sometimes a veritable transformation of consciousness, occurs. The universe turns out to be much more wonderful than one had ever dreamed. The excitement of sociology is usually of a different sort. Sometimes, it is true, the sociologist penetrates into worlds that had previously been quite unknown to him—for instance, the world of crime, or the world of some bizarre religious sect, or the world fashioned by the exclusive concerns of some group such as medical specialists or military leaders or advertising executives. However, much of the time the sociologist moves in sectors of experience that are familiar to him and to most people in his society. He investigates communities, institutions and activities that one can read about every day in the newspapers. Yet there is another excitement of discovery beckoning in his investigations. It is not the excitement of coming upon the totally unfamiliar, but rather the excitement of finding the familiar becoming transformed in its meaning. The fascination of sociology lies in the fact that its perspective makes us see in a new light the very world in which we have lived all our lives. This also constitutes a transformation of consciousness. Moreover, this transformation is more relevant existentially than that of many other intellectual disciplines, because it is more difficult to segregate in some special compartment of the mind. The astronomer does not live in the remote galaxies, and the nuclear physicist can, outside his laboratory, eat and laugh and marry and vote without thinking about the insides of the atom. The geologist looks at rocks only at appropriate times, and the linguist speaks English with his wife. The sociologist lives in society, on the job and off it. His own life, inevitably, is part of his subject matter. Men being what they are, sociologists too manage to segregate their professional insights from their everyday affairs. But it is a rather difficult feat to perform in good faith.

The sociologist moves in the common world of men, close to what most of them would call real. The categories he employs in his analyses are only refinements of the categories by which other men live—power, class, status, race, ethnicity. As a result, there is a deceptive simplicity and obviousness about some sociological investigations. One reads them, nods at the familiar scene, remarks that one has heard all this before and don't people have better things to do than to waste their time on truisms—until one is suddenly brought up against an insight that radically questions everything one had previously assumed about this familiar scene. This is the point at which one begins to sense the excitement of sociology.

Let us take a specific example. Imagine a sociology class in a Southern college where almost all the students are white Southerners. Imagine a lecture on the subject of the racial system of the South. The lecturer is talking here of matters that have been familiar to his students from the time of their infancy. Indeed, it may be that they are much more familiar with the minutiae of this system than he is. They are quite bored as a result. It seems to them that he is only using more pretentious words to describe what they already know. Thus he may use the term "caste," one commonly used now by American sociologists to describe the Southern racial system. But in explaining the term he shifts to traditional Hindu society, to make it clearer. He then goes on to analyze the magical beliefs inherent in caste tabus, the social dynamics of commensalism and connubium, the economic interests concealed within the system, the way in which religious beliefs relate to the tabus, the effects of the caste system upon the industrial development of the society and vice versa—all in India. But suddenly India is not very far away at all. The lecture then goes back to its Southern theme. The familiar now seems not quite so familiar any more. Questions are raised that are new, perhaps raised angrily, but raised all the same. And at least some of the students have begun to understand that there are functions involved in this business of race that they have not read about in the newspapers (at least not those in their hometowns) and that their parents have not told them—partly, at least, because neither the newspapers nor the parents knew about them.

It can be said that the first wisdom of sociology is this—things are not what they seem. This too is a deceptively simple statement. It ceases to be simple after a while. Social reality turns out to have many layers of meaning. The discovery of each new layer changes the perception of the whole.

Anthropologists use the term "culture shock" to describe the impact of a totally new culture upon a newcomer. In an extreme instance such shock will be experienced by the Western explorer who is told, halfway through dinner, that he is eating the nice old lady he had been chatting with the previous day—a shock with predictable physiological if not moral consequences. Most explorers no longer encounter cannibalism in their travels today. However, the first encounters with polygamy or with puberty rites or even with the way some nations drive their automobiles can be quite a shock to an American visitor. With the shock may go not only disapproval or disgust but a sense of excitement that things can *really* be that different from what they are at home. To some extent, at least, this is the excitement of any first travel abroad. The experience of sociological discovery could be described as "culture shock" minus geographical displacement. In other words, the sociologist travels at home—with shocking results. He is unlikely to find that he is eating a nice old lady for dinner. But the discovery, for instance, that his own church has considerable money invested in the missile industry or that a few blocks from his home there are people who engage in cultic orgies may not be drastically different in emotional impact. Yet we would not want to imply that sociological discoveries are always or even usually outrageous to moral sentiment. Not at all. What they have in common with exploration in distant lands, however, is the sudden illumination of new and unsuspected facets of human existence in society. This is the excitement and, as we shall try to show later, the humanistic justification of sociology.

People who like to avoid shocking discoveries, who prefer to believe that society is just what they were taught in Sunday School, who like the safety of the rules and the maxims of what Alfred Schuetz has called the "world-taken-for-granted," should stay away from sociology. People who feel no temptation before closed doors, who have no curiosity about human beings, who are content to admire scenery without wondering about the people who live in those houses on the other side of that river, should probably also stay away from sociology. They will find it unpleasant or, at any rate, unrewarding. People who are interested in human beings only if they can change, convert or reform them should also be warned, for they will find sociology much less useful than they hoped. And people whose interest is mainly in their own conceptual constructions will do just as well to turn to the study of little white mice. Sociology will do just as well to turn to the study of little mice. Sociology will be satisfying, in the long run, only to those who can think of nothing more entrancing than to watch men and to understand things human.

\* \* \*

To be sure, sociology is an individual pastime in the sense that it interests some men and bores others. Some like to observe human beings, others to experiment with mice. The world is big enough to hold all kinds and there is no logical priority for one interest as against another. But the word "pastime" is weak in describing what we mean. Sociology is more like a passion. The sociological perspective is more like a demon that possesses one, that drives one compellingly, again and again, to the questions that are its own. An introduction to sociology is, therefore, an invitation to a very special kind of passion.

# 2

## Personal Experiences and Public Issues*

<small>FROM</small> *The Sociological Imagination*

### C. WRIGHT MILLS

*C. Wright Mills wrote of his own work, "I have tried to be objective; I do not claim to be detached." He argues that sociologists' questions come from the same sources as the important questions everyone asks: their own experiences and the things that perplex, confuse, and inspire them. To be effective, sociology must make a connection between the individual and the social. It must allow the individual to see the larger social context in which his or her life is lived, and in this way give both understanding and meaning to personal experiences.*

Nowadays men often feel that their private lives are a series of traps. They sense that within their everyday worlds, they cannot overcome their troubles, and in this feeling, they are often quite correct: What ordinary men are directly aware of and what they try to do are bounded by the private orbits in which they live; their visions and their powers are limited to the close-up scenes of job, family, neighborhood; in other milieux, they move vicariously and remain spectators. And the more aware they become, however vaguely, of ambitions and of threats which transcend their immediate locales, the more trapped they seem to feel.

Underlying this sense of being trapped are seemingly impersonal changes in the very structure of continent-wide societies. The facts of contemporary history are also facts about the success and the failure of individual men and women. When a society is industrialized, a peasant becomes a worker; a feudal lord is liquidated or becomes a businessman. When classes rise or fall, a man is employed or unemployed; when the rate of investment goes up or down, a man takes new heart or goes broke. When wars happen, an insurance salesman becomes a rocket launcher; a store clerk, a radar man; a wife lives alone; a child grows up without a father. Neither the life of an individual nor the history of a society can be understood without understanding both.

Yet men do not usually define the troubles they endure in terms of historical change and institutional contradiction. The well-being they enjoy, they do not usually impute to the big ups and downs of the societies in which they live.

---

Seldom aware of the intricate connection between the patterns of their own lives and the course of world history, ordinary men do not usually know what this connection means for the kinds of men they are becoming and for the kinds of history-making in which they might take part. They do not possess the quality of mind essential to grasp the interplay of man and society, of biography and history, of self and world. They cannot cope with their personal troubles in such ways as to control the structural transformations that usually lie behind them.

Surely it is no wonder. In what period have so many men been so totally exposed at so fast a pace to such earthquakes of change? That Americans have not known such catastrophic changes as have the men and women of other societies is due to historical facts that are now quickly becoming 'merely history.' The history that now affects every man is world history. Within this scene and this period, in the course of a single generation, one sixth of mankind is transformed from all that is feudal and backward into all that is modern, advanced, and fearful. Political colonies are freed; new and less visible forms of imperialism installed. Revolutions occur; men feel the intimate grip of new kinds of authority. Totalitarian societies rise, and are smashed to bits—or succeed fabulously. After two centuries of ascendancy, capitalism is shown up as only one way to make society into an industrial apparatus. After two centuries of hope, even formal democracy is restricted to a quite small portion of mankind. Everywhere in the underdeveloped world, ancient ways of life are broken up and vague expectations become urgent demands. Everywhere in the overdeveloped world, the means of authority and of violence become total in scope and bureaucratic in form. Humanity itself now lies before us, the super-nation at either pole concentrating its most coordinated and massive efforts upon the preparation of World War Three.

The very shaping of history now outpaces the ability of men to orient themselves in accordance with cherished values. And which values? Even when they do not panic, men often sense that older ways of feeling and thinking have collapsed and that newer beginnings are ambiguous to the point of moral stasis. Is it any wonder that ordinary men feel they cannot cope with the larger worlds with which they are so suddenly confronted? That they cannot understand the meaning of their epoch for their own lives? That—in defense of selfhood—they become morally insensible, trying to remain altogether private men? Is it any wonder that they come to be possessed by a sense of the trap?

It is not only information that they need—in this Age of Fact, information often dominates their attention and overwhelms their capacities to assimilate it. It is not only the skills of reason that they need—although their struggles to acquire these often exhaust their limited moral energy.

What they need, and what they feel they need, is a quality of mind that will help them to use information and to develop reason in order to achieve lucid summations of what is going on in the world and of what may be happening within themselves. It is this quality, I am going to contend, that journalists and scholars, artists and publics, scientists and editors are coming to expect of what may be called the sociological imagination.

## 1

The sociological imagination enables its possessor to understand the larger historical scene in terms of its meaning for the inner life and the external career of a variety of individuals. It enables him to take into account how individuals, in the welter of their daily experience, often become falsely conscious of their social positions. Within that welter, the framework of modern society is sought, and within that framework the psychologies of a variety of men and women are formulated. By such means the personal uneasiness of individuals is focused upon explicit troubles and the indifferences of publics is transformed into involvement with public issues.

The first fruit of this imagination—and the first lesson of the social science that embodies it—is the idea that the individual can understand his own experience and gauge his own fate only by locating himself within his period, that he can know his own chances in life only by becoming aware of those of all individuals in his circumstances. In many ways it is a terrible lesson; in many ways a magnificent one. We do not know the limits of man's capacities for supreme effort or willing degradation, for agony or glee, for pleasurable brutality or the sweetness of reason. But in our time we have come to know that the limits of 'human nature' are frighteningly broad. We have come to know that every individual lives, from one generation to the next, in some society; that he lives out a biography, and that he lives it out within some historical sequence. By the fact of his living he contributes, however minutely, to the shaping of this society and to the course of its history, even as he is made by society and by its historical push and shove.

The sociological imagination enables us to grasp history and biography and the relations between the two within society. That is its task and its promise. To recognize this task and this promise is the mark of the classic social analyst. And it is the signal of what is best in contemporary studies of man and society.

No social study that does not come back to the problems of biography, of history and of their intersections within a society has completed its intellectual journey. Whatever the specific problems of the classic social analysts, however limited or however broad the features of social reality they have examined, those who have been imaginatively aware of the promise of their work have consistently asked three sorts of questions:

1. What is the structure of this particular society as a whole? What are its essential components, and how are they related to one another? How does it differ from other varieties of social order? Within it, what is the meaning of any particular feature for its continuance and for its change?

2. Where does this society stand in human history? What are the mechanics by which it is changing? What is its place within and its meaning for the development of humanity as a whole? How does any particular feature we are examining affect, and how is it affected by, the historical period in which it moves? And this period—what are its essential features? How does it differ from other periods? What are its characteristic ways of history-making?

3. What varieties of men and women now prevail in this society and in this period? And what varieties are coming to prevail? In what ways are they selected and formed, liberated and repressed, made sensitive and blunted? What kinds of 'human nature' are revealed in the conduct and character we observe in this society in this period? And what is the meaning for 'human nature' of each and every feature of the society we are examining?

Whether the point of interest is a great power state or a minor literary mood, a family, a prison, a creed—these are the kinds of questions the best social analysts have asked. They are the intellectual pivots of classic studies of man in society—and they are the questions inevitably raised by any mind possessing the sociological imagination. For that imagination is the capacity to shift from one perspective to another—from the political to the psychological; from examination of a single family to comparative assessment of the national budgets of the world; from the theological school to the military establishment; from considerations of an oil industry to studies of contemporary poetry. It is the capacity to range from the most impersonal and remote transformations to the most intimate features of the human self—and to see the relations between the two. Back of its use there is always the urge to know the social and historical meaning of the individual in the society and in the period in which he has his quality and his being.

That, in brief, is why it is by means of the sociological imagination that men now hope to grasp what is going on in the world, and to understand what is happening in themselves as minute points of the intersections of biography and history within society. In large part, contemporary man's self-conscious view of himself as at least an outsider, if not a permanent stranger, rests upon an absorbed realization of social relativity and of the transformative power of history. The sociological imagination is the most fruitful form of this self-consciousness. By its use men whose mentalities have swept only a series of limited orbits often come to feel as if suddenly awakened in a house with which they had only supposed themselves to be familiar. Correctly or incorrectly, they often come to feel that they can now provide themselves with adequate summations, cohesive assessments, comprehensive orientations. Older decisions that once appeared sound now seem to them products of a mind unaccountably dense. Their capacity for astonishment is made lively again. They acquire a new way of thinking, they experience a transvaluation of values: in a word, by their reflection and by their sensibility, they realize the cultural meaning of the social sciences.

## 2

Perhaps the most fruitful distinction with which the sociological imagination works is between 'the personal troubles of milieu' and 'the public issues of social structure.' This distinction is an essential tool of the sociological imagination and a feature of all classic work in social science.

*Troubles* occur within the character of the individual and within the range of his immediate relations with others; they have to do with his self and with those limited areas of social life of which he is directly and personally aware. Accordingly, the statement and the resolution of troubles properly lie within the individual as a biographical entity and within the scope of his immediate milieu—the social setting that is directly open to his personal experience and to some extent his willful activity. A trouble is a private matter: values cherished by an individual are felt by him to be threatened.

*Issues* have to do with matters that transcend these local environments of the individual and the range of his inner life. They have to do with the organization of many such milieux into the institutions of an historical society as a whole, with the ways in which various milieux overlap and interpenetrate to form the larger structure of social and historical life. An issue is a public matter: some value cherished by publics is felt to be threatened. Often there is a debate about what that value really is and about what it is that really threatens it. This debate is often without focus if only because it is the very nature of an issue, unlike even widespread trouble, that it cannot very well be defined in terms of the immediate and everyday environments of ordinary men. An issue, in fact, often involves a crisis in institutional arrangements, and often too it involves what Marxists call 'contradictions' or 'antagonisms.'

In these terms, consider unemployment. When, in a city of 100,000, only one man is unemployed, that is his personal trouble, and for its relief we properly look to the character of the man, his skills, and his immediate opportunities. But when in a nation of 50 million employees, 15 million men are unemployed, that is an issue, and we may not hope to find its solution within the range of opportunities open to any one individual. The very structure of opportunities has collapsed. Both the correct statement of the problem and the range of possible solutions require us to consider the economic and political institutions of the society, and not merely the personal situation and character of a scatter of individuals.

Consider war. The personal problem of war, when it occurs, may be how to survive it or how to die in it with honor; how to make money out of it; how to climb into the higher safety of the military apparatus; or how to contribute to the war's termination. In short, according to one's values, to find a set of milieux and within it to survive the war or make one's death in it meaningful. But the structural issues of war have to do with its causes; with what types of men it throws up into command; with its effects upon economic and political, family and religious institutions, with the unorganized irresponsibility of a world of nation-states.

Consider marriage. Inside a marriage a man and a woman may experience personal troubles, but when the divorce rate during the first four years of marriage is 250 out of every 1,000 attempts, this is an indication of a structural issue having to do with the institutions of marriage and the family and other institutions that bear upon them.

Or consider the metropolis—the horrible, beautiful, ugly, magnificent sprawl of the great city. For many upper-class people, the personal solution to 'the problem of the city' is to have an apartment with private garage under it in the heart of the city, and forty miles out, a house by Henry Hill, garden by Garrett Eckbo, on a hundred acres of private land. In these two controlled environments—with a small staff at each end and a private helicopter connection—most people could solve many of the problems of personal milieux caused by the facts of the city. But all this, however splendid, does not solve the public issues that the structural fact of the city poses. What should be done with this wonderful monstrosity? Break it all up into scattered units, combining residence and work? Refurbish it as it stands? Or, after evacuation, dynamite it and build new cities according to new plans in new places? What should those plans be? And who is to decide and to accomplish whatever choice is made? These are structural issues; to confront them and to solve them requires us to consider political and economic issues that affect innumerable milieux.

In so far as an economy is so arranged that slumps occur, the problem of unemployment becomes incapable of personal solution. In so far as war is inherent in the nation-state system and in the uneven industrialization of the world, the ordinary individual in his restricted milieu will be powerless—with or without psychiatric aid—to solve the troubles this system or lack of system imposes upon him. In so far as the family as an institution turns women into darling little slaves and men into their chief providers and unweaned dependents, the problem of a satisfactory marriage remains incapable of purely private solution. In so far as the overdeveloped megalopolis and the overdeveloped automobile are built-in features of the overdeveloped society, the issues of urban living will not be solved by personal ingenuity and private wealth.

What we experience in various and specific milieux, I have noted, is often caused by structural changes. Accordingly, to understand the changes of many personal milieux we are required to look beyond them. And the number and variety of such structural changes increase as the institutions within which we live become more embracing and more intricately connected with one another. To be aware of the idea of social structure and to use it with sensibility is to be capable of tracing such linkages among a great variety of milieux. To be able to do that is to possess the sociological imagination.

# 3

## The Tragedy of the Commons*

### GARRETT HARDIN

*Is freedom nothing more than the absence of constraint? This essay, written nearly fifty years ago, has become a classic largely because the issue it poses is perhaps more relevant today than ever. As Émile Durkheim, the great French sociologist, knew, the social world is not simply an accumulation of individual worlds, and what is best for the former is not always determined by what is best for the latter. The author is alarmed by global population growth outstripping Earth's ability to provide enough food. His issue could as easily be global climate change, the depletion of natural resources, or even the pursuit of wealth.*

At the end of a thoughtful article on the future of nuclear war, Wiesner and York concluded that: "Both sides in the arms race are . . . confronted by the dilemma of steadily increasing military power and steadily decreasing national security. *It is our considered professional judgment that this dilemma has no technical solution.* If the great powers continue to look for solutions in the area of science and technology only, the result will be to worsen the situation."

I would like to focus your attention not on the subject of the article (national security in a nuclear world) but on the kind of conclusion they reached, namely that there is no technical solution to the problem. An implicit and almost universal assumption of discussions published in professional and semipopular scientific journals is that the problem under discussion has a technical solution. A technical solution may be defined as one that requires a change only in the techniques of the natural sciences, demanding little or nothing in the way of change in human values or ideas of morality.

In our day (though not in earlier times) technical solutions are always welcome. Because of previous failures in prophecy, it takes courage to assert that a desired technical solution is not possible. Wiesner and York exhibited this courage; publishing in a science journal, they insisted that the solution to the problem was not to be found in the natural sciences. They cautiously qualified their statement with the phrase, "It is our considered professional judgment . . ." Whether they were right or not is not the concern of the present article. Rather, the concern here is with the important concept of a class of

---

*References and footnotes can be found in the original article, published in 1968 in *Science*. [*Editor's note*]

human problems which can be called "no technical solution problems," and, more specifically, with the identification and discussion of one of these.

It is easy to show that the class is not a null class. Recall the game of tick-tack-toe. Consider the problem, "How can I win the game of tick-tack-toe?" It is well known that I cannot, if I assume (in keeping with the conventions of game theory) that my opponent understands the game perfectly. Put another way, there is no "technical solution" to the problem. I can win only by giving a radical meaning to the word "win." I can hit my opponent over the head; or I can drug him; or I can falsify the records. Every way in which I "win" involves, in some sense, an abandonment of the game, as we intuitively understand it. (I can also, of course, openly abandon the game—refuse to play it. This is what most adults do.)

The class of "No technical solution problems" has members. My thesis is that the "population problem," as conventionally conceived, is a member of this class. How it is conventionally conceived needs some comment. It is fair to say that most people who anguish over the population problem are trying to find a way to avoid the evils of overpopulation without relinquishing any of the privileges they now enjoy. They think that farming the seas or developing new strains of wheat will solve the problem—technologically. I try to show here that the solution they seek cannot be found. The population problem cannot be solved in a technical way, any more than can the problem of winning the game of tick-tack-toe.

## WHAT SHALL WE MAXIMIZE?

Population, as Malthus said, naturally tends to grow "geometrically," or, as we would now say, exponentially. In a finite world this means that the per capita share of the world's goods must steadily decrease. Is ours a finite world?

A fair defense can be put forward for the view that the world is infinite; or that we do not know that it is not. But, in terms of the practical problems that we must face in the next few generations with the foreseeable technology, it is clear that we will greatly increase human misery if we do not, during the immediate future, assume that the world available to the terrestrial human population is finite. "Space" is no escape.

A finite world can support only a finite population; therefore, population growth must eventually equal zero. (The case of perpetual wide fluctuations above and below zero is a trivial variant that need not be discussed.) When this condition is met, what will be the situation of mankind? Specifically, can Bentham's goal of "the greatest good for the greatest number" be realized?

No—for two reasons, each sufficient by itself. The first is a theoretical one. It is not mathematically possible to maximize for two (or more) variables at the same time.

The second reason springs directly from biological facts. To live, any organism must have a source of energy (for example, food). This energy is utilized for two purposes: mere maintenance and work. For man, maintenance of life requires about 1600 kilocalories a day ("maintenance calories"). Anything that he does over and above merely staying alive will be defined as work, and is supported by "work calories" which he takes in. Work calories are used not only for what we call work in common speech; they are also required for all forms of enjoyment, from swimming and automobile racing to playing music and writing poetry. If our goal is to maximize population it is obvious what we must do: We must make the work calories per person approach as close to zero as possible. No gourmet meals, no vacations, no sports, no music, no literature, no art. . . . I think that everyone will grant, without argument or proof, that maximizing population does not maximize goods. Bentham's goal is impossible.

In reaching this conclusion I have made the usual assumption that it is the acquisition of energy that is the problem. The appearance of atomic energy has led some to question this assumption. However, given an infinite source of energy, population growth still produces an inescapable problem. The problem of the acquisition of energy is replaced by the problem of its dissipation, as J. H. Fremlin has so wittily shown. The arithmetic signs in the analysis are, as it were, reversed; but Bentham's goal is still unobtainable.

The optimum population is, then, less than the maximum. The difficulty of defining the optimum is enormous; so far as I know, no one has seriously tackled this problem. Reaching an acceptable and stable solution will surely require more than one generation of hard analytical work—and much persuasion.

We want the maximum good per person; but what is good? To one person it is wilderness, to another it is ski lodges for thousands. To one it is estuaries to nourish ducks for hunters to shoot; to another it is factory land. Comparing one good with another is, we usually say, impossible because goods are incommensurable. Incommensurables cannot be compared.

Theoretically this may be true; but in real life incommensurables are commensurable. Only a criterion of judgment and a system of weighting are needed. In nature the criterion is survival. Is it better for a species to be small and hideable, or large and powerful? Natural selection commensurates the incommensurables. The compromise achieved depends on a natural weighting of the values of the variables.

Man must imitate this process. There is no doubt that in fact he already does, but unconsciously. It is when the hidden decisions are made explicit that the arguments begin. The problem for the years ahead is to work out an acceptable theory of weighting. Synergistic effects, nonlinear variation, and difficulties in discounting the future make the intellectual problem difficult, but not (in principle) insoluble.

Has any cultural group solved this practical problem at the present time, even on an intuitive level? One simple fact proves that none has: there is no prosperous population in the world today that has, and has had for some time, a growth rate of zero. Any people that has intuitively identified its optimum point will soon reach it, after which its growth rate becomes and remains zero.

Of course, a positive growth rate might be taken as evidence that a population is below its optimum. However, by any reasonable standards, the most rapidly growing populations on earth today are (in general) the most miserable. This association (which need not be invariable) casts doubt on the optimistic assumption that the positive growth rate of a population is evidence that it has yet to reach its optimum.

We can make little progress in working toward optimum population size until we explicitly exorcize the spirit of Adam Smith in the field of practical demography. In economic affairs, *The Wealth of Nations* (1776) popularized the "invisible hand," the idea that an individual who "intends only his own gain," is, as it were, "led by an invisible hand to promote . . . the public interest." Adam Smith did not assert that this was invariably true, and perhaps neither did any of his followers. But he contributed to a dominant tendency of thought that has ever since interfered with positive action based on rational analysis, namely, the tendency to assume that decisions reached individually will, in fact, be the best decisions for an entire society. If this assumption is correct it justifies the continuance of our present policy of laissez-faire in reproduction. If it is correct we can assume that men will control their individual fecundity so as to produce the optimum population. If the assumption is not correct, we need to reexamine our individual freedoms to see which ones are defensible.

## TRAGEDY OF FREEDOM IN A COMMONS

The rebuttal to the invisible hand in population control is to be found in a scenario first sketched in a little-known pamphlet [written] in 1833 by a mathematical amateur named William Forster Lloyd (1794–1852). We may well call it "the tragedy of the commons," using the word "tragedy" as the philosopher Whitehead used it: "The essence of dramatic tragedy is not unhappiness. It resides in the solemnity of the remorseless working of things." He then goes on to say, "This inevitableness of destiny can only be illustrated in terms of human life by incidents which in fact involve unhappiness. For it is only by them that the futility of escape can be made evident in the drama."

The tragedy of the commons develops in this way. Picture a pasture open to all. It is to be expected that each herdsman will try to keep as many cattle as possible on the commons. Such an arrangement may work reasonably satisfactorily for centuries because tribal wars, poaching, and disease keep the numbers of both man and beast well below the carrying capacity of the land. Finally, however, comes the day of reckoning, that is, the day when the long-desired goal of social stability becomes a reality. At this point, the inherent logic of the commons remorselessly generates tragedy.

As a rational being, each herdsman seeks to maximize his gain. Explicitly or implicitly, more or less consciously, he asks, "What is the utility *to me* of adding one more animal to my herd?" This utility has one negative and one positive component.

1. The positive component is a function of the increment of one animal. Since the herdsman receives all the proceeds from the sale of the additional animal, the positive utility is nearly +1.
2. The negative component is a function of the additional overgrazing created by one more animal. Since, however, the effects of overgrazing are shared by all the herdsmen, the negative utility for any particular decision-making herdsman is only a fraction of –1.

Adding together the component partial utilities, the rational herdsman concludes that the only sensible course for him to pursue is to add another animal to his herd. And another; and another. . . . But this is the conclusion reached by each and every rational herdsman sharing a commons. Therein is the tragedy. Each man is locked into a system that compels him to increase his herd without limit—in a world that is limited. Ruin is the destination toward which all men rush, each pursuing his own best interest in a society that believes in the freedom of the commons. Freedom in a commons brings ruin to all.

Some would say that this is a platitude. Would that it were! In a sense, it was learned thousands of years ago, but natural selection favors the forces of psychological denial. The individual benefits as an individual from his ability to deny the truth even though society as a whole, of which he is a part, suffers.

Education can counteract the natural tendency to do the wrong thing, but the inexorable succession of generations requires that the basis for this knowledge be constantly refreshed.

A simple incident that occurred a few years ago in Leominster, Massachusetts, shows how perishable the knowledge is. During the Christmas shopping season the parking meters downtown were covered with plastic bags that bore tags reading: "Do not open until after Christmas. Free parking courtesy of the mayor and city council." In other words, facing the prospect of an increased demand for already scarce space, the city fathers reinstituted the system of the commons. (Cynically, we suspect that they gained more votes than they lost by this retrogressive act.)

In an approximate way, the logic of the commons has been understood for a long time, perhaps since the discovery of agriculture or the invention of private property in real estate. But it is understood mostly only in special cases which are not sufficiently generalized. Even at this late date, cattlemen leasing national land on the western ranges demonstrate no more than an ambivalent understanding, in constantly pressuring federal authorities to increase the head count to the point where overgrazing produces erosion and weed-dominance. Likewise, the oceans of the world continue to suffer from the survival of the philosophy of the commons. Maritime nations still respond automatically to the shibboleth of the "freedom of the seas." Professing to believe in the "inexhaustible resources of the oceans," they bring species after species of fish and whales closer to extinction.

The National Parks present another instance of the working out of the trag-edy of the commons. At present, they are open to all, without limit. The parks themselves are limited in extent—there is only one Yosemite Valley—whereas population seems to grow without limit. The values that visitors seek in the parks are steadily eroded. Plainly, we must soon cease to treat the parks as com-mons or they will be of no value to anyone.

What shall we do? We have several options. We might sell them off as private property. We might keep them as public property, but allocate the right to enter them. The allocation might be on the basis of wealth, by the use of an auction system. It might be on the basis of merit, as defined by some agreed-upon standards. It might be by lottery. Or it might be on a first-come, first-served basis, administered to long queues. These, I think, are all the reasonable possibilities. They are all objectionable. But we must choose—or acquiesce in the destruction of the commons that we call our National Parks.

## POLLUTION

In a reverse way, the tragedy of the commons reappears in problems of pollu-tion. Here it is not a question of taking something out of the commons, but of putting something in—sewage, or chemical, radioactive, and heat wastes into water; noxious and dangerous fumes into the air, and distracting and unpleas-ant advertising signs into the line of sight. The calculations of utility are much the same as before. The rational man finds that his share of the cost of the wastes he discharges into the commons is less than the cost of purifying his wastes before releasing them. Since this is true for everyone, we are locked into a system of "fouling our own nest," so long as we behave only as indepen-dent, rational, free-enterprisers.

The tragedy of the commons as a food basket is averted by private property, or something formally like it. But the air and waters surrounding us cannot readily be fenced, and so the tragedy of the commons as a cesspool must be prevented by different means, by coercive laws or taxing devices that make it cheaper for the polluter to treat his pollutants than to discharge them untreated. We have not progressed as far with the solution of this problem as we have with the first. Indeed, our particular concept of private property, which deters us from exhausting the positive resources of the earth, favors pollution. The owner of a factory on the bank of a stream—whose property extends to the middle of the stream, often has difficulty seeing why it is not his natural right to muddy the waters flowing past his door. The law, always behind the times, requires elaborate stitching and fitting to adapt it to this newly perceived aspect of the commons.

The pollution problem is a consequence of population. It did not much mat-ter how a lonely American frontiersman disposed of his waste. "Flowing water purifies itself every 10 miles," my grandfather used to say, and the myth was near enough to the truth when he was a boy, for there were not too many people.

But as population became denser, the natural chemical and biological recycling processes became overloaded, calling for a redefinition of property rights. Analysis of the pollution problem as a function of population density uncovers a not generally recognized principle of morality, namely: *the morality of an act is a function of the state of the system at the time it is performed.*

Using the commons as a cesspool does not harm the general public under frontier conditions, because there is no public, the same behavior in a metropolis is unbearable. A hundred and fifty years ago a plainsman could kill an American bison, cut out only the tongue for his dinner, and discard the rest of the animal. He was not in any important sense being wasteful. Today, with only a few thousand bison left, we would be appalled at such behavior.

\* \* \*

## FREEDOM TO BREED IS INTOLERABLE

The tragedy of the commons is involved in population problems in another way. In a world governed solely by the principle of "dog eat dog"—if indeed there ever was such a world—how many children a family had would not be a matter of public concern. Parents who bred too exuberantly would leave fewer descendants, not more, because they would be unable to care adequately for their children. David Lack and others have found that such a negative feedback demonstrably controls the fecundity of birds. But men are not birds, and have not acted like them for millenniums, at least.

If each human family were dependent only on its own resources; if the children of improvident parents starved to death; *if,* thus, overbreeding brought its own "punishment" to the germ line—*then* there would be no public interest in controlling the breeding of families. But our society is deeply committed to the welfare state, and hence is confronted with another aspect of the tragedy of the commons.

In a welfare state, how shall we deal with the family, the religion, the race, or the class (or indeed any distinguishable and cohesive group) that adopts overbreeding as a policy to secure its own aggrandizement?

To couple the concept of freedom to breed with the belief that everyone born has an equal right to the commons is to lock the world into a tragic course of action.

\* \* \*

## CONSCIENCE IS SELF-ELIMINATING

It is a mistake to think that we can control the breeding of mankind in the long run by an appeal to conscience. Charles Galton Darwin made this point when he spoke on the centennial of the publication of his grandfather's great book. The argument is straightforward and Darwinian.

People vary. Confronted with appeals to limit breeding, some people will undoubtedly respond to the plea more than others. Those who have more children will produce a larger fraction of the next generation than those with more susceptible consciences. The difference will be accentuated, generation by generation.

\* \* \*

The argument has here been stated in the context of the population problem, but it applies equally well to any instance in which society appeals to an individual exploiting a commons to restrain himself for the general good—by means of his conscience. To make such an appeal is to set up a selective system that works toward the elimination of conscience from the race.

## PATHOGENIC EFFECTS OF CONSCIENCE

The long-term disadvantage of an appeal to conscience should be enough to condemn it; but has serious short-term disadvantages as well. If we ask a man who is exploiting a commons to desist "in the name of conscience," what are we saying to him? What does he hear?—not only at the moment but also in the wee small hours of the night when, half asleep, he remembers not merely the words we used but also the nonverbal communication cues we gave him unawares? Sooner or later, consciously or subconsciously, he senses that he has received two communications, and that they are contradictory: (i) (intended communication) "If you don't do as we ask, we will openly condemn you for not acting like a responsible citizen"; (ii) (the unintended communication) "If you do behave as we ask, we will secretly condemn you for a simpleton who can be shamed into standing aside while the rest of us exploit the commons."

\* \* \*

If the word responsibility is to be used at all, I suggest that it be in the sense Charles Frankel uses it. "Responsibility," says this philosopher, "is the product of definite social arrangements." Notice that Frankel calls for social arrangements—not propaganda.

## MUTUAL COERCION MUTUALLY AGREED UPON

The social arrangements that produce responsibility are arrangements that create coercion, of some sort. Consider bank-robbing. The man who takes money from a bank acts as if the bank were a commons. How do we prevent such action? Certainly not by trying to control his behavior solely by a verbal appeal to his sense of responsibility. Rather than rely on propaganda we follow Frankel's lead and insist that a bank is not a commons; we seek the definite social arrangements that will keep it from becoming a commons. That we thereby infringe on the freedom of would-be robbers we neither deny nor regret.

The morality of bank-robbing is particularly easy to understand because we accept complete prohibition of this activity. We are willing to say, "Thou shalt not rob banks," without providing for exceptions. But temperance also can be created by coercion. Taxing is a good coercive device. To keep downtown shoppers temperate in their use of parking space we introduce parking meters for short periods, and traffic fines for longer ones. We need not actually forbid a citizen to park as long as he wants to; we need merely make it increasingly expensive for him to do so. Not prohibition, but carefully biased options are what we offer him. A Madison Avenue man might call this persuasion; I prefer the greater candor of the word coercion.

Coercion is a dirty word to most liberals now, but it need not forever be so. As with the four-letter words, its dirtiness can be cleansed away by exposure to the light, by saying it over and over without apology or embarrassment. To many, the word coercion implies arbitrary decisions of distant and irresponsible bureaucrats; but this is not a necessary part of its meaning. The only kind of coercion I recommend is mutual coercion, mutually agreed upon by the majority of the people affected.

To say that we mutually agree to coercion is not to say that we are required to enjoy it, or even to pretend we enjoy it. Who enjoys taxes? We all grumble about them. But we accept compulsory taxes because we recognize that voluntary taxes would favor the conscienceless. We institute and (grumblingly) support taxes and other coercive devices to escape the horror of the commons.

An alternative to the commons need not be perfectly just to be preferable. With real estate and other material goods, the alternative we have chosen is the institution of private property coupled with legal inheritance. Is this system perfectly just? As a genetically trained biologist I deny that it is. It seems to me that, if there are to be differences in individual inheritance, legal possession should be perfectly correlated with biological inheritance—that those who are biologically more fit to be the custodians of property and power should legally inherit more. But genetic recombination continually makes a mockery of the doctrine of "like father, like son" implicit in our laws of legal inheritance. An idiot can inherit millions, and a trust fund can keep his estate intact. We must admit that our legal system of private property plus inheritance is unjust— but we put up with it because we are not convinced, at the moment, that anyone has invented a better system. The alternative of the commons is too horrifying to contemplate. Injustice is preferable to total ruin.

* * *

## RECOGNITION OF NECESSITY

Perhaps the simplest summary of this analysis of man's population problems is this: the commons, if justifiable at all, is justifiable only under conditions of low-population density. As the human population has increased, the commons has had to be abandoned in one aspect after another.

First we abandoned the commons in food gathering, enclosing farm land and restricting pastures and hunting and fishing areas. These restrictions are still not complete throughout the world.

Somewhat later we saw that the commons as a place for waste disposal would also have to be abandoned. Restrictions on the disposal of domestic sewage are widely accepted in the Western world; we are still struggling to close the commons to pollution by automobiles, factories, insecticide sprayers, fertilizing operations, and atomic energy installations.

In a still more embryonic state is our recognition of the evils of the commons in matters of pleasure. There is almost no restriction on the propagation of sound waves in the public medium. The shopping public is assaulted with mindless music, without its consent. Our government is paying out billions of dollars to create supersonic transport which will disturb 50,000 people for every one person who is whisked from coast to coast 3 hours faster. Advertisers muddy the airwaves of radio and television and pollute the view of travelers. We are a long way from outlawing the commons in matters of pleasure. Is this because our Puritan inheritance makes us view pleasure as something of a sin, and pain (that is, the pollution of advertising) as the sign of virtue?

Every new enclosure of the commons involves the infringement of somebody's personal liberty. Infringements made in the distant past are accepted because no contemporary complains of a loss. It is the newly proposed infringements that we vigorously oppose; cries of "rights" and "freedom" fill the air. But what does "freedom" mean? When men mutually agreed to pass laws against robbing, mankind became more free, not less so. Individuals locked into the logic of the commons are free only to bring on universal ruin once they see the necessity of mutual coercion, they become free to pursue other goals. I believe it was Hegel who said, "Freedom is the recognition of necessity."

The most important aspect of necessity that we must now recognize, is the necessity of abandoning the commons in breeding. No technical solution can rescue us from the misery of overpopulation. Freedom to breed will bring ruin to all. At the moment, to avoid hard decisions many of us are tempted to propagandize for conscience and responsible parenthood. The temptation must be resisted, because an appeal to independently acting consciences selects for the disappearance of all conscience in the long run, and an increase in anxiety in the short.

The only way we can preserve and nurture other and more precious freedoms is by relinquishing the freedom to breed, and that very soon. "Freedom is the recognition of necessity"—and it is the role of education to reveal to all the necessity of abandoning the freedom to breed. Only so, can we put an end to this aspect of the tragedy of the commons.

# 4

## The Stranger

### GEORG SIMMEL

*Most students can name the cliques in their high school, but few admit to being in
one, at least full time. They were both inside and outside, involved but detached. Why
does this seem like a good way to be? Georg Simmel (1858–1918) suggests it allows
for intimacies and "confidences," in part because the stranger is not so completely
"bound up" with the group itself. In this sketch of the stranger, and in his other sketches
of social types (e.g., the poor, the miser, the adventurer), Simmel is presenting sociology as the study of relationships and the possibilities—often contradictory—for
different types of interaction. His studies of dyads and triads (two- and three-person
groups) have the same playful but insightful examination of bonds, networks, and
strategies that make society appear to be almost a dance or a game of chess.*

If wandering, considered as a state of detachment from every given point in
space, is the conceptual opposite of attachment to any point, then the sociological form of "the stranger" presents the synthesis, as it were, of both of these
properties. (This is another indication that spatial relations not only are determining conditions of relationships among men, but are also symbolic of those
relationships.) The stranger will thus not be considered here in the usual sense
of the term, as the wanderer who comes today and goes tomorrow, but rather
as the man who comes today and stays tomorrow—the potential wanderer, so
to speak, who, although he has gone no further, has not quite got over the freedom of coming and going. He is fixed within a certain spatial circle—or within
a group whose boundaries are analogous to spatial boundaries—but his position within it is fundamentally affected by the fact that he does not belong in
it initially and that he brings qualities into it that are not, and cannot be, indigenous to it.

In the case of the stranger, the union of closeness and remoteness involved
in every human relationship is patterned in a way that may be succinctly formulated as follows: the distance within this relation indicates that one who is
close by is remote, but his strangeness indicates that one who is remote is near.
The state of being a stranger is of course a completely positive relation; it is a
specific form of interaction. * * *

The following statements about the stranger are intended to suggest how
factors of repulsion and distance work to create a form of being together, a
form of union based on interaction.

In the whole history of economic activity the stranger makes his appearance everywhere as a trader, and the trader makes his as a stranger. As long as production for one's own needs is the general rule, or products are exchanged within a relatively small circle, there is no need for a middleman within the group. A trader is required only for goods produced outside the group. Unless there are people who wander out into foreign lands to buy these necessities, in which case they are themselves "strange" merchants in this other region, the trader *must* be a stranger; there is no opportunity for anyone else to make a living at it.

This position of the stranger stands out more sharply if, instead of leaving the place of his activity, he settles down there. In innumerable cases even this is possible only if he can live by trade as a middleman. Any closed economic group where land and handicrafts have been apportioned in a way that satisfies local demands will still support a livelihood for the trader. For trade alone makes possible unlimited combinations, and through it intelligence is constantly extended and applied in new areas, something that is much harder for the primary producer with his more limited mobility and his dependence on a circle of customers that can be expanded only very slowly. Trade can always absorb more men than can primary production. It is therefore the most suitable activity for the stranger, who intrudes as a supernumerary, so to speak, into a group in which all the economic positions are already occupied. The classic example of this is the history of European Jews. The stranger is by his very nature no owner of land—land not only in the physical sense but also metaphorically as a vital substance which is fixed, if not in space, then at least in an ideal position within the social environment.

Although in the sphere of intimate personal relations the stranger may be attractive and meaningful in many ways, so long as he is regarded as a stranger he is no "landowner" in the eyes of the other. Restriction to intermediary trade and often (as though sublimated from it) to pure finance gives the stranger the specific character of *mobility*. The appearance of this mobility within a bounded group occasions that synthesis of nearness and remoteness which constitutes the formal position of the stranger. The purely mobile person comes incidentally into contact with *every* single element but is not bound up organically, through established ties of kinship, locality, or occupation, with any single one.

Another expression of this constellation is to be found in the objectivity of the stranger. Because he is not bound by roots to the particular constituents and partisan dispositions of the group, he confronts all of these with a distinctly "objective" attitude, an attitude that does not signify mere detachment and non-participation, but is a distinct structure composed of remoteness and nearness, indifference and involvement. I refer to my analysis of the dominating positions gained by aliens, in the discussion of superordination and subordination, typified by the practice in certain Italian cities of recruiting their judges from outside, because no native was free from entanglement in family interests and factionalism.

Connected with the characteristic of objectivity is a phenomenon that is found chiefly, though not exclusively, in the stranger who moves on. This is that he often receives the most surprising revelations and confidences, at times reminiscent of a confessional, about matters which are kept carefully hidden from everybody with whom one is close. Objectivity is by no means nonparticipation, a condition that is altogether outside the distinction between subjective and objective orientations. It is rather a positive and definite kind of participation, in the same way that the objectivity of a theoretical observation clearly does not mean that the mind is a passive tabula rasa on which things inscribe their qualities, but rather signifies the full activity of a mind working according to its own laws, under conditions that exclude accidental distortions and emphases whose individual and subjective differences would produce quite different pictures of the same object.

Objectivity can also be defined as freedom. The objective man is not bound by ties which could prejudice his perception, his understanding, and his assessment of data. This freedom, which permits the stranger to experience and treat even his close relationships as though from a bird's-eye view, contains many dangerous possibilities. From earliest times, in uprisings of all sorts the attacked party has claimed that there has been incitement from the outside, by foreign emissaries and agitators. Insofar as this has happened, it represents an exaggeration of the specific role of the stranger: he is the freer man, practically and theoretically; he examines conditions with less prejudice; he assesses them against standards that are more general and more objective; and his actions are not confined by custom, piety, or precedent.

Finally, the proportion of nearness and remoteness which gives the stranger the character of objectivity also finds practical expression in the more *abstract* nature of the relation to him. That is, with the stranger one has only certain *more general* qualities in common, whereas the relation with organically connected persons is based on the similarity of just those specific traits which differentiate them from the merely universal. In fact, all personal relations whatsoever can be analyzed in terms of this scheme. They are not determined only by the existence of certain common characteristics which the individuals share in addition to their individual differences, which either influence the relationship or remain outside of it. Rather, the kind of effect which that commonality has on the relation essentially depends on whether it exists only among the participants themselves, and thus, although general within the relation, is specific and incomparable with respect to all those on the outside, or whether the participants feel that what they have in common is so only because it is common to a group, a type, or mankind in general. In the latter case, the effect of the common features becomes attenuated in proportion to the size of the group bearing the same characteristics. The commonality provides a basis for unifying the members, to be sure; but it does not specifically direct *these* particular persons to one another. A similarity so widely shared could just as easily unite each person with every possible other. This, too, is evidently a way in which a relationship includes both nearness and remoteness simultaneously. To the extent to which the similarities assume a universal nature, the warmth of the connection based on them will acquire an element of coolness, a sense of the contingent nature of precisely *this* relation—the connecting forces have lost their specific, centripetal character.

In relation to the stranger, it seems to me, this constellation assumes an extraordinary preponderance in principle over the individual elements peculiar to the relation in question. The stranger is close to us insofar as we feel between him and ourselves similarities of nationality or social position, of occupation or of general human nature. He is far from us insofar as these similarities extend beyond him and us, and connect us only because they connect a great many people.

A trace of strangeness in this sense easily enters even the most intimate relationships. In the stage of first passion, erotic relations strongly reject any thought of generalization. A love such as this has never existed before; there is nothing to compare either with the person one loves or with our feelings for that person. An estrangement is wont to set in (whether as cause or effect is hard to decide) at the moment when this feeling of uniqueness disappears from the relationship. A skepticism regarding the intrinsic value of the relationship and its value for us adheres to the very thought that in this relation, after all, one is only fulfilling a general human destiny, that one has had an experience that has occurred a thousand times before, and that, if one had not accidentally met this precise person, someone else would have acquired the same meaning for us.

Something of this feeling is probably not absent in any relation, be it ever so close, because that which is common to two is perhaps never common *only* to them but belongs to a general conception which includes much else besides, many *possibilities* of similarities. No matter how few of these possibilities are realized and how often we may forget about them, here and there, nevertheless, they crowd in like shadows between men, like a mist eluding every designation, which must congeal into solid corporeality for it to be called jealousy. Perhaps this is in many cases a more general, at least more insurmountable, strangeness than that due to differences and obscurities. It is strangeness caused by the fact that similarity, harmony, and closeness are accompanied by the feeling that they are actually not the exclusive property of this particular relation, but stem from a more general one—a relation that potentially includes us and an indeterminate number of others, and therefore prevents that relation which alone was experienced from having an inner and exclusive necessity.

On the other hand, there is a sort of "strangeness" in which this very connection on the basis of a general quality embracing the parties is precluded. The relation of the Greeks to the barbarians is a typical example; so are all the cases in which the general characteristics one takes as peculiarly and merely human are disallowed to the other. But here the expression "the stranger" no longer has any positive meaning. The relation with him is a nonrelation; he is not what we have been discussing here: the stranger as a member of the group itself.

As such, the stranger is near and far *at the same time*, as in any relationship based on merely universal human similarities. Between these two factors of nearness and distance, however, a peculiar tension arises, since the consciousness of having only the absolutely general in common has exactly the effect of putting a special emphasis on that which is not common. For a stranger to the country, the city, the race, and so on, what is stressed is again nothing individual, but alien origin, a quality which he has, or could have, in common with many other strangers. For this reason strangers are not really perceived as individuals, but as strangers of a certain type. Their remoteness is no less general than their nearness.

This form appears, for example, in so special a case as the tax levied on Jews in Frankfurt and elsewhere during the Middle Ages. Whereas the tax paid by Christian citizens varied according to their wealth at any given time, for every single Jew the tax was fixed once and for all. This amount was fixed because the Jew had his social position as a *Jew*, not as the bearer of certain objective contents. With respect to taxes every other citizen was regarded as possessor of a certain amount of wealth, and his tax could follow the fluctuations of his fortune. But the Jew as taxpayer was first of all a Jew, and thus his fiscal position contained an invariable element. This appears most forcefully, of course, once the differing circumstances of individual Jews are no longer considered, limited though this consideration is by fixed assessments, and all strangers pay exactly the same head tax.

Despite his being inorganically appended to it, the stranger is still an organic member of the group. Its unified life includes the specific conditioning of this element. Only we do not know how to designate the characteristic unity of this position otherwise than by saying that it is put together of certain amounts of nearness and of remoteness. Although both these qualities are found to some extent in all relationships, a special proportion and reciprocal tension between them produce the specific form of the relation to the "stranger."

# 5

## The My Lai Massacre: A Crime of Obedience?

FROM *Crimes of Obedience: Toward a Social Psychology
of Authority and Responsibility*

### HERBERT C. KELMAN and V. LEE HAMILTON

*Understanding why people do what they do is never easy. It is especially difficult
when behaviors are contrary to what anyone would expect or want people to do, as
in the case of heinous crimes. In this account of the murder of hundreds of innocent
people—perhaps the most painful episode of a long and unpopular war—Kelman
and Hamilton depart from psychological explanations and focus on the sociology of
men in war. They make a compelling case that the social conditions of these men dramatically weakened the moral inhibitions that otherwise would have prevented their
doing the unthinkable.*

March 16, 1968, was a busy day in U.S. history. Stateside, Robert F.
Kennedy announced his presidential candidacy, challenging a sitting
president from his own party—in part out of opposition to an undeclared
and disastrous war. In Vietnam, the war continued. In many ways, March 16
may have been a typical day in that war. We will probably never know. But we
do know that on that day a typical company went on a mission—which may or
may not have been typical—to a village called Son (or Song) My. Most of what
is remembered from that mission occurred in the subhamlet known to Americans as My Lai 4.

The My Lai massacre was investigated and charges were brought in 1969
and 1970. Trials and disciplinary actions lasted into 1971. Entire books have
been written about the army's year-long cover-up of the massacre (for example, Hersh, 1972), and the cover-up was a major focus of the army's own investigation of the incident. Our central concern here is the massacre itself—a crime
of obedience—and public reactions to such crimes, rather than the lengths to
which many went to deny the event. Therefore this account concentrates on
one day: March 16, 1968.[1]

Many verbal testimonials to the horrors that occurred at My Lai were available. More unusual was the fact that an army photographer, Ronald Haeberle,
was assigned the task of documenting the anticipated military engagement at

---

1. In reconstructing the events of that day, we consulted Hammer (1970), in addition to the
sources cited in the text. Schell (1968) provided information on the region around My Lai.
Concerning Vietnam and peasant rebellions, we consulted FitzGerald (1972), Paige (1975),
Popkin (1979), and Wolf (1969).

My Lai—and documented a massacre instead. Later, as the story of the massacre emerged, his photographs were widely distributed and seared the public conscience. What might have been dismissed as unreal or exaggerated was depicted in photographs of demonstrable authenticity. The dominant image appeared on the cover of *Life*: piles of bodies jumbled together in a ditch along a trail—the dead all apparently unarmed. All were Oriental, and all appeared to be children, women, or old men. Clearly there had been a mass execution, one whose image would not quickly fade.

So many bodies (over twenty in the cover photo alone) are hard to imagine as the handiwork of one killer. These were not. They were the product of what we call a crime of obedience. Crimes of obedience begin with orders. But orders are often vague and rarely survive with any clarity the transition from one authority down a chain of subordinates to the ultimate actors. The operation at Son My was no exception.

"Charlie" Company, Company C, under Lt. Col. Frank Barker's command, arrived in Vietnam in December of 1967. As the army's investigative unit, directed by Lt. Gen. William R. Peers, characterized the personnel, they "contained no significant deviation from the average" for the time. Seymour S. Hersh (1970) described the "average" more explicitly: "Most of the men in Charlie Company had volunteered for the draft; only a few had gone to college for even one year. Nearly half were black, with a few Mexican-Americans. Most were eighteen to twenty-two years old. The favorite reading matter of Charlie Company, like that of other line infantry units in Vietnam, was comic books" (p. 18). The action at My Lai, like that throughout Vietnam, was fought by a cross-section of those Americans who either believed in the war or lacked the social resources to avoid participating in it. Charlie Company was indeed average for that time, that place, and that war.

Two key figures in Charlie Company were more unusual. The company's commander, Capt. Ernest Medina, was an upwardly mobile Mexican-American who wanted to make the army his career, although he feared that he might never advance beyond captain because of his lack of formal education. His eagerness had earned him a nickname among his men: "Mad Dog Medina." One of his admirers was the platoon leader Second Lt. William L. Calley, Jr., an undistinguished, five-foot-three-inch junior-college dropout who had failed four of the seven courses in which he had enrolled his first year. Many viewed him as one of those "instant officers" made possible only by the army's then-desperate need for manpower. Whatever the cause, he was an insecure leader whose frequent claim was "I'm the boss." His nickname among some of the troops was "Surfside 5½," a reference to the swashbuckling heroes of a popular television show, "Surfside 6."

The Son My operation was planned by Lieutenant Colonel Barker and his staff as a search-and-destroy mission with the objective of rooting out the Forty-eighth Viet Cong Battalion from their base area of Son My village. Apparently no written orders were ever issued. Barker's superior, Col. Oran Henderson, arrived at the staging point the day before. Among the issues he reviewed with the assembled officers were some of the weaknesses of prior operations by their units, including their failure to be appropriately aggressive in pursuit of the enemy. Later briefings by Lieutenant Colonel Barker and his staff asserted that no one except Viet Cong was expected to be in the village after 7 A.M. on the following day. The "innocent" would all be at the market. Those present at the briefings gave conflicting accounts of Barker's exact orders, but he conveyed at least a strong suggestion that the Son My area was to be obliterated. As the army's inquiry reported: "While there is some conflict in the testimony as to whether LTC Barker ordered the destruction of houses, dwellings, livestock, and other foodstuffs in the Song My area, the preponderance of the evidence indicates that such destruction was implied, if not specifically directed, by his orders of 15 March" (Peers Report, in Goldstein et al., 1976, p. 94).

Evidence that Barker ordered the killing of civilians is even more murky. What does seem clear, however, is that—having asserted that civilians would be away at the market—he did not specify what was to be done with any who might nevertheless be found on the scene. The Peers Report therefore considered it "reasonable to conclude that LTC Barker's minimal or nonexistent instructions concerning the handling of noncombatants created the potential for grave misunderstandings as to his intentions and for interpretation of his orders as authority to fire, without restriction, on all persons found in target area" (Goldstein et al., 1976, p. 95). Since Barker was killed in action in June 1968, his own formal version of the truth was never available.

Charlie Company's Captain Medina was briefed for the operation by Barker and his staff. He then transmitted the already vague orders to his own men. Charlie Company was spoiling for a fight, having been totally frustrated during its months in Vietnam—first by waiting for battles that never came, then by incompetent forays led by inexperienced commanders, and finally by mines and booby traps. In fact, the emotion-laden funeral of a sergeant killed by a booby trap was held on March 15, the day before My Lai. Captain Medina gave the orders for the next day's action at the close of that funeral. Many were in a mood for revenge.

It is again unclear what was ordered. Although all participants were still alive by the time of the trials for the massacre, they were either on trial or probably felt under threat of trial. Memories are often flawed and self-serving at such times. It is apparent that Medina relayed to the men at least some of Barker's general message—to expect Viet Cong resistance, to burn, and to kill livestock. It is not clear that he ordered the slaughter of the inhabitants, but some of the men who heard him thought he had. One of those who claimed to have heard such orders was Lt. William Calley.

As March 16 dawned, much was expected of the operation by those who had set it into motion. Therefore a full complement of "brass" was present in helicopters overhead, including Barker, Colonel Henderson, and their superior, Major General Koster (who went on to become commandant of West Point before the story of My Lai broke). On the ground the troops were to carry with them one reporter and one photographer to immortalize the anticipated battle.

The action for Company C began at 7:30 as their first wave of helicopters touched down near the subhamlet of My Lai 4. By 7:47 all of Company C was present and set to fight. But instead of the Viet Cong Forty-eighth Battalion, My Lai was filled with the old men, women, and children who were supposed to have gone to market. By this time, in their version of the war, and with whatever orders they thought they had heard, the men from Company C were nevertheless ready to find Viet Cong everywhere. By nightfall, the official tally was 128 VC killed and three weapons captured, although later unofficial body counts ran as high as 500. The operation at Son My was over. And by nightfall, as Hersh reported: "the Viet Cong were back in My Lai 4, helping the survivors bury the dead. It took five days. Most of the funeral speeches were made by the Communist guerrillas. Nguyen Bat was not a Communist at the time of the massacre, but the incident changed his mind. 'After the shooting,' he said, 'all the villagers became Communists'" (1970, p. 74). To this day, the memory of the massacre is kept alive by markers and plaques designating the spots where groups of villagers were killed, by a large statue, and by the My Lai Museum, established in 1975 (Williams, 1985).

But what could have happened to leave American troops reporting a victory over Viet Cong when in fact they had killed hundreds of noncombatants? It is not hard to explain the report of victory; that is the essence of a cover-up. It is harder to understand how the killings came to be committed in the first place, making a cover-up necessary.

## MASS EXECUTIONS AND THE DEFENSE OF SUPERIOR ORDERS

Some of the atrocities on March 16, 1968, were evidently unofficial, spontaneous acts: rapes, tortures, killings. For example, Hersh (1970) describes Charlie Company's Second Platoon as entering "My Lai 4 with guns blazing" (p. 50); more graphically, Lieutenant "Brooks and his men in the second platoon to the north had begun to systematically ransack the hamlet and slaughter the people, kill the livestock, and destroy the crops. Men poured rifle and machine-gun fire into huts without knowing—or seemingly caring—who was inside" (pp. 49–50).

Some atrocities toward the end of the action were part of an almost casual "mopping-up," much of which was the responsibility of Lieutenant LaCross's Third Platoon of Charlie Company. The Peers Report states: "The entire 3rd Platoon then began moving into the western edge of My Lai (4), for the mop-up operation. . . . The squad . . . began to burn the houses in the southwestern portion of the hamlet" (Goldstein et al., 1976, p. 133). They became mingled with other platoons during a series of rapes and killings of survivors for which it was impossible to fix responsibility. Certainly to a Vietnamese all GIs would by this point look alike: "Nineteen-year-old Nguyen Thi Ngoc Tuyet watched a baby trying to open her slain mother's blouse to nurse. A soldier shot the infant while it was struggling with the blouse, and then slashed it with his bayonet." Tuyet also said she saw another baby hacked to death by GIs wielding their bayonets. "Le Tong, a twenty-eight-year-old rice farmer, reported seeing one woman raped after GIs killed her children. Nguyen Khoa, a thirty-seven-year-old peasant, told of a thirteen-year-old girl who was raped before being killed. GIs then attacked Khoa's wife, tearing off her clothes. Before they could rape her, however, Khoa said, their six-year-old son, riddled with bullets, fell and saturated her with blood. The GIs left her alone" (Hersh, 1970, p. 72). All of Company C was implicated in a pattern of death and destruction throughout the hamlet, much of which seemingly lacked rhyme or reason.

But a substantial amount of the killing was *organized* and traceable to one authority: the First Platoon's Lt. William Calley. Calley was originally charged with 109 killings, almost all of them mass executions at the trail and other locations. He stood trial for 102 of these killings, was convicted of 22 in 1971, and at first received a life sentence. Though others—both superior and subordinate to Calley—were brought to trial, he was the only one convicted for the My Lai crimes. Thus, the only actions of My Lai for which *anyone* was ever convicted were mass executions, ordered and committed. We suspect that there are common sense reasons why this one type of killing was singled out. In the midst of rapidly moving events with people running about, an execution of stationary targets is literally a still life that stands out and whose participants are clearly visible. It can be proven that specific people committed specific deeds. An execution, in contrast to the shooting of someone on the run, is also more likely to meet the legal definition of an act resulting from intent—with malice aforethought. Moreover, American military law specifically forbids the killing of unarmed civilians or military prisoners, as does the Geneva Convention between nations. Thus common sense, legal standards, and explicit doctrine all made such actions the likeliest target for prosecution.

When Lieutenant Calley was charged under military law it was for violation of the Uniform Code of Military Justice (UCMJ) Article 118 (murder). This article is similar to civilian codes in that it provides for conviction if an accused:

1. without justification or excuse, unlawfully kills a human being, when he—
2. has a premeditated design to kill;
3. intends to kill or inflict great bodily harm;
4. is engaged in an act which is inherently dangerous to others and evinces a wanton disregard of human life; or
5. is engaged in the perpetration or attempted perpetration of burglary, sodomy, rape, robbery, or aggravated arson. (Goldstein et al., 1976, p. 507)

For a soldier, one legal justification for killing is warfare; but warfare is subject to many legal limits and restrictions, including, of course, the inadmissibility of killing unarmed noncombatants or prisoners whom one has disarmed. The pictures of the trail victims at My Lai certainly portrayed one or the other of these. Such an action would be illegal under military law; ordering another to commit such an action would be illegal; and following such an order would be illegal.

But following an order may provide a second and pivotal justification for an act that would be murder when committed by a civilian. * * * American military law assumes that the subordinate is inclined to follow orders, as that is the normal obligation of the role. Hence, legally, obedient subordinates are protected from unreasonable expectations regarding their capacity to evaluate those orders:

> An order requiring the performance of a military duty may be inferred to be legal. An act performed manifestly beyond the scope of authority, or pursuant to an order that a man of ordinary sense and understanding would know to be illegal, or in a wanton manner in the discharge of a lawful duty, is not excusable. (Par. 216, Subpar. *d*, Manual for Courts Martial, United States, 1969 Rev.)

Thus what *may* be excusable is the good-faith carrying out of an order, as long as that order appears to the ordinary soldier to be a legal one. In military law, invoking superior orders moves the question from one of the action's consequences—the body count*—to one of evaluating the actor's motives and good sense.

In sum, if anyone is to be brought to justice for a massacre, common sense and legal codes decree that the most appropriate targets are those who make themselves executioners. This is the kind of target the government selected in prosecuting Lieutenant Calley with the greatest fervor. And in a military context, the most promising way in which one can redefine one's undeniable deeds into acceptability is to invoke superior orders. This is what Calley did in attempting to avoid conviction. Since the core legal issues involved points of mass execution—the ditches and trail where America's image of My Lai was formed—we review these events in greater detail.

The day's quiet beginning has already been noted. Troops landed and swept unopposed into the village. The three weapons eventually reported as the haul from the operation were picked up from three apparent Viet Cong who fled the village when the troops arrived and were pursued and killed by helicopter gunships. Obviously the Viet Cong did frequent the area. But it appears that by about 8:00 A.M. no one who met the troops was aggressive, and no one was

---

*During the Vietnam War, the success of a military action was often measured by the number of "enemy" killed, relative to allied casualties. [*Editor's note*]

armed. By the laws of war Charlie Company had no argument with such people.

As they moved into the village, the soldiers began to gather its inhabitants together. Shortly after 8:00 A.M. Lieutenant Calley told Pfc. Paul Meadlo that "you know what to do with" a group of villagers Meadlo was guarding. Estimates of the numbers in the group ranged as high as eighty women, children, and old men, and Meadlo's own estimate under oath was thirty to fifty people. As Meadlo later testified, Calley returned after ten or fifteen minutes: "He [Calley] said, 'How come they're not dead?' I said, 'I didn't know we were supposed to kill them.' He said, 'I want them dead.' He backed off twenty or thirty feet and started shooting into the people—the Viet Cong—shooting automatic. He was beside me. He burned four or five magazines. I burned off a few, about three. I helped shoot 'em" (Hammer, 1971, p. 155). Meadlo himself and others testified that Meadlo cried as he fired; others reported him later to be sobbing and "all broke up." It would appear that to Lieutenant Calley's subordinates something was unusual, and stressful, in these orders.

At the trial, the first specification in the murder charge against Calley was for this incident; he was accused of premeditated murder of "an unknown number, not less than 30, Oriental human beings, males and females of various ages, whose names are unknown, occupants of the village of My Lai 4, by means of shooting them with a rifle" (Goldstein et al., 1976, p. 497).

Among the helicopters flying reconnaissance above Son My was that of CWO Hugh Thompson. By 9:00 or soon after Thompson had noticed some horrifying events from his perch. As he spotted wounded civilians, he sent down smoke markers so that soldiers on the ground could treat them. They killed them instead. He reported to headquarters, trying to persuade someone to stop what was going on. Barker, hearing the message, called down to Captain Medina. Medina, in turn, later claimed to have told Calley that it was "enough for today." But it was not yet enough.

At Calley's orders, his men began gathering the remaining villagers—roughly seventy-five individuals, mostly women and children—and herding them toward a drainage ditch. Accompanied by three or four enlisted men, Lieutenant Calley executed several batches of civilians who had been gathered into ditches. Some of the details of the process were entered into testimony in such accounts as Pfc. Dennis Conti's: "A lot of them, the people, were trying to get up and mostly they was just screaming and pretty bad shot up. . . . I seen a woman tried to get up. I seen Lieutenant Calley fire. He hit the side of her head and blew it off" (Hammer, 1971, p. 125).

Testimony by other soldiers presented the shooting's aftermath. Specialist Four Charles Hall, asked by Prosecutor Aubrey Daniel how he knew the people in the ditch were dead, said: "There was blood coming from them. They were just scattered all over the ground in the ditch, some in piles and some scattered out 20, 25 meters perhaps up the ditch. . . . They were very old people, very young children, and mothers. . . . There was blood all over them" (Goldstein et al., 1976, pp. 501–02). And Pfc. Gregory Olson corroborated the general picture of the victims: "They were—the majority were women and children, some babies. I distinctly remember one middle-aged Vietnamese male dressed in white right at my feet as I crossed. None of the bodies were mangled in any way. There was blood. Some appeared to be dead, others followed me with their eyes as I walked across the ditch" (Goldstein et al., 1976, p. 502).

The second specification in the murder charge stated that Calley did "with premeditation, murder an unknown number of Oriental human beings, not less than seventy, males and females of various ages, whose names are unknown, occupants of the village of My Lai 4, by means of shooting them with a rifle" (Goldstein et al., 1976, p. 497). Calley was also charged with and tried for shootings of individuals (an old man and a child); these charges were clearly supplemental to the main issue at trial—the mass killings and how they came about.

It is noteworthy that during these executions more than one enlisted man avoided carrying out Calley's orders, and more than one, by sworn oath, directly refused to obey them. For example, Pfc. James Joseph Dursi testified, when asked if he fired when Lieutenant Calley ordered him to: "No. I just stood there. Meadlo turned to me after a couple of minutes and said 'Shoot! Why don't you shoot! Why don't you fire! He was crying and yelling. I said, 'I can't I won't!' And the people were screaming and crying and yelling. They kept firing for a couple of minutes, mostly automatic and semi-automatic" (Hammer, 1971, p. 143).

Specialist Four Ronald Grzesik reported an even more direct confrontation with Calley, although under oath he hedged about its subject:

GRZESIK: Well, Lieutenant Calley—I walked past the ditch. I was called back by someone, I don't recall who. I had a discussion with Lieutenant Calley. He said to take the fire team back into the village and help the second platoon search.

DANIEL: Did Lieutenant Calley say anything before he gave you that order?

GRZESIK: He said, "Finish them off." I refused.

DANIEL: What did you refuse to do?

GRZESIK: To finish them off.

DANIEL: What did he mean? Who did he mean to finish off?

GRZESIK: I don't know what he meant or who he meant by them. (Hammer, 1971, p. 150)

In preceding months, not under oath, Grzesik had indicated that he had a good idea what was meant but that he simply would not comply. It is likely that the jury at Calley's trial did not miss the point.

Disobedience of Lieutenant Calley's own orders to kill represented a serious legal and moral threat to a defense *based* on superior orders, such as Calley was attempting. This defense had to assert that the orders seemed reasonable enough to carry out, that they appeared to be legal orders. Even if the orders in question were not legal, the defense had to assert that an ordinary individual could not and should not be expected to see the distinction. In short, if what happened was "business as usual," even though it might be bad business, then the defendant stood a chance of acquittal. But under direct command from "Surfside 5½," some ordinary enlisted men managed to refuse, to avoid, or at least to stop doing what they were ordered to do. As "reasonable men" of "ordinary sense and understanding," they had apparently found something awry that morning; and it would have been hard for an officer to plead successfully that he was more ordinary than his men in his capacity to evaluate the reasonableness of orders.

Even those who obeyed Calley's orders showed great stress. For example, Meadlo eventually began to argue and cry directly in front of Calley. Pfc. Herbert Carter shot himself in the foot, possibly because he could no longer take what he was doing. We were not destined to hear a sworn version of the incident, since neither side at the Calley trial called him to testify.

The most unusual instance of resistance to authority came from the skies. CWO Hugh Thompson, who had protested the apparent carnage of civilians, was Calley's inferior in rank but was not in his line of command. He was also watching the ditch from his helicopter and noticed some people moving after the first round of slaughter—chiefly children who had been shielded by their mothers' bodies. Landing to rescue the wounded, he also found some villagers hiding in a nearby bunker. Protecting the Vietnamese with his own body, Thompson ordered his men to train their guns on the Americans and to open fire if the Americans fired on the Vietnamese. He then radioed for additional rescue helicopters and stood between the Vietnamese and the Americans under Calley's command until the Vietnamese could be evacuated. He later returned to the ditch to unearth a child buried, unharmed, beneath layers of bodies. In October 1969, Thompson was awarded the Distinguished Flying Cross for heroism at My Lai, specifically (albeit inaccurately) for the rescue of children hiding in a bunker "between Viet Cong forces and advancing friendly forces" and for the rescue of a wounded child "caught in the intense crossfire" (Hersh, 1970, p. 119). Four months earlier, at the Pentagon, Thompson had identified Calley as having been at the ditch.

By about 10:00 A.M., the massacre was winding down. The remaining actions consisted largely of isolated rapes and killings, "clean-up" shootings of the wounded, and the destruction of the village by fire. We have already seen some examples of these more indiscriminate and possibly less premeditated acts. By the 11:00 A.M. lunch break, when the exhausted men of Company C were relaxing, two young girls wandered back from a hiding place only to be invited to share lunch. This surrealist touch illustrates the extent to which the soldiers' action had become dissociated from its meaning. An hour earlier, some of these men were making sure that not even a child would escape the executioner's bullet. But now the job was done and it was time for lunch—and in this new context it seemed only natural to ask the children who had managed to escape execution to join them. The massacre had ended. It remained only for the Viet Cong to reap the political rewards among the survivors in hiding.

The army command in the area knew that something had gone wrong. Direct commanders, including Lieutenant Colonel Barker, had firsthand reports, such as Thompson's complaints. Others had such odd bits of evidence as the claim of 128 Viet Cong dead with a booty of only three weapons. But the cover-up of My Lai began at once. The operation was reported as a victory over a stronghold of the Viet Cong Forty-eighth.

My Lai might have remained a "victory" but for another odd twist. A soldier who had not even been at the massacre, Ronald Ridenhour, talked to several friends and acquaintances who had been. As he later wrote: "It was late in April, 1968 that I first heard of 'Pinkville' [a nickname reflecting the villagers' reputed Communist sympathies] and what allegedly happened there. I received that first report with some skepticism, but in the following months I was to hear similar stories from such a wide variety of people that it became impossible for me to disbelieve that something rather dark and bloody did indeed occur sometime in March, 1968 in a village called 'Pinkville' in the Republic of Viet Nam" (Goldstein et al., 1976, p. 34). Ridenhour's growing conviction that a massacre—or something close to it—had occurred was reinforced by his own travel over the area by helicopter soon after the event. My Lai was desolate. He gradually concluded that someone was covering up the incident within the army and that an independent investigation was needed.

At the end of March 1969, he finally wrote a letter detailing what he knew about "Pinkville." The letter, beginning with the paragraph quote above, was sent to thirty individuals—the president, Pentagon officials, and some members of the Senate and House. Ridenhour's congressman, fellow Arizonian Morris Udall, gave it particular heed. The slow unraveling of the cover-up began. During the following months, the army in fact initiated an investigation but carried it out in strict secrecy. Ridenhour, convinced that the cover-up was continuing, sought journalistic help and finally, by coincidence, connected with Seymour Hersh. Hersh followed up and broke the story, which eventually brought him a Pulitzer Prize and other awards for his investigative reporting. The cover-up collapsed, leaving only the question of the army's resolve to seek justice in the case: Against whom would it proceed, with how much speed and vigor, and with what end in mind?

William Calley was not the only man tried for the events at My Lai. The actions of over thirty soldiers and civilians were scrutinized by investigators; over half of these had to face charges or disciplinary action of some sort. Targets of investigation included Captain Medina, who was tried, and various higher-ups, including General Koster. But Lieutenant Calley was the only person convicted, the only person to serve time.

\* \* \*

## SANCTIONED MASSACRES

The slaughter at My Lai is an instance of a class of violent acts that can be described as sanctioned massacres (Kelman, 1973): acts of indiscriminate, ruthless, and often systematic mass violence, carried out by military or paramilitary personnel while engaged in officially sanctioned campaigns, the victims of which are defenseless and unresisting civilians, including old men, women, and children. Sanctioned massacres have occurred throughout history. Within American history, My Lai had its precursors in the Philippine war around the turn of the century (Schirmer, 1971) and in the massacres of American Indians. Elsewhere in the world, one recalls the Nazis' "final solution" for European Jews, the massacres and deportations of Armenians by Turks, the liquidation of the kulaks and the great purges in the Soviet Union, and more recently the massacres in Indonesia and Bangladesh, in Biafra and Burundi, in South Africa and Mozambique, in Cambodia and Afghanistan, in Syria and Lebanon. Sanctioned massacres may vary on a number of dimensions. For present purposes, however, we want to focus on features they share. Two of these are the *context* and the *target* of the violence.

Sanctioned massacres tend to occur in the context of an overall policy that is explicitly or implicitly genocidal: designed to destroy all or part of a category of people defined in ethnic, national, racial, religious, or other terms. Such a policy may be deliberately aimed at the systematic extermination of a population group as an end in itself, as was the case with the Holocaust during World War II. In the Nazis' "final solution" for European Jewry, a policy aimed at exterminating millions of people was consciously articulated and executed (see Levinson, 1973), and the extermination was accomplished on a mass-production basis through the literal establishment of a well-organized, efficient death industry. Alternatively, such a policy may be aimed at an objective other than extermination—such as the pacification of the rural population of South Vietnam, as was the case in U.S. policy for Indochina—but may include the deliberate decimation of large segments of a population as an acceptable means to that end.

We agree with Bedau's (1974) conclusion from his carefully reasoned argument that the charge of U.S. genocide in Vietnam has not been definitively proven, since such a charge requires evidence of a specific genocidal *intent*. Although the evidence suggests that the United States committed war crimes and crimes against humanity in Indochina (see Sheehan, 1971; Browning and Forman, 1972), it does not show that extermination was the conscious purpose of U.S. policy. The evidence reviewed by Bedau, however, suggests that the United States did commit genocidal acts in Vietnam as a means to other ends. Central to U.S. strategy in South Vietnam were such actions as unrestricted air and artillery bombardments of peasant hamlets, search-and-destroy missions by ground troops, crop destruction programs, and mass deportation of rural populations. These actions (and similar ones in Laos and Cambodia) were clearly and deliberately aimed at civilians and resulted in the death, injury, and/or uprooting of large numbers of that population and in the destruction of their countryside, their source of livelihood, and their social structure. These consequences were anticipated by policymakers and indeed were intended as part of their pacification effort; the actions were designed to clear the countryside and deprive guerrillas of their base of operations, even if this meant destroying the civilian population. Massacres of the kind that occurred at My Lai were not deliberately planned, but they took place in an atmosphere in which the rural Vietnamese population was viewed as expendable and actions that resulted in the killing of large numbers of that population as strategic necessities.

A second feature of sanctioned massacres is that their targets have not themselves threatened or engaged in hostile actions toward the perpetrators of the violence. The victims of this class of violence are often defenseless civilians, including old men, women, and children. By all accounts, at least after the first moments at My Lai, the victims there fit this description, although in guerrilla warfare there always remains some ambiguity about the distinction between armed soldiers and unarmed civilians. * * *

There are, of course, historical and situational reasons particular groups become victims of sanctioned massacres, but these do not include their own immediate harmfulness or violence toward the attackers. Rather, their selection as targets for massacre at a particular time can ultimately be traced to their relationship to the pursuit of larger policies. Their elimination may be seen as a useful tool† of their continued existence as an irritating obstacle in the execution of policy.

* * *

In searching for a psychological explanation for mass violence under these conditions, one's first inclination is to look for forces that might impel people toward such murderous acts. Can we identify, in massacre situations, psychological forces so powerful that they outweigh the moral restraints that would normally inhibit unjustifiable violence?

The most obvious approach—searching for psychological dispositions within those who perpetrate these acts—does not yield a satisfactory explanation of the phenomenon, although it may tell us something about the types of individuals most readily recruited for participation. For example, any explanation involving the attackers' strong sadistic impulses is inadequate. There is no evidence that the majority of those who participate in such killings are sadistically inclined. Indeed, speaking of the participants in the Nazi slaughters, Arendt (1964) points out that they "were not sadists or killers by nature; on the contrary,

---

†Committing violence against innocents as a tool to achieve political goals is the hallmark of terrorism. [*Editor's note*]

a systematic effort was made to weed out all those who derived physical pleasure from what they did" (p. 105). To be sure, some of the commanders and
guards of concentration camps could clearly be described as sadists, but
what has to be explained is the existence of concentration camps in which
these individuals could give play to their sadistic fantasies. These opportunities were provided with the participation of large numbers of individuals to
whom the label of sadist could not be applied.

A more sophisticated type of dispositional approach seeks to identify certain characterological themes that are dominant within a given culture. An
early example of such an approach is Fromm's (1941) analysis of the appeals of
Nazism in terms of the prevalence of sadomasochistic strivings, particularly
among the German lower middle class. It would be important to explore whether
similar kinds of characterological dispositions can be identified in the very wide
range of cultural contexts in which sanctioned massacres have occurred. However general such dispositions turn out to be, it seems most likely that they
represent states of readiness to participate in sanctioned massacres when the
opportunity arises rather than major motivating forces in their own right. Similarly, high levels of frustration within a population are probably facilitators
rather than instigators of sanctioned massacres. * * *

Could participation in sanctioned massacres be traced to an inordinately
intense hatred toward those against whom the violence is directed? The evidence does not seem to support such an interpretation. Indications are that
many of the active participants in the extermination of European Jews, such
as Adolf Eichmann (Arendt, 1964), did not feel any passionate hatred of Jews.
There is certainly no reason to believe that those who planned and executed
American policy in Vietnam felt a profound hatred of the Vietnamese population, although deeply rooted racist attitudes may conceivably have played a role.

To be sure, hatred and rage *play a part* in sanctioned massacres. Typically
there is a long history of profound hatred against the groups targeted for
violence—the Jews in Christian Europe, the Chinese in Southeast Asia, the
Ibos in northern Nigeria—which helps establish them as suitable victims. Hostility also plays an important part at the point at which the killings are actually perpetrated, even if the official planning and the bureaucratic preparations
that ultimately lead up to this point are carried out in a passionless and busi-
nesslike atmosphere. For example, Lifton's (1973) descriptions of My Lai, based
on eyewitness reports, suggest that the killings were accompanied by generalized rage and by expressions of anger and revenge toward the victims. Hostility toward the target, however, does not seem to be the *instigator* of these
violent actions. The expressions of anger in the situation itself can more properly be viewed as outcomes rather than causes of the violence. They serve to
provide the perpetrators with an explanation and rationalization for their violent actions and appropriate labels for their emotional state. They also help
reinforce, maintain, and intensify the violence, but the anger is not the primary
source of the violence. Hostility toward the target, historically rooted or

situationally induced, contributes heavily toward the violence, but it does so largely by dehumanizing the victims rather than by motivating violence against them in the first place.

In sum, the occurrence of sanctioned massacres cannot be adequately explained by the existence of psychological forces—whether these be characterological dispositions to engage in murderous violence or profound hostility against the target—so powerful that they must find expression in violent acts unhampered by moral restraints. Instead, the major instigators for this class of violence derive from the policy process. The question that really calls for psychological analysis is why so many people are willing to formulate, participate in, and condone policies that call for the mass killings of defenseless civilians. Thus it is more instructive to look not at the motives for violence but at the conditions under which the usual moral inhibitions against violence become weakened. Three social processes that tend to create such conditions can be identified: authorization, routinization, and dehumanization. Through authorization, the situation becomes so defined that the individual is absolved of the responsibility to make personal moral choices. Through routinization, the action becomes so organized that there is no opportunity for raising moral questions. Through dehumanization, the actors' attitudes toward the target and toward themselves become so structured that it is neither necessary nor possible for them to view the relationship in moral terms.

## AUTHORIZATION

Sanctioned massacres by definition occur in the context of an authority situation, a situation in which, at least for many of the participants, the moral principles that generally govern human relationships do not apply. Thus, when acts of violence are explicitly ordered, implicitly encouraged, tacitly approved, or at least permitted by legitimate authorities, people's readiness to commit or condone them is enhanced. That such acts are authorized seems to carry automatic justification for them. Behaviorally, authorization obviates the necessity of making judgments or choices. Not only do normal moral principles become inoperative, but—particularly when the actions are explicitly ordered—a different kind of morality linked to the duty to obey superior orders, tends to take over.

In an authority situation, individuals characteristically feel obligated to obey the orders of the authorities, whether or not these correspond with their personal preferences. They see themselves as having no choice as long as they accept the legitimacy of the orders and of the authorities who give them. Individuals differ considerably in the degree to which—and the conditions under which—they are prepared to challenge the legitimacy of an order on the grounds that the order itself is illegal, or that those giving it have overstepped their authority, or that it stems from a policy that violates fundamental societal values. Regardless of subtle individual differences, however, the basic structure of a situation of legitimate authority requires subordinates to respond in terms of their role obligations rather than their personal preferences; they can openly disobey only by challenging the legitimacy of the authority. Often people obey without question even though the behavior they engage in may entail great personal sacrifice or great harm to others.

An important corollary of the basic structure of the authority situation is that actors often do not see themselves as personally responsible for the consequences of their actions. Again, there are individual differences, depending on actors' capacity and readiness to evaluate the legitimacy of orders received. Insofar as they see themselves as having had no choice in their actions, however, they do not feel personally responsible for them. They were not personal agents, but merely extensions of the authority. Thus, when their actions cause harm to others, they can feel relatively free of guilt. A similar mechanism operates when a person engages in antisocial behavior that was not ordered by the authorities but was tacitly encouraged and approved by them—even if only by making it clear that such behavior will not be punished. In this situation, behavior that was formerly illegitimate is legitimized by the authorities' acquiescence.

In the My Lai massacre, it is likely that the structure of the authority situation contributed to the massive violence in both ways—that is, by conveying the message that acts of violence against Vietnamese villagers were *required*, as well as the message that such acts, even if not ordered, were *permitted* by the authorities in charge. The actions at My Lai represented, at least in some respects, responses to explicit or implicit orders. Lieutenant Calley indicated, by orders and by example, that he wanted large numbers of villagers killed. Whether Calley himself had been ordered by his superiors to "waste" the whole area, as he claimed, remains a matter of controversy. Even if we assume, however, that he was not explicitly ordered to wipe out the village, he had reason to believe that such actions were expected by his superior officers. Indeed, the very nature of the war conveyed this expectation. The principal measure of military success was the "body count"—the number of enemy soldiers killed—and any Vietnamese killed by the U.S. military was commonly defined as a "Viet Cong." Thus, it was not totally bizarre for Calley to believe that what he was doing at My Lai was to increase his body count, as any good officer was expected to do.

Even to the extent that the actions at My Lai occurred spontaneously, without reference to superior orders, those committing them had reason to assume that such actions might be tacitly approved of by the military authorities. Not only had they failed to punish such acts in most cases, but the very strategies and tactics that the authorities consistently devised were based on the proposition that the civilian population of South Vietnam—whether "hostile" or "friendly"—was expendable. Such policies as search-and-destroy missions, the establishment of free-shooting zones, the use of antipersonnel weapons, the bombing of entire villages if they were suspected of harboring guerrillas, the forced migration of masses of the rural population, and the defoliation of vast forest areas helped legitimize acts of massive violence of the kind occurring at My Lai.

Some of the actions at My Lai suggest an orientation to authority based on unquestioning obedience to superior orders, no matter how destructive the actions these orders call for. Such obedience is specifically fostered in the course of military training and reinforced by the structure of the military authority situation. It also reflects, however, an ideological orientation that may be more widespread in the general population. * * *

## ROUTINIZATION

Authorization processes create a situation in which people become involved in an action without considering its implications and without really making a decision. Once they have taken the initial step, they are in a new psychological and social situation in which the pressures to continue are powerful. As Lewin (1947) has pointed out, many forces that might originally have kept people out of a situation reverse direction once they have made a commitment (once they have gone through the "gate region") and now serve to keep them in the situation. For example, concern about the criminal nature of an action, which might originally have inhibited a person from becoming involved, may now lead to deeper involvement in efforts to justify the action and to avoid negative consequences.

Despite these forces, however, given the nature of the actions involved in sanctioned massacres, one might still expect moral scruples to intervene; but the likelihood of moral resistance is greatly reduced by transforming the action into routine, mechanical, highly programmed operations. Routinization fulfills two functions. First, it reduces the necessity of making decisions, thus minimizing the occasions in which moral questions may arise. Second, it makes it easier to avoid the implications of the action, since the actor focuses on the details of the job rather than on its meaning. The latter effect is more readily achieved among those who participate in sanctioned massacres from a distance—from their desks or even from the cockpits of their bombers.

Routinization operates both at the level of the individual actor and at the organizational level. Individual job performance is broken down into a series of discrete steps, most of them carried out in automatic, regularized fashion. It becomes easy to forget the nature of the product that emerges from this process. When Lieutenant Calley said of My Lai that it was "no great deal," he probably implied that it was all in a day's work. Organizationally, the task is divided among different offices, each of which has responsibility for a small portion of it. This arrangement diffuses responsibility and limits the amount and scope of decision making that is necessary. There is no expectation that the moral implications will be considered at any of these points, nor is there any opportunity to do so. The organizational processes also help further legitimize the actions of each participant. By proceeding in routine fashion—processing papers, exchanging memos, diligently carrying out their assigned tasks—the different units mutually reinforce each other in the view that what is going on must be perfectly normal, correct, and legitimate. The shared illusion that they are engaged in a legitimate enterprise helps the participants assimilate their activities to other purposes, such as the efficiency of their performance, the productivity of their unit, or the cohesiveness of their group (see Janis, 1972).

Normalization of atrocities is more difficult to the extent that there are constant reminders of the true meaning of the enterprise. Bureaucratic inventiveness in the use of language helps to cover up such meaning. For example, the SS had a set of *Sprachregelungen*, or "language rules," to govern descriptions of their extermination program. As Arendt (1964) points out, the term *language rule* in itself was "a code name; it meant what in ordinary language would be called a lie" (p. 85). The code names for killing and liquidation were "final solution," "evacuation," and "special treatment." The war in Indochina produced its own set of euphemisms, such as "protective reaction," "pacification," and "forced-draft urbanization and modernization." The use of euphemisms allows participants in sanctioned massacres to differentiate their actions from ordinary killing and destruction and thus to avoid confronting their true meaning.

## DEHUMANIZATION

Authorization processes override standard moral considerations; routinization processes reduce the likelihood that such considerations will arise. Still, the inhibitions against murdering one's fellow human beings are generally so strong that the victims must also be stripped of their human status if they are to be subjected to systematic killing. Insofar as they are dehumanized, the usual principles of morality no longer apply to them.

Sanctioned massacres become possible to the extent that the victims are deprived in the perpetrators' eyes of the two qualities essential to being perceived as fully human and included in the moral compact that governs human relationships: *identity*—standing as independent, distinctive individuals, capable of making choices and entitled to live their own lives—and *community*—fellow membership in an interconnected network of individuals who care for each other and respect each other's individuality and rights (Kelman, 1973; see also Bakan, 1966, for a related distinction between "agency" and "communion"). Thus, when a group of people is defined entirely in terms of a category to which they belong, and when this category is excluded from the human family, moral restraints against killing them are more readily overcome.

Dehumanization of the enemy is a common phenomenon in any war situation. Sanctioned massacres, however, presuppose a more extreme degree of dehumanization, insofar as the killing is not in direct response to the target's threats or provocations. It is not what they have done that marks such victims for death but who they are—the category to which they happen to belong. They are the victims of policies that regard their systematic destruction as a desirable end or an acceptable means. Such extreme dehumanization becomes possible when the target group can readily be identified as a separate category of people who have historically been stigmatized and excluded by the victimizers; often the victims belong to a distinct racial, religious, ethnic, or political group regarded as inferior or sinister. The traditions, the habits, the images, and the vocabularies for dehumanizing such groups are already well established and can be drawn upon when the groups are selected for massacre. Labels help deprive the victims of identity and community, as in the epithet "gooks" that was commonly used to refer to Vietnamese and other Indochinese peoples.

The dynamics of the massacre process itself further increase the participants' tendency to dehumanize their victims. Those who participate as part of the bureaucratic apparatus increasingly come to see their victims as bodies to be counted and entered into their reports, as faceless figures that will determine their productivity rates and promotions. Those who participate in the massacre directly—in the field, as it were—are reinforced in their perception of the victims as less than human by observing their very victimization. The only way they can justify what is being done to these people—both by others and by themselves—and the only way they can extract some degree of meaning out of the absurd events in which they find themselves participating (see Lifton, 1971, 1973) is by coming to believe that the victims are subhuman and deserve to be rooted out. And thus the process of dehumanization feeds on itself.

\* \* \*

## REFERENCES

Arendt, H. (1964). *Eichmann in Jerusalem: A report on the banality of evil.* New York: Viking Press.

Bakan, D. (1966). *The duality of human existence.* Chicago: Rand McNally.

Bedau, H. A. (1974). Genocide in Vietnam? The line between legal argument and moral judgment. In *Philosophy, morality, and international affairs.* Ed. Virginia Held, Sidney Morgenbesser, and Thomas Nagel. New York: Oxford University Press.

Browning, F., & Forman, D. (Eds.). (1972). *The wasted nations: Report of the International Commission of Enquiry into United States Crimes in Indochina, June 20–25, 1971.* New York: Harper & Row.

FitzGerald, F. (1972). *Fire in the lake: The Vietnamese and the Americans in Vietnam.* Boston: Atlantic-Little, Brown.

Fromm, E. (1941). *Escape from freedom.* New York: Rinehart.

Goldstein, J.; Marshall, B.; & Schwartz, J. (Eds.). (1976). *The My Lai massacre and its cover-up: Beyond the reach of law?* (The Peers report with a supplement and introductory essay on the limits of law.) New York: Free Press.

Hammer, R. (1970). *One morning in the war.* New York: Coward-McCann.

_____. (1971). *The court-martial of Lt. Calley.* New York: Coward, McCann, & Geoghegan.

Hersh, S. (1970). *My Lai 4: A report on the massacre and its aftermath.* New York: Vintage Books.

Janis, I. L. (1972). *Victims of groupthink: A psychological study of foreign-policy decisions and fiascoes.* Boston: Houghton Mifflin.

Kelman, H. C. (1958). Compliance, identification, and internalization: Three processes of attitude change. *Journal of Conflict Resolution,* 2, 51–60.

_____. (1972). The rights of the subject in social research: An analysis in terms of relative power and legitimacy. *American Psychologist,* 27, 989–1016.

_____. (1973). Violence without moral restraint: Reflections on the dehumanization of victims and victimizers. *Journal of Social Issues,* 29(4), 25–61.

Levinson, S. (1973). Responsibility for crimes of war. *Philosophy and Public Affairs,* 2, 244–273.

Lewin, K. (1947). Frontiers in group dynamics: Concept, method and reality in social science, social equilibria and social change. *Human Relations,* 1(1), 5–41.

Lifton, R. J. (1971). Existential evil. In N. Sanford, C. Comstock, & Associates, *Sanctions for evil: Sources of social destructiveness.* San Francisco: Jossey-Bass.

_____. (1973). *Home from the war—Vietnam veterans: Neither victims nor executioners.* New York: Simon & Schuster.

Paige, J. (1975). *Agrarian revolution: Social movements and export agriculture in the underdeveloped world.* New York: Free Press.

Popkin, S. L. (1979). *The rational peasant: The political economy of rural society in Vietnam.* Berkeley: University of California Press.

Schell, J. (1968). *The military half.* New York: Vintage Books.

Schirmer, D. B. (1971, April 24). My Lai was not the first time. *New Republic,* pp. 18–21.

Sheehan, N. (1971, March 28). Should we have war crime trials? *The New York Times Book Review,* pp. 1–3, 30–34.

Williams, B. (1985, April 14–15). "I will never forgive," says My Lai survivor. *Jordan Times* (Amman), p. 4.

Wolf, E. (1969). *Peasant wars of the twentieth century.* New York: Harper & Row.

# 6

## Telling the Truth about Damned Lies and Statistics

### JOEL BEST

*Many people feel they live in a world of information overload. Statistics are a big part of this feeling, continually thrown about to impress, sell, or convince. In many cases the statistics are not accurate, leading to distrust of all statistics. But as Joel Best explains, we need good statistics, and he shows why. Part of the "sociological imagination" is the capacity to think critically about information, including statistics, in order to answer questions and solve problems. As you read this essay, think of the last time you heard someone misuse a statistic. Better yet, think of the last time you did.*

The dissertation prospectus began by quoting a statistic—a "grabber" meant to capture the reader's attention. The graduate student who wrote this prospectus undoubtedly wanted to seem scholarly to the professors who would read it; they would be supervising the proposed research. And what could be more scholarly than a nice, authoritative statistic, quoted from a professional journal in the student's field?

So the prospectus began with this (carefully footnoted) quotation: "Every year since 1950, the number of American children gunned down has doubled." I had been invited to serve on the student's dissertation committee. When I read the quotation, I assumed the student had made an error in copying it. I went to the library and looked up the article the student had cited. There, in the journal's 1995 volume, was exactly the same sentence: "Every year since 1950, the number of American children gunned down has doubled."

This quotation is my nomination for a dubious distinction: I think it may be the worst—that is, the most inaccurate—social statistic ever.

What makes this statistic so bad? Just for the sake of argument, let's assume that "the number of American children gunned down" in 1950 was one. If the number doubled each year, there must have been two children gunned down in 1951, four in 1952, eight in 1953, and so on. By 1960, the number would have been 1,024. By 1965, it would have been 32,768 (in 1965, the F.B.I. identified only 9,960 criminal homicides in the entire country, including adult as well as child victims). By 1970, the number would have passed one million; by 1980, one billion (more than four times the total U.S. population in that year). Only three years later, in 1983, the number of American children gunned down would have been 8.6 billion (nearly twice the earth's population at the time). Another milestone would have been passed in 1987, when the number of gunned-down American children (137 billion) would have surpassed the best estimates for the total human population throughout history (110 billion). By 1995, when the article was published, the annual number of victims would have been over 35 trillion—a really big number, of a magnitude you rarely encounter outside economics or astronomy.

Thus my nomination: estimating the number of American child gunshot victims in 1995 at 35 trillion must be as far off—as hilariously, wildly wrong—as a social statistic can be. (If anyone spots a more inaccurate social statistic, I'd love to hear about it.)

Where did the article's author get this statistic? I wrote the author, who responded that the statistic came from the Children's Defense Fund, a well-known advocacy group for children. The C.D.F.'s *The State of America's Children Yearbook 1994* does state: "The number of American children killed each year by guns has doubled since 1950." Note the difference in the wording—the C.D.F. claimed there were twice as many deaths in 1994 as in 1950; the article's author reworded that claim and created a very different meaning.

It is worth examining the history of this statistic. It began with the C.D.F. noting that child gunshot deaths had doubled from 1950 to 1994. This is not quite as dramatic an increase as it might seem. Remember that the U.S. population also rose throughout this period; in fact, it grew about 73 percent—or nearly double. Therefore, we might expect all sorts of things—including the number of child gunshot deaths—to increase, to nearly double, just because the population grew. Before we can decide whether twice as many deaths indicates that things are getting worse, we'd have to know more. The C.D.F. statistic raises other issues as well: Where did the statistic come from? Who counts child gunshot deaths, and how? What is meant by a "child" (some C.D.F. statistics about violence include everyone under age 25)? What is meant by "killed by guns" (gunshot-death statistics often include suicides and accidents, as well as homicides)? But people rarely ask questions of this sort when they encounter statistics. Most of the time, most people simply accept statistics without question.

Certainly, the article's author didn't ask many probing, critical questions about the C.D.F.'s claim. Impressed by the statistic, the author repeated it—well, meant to repeat it. Instead, by rewording the C.D.F.'s claim, the author created a mutant statistic, one garbled almost beyond recognition.

But people treat mutant statistics just as they do other statistics—that is, they usually accept even the most implausible claims without question. For example, the journal editor who accepted the author's article for publication did not bother to consider the implications of child victims doubling each year. And people repeat bad statistics: The graduate student copied the garbled statistic and inserted it into the dissertation prospectus. Who knows whether still other readers were impressed by the author's statistic and remembered it or repeated it? The article remains on the shelf in hundreds of libraries, available to anyone who needs a dramatic quote. The lesson should be clear: Bad statistics live on; they take on lives of their own.

Some statistics are born bad—they aren't much good from the start, because they are based on nothing more than guesses or dubious data. Other statistics mutate; they become bad after being mangled (as in the case of the author's creative rewording). Either way, bad statistics are potentially important: They can be used to stir up public outrage or fear; they can distort our understanding of our world; and they can lead us to make poor policy choices.

The notion that we need to watch out for bad statistics isn't new. We've all heard people say, "You can prove anything with statistics." The title of my book, *Damned Lies and Statistics*, comes from a famous aphorism (usually attributed to Mark Twain or Benjamin Disraeli): "There are three kinds of lies: lies, damned lies, and statistics." There is even a useful little book, still in print after more than 40 years, called *How to Lie With Statistics.*

Statistics, then, have a bad reputation. We suspect that statistics may be wrong, that people who use statistics may be "lying"—trying to manipulate us by using numbers to somehow distort the truth. Yet, at the same time, we need statistics; we depend upon them to summarize and clarify the nature of our complex society. This is particularly true when we talk about social problems. Debates about social problems routinely raise questions that demand statistical answers: Is the problem widespread? How many people—and which people—does it affect? Is it getting worse? What does it cost society? What will it cost to deal with it? Convincing answers to such questions demand evidence, and that usually means numbers, measurements, statistics.

But can't you prove anything with statistics? It depends on what "prove" means. If we want to know, say, how many children are "gunned down" each year, we can't simply guess—pluck a number from thin air: 100, 1,000, 10,000, 35 trillion, whatever. Obviously, there's no reason to consider an arbitrary guess "proof" of anything. However, it might be possible for someone—using records kept by police departments or hospital emergency rooms or coroners—to keep track of children who have been shot; compiling careful, complete records might give us a fairly accurate idea of the number of gunned-down children. If that number seems accurate enough, we might consider it very strong evidence—or proof.

The solution to the problem of bad statistics is not to ignore all statistics, or to assume that every number is false. Some statistics are bad, but others are pretty good, and we need statistics—good statistics—to talk sensibly about social problems. The solution, then, is not to give up on statistics, but to become better judges of the numbers we encounter. We need to think critically about statistics—at least critically enough to suspect that the number of children gunned down hasn't been doubling each year since 1950.

A few years ago, the mathematician John Allen Paulos wrote *Innumeracy,* a short, readable book about "mathematical illiteracy." Too few people, he argued, are comfortable with basic mathematical principles, and this makes them poor judges of the numbers they encounter. No doubt this is one reason we have so many bad statistics. But there are other reasons, as well.

Social statistics describe society, but they are also products of our social arrangements. The people who bring social statistics to our attention have reasons for doing so; they inevitably want something, just as reporters and the other media figures who repeat and publicize statistics have their own goals. Statistics are tools, used for particular purposes. Thinking critically about statistics requires understanding their place in society.

While we may be more suspicious of statistics presented by people with whom we disagree—people who favor different political parties or have different beliefs—bad statistics are used to promote all sorts of causes. Bad statistics come from conservatives on the political right and liberals on the left, from wealthy corporations and powerful government agencies, and from advocates of the poor and the powerless.

In order to interpret statistics, we need more than a checklist of common errors. We need a general approach, an orientation, a mind-set that we can use to think about new statistics that we encounter. We ought to approach statistics thoughtfully. This can be hard to do, precisely because so many people in our society treat statistics as fetishes. We might call this the mind-set of the Awestruck—the people who don't think critically, who act as though statistics have magical powers. The awestruck know they don't always understand the statistics they hear, but this doesn't bother them. After all, who can expect to understand magical numbers? The reverential fatalism of the awestruck is not thoughtful—it is a way of avoiding thought. We need a different approach.

One choice is to approach statistics critically. Being critical does not mean being negative or hostile—it is not cynicism. The critical approach statistics thoughtfully; they avoid the extremes of both naive acceptance and cynical rejection of the numbers they encounter. Instead, the critical attempt to evaluate numbers, to distinguish between good statistics and bad statistics.

The critical understand that, while some social statistics may be pretty good, they are never perfect. Every statistic is a way of summarizing complex information into relatively simple numbers. Inevitably, some information, some of the complexity, is lost whenever we use statistics. The critical recognize that this is an inevitable limitation of statistics. Moreover, they realize that every statistic is the product of choices—the choice between defining a category broadly or narrowly, the choice of one measurement over another, the choice of a sample. People choose definitions, measurements, and samples for all sorts of reasons: Perhaps they want to emphasize some aspect of a problem; perhaps it is easier or cheaper to gather data in a particular way—many considerations can come into play. Every statistic is a compromise among choices. This means that every definition—and every measurement and every sample— probably has limitations and can be criticized.

Being critical means more than simply pointing to the flaws in a statistic. Again, every statistic has flaws. The issue is whether a particular statistic's flaws are severe enough to damage its usefulness. * * * Similarly, how do the choices of measurements and samples affect the statistic? What would happen if different measures or samples were chosen? And how is the statistic used? Is it being interpreted appropriately, or has its meaning been mangled to create a mutant statistic? Are the comparisons that are being made appropriate, or are apples being confused with oranges? How do different choices produce the conflicting numbers found in stat wars? These are the sorts of questions the critical ask.

As a practical matter, it is virtually impossible for citizens in contemporary society to avoid statistics about social problems. Statistics arise in all sorts of ways, and in almost every case the people promoting statistics want to persuade us. Activists use statistics to convince us that social problems are serious and deserve our attention and concern. Charities use statistics to encourage donations. Politicians use statistics to persuade us that they understand society's problems and that they deserve our support. The media use statistics to make their reporting more dramatic, more convincing, more compelling. Corporations use statistics to promote and improve their products. Researchers use statistics to document their findings and support their conclusions. Those with whom we agree use statistics to reassure us that we're on the right side, while our opponents use statistics to try and convince us that we are wrong. Statistics are one of the standard types of evidence used by people in our society.

It is not possible simply to ignore statistics, to pretend they don't exist. That sort of head-in-the-sand approach would be too costly. Without statistics, we limit our ability to think thoughtfully about our society; without statistics, we have no accurate ways of judging how big a problem may be, whether it is getting worse, or how well the policies designed to address that problem actually work. And awestruck or naive attitudes toward statistics are no better than ignoring statistics; statistics have no magical properties, and it is foolish to assume that all statistics are equally valid. Nor is a cynical approach the answer; statistics are too widespread and too useful to be automatically discounted.

It would be nice to have a checklist, a set of items we could consider in evaluating any statistic. The list might detail potential problems with definitions, measurements, sampling, mutation, and so on. These are, in fact, common sorts of flaws found in many statistics, but they should not be considered a formal, complete checklist. It is probably impossible to produce a complete list of statistical flaws—no matter how long the list, there will be other possible problems that could affect statistics.

The goal is not to memorize a list, but to develop a thoughtful approach. Becoming critical about statistics requires being prepared to ask questions about numbers. When encountering a new statistic in, say, a news report, the critical try to assess it. What might be the sources for this number? How could one go about producing the figure? Who produced the number, and what interests might they have? What are the different ways key terms might have been defined, and which definitions have been chosen? How might the phenomena be measured, and which measurement choices have been made? What sort of sample was gathered, and how might that sample affect the result? Is the statistic being properly interpreted? Are comparisons being made, and if so, are the comparisons appropriate? Are there competing statistics? If so, what stakes do the opponents have in the issue, and how are those stakes likely to affect their use of statistics? And is it possible to figure out why the statistics seem to disagree, what the differences are in the ways the competing sides are using figures?

At first, this list of questions may seem overwhelming. How can an ordinary person—someone who reads a statistic in a magazine article or hears it on a news broadcast—determine the answers to such questions? Certainly news reports rarely give detailed information on the process by which statistics are created. And few of us have time to drop everything and investigate the background of some new number we encounter. Being critical, it seems, involves an impossible amount of work.

In practice, however, the critical need not investigate the origin of every statistic. Rather, being critical means appreciating the inevitable limitations that affect all statistics, rather than being awestruck in the presence of numbers. It means not being too credulous, not accepting every statistic at face value. But it also means appreciating that statistics, while always imperfect, can be useful. Instead of automatically discounting every statistic, the critical reserve judgment. When confronted with an interesting number, they may try to learn more, to evaluate, to weigh the figure's strengths and weaknesses.

Of course, this critical approach need not—and should not—be limited to statistics. It ought to apply to all the evidence we encounter when we scan a news report, or listen to a speech—whenever we learn about social problems. Claims about social problems often feature dramatic, compelling examples; the critical might ask whether an example is likely to be a typical case or an extreme, exceptional instance. Claims about social problems often include quotations from different sources, and the critical might wonder why those sources have spoken and why they have been quoted: Do they have particular expertise? Do they stand to benefit if they influence others? Claims about social problems usually involve arguments about the problem's causes and potential solutions. The critical might ask whether these arguments are convincing. Are they logical? Does the proposed solution seem feasible and appropriate? And so on. Being critical—adopting a skeptical, analytical stance when confronted with claims—is an approach that goes far beyond simply dealing with statistics.

Statistics are not magical. Nor are they always true—or always false. Nor need they be incomprehensible. Adopting a critical approach offers an effective way of responding to the numbers we are sure to encounter. Being critical requires more thought, but failing to adopt a critical mind-set makes us powerless to evaluate what others tell us. When we fail to think critically, the statistics we hear might just as well be magical.

# 7

## Public Sociologies: Contradictions, Dilemmas, and Possibilities*

### MICHAEL BURAWOY

*Since the middle of the nineteenth century, social scientists have been asking about the influence of their work on society. Should it contribute to social order and stability? Should it address problems and seek to devise solutions? Or should it promote social change that could lead to a new and more progressive form of society? One view of science is that the best research is guided by idle curiosity, while another argues that necessity and crisis spur the greatest discoveries. Some scholars embrace their work with personal passion, while others believe scientific objectivity is compromised by too much emotional investment. Sociology is not immune to these debates. This article, a version of the presidential address to the American Sociological Association, again raises the question the great sociologist Howard Becker asked years ago, "Whose side are you on?"*

In 2003 the members of the American Sociological Association (ASA) were asked to vote on a member resolution opposing the war in Iraq. The resolution included the following justification: "[F]oreign interventions that do not have the support of the world community create more problems than solutions . . . Instead of lessening the risk of terrorist attacks, this invasion could serve as the spark for multiple attacks in years to come." It passed by a two-thirds majority (with 22% of voting members abstaining) and became the association's official position. In an opinion poll on the same ballot, 75% of the members who expressed an opinion were opposed to the war. To assess the ethos of sociologists today, it is worthwhile comparing these results with those of 1968 when a similar double item was presented to the membership with respect to the Vietnam war. Then two-thirds of the votes cast *opposed* the ASA adopting a resolution against the war and only 54% were individually opposed to the war (Rhoades 1981:60).

It is complicated to interpret this apparent shift in political orientation, given the different national and military contexts within which the voting took place, given the different wording of the questions. Still two hypotheses present themselves. First, the membership of the ASA, always leaning toward the liberal

*"Public Sociologies: Contradiction, Dilemmas, and Possibilities," by Michael Burawoy. From *Social Forces*, Vol. 82, No. 4, pp. 1603–1618. Copyright © 2004 by the University of North Carolina Press. Used by permission of Oxford University Press.

end of the political spectrum, has moved much further to the left. In 1968 the opinion of sociologists was close to the rest of the population (54% of sociologists opposed the war as compared to between 46% and 54% of the general public), whereas in 2003 the two distributions were the inverse of each other—75% of voting sociologists opposed the war at the end of April, 2003, while at the same time 75% of the public supported the war. One might conjecture that in 1968 a very different generation dominated the profession—a postwar generation celebratory of the U.S. and its "victory over fascism," among them pioneers of professional sociology. Today's post-Vietnam generations are more accustomed to criticizing the U.S. government and in particular its foreign policy. They are also less concerned about the purity of sociology as science and more likely to assume that our accumulated knowledge should be put to public use, whether in the form of member resolutions or policy interventions.

Second, the world itself is different. In 1968 the world seemed ripe for change for the better. The civil rights movements, the women's movement, student movements around the world, antiwar marches and sit-ins captured the imagination of a new generation of sociologists who saw conventional sociology as lagging behind the most progressive movements; whereas today the world is lagging behind sociology, unapologetic about its drift into political and economic fundamentalism. Sociologists shift their critical eye ever more away from sociology toward the world it describes, a shift reflected in the insurgent interest in public sociology. In short, over the last 35 years there has been a scissors movement. The political context and the sociological conscience have moved in opposite directions, so that the world we inhabit is increasingly in conflict with the ethos and principles that animate sociologists—an ethos opposed to inequality, to the erosion of civil liberties, to the destruction of public life, and to discrimination and exclusion.

This shift in sociological ethos is not uncontroversial. It has, indeed, generated its own opposition. Dissatisfied with the political winds, 102 ASA members signed a petition, sent to the association's Committee on Professional Ethics, charging that the anti-Iraq-war resolution violated the ASA's code of conduct. Why? Because it did not rely on "scientifically and professionally derived knowledge." The complaint did not get far because, unlike other professional associations, there are no clear rules that limit the types of resolutions the ASA can endorse. Nonetheless, the 102 (and presumably many others) did take a principled position: scientific sociologists have no business making moral or political pronouncements. Taking a moral or political position is incompatible with scientific objectivity. Opposition to the resolution also took a more pragmatic form, fears that such a visible and public stance against the war (and I have not found another association to have taken such a stance) would undermine what legitimacy we have as sociologists, conceivably threaten research funding, and even prompt political reprisals. Alas, this is not so far fetched. * * *

The "pure science" position that research must be completely insulated from politics is untenable since antipolitics is no less political than *public engagement*. The more usual "abstentionist" position limits politics to *professional self-defense*: that we should enter the political arena only to defend our immediate professional interests. Thus, we might mobilize resources to oppose the defunding of research into sexual behavior (as was attempted in Congress recently), or to protest the closure or dramatic cuts in a sociology department (as in Germany today), or to protect the human rights of an individual (e.g., Egyptian sociologist, Saad Eddin Ibrahim), or, most recently, to defend a journal's right to review and edit articles from "enemy" countries. In all these instances we enter the political arena, but solely to defend the integrity of our professional activities.

Between professional self-defense and public engagement there is a compromise position that moves from the defense of professional interests to *policy interventions*. Here the association takes a political position on the basis of an accumulated body of evidence whose validity is widely accepted and whose interpretation is unambiguous. One such example is the ASA's recent statement that summarized the sociological literature on race: race exists, it has social causes, and it has social consequences. An extension of this was the ASA's Amicus Curiae brief to the Supreme Court in the 2003 Michigan Law School affirmative action case, *Grutter* v. *Bollinger*. Again a body of sociological research was mobilized to show that racial discrimination exists and that efforts to diversify the student body would improve the educational experience of all.

So far, then, we have three possible political stances: "professional self-defense," "policy intervention" and "public engagement." There is, however, a fourth stance. The association is a political venue unto itself—a place to debate the stances we might adopt. We cannot advocate democracy for others if we are not internally democratic, if we do not attempt to arrive at public stances through maximal participation in collective deliberation. It is just such a critical debate that we are involved in today. The resolution against the Iraq War is but a dramatic instance of the broader issue we are discussing: what should be our involvement in the world beyond the academy? Recognizing we are part of the world we study, we must take some *stance* with respect to that world. To fail to do so is to take a stance by default.

We can problematize our place in society by asking two questions. The first was posed by Alfred McClung Lee in his 1976 Presidential Address to the American Sociological Association: "Knowledge for Whom?" As sociologists are we just talking to ourselves? Are we to remain locked up in the antechambers of society, never really entering its tumultuous currents, hiding behind the barricades of professional insularity? Or can we, ever cautious, ever vigilant, wade forth into society, armed with our sociological expertise? If we are going to talk to others, which others and how shall we do it? This leads directly to the second question, famously posed by Robert Lynd (1939): Knowledge for What? Do we take the values and goals of our research for granted, handed down to us by some external (funding or policy) agency? Should we only concentrate on providing solutions to predefined problems, focusing on the means to achieve predetermined ends, on what Weber called technical rationality and what I call *instrumental knowledge*? In other words, should we repress the question of ends and pretend that knowledge and laws spring spontaneously from the data, if only we can develop the right methods? Or should we be concerned explicitly with the goals for which our research may be mobilized, and with the values that underpin and guide our research? Going further afield, should sociologists be in the business of stimulating public discussions about the possible meanings of the "good society"? Like Weber, I believe that without value commitments there can be no sociology, no basis for the questions that guide our research programs. Without values social science is blind. * * * Thus, empirical science can only take us so far: it can help us understand the consequences of our value commitments and inform our value discussions, but it cannot determine those values. Determining values should take place through democratic and collective deliberation.

* * * Professional and policy sociology are forms of instrumental knowledge focusing respectively on academic and extra-academic audiences. Critical and public sociology are forms of reflexive knowledge focusing respectively on academic and extra-academic audiences. Let me consider each in turn.

*Public sociology* engages publics beyond the academy in dialogue about matters of political and moral concern. It has to be relevant to such publics without being faddish, that is subservient to publics. * * *

* * *

Public sociology should be distinguished from *policy sociology*. While public sociology generates conversation or debate between sociologist and public on a terrain of reciprocal engagement, policy sociology focuses on solutions to specific problems defined by clients. The relation between sociologist and client is often of a contractual character in which expertise is sold for a fee. The sociologist, thereby, cedes independence to the client. All manner of organizations may contract sociological expertise, from business to state, from multilateral organization to the small NGO [nongovernmental organization]. What makes the relation instrumental is that the research terrain is not defined by the sociologist. It is defined narrowly in the case of a "client" or broadly in the case of a "patron."

* * *

Public and policy sociologies could not exist without *professional sociology*, which provides legitimacy, expertise, distinctive problem definitions, relevant bodies of knowledge, and techniques for analyzing data. An effective public or policy sociology is not hostile to, but depends upon the professional sociology that lies at the core of our disciplinary field. Why do I call our disciplinary knowledge instrumental? As professional sociologists we are located in research traditions, sometimes going back to founding fathers (Weber, Durkheim, and

Marx) and otherwise of a more recent pedigree (feminism, poststructuralism). These research traditions may be elaborated into self-conscious research programs—structural functionalism, stratification theory, sex-gender systems, experimental social psychology—with their grounding assumptions, distinctive questions, exemplary models and appropriate techniques of research. Research programs (Lakatos 1978) advance by resolving internal contradictions and absorbing anomalies (discrepancies between theoretical expectation and empirical observations). They require a community of scientists committed to working on the important (collectively defined) *puzzles* that the research program generates. Flourishing public and policy sociologies increase the stakes of our knowledge and thus makes the vigilant pursuit of coherent research programs all the more important.

In the world of normal science we cannot push forward the frontiers of knowledge and at the same time question its foundations. The latter task is the province of *critical sociology*. In much the same way that public sociology interrogates the value assumptions of policy sociology, so in a similar and more direct way critical sociology is the conscience of professional sociology.

\* \* \*

As sociology grew, its institutional base differentiated, so that today sociologists work both inside and outside academia. Those outside tend to occupy positions in government agencies, such as the census bureau or the department of corrections; in consulting companies for human resource management; or in international NGOs. Then, there are sociologists who are employed in professional schools—business schools, public administration, educational schools, agricultural extension, and so forth—where they may engage nonacademic audiences. Equally important is the complex hierarchy of the university system which ranges from elite private universities, to the different tiers of state university systems, liberal arts colleges, and two-year community colleges. The configuration of the division of sociological labor will vary with a department's location in this system. Thus, in state colleges where teaching takes up so much of one's time, research has a public or policy dimension, often driven by local issues. Based on my attendance at the meetings of state associations, such as the North Carolina Sociological Association, I have found public sociology to be both more widely practiced and more highly valued in state colleges than in most elite departments. I have found projects ranging from research on displaced workers, toxic waste, housing inequalities, and educational reform, to advocacy for public health campaigns around HIV-AIDS or needle exchange to training community organizers to deal with the media. Sadly, all too often, this public (and policy) sociology, widespread though it may be, remains invisible and unrecognized because its practitioners lack the time or incentive to write it up.

History and hierarchy give one sense of the possible variation in the configuration of the disciplinary field, international comparisons give another. When one travels the world talking about public sociology, one quickly learns just how distinctively American the concept is, marking the unique strength of professional sociology in the U.S. In many countries it is taken for granted that sociology has a public face. Why else be a sociologist? The career of sociology in many Third World countries reflects the succession of different political regimes. One of the first acts of the Pinochet regime in Chile was to abolish sociology. In South Africa sociology flourished in the late 1970s and 1980s as the anti-apartheid movement grew in strength, just as it has suffered amalgamation and budgetary cuts in the postapartheid period. Soviet sociology, nonexistent under Stalinism, reappeared in the 1950s as an ideological and surveillance arm of the party state. Sociological opinion research was deployed as a weapon of critique, revealing public discontent in order to justify swings in policy. This instrumental use of sociology comes home to roost in the post-Soviet period where, increasingly, it has become a form of market research. If it is not co-opted or repressed by authoritarian regimes, sociology's reflexive side may sustain critical opposition, as was often the case in Eastern Europe. In the social democratic countries of Scandinavia, by contrast, it is the policy dimension that often stands out. Although when conservative parties assume power, the sociological winds shift direction from policy to public.

Here then are just a few hints at national variation, underlining once again just how peculiar is U.S. sociology. It is not just peculiar, it is also very powerful, dominating the world scene. Accordingly in the international division of sociological labor, professional sociology is concentrated in the resource rich United States, and to a lesser extent in Western Europe, while public sociology has relatively greater strength in the poorer countries—a distribution that mirrors the hierarchy within the U.S.

\* \* \*

Finally, we come to the critical question: what are the grounds for claiming sociology's affinity to the public? If political science's distinctive object of study is the state and its value the protection of political order, and if economics has as it distinctive object the economy and its value is the expansion of the market, then sociology's distinctive object is civil society and its value is the resilience and autonomy of the social. Sociology is born with civil society and dies with civil society. The classical sociology of Weber, Durkheim, Simmel, and Pareto arose with the expansion of trade unions, political parties, mass education, voluntary associations at the end of the nineteenth century, just as U.S. sociology was born amidst reform and religious organizations. Sociology disappears with the eclipse of civil society as in fascism, Stalinism or Pinochet's Chile, just as it quickly bubbles to the surface with the unfurling of perestroika in the Soviet Union or the civic and labor associations of South Africa's anti-apartheid movement.

\* \* \*

The burgeoning interest in public sociology and the unanticipated vote against the war in Iraq suggest to me that the stakes are indeed becoming clearer. In a world tending toward market tyranny and state unilateralism, civil society is at once threatened with extinction and at the same time a major possible hold-out against deepening inequalities and multiplying threats to all manner of human rights. The interest of sociology in the very existence, let alone expansion, of civil society (even with all its warts) becomes the interest of humanity—locally, nationally and globally. If we can transcend our parochialism and recognize our distinctive relation to diverse publics within and across borders, sociologists could yet create the fulcrum around which a critical social science might evolve, one responsive to public issues while at the same time committed to professional excellence.

## REFERENCES

Lakatos, Imre. 1978. *The Methodology of Scientific Research Programmes.* Cambridge University Press.

Lee, Alfred McClung. 1976. "Sociology for Whom?" *American Sociological Review* 44: 925–36.

Lynd, Robert. 1939. *Knowledge for What? The Place of Social Sciences in American Culture.* Princeton University Press.

Rhoades, Lawrence. 1981. *A History of the American Sociological Association, 1905–1980.* American Sociological Association, Washington D.C.

# 8

## Racism and Research: The Case of the Tuskegee Syphilis Study

### ALLAN M. BRANDT

*Was it scientific zeal and the search for medical knowledge? Or was it a callous disregard for the lives and suffering of persons thought to be inferior in a racist society? Probably both, and the lessons remain important for everyone. This tragic study has become a classic example of how to do unethical research. Perhaps the lessons to be learned from it can somehow begin to make amends for the harm it did.*

In 1932 the U.S. Public Health Service (USPHS) initiated an experiment in Macon County, Alabama, to determine the natural course of untreated, latent syphilis in black males. The test comprised 400 syphilitic men, as well as 200 uninfected men who served as controls. The first published report of the study appeared in 1936 with subsequent papers issued every four to six years, through the 1960s. When penicillin became widely available by the early 1950s as the preferred treatment for syphilis, the men did not receive therapy. In fact on several occasions, the USPHS actually sought to prevent treatment. Moreover, a committee at the federally operated Center for Disease Control decided in 1969 that the study should be continued. Only in 1972, when accounts of the study first appeared in the national press, did the Department of Health, Education, and Welfare halt the experiment. At that time seventy-four of the test subjects were still alive; at least twenty-eight, but perhaps more than 100, had died directly from advanced syphilitic lesions. In August 1972, HEW appointed an investigatory panel, which issued a report the following year. The panel found the study to have been "ethically unjustified," and argued that penicillin should have been provided to the men.

This article attempts to place the Tuskegee Study in a historical context and to assess its ethical implications. Despite the media attention which the study received, the HEW *Final Report*, and the criticism expressed by several professional organizations, the experiment has been largely misunderstood. The most basic questions of *how* the study was undertaken in the first place and *why* it continued for forty years were never addressed by the HEW investigation. Moreover, the panel misconstrued the nature of the experiment, failing to consult important documents available at the National Archives which bear significantly on its ethical assessment. Only by examining the specific ways in which values are engaged in scientific research can the study be understood.

## RACISM AND MEDICAL OPINION

A brief review of the prevailing scientific thought regarding race and heredity in the early twentieth century is fundamental for an understanding of the Tuskegee Study. By the turn of the century, Darwinism had provided a new rationale for American racism. Essentially primitive peoples, it was argued, could not be assimilated into a complex, white civilization. Scientists speculated that in the struggle for survival the Negro in America was doomed. Particularly prone to disease, vice, and crime, black Americans could not be helped by education or philanthropy. Social Darwinists analyzed census data to predict the virtual extinction of the Negro in the twentieth century, for they believed the Negro race in America was in the throes of a degenerative evolutionary process.

The medical profession supported these findings of late nineteenth- and early twentieth-century anthropologists, ethnologists, and biologists. Physicians studying the effects of emancipation on health concluded almost universally that freedom had caused the mental, moral, and physical deterioration of the black population. They substantiated this argument by citing examples in the comparative anatomy of the black and white races. As Dr. W. T. English wrote: "A careful inspection reveals the body of the negro a mass of minor defects and imperfections from the crown of the head to the soles of the feet. . . ." Cranial structures, wide nasal apertures, receding chins, projecting jaws, all typed the Negro as the lowest species in the Darwinian hierarchy.

Interest in racial differences centered on the sexual nature of blacks. The Negro, doctors explained, possessed an excessive sexual desire, which threatened the very foundations of white society. As one physician noted in the *Journal of the American Medical Association*, "The negro springs from a southern race, and as such his sexual appetite is strong; all of his environments stimulate this appetite, and as a general rule his emotional type of religion certainly does not decrease it." Doctors reported a complete lack of morality on the part of blacks:

> Virtue in the negro race is like angels' visits—few and far between. In a practice of sixteen years I have never examined a virgin negro over fourteen years of age.

A particularly ominous feature of this overzealous sexuality, doctors argued, was the black males' desire for white women. "A perversion from which most races are exempt," wrote Dr. English, "prompts the negro's inclination towards white women, whereas other races incline towards females of their own." Though English estimated the "gray matter of the negro brain" to be at least a thousand years behind that of the white races, his genital organs were overdeveloped. As Dr. William Lee Howard noted:

> The attacks on defenseless white women are evidences of racial instincts that are about as amenable to ethical culture as is the inherent odor of the race. . . .

> When education will reduce the size of the negro's penis as well as bring about
> the sensitiveness of the terminal fibers which exist in the Caucasian, then will it
> also be able to prevent the African's birth-right to sexual madness and excess.

One southern medical journal proposed "Castration Instead of Lynching," as retribution for black sexual crimes. "An impressive trial by a ghost-like kuk-lux klan [sic] and a 'ghost' physician or surgeon to perform the operation would make it an event the 'patient' would never forget," noted the editorial.

According to these physicians, lust and immorality, unstable families, and reversion to barbaric tendencies made blacks especially prone to venereal diseases. One doctor estimated that over 50 percent of all Negroes over the age of twenty-five were syphilitic. Virtually free of disease as slaves, they were now overwhelmed by it, according to informed medical opinion. Moreover, doctors believed that treatment for venereal disease among blacks was impossible, particularly because in its latent stage the symptoms of syphilis become quiescent. As Dr. Thomas W. Murrell wrote:

> They come for treatment at the beginning and at the end. When there are visi-
> ble manifestations or when harried by pain, they readily come, for as a race they
> are not averse to physic; but tell them not, though they look well and feel well,
> that they are still diseased. Here ignorance rates science a fool . . .

Even the best-educated black, according to Murrell, could not be convinced to seek treatment for syphilis. Venereal disease, according to some doctors, threatened the future of the race. The medical profession attributed the low birth rate among blacks to the high prevalence of venereal disease, which caused stillbirths and miscarriages. Moreover, the high rates of syphilis were thought to lead to increased insanity and crime. One doctor writing at the turn of the century estimated that the number of insane Negroes had increased thirteen-fold since the end of the Civil War. Dr. Murrell's conclusion echoed the most informed anthropological and ethnological data:

> So the scourge sweeps among them. Those that are treated are only half cured,
> and the effort to assimilate a complex civilization driving their diseased minds
> until the results are criminal records. Perhaps here, in conjunction with tuber-
> culosis, will be the end of the negro problem. Disease will accomplish what man
> cannot do.

This particular configuration of ideas formed the core of medical opinion concerning blacks, sex, and disease in the early twentieth century. Doctors generally discounted socioeconomic explanations of the state of black health, arguing that better medical care could not alter the evolutionary scheme. These assumptions provide the backdrop for examining the Tuskegee Syphilis Study.

## THE ORIGINS OF THE EXPERIMENT

In 1929, under a grant from the Julius Rosenwald Fund, the USPHS conducted studies in the rural South to determine the prevalence of syphilis among blacks and explore possibilities for mass treatment. The USPHS found Macon County, Alabama, in which the town of Tuskegee is located, to have the highest syphilis rate of the six counties surveyed. The Rosenwald Study concluded that mass treatment could be successfully implemented among rural blacks. Although it is doubtful that the necessary funds would have been allocated even in the best economic conditions, after the economy collapsed in 1929, the findings were ignored. It is, however, ironic that the Tuskegee Study came to be based on findings of the Rosenwald Study that demonstrated the possibilities of mass treatment.

Three years later, in 1932, Dr. Taliaferro Clark, Chief of the USPHS Venereal Disease Division and author of the Rosenwald Study report, decided that conditions in Macon County merited renewed attention. Clark believed the high prevalence of syphilis offered an "unusual opportunity" for observation. From its inception, the USPHS regarded the Tuskegee Study as a classic "study in nature,"[1] rather than an experiment. As long as syphilis was so prevalent in Macon and most of the blacks went untreated throughout life, it seemed only natural to Clark that it would be valuable to observe the consequences. He described it as a "ready-made situation." Surgeon General H. S. Cumming wrote to R. R. Moton, Director of the Tuskegee Institute:

> The recent syphilis control demonstration carried out in Macon County, with the financial assistance of the Julius Rosenwald Fund, revealed the presence of an unusually high rate in this county and, what is more remarkable, the fact that 99 percent of this group was entirely without previous treatment. This combination, together with the expected cooperation of your hospital, offers an unparalleled opportunity for carrying on this piece of scientific research which probably cannot be duplicated anywhere else in the world.

Although no formal protocol appears to have been written, several letters of Clark and Cumming suggest what the USPHS hoped to find. Clark indicated that it would be important to see how disease affected the daily lives of the men:

---

1. In 1865, Claude Bernard, the famous French physiologist, outlined the distinction between a "study in nature" and experimentation. A study in nature required simple observation, an essentially passive act, while experimentation demanded intervention which altered the original condition. The Tuskegee Study was thus clearly not a study in nature. The very act of diagnosis altered the original conditions. "It is on this very possibility of acting or not acting on a body," wrote Bernard, "that the distinction will exclusively rest between sciences called sciences of observation and sciences called experimental."

The results of these studies of case records suggest the desirability of making a further study of the effect of untreated syphilis on the human economy among people now living and engaged in their daily pursuits.

It also seems that the USPHS believed the experiment might demonstrate that antisyphilitic treatment was unnecessary. As Cumming noted: "It is expected the results of this study may have a marked bearing on the treatment, or conversely the non-necessity of treatment, of cases of latent syphilis. . . ."

## SELECTING THE SUBJECTS

Clark sent Dr. Raymond Vonderlehr to Tuskegee in September 1932 to assemble a sample of men with latent syphilis for the experiment. The basic design of the study called for the selection of syphilitic black males between the ages of twenty-five and sixty, a thorough physical examination including x-rays, and finally, a spinal tap to determine the incidence of neuro-syphilis. They had no intention of providing any treatment for the infected men. The USPHS originally scheduled the whole experiment to last six months; it seemed to be both a simple and inexpensive project.

The task of collecting the sample, however, proved to be more difficult than the USPHS had supposed. Vonderlehr canvassed the largely illiterate, poverty-stricken population of sharecroppers and tenant farmers in search of test subjects. If his circulars requested only men over twenty-five to attend his clinics, none would appear, suspecting he was conducting draft physicals. Therefore, he was forced to test large numbers of women and men who did not fit the experiments specifications. This involved considerable expense since the USPHS had promised the Macon County Board of Health that it would treat those who were infected, but not included in the study. Clark wrote to Vonderlehr about the situation: "It never once occured to me that we would be called upon to treat a large part of the county as return for the privilege of making this study. . . . I am anxious to keep the expenditures for treatment down to the lowest possible point because it is the one item of expenditure in connection with the study most difficult to defend despite our knowledge of the need therefor." Vonderlehr responded: "If we could find from 100 to 200 cases . . . we would not have to do another Wassermann on useless individuals. . . ."

Significantly, the attempt to develop the sample contradicted the prediction the USPHS had made initially regarding the prevalence of the disease in Macon County. Overall rates of syphilis fell well below expectations; as opposed to the USPHS projection of 35 percent, 20 percent of those tested were actually diseased. Moreover, those who had sought and received previous treatment far exceeded the expectations of the USPHS. Clark noted in a letter to Vonderlehr:

> I find your report of March 6th quite interesting but regret the necessity for Wassermanning [sic] . . . such a large number of individuals in order to uncover this relatively limited number of untreated cases.

Further difficulties arose in enlisting the subjects to participate in the experiment, to be "Wassermanned," and to return for a subsequent series of examinations. Vonderlehr found that only the offer of treatment elicited the cooperation of the men. They were told they were ill and were promised free care. Offered therapy, they became willing subjects. The USPHS did not tell the men that they were participants in an experiment; on the contrary, the subjects believed they were being treated for "bad blood"—the rural South's colloquialism for syphilis. They thought they were participating in a public health demonstration similar to the one that had been conducted by the Julius Rosenwald Fund in Tuskegee several years earlier. In the end, the men were so eager for medical care that the number of defaulters in the experiment proved to be insignificant.

To preserve the subjects' interest, Vonderlehr gave most of the men mercurial ointment, a noneffective drug, while some of the younger men apparently received inadequate dosages of neoarsphenamine. This required Vonderlehr to write frequently to Clark requesting supplies. He feared the experiment would fail if the men were not offered treatment.

\* \* \*

The readiness of the test subjects to participate of course contradicted the notion that blacks would not seek or continue therapy.

The final procedure of the experiment was to be a spinal tap to test for evidence of neuro-syphilis. The USPHS presented this purely diagnostic exam, which often entails considerable pain and complications, to the men as a "special treatment." Clark explained to Moore:

> We have not yet commenced the spinal punctures. This operation will be deferred to the last in order not to unduly disturb our field work by any adverse reports by the patients subjected to spinal puncture because of some disagreeable sensations following this procedure. These negroes are very ignorant and easily influenced by things that would be of minor significance in a more intelligent group.

The letter to the subjects announcing the spinal tap read:

> Some time ago you were given a thorough examination and since that time we hope you have gotten a great deal of treatment for bad blood. You will now be given your last chance to get a second examination. This examination is a very special one and after it is finished you will be given a special treatment if it is believed you are in a condition to stand it. . . .
> Remember This Is Your Last Chance For Special Free Treatment. Be Sure to Meet The Nurse.

The HEW investigation did not uncover this crucial fact: the men participated in the study under the guise of treatment.

Despite the fact that their assumption regarding prevalence and black attitudes toward treatment had proved wrong, the USPHS decided in the summer of 1933 to continue the study. Once again, it seemed only "natural" to pursue
the research since the sample already existed, and with a depressed economy,
the cost of treatment appeared prohibitive—although there is no indication it
was ever considered. Vonderlehr first suggested extending the study in letters
to Clark and Wenger:

> At the end of this project we shall have a considerable number of cases present-
> ing various complications of syphilis, who have received only mercury and may
> still be considered untreated in the modern sense of therapy. Should these cases
> be followed over a period of from five to ten years many interesting facts could
> be learned regarding the course and complications of untreated syphilis.

"As I see it," responded Wenger, "we have no further interest in these
patients *until they die.*" Apparently, the physicians engaged in the experiment
believed that only autopsies could scientifically confirm the findings of the
study.

Bringing the men to autopsy required the USPHS to devise a further series
of deceptions and inducements. Wenger warned Vonderlehr that the men must
not realize that they would be autopsied:

> There is one danger in the latter plan and that is if the colored population become
> aware that accepting free hospital care means a postmortem; every darkey will
> leave Macon County and it will hurt [Dr. Eugene] Dibble's hospital.

The USPHS offered several inducements to maintain contact and to pro-
cure the continued cooperation of the men. Eunice Rivers, a black nurse, was
hired to follow their health and to secure approval for autopsies. She gave the
men non-effective medicines—"spring tonic" and aspirin—as well as transportation and hot meals on the days of their examinations. More important, Nurse
Rivers provided continuity to the project over the entire forty-year period. By
supplying "medicinals," the USPHS was able to continue to deceive the participants, who believed that they were receiving therapy from the government
doctors. Deceit was integral to the study. When the test subjects complained
about spinal taps one doctor wrote:

> They simply do not like spinal punctures. A few of those who were tapped are
> enthusiastic over the results but to most, the suggestion causes violent shaking
> of the head; others claim they were robbed of their procreative powers (regard-
> less of the fact that I claim it stimulates them).

Letters to the subjects announcing an impending USPHS visit to Tuskegee
explained: "[The doctor] wants to make a special examination to find out how

you have been feeling and whether the treatment has improved your health." In fact, after the first six months of the study, the USPHS had furnished no treatment whatsoever.

Finally, because it proved difficult to persuade the men to come to the hospital when they became severely ill, the USPHS promised to cover their burial expenses. The Milbank Memorial Fund provided approximately $50 per man for this purpose beginning in 1935. This was a particularly strong inducement as funeral rites constituted an important component of the cultural life of rural blacks. One report of the study concluded. "Without this suasion it would, we believe, have been impossible to secure the cooperation of the group and their families."

Reports of the study's findings, which appeared regularly in the medical press beginning in 1936, consistently cited the ravages of untreated syphilis. The first paper, read at the 1936 American Medical Association annual meeting, found "that syphilis in this period [latency] tends to greatly increase the frequency of manifestations of cardiovascular disease." Only 16 percent of the subjects gave no sign of morbidity as opposed to 61 percent of the controls. Ten years later, a report noted coldly, "The fact that nearly twice as large a proportion of the syphilitic individuals as of the control group has died is a very striking one." Life expectancy, concluded the doctors, is reduced by about 20 percent.

A 1955 article found that slightly more than 30 percent of the test group autopsied had died *directly* from advanced syphilitic lesions of either the cardiovascular or the central nervous system. Another published account stated, "Review of those still living reveals that an appreciable number have late complications of syphilis which probably will result, for some at least, in contributing materially to the ultimate cause of death." In 1950, Dr. Wenger had concluded, "We now know, where we could only surmise before, that we have contributed to their ailments and shortened their lives." As black physician Vernal Cave, a member of the HEW panel, later wrote, "They proved a point, then proved a point, then proved a point."

During the forty years of the experiment the USPHS had sought on several occasions to ensure that the subjects did not receive treatment from other sources. To this end, Vonderlehr met with groups of local black doctors in 1934, to ask their cooperation in not treating the men. Lists of subjects were distributed to Macon County physicians along with letters requesting them to refer these men back to the USPHS if they sought care. The USPHS warned the Alabama Health Department not to treat the test subjects when they took a mobile VD unit into Tuskegee in the early 1940s. In 1941, the Army drafted several subjects and told them to begin antisyphilitic treatment immediately. The USPHS supplied the draft board with a list of 256 names they desired to have excluded from treatment, and the board complied.

In spite of these efforts, by the early 1950s many of the men had secured some treatment on their own. By 1952, almost 30 percent of the test subjects had received some penicillin, although only 7.5 percent had received what could be considered adequate doses. Vonderlehr wrote to one of the participating physicians, "I hope that the availability of antibiotics has not interfered too much with this project." A report published in 1955 considered whether the treatment that some of the men had obtained had "defeated" the study. The article attempted to explain the relatively low exposure to penicillin in an age of antibiotics, suggesting as a reason: "the stoicism of these men as a group; they still regard hospitals and medicines with suspicion and prefer an occasional dose of time-honored herbs or tonics to modern drugs." The authors failed to note that the men believed they already were under the care of the government doctors and thus saw no need to seek treatment elsewhere. Any treatment which the men might have received, concluded the report, had been insufficient to compromise the experiment.

When the USPHS evaluated the status of the study in the 1960s they continued to rationalize the racial aspects of the experiment. For example, the minutes of a 1965 meeting at the Center for Disease Control recorded:

> Racial issue was mentioned briefly. Will not affect the study. Any questions can be handled by saying these people were at the point that therapy would no longer help them. They are getting better medical care than they would under any other circumstances.

A group of physicians met again at the CDC in 1969 to decide whether or not to terminate the study. Although one doctor argued that the study should be stopped and the men treated, the consensus was to continue. Dr. J. Lawton Smith remarked, "You will never have another study like this; take advantage of it." A memo prepared by Dr. James B. Lucas, Assistant Chief of the Venereal Disease Branch, stated: "Nothing learned will prevent, find, or cure a single case of infectious syphilis or bring us closer to our basic mission of controlling veneral disease in the United States." He concluded, however, that the study should be continued "along its present lines." When the first accounts of the experiment appeared in the national press in July 1972, data were still being collected and autopsies performed.

## THE NEW FINAL REPORT

HEW finally formed the Tuskegee Syphilis Study Ad Hoc Advisory Panel on August 28, 1972, in response to criticism that the press descriptions of the experiment had triggered. The panel, composed of nine members, five of them black, concentrated on two issues. First, was the study justified in 1932 and had the men given their informed consent? Second, should penicillin have been provided when it became available in the early 1950s? The panel was also charged with determining if the study should be terminated and assessing current policies regarding experimentation with human subjects. The group issued their report in June 1973.

By focusing on the issues of penicillin therapy and informed consent, the *Final Report* and the investigation betrayed a basic misunderstanding of the experiment's purposes and design. The HEW report implied that the failure to provide penicillin constituted the study's major ethical misjudgment; implicit was the assumption that no adequate therapy existed prior to penicillin. Nonetheless medical authorities firmly believed in the efficacy of arsenotherapy for treating syphilis at the time of the experiment's inception in 1932. The panel further failed to recognize that the entire study had been predicated on nontreatment. Provision of effective medication would have violated the rationale of the experiment—to study the natural course of the disease until death. On several occasions, in fact, the USPHS had prevented the men from receiving proper treatment. Indeed, there is no evidence that the USPHS ever considered providing penicillin.

The other focus of the *Final Report*—informed consent—also served to obscure the historical facts of the experiment. In light of the deceptions and exploitations which the experiment perpetrated, it is an understatement to declare, as the *Report* did, that the experiment was "ethically unjustified," because it failed to obtain informed consent from the subjects. The *Final Report's* statement, "Submitting voluntarily is not informed consent," indicated that the panel believed that the men had volunteered *for the experiment.* The records in the National Archives make clear that the men did not submit voluntarily to an experiment; they were told and they believed that they were getting free treatment from expert government doctors for a serious disease. The failure of the HEW *Final Report* to expose this critical fact—that the USPHS lied to the subjects—calls into question the thoroughness and credibility of their investigation.

Failure to place the study in a historical context also made it impossible for the investigation to deal with the essentially racist nature of the experiment. The panel treated the study as an aberration, well-intentioned but misguided. Moreover, concern that the *Final Report* might be viewed as a critique of human experimentation in general seems to have severely limited the scope of the inquiry. The *Final Report* is quick to remind the reader on two occasions: "The position of the Panel must not be construed to be a general repudiation of scientific research with human subjects." The *Report* assures us that a better-designed experiment could have been justified:

> It is possible that a scientific study in 1932 of untreated syphilis, properly conceived with a clear protocol and conducted with suitable subjects who fully understood the implications of their involvement, might have been justified in the pre-penicillin era. This is especially true when one considers the uncertain nature of the results of treatment of late latent syphilis and the highly toxic nature of therapeutic agents then available.

This statement is questionable in view of the proven dangers of untreated syphilis known in 1932.

Since the publication of the HEW *Final Report*, a defense of the Tuskegee Study has emerged. These arguments, most clearly articulated by Dr. R. H. Kampmeier in the *Southern Medical Journal*, center on the limited knowledge of effective therapy for latent syphilis when the experiment began. Kampmeier argues that by 1950, penicillin would have been of no value for these men. Others have suggested that the men were fortunate to have been spared the highly toxic treatments of the earlier period. Moreover, even these contemporary defenses assume that the men never would have been treated anyway. As Dr. Charles Barnett of Stanford University wrote in 1974, "The lack of treatment was not contrived by the USPHS but was an established fact of which they proposed to take advantage." Several doctors who participated in the study continued to justify the experiment. Dr. J. R. Heller, who on one occasion had referred to the test subjects as the "Ethiopian population," told reporters in 1972:

> I don't see why they should be shocked or horrified. There was no racial side to this. It just happened to be in a black community. I feel this was a perfectly straightforward study, perfectly ethical, with controls. Part of our mission as physicians is to find out what happens to individuals with disease and without disease.

These apologies, as well as the HEW *Final Report*, ignore many of the essential ethical issues which the study poses. The Tuskegee Study reveals the persistence of beliefs within the medical profession about the nature of blacks, sex, and disease—beliefs that had tragic repercussions long after their alleged "scientific" bases were known to be incorrect. Most strikingly, the entire health of a community was jeopardized by leaving a communicable disease untreated. There can be little doubt that the Tuskegee researchers regarded their subjects as less than human. As a result, the ethical canons of experimenting on human subjects were completely disregarded.

The study also raises significant questions about professional self-regulation and scientific bureaucracy. Once the USPHS decided to extend the experiment in the summer of 1933, it was unlikely that the test would be halted short of the men's deaths. The experiment was widely reported for forty years without evoking any significant protest within the medical community. Nor did any bureaucratic mechanism exist within the government for the periodic reassessment of the Tuskegee experiment's ethics and scientific value. The USPHS sent physicians to Tuskegee every several years to check on the study's progress, but never subjected the morality or usefulness of the experiment to serious scrutiny. Only the press accounts of 1972 finally punctured the continued rationalizations of the USPHS and brought the study to an end. Even the HEW investigation was compromised by fear that it would be considered a threat to future human experimentation.

In retrospect the Tuskegee Study revealed more about the pathology of racism than it did about the pathology of syphilis; more about the nature of scientific inquiry than the nature of the disease process. The injustice committed by the experiment went well beyond the facts outlined in the press and the HEW *Final Report.* The degree of deception and damages have been seriously underestimated. As this history of the study suggests, the notion that science is a value-free discipline must be rejected. The need for greater vigilance in assessing the specific ways in which social values and attitudes affect professional behavior is clearly indicated.*

---

*In the summer of 2010 Susan Reverby, history professor at Wellesley College, revealed that from 1946 to 1948 doctors from the United States deliberately infected Guatemalans with venereal diseases, ostensibly to study the use of penicillin as a preventative as well as a curative for syphilis. Dr. John C. Cutler, involved in the Tuskegee experiments, led the experiment in Guatemala. It is unclear if the Guatemalan subjects were effectively treated once they were infected with venereal diseases. See Donald G. McNeil's article, "U.S. Infected Guatemalans with Syphilis in '40s," *New York Times,* October 1, 2010, page A1 and A6. [*Editor's note*]

# 9

## One Thousand and Forty-Nine Reasons Why It's Hard to Know When a Fact Is a Fact*

FROM *Families as They Really Are*

### ANDREW J. CHERLIN

*In a world filled with noisy voices insisting that we see the world their way, encouraging us to shut our eyes to facts that challenge our comfort zone, critical thinking is more important than ever. No one has a monopoly on the truth, including sociologists. But the sociological perspective insists on going beyond everyone's taken-for-granted understanding, to ask: Whose facts? and What are you not telling me?*

When is a fact a fact? If you are a postmodernist, the answer is clear: never. Postmodern critics of standard social science argue that the conclusions we draw are not, and cannot be, genuinely objective. Rather, they say, our findings are contaminated in several ways. First, the questions we ask and the point of view we take often reflect our values, whether those are an enthusiasm for feminist or civil rights-inspired activism or a belief in the importance of marriage and premarital chastity. Even the categories and labels we use often reflect values-based assumptions.

Here is an example from my field, family demography: In 1941, Paul Glick, the Bureau of the Census demographer who virtually created the field, wrote a pioneering article entitled "Types of Families: An Analysis of Census Data." Glick divided American families into three groups: (1) normal families, a category that consisted of all two-parent families; (2) other male-headed families; and (3) other female-headed families. The implication, of course, was that all single-parent families were abnormal.

Or consider contemporary debates over immigration, which may be shaped by whether one uses the term "illegal alien" or "undocumented immigrant." The first conjures up an image of a law-breaking invader from outer space; the second conveys an image of a striving newcomer who merely lacks the right papers.

Recognizing that most researchers draw upon particular values when they choose what categories to use and what questions to ask does not mean that all data are suspect or that all interpretations of data are equally valid. But it does drive home the importance of treating so-called facts critically and of questioning their origins and purposes. When we read facts, we should ask ourselves a few key questions: Who produced this fact? Was it a person or an

---

*References and footnotes can be found in the original article, pages 10–14 of *Families as They Really Are*. [*Editor's note*]

organization that promotes a particular point of view? What was the purpose of making this fact known? What do we know about the relationship of this fact to other facts or trends?

Consider familyfacts.org, a website operated by the Heritage Foundation. It publicizes findings from social scientific research on family life. On its home page (www.familyfacts.org), familyfacts.org presents itself as a neutral clearing-house for family research: "The Heritage Foundation's familyfacts.org catalogs social science findings on the family, society and religion gleaned from peer-reviewed journals, books and government surveys. Serving policymakers, journalists, scholars and the general public, familyfacts.org makes social science research easily accessible to the non-specialist."

In 2008, this site featured a "top ten" list of findings about how children in different kinds of families fare in school. According to each finding, children living with two parents were doing better than children living with one parent or with stepparents. Here are two of the findings: "Kindergartners in intact families have higher average reading scores than peers in stepfamilies or cohabiting families" and "First-graders whose mothers were married when they were born are less likely to engage in disruptive behavior with peers and teachers than those whose mothers were single or cohabiting." In fact, virtually all of the thousands of findings on the site support the view that marriage is best for children and that religion improves family outcomes.

These findings are not falsified. They are taken from reputable studies published in well-regarded journals such as the *Journal of Marriage and Family* and, by and large, are described accurately. A naive user might think that this is all social scientists know. But the facts reported on this site have been selected to support a particular conclusion, while facts that modify, complicate, or challenge that conclusion are not reported.

For example, the site quotes a 1998 article that I co-wrote about a study showing that children whose parents had divorced had a higher risk of emotional problems in adulthood. Yet that same article also showed that some of the emotional problems had been visible in childhood before the parents even divorced, but this additional finding was not mentioned. Nor does the site mention a 1991 article that I co-wrote that also suggested that some of the problems experienced by children from divorced families might have occurred even had the parents stayed together. This is not a fact that familyfacts.org thinks you need to know.

Which findings are included and which are excluded make sense if one knows that the Heritage Foundation, a conservative think tank, promotes the values of institutions such as "traditional" marriage and religion. This is not to say that one should disregard the findings on familyfacts.org; in fact, much evidence does suggest that growing up with two parents is beneficial to children. But the informed reader will know that it is necessary to go elsewhere to see whether the kinds of findings that are cataloged at familyfacts.org tell the whole story.

Conservatives are not the only ones who use facts in ways that reflect their values. In the 1980s, when homelessness was first being recognized as a social problem, many news stories included the information that 2 to 3 million Americans were homeless. Soon this figure became an accepted fact. Yet it subsequently came to light that this fact had been provided by a leading advocate for the homeless, Mitch Snyder, who basically made a guess. He said in a television interview:

> Everybody demanded it. Everybody said we want a number. . . . We got on the phone, we made a lot of calls, we talked to a lot of people, and we said, "Okay, here are some numbers."

Snyder was just doing what advocates usually do: providing the largest credible estimate of how many people are affected by the problem they want to alleviate or by the disease they would like to cure or by the injustice they want to remedy. In counting the homeless, as in estimating the number of women who have been raped or who experience eating disorders, advocates often take the most expansive definition of the problem and adjust for underreporting. But such estimates are especially susceptible to manipulation for dramatic effect.

More recently, we have heard much in debates over same-sex partnerships about the 1,049 federal benefits and rights that marriage supposedly confers on husbands and wives. This number appeared in the late 1990s and was soon cited everywhere as a fact about the legal benefits of marriage. In 1999, advocates of same-sex marriage, while welcoming the Vermont legislation that created the nation's first civil unions, noted that state-level recognition of gay unions would not provide the partners with the federal benefits of marriage. Hanna Rosin reported in the *Washington Post*:

> The plaintiffs in the Vermont case documented a long list of benefits granted to married couples but denied to gay ones. The 300 state and 1,049 federal laws cover such matters as the right to pay taxes jointly, and social security benefits.

Ever since, reputable newspapers around the country and politicians on both sides of the political spectrum have accepted this claim as fact, derived from a federal study conducted by the General Accounting Office. The precision of this fact—not 1,048 or 1,050 but exactly 1,049—gave it such verisimilitude that no one challenged it. And its magnitude suggested an overwhelming bias in favor of marriage, making it an attractive "fact" that could be used by proponents of same-sex marriage, just as the people who constructed the Heritage website were attracted to only some of the "facts" reported by family researchers on divorce. But in hindsight, its precision and size are the very factors that should have suggested caution in using this fact.

The source of this "fact" was indeed a federal study, but the study did not establish what these and many other news reports have since claimed. In 1996, when Congress enacted the Defense of Marriage Act,* Represenative Henry Hyde requested that the General Accounting Office identify all federal laws that involved benefits, rights, and privileges that depend on being married. As the GAO staff discussed this request with Hyde's staff, they agreed to broaden the scope of the study to include "all those laws in the United States Code in which marital status is a factor, even though some of those laws may not directly create benefits, rights, or privileges." In other words, the GAO counted all laws that involved marriage, including those that *penalized* married couples.

One of the 1,049 laws, for example, is a statute that limits the amount of certain crop support payments that one person can receive. For this purpose, a married couple is considered to be one person. But an unmarried couple can apparently escape this restriction and each receive the maximum amount. Another law mandates that a candidate may not spend more than $50,000 of his or her own money, or the money of his or her immediate family, on a political campaign and still be eligible for federal funding; but there's nothing to prevent the candidate's unmarried partner from kicking in additional funds.

Many of the so-called benefits of marriage, furthermore, are trivial. It is true that one law discriminates against cohabiting couples by making it a federal crime to try to influence United States officials by threatening to kill their spouses, whereas it seems not to be a federal crime to threaten to kill their cohabiting partners. But this "benefit" of marriage applies to very few couples.

It did not take weeks of research in dusty government archives to get to the bottom of this; rather, I found the information on the Internet in less than an hour. That so many people had quoted the number without checking it shows how easily a "fact" can become part of the dialogue about social and political issues.

What happens to a fact of this kind is that it becomes a symbol of the issue in dispute. Clearly, marriage does provide some important federal benefits. Only married couples can file their federal tax returns jointly; and only married people can continue to receive part of their partner's Social Security benefits after the partner dies. But the figure of 1,049 benefits became a dramatic, and at first glance convincing, stand-in for the general privilege of being married in American society. It was this general privilege that really was the point of the debate. This was the reasoning of the Massachusetts Supreme Court in ruling that restricting marriage to heterosexuals was unacceptable even if same-sex partners were given the same legal status. Marriage, the judges wrote, is more than a collection of benefits; rather, it is a "status that is specially recognized in society." Denying same-sex couples that special status, the justices argued would create a "stigma of exclusion."

Debating the abstract notion of social status is, however, more difficult than debating legal benefits. Advocates therefore focused on the 1,049 benefits as a

---

*In 2013 the United States Supreme Court ruled the Defense of Marriage Act unconstitutional. [*Editor's note*]

way of building support for their more general position. Many debates over social and political issues revolve around symbols such as this one, and it is in the interest of each side to define the symbol in the largest or the smallest terms possible to bolster their case.

Whether everyone knows where the supposed facts come from, as is the case with the findings displayed on the familyfacts.org website, or whether no one seems to know, as with the apocryphal 1,049 benefits, the careful user of facts will not take them at face value. At the least, the user must examine (or uncover) the source and determine its position on the issues. Even your most trusted friends probably care about the social and political issues they discuss, which makes it difficult for them to be truly balanced in the facts they tell you about. And as a rule, no organization that takes sides in a public debate will provide facts that should be considered fully objective and balanced. To be sure, some organizations may be more transparent and balanced, and others more opaque and one-sided, in their use of facts. But even the fairest will have made choices about what questions to ask, what counts as good research, and on what basis one draws conclusions. Unless you understand where the source is coming from, it's hard to evaluate the information it provides. And that's a fact.

PART TWO

## CULTURE AND SOCIETY

# 10

## Shadows on the Wall

FROM *Channels of Desire: Mass Images and the Shaping*
*of American Consciousness*

### STUART EWEN and ELIZABETH EWEN

*Traditional societies lived in their culture the way fish live in a watery aquarium. The way of seeing and understanding the world was a given, a constant, ever present and unquestioned. Not so today. We are continually reminded that others live in cultural systems different from our own, and we draw freely from these when we eat, travel internationally, and watch foreign films. We also experience today a rapidly changing culture, so much of which is the product of large corporations seeking to configure the cultural world to advantage their interests. Much of this involves creating images of reality (e.g., the experience of eating at Applebee's or the thrill of driving a new BMW) that have become not only icons of "the good life" but configure who we are, what we do, how we relate to one another, and how we see the world. For the authors of this essay, this technology for creating culture has serious implications for democratic society.*

> *Secure the shadow ere the substance fade*
> —Advertising slogan for a photographer's studio (1840s)

The tension between the "real" world, and the ways people perceive it has been a problem that has confounded Western culture since antiquity. This question stands at the heart of Plato's often-cited "parable of the cave," which appears in *The Republic*. In the parable, Plato describes human life as if it were lived "in a sort of underground den." Inside the den, people's eyes are averted from the mouth of the cave, turned toward its innermost wall. Their perception of the world outside is perpetually indirect, limited to the shadows that play upon the wall. Though only a mediation of the actual world, to the person inside the den these shadows constitute "reality."

The inability to know the world, except through its representations, has continued to plague philosophy into the modern era. This dilemma posed a pivotal issue for Immanuel Kant in his *Critique of Pure Reason*. While Hegel, and then Marx, envisioned a future in which *concept* and *reality* would come together in the unfolding of human history, the twentieth century, once again, has witnessed the resuscitation of this persistent paradox. The spell that *the image* casts upon the human imagination has reemerged as a preoccupation of contemporary existence.

There is something about twentieth-century life that dramatizes the division between the material world and its aspect, between form and substance. In large part it stems from the exponential growth of a modern media system, a profound apparatus of representation that has come to permeate nearly all facets of life. In an increasingly global market society, the chasm between immediate experience, and mediations of a "world at large" grows greater. Life is lived deeper and deeper within the cave, while the shadows cast by the media grow more numerous, more authoritative, more alluring. It is little wonder that historians and cultural analysts have, in the past twenty-five years, zeroed in on "the problem of representation" as the cardinal issue of our time.

\* \* \*

What was it about this fantastic world, standing beyond the edges of common sense, that made it so believable? Clearly, the answer to this question is historical. It is connected to the emergence of the media of communication, and to common patterns of perception that have developed since the beginnings of the industrial revolution. It is also wedded to a market society in which worlds beyond the orbit of immediate experience were of increasing relevance to people's lives.

The media provided a powerful lens through which this broader universe might be seen and interpreted. As we have seen, the ability to communicate a persuasive rendition of reality was an early capacity of print. This capacity has been constantly enlarged by new devices for collecting, maintaining, and disseminating information. As *the word* or *the image* is reproduced, again and again, it becomes *fact*, known simultaneously by strangers, a common, if sometimes deceptive, bond. It is the lifeblood of a mobile world-system employing standardized meanings and requiring uniform understandings. *Fact!* is seen, over and over again, repeated by itself, repeated by others. When it is stored, it becomes *a history*, a common heritage. Against the random and irretrievable quality of daily life lies the tangible evidence of the printed word, of the graven image, of the fact.

\* \* \*

In the decades since the twenties, vast industries have emerged whose primary intent is the packaging of image and information for the purpose of influencing attitudes and behavior. In merchandising, in finance, in politics, in everyday life, the primacy of representation has escalated; the ability to shape perception has become the bottom line. Even in entertainment, ostensibly a respite from the workaday world, the durability of an image or an idea is inseparable from its ability to garner a "significant" market share.

Together, these developments convene to offer a detailed portrait of the world. At the same time, it must be noted, it is a portrait that is perpetually shifting. In a society where novelty and disposability make up the backbone of the market, images and ideas fall into disuse as soon as new ones enter the scene. Yet within the ephemera there is, perhaps, a logic. Our shadows on the wall are projected by the social, cultural, economic, and political currents that mark our time.

\* \* \*

## THE CULTURE OF IGNORANCE

On a hot summer day, two men convene at a newsstand and discuss the front page of the *New York Post*.

Looming above a photograph of Donald and Ivana Trump, turned away from each other, is a banner headline: "IVANA AND DONALD UNTIE THE KNOT." The announcement, with its extreme sense of moment, overwhelms the page. At the bottom of the page, a small headline reports: "Nelson Mandela is Free."

One man shrugs his shoulders and remarks to the other, "Freedom doesn't seem very important these days." "Yeah," notes the other with irony, "today we're only interested in the freedom of the rich and famous."

This is a quintessential encounter of our time. It is often said that we are living in the middle of an "information age." The media are everywhere. Computer technology permeates more and more of the fibers of life. More and more industries are involved in the traffic of information: collecting, processing, and disseminating data. Yet while pundits and futurists celebrate the information age, much of the information that circulates throughout society leaves people profoundly ignorant of their world.

To a large extent, this unawareness is a by-product of media driven by market considerations. In a world where attracting ever-larger audiences is the key to survival, the media tend to package "truth" in such away that will sell. The "age of information" is, for most of us, an age of sensationalism. It plays on emotions, placing feeling above intellect, and elicits visceral responses above rational considerations. Alongside the spectacles of choice, and of violence, the popular media present a picture of what is important by fixating on the phenomenon of celebrity. Celebrity faces dot the media landscape. \* \* \* Fatuous soap operas of private life provide more gripping drama than the complexity of consequential public issues. Amid the rhetoric of "information," the ability to think is overcome by waves of trivia and superficiality.

Nowhere is this cultural trend more disturbing than in the ways it compromises the arena of politics, the possibilities of democratic life. In his first inaugural address, delivered in 1801, Thomas Jefferson spoke of democracy as a system that depends upon an informed and intelligent citizenry, capable of evaluating and acting upon the issues before them. "The diffusion of information and the arraignment of all abuses at the bar of public reason," he intoned, "should be the creed of our political faith—the text of civil instruction." In our era, the *text of civil instruction* is the sound bite. The *bar of public reason* is the photo opportunity.

At the center of this development lies the evolution of the mass media as the prime apparatus of public address. Building on developments that unfolded from the mid-nineteenth century onward, a reciprocal relationship between politics and the mass media has marked the dynamics of power in twentieth-century American life. From the time he was Police Commissioner in New York City, Theodore Roosevelt curried an unprecedented familiarity between himself and newspaper reporters, assuring constant and favorable coverage of his activities. His distant cousin Franklin D. Roosevelt continued to cultivate the press corps, ingeniously using radio and other media to promote New Deal policies. It is part of the folklore of modern politics that without television John F. Kennedy would never have been elected president.

The 1980s, however, witnessed a sea change in the relationship between media and politics. Advertising and public relations experts, pollsters and spin doctors, political consultants and cosmeticians were now beginning to script the political process itself. With the decline of ward heelers and old-style party machines, the mass media, with television as the prime venue, were emerging as the environment in which all public politics were taking place. As the late Lee Atwater, a point man in the Reagan offense, noted, television "drives the system now." If in the era of FDR, or even of Kennedy, economists, intellectuals, and engineers constituted the requisite "brain trust," today's inner circle is made up of pollsters and image consultants.

With such advisers, political wisdom is increasingly infused with a Nielsen ratings mentality. This environment accomplishes the idea that an image *that will sell* overrides considerations of fundamental issues or long-term social objectives. Representative David Obey, Democrat from Wisconsin, describes the way in which media considerations not only affect, but shape and ultimately debilitate the political process:

> When the main question in a member's mind every time he votes is, "What kind of a thirty-second spot are they going to make out of this vote?," then truly the ability of the political system to make tough decisions in the long-range interest of the United States is atomized.

At a time when a wide range of social issues demands serious deliberation and action, the context for substantive political discussion has given way to an image-laden ratings war. This development, however, is not merely the intrinsic outcome of the media themselves. It is intimately connected to the increasing use of the media as a weapon of political power.

The rise of comprehensive strategies of image management coincided with the reemergence of the political right wing in the period following the Watergate debacle. In a society permeated by doubts regarding its political ethics, the right wing rose to power following a blueprint for the reconstruction of public imagination. Building on people's frustrations and mistrust, and drawing upon a panoply of maudlin symbols—most of which had been market-tested by Hollywood and the *Saturday Evening Post* for decades—an iconography aimed at *gut feeling* began to assemble a new political constituency. While commentators initially made light of this politics of image, and the intelligentsia decried crass appeals to sentiment, the landslide election of Ronald Reagan demonstrated the effectiveness of this game plan. Watergate might well have led to the destruction of the Republican party. Instead, the very disaffection and cynicism that Watergate helped to engender became capital out of which a Republican revival was manufactured.

Reagan didn't just use *image*, he was *image*. A likable, not particularly bright, sometimes bumbling man, he was like somebody's uncle. He had a lot of weird ideas, but he was familiar, comforting to many. His lapses and his confusions could always be excused. When members of the public objected to his policies, it was a problem of "perception," he had merely been misunderstood. The tilt of his head and his way of speaking as if he were always about to spin a yarn ("Well . . .") provided a tolerable facade for social policies that, meanwhile, were destroying the nation. Fortunes were built on pyramids of thin air, while many Americans lost their livelihoods and their homes.

Reaganism set a dangerous tone in the United States. It established the legitimacy of pure, disembodied symbolism as the prime political instrument. Democracy was no longer a process, it was but one in a grab bag of catch words. Conviction was no longer something that resulted from thought and contemplation, it was a feeling that welled up in the eyes and left a pleasant ache in the pit of the stomach. As this became the triumphant norm, political consultants became ever more avid students of trigger-point rhetoric and telegenic images. Writing in the *New York Times* in 1990, Robin Toner corroborated the trend, reporting that "political strategists are on an increasing quest for the image, the code, the word, the value, the picture that moves voters." The semiotics of influence were emerging as the prime political exercise.

# 11

## McDonald's in Hong Kong: Consumerism, Dietary Change, and the Rise of a Children's Culture

FROM *Golden Arches East*

### JAMES L. WATSON

*McDonald's has not only become the symbol of globalization. It is emblematic of the influence of the West, and particularly the United States, on the rest of the world. Many people question the value of this bequest, seeing fast food as a corrosive and crude intrusion on traditional practices, to say nothing of its questionable nutritional value. James Watson takes exception, not because he necessarily loves fast food and wants to speed up the erosion of local practices, but because he finds in those who are encouraged to take up Western practices—in this case the McDonald's "experience"—more selectivity and creativity. Although South Koreans openly oppose and reject McDonald's, many in Hong Kong have redefined McDonald's in ways that reveal the human capacity to shape culture and find compatibility between the old and the new.*

### TRANSNATIONALISM AND THE FAST FOOD INDUSTRY

Does the roaring success of McDonald's and its rivals in the fast food industry mean that Hong Kong's local culture is under siege? Are food chains helping to create a homogeneous, "global" culture better suited to the demands of a capitalist world order? Hong Kong would seem to be an excellent place to test the globalization hypothesis, given the central role that cuisine plays in the production and maintenance of a distinctive local identity. Man Tso-chuen's great-grandchildren are today avid consumers of Big Macs, pizza, and Coca-Cola; does this somehow make them less "Chinese" than their grandfather?

It is my contention that the cultural arena in places like Hong Kong is changing with such breathtaking speed that the fundamental assumptions underlining such questions are themselves questionable. Economic and social realities make it necessary to construct an entirely new approach to global issues, one that takes the consumers' own views into account. Analyses based on neomarxian and dependency (center/periphery) models that were popular in the 1960s and 1970s do not begin to capture the complexity of emerging transnational systems.

This chapter represents a conscious attempt to bring the discussion of globalism down to earth, focusing on one local culture. The people of Hong Kong have embraced American-style fast foods, and by so doing they might appear to be in the vanguard of a worldwide culinary revolution. But they have not been stripped of their cultural traditions, nor have they become "Americanized" in any but the most superficial of ways. Hong Kong in the late 1990s constitutes one of the world's most heterogeneous cultural environments. Younger people, in particular, are fully conversant in transnational idioms, which include language, music, sports, clothing, satellite television, cyber-communications, global travel, and—of course—cuisine. It is no longer possible to distinguish what is local and what is not. In Hong Kong, as I hope to show in this chapter, the transnational *is* the local.

## EATING OUT: A SOCIAL HISTORY OF CONSUMPTION

By the time McDonald's opened its first Hong Kong restaurant in 1975, the idea of fast food was already well established among local consumers. Office workers, shop assistants, teachers, and transport workers had enjoyed various forms of take-out cuisine for well over a century; an entire industry had emerged to deliver mid-day meals direct to workplaces. In the 1960s and 1970s thousands of street vendors produced snacks and simple meals on demand, day or night. Time has always been money in Hong Kong; hence, the dual keys to success in the catering trade were speed and convenience. Another essential characteristic was that the food, based primarily on rice or noodles, had to be hot. Even the most cosmopolitan or local consumers did not (and many still do not) consider cold foods, such as sandwiches and salads, to be acceptable meals. Older people in South China associate cold food with offerings to the dead and are understandably hesitant to eat it.

The fast food industry in Hong Kong had to deliver hot items that could compete with traditional purveyors of convenience foods (noodle shops, dumpling stalls, soup carts, portable grills). The first modern chain to enter the fray was Café de Coral, a local corporation that began operation in 1969 and is still a dominant player in the Hong Kong fast food market (with 109 outlets and a 25 percent market share, compared to McDonald's 20 percent market share in 1994).[1] Café de Coral's strategy was simple: It moved Hong Kong's street foods indoors, to a clean, well-lighted cafeteria that offered instant service and moderate prices; popular Cantonese items were then combined with (sinicized) "Western" foods that had been popular in Hong Kong for decades. Café de Coral's menu reads like the *locus classicus* of Pacific Rim cuisine: deep-fried chicken wings, curry on rice, hot dogs, roast pork in soup noodles, spaghetti with meat balls, barbecued ribs, red bean sundaes, Oval-tine, Chinese tea, and Coca-Cola (with lemon, hot or cold). The formula was so successful it spawned dozens of imitators, including three full-scale chains.

\* \* \*

1. Seven of the world's ten busiest McDonald's restaurants are located in Hong Kong. When McDonald's first opened in 1975, few thought it would survive more than a few months. By January 1, 1997, Hong Kong had 125 outlets, which means that there was one McDonald's for every 51,200 residents, compared to one for every 30,000 people in the United States.

McDonald's mid-1970s entry also corresponded to an economic boom associated with Hong Kong's conversion from a low-wage, light-industrial outpost to a regional center for financial services and high-technology industries. McDonald's' takeoff thus paralleled the rise of a new class of highly educated, affluent consumers who thrive in Hong Kong's ever-changing urban environment—one of the most stressful in the world. These new consumers eat out more often than their parents and have created a huge demand for fast, convenient foods of all types. In order to compete in this market, McDonald's had to offer something different. That critical difference, at least during the company's first decade of operation, was American culture packaged as all-American, middle-class food.

\* \* \*

## MENTAL CATEGORIES: SNACK VERSUS MEAL

As in other parts of East Asia, McDonald's faced a serious problem when it began operation in Hong Kong: Hamburgers, fries, and sandwiches were perceived as snacks (Cantonese *siu sihk*, literally "small eats"); in the local view these items did not constitute the elements of a proper meal. This perception is still prevalent among older, more conservative consumers who believe that hamburgers, hot dogs, and pizza can never be "filling." Many students stop at fast food outlets on their way home from school; they may share hamburgers and fries with their classmates and then eat a full meal with their families at home. This is not considered a problem by parents, who themselves are likely to have stopped for tea and snacks after work. Snacking with friends and colleagues provides a major opportunity for socializing (and transacting business) among southern Chinese. Teahouses, coffee shops, bakeries, and ice cream parlors are popular precisely because they provide a structured yet informal setting for social encounters. Furthermore, unlike Chinese restaurants and banquet halls, snack centers do not command a great deal of time or money from customers.

Contrary to corporate goals, therefore, McDonald's entered the Hong Kong market as a purveyor of snacks. Only since the late 1980s has its fare been treated as the foundation of "meals" by a generation of younger consumers who regularly eat non-Chinese food. Thanks largely to McDonald's, hamburgers and fries are now a recognized feature of Hong Kong's lunch scene. The evening hours remain, however, the weak link in McDonald's marketing plan; the real surprise was breakfast, which became a peak traffic period.

The mental universe of Hong Kong consumers is partially revealed in the everyday use of language. Hamburgers are referred to, in colloquial Cantonese, as *han bou bao*—*han* being a homophone for "ham" and *bao* the common term for stuffed buns or bread rolls. *Bao* are quintessential snacks, and however excellent or nutritious they might be, they do not constitute the basis of a satisfying (i.e., filling) meal. In South China that honor is reserved for culinary arrangements that rest, literally, on a bed of rice (*fan*). Foods that accompany rice are referred to as *sung*, probably best translated as "toppings" (including meat, fish, and vegetables). It is significant that hamburgers are rarely categorized as meat (*yuk*); Hong Kong consumers tend to perceive anything that is served between slices of bread (Big Macs, fish sandwiches, hot dogs) as *bao*. In American culture the hamburger is categorized first and foremost as a meat item (with all the attendant worries about fat and cholesterol content), whereas in Hong Kong the same item is thought of primarily as bread.

## FROM EXOTIC TO ORDINARY: MCDONALD'S BECOMES LOCAL

Following precedents in other international markets, the Hong Kong franchise promoted McDonald's basic menu and did not introduce items that would be more recognizable to Chinese consumers (such as rice dishes, tropical fruit, soup noodles). Until recently the food has been indistinguishable from that served in Mobile, Alabama, or Moline, Illinois. There are, however, local preferences: the best-selling items in many outlets are fish sandwiches and plain hamburgers; Big Macs tend to be the favorites of children and teenagers. Hot tea and hot chocolate outsell coffee, but Coca-Cola remains the most popular drink.

McDonald's conservative approach also applied to the breakfast menu. When morning service was introduced in the 1980s, American-style items such as eggs, muffins, pancakes, and hash brown potatoes were not featured. Instead, the local outlets served the standard fare of hamburgers and fries for breakfast. McDonald's initial venture into the early morning food market was so successful that Mr. Ng hesitated to introduce American-style breakfast items, fearing that an abrupt shift in menu might alienate consumers who were beginning to accept hamburgers and fries as a regular feature of their diet. The transition to eggs, muffins, and hash browns was a gradual one, and today most Hong Kong customers order breakfasts that are similar to those offered in American outlets. But once established, dietary preferences change slowly: McDonald's continues to feature plain hamburgers (but not the Big Mac) on its breakfast menu in most Hong Kong outlets.

Management decisions of the type outlined above helped establish McDonald's as an icon of popular culture in Hong Kong. From 1975 to approximately 1985, McDonald's became the "in" place for young people wishing to associate themselves with the laid-back, nonhierarchical dynamism they perceived American society to embody. The first generation of consumers patronized McDonald's precisely because it was *not* Chinese and was *not* associated with Hong Kong's past as a backward-looking colonial outpost where (in their view) nothing of consequence ever happened. Hong Kong was changing and, as noted earlier, a new consumer culture was beginning to take shape. McDonald's caught the wave of this cultural movement and has been riding it ever since.

* * *

Today, McDonald's restaurants in Hong Kong are packed—wall-to-wall—with people of all ages, few of whom are seeking an American cultural experience. Twenty years after Mr. Ng opened his first restaurant, eating at McDonald's has become an ordinary, everyday experience for hundreds of thousands of Hong Kong residents. The chain has become a local institution in the sense that it has blended into the urban landscape; McDonalds outlets now serve as rendezvous points for young and old alike.

* * *

## WHAT'S IN A SMILE? FRIENDLINESS AND PUBLIC SERVICE

American consumers expect to be served "with a smile" when they order fast food, but this is not true in all societies. In Hong Kong people are suspicious of anyone who displays what is perceived to be an excess of congeniality, solicitude, or familiarity. The human smile is not, therefore, a universal symbol of openness and honesty. "If you buy an apple from a hawker and he smiles at you," my Cantonese tutor once told me, "you know you're being cheated."

Given these cultural expectations, it was difficult for Hong Kong management to import a key element of the McDonald's formula—service with a smile—and make it work. Crew members were trained to treat customers in a manner that approximates the American notion of "friendliness." Prior to the 1970s, there was not even an indigenous Cantonese term to describe this form of behavior. The traditional notion of friendship is based on loyalty to close associates, which by definition cannot be extended to strangers. Today the concept of *public* friendliness is recognized—and verbalized—by younger people in Hong Kong, but the term many of them use to express this quality is "friendly," borrowed directly from English. McDonald's, through its television advertising, may be partly responsible for this innovation, but to date it has had little effect on workers in the catering industry.

During my interviews it became clear that the majority of Hong Kong consumers were uninterested in public displays of congeniality from service personnel. When shopping for fast food, most people cited convenience, cleanliness, and table space as primary considerations; few even mentioned service except to note that the food should be delivered promptly. Counter staff in Hong Kong's fast food outlets (including McDonald's) rarely make great efforts to smile or to behave in a manner Americans would interpret as friendly. Instead, they project qualities that are admired in the local culture: competence, directness, and unflappability. In a North American setting the facial expression that Hong

Kong employees use to convey these qualities would likely be interpreted as a deliberate attempt to be rude or indifferent. Workers who smile on the job are assumed to be enjoying themselves at the consumer's (and management's) expense: In the words of one diner I overheard while standing in a queue, "They must be playing around back there. What are they laughing about?"

## CONSUMER DISCIPLINE?

[A] hallmark of the American fast food business is the displacement of labor costs from the corporation to the consumers. For the system to work, consumers must be educated—or "disciplined"—so that they voluntarily fulfill their side of an implicit bargain: We (the corporation) will provide cheap, fast service, if you (the customer) carry your own tray, seat yourself, and help clean up afterward. Time and space are also critical factors in the equation: Fast service is offered in exchange for speedy consumption and a prompt departure, thereby making room for others. This system has revolutionized the American food industry and has helped to shape consumer expectations in other sectors of the economy. How has it fared in Hong Kong? Are Chinese customers conforming to disciplinary models devised in Oak Brook, Illinois?

The answer is both yes and no. In general Hong Kong consumers have accepted the basic elements of the fast food formula, but with "localizing" adaptations. For instance, customers generally do not bus their own trays, nor do they depart immediately upon finishing. Clearing one's own table has never been an accepted part of local culinary culture, owing in part to the low esteem attaching to this type of labor. During McDonald's' first decade in Hong Kong, the cost of hiring extra cleaners was offset by low wages. A pattern was thus established, and customers grew accustomed to leaving without attending to their own rubbish. Later, as wages escalated in the late 1980s and early 1990s McDonald's tried to introduce self-busing by posting announcements in restaurants and featuring the practice in its television advertisements. As of February 1997, however, little had changed. Hong Kong consumers * * * have ignored this aspect of consumer discipline.

What about the critical issues of time and space? Local managers with whom I spoke estimated that the average eating time for most Hong Kong customers was between 20 and 25 minutes, compared to 11 minutes in the United States fast food industry. This estimate confirms my own observations of McDonald's consumers in Hong Kong's central business district (Victoria and Tsimshatsui). A survey conducted in the New Territories city of Yuen Long—an old market town that has grown into a modern urban center—revealed that local McDonalds consumers took just under 26 minutes to eat.

Perhaps the most striking feature of the American-inspired model of consumer discipline is the queue. Researchers in many parts of the world have reported that customers refuse, despite "education" campaigns by the chains involved, to form neat lines in front of cashiers. Instead, customers pack themselves into disorderly scrums and jostle for a chance to place their orders. Scrums of this nature were common in Hong Kong when McDonalds opened in 1975. Local managers discouraged this practice by stationing queue monitors near the registers during busy hours and, by the 1980s, orderly lines were the norm at McDonald's. The disappearance of the scrum corresponds to a general change in Hong Kong's public culture as a new generation of residents, the children of refugees, began to treat the territory as their home. Courtesy toward strangers was largely unknown in the 1960s: Boarding a bus during rush hour could be a nightmare and transacting business at a bank teller's window required brute strength. Many people credit McDonald's with being the first public institution in Hong Kong to enforce queuing, and thereby helping to create a more "civilized" social order. McDonald's did not, in fact, introduce the queue to Hong Kong, but this belief is firmly lodged in the public imagination.

## HOVERING AND THE NAPKIN WARS

Purchasing one's food is no longer a physical challenge in Hong Kong's McDonald's but finding a place to sit is quite another matter. The traditional practice of "hovering" is one solution: Choose a group of diners who appear to be on the verge of leaving and stake a claim to their table by hovering nearby, sometimes only inches away. Seated customers routinely ignore the intrusion; it would, in fact, entail a loss of face to notice. Hovering was the norm in Hong Kong's lower- to middle-range restaurants during the 1960s and 1970s, but the practice has disappeared in recent years. Restaurants now take names or hand out tickets at the entrance; warning signs, in Chinese and English, are posted: "Please wait to be seated." Customers are no longer allowed into the dining area until a table is ready.

Fast food outlets are the only dining establishments in Hong Kong where hovering is still tolerated, largely because it would be nearly impossible to regulate. Customer traffic in McDonald's is so heavy that the standard restaurant design has failed to reproduce American-style dining routines: Rather than ordering first and finding a place to sit afterward, Hong Kong consumers usually arrive in groups and delegate one or two people to claim a table while someone else joins the counter queues. Children make ideal hoverers and learn to scoot through packed restaurants, zeroing in on diners who are about to finish. It is one of the wonders of comparative ethnography to witness the speed with which Hong Kong children perform this reconnaissance duty. Foreign visitors are sometimes unnerved by hovering, but residents accept it as part of everyday life in one of the worlds most densely populated cities. It is not surprising, therefore, that Hong Kong's fast food chains have made few efforts to curtail the practice.

Management is less tolerant of behavior that affects profit margins. In the United States fast food companies save money by allowing (or requiring) customers to collect their own napkins, straws, plastic flatware, and condiments.

Self-provisioning is an essential feature of consumer discipline, but it only works if the system is not abused. In Hong Kong napkins are dispensed, one at a time, by McDonalds crew members who work behind the counter; customers who do not ask for napkins do not receive any. This is a deviation from the corporation's standard operating procedure and adds a few seconds to each transaction, which in turn slows down the queues. Why alter a well-tested routine? The reason is simple: napkins placed in public dispensers disappear faster than they can be replaced.

* * *

Buffets, like fast food outlets, depend upon consumers to perform much of their own labor in return for reduced prices. Abuse of the system—wasting food or taking it home—is taken for granted and is factored into the price of buffet meals. Fast food chains, by contrast, operate at lower price thresholds where consumer abuse can seriously affect profits.

Many university students of my acquaintance reported that they had frequently observed older people pocketing wads of paper napkins, three to four inches thick, in restaurants that permit self-provisioning. Management efforts to stop this behavior are referred to, in the Cantonese-English slang of Hong Kong youth, as the "Napkin Wars." Younger people were appalled by what they saw as the waste of natural resources by a handful of customers. As they talked about the issue, however, it became obvious that the Napkin Wars represented more—in their eyes—than a campaign to conserve paper. The sight of diners abusing public facilities reminded these young people of the bad old days of their parents and grandparents, when Hong Kong's social life was dominated by refugees who had little stake in the local community. During the 1960s and 1970s, economic insecurities were heightened by the very real prospect that Red Guards might take over the colony at any moment. The game plan was simple during those decades: Make money as quickly as possible and move on. In the 1980s a new generation of local-born youth began treating Hong Kong as home and proceeded to build a public culture better suited to their vision of life in a cosmopolitan city. In this new Hong Kong, consumers are expected to be sophisticated and financially secure, which means that it would be beneath their dignity to abuse public facilities. Still, McDonalds retains control of its napkins.

## CHILDREN AS CONSUMERS

During the summer of 1994, while attending a business lunch in one of Hong Kong's fanciest hotels, I watched a waiter lean down to consult with a customer at an adjoining table. The object of his attention was a six-year-old child who studied the menu with practiced skill. His parents beamed as their prodigy performed; meanwhile, sitting across the table, a pair of grandparents sat bolt upright, scowling in obvious disapproval. Twenty years ago the sight of a child commanding such attention would have shocked the entire restaurant into silence. No one, save the immediate party (and this observer), even noticed in 1994.

Hong Kong children rarely ate outside their home until the late 1970s, and when they did, they were expected to eat what was put in front of them. The idea that children might actually order their own food or speak to a waiter would have outraged most adults; only foreign youngsters (notably the off-spring of British and American expatriates) were permitted to make their preferences known in public. Today, Hong Kong children as young as two or three participate in the local economy as full-fledged consumers, with their own tastes and brand loyalties. Children now have money in their pockets and they spend it on personal consumption, which usually means snacks. In response, new industries and a specialized service sector has emerged to "feed" these discerning consumers. McDonald's was one of the first corporations to recognize the potential of the children's market; in effect, the company started a revolution by making it possible for even the youngest consumers to *choose* their own food.

\* \* \*

Many Hong Kong children of my acquaintance are so fond of McDonald's that they refuse to eat with their parents or grandparents in Chinese-style restaurants or *dim sam* teahouses. This has caused intergenerational distress in some of Hong Kong's more conservative communities. In 1994, a nine-year-old boy, the descendant of illustrious ancestors who settled in the New Territories eight centuries ago, talked about his concerns as we consumed Big Macs, fries, and shakes at McDonald's: "A-bak [uncle], I like it here better than any place in the world. I want to come here every day." His father takes him to McDonald's at least twice a week, but his grandfather, who accompanied them a few times in the late 1980s, will no longer do so. "I prefer to eat *dim sam*," the older man told me later. "That place [McDonald's] is for kids." Many grandparents have resigned themselves to the new consumer trends and take their preschool grandchildren to McDonald's for midmorning snacks—precisely the time of day that local teahouses were once packed with retired people. Cantonese grandparents have always played a prominent role in child minding, but until recently the children had to accommodate to the proclivities of their elders. By the 1990s grandchildren were more assertive and the mid-morning *dim sam* snack was giving way to hamburgers and Cokes.

\* \* \*

## RONALD MCDONALD AND THE INVENTION OF BIRTHDAY PARTIES

Until recently most people in Hong Kong did not even know, let alone celebrate, their birthdates in the Western calendrical sense; dates of birth according to the lunar calendar were recorded for divinatory purposes but were not noted in annual rites. By the late 1980s, however, birthday parties, complete with cakes and candles, were the rage in Hong Kong. Any child who was anyone had to have a party, and the most popular venue was a fast food restaurant, with McDonald's ranked above all competitors. The majority of Hong Kong people live in overcrowded flats, which means that parties are rarely held in private homes.

Except for the outlets in central business districts, McDonald's restaurants are packed every Saturday and Sunday with birthday parties, cycled through at the rate of one every hour. A party hostess, provided by the restaurant, leads the children in games while the parents sit on the sidelines, talking quietly among themselves. For a small fee celebrants receive printed invitation cards, photographs, a gift box containing toys and a discount coupon for future trips to McDonald's. Parties are held in a special enclosure, called the Ronald Room, which is equipped with low tables and tiny stools—suitable only for children. Television commercials portray Ronald McDonald leading birthday celebrants on exciting safaris and expeditions. The clown's Cantonese name, Mak Dong Lou Suk-Suk ("Uncle McDonald"), plays on the intimacy of kinship and has helped transform him into one of Hong Kong's most familiar cartoon figures.

\* \* \*

## MCDONALD'S AS A YOUTH CENTER

Weekends may be devoted to family dining and birthday parties for younger children, but on weekday afternoons, from 3:00 to 6:00 P.M., McDonald's restaurants are packed with teenagers stopping for a snack on their way home from school. In many outlets 80 percent of the late afternoon clientele appear in school uniforms, turning the restaurants into a sea of white frocks, light blue shirts, and dark trousers. The students, aged between 10 and 17, stake out tables and buy snacks that are shared in groups. The noise level at this time of day is deafening; students shout to friends and dart from table to table. Few adults, other than restaurant staff, are in evidence. It is obvious that McDonald's is treated as an informal youth center, a recreational extension of school where students can unwind after long hours of study.

\* \* \*

In contrast to their counterparts in the United States, where fast food chains have devised ways to discourage lingering, McDonald's in Hong Kong does not set a limit on table time. When I asked the managers of several Hong Kong outlets how they coped with so many young people chatting at tables that might otherwise be occupied by paying customers, they all replied that the students were "welcome." The obvious strategy is to turn a potential liability into an asset: "Students create a good atmosphere which is good for our business," said one manager as he watched an army of teenagers—dressed in identical school uniforms—surge into his restaurant. Large numbers of students also use McDonald's as a place to do homework and prepare for exams, often in groups. Study space of any kind, public or private, is hard to find in overcrowded Hong Kong. * * *

## CONCLUSIONS: WHOSE CULTURE IS IT?

In concluding this chapter, I would like to return to the questions raised in my opening remarks: In what sense, if any, is McDonald's involved in these cultural transformations (the creation of a child-centered consumer culture, for instance)? Has the company helped to create these trends, or merely followed the market? Is this an example of American-inspired, transnational culture crowding out indigenous cultures?

* * *

The deeper I dig into the lives of consumers themselves, in Hong Kong and elsewhere, the more complex the picture becomes. Having watched the processes of culture change unfold for nearly thirty years, it is apparent to me that the ordinary people of Hong Kong have most assuredly *not* been stripped of their cultural heritage, nor have they become the uncomprehending dupes of transnational corporations. Younger people—including many of the grandchildren of my former neighbors in the New Territories—are avid consumers of transnational culture in all of its most obvious manifestations: music, fashion, television, and cuisine. At the same time, however, Hong Kong has itself become a major center for the *production* of transnational culture, not just a sinkhole for its *consumption*. Witness, for example, the expansion of Hong Kong popular culture into China, Southeast Asia, and beyond: "Cantopop" music is heard on radio stations in North China, Vietnam, and Japan; the Hong Kong fashion industry influences clothing styles in Los Angeles, Bangkok, and Kuala Lumpur; and, perhaps most significant of all, Hong Kong is emerging as a center for the production and dissemination of satellite television programs throughout East, Southeast, and South Asia.

A lifestyle is emerging in Hong Kong that can best be described as postmodern, postnationalist, and flamboyantly transnational. The wholesale acceptance and appropriation of Big Macs, Ronald McDonald and birthday parties are small but significant aspects of this redefinition of Chinese cultural identity. In closing, therefore, it seems appropriate to pose an entirely new set of questions: Where does the transnational end and the local begin? Whose culture is it, anyway? In places like Hong Kong the postcolonial periphery is fast becoming the metropolitan center, where local people are consuming and simultaneously producing new cultural systems.

* * *

# 12

## The Code of the Streets

### ELIJAH ANDERSON

*The capacity of sociology to look beyond the headlines is captured in this ethnographic account of a culture of respect, violence, and control on urban streets. Anderson describes this as "a cultural adaptation" to poverty, discrimination in public services, and social marginality. The "presentation of self" examined in this essay is a fascinating social construction and one with deadly serious consequences for everyone, not only for those who embrace the code of the street. The rich complexity of social life is revealed in Anderson's account, as is the difficulty in altering cultural practices without changing the circumstances of those who live the code.*

Of all the problems besetting the poor inner-city black community, none is more pressing than that of interpersonal violence and aggression. It wreaks havoc daily with the lives of community residents and increasingly spills over into downtown and residential middle-class areas. Muggings, burglaries, carjackings, and drug-related shootings, all of which may leave their victims or innocent bystanders dead, are now common enough to concern all urban and many suburban residents. The inclination to violence springs from the circumstances of life among the ghetto poor—the lack of jobs that pay a living wage, the stigma of race, the fallout from rampant drug use and drug trafficking, and the resulting alienation and lack of hope for the future.

Simply living in such an environment places young people at special risk of falling victim to aggressive behavior. Although there are often forces in the community which can counteract the negative influences, by far the most powerful being a strong, loving, "decent" (as inner-city residents put it) family committed to middle-class values, the despair is pervasive enough to have spawned an oppositional culture, that of "the streets," whose norms are often consciously opposed to those of mainstream society. These two orientations—decent and street—socially organize the community, and their coexistence has important consequences for residents, particularly children growing up in the inner city. Above all, this environment means that even youngsters whose home lives reflect mainstream values—and the majority of homes in the community do—must be able to handle themselves in a street-oriented environment.

This is because the street culture has evolved what may be called a code of the streets, which amounts to a set of informal rules governing interpersonal public behavior, including violence. The rules prescribe both a proper comportment and a proper way to respond if challenged. They regulate the use of violence and so allow those who are inclined to aggression to precipitate violent encounters in an approved way. The rules have been established and are enforced mainly by the street-oriented, but on the streets the distinction between street and decent is often irrelevant; everybody knows that if the rules are violated, there are penalties. Knowledge of the code is thus largely defensive; it is literally necessary for operating in public. Therefore, even though families with a decency orientation are usually opposed to the values of the code, they often reluctantly encourage their children's familiarity with it to enable them to negotiate the inner-city environment.

At the heart of the code is the issue of respect—loosely defined as being treated "right," or granted the deference one deserves. However, in the troublesome public environment of the inner city, as people increasingly feel buffeted by forces beyond their control, what one deserves in the way of respect becomes more and more problematic and uncertain. This in turn further opens the issue of respect to sometimes intense interpersonal negotiation. In the street culture, especially among young people, respect is viewed as almost an external entity that is hard-won but easily lost, and so must constantly be guarded. The rules of the code in fact provide a framework for negotiating respect. The person whose very appearance—including his clothing, demeanor, and way of moving—deters transgressions feels that he possesses, and may be considered by others to possess, a measure of respect. With the right amount of respect, for instance, he can avoid "being bothered" in public. If he is bothered, not only may he be in physical danger but he has been disgraced or "dissed" (disrespected). Many of the forms that dissing can take might seem petty to middle-class people (maintaining eye contact for too long, for example), but to those invested in the street code, these actions become serious indications of the other person's intentions. Consequently, such people become very sensitive to advances and slights, which could well serve as warnings of imminent physical confrontation.

This hard reality can be traced to the profound sense of alienation from mainstream society and its institutions felt by many poor inner-city black people, particularly the young. The code of the streets is actually a cultural adaptation to a profound lack of faith in the police and the judicial system. The police are most often seen as representing the dominant white society and not caring to protect inner-city residents. When called, they may not respond, which is one reason many residents feel they must be prepared to take extraordinary measures to defend themselves and their loved ones against those who are inclined to aggression. Lack of police accountability has in fact been incorporated into the status system: the person who is believed capable of "taking care of himself" is accorded a certain deference, which translates into a sense of physical and psychological control. Thus the street code emerges where the influence of the police ends and personal responsibility for one's safety is felt to begin. Exacerbated by the proliferation of drugs and easy access to guns, this volatile situation results in the ability of the street-oriented minority (or those who effectively "go for bad") to dominate the public spaces.

## DECENT AND STREET FAMILIES

Although almost everyone in poor inner-city neighborhoods is struggling financially and therefore feels a certain distance from the rest of America, the decent and the street family in a real sense represent two poles of value orientation, two contrasting conceptual categories. The labels "decent" and "street," which the residents themselves use, amount to evaluative judgments that confer status on local residents. The labeling is often the result of a social contest among individuals and families of the neighborhood. Individuals of the two orientations often coexist in the same extended family. Decent residents judge themselves to be so while judging others to be of the street, and street individuals often present themselves as decent, drawing distinctions between themselves and other people. In addition, there is quite a bit of circumstantial behavior—that is, one person may at different times exhibit both decent and street orientations, depending on the circumstances. Although these designations result from so much social jockeying, there do exist concrete features that define each conceptual category.

Generally, so called decent families tend to accept mainstream values more fully and attempt to instill them in their children. Whether married couples with children or single-parent (usually female) households, they are generally "working poor" and so tend to be better off financially than their street-oriented neighbors. They value hard work and self-reliance and are willing to sacrifice for their children. Because they have a certain amount of faith in mainstream society, they harbor hopes for a better future for their children, if not for themselves. Many of them go to church and take a strong interest in their children's schooling. Rather than dwelling on the real hardships and inequities facing them, many such decent people, particularly the increasing number of grandmothers raising grandchildren, see their difficult situation as a test from God and derive great support from their faith and from the church community.

Extremely aware of the problematic and often dangerous environment in which they reside, decent parents tend to be strict in their child-rearing practices, encouraging children to respect authority and walk a straight moral line. They have an almost obsessive concern about trouble of any kind and remind their children to be on the lookout for people and situations that might lead to it. At the same time, they are themselves polite and considerate of others, and teach their children to be the same way. At home, at work, and in church, they strive hard to maintain a positive mental attitude and a spirit of cooperation.

So-called street parents, in contrast, often show a lack of consideration for other people and have a rather superficial sense of family and community. Though they may love their children, many of them are unable to cope with the physical and emotional demands of parenthood, and find it difficult to reconcile their needs with those of their children. These families, who are more fully invested in the code of the streets than the decent people are, may aggressively socialize their children into it in a normative way. They believe in the code and judge themselves and others according to its values.

In fact the overwhelming majority of families in the inner-city community try to approximate the decent-family model, but there are many others who clearly represent the worst fears of the decent family. Not only are their financial resources extremely limited, but what little they have may easily be misused. The lives of the street-oriented are often marked by disorganization. In the most desperate circumstances people frequently have a limited understanding of priorities and consequences, and so frustrations mount over bills, food, and, at times, drink, cigarettes, and drugs. Some tend toward self-destructive behavior; many street-oriented women are crack-addicted ("on the pipe"), alcoholic, or involved in complicated relationships with men who abuse them. In addition, the seeming intractability of their situation, caused in large part by the lack of well-paying jobs and the persistence of racial discrimination, has engendered deep-seated bitterness and anger in many of the most desperate and poorest blacks, especially young people. The need both to exercise a measure of control and to lash out at somebody is often reflected in the adults' relations with their children. At the least, the frustrations of persistent poverty shorten the fuse in such people—contributing to a lack of patience with anyone, child or adult, who irritates them.

In these circumstances a woman—or a man, although men are less consistently present in children's lives—can be quite aggressive with children, yelling at and striking them for the least little infraction of the rules she has set down. Often little if any serious explanation follows the verbal and physical punishment. This response teaches children a particular lesson. They learn that to solve any kind of interpersonal problem one must quickly resort to hitting or other violent behavior. Actual peace and quiet, and also the appearance of calm, respectful children conveyed to her neighbors and friends, are often what the young mother most desires, but at times she will be very aggressive in trying to get them. Thus she may be quick to beat her children, especially if they defy her law, not because she hates them but because this is the way she knows to control them. In fact, many street-oriented women love their children dearly. Many mothers in the community subscribe to the notion that there is a "devil in the boy" that must be beaten out of him or that socially "fast girls need to be whupped." Thus much of what borders on child abuse in the view of social authorities is acceptable parental punishment in the view of these mothers.

Many street-oriented women are sporadic mothers whose children learn to fend for themselves when necessary, foraging for food and money any way they can get it. The children are sometimes employed by drug dealers or become addicted themselves. These children of the street, growing up with little supervision, are said to "come up hard." They often learn to fight at an early age, sometimes using short-tempered adults around them as role models. The street-oriented home may be fraught with anger, verbal disputes, physical aggression, and even mayhem. The children observe these goings-on, learning the lesson that might makes right. They quickly learn to hit those who cross them, and the dog-eat-dog mentality prevails. In order to survive, to protect oneself, it is necessary to marshal inner resources and be ready to deal with adversity in a hands-on way. In these circumstances physical prowess takes on great significance. * * *

## CAMPAIGNING FOR RESPECT

These realities of inner-city life are largely absorbed on the streets. At an early age, often even before they start school, children from street-oriented homes gravitate to the streets, where they "hang"—socialize with their peers. Children from these generally permissive homes have a great deal of latitude and are allowed to "rip and run" up and down the street. They often come home from school, put their books down, and go right back out the door. On school nights eight- and nine-year-olds remain out until nine or ten o'clock (and teenagers typically come in whenever they want to). On the streets they play in groups that often become the source of their primary social bonds. Children from decent homes tend to be more carefully supervised and are thus likely to have curfews and to be taught how to stay out of trouble.

When decent and street kids come together, a kind of social shuffle occurs in which children have a chance to go either way. Tension builds as a child comes to realize that he must choose an orientation. The kind of home he comes from influences but does not determine the way he will ultimately turn out—although it is unlikely that a child from a thoroughly street-oriented family will easily absorb decent values on the streets. Youths who emerge from street-oriented families but develop a decency orientation almost always learn those values in another setting—in school, in a youth group, in church. Often it is the result of their involvement with a caring "old head" (adult role model).

In the street, through their play, children pour their individual life experiences into a common knowledge pool, affirming, confirming, and elaborating on what they have observed in the home and matching their skills against those of others. And they learn to fight. Even small children test one another, pushing and shoving, and are ready to hit other children over circumstances not to their liking. In turn, they are readily hit by other children, and the child who is toughest prevails. Thus the violent resolution of disputes, the hitting and cursing, gains social reinforcement. The child in effect is initiated into a system that is really a way of campaigning for respect.

In addition, younger children witness the disputes of older children, which are often resolved through cursing and abusive talk, if not aggression or outright violence. They see that one child succumbs to the greater physical and mental abilities of the other. They are also alert and attentive witnesses to the verbal and physical fights of adults, after which they compare notes and share their interpretations of the event. In almost every case the victor is the person who physically won the altercation, and this person often enjoys the esteem and respect of onlookers. These experiences reinforce the lessons the children have learned at home: might makes right, and toughness is a virtue, while humility is not. In effect they learn the social meaning of fighting. When it is left virtually unchallenged, this understanding becomes an ever more important part of the child's working conception of the world. Over time the code of the streets becomes refined.

Those street-oriented adults with whom children come in contact—including mothers, fathers, brothers, sisters, boyfriends, cousins, neighbors, and friends—help them along in forming this understanding by verbalizing the messages they are getting through experience: "Watch your back." "Protect yourself." "Don't punk out." "If somebody messes with you, you got to pay them back." "If someone disses you, you got to straighten them out." Many parents actually impose sanctions if a child is not sufficiently aggressive. For example, if a child loses a fight and comes home upset, the parent might respond, "Don't you come in here crying that somebody beat you up; you better get back out there and whup his ass. I didn't raise no punks! Get back out there and whup his ass. If you don't whup his ass, I'll whup your ass when you come home." Thus the child obtains reinforcement for being tough and showing nerve.

* * *

## SELF-IMAGE BASED ON "JUICE"

By the time they are teenagers, most youths have either internalized the code of the streets or at least learned the need to comport themselves in accordance with its rules, which chiefly have to do with interpersonal communication. The code revolves around the presentation of self. Its basic requirement is the display of a certain predisposition to violence. Accordingly, one's bearing must send the unmistakable if sometimes subtle message to "the next person" in public that one is capable of violence and mayhem when the situation requires it, that one can take care of oneself. The nature of this communication is largely determined by the demands of the circumstances but can include facial expressions, gait, and verbal expressions—all of which are geared mainly to deterring aggression. Physical appearance, including clothes, jewelry, and grooming, also plays an important part in how a person is viewed; to be respected, it is important to have the right look.

Even so, there are no guarantees against challenges, because there are always people around looking for a fight to increase their share of respect—or "juice," as it is sometimes called on the street. Moreover, if a person is assaulted, it is important, not only in the eyes of his opponent but also in the eyes of his "running buddies," for him to avenge himself. Otherwise he risks being "tried" (challenged) or "moved on" by any number of others. To maintain his honor he must show he is not someone to be "messed with" or "dissed." In general, the person must "keep himself straight" by managing his position of respect among others; this involves in part his self-image, which is shaped by what he thinks others are thinking of him in relation to his peers.

Objects play an important and complicated role in establishing self-image. Jackets, sneakers, gold jewelry, reflect not just a person's taste, which tends to be tightly regulated among adolescents of all social classes, but also a willingness to possess things that may require defending. A boy wearing a fashionable, expensive jacket, for example, is vulnerable to attack by another who covets the jacket and either cannot afford to buy one or wants the added satisfaction of depriving someone else of his. However, if the boy forgoes the desirable jacket and wears one that isn't "hip," he runs the risk of being teased and possibly even assaulted as an unworthy person. To be allowed to hang with certain prestigious crowds, a boy must wear a different set of expensive clothes—sneakers and athletic suit—every day. Not to be able to do so might make him appear socially deficient. The youth comes to covet such items—especially when he sees easy prey wearing them.

In acquiring valued things, therefore, a person shores up his identity—but since it is an identity based on having things, it is highly precarious. This very precariousness gives a heightened sense of urgency to staying even with peers, with whom the person is actually competing. Young men and women who are able to command respect through their presentation of self—by allowing their possessions and their body language to speak for them—may not have to campaign for regard but may, rather, gain it by the force of their manner. Those who are unable to command respect in this way must actively campaign for it—and are thus particularly alive to slights.

One way of campaigning for status is by taking the possessions of others. In this context, seemingly ordinary objects can become trophies imbued with symbolic value that far exceeds their monetary worth. Possession of the trophy can symbolize the ability to violate somebody—to "get in his face," to take something of value from him, to "dis" him, and thus to enhance one's own worth by stealing someone else's. The trophy does not have to be something material. It can be another person's sense of honor, snatched away with a derogatory remark. It can be the outcome of a fight. It can be the imposition of a certain standard, such as a girl's getting herself recognized as the most beautiful. Material things, however, fit easily into the pattern. Sneakers, a pistol, even somebody else's girlfriend, can become a trophy. When a person can take something from another and then flaunt it, he gains a certain regard by being the owner, or the controller, of that thing. But this display of ownership can then provoke other people to challenge him. This game of who controls what is thus constantly being played out on inner-city streets, and the trophy—extrinsic or intrinsic, tangible or intangible—identifies the current winner.

An important aspect of this often violent give-and-take is its zero-sum quality. That is, the extent to which one person can raise himself up depends on his ability to put another person down. This underscores the alienation that permeates the inner-city ghetto community. There is a generalized sense that very little respect is to be had, and therefore everyone competes to get what affirmation he can of the little that is available. The craving for respect that results gives people thin skins. Shows of deference by others can be highly soothing, contributing to a sense of security, comfort, self-confidence, and self-respect. Transgressions by others which go unanswered diminish these feelings and are believed to encourage further transgressions. Hence one must be ever vigilant against the transgressions of others or even *appearing* as if transgressions will be tolerated. Among young people, whose sense of self-esteem is particularly vulnerable, there is an especially heightened concern with being disrespected. Many inner-city young men in particular crave respect to such a degree that they will risk their lives to attain and maintain it.

The issue of respect is thus closely tied to whether a person has an inclination to be violent, even as a victim. In the wider society people may not feel required to retaliate physically after an attack, even though they are aware that they have been degraded or taken advantage of. They may feel a great need to defend themselves *during* an attack, or to behave in such a way as to deter aggression (middle-class people certainly can and do become victims of street-oriented youths), but they are much more likely than street-oriented people to feel that they can walk away from a possible altercation with their self-esteem intact. Some people may even have the strength of character to flee, without any thought that their self-respect or esteem will be diminished.

In impoverished inner-city black communities, however, particularly among young males and perhaps increasingly among females, such flight would be extremely difficult. To run away would likely leave one's self-esteem in tatters. Hence people often feel constrained not only to stand up and at least attempt to resist during an assault but also to "pay back"—to seek revenge—after a successful assault on their person. This may include going to get a weapon or even getting relatives involved. Their very identity and self-respect, their honor, is often intricately tied up with the way they perform on the streets during and after such encounters. This outlook reflects the circumscribed opportunities of the inner-city poor. Generally people outside the ghetto have other ways of gaining status and regard, and thus do not feel so dependent on such physical displays.

## BY TRIAL OF MANHOOD

On the street, among males these concerns about things and identity have come to be expressed in the concept of "manhood." Manhood in the inner city means taking the prerogatives of men with respect to strangers, other men, and women—being distinguished as a man. It implies physicality and a certain ruthlessness. Regard and respect are associated with this concept in large part because of its practical application: if others have little or no regard for a person's manhood, his very life and those of his loved ones could be in jeopardy. But there is a chicken-and-egg aspect to this situation: one's physical safety is more likely to be jeopardized in public *because* manhood is associated with respect. In other words, an existential link has been created between the idea of manhood and one's self-esteem, so that it has become hard to say which is primary. For many inner-city youths, manhood and respect are flip sides of the same coin; physical and psychological well-being are inseparable, and both require a sense of control, of being in charge.

The operating assumption is that a man, especially a real man, knows what other men know—the code of the streets. And if one is not a real man, one is somehow diminished as a person, and there are certain valued things one simply does not deserve. There is thus believed to be a certain justice to the code, since it is considered that everyone has the opportunity to know it. Implicit in this is that everybody is held responsible for being familiar with the code. If the victim of a mugging, for example, does not know the code and so responds "wrong," the perpetrator may feel justified even in killing him and may feel no remorse. He may think, "Too bad, but it's his fault. He should have known better."

So when a person ventures outside, he must adopt the code—a kind of shield, really—to prevent others from "messing with" him. In these circumstances it is easy for people to think they are being tried or tested by others even when this is not the case. For it is sensed that something extremely valuable is at stake in every interaction, and people are encouraged to rise to the occasion, particularly with strangers. For people who are unfamiliar with the code—generally people who live outside the inner city—the concern with respect in the most ordinary interactions can be frightening and incomprehensible. But for those who are invested in the code, the clear object of their demeanor is to discourage strangers from even thinking about testing their manhood. And the sense of power that attends the ability to deter others can be alluring even to those who know the code without being heavily invested in it—the decent inner-city youths. Thus a boy who has been leading a basically decent life can, in trying circumstances, suddenly resort to deadly force.

Central to the issue of manhood is the widespread belief that one of the most effective ways of gaining respect is to manifest "nerve." Nerve is shown when one takes another persons possessions (the more valuable the better), "messes with" someone's woman, throws the first punch, "gets in someone's face," or pulls a trigger. Its proper display helps on the spot to check others who would violate one's person and also helps to build a reputation that works to prevent future challenges. But since such a show of nerve is a forceful expression of disrespect toward the person on the receiving end, the victim may be greatly offended and seek to retaliate with equal or greater force. A display of nerve, therefore, can easily provoke a life-threatening response, and the background knowledge of that possibility has often been incorporated into the concept of nerve.

True nerve exposes a lack of fear of dying. Many feel that it is acceptable to risk dying over the principle of respect. In fact, among the hard-core street-oriented, the clear risk of violent death may be preferable to being "dissed" by another. The youths who have internalized this attitude and convincingly display it in their public bearing are among the most threatening people of all, for it is commonly assumed that they fear no man. As the people of the community say, "They are the baddest dudes on the street." They often lead an existential life that may acquire meaning only when they are faced with the possibility of imminent death. Not to be afraid to die is by implication to have few compunctions about taking another's life. Not to be afraid to die is the quid pro quo of being able to take somebody else's life—for the right reasons, if the situation demands it. When others believe this is one's position, it gives one a real sense of power on the streets. Such credibility is what many inner-city youths strive to achieve, whether they are decent or street-oriented, both because of its practical defensive value and because of the positive way it makes them feel about themselves. The difference between the decent and the street-oriented youth is often that the decent youth makes a conscious decision to appear tough and manly; in another setting—with teachers, say, or at his part-time job—he can be polite and deferential. The street-oriented youth, on the other hand, has made the concept of manhood a part of his very identity; he has difficulty manipulating it—it often controls him.

## GIRLS AND BOYS

Increasingly, teenage girls are mimicking the boys and trying to have their own version of "manhood." Their goal is the same—to get respect, to be recognized as capable of setting or maintaining a certain standard. They try to achieve this end in the ways that have been established by the boys, including posturing, abusive language, and the use of violence to resolve disputes, but the issues for the girls are different. Although conflicts over turf and status exist among the girls, the majority of disputes seem rooted in assessments of beauty (which girl in a group is "the cutest"), competition over boyfriends, and attempts to regulate other people's knowledge of and opinions about a girl's behavior or that of someone close to her, especially her mother.

A major cause of conflicts among girls is "he say, she say." This practice begins in the early school years and continues through high school. It occurs when "people," particularly girls, talk about others, thus putting their "business in the streets." Usually one girl will say something negative about another in the group, most often behind the person's back. The remark will then get back to the person talked about. She may retaliate or her friends may feel required to "take up for" her. In essence this is a form of group gossiping in which individuals are negatively assessed and evaluated. As with much gossip, the things said may or may not be true, but the point is that such imputations can cast aspersions on a person's good name. The accused is required to defend herself against the slander, which can result in arguments and fights, often over little of real substance. Here again is the problem of low self-esteem, which encourages youngsters to be highly sensitive to slights and to be vulnerable to feeling easily "dissed." To avenge the dissing, a fight is usually necessary.

Because boys are believed to control violence, girls tend to defer to them in situations of conflict. Often if a girl is attacked or feels slighted, she will get a brother, uncle, or cousin to do her fighting for her. Increasingly, however, girls are doing their own fighting and are even asking their male relatives to teach them how to fight. Some girls form groups that attack other girls or take things from them. A hard-core segment of inner-city girls inclined toward violence seems to be developing. As one thirteen-year-old girl in a detention center for youths who have committed violent acts told me, "To get people to leave you alone, you gotta fight. Talking don't always get you out of stuff." One major difference between girls and boys: girls rarely use guns. Their fights are therefore not life-or-death struggles. Girls are not often willing to put their lives on the line for "manhood." The ultimate form of respect on the male-dominated inner-city street is thus reserved for men.

### "GOING FOR BAD"

In the most fearsome youths such a cavalier attitude toward death grows out of a very limited view of life. Many are uncertain about how long they are going to live and believe they could die violently at any time. They accept this fate; they live on the edge. Their manner conveys the message that nothing intimidates them; whatever turn the encounter takes, they maintain their attack—rather like a pit bull, whose spirit many such boys admire. The demonstration of such tenacity "shows heart" and earns their respect.

This fearlessness has implications for law enforcement. Many street-oriented boys are much more concerned about the threat of "justice" at the hands of a peer than at the hands of the police. Moreover, many feel not only that they have little to lose by going to prison but that they have something to gain. The toughening-up one experiences in prison can actually enhance one's reputation on the streets. Hence the system loses influence over the hard core who are without jobs, with little perceptible stake in the system. If mainstream society has done nothing *for* them, they counter by making sure it can do nothing *to* them.

At the same time, however, a competing view maintains that true nerve consists in backing down, walking away from a fight, and going on with one's business. One fights only in self-defense. This view emerges from the decent philosophy that life is precious, and it is an important part of the socialization process common in decent homes. It discourages violence as the primary means of resolving disputes and encourages youngsters to accept nonviolence and talk as confrontational strategies. But "if the deal goes down," self-defense is greatly encouraged. When there is enough positive support for this orientation, either in the home or among one's peers, then nonviolence has a chance to prevail. But it prevails at the cost of relinquishing a claim to being bad and tough, and therefore sets a young person up as at the very least alienated from street-oriented peers and quite possibly a target of derision or even violence.

Although the nonviolent orientation rarely overcomes the impulse to strike back in an encounter, it does introduce a certain confusion and so can prompt a measure of soul-searching, or even profound ambivalence. Did the person back down with his respect intact or did he back down only to be judged a "punk"—a person lacking manhood? Should he or she have acted? Should he or she have hit the other person in the mouth? These questions beset many young men and women during public confrontations. What is the "right" thing to do? In the quest for honor, respect, and local status—which few young people are uninterested in—common sense most often prevails, which leads many to opt for the tough approach, enacting their own particular versions of the display of nerve. The presentation of oneself as rough and tough is very often quite acceptable until one is tested. And then that presentation may help the person pass the test, because it will cause fewer questions to be asked about what he did and why. It is hard for a person to explain why he lost the fight or why he backed down. Hence many will strive to appear to "go for bad," while hoping they will never be tested. But when they are tested, the outcome of the situation may quickly be out of their hands, as they become wrapped up in the circumstances of the moment.

## AN OPPOSITIONAL CULTURE

The attitudes of the wider society are deeply implicated in the code of the streets. Most people in inner-city communities are not totally invested in the code, but the significant minority of hard-core street youths who are have to maintain the code in order to establish reputations, because they have—or feel they have—few other ways to assert themselves. For these young people the standards of the street code are the only game in town. The extent to which some children—particularly those who through upbringing have become most alienated and those lacking in strong and conventional social support—experience, feel, and internalize racist rejection and contempt from mainstream society may strongly encourage them to express contempt for the more conventional society in turn. In dealing with this contempt and rejection, some youngsters will consciously invest themselves and their considerable mental resources in what amounts to an oppositional culture to preserve themselves and their self-respect. Once they do, any respect they might be able to garner in the wider system pales in comparison with the respect available in the local system; thus they often lose interest in even attempting to negotiate the mainstream system.

At the same time, many less alienated young blacks have assumed a street-oriented demeanor as a way of expressing their blackness while really embracing a much more moderate way of life; they, too, want a nonviolent setting in which to live and raise a family. These decent people are trying hard to be part of the mainstream culture, but the racism, real and perceived, that they encounter helps to legitimate the oppositional culture. And so on occasion they adopt street behavior. In fact, depending on the demands of the situation, many people in the community slip back and forth between decent and street behavior.

A vicious cycle has thus been formed. The hopelessness and alienation many young inner-city black men and women feel, largely as a result of endemic joblessness and persistent racism, fuels the violence they engage in. This violence serves to confirm the negative feelings many whites and some middle-class blacks harbor toward the ghetto poor, further legitimating the oppositional culture and the code of the streets in the eyes of many poor young blacks. Unless this cycle is broken, attitudes on both sides will become increasingly entrenched, and the violence, which claims victims black and white, poor and affluent, will only escalate.

# 13

## America's National Eating Disorder

FROM *The Omnivore's Dilemma: A Natural History of Four Meals*

### MICHAEL POLLAN

*One of the most popular and talked-about books of recent years,* The Omnivore's Dilemma, *includes this essay, which asks, What should I eat? In an affluent society where grocery items come from all over the world, everything is available. Or, I can skip the grocery store and just eat out. But in either case, I may not know what I'm eating. Michael Pollan has tapped the root of food insecurity and come up with a critique of both American culture and corporate capitalism. It is certainly food for thought.*

All the customs and rules culture has devised to mediate the clash of human appetite and society probably bring greater comfort to us as eaters than as sexual beings. Freud and others lay the blame for many of our sexual neuroses at the door of an overly repressive culture, but that doesn't appear to be the principal culprit in our neurotic eating. To the contrary, it seems as though our eating tends to grow more tortured as our culture's power to manage our relationship to food weakens.

This seems to me precisely the predicament we find ourselves in today as eaters, particularly in America. America has never had a stable national cuisine; each immigrant population has brought its own foodways to the American table, but none has ever been powerful enough to hold the national diet very steady. We seem bent on reinventing the American way of eating every generation, in great paroxysms of neophilia and neophobia. That might explain why Americans have been such easy marks for food fads and diets of every description.

This is the country, after all, where at the turn of the last century Dr. John Harvey Kellogg persuaded great numbers of the country's most affluent and best educated to pay good money to sign themselves into his legendarily nutty sanitarium at Battle Creek, Michigan, where they submitted to a regime that included all-grape diets and almost hourly enemas. Around the same time millions of Americans succumbed to the vogue for "Fletcherizing"—chewing each bite of food as many as one hundred times—introduced by Horace Fletcher, also known as the Great Masticator.

This period marked the first golden age of American food faddism, though of course its exponents spoke not in terms of fashion but of "scientific eating," much as we do now. Back then the best nutritional science maintained that carnivory promoted the growth of toxic bacteria in the colon; to battle these evil-doers Kellogg vilified meat and mounted a two-fronted assault on his patients' alimentary canals, introducing quantities of Bulgarian yogurt at both ends. It's easy to make fun of people who would succumb to such fads, but it's not at all clear that we're any less gullible. It remains to be seen whether the current Atkins school theory of ketosis—the process by which the body resorts to burning its own fat when starved of carbohydrates—will someday seem as quaintly quackish as Kellogg's theory of colonic autointoxication.

What is striking is just how little it takes to set off one of these applecart-toppling nutritional swings in America; a scientific study, a new government guideline, a lone crackpot with a medical degree can alter this nation's diet overnight. One article in the *New York Times Magazine* in 2002 almost single-handedly set off the recent spasm of carbophobia in America. But the basic pattern was fixed decades earlier, and suggests just how vulnerable the lack of stable culinary traditions leaves us to the omnivore's anxiety, and the companies and quacks who would prey on it. So every few decades some new scientific research comes along to challenge the prevailing nutritional orthodoxy; some nutrient that Americans have been happily chomping for decades is suddenly found to be lethal; another nutrient is elevated to the status of health food; the industry throws its weight behind it; and the American way of dietary life undergoes yet another revolution.

Harvey Levenstein, a Canadian historian who has written two fascinating social histories of American foodways, neatly sums up the beliefs that have guided the American way of eating since the heyday of John Harvey Kellogg: "that taste is not a true guide to what should be eaten; that one should not simply eat what one enjoys; that the important components of food cannot be seen or tasted, but are discernible only in scientific laboratories; and that experimental science has produced rules of nutrition that will prevent illness and encourage longevity." The power of any orthodoxy resides in its ability not to seem like one and, at least to a 1906 or 2006 genus American, these beliefs don't seem in the least bit strange or controversial.

It's easy, especially for Americans, to forget just how novel this nutritional orthodoxy is, or that there are still cultures that have been eating more or less the same way for generations, relying on such archaic criteria as taste and tradition to guide them in their food selection. We Americans are amazed to learn that some of the cultures that set their culinary course by the lights of habit and pleasure rather than nutritional science and marketing are actually healthier than we are—that is, suffer a lower incidence of diet-related health troubles.

The French paradox is the most famous such case, though as Paul Rozin points out, the French don't regard the matter as paradoxical at all. We Americans resort to that term because the French experience—a population of wine-swilling cheese eaters with lower rates of heart disease and obesity—confounds our orthodoxy about food. That orthodoxy regards certain tasty foods as poisons (carbs now, fats then), failing to appreciate that how we eat, and even how we feel about eating, may in the end be just as important as what we eat. The French eat all sorts of supposedly unhealthy foods, but they do it according to a strict and stable set of rules: They eat small portions and don't go back for seconds; they don't snack; they seldom eat alone; and communal meals are long, leisurely affairs. In other words, the French culture of food successfully negotiates the omnivore's dilemma, allowing the French to enjoy their meals without ruining their health.

Perhaps because we have no such culture of food in America almost every question about eating is up for grabs. Fats or carbs? Three squares or continuous grazing? Raw or cooked? Organic or industrial? Veg or vegan? Meat or mock meat? Foods of astounding novelty fill the shelves of our supermarket, and the line between a food and a "nutritional supplement" has fogged to the point where people make meals of protein bars and shakes. Consuming these neo-pseudo-foods alone in our cars, we have become a nation of antinomian eaters, each of us struggling to work out our dietary salvation on our own. Is it any wonder Americans suffer from so many eating disorders? In the absence of any lasting consensus about what and how and where and when to eat, the omnivore's dilemma has returned to America with an almost atavistic force.

This situation suits the food industry just fine, of course. The more anxious we are about eating, the more vulnerable we are to the seductions of the marketer and the expert's advice. Food marketing in particular thrives on dietary instability and so tends to exacerbate it. Since it's difficult to sell more food to such a well-fed population (though not, as we're discovering, impossible), food companies put their efforts into grabbing market share by introducing new kinds of highly processed foods, which have the virtue of being both highly profitable and infinitely adaptable. Sold under the banner of "convenience," these processed foods are frequently designed to create whole new eating occasions, such as in the bus on the way to school (the protein bar or Pop-Tart) or in the car on the way to work (Campbell's recently introduced a one-handed microwaveable microchunked soup in a container designed to fit a car's cup holder).

The success of food marketers in exploiting shifting eating patterns and nutritional fashions has a steep cost. Getting us to change how we eat over and over again tends to undermine the various social structures that surround and steady our eating, institutions like the family dinner, for example, or taboos on snacking between meals and eating alone. In their relentless pursuit of new markets, food companies (with some crucial help from the microwave oven, which made "cooking" something even small children could do) have broken Mom's hold over the American menu by marketing to every conceivable demographic—and especially to children.

A vice president of marketing at General Mills once painted for me a picture of the state of the American family dinner, courtesy of video cameras that the company's consulting anthropologists paid families to let them install in the ceiling above the kitchen and dining room tables. Mom, perhaps feeling sentimental about the dinners of her childhood, still prepares a dish and a salad that she usually winds up eating by herself. Meanwhile, the kids, and Dad, too, if he's around, each fix something different for themselves, because Dad's on a low-carb diet, the teenager's become a vegetarian, and the eight-year-old is on a strict ration of pizza that the shrink says it's best to indulge (lest she develop eating disorders later on in life). So over the course of a half hour or so each family member roams into the kitchen, removes a single-portion entree from the freezer, and zaps it in the microwave. (Many of these entrees have been helpfully designed to be safely "cooked" by an eight-year-old.) After the sound of the beep each diner brings his microwaveable dish to the dining room table, where he or she may or may not cross paths with another family member at the table for a few minutes. Families who eat this way are among the 47 percent of Americans who report to pollsters that they still sit down to a family meal every night.

Several years ago, in a book called *The Cultural Contradictions of Capitalism*, sociologist Daniel Bell called attention to the tendency of capitalism, in its single-minded pursuit of profit, to erode the various cultural underpinnings that steady a society but often impede the march of commercialization. The family dinner, and more generally a cultural consensus on the subject of eating, appears to be the latest such casualty of capitalism. These rules and rituals stood in the way of the food industry's need to sell a well-fed population more food through ingenious new ways of processing, packaging, and marketing it. Whether a stronger set of traditions would have stood up better to this relentless economic imperative is hard to say; today America's fast-food habits are increasingly gaining traction even in places like France.

So we find ourselves as a species almost back where we started: anxious omnivores struggling once again to figure out what it is wise to eat. Instead of relying on the accumulated wisdom of a cuisine, or even on the wisdom of our senses, we rely on expert opinion, advertising, government food pyramids, and diet books, and we place our faith in science to sort out for us what culture once did with rather more success. Such has been the genius of capitalism, to re-create something akin to a state of nature in the modern supermarket or fast-food outlet, throwing us back on a perplexing, nutritionally perilous landscape deeply shadowed again by the omnivore's dilemma.

PART THREE

GROWING UP SOCIAL

# 14

## Boyhood, Organized Sports, and the Construction of Masculinities

### MICHAEL A. MESSNER

*Though young women are now participating in sports in unprecedented numbers, the influence of sports activity on boys' identity and socialization experience remains a major interest in gender studies. Michael Messner, one of the pioneers and most prominent researchers of this topic, examines the way sports focus and define what it is to be masculine, the variations in sports' influence across social classes, and some unsuspected lessons sports participation imparts for relationships beyond the gym, pool, and fields of play. In reading this article, you might want to ask yourself: What would this article be saying if the subject was young women?*

In this study I explore and interpret the meanings that males themselves attribute to their boyhood participation in organized sport. In what ways do males construct masculine identities within the institution of organized sports? In what ways do class and racial differences mediate this relationship and perhaps lead to the construction of different meanings, and perhaps different masculinities? And what are some of the problems and contradictions within these constructions of masculinity?

### DESCRIPTION OF RESEARCH

Between 1983 and 1985, I conducted interviews with 30 male former athletes. Most of the men I interviewed had played the (U.S.) "major sports"—football, basketball, baseball, track. At the time of the interview, each had been retired from playing organized sports for at least five years. Their ages ranged from 21 to 48, with the median, 33; 14 were black, 14 were white, and two were Hispanic; 15 of the 16 black and Hispanic men had come from poor or working-class families, while the majority (9 of 14) of the white men had come from middle-class or professional families. All had at some time in their lives based their identities largely on their roles as athletes and could therefore be said to have had "athletic careers." Twelve had played organized sports through high school, 11 through college, and seven had been professional athletes. Though the sample was not randomly selected, an effort was made to see that the sample had a range of difference in terms of race and social class backgrounds, and that there was some variety in terms of age, types of sports played and levels of success in athletic careers. Without exception each man contacted agreed to be interviewed.

The tape-recorded interviews were semi-structured and took from one and one-half to six hours, with most taking about three hours. I asked each man to talk about four broad eras in his life: (1) his earliest experiences with sports in boyhood, (2) his athletic career, (3) retirement or disengagement from the athletic career, and (4) life after the athletic career. In each era, I focused the interview on the meanings of "success and failure," and on the boy's/man's relationships with family, with other males, with women, and with his own body.

In collecting what amounted to life histories of these men, my overarching purpose was to use feminist theories of masculine gender identity to explore how masculinity develops and changes as boys and men interact within the socially constructed world of organized sports. In addition to using the data to move toward some generalizations about the relationship between "masculinity and sport," I was also concerned with sorting out some of the variations among boys, based on class and racial inequalities, that led them to relate differently to athletic careers. I divided my sample into two comparison groups. The first group was made up of 10 men from higher-status backgrounds, primarily white, middle-class, and professional families. The second group was made up of 20 men from lower status backgrounds, primarily minority, poor, and working-class families.

## BOYHOOD AND THE PROMISE OF SPORTS

Zane Grey once said, "All boys love baseball. If they don't they're not real boys" (as cited in Kimmel 1990). This is, of course, an ideological statement; in fact, some boys do *not* love baseball, or any other sports, for that matter. There are millions of males who at an early age are rejected by, become alienated from, or lose interest in organized sports. Yet all boys are, to a greater or lesser extent, judged according to their ability, or lack of ability, in competitive sports (Eitzen 1975; Sabo 1985). In this study I focus on those males who did become athletes—males who eventually poured thousands of hours into the development of specific physical skills. It is in boyhood that we can discover the roots of their commitment to athletic careers.

How did organized sports come to play such a central role in these boy's lives? When asked to recall how and why they initially got into playing sports, many of the men interviewed for this study seemed a bit puzzled: after all, playing sports was "just the thing to do." A 42-year-old black man who had played college basketball put it this way:

> It was just what you did. It's kind of like, you went to school, you played athletics, and if you didn't, there was something wrong with you. It was just like brushing your teeth: it's just what you did. It's part of your existence.

Spending one's time playing sports with other boys seemed as natural as the cycle of the seasons: baseball in the spring and summer, football in the fall, basketball in the winter—and then it was time to get out the old baseball glove and begin again. As a black 35-year-old former professional football star said:

> I'd say when I wasn't in school, 95% of the time was spent in the park playing. It was the only thing to do. It just came as natural.

And a black, 34-year-old professional basketball player explained his early experiences in sports:

> My principal and teacher said, "Now if you work at this you might be pretty damned good." So it was more or less a community thing—everybody in the community said, "Boy, if you work hard and keep your nose clean, you gonna be good." 'Cause it was natural instinct.

"It was natural instinct." "I was a natural." Several athletes used words such as these to explain their early attraction to sports. But certainly there is nothing "natural" about throwing a ball through a hoop, hitting a ball with a bat, or jumping over hurdles. A boy, for instance, may have amazingly dexterous inborn hand-eye coordination, but this does not predispose him to a career of hitting baseballs any more than it predisposes him to a life as a brain surgeon. When one listens closely to what these men said about their early experiences in sports, it becomes clear that their adoption of the self-definition of "natural athlete" was the result of what Connell (1990) has called "a collective practice" that constructs masculinities. The boyhood development of masculine identity and status—truly problematic in a society that offers no official rite of passage into adulthood—results from a process of interaction with people and social institutions. Thus, in discussing early motivations in sports, men commonly talk of the importance of relationships with family members, peers, and the broader community.

## FAMILY INFLUENCES

Though most of the men in this study spoke of their mothers with love, respect, even reverence, their descriptions of their earliest experiences in sports are stories of an exclusively male world. The existence of older brothers or uncles who served as teachers and athletic role models—as well as sources of competition for attention and status within the family—was very common. An older brother, uncle, or even close friend of the family who was a successful athlete appears to have acted as a sort of standard of achievement against whom to measure oneself. A 34-year-old black man who had been a three-sport star in high school said:

> My uncles—my Uncle Harold went to the Detroit Tigers, played pro ball—all of 'em, everybody played sports, so I wanted to be better than anybody else. I knew

that everybody in this town knew them—their names were something. I wanted my name to be just like theirs.

Similarly, a black 41-year-old former professional football player recalled:

I was the younger of three brothers and everybody played sports, so consequently I was more or less forced into it. 'Cause one brother was always better than the next brother and then I came along and had to show them that I was just as good as them. My oldest brother was an all-city ballplayer, then my other brother comes along he's all-city and all-state, and then I have to come along.

For some, attempting to emulate or surpass the athletic accomplishments of older male family members created pressures that were difficult to deal with. A 33-year-old white man explained that he was a good athlete during boyhood, but the constant awareness that his two older brothers had been better made it difficult for him to feel good about himself, or to have fun in sports:

I had this sort of reputation that I followed from the playgrounds through grade school, and through high school. I followed these guys who were all-conference and all-state.

Most of these men, however, saw their relationships with their athletic older brothers and uncles in a positive light; it was within these relationships that they gained experience and developed motivations that gave them a competitive "edge" within their same-aged peer group. As a 33-year-old black man describes his earliest athletic experiences:

My brothers were role models. I wanted to prove—especially to my brothers— that I had heart, you know, that I was a man.

When asked, "What did it mean to you to be 'a man' at that age?" he replied:

Well, it meant that I didn't want to be a so-called scaredy-cat. You want to hit a guy even though he's bigger than you to show that, you know, you've got this macho image. I remember that at that young an age, that feeling was exciting to me. And that carried over, and as I got older, I got better and I began to look around me and see, well hey! I'm competitive with these guys, even though I'm younger, you know? And then of course all the compliments come—and I began to notice a change, even in my parents—especially in my father—he was proud of that, and that was very important to me. He was extremely important . . . he showed me more affection, now that I think of it.

As this man's words suggest, if men talk of their older brothers and uncles mostly as role models, teachers, and "names" to emulate, their talk of their relationships with their fathers is more deeply layered and complex. Athletic skills and competition for status may often be learned from older brothers, but it is in boys' relationships with fathers that we find many of the keys to the emotional salience of sports in the development of masculine identity.

## RELATIONSHIPS WITH FATHERS

The fact that boys' introductions to organized sports are often made by fathers who might otherwise be absent or emotionally distant adds a powerful emotional charge to these early experiences (Osherson 1986). Although playing organized sports eventually came to feel "natural" for all of the men interviewed in this study, many needed to be "exposed" to sports, or even gently "pushed" by their fathers to become involved in activities like Little League baseball. A white, 33-year-old-man explained:

> I still remember it like it was yesterday—Dad and I driving up in his truck, and I had my glove and my hat and all that—and I said, "Dad, I don't want to do it." He says, "What?" I says, "I don't want to do it." I was nervous. That I might fail. And he says, "Don't be silly. Lookit: There's Joey and Petey and all your friends out there." And so Dad says, "You're gonna do it, come on." And in my memory he's never said that about anything else; he just knew I needed a little kick in the pants and I'd do it. And once you're out there and you see all the other kids making errors and stuff, and you know you're better than those guys, you know: Maybe I *do* belong here. As it turned out, Little League was a good experience.

Some who were similarly "pushed" by their fathers were not so successful as the aforementioned man had been in Little League baseball, and thus the experience was not altogether a joyous affair. One 34-year-old white man, for instance, said he "inherited" his interest in sports from his father, who started playing catch with him at the age of four. Once he got into Little League, he felt pressured by his father, one of the coaches, who expected him to be the star of the team:

> I'd go 0-for-four sometimes, strike out three times in a Little League game, and I'd dread the ride home. I'd come home and he'd say, "Go in the bathroom and swing the bat in the mirror for an hour," to get my swing level . . . It didn't help much, though, I'd go out and strike out three or four times again the next game too [laughs ironically].

When asked if he had been concerned with having his father's approval, he responded:

Failure in his eyes? Yeah, I always thought that he wanted me to get some kind of [athletic] scholarship. I guess I was afraid of him when I was a kid. He didn't hit that much, but he had a rage about him—he'd rage, and that voice would just rattle you.

Similarly, a 24-year-old black man described his awe of his father's physical power and presence, and his sense of inadequacy in attempting to emulate him:

My father had a voice that sounded like rolling thunder. Whether it was intentional on his part or not, I don't know, but my father gave me a sense, an image of him being the most powerful being on earth, and that no matter what I ever did I would never come close to him . . . There were definite feelings of physical inadequacy that I couldn't work around.

It is interesting to note how these feelings of physical inadequacy relative to the father lived on as part of this young man's permanent internalized image. He eventually became a "feared" high school football player and broke school records in weight-lifting, yet,

As I grew older, my mother and friends told me that I had actually grown to be a larger man than my father. Even though in time I required larger clothes than he, which should have been a very concrete indication, neither my brother nor I could ever bring ourselves to say that I was bigger. We simply couldn't conceive of it.

Using sports activities as a means of identifying with and "living up to" the power and status of one's father was not always such a painful and difficult task for the men I interviewed. Most did not describe fathers who "pushed" them to become sports stars. The relationship between their athletic strivings and their identification with their fathers was more subtle. A 48-year-old black man, for instance, explained that he was not pushed into sports by his father, but was aware from an early age of the community status his father had gained through sports. He saw his own athletic accomplishments as a way to connect with and emulate his father:

I wanted to play baseball because my father had been quite a good baseball player in the Negro leagues before baseball was integrated, and so he was kind of a model for me. I remember, quite young, going to a baseball game he was in— this was before the war and all—I remember being in the stands with my mother and seeing him on first base, and being aware of the crowd . . . I was aware of people's confidence in him as a serious baseball player. I don't think my father ever said anything to me like "play sports" . . . [But] I knew he would like it if I did well. His admiration was important . . . he mattered.

Similarly, a 24-year-old white man described his father as a somewhat distant "role model" whose approval mattered:

> My father was more of an example . . . he definitely was very much in touch with and still had very fond memories of being an athlete and talked about it, bragged about it. . . . But he really didn't do that much to teach me skills, and he didn't always go to every game I played like some parents. But he approved and that was important, you know. That was important to get his approval. I always knew that playing sports was important to him, so I knew implicitly that it was good and there was definitely a value on it.

First experiences in sports might often come through relationships with brothers or older male relatives, and the early emotional salience of sports was often directly related to a boy's relationship with his father. The sense of commitment that these young boys eventually made to the development of athletic careers is best explained as a process of development of masculine gender identity and status in relation to same-sex peers.

## MASCULINE IDENTITY AND EARLY COMMITMENT TO SPORTS

When many of the men in this study said that during childhood they played sports because "it's just what everybody did," they of course meant that it was just what *boys* did. They were introduced to organized sports by older brothers and fathers, and once involved, found themselves playing within an exclusively male world. Though the separate (and unequal) gendered worlds of boys and girls came to appear as "natural," they were in fact socially constructed. Thorne's observations of children's activities in schools indicated that rather than "naturally" constituting "separate gendered cultures," there is considerable interaction between boys and girls in classrooms and on playgrounds. When adults set up legitimate contact between boys and girls, Thorne observed, this usually results in "relaxed interactions." But when activities in the classroom or on the playground are presented to children as sex-segregated activities and gender is marked by teachers and other adults ("boys line up here, girls over there"), "gender boundaries are heightened, and mixed-sex interaction becomes an explicit arena of risk" (Thorne 1986; 70). Thus sex-segregated activities such as organized sports as structured by adults, provide the context in which gendered identities and separate "gendered cultures" develop and come to appear natural. For the boys in this study, it became "natural" to equate masculinity with competition, physical strength, and skills. Girls simply did not (could not, it was believed) participate in these activities.

Yet it is not simply the separation of children, by adults, into separate activities that explains why many boys came to feel such a strong connection with sports activities, while so few girls did. As I listened to men recall their earliest experiences in organized sports, I heard them talk of insecurity, loneliness, and especially a need to connect with other people as a primary motivation in their early sports strivings. As a 42-year-old white man stated, "The most important thing was just being out there with the rest of the guys—being friends." Another 32-year-old interviewee was born in Mexico and moved to the United States at a fairly young age. He never knew his father, and his mother died when he was only nine years old. Suddenly he felt rootless, and threw himself into sports. His initial motivations, however, do not appear to be based on a need to compete and win:

> Actually, what I think sports did for me is it brought me into kind of an instant family. By being on a Little League team, or even just playing with all kinds of different kids in the neighborhood, it brought what I really wanted, which was some kind of closeness. It was just being there, and being friends.

Clearly, what these boys needed and craved was that which was most problematic for them: connection and unity with other people. But why do these young males find *organized sports* such an attractive context in which to establish "a kind of closeness" with others? Comparative observations of young boys' and girls' game-playing behaviors yield important insights into this question. Piaget (1965) and Lever (1976) both observed that girls tend to have more "pragmatic" and "flexible" orientations to the rules of games; they are more prone to make exceptions and innovations in the middle of a game in order to make the game more "fair." Boys, on the other hand, tend to have a more firm, even inflexible orientation to the rules of a game; to them, the rules are what protects any fairness. This difference, according to Gilligan (1982), is based on the fact that early developmental experiences have yielded deeply rooted differences between males' and females' developmental tasks, needs, and moral reasoning. Girls, who tend to define themselves primarily through connection with others, experience highly competitive situations (whether in organized sports or in other hierarchical institutions) as threats to relationships, and thus to their identities. For boys, the development of gender identity involves the construction of positional identities, where a sense of self is solidified through separation from others (Chodorow 1978). Yet feminist psychoanalytic theory has tended to oversimplify the internal lives of men (Lichterman 1986). Males do appear to develop positional identities, yet despite their fears of intimacy, they also retain a human need for closeness and unity with others. This ambivalence toward intimate relationships is a major thread running through masculine development throughout the life course. Here we can conceptualize what Craib (1987) calls the "elective affinity" between personality and social structure: For the boy who both seeks and fears attachment with others, the rule-bound structure of organized sports can promise to be a safe place in which to seek nonintimate attachment with others within a context that maintains clear boundaries, distance, and separation.

## COMPETITIVE STRUCTURES AND CONDITIONAL SELF-WORTH

Young boys may initially find that sports gives them the opportunity to experience "some kind of closeness" with others, but the structure of sports and athletic careers often undermines the possibility of boys learning to transcend their fears of intimacy, thus becoming able to develop truly close and intimate relationships with others (Kidd 1990; Messner 1987). The sports world is extremely hierarchical, and an incredible amount of importance is placed on winning, on "being number one." For instance, a few years ago I observed a basketball camp put on for boys by a professional basketball coach and his staff. The youngest boys, about eight years old (who could barely reach the basket with their shots) played a brief scrimmage. Afterwards, the coaches lined them up in a row in front of the older boys who were sitting in the grandstands. One by one, the coach would stand behind each boy, put his hand on the boy's head (much in the manner of a priestly benediction), and the older boys in the stands would applaud and cheer, louder or softer, depending on how well or poorly the young boy was judged to have performed. The two or three boys who were clearly the exceptional players looked confident that they would receive the praise they were due. Most of the boys, though, had expressions ranging from puzzlement to thinly disguised terror on their faces as they awaited the judgments of the older boys.

This kind of experience teaches boys that it is not "just being out there with the guys—being friends," that ensures the kind of attention and connection that they crave; it is being *better* than the other guys—*beating* them—that is the key to acceptance. Most of the boys in this study did have some early successes in sports, and thus their ambivalent need for connection with others was met, at least for a time. But the institution of sport tends to encourage the development of what Schafer (1975) has called "conditional self-worth" in boys. As boys become aware that acceptance by others is contingent upon being good—a "winner"—narrow definitions of success, based upon performance and winning become increasingly important to them. A 33-year-old black man said that by the time he was in his early teens:

> It was expected of me to do well in all my contests—I mean by my coaches, my peers, and my family. So I in turn expected to do well, and if I didn't do well, then I'd be very disappointed.

The man from Mexico, discussed above, who said that he had sought "some kind of closeness" in his early sports experiences began to notice in his early teens that if he played well, was a *winner*, he would get attention from others:

It got to the point where I started realizing, noticing that people were always there for me, backing me all the time—sports got to be really fun because I always had some people there backing me. Finally my oldest brother started going to all my games, even though I had never really seen who he was [laughs]—after the game, you know, we never really saw each other, but he was at all my base-ball games, and it seemed like we shared a kind of closeness there, but only in those situations. Off the field, when I wasn't in uniform, he was never around.

By high school, he said, he felt "up against the wall." Sports hadn't deliv-ered what he had hoped it would, but he thought if he just tried harder, won one more championship trophy, he would get the attention he truly craved. Despite his efforts, this attention was not forthcoming. And, sadly, the pres-sures he had put on himself to excel in sports had taken most of the fun out of playing.

For many of the men in this study, throughout boyhood and into adolescence, this conscious striving for successful achievement became the primary means through which they sought connection with other people (Messner 1987). But it is important to recognize that young males' internalized ambivalences about intimacy do not fully determine the contours and directions of their lives. Mas-culinity continues to develop through interaction with the social world—and because boys from different backgrounds are interacting with substantially different familial, educational, and other institutions, these differences will lead them to make different choices and define situations in different ways. Next, I examine the differences in the ways that boys from higher- and lower-status families and communities related to organized sports.

## STATUS DIFFERENCES AND COMMITMENTS TO SPORTS

In discussing early attractions to sports, the experiences of boys from higher- and lower-status backgrounds are quite similar. Both groups indicate the importance of fathers and older brothers in introducing them to sports. Both groups speak of the joys of receiving attention and acceptance among family and peers for early successes in sports. Note the similarities, for instance, in the following descriptions of boyhood athletic experiences of two men. First, a man born in a white, middle-class family:

I loved playing sports so much from a very early age because of early exposure. A lot of the sports came easy at an early age, and because they did, and because you were successful at something, I think that you're inclined to strive for that gratification. It's like, if you're good, you like it, because it's instant gratification. I'm doing something that I'm good at and I'm gonna keep doing it.

Second, a black man from a poor family:

Fortunately I had some athletic ability, and, quite naturally, once you start doing good in whatever it is—I don't care if it's jacks—you show off what you do. That's your ability, that's your blessing, so you show it off as much as you can.

For boys from both groups, early exposure to sports, the discovery that they had some "ability," shortly followed by some sort of family, peer, and community recognition, all eventually led to the commitment of hundreds and thousands of hours of playing, practicing, and dreaming of future stardom. Despite these similarities, there are also some identifiable differences that begin to explain the tendency of males from lower-status backgrounds to develop higher levels of commitment to sports careers. The most clear-cut differences was that while men from higher-status backgrounds are likely to describe their earliest athletic experiences and motivations almost exclusively in terms of immediate family, men from lower-status backgrounds more commonly describe the importance of a broader community context. For instance, a 46-year-old man who grew up in a "poor working class" black family in a small town in Arkansas explained:

> In that community, at the age of third or fourth grade, if you're a male, they expect you to show some kind of inclination, some kind of skill in football or basketball. It was an expected thing, you know? My mom and my dad, they didn't push at all. It was the general environment.

A 48-year-old man describes sports activities as a survival strategy in his poor black community:

> Sports protected me from having to compete in gang stuff, or having to be good with my fists. If you were an athlete and got into the fist world, that was your business, and that was okay—but you didn't have to if you didn't want to. People would generally defer to you, give you your space away from trouble.

A 35-year-old man who grew up in "a poor black ghetto" described his boyhood relationship to sports similarly:

> Where I came from, either you were one of two things: you were in sports or you were out on the streets being a drug addict, or breaking into places. The guys who were in sports, we had it a little easier, because we were accepted by both groups. . . . So it worked out to my advantage, cause I didn't get into a lot of trouble—some trouble, but not a lot.

The fact that boys in lower-status communities faced these kinds of realities gave salience to their developing athletic identities. In contrast, sports were important to boys from higher-status backgrounds, yet the middle-class environment seemed more secure, less threatening, and offered far more options. By the time most of these boys got into junior high or high school, many had made conscious decisions to shift their attentions away from athletic careers to educational and (nonathletic) career goals. A 32-year-old white college athletic director told me that he had seen his chance to pursue a pro baseball career as "pissing in the wind," and instead, focused on education. Similarly, a 33-year-old white dentist who was a three-sport star in high school, decided not to play sports in college, so he could focus on getting into dental school. As he put it,

> I think I kind of downgraded the stardom thing. I thought it was small potatoes. And sure, that's nice in high school and all that, but on a broad scale, I didn't think it amounted to all that much.

This statement offers an important key to understanding the construction of masculine identity within a middle-class context. The status that this boy got through sports had been *very* important to him, yet he could see that "on a broad scale," this sort of status was "small potatoes." This sort of early recognition is more than a result of the oft-noted middle-class tendency to raise "future-oriented" children (Rubin 1976; Sennett and Cobb 1973). Perhaps more important, it is that the *kinds* of future orientations developed by boys from higher-status backgrounds are consistent with the middle-class context. These men's descriptions of their boyhoods reveal that they grew up immersed in a wide range of institutional frameworks, of which organized sports was just one. And—importantly—they could see that the status of adult males around them was clearly linked to their positions within various professions, public institutions, and bureaucratic organizations. It was clear that access to this sort of institutional status came through educational achievement, not athletic prowess. A 32-year-old black man who grew up in a professional-class family recalled that he had idolized Wilt Chamberlain and dreamed of being a pro basketball player, yet his father discouraged his athletic strivings:

> He knew I liked the game. I *loved* the game. But basketball was not recommended; my dad would say, "That's a stereotyped image for black youth. . . . When your basketball is gone and finished, what are you gonna do? One day, you might get injured. What are you gonna look forward to?" He stressed education.

Similarly, a 32-year-old man who was raised in a white, middle-class family, had found in sports a key means of gaining acceptance and connection in his peer group. Yet he was simultaneously developing an image of himself as a "smart student," and becoming aware of a wide range of nonsport life options:

> My mother was constantly telling me how smart I was, how good I was, what a nice person I was, and giving me all sorts of positive strokes, and those positive

strokes became a self-motivating kind of thing. I had this image of myself as smart, and I lived up to that image.

It is not that parents of boys in lower-status families did not also encourage their boys to work hard in school. Several reported that their parents "stressed books first, sports second." It's just that the broader social context—education, economy, and community—was more likely to *narrow* lower-status boys' perceptions of real-life options, while boys from higher-status backgrounds faced an expanding world of options. For instance, with a different socioeconomic background, one 35-year-old black man might have become a great musician instead of a star professional football running back. But he did not. When he was a child, he said, he was most interested in music:

> I wanted to be a drummer. But we couldn't afford drums. My dad couldn't go out and buy me a drum set or a guitar even—it was just one of those things; he was just trying to make ends meet.

But he *could* afford, as could so many in his socioeconomic condition, to spend countless hours at the local park, where he was told by the park supervisor

> that I was a natural—not only in gymnastics or baseball—whatever I did, I was a natural. He told me I shouldn't waste this talent, and so I immediately started watching the big guys then.

In retrospect, this man had potential to be a musician or any number of things, but his environment limited his options to sports, and he made the best of it. Even within sports, he, like most boys in the ghetto, was limited:

> We didn't have any tennis courts in the ghetto—we used to have a lot of tennis balls, but no racquets. I wonder today how good I might be in tennis if I had gotten a racquet in my hands at an early age.

It is within this limited structure of opportunity that many lower-status young boys found sports to be *the* place, rather than *a* place, within which to construct masculine identity, status, the relationships. A 36-year-old white man explained that his father left the family when he was very young and his mother faced a very difficult struggle to make ends meet. As his words suggest, the more limited a boy's options, and the more insecure his family situation, the more likely he is to make an early commitment be an athletic career.

> I used to ride my bicycle to Little League practice—if I'd waited for someone to pick me up and take me to the ball park I'd have never played. I'd get to the ball park and all the other kids would have their dad bring them to practice or games. But I'd park my bike to the side and when it was over I'd get on it and go home.

Sports was the way for me to move everything to the side—family problems, just all the embarrassments—and think about one thing, and that was sports . . . In the third grade, when the teacher went around the classroom and asked everybody, "What do you want to be when you grow up?," I said, "I want to be a major league baseball player," and everybody laughed their heads off.

This man eventually did enjoy a major league baseball career. Most boys from lower-status backgrounds who make similar early commitments to athletic careers are not so successful. As stated earlier, the career structure of organized sports is highly competitive and hierarchical. In fact, the chances of attaining professional status in sports are approximately 4:100,000 for a white man, 2:100,000 for a black man, and 3:1 million for a Hispanic man in the United States (Leonard and Reyman 1988). Nevertheless, the immediate rewards (fun, status, attention), along with the constricted (nonsports) structure of opportunity, attract disproportionately large numbers of boys from lower-status backgrounds to athletic careers as their major means of constructing a masculine identity. These are the boys who later, as young men, had to struggle with "conditional self-worth," and, more often than not, occupational dead ends. Boys from higher-status backgrounds, on the other hand, bolstered their boyhood, adolescent, and early adult status through their athletic accomplishments. Their wider range of experiences and life chances led to an early shift away from sports careers as the major basis of identity (Messner 1989).

## CONCLUSION

The conception of the masculinity-sports relationship developed here begins to illustrate the idea of an "elective affinity" between social structure and personality. Organized sports is a "gendered institution"—an institution constructed by gender relations. As such, its structure and values (rules, formal organization, sex composition, etc.), reflect dominant conceptions of masculinity and femininity. Organized sports is also a "gendering institution"—an institution that helps to construct the current gender order. Part of this construction of gender is accomplished through the "masculinizing" of male bodies and minds.

Yet boys do not come to their first experiences in organized sports as "blank slates," but arrive with already "gendering" identities due to early developmental experiences and previous socialization. I have suggested here that an important thread running through the development of masculine identity is males' ambivalence toward intimate unity with others. Those boys who experience early athletic successes find in the structure of organized sport an affinity with this masculine ambivalence toward intimacy: The rule-bound, competitive, hierarchical world of sport offers boys an attractive means of establishing an emotionally distant (and thus "safe") connection with others. Yet as boys begin to define themselves as "athletes," they learn that in order to be accepted (to have connection) through sports, they must be winners. And in order to be winners, they must construct relationships with others (and with themselves) that are consistent with the competitive and hierarchical values and structure of the sports world. As a result, they often develop a "conditional self-worth" that leads them to construct more instrumental relationships with themselves and others. This ultimately exacerbates their difficulties in constructing intimate relationships with others. In effect, the interaction between the young male's preexisting internalized ambivalence toward intimacy with the competitive hierarchical institution of sport has resulted in the construction of a masculine personality that is characterized by instrumental rationality, goal-orientation, and difficulties with intimate connection and expression (Messner 1987).

This theoretical line of inquiry invites us not simply to examine how social institutions "socialize" boys, but also to explore the ways that boys' already-gendering identities interact with social institutions (which, like organized sport, are themselves the product of gender relations). This study has also suggested that it is not some singular "masculinity" that is being constructed through athletic careers. It may be correct, from a psychoanalytic perspective, to suggest that all males bring ambivalences toward intimacy to their interactions with the world, but "the world" is a very different place for males from different racial and socioeconomic backgrounds. Because males have substantially different interactions with the world, based on class, race, and other differences and inequalities, we might expect the construction of masculinity to take on different meanings for boys and men from differing backgrounds (Messner 1989). Indeed, this study has suggested that boys from higher-status backgrounds face a much broader range of options than do their lower-status counterparts. As a result, athletic careers take on different meanings for these boys. Lower-status boys are likely to see athletic careers as *the* institutional context for the construction of their masculine status and identities, while higher-status males make an early shift away from athletic careers toward other institutions (usually education and nonsports careers). A key line of inquiry for future studies might begin by exploring this irony of sports careers: Despite the fact that "the athlete" is currently an example of an exemplary form of masculinity in public ideology, the vast majority of boys who become most committed to athletic careers are never well-rewarded for their efforts. The fact that class and racial dynamics lead boys from higher-status backgrounds, unlike their lower status counterparts to move into non-sports careers illustrates how the construction of different kinds of masculinities is a key component of the overall construction of the gender order.

## REFERENCES

Chodorow, N. (1978). *The Reproduction of Mothering.* Berkeley: Univ. of California Press.
Connell, R. W. (1987). *Gender and Power.* Stanford, CA: Stanford Univ. Press.

Connell, R. W. (1990). "An iron man: the body and some contradictions of hegemonic masculinity." In M. A. Messner and D. F. Sabo (eds.) *Sport, Men and the Gender Order: Critical Feminist Perspectives.* Champaign, IL: Human Kinetics.

Craib, I. (1987). "Masculinity and male dominance." *Soc. Rev.* 38: 721–743.

Eitzen, D. S. (1975). "Athletics in the status system of male adolescents: a replication of Coleman's *The Adolescent Society." Adolescence* 10: 268–276.

Gilligan, C. (1982). *In a Different Voice: Psychological Theory and Women's Development.* Cambridge, MA: Harvard Univ. Press.

Kidd, B. (1990). "The men's cultural center: sports and the dynamic of women's oppression/men's repression," In M. A. Messner and D. F. Sabo (eds.) *Sport, Men and the Gender Order: Critical Feminist Perspectives.* Champaign, IL: Human Kinetics.

Kimmel, M. S. (1990). "Baseball and the reconstitution of American masculinity: 1880–1920." In M. A. Messner and D. F. Sabo (eds.) *Sport, Men and the Gender Order: Critical Feminist Perspectives.* Champaign, IL: Human Kinetics.

Leonard, W. M. II and J. M. Reyman (1988). "The odds of attaining professional athlete status: refining the computations." *Sociology of Sport J.* 5: 162–169.

Lever, J. (1976). "Sex differences in the games children play." *Social Problems* 23: 478–487.

Lichterman, P. (1986). "Chodorow's psychoanalytic sociology: a project half-completed." *California Sociologist* 9: 147–166.

Messner, M. (1987). "The meaning of success: the athletic experience and the development of male identity," pp. 193–210 in H. Brod (ed.) *The Making of Masculinities: The New Men's Studies.* Boston: Allen and Unwin.

Messner, M. (1989). "Masculinities and athletic careers." *Gender and Society* 3: 71–88.

Osherson, S. (1986). *Finding Our Fathers: How a Man's Life Is Shaped by His Relationship with His Father.* New York: Fawcett Columbine.

Piaget, J. H. (1965). *The Moral Judgment of the Child.* New York: Free Press.

Rubin, L. B. (1976). *Worlds of Pain: Life in the Working Class Family.* New York: Basi Books.

Sabo, D. (1985). "Sport, patriarchy and male identity: new questions about men and sport." *Arena Rev.* 9: 2.

Schafer, W. E. (1975). "Sport and male sex role socialization." *Sport Sociology Bull* 47–54.

Sennett, R. and J. Cobb (1973). *The Hidden Injuries of Class.* New York: Random House.

Thorne, B. (1986). "Girls and boys together . . . but mostly apart: gender arrangement in elementary schools," pp. 167–184 in W. W. Hartup and Z. Rubin (eds.) *Relationships and Development.* Hillsdale, NJ: Lawrence Erlbaum.

# 15

## Concerted Cultivation and the Accomplishment of Natural Growth

FROM *Unequal Childhoods: Class, Race, and Family Life*

### ANNETTE LAREAU

*For many years sociologists have studied differing socialization (child-rearing) practices. These studies often negatively contrast working-class practices against middle-class ones, especially in terms of preparation for success in a rapidly changing society and world. Annette Lareau implicitly challenges this bias, suggesting that the "concerted cultivation" practices of more affluent middle-class families may have their drawbacks. She and her students observed the lives of children across a range of social classes for several years and determined not only fairly distinct class differences but the benefits of a contrasting "accomplishment of natural growth" among the nonaffluent.*

Laughing and yelling, a white fourth-grader named Garrett Tallinger splashes around in the swimming pool in the backyard of his four-bedroom home in the suburbs on a late spring afternoon. As on most evenings, after a quick dinner his father drives him to soccer practice. This is only one of Garrett's many activities. His brother has a baseball game at a different location. There are evenings when the boys' parents relax, sipping a glass of wine. Tonight is not one of them. As they rush to change out of their work clothes and get the children ready for practice, Mr. and Mrs. Tallinger are harried.

Only ten minutes away, a Black fourth-grader, Alexander Williams, is riding home from a school open house. His mother is driving their beige, leather-upholstered Lexus. It is 9:00 P.M. on a Wednesday evening. Ms. Williams is tired from work and has a long Thursday ahead of her. She will get up at 4:45 A.M. to go out of town on business and will not return before 9:00 P.M. On Saturday morning, she will chauffeur Alexander to a private piano lesson at 8:15 A.M., which will be followed by a choir rehearsal and then a soccer game. As they ride in the dark, Alexander's mother, in a quiet voice, talks with her son, asking him questions and eliciting his opinions.

Discussions between parents and children are a hallmark of middle-class child rearing. Like many middle-class parents, Ms. Williams and her husband see themselves as "developing" Alexander to cultivate his talents in a concerted fashion. Organized activities, established and controlled by mothers and fathers, dominate the lives of middle-class children such as Garrett and Alexander. By making certain their children have these and other experiences, middle-class parents engage in a process of *concerted cultivation*. From this, a robust sense of entitlement takes root in the children. This sense of entitlement plays an especially important role in institutional settings, where middle-class children learn to question adults and address them as relative equals.

Only twenty minutes away, in blue-collar neighborhoods, and slightly farther away, in public housing projects, childhood looks different. Mr. Yanelli, a white working-class father, picks up his son Little Billy, a fourth-grader, from an after-school program. They come home and Mr. Yanelli drinks a beer while Little Billy first watches television, then rides his bike and plays in the street. Other nights, he and his Dad sit on the sidewalk outside their house and play cards. At about 5:30 P.M. Billys mother gets home from her job as a house cleaner. She fixes dinner and the entire family sits down to eat together. Extended family are a prominent part of their lives. Ms. Yanelli touches base with her "entire family every day" by phone. Many nights Little Billy's uncle stops by, sometimes bringing Little Billy's youngest cousin. In the spring, Little Billy plays baseball on a local team. Unlike for Garrett and Alexander, who have at least four activities a week, for Little Billy, baseball is his only organized activity outside of school during the entire year. Down the road, a white working-class girl, Wendy Driver, also spends the evening with her girl cousins, as they watch a video and eat popcorn, crowded together on the living room floor.

Farther away, a Black fourth-grade boy, Harold McAllister, plays outside on a summer evening in the public housing project in which he lives. His two male cousins are there that night, as they often are. After an afternoon spent unsuccessfully searching for a ball so they could play basketball, the boys had resorted to watching sports on television. Now they head outdoors for a twilight water balloon fight. Harold tries to get his neighbor, Miss Latifa, wet. People sit in white plastic lawn chairs outside the row of apartments. Music and television sounds waft through the open windows and doors.

The adults in the lives of Billy, Wendy, and Harold want the best for them. Formidable economic constraints make it a major life task for these parents to put food on the table, arrange for housing, negotiate unsafe neighborhoods, take children to the doctor (often waiting for city buses that do not come), clean children's clothes, and get children to bed and have them ready for school the next morning. But unlike middle-class parents, these adults do not consider the concerted development of children, particularly through organized leisure activities, an essential aspect of good parenting. Unlike the Tallingers and Williamses, these mothers and fathers do not focus on concerned cultivation. For them, the crucial responsibilities of parenthood do not lie in eliciting their children's feelings, opinions, and thoughts. Rather, they see a clear boundary between adults and children. Parents tend to use directives: they tell their children what to do rather than persuading them with reasoning. Unlike their middle-class counterparts, who have a steady diet of adult organized activities, the working-class and poor children have more control over the character of their leisure activities. Most children are free to go out and play with friends and relatives who typically live close by. Their parents and guardians facilitate the *accomplishment of natural growth*. Yet these children and their parents interact with central institutions in the society, such as schools, which firmly and decisively promote strategies of concerted cultivation in child rearing. For working-class and poor families, the cultural logic of child rearing at home is out of synch with the standards of institutions. As a result, while children whose parents adopt strategies of concerted cultivation appear to gain a sense of entitlement, children such as Billy Yanelli, Wendy Driver, and Harold McAllister appear to gain an emerging sense of distance, distrust, and constraint in their institutional experiences.

## CULTURAL REPERTOIRES

Professionals who work with children, such as teachers, doctors, and counselors, generally agree about how children should be raised. Of course, from time to time they may disagree on the ways standards should be enacted for an individual child or family. For example, teachers may disagree about whether or not parents should stop and correct a child who mispronounces a word while reading. Counselors may disagree over whether a mother is being too protective of her child. Still, there is little dispute among professionals on the broad principles for promoting educational development in children through proper parenting. These standards include the importance of talking with children, developing their educational interests, and playing an active role in their schooling. Similarly, parenting guidelines typically stress the importance of reasoning with children and teaching them to solve problems through negotiation rather than with physical force. Because these guidelines are so generally accepted, and because they focus on a set of practices concerning how parents should raise children, they form a *dominant set of cultural repertoires* about how children should be raised. This widespread agreement among professionals about the broad principles for child rearing permeates our society. A small number of experts thus potentially shape the behavior of a large number of parents.

Professionals' advice regarding the best way to raise children has changed regularly over the last two centuries. From strong opinions about the merits of bottle feeding, being stern with children, and utilizing physical punishment (with dire warnings of problematic outcomes should parents indulge children), there have been shifts to equally strongly worded recommendations about the benefits of breast feeding, displaying emotional warmth toward children, and using reasoning and negotiation as mechanisms of parental control. Middle-class parents appear to shift their behaviors in a variety of spheres more rapidly and more thoroughly than do working-class or poor parents. As professionals have shifted their recommendations from bottlefeeding to breast feeding, from stern approaches to warmth and empathy, and from spanking to time-outs, it is middle-class parents who have responded most promptly. Moreover, in recent decades, middle-class children in the United States have had to face the prospect of "declining fortunes." Worried about how their children will get ahead, middle-class parents are increasingly determined to make sure that their children are not excluded from any opportunity that might eventually contribute to their advancement.

Middle-class parents who comply with current professional standards and engage in a pattern of concerted cultivation deliberately try to stimulate their children's development and foster their cognitive and social skills. The commitment among working-class and poor families to provide comfort, food, shelter, and other basic support requires ongoing effort, given economic challenges and the formidable demands of child rearing. But it stops short of the deliberate cultivation of children and their leisure activities that occurs in middle-class families. For working-class and poor families, sustaining children's natural growth is viewed as an accomplishment.

What is the outcome of these different philosophies and approaches to child rearing? Quite simply, they appear to lead to the *transmission of differential advantages* to children. In this study, there was quite a bit more talking in middle-class homes than in working-class and poor homes, leading to the development of greater verbal agility, larger vocabularies, more comfort with authority figures, and more familiarity with abstract concepts. Importantly, children also developed skill differences in interacting with authority figures in institutions and at home. Middle-class children such as Garrett Tallinger and Alexander Williams learn, as young boys, to shake the hands of adults and look them in the eye. In studies of job interviews, investigators have found that potential employees have less than one minute to make a good impression. Researchers stress the importance of eye contact, firm handshakes, and displaying comfort with bosses during the interview. In poor families like Harold McAllister's, however, family members usually do not look each other in the eye when conversing. In addition, as Elijah Anderson points out, they live in neighborhoods where it can be dangerous to look people in the eye too long. The types of social competence transmitted in the McAllister family are valuable, but they are potentially less valuable (in employment interviews, for example) than those learned by Garrett Tallinger and Alexander Williams.

The white and Black middle-class children in this study also exhibited an emergent version of the *sense of entitlement* characteristic of the middle-class. They acted as though they had a right to pursue their own individual preferences and to actively manage interactions in institutional settings. They appeared comfortable in these settings; they were open to sharing information and asking for attention. Although some children were more outgoing than others, it was common practice among middle-class children to shift interactions to suit *their* preferences. Alexander Williams knew how to get the doctor to listen to his concerns (about the bumps under his arm from his new deodorant). His mother explicitly trained and encouraged him to speak up with the doctor. Similarly, a Black middle-class girl, Stacey Marshall, was taught by her mother to expect the gymnastics teacher to accommodate her individual learning style. Thus, middle-class children were trained in "the rules of the game" that govern interactions with institutional representatives. They were not conversant in other important social skills, however, such as organizing their time for hours on end during weekends and summers, spending long periods of time away from adults, or hanging out with adults in a nonobtrusive, subordinate fashion. Middle-class children also learned (by imitation and by direct training) how to make the rules work in their favor. Here, the enormous stress on reasoning and negotiation in the home also has a potential advantage for future institutional negotiations. Additionally, those in authority responded positively to such interactions. Even in fourth grade, middle-class children appeared to be acting on their own behalf to gain advantages. They made special requests of teachers and doctors to adjust procedures to accommodate their desires.

The working-class and poor children, by contrast, showed an emerging *sense of constraint* in their interactions in institutional settings. They were less likely to try to customize interactions to suit their own preferences. Like their parents, the children accepted the actions of persons in authority (although at times they also covertly resisted them). Working-class and poor parents sometimes were not as aware of their children's school situation (as when their children were not doing homework). Other times, they dismissed the school rules as unreasonable. For example, Wendy Driver's mother told her to "punch" a boy who was pestering her in class; Billy Yanelli's parents were proud of him when he "beat up" another boy on the playground, even though Billy was then suspended from school. Parents also had trouble getting "the school" to respond to their concerns. When Ms. Yanelli complained that she "hates" the school, she gave her son a lesson in powerlessness and frustration in the face of an important institution. Middle-class children such as Stacey Marshall learned to make demands on professionals, and when they succeeded in making the rules work in their favor they augmented their "cultural capital" (i.e., skills individuals inherit that can then be translated into different forms of value as they move through various institutions) for the future. When working-class and poor children confronted institutions, however, they generally were unable to make the rules work in their favor nor did they obtain capital for adulthood. Because of these patterns of legitimization, children raised according to the logic of concerted cultivation can gain advantages, in the form of an emerging sense of entitlement, while children raised according to the logic of natural growth tend to develop an emerging sense of constraint.

In this study, the research assistants and I followed a small number of families around in an intensive fashion to get a sense of the rhythms of their everyday lives. On the basis of the data collected, I develop the claim that common economic position in the society, defined in terms of social class membership, is closely tied to differences in the cultural logic of child-rearing. Following a well-established Western European tradition, I provide a categorical analysis, grouping families into the social categories of middle class, working class, and poor. * * * I see this approach as more valuable than the gradational analysis

TABLE I. TYPOLOGY OF DIFFERENCES IN CHILD REARING

| | Child-Rearing Approach | |
| --- | --- | --- |
| | Concerted Cultivation | Accomplishment of Natural Growth |
| Key Elements | Parent actively fosters and assesses child's talents, opinions, and skills | Parent cares for child and allows child to grow |
| Organization of Daily Life | Multiple child leisure activities orchestrated by adults | "Hanging out," particularly with kin, by child |
| Language Use | Reasoning/directives Child contestation of adult statements Extended negotiations between parents and child | Directives Rare questioning or challenging of adults by child General acceptance by child of directives |
| Interventions in Institutions | Criticisms and interventions on behalf of child Training of child to take on this role | Dependence on institutions Sense of powerlessness and frustration Conflict between child-rearing practices at home and at school |
| Consequences | Emerging sense of entitlement on the part of the child | Emerging sense of constraint on the part of the child |

often adopted by American scholars. In addition, I demonstrate that class differences in family life cut across a number of different and distinct spheres, which are usually not analyzed together by social scientists.

In particular, I delineate a pattern of concerted cultivation in middle-class families and a pattern of the accomplishment of natural growth in working-class and poor families. Table I provides an overview of the main points of the book. It indicates that concerted cultivation entails an emphasis on children's structured activities, language development and reasoning in the home, and active intervention in schooling. By contrast, the accomplishment of natural growth describes a form of child rearing in which children "hang out" and play, often with relatives, are given clear directives from parents with limited negotiation, and are granted more autonomy to manage their own affairs in institutions outside of the home. These patterns help us unpack the mechanisms through which social class conveys an advantage in daily life.

\* \* \*

Social class differences in children's life experiences can be seen in the details of life. In our study, the pace of life was different for middle-class families compared to working-class and poor families. In the middle class, life was hectic. Parents were racing from activity to activity. In families with more than one child, parents often juggled conflicts between children's activities. In these families, economic resources for food, clothing, shelter, transportation, children's activities, and other routine expenses were in ample supply. Of course, some parents often *felt* short of money. At times they were not able to enjoy the vacations that they would have liked. But, as I show, families routinely spent hundreds and even thousands of dollars per year promoting children's activities.

Because there were so many children's activities, and because they were accorded so much importance, children's activities determined the schedule for the entire family. Siblings tagged along, sometimes willingly and sometimes not. Adults' leisure time was absorbed by children's activities. Children also spent much of their time in the company of adults or being directed by adults. They also had informal free time, but generally it was sandwiched between structured activities. In the organization of daily life, children's interests and activities were treated as matters of consequence.

In working-class and poor families, the organization of daily life differed from that of middle-class families. Here, there was economic strain not felt by many middle-class families. Particularly in poor families, it took enormous labor to get family members through the day, as mothers scrimped to make food last until they were able to buy more, waited for buses that didn't come, carried children's laundry out to public washers, got young children up, fed, dressed, and ready for school and oversaw children's daily lives. Children were aware of the economic strain. Money matters were frequently discussed.

Although money was in short supply, children's lives were more relaxed and, more importantly, the pace of life was slower. Children played with other children outside of the house. They frequently played with their cousins. Some children had organized activities, but they were far fewer than in middle-class families. Other times, children wanted to be in organized activities, but economic constraints, compounded by lack of transportation, made participation prohibitive. When children sought to display their budding talents and pursue activities more informally around the house, adults often treated children's interests as inconsequential. In addition, since they were not riding around in cars with parents going to organized activities or being directed by adults in structured activities, children in working-class and poor families had more autonomy from adults. Working-class and poor children had long stretches of free time during which they watched television and played with relatives and friends in the neighborhood, creating ways to occupy themselves. In these activities, there was more of a separation between adults' worlds and children's worlds.

In sum, there were social class differences in the number of organized activities, pace of family life, economic strain of family life, time spent in informal play, interest on the part of adults in children's activities, domination by children's activities of adult lives, and the amount of autonomy children had from adults. To be sure, other things also mattered in addition to social class. Gender differences were particularly striking. Girls and boys enjoyed different types of activities. Girls had more sedentary lives compared to boys. They also played closer to home. Race also played a role, particularly as racial segregation of residential neighborhoods divided children into racially segregated informal play groups (although race did not influence the number of activities children had).

## THE POWER OF SOCIAL CLASS

In the United States, people disagree about the importance of social class in daily life. Many Americans believe that this country is fundamentally *open*. They assume the society is best understood as a collection of individuals. They believe that people who demonstrate hard work, effort, and talent are likely to achieve upward mobility. Put differently, many Americans believe in the American Dream. In this view, children should have roughly equal life chances. The extent to which life chances vary can be traced to differences in aspirations, talent, and hard work on the part of individuals. This perspective rejects the notion that parents' social location systematically shapes children's life experiences and outcomes. Instead, outcomes are seen as resting more in the hands of individuals.

In a distinctly different but still related vein, some social scientists acknowledge that there are systemic forms of inequality, including, for example, differences in parents' educational levels, occupational prestige, and income, as well as in their child-rearing practices. These scholars, however, see such differences within society as a matter of *graduation*. To explain unequal life outcomes, they see it as helpful to look at, for example, differences in mothers' years of education or the range of incomes by households in a particular city. These different threads are interwoven in an intricate and often baffling pattern. Scholars who take this perspective on inequality typically focus on the ways specific patterns are related (e.g., the number of years of mothers' schooling and the size of children's vocabularies, or the number of years of mothers' education and parental involvement in schooling). Implicitly and explicitly, social scientists who share this perspective do not accept the position that there are identifiable, categorical differences in groups. They do not believe that the differences that do exist across society cohere into patterns recognizable as social classes.

* * * I have challenged both views. Rather than seeing society as a collection of individuals, I stressed the importance of individuals' social structural location in shaping their daily lives. Following a well-established European tradition, I rejected analyses that see differences in American families as best interpreted as a matter of fine gradations. Instead, I see as more valuable a

*categorical* analysis, wherein families are grouped into social categories such as poor, working class, and middle class. I argued that these categories are helpful in understanding the behavior of family members, not simply in one particular aspect but across a number of spheres. Family practices cohere by social class. Social scientists who accept this perspective may disagree about the number and type of categories and whether there should be, for example, an upper-middle-class category as well as a lower-middle-class one. Still, they agree that the observed differences in how people act can be meaningfully and fruitfully grouped into categories, without violating the complexity of daily life. My own view is that seeing selected aspects of family life as differentiated by social class is simply a better way to understand the reality of American family life. I also believe that social location at birth can be very important in shaping the routines of daily life, even when family members are not particularly conscious of the existence of social classes.

Thus, I have stressed how social class dynamics are woven into the texture and rhythm of children and parents' daily lives. Class position influences critical aspects of family life: time use, language use, and kin ties. Working-class and middle-class mothers may express beliefs that reflect a similar notion of "intensive mothering," but their behavior is quite different.

When children and parents move outside the home into the world of social institutions, they find that these cultural practices are not given equal value. There are signs that middle-class children benefit, in ways that are invisible to them and to their parents, from the degree of similarity between the cultural repertoires in the home and those standards adopted by institutions. * * *

## CONCERTED CULTIVATION AND THE ACCOMPLISHMENT OF NATURAL GROWTH

* * * [S]ocial class made a significant difference in the routines of children's daily lives. The white and Black middle-class parents engaged in practices of *concerted cultivation*. In these families, parents actively fostered and assessed their children's talents, opinions, and skills. They scheduled their children for activities. They reasoned with them. They hovered over them and outside the home they did not hesitate to intervene on the children's behalf. They made a deliberate and sustained effort to stimulate children's development and to cultivate their cognitive and social skills. The working-class and poor parents viewed children's development as unfolding spontaneously, as long as they were provided with comfort, food, shelter, and other basic support. I have called this cultural logic of child rearing the *accomplishment of natural growth*. As with concerted cultivation, this commitment, too, required ongoing effort; sustaining children's natural growth despite formidable life challenges is properly viewed as accomplishment. Parents who relied on natural growth generally organized their children's lives so they spent time in and around home, in informal play with peers, siblings, and cousins. As a result, the children had more autonomy

regarding leisure time and more opportunities for child-initiated play. They also were more responsible for their lives outside the home. Unlike in middle-class families, adult-organized activities were uncommon. Instead of the relentless focus on reasoning and negotiation that took place in middle-class families, there was less speech (including less whining and badgering) in working-class and poor homes. Boundaries between adults and children were clearly marked; parents generally used language not as an aim in itself but more as a conduit for social life. Directives were common. In their institutional encounters, working-class and poor parents turned over responsibility to professionals; when parents did try to intervene, they felt that they were less capable and less efficacious than they would have liked. While working-class and poor children differed in important ways, particularly in the stability of their lives, surprisingly there was not a major difference between them in their cultural logic of child rearing. Instead, in this study the cultural divide appeared to be between the middle class and everyone else.

# 16

## Deviance and Liminality

FROM *Something Old, Something Bold: Bridal Showers and Bachelorette Parties*

BETH MONTEMURRO

*Some cultural practices are secular rituals, especially those marking passages in the life cycle. The way societies—our own included—recognize and ritualize birth, the onset of puberty (adulthood), marriage, and death are sometimes seen as curious events. The author's term liminality refers to being "neither here nor there" in passing from one status to another, e.g., youth to married person. Liminality provides a moment, an opportunity, for deviant behavior in a socially approved if often embarrassing way. It also reveals the continuing struggle of young women to find greater gender equality, however imperfectly pursued.*

## DEVIANCE AND LIMINALITY

For some women, the deviant activity consistent at bachelorette parties—going to see strippers, kissing or flirting with strange men, getting intoxicated—was part of the fun. John Lofland (1969) suggested that some deviance is performed for the fun or thrill generated from participating in what he called "the adventurous deviant act." He wrote, "Some kinds of prohibited activities are claimed by some parts of the population to be *in themselves* fun, exciting, and adventurous. More than simply deriving pleasant fearfulness from violating the prohibition per se, there can exist claims that the prohibited activity itself produces a pleasant level of excitation" (Lofland 1969, 109). Drinking was clearly fun for many of the women at bachelorette parties. Brides-to-be were more comfortable engaging in embarrassing and otherwise deviant acts, such as being dressed up in a costume or watching a dance by a stripper, when they had consumed a substance that made them less self-conscious. Dwight Heath suggested that because alcohol is associated with lowered inhibitions, it is sometimes used as an excuse to deviate: "Others who claim to drink, 'just to get drunk' or 'to be totally out of it' subsequently take great pleasure in recounting their outlandish behavior, suggesting that they may . . . have been drinking primarily in order to misbehave while enjoying the temporary suspension of certain social expectations (time-out) that is often accorded to the inebriate" (2000, 171). Though for some women the subsequent hangover was described as the worst part of the party, it was clear that drinking with friends and feeling the effects of alcohol were quite pleasurable. Alcohol is associated with increased sociability and solidarity (Trice 1966), and this heightened

feeling of camaraderie was enjoyable for and important to women on bachelorette parties.

Since play is seen as time off or time out from the responsibilities of everyday life and adulthood, the focus on having a good time or giving the bride-
to-be a night she will never forget may imply that she sacrifices this type of
play when she is married. Play, particularly in the form of binge drinking and
having a "girls' night," is associated with youthfulness and a more carefree lifestyle. To some extent, the freedom to do this frequently is something that is
given up upon marriage. The idea of going all out for the bachelorette party
can be explained in part, then, by the idea that this is the bride's last chance
to free herself of urges to do so in the future. As Jamie, aged twenty-eight and
engaged, noted, "Your bachelorette party is supposed to be a crazy, uninhib-
ited time, and you're supposed to act like you wouldn't normally act. . . . [I]t's
kind of like your free pass for the night. . . . As we become adults, we don't do
that, and we can't because we have to get up the next morning. We have to go
to work. . . . Like every other night, you really can't because—not because you
have a husband at home, but because you have a job or you have kids." For many
women this transition from single to married is not merely that but also a symbolic transition from childhood to adulthood. Since we do not have any secular rituals expressly designated to mark this status passage, exactly when this
transition is completed is ambiguous. Not only is marriage about the union of
two individuals; it also functions as recognition of adulthood. In this sense, the
drinking and play of the bachelorette party are opportunities for brides-to-be
to act not as children or responsible adults, but somewhere in between.

There is little doubt that the activities engaged in at bachelorette parties
are defined as deviant by the participants in this ritual because this is exactly
the point of these parties. Although some women called their own behavior
"bad" or "naughty," they did so while grinning, seemingly proud of their transgressions because such acts meant they had accomplished the goals of the bachelorette party. However, a couple of women said they felt regret for what
happened or described friends who felt guilty about what they did on their bachelorette parties. April, for example, described the aftermath of a friend's bachelorette party in which pictures were taken of the bride-to-be kissing random
men. She described her friend's feelings of remorse, saying "When she showed
me the photos at work the next week and she had to censor them for her fiancé,
you know, I think she felt bad about that. I'm sure there's a lot worse things
that happen at bachelorette parties then just kissing a couple of guys because
your friends egg you on to do it. I'm sure horrible things happen. But she felt
guilty, I think, about that part of it. I think overall she had a good time . . . but
I do think she had a little bit of regret."

Most women, however, recognized their behavior as deviant but felt it was
excused or legitimated within the context of the bachelorette party. David
Matza (1969) argued that all members of society have periods of nonconfor-
mity and, as a result, develop justifications or accounts in order to explain why

they violate the norms, rules, and laws of society at certain points in their lives. Matza argued that we all "drift" in and out of conformity; yet, we still like to consider ourselves conforming, moral members of society. Since these deviant acts are subject to evaluation and judgment by others, when otherwise rule-following members of society deviate, they account for or defend their rule or norm breaking by using what Sykes and Matza (1957) called "techniques of neutralization." Jamie employed the "denial of responsibility" technique in her comment above when she called the bachelorette party a "free pass," indicating that because it is the bride's special night, she is not responsible for her actions. One way women employed this technique was by saying that their actions were the result of their friends' pressure or instruction. The friends at the bachelorette party create the task list or scavenger hunt and the bachelorette, as the submissive initiate, knows it is her duty to play along. Pam, for example, was instructed to have two dozen men sign her shirt. When her fiancé saw her shirt after the bachelorette party and asked about it, she responded, "Hey, it wasn't my doing." April, who was quoted above regarding the guilt her friend felt after her bachelorette party, defended her friend, explaining to me that her behavior was not really her fault. She said, "I mean she was forced to wear and do these things, but she's such an easy going person that she just went along with it. . . . She has this group of friends and they do a lot of things together, and I guess a few of them were married and they had gone through this exact same thing, so they were determined to put [this bride] through it all. . . . But it was very familiar and there was a whole set way they had to do all of this." In this case, April attempted to neutralize her friend's deviant behavior by suggesting that she did what she did because her friends pressured her to do so. Related to this, the bachelorette party calls attention to the transitory or liminal status of the bride-to-be at this point in time. Victor Turner argued that liminality is when one is between statuses, and those who experience it "elude or slip through the network of classifications that normally locate states and positions in cultural space. Liminal entities are neither here nor there; they are betwixt and between" (1969, 95). At the bachelorette party the bride-to-be is no longer single but not yet married. She is spoken for but not legally committed. As Tye and Powers suggested, part of the successful bachelorette role is the communal understanding that "while she is available, she is not available" (1998, 58). Because of this special and ambiguous status, the bride-to-be has a degree of freedom that she will not have again.

Erikson (1966) noted that some societies, like ours, sanction this type of behavior, what I call "liminal deviance." He stated, "There are societies which appoint special days or occasions as periods of general license, during which members of the group are permitted (if not expected) to violate rules they have observed during the preceding season and will again observe during the coming season" (Erikson 1966, 27). The bride-to-be is not in a constant state of back and forth during the engagement period, kissing strange men, going to strip clubs, and then being devoted to her fiancé. Rather, she is offered one opportunity during this time to act out feelings of ambivalence or doubt (whether she has them or not). She is given one chance to play and behave as a single woman before returning to her role as a faithful, committed romantic partner. This "special period of license" is when the bride-to-be is both allowed and expected to cross the boundaries of acceptable behavior for a girlfriend, fiancée, or (especially) wife. Thus, the bachelorette party itself, given the liminal status of its central participant, functions as an excuse for deviant and excessive behavior.

## STRIPPERS AND SEDUCTION: INTERPRETING THE MEANINGS OF SEX SYMBOLS

The majority of bachelorette parties described (81 percent, or 115) and all parties that I observed included a sexual element or theme. Sex was a major component of the bachelorette party, and some of the women I interviewed questioned the legitimacy of bachelorette parties that omitted it entirely. Much of the deviant behavior at bachelorette parties involved sexualized interaction and play. Brides-to-be danced with strippers. Random men sucked candy pieces that were suggestively attached to brides' shirts. Women carried around giant phallic-shaped novelty items. Why is the bachelorette party sexualized? How can the use of sex symbols and props be interpreted? The association between sex and marriage is certainly a partial explanation. Traditionally, sex was expected to be reserved for marriage, and thus the bachelorette party could be interpreted as a means of socializing women into marriage by giving them sexual advice and showering them with symbols of sexuality so that they are prepared for a sexual relationship with their husbands. However, since the majority of women who marry in contemporary American society are not virgins (Laumann et al. 1994), and since the bachelorette party appears to have emerged in the United States after the sexual revolution of the 1960s, this rationale is insufficient.

A modern explanation would be what I have suggested thus far, that women have dated different men prior to marriage and that many have had more than one sexual partner. Like men have for decades with bachelor parties, they see the bachelorette party as a way to acknowledge the termination of their single life. It is a symbolic means of showing that they are "off the market." Similarly, part of the sexual element comes directly from bachelor parties, from which the bachelorette party is certainly derived. Stereotypes about bachelor parties suggest that they are hyper-sexualized and that men frequent strip clubs or view pornography as a part of their "last night of freedom" (Schultz 1995). Luanne, a bride-to-be in her mid-twenties, expressed this when she stated why she felt sex talk and imagery are involved. She said, "When . . . girls were copying the bachelor party into the bachelorette party, they really were just kind of copying the same thing. It's not that girls are as interested in [sex] when they're just sitting around—not that, I mean shoot, [you] can't get a group of girls together without it coming up eventually, too. But I think . . . we can certainly find other things to talk about. I think it was more copycatting the whole bachelor party thing." Luanne's comments, coupled with an examination of the structure of the bachelorette party, particularly the Women's Bachelor Party or Anything Goes types, suggest that a major reason women include sexual elements is that they are purposefully replicating their image of the bachelor party.

One prominent element of bachelorette parties, the inclusion of a stripper, seems to have been copied from women's perceptions of men's parties. The stereotype of strippers as a part of bachelor parties is certainly dominant in our cultural history. Films depicting bachelor parties, such as *Bachelor Party* (1984) and *Very Bad Things* (1999), include strippers as central elements. However, while strippers were often included in bachelorette parties, and bachelorette parties made up a large portion of patrons of strip clubs like the Hideaway and the Regal Room (Montemurro 2001), women's interactions with and feelings about strippers conveyed ambivalence. In trying to replicate the bachelor party, it seems that some women ignored their own indifference to or even dislike of strippers in order to do what they felt was appropriate for a bachelorette party. Several women admitted that they really did not want to have strippers at their parties or did not care about having strippers but did so because they thought that was what was supposed to be done. Luanne communicated this as she told me about the first bachelorette party she attended. She said, "It almost seemed like we were trying to chase down that novel idea, but weren't really having a good time with it. Like you think you are going into a strip club with a bunch of girls and you're going to hoot and holler and it's going to be great. And we did, but after about thirty minutes it's like, 'This is getting boring. Let's go and meet some real men.'"

\* \* \*

The games played at most bachelorette parties were notably different from those at the bridal shower. Even though some of the bridal shower games were laced with sexual innuendo, most were dated and sustained the assumption of the virgin bride. As in the game where the maid of honor records the bride's reactions as she opens her presents, then reads the list back as if it is what she might say on her wedding night, the bride at the shower is sexually naive. Knowing older relatives and married peers introduce her to the adult world with advice or lingerie, communicating their approval of sexual activity within the bounds of marriage. These older family members often tease the bride about her future sexual activity, communicating that they hope it will soon lead to procreation. When the bride-to-be is told that the number of ribbons she breaks when she opens her gifts is equivalent to the number of children she will have, she receives the message that motherhood follows marriage. Simply, the sexualized games at the shower connect sex to marriage and childbearing. In contrast, the games at the bachelorette party assume an opposite identity for the bride-to-be.

\* \* \*

Furthermore, women may have found the sexualized atmosphere of the bachelorette party to be awkward given the cultural ambivalence about women's sexuality in contemporary society. As Susan Douglas articulated in her study of images of women in popular culture, American media have presented conflicting images of girls and women, images that paint them as either innocent or promiscuous, resulting in "schizophrenic [ideas] about women's sexuality" (1995, 15). The women in this study have grown up with a sexual double standard that suggests that men who have multiple sexual partners are to be congratulated while women who do so are to be punished. They also have learned from American culture, through media and other agents of socialization, that men are the sexual aggressors while women should be sexually passive (Spade and Valentine 2004). At parties, engaging in the various tasks positioned the bride-to-be as object more often than aggressor. When women played the Suck for a Buck game or had men remove pieces of candy from necklaces, or when they had men sign their underwear, this placed them as sexual objects, selling or making themselves available for men's pleasure. Rather than representing their sexual confidence or participating in acts that were sexually titillating as a means of celebrating their last night of sexual freedom, instead, some of the bachelorette party games were about offering themselves up one last time to interested men. Some tasks called for brides-to-be to play aggressor by approaching random men and asking for their phone numbers or other items on a scavenger hunt. Thus, it is not surprising that the women's response to exotic dancers and the general sexualized atmosphere of the party was ambivalence because, on one hand, women are told to claim and embrace their sexuality, but, on the other hand, much of the expected sexual expression is based on making themselves available to arouse and entertain men.

The bachelorette party is based on the idea of the non-virgin bride who has had sexual experiences and is acknowledging, even lamenting, the end of her freedom. Yet the sexually experienced woman is not a privileged position in Western society. Leora Tanenbaum (2000) argued as much in her study of female sexual activity. She noted that teenage girls and women face pressure both to have sex and to preserve their reputation as "good girls." Having grown up in the wake of the feminist movement, the women I interviewed received the message that they can do what boys or men do. But in terms of sexuality, when women of this generation listened to such rhetoric, they would quickly be made aware of the consequences of promiscuity (Tanenbaum 2000). Furthermore, women received mixed messages about how they should express this sexual liberation. The bride-to-be at the bachelorette party exemplifies this contradiction with the props she carries, the way she is costumed, and the expectations for her behavior. The party itself is indicative of this incongruity as women play along with a male-defined image of feminine sexuality in terms of the show or performative aspect of bachelorette parties.

\* \* \*

## REFERENCES

Douglas, Susan. 1995. *Where the Girls Are: Growing up Female with the Mass Media.* New York: Times Books.

Erikson, Kai T. 1966. *Wayward Puritans: A Study in the Sociology of Deviance.* New York: John Wiley and Sons.

Heath, Dwight B. 2000. *Drinking Occasions: Comparative Perspectives on Alcohol and Culture.* Philadelphia: Brunner/Mazel.

Laumann, Edward O., John H. Gagnon, Robert T. Micháel, and Stuart Michaels. 1994. *The Social Organization of Sexuality: Sexual Practices in the United States.* Chicago: University of Chicago Press.

Lofland, John, 1969. *Deviance and Identity.* Englewood Cliffs, NJ: Prentice Hall.

Matza, David. 1969. *Becoming Deviant.* Englewood Cliffs, NJ: Prentice Hall.

Montemurro, Beth. 2001. Strippers and Screamers: The Emergence of Social Control in a Non-Institutionalized Setting. *Journal of Contemporary Ethnography* 30: 275–304.

Schultz, Jason. 1995. Getting off on Feminism. In *To Be Real: Telling the Truth and Changing the Face of Feminism*, edited by Rebecca Walker, 107–126. New York: Anchor Books.

Spade, Joan Z., and Catherine G. Valentine. 2004. Tracing Gender's Mark on Bodies, Sexualities, and Emotions. In *The Kaleidoscope of Gender: Prisms, Patterns, and Possibilities*, edited by Joan Z. Spade and Catherine G. Valentine, 279–285. Belmont, CA: Wadsworth.

Sykes, Gresham, and David Matza. 1957. Techniques of Neutralization: A Theory of Delinquency. *American Sociological Review* 22: 664–670.

Tanenbaum, Leora. 2000. *Slut! Growing up Female with a Bad Reputation.* New York: HarperCollins.

Trice, Harrison. 1966. *Alcoholism in America.* New York: McGraw-Hill.

Turner, Victor. 1969. *The Ritual Process: Structure and Anti-structure.* Repr., New York: Aldine de Gruyter, 1995.

Tye, Diane, and Ann Marie Powers. 1998. Gender, Resistance, and Play: Bachelorette Parties in Atlantic Canada. *Women's Studies International Forum* 21:551–561.

# 17

## Falling Back on Plan B: The Children of the Gender Revolution Face Uncharted Territory*

FROM *Families as They Really Are*

### KATHLEEN GERSON

*Since the 1960s, there has been a steady rise in young women's expectations for mean-ingful work outside the home. As young men and women today—many of whom are growing up in single-parent households—work to have the things their parents and grandparents also sought, they face challenges unmatched by earlier generations. What happens if things don't work out according to plan? In the absence of what the author calls gender flexibility, young men and women have different ideas about the "second-best option."*

Young adults today grew up with mothers who broke barriers in the work-place and parents who forged innovative alternatives to traditional mar-riage. These "children of the gender revolution" now face a world that is far different from that of their parents or grandparents. While massive changes in work and family arrangements have expanded their options, these changes also pose new challenges to crafting a marriage, rearing children, and build-ing a career. Members of this new generation walk a fine line between their desire to achieve egalitarian, sharing relationships that can meld with satis-fying work, and succumbing to the realities of gender conflict, fragile relation-ships, and uncertain job prospects. The choices they make will shape work and family life for decades to come.

Social forecasters have reached starkly different conclusions about what these choices will be. Some proclaim that the recent upturn in "opt-out" moth-ers foreshadows a wider return to tradition among younger women. Others believe the rising number of single adults foretells a deepening "decline of com-mitment" that is threatening family life and the social fabric. While there is little doubt that tumultuous changes have shaped the lives of a new genera-tion, there is great disagreement about how. Does the diversification of fami-lies into two-earner, single-parent, and cohabiting forms represent a waning of family life or the growth of more flexible relationships? Will this new gen-eration integrate family and work in new ways, or will older patterns inexora-bly pull them back?

---

*References and footnotes can be found in the original article, pages 378–392 of *Families as They Really Are*. [*Editor's note*]

To find out how members of the first generation to grow up in these diversifying families look back on their childhoods and forward to their own futures, I conducted in-depth, life history interviews with a carefully selected group of young people between eighteen and thirty-two. These young women and men experienced the full range of changes that have taken place in family life, and most lived in some form of "nontraditional" arrangement at some point in their childhood. My interviews reveal a generation that does not conform to prevailing media stereotypes, whether they depict declining families or a return to strict gender divisions in caretaking and breadwinning.

In contrast to popular images of twenty- and thirty-somethings who wish to return to tradition or reject family life altogether, the young women and men I interviewed are more focused on *how well* their parents met the challenges of providing economic and emotional support than on *what form* their families took. Now making their own way in early adulthood, women and men share a set of lofty aspirations. Despite their varied family experiences, most hope to blend the traditional value of a lifelong relationship with the modern value of flexibly sharing work, child care, and domestic chores. In the best of all possible worlds, the majority would like to create a lasting marriage (or a "marriage-like" relationship) that allows them to balance home and work in a flexible, egalitarian way.

Yet young people are also developing strategies to prepare for "second-best" options in a world where time-demanding workplaces, a lack of child care, and fragile relationships may place their ideals out of reach. Concerned about the difficulty of finding a reliable and egalitarian partner to help them integrate work with family caretaking, most women see work as essential to their own and their children's survival, whether or not they marry. Worried about time-greedy workplaces, most men feel they must place work first and will need to count on a partner at home. As they prepare for second-best options, the differing fallback positions of "self-reliant" women and "neo-traditional" men may point to a new gender divide. But this divide does not reflect a new generation's highest aspirations for blending lifelong commitment and flexible, egalitarian sharing in their relationships.

## GROWING UP IN CHANGING FAMILIES

Even though theorists and social commentators continue to debate the merits of various family forms, my interviewees did not focus on their family's "structure." Instead, I found large variation among children who grew up in apparently similar family types. Those who grew up in families with a homemaking mother and breadwinning father were divided in their assessments of this arrangement. While a little more than half thought this was the best arrangement, close to half reached a different conclusion. When being a homemaker and out of the workforce appeared to undermine a mother's satisfaction, disturb the household's harmony, or threaten its economic security, the children concluded that it would have been better if their mothers had pursued a sustained commitment to work.

Many of those who grew up in a single-parent home also expressed ambivalence about their parents' breakups. Slightly more than half wished their parents had stayed together, but close to half believed that a breakup, while not ideal, was better than continuing to live in a conflict-ridden or silently unhappy home. The longer-term consequences of a breakup shaped the lessons children drew. If their parents got back on their feet and created better lives, children developed surprisingly positive outlooks on the decision to separate.

Those who grew up in a dual-earner home were the least ambivalent about their parents' arrangements. More than three-fourths believed that having two work-committed parents provided increased economic resources and also promoted marriages that seemed more egalitarian and satisfying. If the pressures of working long hours or coping with blocked opportunities and family-unfriendly workplaces took their toll, however, some children concluded that having over-burdened, time-stressed caretakers offset these advantages.

In short, growing up in this era of diverse families led children to focus more on how well—or poorly—parents (and other caretakers) were able to meet the twin challenges of providing economic and emotional support rather than on its form. Even more important, children experienced family life as a dynamic process that changed over time. Since family life is best seen as a film, not a snapshot, the key to understanding young people's views lies in charting the diverse paths their families took.

## FAMILY PATHS AND GENDER FLEXIBILITY

Families can take different paths from seemingly common starting points, and similar types of families can travel toward different destinations. When young adults reflect on their families, they focus on how their homes either came to provide stability and support or failed to do so. About a third of my interviewees reported growing up in a stable home, while a quarter concluded that their families grew more supportive as time passed. In contrast, just under one in ten reported living in a chronically insecure home, while a bit more than a third felt that family support eroded as they grew up. Why, then, do some children look back on families that became more supportive and secure, while others experienced a decline in their family's support?

Parents' strategies for organizing breadwinning and caretaking hold the key to understanding a family's pathway: Flexible strategies, which allowed mothers, fathers, and other caretakers to transcend rigid gender boundaries, helped families prevail in the face of unexpected economic and interpersonal crises. Inflexible responses, in contrast, left families ill-equipped to cope with eroding supports for a strict division in mothers' and fathers' responsibilities.

## RISING FAMILY FORTUNES

The sources of expanding support differed by family situation, but all reflected a flexible response to unexpected difficulties. Sometimes marriages became more equal as demoralized mothers went to work and pushed for change or helped overburdened fathers. Josh, for example, reported that his mother's decision to go to work gave her the courage to insist that his father tackle his drug addiction.

> My parents fought almost constantly. Then my mom got a job. They separated for about five, six, seven months. Even though I was upset, I thought it was for the best. That's when (my dad) got into some kind of program and my mom took him back. That changed the whole family dynamic. We got extremely close. A whole new relationship developed with my father.

Chris recalled how his mother's job allowed his father to quit a dead-end job and train for a more satisfying career:

> Between 7th and 8th grade, my dad had a business which didn't work. It was a dead-end thing, and he came home frustrated, so my mom got him to go to school. It was hard financially, but it was good because he was actually enjoying what he was doing. He really flourished. A lot of people say, "Wow, your mom is the breadwinner, and that's strange." It's not. It is a very joint thing.

Parental breakups that relieved domestic conflict or led to the departure of an unstable parent also helped caretaking parents get back on their feet. Connie recounted how her mother was able to create a more secure home after separating from an alcoholic husband and finding a job that offered a steady income and a source of personal esteem:

> My father just sat in the corner and once in a while got angry at us, but [my mom]—I don't know if it was him or the money, but she didn't stand up for herself as much as I think she should. The tension with my dad never eased, and my mom had gotten sick with multiple bleeding ulcers. That was her real turning point. It was building inside of her to leave, 'cause she'd got a job and started to realize she had her own money . . . [She] became a much happier person. And because she was better, I was better. I had a weight taken off of me.

More stable and egalitarian remarriages could also give children the economic and emotional support they had not previously received. Having never known her biological father, Shauna recalled how her stepfather became a devoted caretaker and the "real" father she always wanted:

> At first, I was feeling it was a bad change because I wanted my mom to myself. Then my mom said, "Why don't you call him daddy?" The next thing I was

saying "Daddy!" I remember the look on his face and his saying "She called me daddy!" I was so happy. After that, he's always been my dad, and there's never been any question about it. . . . [He] would get home before my mom, so he would cook the dinner and clean. My dad spoiled me for any other man, because this is the model I had.

When Isabella's parents divorced, her grandfather became a treasured caretaker:

It's not like I didn't have a father, because my grandfather was always there. He was there to take me to after-school clubs and pick me up. I was sheltered—he had to take me to the library, wait till I finished all my work, take me home. I call him dad. Nobody could do better.

And when Antonio's single mother lost her job, his grandparents provided essential income that kept the family afloat:

My mom and grandparents were the type of people that even if we didn't have [money], we was gonna get it. Their ideal is, "I want to give you all the things I couldn't have when I was young." My grandparents and my mother thought like that, so no matter how much in poverty we were living, I was getting everything I wanted.

Despite their obvious differences, the common ingredient in these narratives is the ability of parents and other caretakers to reorganize child rearing and breadwinning in a more flexible, less gender-divided way, Mothers going to work, fathers becoming more involved in child rearing, and others joining in the work of family life—all of these strategies helped families overcome unexpected difficulties and create more economically secure, emotionally stable homes. Growing flexibility in how parents met the challenges of earning needed income and caring for children nourished parental morale, increased a home's financial security, and provided inspiring models of adult resilience. While children acknowledged the costs, they valued these second chances and gleaned lessons from watching parents find ways to create a better life. Looking back, they could conclude that "all's well that ends well."

## DECLINING FAMILY FORTUNES

For some children, home life followed a downward slope. Here, too, the key to their experiences lay in the work and caretaking strategies of those entrusted with their care, but here gender inflexibility in the face of domestic difficulties left children with less support than they had once taken for granted. Faced with a father's abandonment or a stay-at-home mother's growing frustration, children described how their parents' resistance to more flexible strategies for apportioning paid and domestic work left them struggling to meet children's economic and emotional needs. Over time, deteriorating marriages, declining parental morale, and financial insecurity shattered a once rosy picture of family stability and contentment.

When parents became stuck in a rigid division of labor, with unhappy mothers and fathers ill-equipped to support the household, traditional marriages could deteriorate. Sarah explains how her mother became increasingly depressed and "over-involved" after relinquishing a promising career to devote all of her time to child rearing:

> When my sister was born, [my mom's] job had started up, career-wise, so she wasn't happy [but] she felt she had to be home. She had a lot of conflicts about work and home and opted to be really committed to family, but also resented it. . . . She was the supermom, but just seemed really depressed a lot of time . . . [It came] with an edge to it—"in return, I want you to be devoted to me." If we did something separate from her, that was a major problem. So I was making distance because I felt I had to protect myself from this invasion. . . . She thought she was doing something good to sacrifice for us . . . but it would have been better if my mother was happier working.

Megan recalls her father's mounting frustration as his income stagnated and he endured the complaints of a wife who expected to him to provide a "better lifestyle":

> My mother was always dissatisfied. She wanted my father to be more ambitious, and he wasn't an ambitious man. As long as he was supporting the family, it didn't matter if it was a bigger house or a bigger car. Forty years of being married to a woman saying, "Why don't we have more money?"—I think that does something to your self-esteem.

Unresolved power struggles in dual-earner marriages could also cause problems, as wives felt the weight of "doing it all" and fathers resisted egalitarian sharing. Juggling paid and domestic work left Justin's mother exhausted, while a high-pressured job running a restaurant left his father with no time to attend nightly dinners or even Little League games. Justin describes the strain his parents experienced and its effect on him:

> I was slightly disappointed that I could not see my father more—because I understood but also because it depends on the mood he's in. And it got worse as work [went] downhill . . . [So] I can't model my relationship on my parents. My mother wasn't very happy. There was a lot of strain on her.

Harmful breakups, where fathers abandoned their children and mothers could not find new ways to support the family or create an identity beyond wife and mother, also eroded family support. Nina remembers how her father's disappearance, combined with her mother's reluctance to seek a job and create a more independent life, triggered the descent from a comfortable middle-class existence to one of abiding poverty:

> My mother ended up going on welfare. We went from a nice place to living in a really cruddy building. And she's still in the same apartment. To this day, my sister will not speak to my father because of what he's done to us.

Children (and their parents) sometimes lost the support of other caretakers. Shortly after Jasmine's father left to live with another woman and her mother fell into a deep depression, she suffered the loss of a "third parent" when her beloved grandmother died. Her grandmother's loss left her feeling especially bereft after her father's departure:

> It was so great when my parents were together and my grandmother was alive, so when she died, it was really hard. I lost [the money], and I lost her just being there. We were going through a real trauma in my whole family, so when [my father] left, it was like another death. I don't think it would have been any better if they'd stayed together, but my grandmother being alive would have been much more of a difference.

The events that propelled families on a downward track—including rising financial instability, declining parental involvement and morale, and a dearth of other supportive caretakers—share a common element. Whether parents faced marital impasses or difficult breakups, resistance to more flexible gender arrangements left them unable to sustain an emotionally or economically secure home. Their children concluded that all did *not* end well.

In sum, sustained parental support and economic security were more important to my informants than the form their families took. Since any family type holds potential pitfalls if parents do not or cannot prevail over the difficulties that arise, conventional categories that see families as static "forms" cannot account for the ways that families change as children grow to adulthood. Instead, young women and men from diverse family backgrounds recounted how parents and other family members who transcended gender boundaries and developed flexible strategies for breadwinning and caretaking were better able to cope with marital crises, economic insecurities, and other unanticipated challenges.

A range of social trends—including the erosion of single-earner paychecks, the fragility of modern marriages, and the expanding options and pressures for women to work—require varied and versatile ways of earning and caring. These institutional shifts make gender flexibility increasingly desirable and even essential. Flexible approaches to work and parenting help families adapt, while inflexible ones leave them ill-prepared to cope with new economic and social realities.

## CONVERGING IDEALS, DIVERGING FALLBACKS

How do young adults use the lessons of growing up in changing families to formulate their own plans for the future? Women and men from diverse family backgrounds share a set of lofty aspirations. Whether or not their parents stayed together, more than nine out of ten hope to rear children in the context of a satisfying lifelong bond. Far from rejecting the value of commitment, almost everyone wants to create a lasting marriage or "marriage-like" partnership. This does not, however, reflect a desire for a traditional relationship. Most also aspire to build a committed bond where both paid work and family caretaking are shared. Three-fourths of those who grew up in dual-earner homes want their spouse to share breadwinning and caretaking, but so do more than two-thirds of those from traditional homes, and close to nine-tenths of those with single parents. While four-fifths of women want an egalitarian relationship, so do two-thirds of men. In short, most share an ideal that stresses the value of a lasting, flexible, and egalitarian partnership with considerable room for personal autonomy. Amy, an Asian American with two working parents, thus explains that:

> I want a fifty-fifty relationship, where we both have the potential of doing everything—both of us working and dealing with kids. With regard to career, if neither has flexibility, then one of us will have to sacrifice for one period, and the other for another.

And Wayne, an African American raised by a single mother, expresses the essentially same hopes when he says that:

> I don't want the '50s type of marriage, where I come home and she's cooking. I want her to have a career of her own. I want to be able to set my goals, and she can do what she wants, too.

While most of my interviewees hope to strike a flexible breadwinning and caretaking balance with an egalitarian partner, they are also skeptical about their chances of achieving this ideal. Women and men both worry that work demands, a lack of child-rearing supports, and the fragility of modern relationships will undermine their aspirations to forge an enduring, egalitarian partnership. In the face of barriers to equality, most have concluded that they have little choice but to prepare for options that may fall substantially short of their ideals. Despite their shared aspirations, however, men and women face different institutional obstacles and cultural pressures, which are prompting divergent fallback strategies. If they cannot find a supportive partner, most women prefer self-reliance over economic dependence within a traditional marriage. Most men, if they cannot strike an equal balance between work and parenting, prefer a neo-traditional arrangement that allows them to put work first and rely on a partner for the lion's share of caregiving.

In the event that Plan A proves unreachable, women and men are thus pursuing a different Plan B as insurance against their "worst case" fears. These divergent fallback strategies point toward the emergence of a new gender divide between young women, most of whom see a need for self-reliance, and young men, who are more inclined to retain a modified version of traditional expectations.

### Women's Plan B

Torn between high hopes for combining work and family and worries about sustaining a lasting and satisfying partnership, young women are navigating uncertain waters. While some are falling back on domesticity, most prefer to find a more independent base than traditional marriage provides. In contrast to the media-driven message that young women are turning away from work and career in favor of domestic pursuits, the majority of my interviewees are determined to seek financial and emotional self-reliance, whether or not they also forge a committed relationship. Regardless of class, race, or ethnicity, most are reluctant to surrender their autonomy in a traditional marriage. When the bonds of marriage are so fragile, relying on a husband for economic security seems foolhardy. And if a relationship deteriorates, economic dependence on a man leaves few means of escape. Danisha, an African American who grew up in an inner-city, working-class neighborhood, and Jennifer, who was raised in a middle-class, predominantly white suburb, agree. Danisha proclaims that:

> Let's say that my marriage doesn't work. Just in case, I want to establish myself, because I don't ever want to end up, like, "What am I going to do?" I want to be able to do what I have to do and still be okay.

Jennifer concurs:

> I will have to have a job and some kind of stability before considering marriage. Too many of my mother's friends went for that—"Let him provide everything"— and they're stuck in a very unhappy relationship, but can't leave because they can't provide for themselves or the children they now have. So it's either welfare or putting up with somebody else's c—p.

Hoping to avoid being trapped in an unhappy marriage or left by an unreliable partner without a way to survive, almost three-fourths of women plan to build a non-negotiable base of self-reliance and an independent identity in the world of paid work. But they do not view this strategy as incompatible with the search for a life partner. Instead, it reflects their determination to set a high standard for a worthy relationship. Economic self-reliance and personal independence make it possible to resist "settling" for anything less than a satisfying, mutually supportive bond.

Women from all backgrounds have concluded that work provides indispensable economic, social, and emotional resources. They have drawn lessons about the rewards of self-reliance and the perils of domesticity from their mothers, other women, and their own experiences growing up. When the bonds of marriage are fragile, relying on a husband for economic security seems foolhardy. They are thus seeking alternatives to traditional marriage by establishing a firm tie to paid work, by redesigning motherhood to better fit their work aspirations, and by looking to kin and friends as a support network to enlarge and, if needed, substitute, for an intimate relationship. These strategies do not preclude finding a life partner, but they reflect a determination to set a high standard for choosing one. Maria, who grew up in a two-parent home in a predominantly white, working-class suburb, declares:

> I want to have this person to share [my] life with—[someone] that you're there for as much as they're there for you. But I can't settle.

And Rachel, whose Latino parents separated when she was young, shares this view:

> I'm not afraid of being alone, but I am afraid of being with somebody's who's a jerk. I want to get married and have children, but it has to be under the right circumstances, with the right person.

Maria and Rachel also agree that if a worthy relationship ultimately proves out of reach, then remaining single need not mean social disconnection. Kin and friends provide a support network that enlarges and, if needed, even substitutes for an intimate relationship. Maria explains:

> If I don't find [a relationship], then I cannot live in sorrow. It's not the only thing that's ultimately important. If I didn't have my family, if I didn't have a career, if I didn't have friends, I would be equally unhappy. [A relationship] is just one slice of the pie.

And Rachel concurs:

> I can spend the rest of my life on my own, and as long as I have my sisters and my friends, I'm okay.

By blending support from friends and kin with financial self-sufficiency, these young women are pursuing a strategy of autonomy rather than placing their own fate or their children's fate in the hands of a traditional relationship. Whether or not this strategy ultimately leads to marriage, it appears to offer the safest and most responsible way to prepare for the uncertainties of relationships and the barriers to men's equal sharing.

## Men's Plan B

Young men face a different dilemma: Torn between women's pressures for an egalitarian partnership and their own desire to succeed—or at least survive—in time-demanding workplaces, they are more inclined to fall back on a modified traditionalism that contrasts vividly with women's search for self-reliance. While they do not want or expect to return to a 1950s model of fathers as the only breadwinner, most men prefer a modified traditionalism that recognizes a mother's right (and need) to work, but puts his own career first. Although Andrew grew up in a consistently two-income home, he distinguished between a woman's "choice" to work and a man's "responsibility" to support his family:

> I would like to have it be equal—just from what I was exposed to and what attracts me—but I don't have a set definition for what that would be like. I would be fine if both of us were working, but if she thought, "At this point in my life, I don't want to work," then it would be fine.

Because equality may prove to be too costly to their careers, seven out of ten men are pursuing a strategy that positions them as the main breadwinner, even if it allows for two working spouses. When push comes to shove, and the demands of work collide with the needs of children, this approach allows men to resist equal caretaking, even in a two-earner context. Like women, men from a range of family, class, and ethnic backgrounds fall back on neotraditionalism. They favor retaining a clear boundary between a breadwinning father and a caretaking mother, even when she holds a paid job. This neo-traditional strategy stresses women's primary status as mothers and defines equality as a woman's "choice" to add work onto mothering.

By making room for two earners, this strategy offers the financial cushion of a second income, acknowledges women's desire for a life beyond the home, and allows for more involved fatherhood. Yet, by claiming separate spheres of responsibility for women and men, it does not challenge a man's position as the primary earner or undermine the claim that his work prospects should come first. Although James's mother became too mentally ill to care for her children or herself, Josh plans to leave the lion's share of caretaking to his wife:

> All things being equal, it [caretaking] should be shared. It may sound sexist, but if somebody's going to be the breadwinner, it's going to be me. First of all, I make a better salary, and I feel the need to work, and I just think the child really needs the mother more than the father at a young age.

Men are thus more likely to favor a fallback arrangement that retains the gender boundary between breadwinning and caretaking, even when mothers hold paid jobs. From young men's perspective, this modified but still gendered household offers women the chance to earn income and establish an identity at the workplace without imposing the costs of equal parenting on men. Granting a mother's "choice" to work supports women's claims for independence, but it does not undermine men's claim that their work prospects should come first. Acknowledging men's responsibilities at home provides for more involved fatherhood, but it does not envision domestic equality. And making room for two earners provides a buffer against the difficulties of living on one income, but it does not challenge men's position as the primary earner. Modified traditionalism thus appears to be a good compromise when the career costs of equality remain so high. New economic insecurities, coupled with women's growing desire for equality, are creating dilemmas for men, even if they take a different form than the ones confronting women. Ultimately, however, men's desire to protect work prerogatives collides with women's growing desire for equality and need for independence.

## ACROSS THE GENDER DIVIDE

In contrast to the popular images of a generation that feels neglected by working mothers, unsettled by parental breakups, and wary of equality, these life stories show strong support for working mothers, a focus on the quality of a relationship, and a shared desire to create lasting, flexible, and egalitarian partnerships. The good news is that most young women and men had largely positive experiences with mothers who worked and parents who strove for flexibility and equality. Those who grew up with a caring support network and sufficient economic security, whether in a single- or a two-parent household, did well. Young women and men both recounted how gender flexibility in breadwinning and caretaking helped their parents (and other caretakers) overcome such increasingly prevalent family crises as the loss of a father's income or the decline of a mother's morale. By letting go of rigid patterns that once narrowly defined women's and men's "proper" places in the family and the wider world, all kinds of families were able to overcome unexpected challenges and create more financially stable and emotionally supportive homes. And most, even among those who grew up in less flexible families, hope to build on the struggles and gains of their parents' generation by seeking equality and flexibility in their own lives.

The bad news, however, is that most young adults remain skeptical about their chances of achieving their ideals. Amid their shared desire to transcend gender boundaries and achieve flexibility in their own lives, young women and men harbor strong concerns that their aspirations will prove impossible to reach. Faced with the many barriers to egalitarian relationships and fearful that they will not find the right partner to help them integrate work with family caretaking, they are also preparing for options that may fall substantially short of their ideals. Reversing the argument that women are returning to tradition, however, these divergent fallback strategies suggest that a new divide is emerging between "self-reliant" women, who see work, an independent income, and personel autonomy as essential to their survival, and "neo-traditional" men, who grant women's "choice" to work but also feel the need and pressure to be a primary breadwinner.

While women are developing more innovative strategies than are men, the underlying story is one of a resilient, but realistic generation that has changed far more than the institutions it has inherited. Whether they grew up in a flexible home or one with more rigid definitions of women's and men's proper places, their hard-won lessons about the need for new, more egalitarian options for building relationships and caring for children are outpacing their ability to implement these goals.

Yet, young men and women still hope to reach across the divide that separates them. Aware that traditional job ladders and traditional marriages are both waning, they are seeking more flexible ways to build careers, care for families, and integrate the two. Convinced that the traditional career, defined by orderly steps up an organizational chart, is a relic of the past, most hope to craft a "personal career" that is not bound by a single employer or work organization. Most men as well as women are trying to redefine the "ideal worker" to accommodate the ebb and flow of family life, even if that means sacrificing some income for a more balanced life. They hope to create a shared "work-family" career that interweaves breadwinning and caretaking.

Growing up in changing families and facing uncertainty in their own lives has left this generation weary of rigid, narrowly framed "family values" that moralize about their personal choices or those of others. They are searching for a morality without moralism that balances an ethic of tolerance and inclusiveness with the core values of behaving responsibly and caring for others. The clash between self-reliant women and neo-traditional men may signal a new divide, but it stems from intensifying work-family dilemmas, not from a decline of laudable values.

Since new social realities are forcing young adults to seek new ways to combine love and work, the best hope for bridging gender divides lies in creating social policies that will allow twenty-first-century Americans to pursue the flexible, egalitarian strategies they want rather than forcing them to fall back on less desirable—and ultimately less workable—options. Whether the goal is equal opportunity or a healthy family landscape, the best family values can only be achieved by creating the social supports for gender flexibility in our communities, homes, and workplaces.

# PART FOUR

# SOCIAL INTERACTION AND IDENTITY

# 18

## On Face-Work

### ERVING GOFFMAN

*Many students find the idea of a "self-presentation" to be manipulative, insincere, and inauthentic. What Goffman's work shows is that we cannot avoid the work of presenting a "face" or identity in social interaction. We can deny that this activity goes on and we can be unaware of what we are doing, but all of us must do this work in order to carry on social interaction. Goffman takes sociology into the deepest realm of social life: our most intimate relations and our most private ideas about who we are.*

Every person lives in a world of social encounters, involving him either in face-to-face or mediated contact with other participants. In each of these contacts, he tends to act out what is sometimes called a *line*—that is, a pattern of verbal and nonverbal acts by which he expresses his view of the situation and through this his evaluation of the participants, especially himself. Regardless of whether a person intends to take a line, he will find that he has done so in effect. The other participants will assume that he has more or less willfully taken a stand, so that if he is to deal with their response to him he must take into consideration the impression they have possibly formed of him.

The term *face* may be defined as the positive social value a person effectively claims for himself by the line others assume he has taken during a particular contact. Face is an image of self-delineation in terms of approved social attributes—albeit an image that others may share, as when a person makes a good showing for his profession or religion by making a good showing for himself.

A person tends to experience an immediate emotional response to the face which a contact with others allows him; he cathects his face; his "feelings" become attached to it. If the encounter sustains an image of him that he has long taken for granted, he probably will have few feelings about the matter. If events establish a face for him that is better than he might have expected, he is likely to "feel good"; if his ordinary expectations are not fulfilled, one expects that he will "feel bad" or "feel hurt." In general, a person's attachment to a particular face, coupled with the ease with which disconfirming information can be conveyed by himself and others, provides one reason why he finds that participation in any contact with others is a commitment. A person will also have feelings about the face sustained for the other participants, and while these feelings may differ in quantity and direction from those he has for his own face, they constitute an involvement in the face of others that is as immediate and spontaneous as the involvement he has in his own face. One's own face and the face of others are constructs of the same order; it is the rules of the group and the definition of the situation which determine how much feeling one is to have for face and how this feeling is to be distributed among the faces involved.

A person may be said to *have,* or *be in,* or *maintain* face when the line he effectively takes presents an image of him that is internally consistent, that is supported by judgments and evidence conveyed by other participants, and that is confirmed by evidence conveyed through impersonal agencies in the situation. At such times the person's face clearly is something that is not lodged in or on his body, but rather something that is diffusely located in the flow of events in the encounter and becomes manifest only when these events are read and interpreted for the appraisals expressed in them.

The line maintained by and for a person during contact with others tends to be of a legitimate institutionalized kind. During a contact of a particular type, an interactant of known or visible attributes can expect to be sustained in a particular face and can feel that it is morally proper that this should be so. Given his attributes and the conventionalized nature of the encounter, he will find a small choice of lines will be open to him and a small choice of faces will be waiting for him. Further, on the basis of a few known attributes, he is given the responsibility of possessing a vast number of others. His coparticipants are not likely to be conscious of the character of many of these attributes until he acts perceptibly in such a way as to discredit his possession of them; then everyone becomes conscious of these attributes and assumes that he willfully gave a false impression of possessing them.

\* \* \*

A person may be said to *be in wrong face* when information is brought forth in some way about his social worth which cannot be integrated, even with effort, into the line that is being sustained for him. A person may be said to *be out of face* when he participates in a contact with others without having ready a line of the kind participants in such situations are expected to take. The intent of many pranks is to lead a person into showing a wrong face or no face, but there will also be serious occasions, of course, when he will find himself expressively out of touch with the situation.

When a person senses that he is in face, he typically responds with feelings of confidence and assurance. Firm in the line he is taking, he feels that he can hold his head up and openly present himself to others. He feels some security and some relief—as he also can when the others feel he is in wrong face but successfully hide these feelings from him.

When a person is in wrong face or out of face, expressive events are being contributed to the encounter which cannot be readily woven into the expressive fabric of the occasion. Should he sense that he is in wrong face or out of face, he is likely to feel ashamed and inferior because of what has happened to the activity on his account and because of what may happen to his reputation as a participant. Further, he may feel bad because he had relied upon the encounter to support an image of self to which he has become emotional attached and which he now finds threatened. Felt lack of judgmental support from the encounter may take him aback, confuse him, and momentarily incapacitate him as an interactant. His manner and bearing may falter, collapse and crumble. He may become embarassed and chagrined; he may become shamefaced. The feeling, whether warranted or not, that he is perceived in flustered state by others, and that he is presenting no usable line, may add further injuries to his feelings, just as his change from being in wrong face or out of face to being shamefaced can add further disorder to the expressive organization of the situation. Following common usage, I shall employ the term _poise_ to refer to the capacity to suppress and conceal any tendency to become shamefaced during encounters with others.

In our Anglo-American society, as in some others, the phrase "to lose face" seems to mean to be in wrong face, to be out of face, or to be shamefaced. The phrase "to save one's face" appears to refer to the process by which the person sustains an impression for others that he has not lost face. Following Chinese usage, one can say that "to give face" is to arrange for another to take a better line than he might otherwise have been able to take, the other thereby gets face given him, this being one way in which he can gain face.

\* \* \*

Just as the member of any group is expected to have self-respect, so also he is expected to sustain a standard of considerateness; he is expected to go to certain lengths to save the feelings and the face of others present, and he is expected to do this willingly and spontaneously because of emotional identification with the others and with their feelings. In consequence, he is disinclined to witness the defacement of others. The person who can witness another's humiliation and unfeelingly retain a cool countenance himself is said in our society to be "heartless," just as he who can unfeelingly participate in his own defacement is thought to be "shameless."

The combined effect of the rule of self-respect and the rule of considerateness is that the person tends to conduct himself during an encounter so as to maintain both his own face and the face of the other participants. This means that the line taken by each participant is usually allowed to prevail, and each participant is allowed to carry off the role he appears to have chosen for himself. A state where everyone temporarily accepts everyone else's line is established. This kind of mutual acceptance seems to be a basic structural feature of interaction, especially the interaction of face-to-face talk. It is typically a "working" acceptance, not a "real" one, since it tends to be based not on agreement of candidly expressed heart-felt evaluations, but upon a willingness to give temporary lip service to judgments with which the participants do not really agree.

The mutual acceptance of lines has an important conservative effect upon encounters. Once the person initially presents a line, he and the others tend to build their later responses upon it, and in a sense become stuck with it. Should the person radically alter his line, or should it become discredited, then confusion results, for the participants will have prepared and committed themselves for actions that are now unsuitable.

Ordinarily, maintenance of face is a condition of interaction, not its objective. Usual objectives, such as gaining face for oneself, giving free expression to one's true beliefs, introducing depreciating information about the others, or solving problems and performing tasks, are typically pursued in such a way as to be consistent with the maintenance of face. To study face-saving is to study the traffic rules of social interaction; one learns about the code the person adheres to in his movement across the paths and designs of others, but not where he is going, or why he wants to get there. One does not even learn why he is ready to follow the code, for a large number of different motives can equally lead him to do so. He may want to save his own face because of his emotional attachment to the image of self which it expresses, because of his pride or honor, because of the power his presumed status allows him to exert over the other participants, and so on. He may want to save the others' face because of his emotional attachment to an image of them, or because he feels that his coparticipants have a moral right to this protection, or because he wants to avoid the hostility that may be directed toward him if they lose their face. He may feel that an assumption has been made that he is the sort of person who shows compassion and sympathy toward others, so that to retain his own face, he may feel obliged to be considerate of the line taken by the other participants.

* * *

## THE BASIC KINDS OF FACE-WORK

*The Avoidance Process.* The surest way for a person to prevent threats to his face is to avoid contacts in which these threats are likely to occur. In all societies one can observe this in the avoidance relationship and in the tendency for certain delicate transactions to be conducted by go-betweens. Similarly, in many societies, members know the value of voluntarily making a gracious withdrawal before an anticipated threat to face has had a chance to occur.

Once the person does chance an encounter, other kinds of avoidance practices come into play. As defensive measures, he keeps off topics and away from activities that would lead to the expression of information that is inconsistent with the line he is maintaining. At opportune moments he will change the top of conversation or the direction of activity. He will often present initially a front of diffidence and composure, suppressing any show of feeling until he has found out what kind of line the others will be ready to support for him. Any claims regarding self may be made with belittling modesty, with strong qualifications, or with a note of unseriousness; by hedging in these ways he will have prepared a self for himself that will not be discredited by exposure, personal failure, or the unanticipated acts of others. And if he does not hedge his claims about self, he will at least attempt to be realistic about them, knowing that otherwise events may discredit him and make him lose face.

Certain protective maneuvers are as common as these defensive ones. The person shows respect and politeness, making sure to extend to others any ceremonial treatment that might be their due. He employs discretion; he leaves unstated facts that might implicitly or explicitly contradict and embarrass the positive claims made by others. He employs circumlocutions and deceptions, phrasing his replies with careful ambiguity so that the others' face is preserved even if their welfare is not. He employs courtesies, making slight modifications of his demands on or appraisals of the others so that they will be able to define the situation as one in which their self-respect is not threatened. In making a belittling demand upon the others, or in imputing uncomplimentary attributes to them, he may employ a joking manner, allowing them to take the line that they are good sports, able to relax from their ordinary standards of pride and honor. And before engaging in a potentially offensive act, he may provide explanations as to why the others ought not to be affronted by it. For example, if he knows that it will be necessary to withdraw from the encounter before it has terminated, he may tell the others in advance that it is necessary for him to leave, so that they will have faces that are prepared for it. But neutralizing the potentially offensive act need not be done verbally; he may wait for a propitious moment or natural break—for example, in conversation, a momentary lull when no one speaker can be affronted— and then leave, in this way using the context instead of his words as a guarantee of inoffensiveness.

When a person fails to prevent an incident, he can still attempt to maintain the fiction that no threat to face has occurred. The most blatant example of this is found where the person acts as if an event that contains a threatening expression has not occurred at all. He may apply this studied nonobservance to his own acts—as when he does not by any outward sign admit that his stomach is rumbling—or to the acts of others, as when he does not "see" that another has stumbled. Social life in mental hospitals owes much to this process; patients employ it in regard to their own peculiarities, and visitors employ it, often with tenuous desperation, in regard to patients. In general, tactful blindness of this kind is applied only to events that, if perceived at all, could be perceived and interpreted only as threats to face.

\* \* \*

Another kind of avoidance occurs when a person loses control of his expressions during an encounter. At such times he may try not so much to overlook the incident as to hide or conceal his activity in some way, thus making it possible for the others to avoid some of the difficulties created by a participant who has not maintained face. Correspondingly, when a person is caught out of face because he had not expected to be thrust into interaction, or because strong feelings have disrupted his expressive mask, the others may protectively turn away from him or his activity for a moment, to give him time to assemble himself.

*The Corrective Process.* When the participants in an undertaking or encounter fail to prevent the occurrence of an event that is expressively incompatible with the judgments of social worth that are being maintained, and when the event is of the kind that is difficult to overlook, then the participants are likely to give it accredited status as an incident—to ratify it as a threat that deserves direct official attention—and to proceed to try to correct for its effects. At this point one or more participants find themselves in an established state of ritual disequilibrium or disgrace, and an attempt must be made to reestablish a satisfactory ritual state for them. I use the term *ritual* because I am dealing with acts through whose symbolic component the actor shows how worthy he is of respect or how worthy he feels others are of it. The imagery of equilibrium is apt here because the length and intensity of the corrective effort is nicely adapted to the persistence and intensity of the threat. One's face, then, is a sacred thing, and the expressive order required to sustain it is therefore a ritual one.

The sequence of acts set in motion by an acknowledged threat to face, and terminating in the re-establishment of ritual equilibrium, I shall call an *interchange.* Defining a message or move as everything conveyed by an actor during a turn at taking action, one can say that an interchange will involve two or more moves and two or more participants. Obvious examples in our society may be found in the sequence of "Excuse me" and "Certainly," and in the exchange of presents or visits. The interchange seems to be a basic concrete unit of social activity and provides one natural empirical way to study interaction of all kinds. Face-saving practices can be usefully classified according to their position in the natural sequence of moves that comprise this unit. Aside from the event which introduces the need for a corrective interchange, four classic moves seem to be involved.

There is, first, the challenge, by which participants take on the responsibility of calling attention to the misconduct; by implication they suggest that the threatened claims are to stand firm and that the threatening event itself will have to be brought back into line.

The second move consists of the offering, whereby a participant, typically the offender, is given a chance to correct for the offense and reestablish the expressive order. Some classic ways of making this move are available. On the one hand, an attempt can be made to show that what admittedly appeared to be a threatening expression is really a meaningless event, or an unintentional act, or a joke not meant to be taken seriously, or an unavoidable, "understandable" product of extenuating circumstances. On the other hand, the meaning of the event may be granted and effort concentrated on the creator of it. Information may be provided to show that the creator was under the influence of something and not himself, or that he was under the command of somebody else and not acting for himself. When a person claims that an act was meant in jest, he may go on and claim that the self that seemed to lie behind the act was also projected as a joke. When a person suddenly finds that he has demonstrably failed in capacities that the others assumed him to have and to claim for himself—such as the capacity to spell, to perform minor tasks, to talk without malapropisms, and so on—he may quickly add, in a serious or unserious way, that he claims these incapacities as part of his self. The meaning of the threatening incident thus stands, but it can now be incorporated smoothly into the flow of expressive events.

As a supplement to or substitute for the strategy of redefining the offensive act or himself, the offender can follow two other procedures: he can provide compensations to the injured—when it is not his own face that he has threatened; or he can provide punishment, penance, and expiation for himself. These are important moves or phases in the ritual interchange. Even though the offender may fail to prove his innocence, he can suggest through these means that he *is* now a renewed person, a person who has paid for his sin against the expressive order and is once more to be trusted in the judgmental scene. Further, he can show that he does not treat the feelings of the others lightly, and that if their feelings have been injured by him, however innocently he is prepared to pay a price for his action. Thus he assures the others that they can accept his explanations without this acceptance constituting a sign of weakness and a lack of pride on their part. Also, by his treatment of himself, by his self-castigation, he shows that he is clearly aware of the kind of crime he would have committed had the incident been what it first appeared to be, and that he knows the kind of punishment that ought to be accorded to one who would commit such a crime. The suspected person thus shows that he is thoroughly capable of taking the role of the others toward his own activity, that he can still be used as a responsible participant in the ritual process, and that the rules of conduct which he appears to have broken are still sacred, real, and unweakened. An offensive act may arouse anxiety about the ritual code; the offender allays this anxiety by showing that both the code and he as an upholder of it are still in working order.

After the challenge and the offering have been made, the third move can occur: the persons to whom the offering is made can accept it as a satisfactory means of reestablishing the expressive order and the faces supported by this order. Only then can the offender cease the major part of his ritual offering.

In the terminal move of the interchange, the forgiven person conveys a sign of gratitude to those who have given him the indulgence of forgiveness.

The phases of the corrective process—challenge, offering, acceptance, and thanks—provide a model for interpersonal ritual behavior, but a model that may be departed from in significant ways. For example, the offended parties may give the offender a chance to initiate the offering on his own before a challenge is made and before they ratify the offense as an incident. This is a common courtesy, extended on the assumption that the recipient will introduce a self-challenge. Further, when the offended persons accept the corrective offering, the offender may suspect that this has been grudgingly done from tact, and so he may volunteer additional corrective offerings, not allowing the matter to rest until he has received a second or third acceptance of his repeated apology. Or the offended persons may tactfully take over the role of the offender and volunteer excuses for him that will, perforce, be acceptable to the offended persons.

An important departure from the standard corrective cycle occurs when a challenged offender patently refuses to heed the warning and continues with his offending behavior, instead of setting the activity to rights. This move shifts the play back to the challengers. If they countenance the refusal to meet their demands, then it will be plain that their challenge was a bluff and that the bluff has been called. This is an untenable position; a face for themselves cannnot be derived from it, and they are left to bluster. To avoid this fate, some classic moves are open to them. For instance, they can resort to tactless, violent retaliation, destroying either themselves or the person who had refused to heed their warning. Or they can withdraw from the undertaking in a visible huff—righteously indignant, outraged, but confident of ultimate vindication. Both tacks provide a way of denying the offender his status as an interactant, and hence denying the reality of the offensive judgment he has made. Both strategies are ways of salvaging face, but for all concerned the costs are usually high. It is partly to forestall such scenes that an offender is usually quick to offer apologies; he does not want the affronted persons to trap themselves into the obligation to resort to desperate measures.

It is plain that emotions play a part in these cycles of response, as when anguish is expressed because of what one has done to another's face, or anger because of what has been done to one's own. I want to stress that these emotions function as moves, and fit so precisely into the logic of the ritual game that it would seem difficult to understand them without it.[1] In fact, spontaneously expressed feelings are likely to fit into the formal pattern of the ritual interchange more elegantly than consciously designed ones.

---

1. Even when a child demands something and is refused, he is likely to cry and sulk not as an irrational expression of frustration but as a ritual move, conveying that he already has a face to lose and that its loss is not to be permitted lightly. Sympathetic parents may even allow for such display, seeing in these crude strategies the beginnings of a social self.

## COOPERATION IN FACE-WORK

When a face has been threatened, face-work must be done, but whether this is initiated and primarily carried through by the person whose face is threatened, or by the offender, or by a mere witness, is often of secondary importance. Lack of effort on the part of one person induces compensatory effort from others; a contribution by one person relieves the others of the task. In fact, there are many minor incidents in which the offender and the offended simultaneously attempt to initiate an apology. Resolution of the situation to everyone's apparent satisfaction is the first requirement; correct apportionment of blame is typically a secondary consideration.

Since each participant in an undertaking is concerned, albeit for differing reasons, with saving his own face and the face of the others, then tacit cooperation will naturally arise so that the participants together can attain their shared but differently motivated objectives.

One common type of tacit cooperation in face-saving is the tact exerted in regard to face-work itself. The person not only defends his own face and protects the face of the others, but also acts so as to make it possible and even easy for the others to employ face-work for themselves and him. He helps them to help themselves and him. Social etiquette, for example, warns men against asking for New Year's Eve dates too early in the season, lest the girl find it difficult to provide a gentle excuse for refusing. This second-order tact can be further illustrated by the widespread practice of negative-attribute etiquette. The person who has an unapparent negatively valued attribute often finds it expedient to begin an encounter with an unobtrusive admission of his failing, especially with persons who are uninformed about him. The others are thus warned in advance against making disparaging remarks about his kind of person and are saved from the contradiction of acting in a friendly fashion to a person toward whom they are unwittingly being hostile. This strategy also prevents the others from automatically making assumptions about him which place him in a false position and saves him from painful forbearance or embarrassing remonstrances.

\* \* \*

Another form of tacit cooperation, and one that seems to be much used in many societies, is reciprocal self-denial. Often the person does not have a clear idea of what would be a just or acceptable apportionment of judgments during the occasion, and so he voluntarily deprives or depreciates himself while indulging and complimenting the others, in both cases carrying the judgments safely past what is likely to be just. The favorable judgments about himself he allows to come from the others; the unfavorable judgments of himself are his own contributions. This "after you, Alphonse" technique works, of course, because in depriving himself he can reliably anticipate that the others will compliment or indulge him. Whatever allocation of favors is eventually established, all participants are first given a chance to show that they are not bound or constrained by their own desires and expectations, that they have a properly modest view of themselves, and that they can be counted upon to support the ritual code. Negative bargaining, through which each participant tries to make the terms of trade more favorable to the other side, is another instance; as a form of exchange perhaps it is more widespread than the economist's kind.

A person's performance of face-work, extended by his tacit agreement to help others perform theirs, represents his willingness to abide by the ground rules of social interaction. Here is the hallmark of his socialization as an interactant. If he and the others were not socialized in this way, interaction in most societies and most situations would be a much more hazardous thing for feelings and faces. The person would find it impractical to be oriented to symbolically conveyed appraisals of social worth, or to be possessed of feelings—that is, it would be impractical for him to be a ritually delicate object. And as I shall suggest, if the person were not a ritually delicate object, occasions of talk could not be organized in the way they usually are. It is no wonder that trouble is caused by a person who cannot be relied upon to play the face-saving game.

## THE RITUAL ROLES OF THE SELF

So far I have implicitly been using a double definition of self: the self as an image pieced together from the expressive implications of the full flow of events in an undertaking; and the self as a kind of player in a ritual game who copes honorably or dishonorably, diplomatically or undiplomatically, with the judgmental contingencies of the situation. A double mandate is involved. As sacred objects, men are subject to slights and profanation; hence as players of the ritual game they have had to lead themselves into duels, and wait for a round of shots to go wide of the mark before embracing their opponents.

\* \* \*

Further, within limits the person has a right to forgive other participants for affronts to his sacred image. He can forbearantly overlook minor slurs upon his face, and in regard to somewhat greater injuries he is the one person who is in a position to accept apologies on behalf of his sacred self. This is a relatively safe prerogative for the person to have in regard to himself, for it is one that is exercised in the interests of the others or of the undertaking. Interestingly enough, when the person commits a *gaffe* against himself, it is not he who has the license to forgive the event; only the others have that prerogative, and it is a safe prerogative for them to have because they can exercise it only in his interests or in the interests of the undertaking. One finds, then, a system of checks and balances by which each participant tends to be given the right to handle only those matters which he will have little motivation for mishandling. In short, the rights and obligations of an interactant are designed to prevent him from abusing his role as an object of sacred value.

When a person begins a mediated or immediate encounter, he already stands in some kind of social relationship to the others concerned, and expects to stand in a given relationship to them after the particular encounter ends. This, of course, is one of the ways in which social contacts are geared into the wider society. Much of the activity occurring during an encounter can be understood as an effort on everyone's part to get through the occasion and all the unanticipated and unintentional events that can cast participants in an undesirable light, without disrupting the relationships of the participants. And if relationships are in the process of change, the object will be to bring the encounter to a satisfactory close without altering the expected course of development. This perspective nicely accounts, for example, for the little ceremonies of greeting and farewell which occur when people begin a conversational encounter or depart from one. Greetings provide a way of showing that a relationship is still what it was at the termination of the previous coparticipation and, typically, that this relationship involves sufficient suppression of hostility for the participants temporarily to drop their guards and talk. Farewells sum up the effect of the encounter upon the relationship and show what the participants may expect of one another when they next meet. The enthusiasm of greetings compensates for the weakening of the relationship caused by the absence just terminated, while the enthusiasm of farewells compensates the relationship for the harm that is about to be done to it by separation.

# 19

## To Veil or Not to Veil? A Case Study of Identity Negotiation among Muslim Women in Austin, Texas*

### JEN'NAN GHAZAL READ and JOHN P. BARTKOWSKI

*There is much controversy in England, France, and other European countries about the clothes Muslim women wear. Some people object to the scarf (in Arabic, hijab) worn to cover women's hair. As a cultural object, Orthodox Jewish women, too, cover their natural hair. Many women in traditional groups (e.g., Mennonites, Amish) and fundamentalist Mormons do the same. Catholic nuns until a few years ago wore a habit that covered all but their faces. Interestingly, millions of Muslim women worldwide do not wear the* hijab, *in Indonesia, Malaysia, Turkey, Tunisia, Senegal, and elsewhere. In the United States it is a choice that carries both social implications and personal meanings, for those who wear the* hijab *and those who do not.*

In light of expanded social opportunities for women in Western industrialized countries, scholars have turned their attention to the status of women in other parts of the world. This burgeoning research literature has given rise to a debate concerning the social standing of Muslim women in the Middle East. On one hand, some scholars contend that Muslim women occupy a subordinate status within many Middle Eastern countries. Some empirical evidence lends support to this view, as many researchers have highlighted the traditional and gendered customs prescribed by Islam—most notably, the veiling and shrouding of Muslim women.

On the other hand, a growing number of scholars now argue that claims about the oppression and subjugation of veiled Muslim women may, in many regards, be overstated. Scholars who have generated insider portraits of Islamic gender relations have revealed that Muslim women's motivations for veiling can vary dramatically. Some Muslim women veil to express their strongly held convictions about gender difference, others are motivated to do so more as a means of critiquing Western colonialism in the Middle East. It is this complexity surrounding the veil that leads Elizabeth Fernea (1993, 122) to conclude that the veil (or *hijab*†) "means different things to different people within [Muslim]

---

*Footnotes and references can be found in the original article, published in *Gender and Society*, June 2000. [*Editor's note*]

†The *hijab* is called a veil but is, in fact, a hair covering, usually a scarf. It "screens" (the literal meaning of *hijab*) the beauty of a woman's hair from the untoward gaze of males. The face covering, *niqab*, comes to mind when the word "veil" is used but is not the subject of this essay. Curious students can Google "images" to see the variety of forms of the *hijab*. [*Editor's note*]

society, and it means different things to Westerners than it does to Middle Easterners."

Our study takes as its point of departure the conflicting meanings of the veil among both Muslim religious elites and rank-and-file Islamic women currently living in the United States. In undertaking this investigation, we supplement the lone study (published in Arabic) that compares the gender attitudes of veiled and unveiled women. That study, based largely on survey data collected from university women living in the Middle East, demonstrates that while veiled women evince somewhat conservative gender attitudes, the vast majority of them support women's rights in public life and a substantial proportion subscribe to marital equality. We seek to extend these suggestive findings by using in-depth, personal interviews, because data from such interviews are more able to capture the negotiation of cultural meanings by veiled and unveiled respondents, as well as the nuances of these women's gender identities.

The importance of our study is further underscored by the influx of Muslims into the United States during recent decades and the increasing prominence of Muslim Americans and Islamic women on the domestic scene. Although population estimates of Muslim Americans vary (ranging from 5 to 8 million), many observers consider Islam to be one of the fastest growing religions in the United States. Moreover, recent research indicates that a majority of Muslims in the United States are university graduates firmly situated within the American middle class. Yet, even as this religious subculture has enjoyed such rapid growth and economic privilege throughout much of the West, Muslims in the United States and abroad have become the target of pejorative stereotypes. Caricatures that portray Islamic women as submissive and backward have become more pervasive within recent years, but recent research on Muslim women living in the United States has called such unflattering depictions into question. Such research has revealed that Muslim American women creatively negotiate their gender, religious, and ethnic identities in light of dominant U.S. social norms and modernist discourses that often define these women as "other."

Our investigation therefore aims to enrich this growing research literature, while critically evaluating negative stereotypes about Muslim women. After outlining our theoretical perspective, we review the debates that currently characterize Muslim elite discourse concerning the veil. Then, to discern the impact of these broad cultural disputes on the gender identities of women of Islam located in the United States, we analyze interview data collected from a sample of religiously active Muslim women—both veiled and unveiled—currently living in Austin, Texas. Our analysis highlights salient points of ideological divergence, as well as unanticipated points of congruence, between these veiled and unveiled Muslim women concerning this controversial cultural practice.

## THEORY AND CONTEXT: DISCOURSE, IDENTITY, AND THE LANDSCAPE OF ISLAM

How can scholars effectively explore the interconnections between broad-based cultural constructions of gender on one hand and the more circumscribed (inter)subjective (i.e., personal) negotiation of gender relations on the other? In an effort to address these issues, a large number of contemporary feminist theorists and gender scholars have begun to examine discourse as one important medium through which gender is constructed. Our study is informed by these theoretical insights and by feminist standpoint theories and notions of subjectivity that take seriously women's agency, as well as their bodily practices and everyday experiences, in the negotiation of their gender identities.

Theories of discourse suggest that cultural forms (e.g., gender, religion, ethnicity) are best understood as *constructed, contested*, and *intersecting* social phenomena. First, the meanings attributed to the Muslim veil are not endemic to the veil itself; rather, they are produced through cultural discourse and vast networks of social relationships. Social practices that imbue the veil with cultural significance include the rhetoric of religious elites who equate veiling with religious devotion, as well as the actual ostracism of unveiled Muslim women from some Islamic institutions. Second, theories of discourse call attention to the contested character of cultural forms. Cultural symbols are capable of being interpreted in a variety of different ways and often become a site of struggle and contestation. Divergent interpretations of the same cultural practice may be advanced by groups who share a common religious heritage. As evidenced in our analysis below, various factions of Muslim elites offer strikingly different interpretations of the veil and the Qur'anic passages pertaining to this cultural practice. Finally, theories of discourse attune researchers to the multidimensional and overlapping character of cultural forms. Discourses are not discrete ideologies; rather, they are culturally specific modes of understanding the world that intersect with competing viewpoints. As we reveal below, religiously active Muslim women living in the United States are exposed not only to the internecine gender debates waged within Islamic circles mentioned above. These women also construct their gender identities in light of non-Muslim discourses of gender and ethnicity prevalent in late-twentieth-century America.

As noted, we complement these insights with feminist notions of standpoint, subjectivity, and bodily practice. Taken together, these theoretical perspectives suggest that discursive regimes provide social actors with important symbolic resources for identity negotiation and for the legitimation of everyday social and bodily practices. Current gender scholarship construes identity negotiation as a *process* and everyday *practice* that is fraught with ambiguity, contradiction, and struggle. These perspectives stand in bold contrast to more static psychological conceptualizations of *personality* as divorced from lived experience and bodily practice. Therefore, we are careful to recognize how competing discourses of the veil enable veiled Muslim women to legitimate their decision to veil on a variety of grounds—from explicitly antifeminist rationales to feminist justifications for veiling. Yet, at the same time, we reveal how the respondents use their everyday experiences to lend a practical edge to their understanding of the veil and their perceptions of themselves as Muslim women.

The most germane aspects of Muslim theology for this study concern two sets of Islamic sacred texts, the Qur'an and the hidiths. The Qur'an is held in high esteem by virtually all Muslims. Not unlike the "high view" of the Bible embraced by various conservative Christian groups, many contemporary Muslims believe that the Qur'an is the actual Word of God that was ably recorded by Muhammed during the early portion of the seventh century. In addition to the Qur'an, many Muslims also look to the hadiths for moral and spiritual guidance in their daily lives. The hadiths, second-hand reports of Muhammed's personal traditions and lifestyle, began to be collected shortly after his death because of the difficulty associated with applying the dictates of the Qur'an to changing historical circumstances. The full collection of these hadiths has come to be known as the *sunna*. Along with the Qur'an, the hadiths constitute the source of law that has shaped the ethics and values of many Muslims.

Within Islam, the all-male Islamic clergy (variously called *faghihs, imams,* [*maribors*], *muftis, mullahs,* or *ulumas*) often act as interpretive authorities who are formally charged with distilling insights from the Qur'an or hadiths and with disseminating these scriptural interpretations to the Muslim laity. Given that such positions of structural privilege are set aside for Muslim men, Islam is a patriarchal religious institution. Yet, patriarchal institutions do not necessarily produce homogeneous gender ideologies, a fact underscored by the discursive fissures [arguments] that divide Muslim religious authorities and elite commentators concerning the veil.

## COMPETING DISCOURSES OF THE VEIL IN CONTEMPORARY ISLAM

Many Muslim clergy and Islamic elites currently prescribe veiling as a custom in which "good" Muslim women should engage. Proponents of veiling often begin their defense of this cultural practice by arguing that men are particularly vulnerable to corruption through unregulated sexual contact with women. These experts contend that the purpose of the hijab or veil is the regulation of such contact:

> The society that Islam wants to establish is not a sensate, sex-ridden society. . . . The Islamic system of *Hijab* is a wide-ranging system which protects the family and closes those avenues that lead toward illicit sex relations or even indiscriminate contact between the sexes in society. . . . To protect her virtue and to safeguard her chastity from lustful eyes and covetous hands, Islam has provided

for purdah which sets norms of dress, social get-together . . . and going out of
the four walls of one's house in hours of need. (Siddiqi 1983, vii–viii)

Many expositors of the pro-veiling discourse call attention to the uniquely
masculine penchant for untamed sexual activity and construe the veil as a God-
ordained solution to the apparent disparities in men's and women's sexual appe-
tites. Women are therefore deemed responsible for the management of men's
sexuality. Some contend that the Muslim woman who veils should be sure that
the hijab covers her whole body (including the palms of her hands), should be
monotone in color ("so as not to be attractive to draw the attentions to"), and
should be opaque and loose so as not to reveal "the woman's shape or what
she is wearing underneath" (Al-Swailem 1995, 24–25).

Pro-veiling Muslim luminaries also defend veiling on a number of nonsex-
ual grounds. The veil, according to these commentators, serves as (1) a demonstration of the Muslim woman's unwavering obedience to the tenets of Islam;
(2) a clear indication of the essential differences distinguishing men from
women; (3) a reminder to women that their proper place is in the home rather
than in pursuing public-sphere activities; and (4) a sign of the devout Muslim
woman's disdain for the profane, immodest, and consumerist cultural customs
of the West. In this last regard, veiling is legitimated as an anti-imperialist statement of ethnic and cultural distinctiveness.

Nevertheless, the most prominent justifications for veiling entail, quite simply, the idea that veiling is prescribed in the Qur'an. Several Muslim clergy
place a strong interpretive emphasis on a Qur'anic passage (S. 24:31) that urges
women "not [to] display their beauty and adornments" but rather to "draw their
head cover over their bosoms and not display their ornament." Many of these
same defenders of the veil marshal other Qur'anic passages that bolster their
proveiling stance: "And when you ask them [the Prophet's wives] for anything
you want ask them from before a screen (*hijab*); that makes for greater purity
for your hearts and for them" (S. 33:53); "O Prophet! Tell your wives and daughters and the believing women that they should cast their outer garments over
themselves, that is more convenient that they should be known and not
molested" (S. 33:59).

In addition to these Qur'anic references, pro-veiling Muslim clergy highlight
hadiths intended to support the practice of veiling. Many pro-veiling Muslim
clergy maintain that the veil verse was revealed to Muhammad at a wedding
five years before the Prophet's death. As the story goes, three tactless guests
overstayed their welcome after the wedding and continued to chat despite the
Prophet's desire to be alone with his new wife. To encourage their departure,
Muhammad drew a curtain between the nuptial chamber and one of his incon-
siderate companions while ostensibly uttering "the verse of the hijab" (S. 33:53,
cited above). A second set of hadiths claim that the verse of hijab was prompted
when one of the Prophet's companions accidentally touched the hand of one of
Muhammad's wives while eating dinner. Yet a third set of hadiths suggests that

the verse's objective was to stop the visits of an unidentified man who tarried with the wives of the Prophet, promising them marriage after Muhammad's death.

In stark contrast to the pro-veiling apologias discussed above, an oppositional discourse against veiling has emerged within Islamic circles in recent years. Most prominent among these opponents of veiling are Islamic feminists. Although Islamic feminists are marginalized from many of the institutional apparatuses available to the all-male Muslim clergy, they nevertheless exercise considerable influence via the dissemination of dissident publications targeted at Islamic women and through grassroots social movements. Fatima Mernissi, arguably the most prominent Muslim feminist, is highly critical of dominant gender conceptualizations that construe veiling as the ultimate standard by which the spiritual welfare and religious devoutness of Muslim women should be judged. In *The Veil and the Male Elite: A Feminist Interpretation of Women's Rights in Islam*, Mernissi (1991, 194) queries her readers:

> What a strange fate for Muslim memory, to be called upon in order to censure and punish [Islamic women]! What a strange memory, where even dead men and women do not escape attempts at assassination, if by chance they threaten to raise the *hijab* [veil] that covers the mediocrity and servility that is presented to us [Muslim women] as tradition. How did the tradition succeed in transforming the Muslim woman into that submissive, marginal creature who buries herself and only goes out into the world timidly and huddled in her veils? Why does the Muslim man need such a mutilated companion?

Mernissi and other Muslim commentators who oppose veiling do so on a number of grounds. First, Mernissi seeks to reverse the sacralization of the veil by linking the hijab with oppressive social hierarchies and male domination. She argues that the veil represents a tradition of "mediocrity and servility" rather than a sacred standard against which to judge Muslim women's devotion to Allah. Second, antiveiling Muslim commentators are quick to highlight the historical fact that veiling is a cultural practice that originated from outside of Islamic circles. Although commonly assumed to be of Muslim origin, historical evidence reveals that veiling was actually practiced in the ancient Near East and Arabia long before the rise of Islam. Using this historical evidence to bolster their antiveiling stance, some Muslim feminists conclude that because the veil is not a Muslim invention, it cannot be held up as the standard against which Muslim women's religiosity is to be gauged.

Finally, Islamic feminists such as Mernissi point to the highly questionable scriptural interpretations on which Muslim clergy often base their pro-veiling edicts. Dissident Islamic commentators call attention to the fact that the Qur'an refers cryptically to a "curtain" and never directly instructs women to wear a veil. Although proponents of veiling interpret Qur'anic edicts as Allah's directive to all Muslim women for all time, Islamic critics of veiling counter this interpretive strategy by placing relatively greater weight on the "occasions of revelation" (*asbab nuzul al-Qur'an*)—that is, the specific social circumstances under which key Qur'anic passages were revealed. It is with this interpretive posture that many Islamic feminists believe the veil verse (S. 33:53) to be intended solely for the wives of Muhammad. Muslim critics of veiling further counter many of the pro-veiling hadith citations by arguing that they are interpretations of extrascriptural texts whose authenticity is highly questionable. Finally, critics of hijab point to select verses in the Qur'an that invoke images of gender egalitarianism, including one passage that refers to the "vast reward" Allah has prepared for both "men who guard their modesty and women who guard their modesty" (S. 33:35).

## THE VEIL AND GENDER IDENTITY NEGOTIATION AMONG MUSLIM WOMEN IN AUSTIN

To this point, we have drawn comparisons between pro-veiling edicts that link devout, desexualized Muslim womanhood to the practice of veiling and anti-veiling discourses that reject this conflation of hijab and women's religious devotion. We now attempt to gauge the impact of these debates on the gender identities of a sample of 24 Muslim women—12 of whom veil, 12 of whom do not. All women in our sample define themselves as devout Muslims (i.e., devoted followers of Muhammad who actively practice their faith). These women were recruited through a combination of snowball and purposive sampling. Taken together, the respondents identify with a range of different nationalities (e.g., Iranian, Pakistani, Kuwaiti) and Muslim sects. Nineteen women have lived 10 or more years in the United States, while five women in our sample have immigrated in the past 5 years. Their ages range from 21 to 55 years old, and they occupy a range of social roles (e.g., college students, professional women, homemakers). Consistent with the demographic characteristics of U.S. Muslim immigrants at large, our sample is composed of middle-class women with some postsecondary education (either a college degree or currently attending college). Class homogeneity among the respondents is also partly a product of the locale from which the sample was drawn, namely, a university town. Consequently, this study extends cross-cultural scholarship on the intersection of veiling, ethnicity, and nationality for middle-class Muslim women living in Western and largely modernized societies.

In-depth interviews with these Muslim women were conducted by the first author during 1996 and 1997. The interview questionnaire covered a range of topics, including the women's practical experiences with veiling, the meaning of the veil to them, their reasons for wearing or not wearing the veil and the impact of this decision on their social relationships, their perceptions about the significance of the veil in their country of origin, and the importance of Islamic beliefs and devotional activities (e.g., prayer, scriptural study) to these women. In light of our topic's sensitivity, as well as cultural differences between our respondents and the first author (a non-Muslim unveiled woman), the interviews were not audiotaped. Because many of the women were forthright about their opposition to participating in a study based on tape-recorded interviews, the tenor, depth, and candor of these interviews would have been seriously inhibited if conversations were tape-recorded. Consequently, with the women's consent, handwritten notes were recorded during the course of each interview. Immediately after the interview, these notes were then elaborated into a more detailed set of transcripts. Each transcript was initially evaluated as an independent conversation concerning the significance of the veil and its relationship to the respondent's religious and gender identity. Emergent themes from each interview were flagged and coded during this stage of the analysis. Then, during a second stage of analysis, we compared the themes that emerged from interviews conducted with each of the two different subgroups of Muslim women (veiled and unveiled).

Interview data collected from these women, identified below by pseudonyms, are designed to address several interrelated issues: What does the veil itself and the practice of veiling mean to these women? Among the women who veil, why do they do so? Among the women who do not veil, how have they arrived at the decision to remain unveiled? Finally, how does each group of our respondents feel about women who engage in the "opposite" cultural practice?

## VEILED CONTRADICTIONS: PERCEPTIONS OF HIJAB AND GENDER PRACTICES AMONG VEILED MUSLIM WOMEN

### Religious Edicts and Social Bonds

In several respects, the veiled respondents' accounts of wearing hijab conform to the pro-veiling gender discourse explicated above. Many of the veiled women invoke various sorts of religious imagery and theological edicts when asked about their motivations for veiling. One respondent in her early twenties, Huneeya, states flatly: "I wear the hijab because the Qur'an says it's better [for women to be veiled]." Yet another veiled woman, Najette, indicates that hijab "makes [her] more special" because it symbolizes her commitment to Islam. Mona says outright: "The veil represents submission to God," and Masouda construes the veil as a "symbol of worship" on the part of devout Muslim women to Allah and the teachings of the Prophet Muhammad. Not surprisingly, many veiled women contend that veiling is commanded in the Qur'an.

Of course, this abundance of theological rationales is not the only set of motivations that the veiled women use to justify this cultural practice. For many of the veiled respondents, the scriptural edicts and the religious symbolism surrounding the veil are given palpable force through their everyday gender practices and the close-knit social networks that grow out of this distinctive cultural practice. Indeed, narratives about some women's deliberate choice to begin veiling at a particular point in their lives underscore how religious edicts stand in tension with the women's strategic motivations. Several women recount that they began to veil because they had friends who did so or because they felt more closely connected to significant others through this cultural practice. Aisha, for example, longed to wear the veil while she attended high school in the Middle East approximately three decades ago. Reminiscent of issues faced by her teen counterparts in the United States, Aisha's account suggests that high school was a crucial time for identity formation and the cultivation of peer group relationships. The veil served Aisha as a valuable resource in resolving many of the dilemmas she faced 30 years ago as a maturing high school student. She decided to begin veiling at that time after hearing several prominent Muslim speakers at her school "talk[ing] about how good veiling is." The veil helped Aisha not only to form meaningful peer relationships at that pivotal time in her life (i.e., adolescence) but also continues to facilitate for her a feeling of connectedness with a broader religious community of other veiled Muslim women. During her recent trip to Egypt during the summer, Aisha says that the veil helped her "to fit in" there in a way that she would not have if she were unveiled.

Several other respondents also underscore the significance of Islamic women's friendship networks that form around the veil, which are particularly indispensable because they live in a non-Muslim country (i.e., the United States). In recounting these friendship circles that are cultivated around hijab in a "foreign" land, our veiled respondents point to an important overlay between their gender identities (i.e., good Muslim women veil) and their ethnic identities (i.e., as Middle Easterners). The common foundation on which these twin identities are negotiated is distinctively religious in nature. Hannan touts the personal benefits of veiling both as a *woman*—"the veil serves as an identity for [Islamic] women"—and as a *Muslim*: "[Because I veil,] Muslim people know I am Muslim, and they greet me in Arabic." This interface between gender and ethnicity is also given voice by Aisha, whose initial experiences with the veil were noted above. Aisha maintains, "The veil differentiates Muslim women from other women. When you see a woman in hijab, you know she's a Muslim." Much like the leading Muslim commentators who encourage Islamic women to "wear" their religious convictions (literally, via the veil) for all to see, these veiled respondents find comfort in the cultural and ethnic distinctiveness that the veil affords them. In this way, hijab is closely connected with their overlapping religious-gender-ethnic identities and links them to the broader community (*ummah*) of Islamic believers and Muslim women.

### Gender Difference and Women's "Emancipation"

In addition to providing religious rationales for wearing the veil, many of the women who wear hijab also invoke the discourse of masculine-feminine difference to defend the merits of veiling. For several women, the idea of masculine hypersexuality and feminine vulnerability to the male sex drive is crucial to this essentialist rationale for veiling. Despite the fact that veiled women were rather guarded in their references to sex, their nods in that direction are difficult to interpret in any other fashion. In describing the veil's role in Islam and in the lives of Muslim men and women (such as herself), Sharadda states, "Islam is natural and men need some things naturally. If we abide by these needs [and veil accordingly], we will all be happy." She continues, "If the veil did not exist, many evil things would happen. Boys would mix with girls, which will result in evil things."

Similarly, Hannan describes what she perceives to be women's distinctive attributes and their connection to the veil: "Women are like diamonds; they are so precious. They should not be revealed to everyone—just to their husbands and close kin." Like Qur'anic references to women's "ornaments," Hannan is contrasting the "precious" diamond-like feminine character to the ostensibly less refined, less distinctive masculine persona. Interestingly, it is by likening women to diamonds that Hannan rhetorically inverts traditional gender hierarchies that privilege "masculine" traits over their "feminine" counterparts. In the face of those who would denigrate feminine qualities, Hannan reinterprets the distinctiveness of womanhood as more "precious" (i.e., more rare and valuable) than masculine qualities. Women's inherent difference from men, then, is perceived to be a source of esteem rather than denigration.

It is important to recognize, however, that the respondents who invoke this rhetoric of gender difference are not simply reproducing the pro-veiling discourse advanced by Muslim elites [clerics]. Despite their essentialist convictions, many of the veiled respondents argue that the practice of wearing hijab actually liberates them from men's untamed, potentially explosive sexuality and makes possible for them various sorts of public-sphere pursuits. So, whereas pro-veiling Islamic elites often reason that women's sexual vulnerability (and, literally, their fragile bodily "ornaments") should restrict them to the domestic sphere, many of the veiled women in this study simply do not support this view of domesticized femininity. To the contrary, these women—many of whom are themselves involved in occupational or educational pursuits—argue that the veil is a great equalizer that enables women to work alongside of men. In the eyes of Hannan, women's "preciousness" should not be used to cajole them to remain in the home: "Women who wear the hijab are not excluded from society. They are freer to move around in society because of it."

Rabbab, who attends to various public-sphere pursuits, offers a similar appraisal. She argues that the veil (hijab) is an invaluable aid for Muslim women who engage in extradomestic pursuits. In advancing this claim, Rabbab uses women who veil their whole bodies (such body garments are called *abaya*) as a counterpoint of excessive traditionalism. When asked what the veil means to her personally, as well as to Muslim women and Islamic culture at large, she says,

> It depends on the extent of the hijab [that is worn]. . . . Women who wear face
> veils and cover their whole bodies [with abaya] are limited to the home. They

are too dependent on their husbands. How can they interact when they are so secluded? . . . [However,] taking away the hijab would make women have to fight to be taken seriously [in public settings]. . . . With hijab, men take us more seriously.

This hijab-as-liberator rationale for veiling was repeated by many of the veiled women who pursued educational degrees in schools and on college campuses where young predatorial men ostensibly rove in abundance. Aisha, a 41-year-old former student, recounts how the veil emancipated her from the male gaze during her school years:

> There was a boy who attended my university. He was very rude to all of the girls, always whistling and staring at them. One day, I found myself alone in the hallway with him. I was very nervous because I had to walk by him. But because I was wearing the hijab, he looked down when I walked past. He did not show that respect to the unveiled girls.

Drawing on experiences such as these, Aisha concludes succinctly: "The veil gives women advantages. . . . They can go to coeducational schools and feel safe." A current student, Najette, says that the veil helps her to "feel secure" in going about her daily activities. Finally, the account of a young female student who is 22 years of age sheds further light on the hijab's perceived benefits in the face of men's apparent propensity to objectify women: "If you're in hijab, then someone sees you and treats you accordingly. I feel more free. Especially men, they don't look at your appearance—they appreciate your intellectual abilities. They respect you." For many of the veiled women in this study, the respect and protection afforded them by the hijab enables them to engage in extradomestic pursuits that would ironically generate sharp criticism from many pro-veiling Muslim elites.

## The Discontents of Hijab and Tolerance for the Unveiled

While the foregoing statements provide clear evidence of these women's favorable feelings about hijab, many of the veiled women also express mixed feelings about this controversial cultural symbol. It was not uncommon for the veiled respondents to recount personal difficulties that they have faced because of their decision to wear hijab. Some dilemmas associated with the veil emanate from the fact that these women live in a secular society inhabited predominantly by Christians rather than Muslims. Najette, the same respondent who argued that veiling makes her feel "special," was quick to recognize that this esteem is purchased at the price of being considered "weird" by some Americans who do not understand her motivations for veiling. For women like her, engaging in a dissident cultural practice underscores Najette's cultural distinctiveness in a way that some people find refreshing and others find threatening.

Such points of tension surrounding the veil are evident not only in cross-cultural encounters such as that mentioned above. Even within Muslim circles, the practice of veiling has generated enough controversy to produce rifts among relatives and friends when some of the veiled respondents appear publicly in hijab. Huneeya, a student who veils because she wishes to follow Qur'anic edicts and enjoys being treated as an intellectual equal by her male peers, highlighted just this point of friction with her family members, all of whom except her are "against hijab. [My family members] think it is against modernity."

For some women, the tensions produced within intimate relationships by the veil move beyond the realm of intermittent family squabbles. One veiled respondent, Asma, revealed that extended family difficulties surrounding the veil have caused her to alter the practice of veiling itself, if only temporarily. Her recent experiences underscore the complex machinations of power involved in the contested arenas of family relations and friendships where veiling is concerned. Asma moved to the United States with her husband only two years ago. Asma was quite conscientious about veiling. She relished the sense of uniqueness and cultural distinctiveness afforded to her by the hijab while living in a non-Muslim country. Yet, recent summer-long visits from her mother-in-law presented her with a dilemma. Asma's mother-in-law had arranged the marriage between her son and daughter-in-law. At the time, the mother-in-law greatly appreciated the conservative religious values embraced by her future daughter-in-law, evidenced in Asma's attentiveness to wearing the veil. Yet, since that time, Asma's mother-in-law had undergone a conversion of sorts concerning the practice of veiling. Quite recently, Asma's mother-in-law stopped wearing the veil and wanted her daughter-in-law to follow suit by discarding the veil as well. Indeed, this mother-in-law felt that Asma was trying to upstage her by using the veil to appear more religiously devout than her elder. Asma's short-term solution to this dilemma is to submit to the wishes of her mother-in-law during her summer visits to the United States. Consequently, for two months each summer, Asma discards her veil. Yet, this solution is hardly satisfactory to her and does not placate Asma's veiled friends who think less of her for unveiling:

> I feel very uncomfortable without the veil. The veil keeps us [Muslim women] from getting mixed up in American culture. But I don't want to make my mother-in-law feel inferior, so I take it off while she is here. I know my friends think I am a hypocrite.

Although Asma is sanctioned by her friends for unveiling temporarily during her mother-in-law's visit, our interview data suggest that the preponderance of veiled women in this study harbor no ill will toward their Muslim sisters who choose not to veil. Despite these veiled women's enthusiastic defenses of hijab, they are willing to define what it means to be a good Muslim broadly enough to include Islamic women who do not veil. When asked, for instance, what she thought being a good Muslim entails, one of our veiled respondents (Najette) states simply: "You must be a good person and always be honest." Echoing these sentiments, Masouda suggests, "Your attitude towards God is most important for being a good Muslim—your personality. You must be patient, honest, giving." Even when asked point-blank if veiling makes a woman a good Muslim, another veiled respondent answers, "Hijab is not so important for being a good Muslim. Other things are more important, like having a good character and being honest." One respondent even took on a decidedly ecumenical tone in detaching veiling from Islamic devotion: "Being a good Muslim is the same as being a good Christian or a good Jew—treat others with respect and dignity. Be considerate and open-minded." In the end, then, these women in hijab are able to distinguish between what veiling means to them at a personal level (i.e., a sign of religious devotion) versus what the veil says about Muslim women in general (i.e., a voluntary cultural practice bereft of devotional significance). These veiled women's heterogeneous lived experiences with the hijab—both comforting and uncomfortable, affirming and tension producing, positive and negative—seem to provide them with a sensitivity to cultural differences that often seems lacking in the vitriolic debates about veiling currently waged by leading Muslims.

## ISLAMIC FEMINISM MODIFIED: PERCEPTIONS OF HIJAB AND GENDER PRACTICES AMONG THE UNVEILED

### Patriarchal Oppression and Religious Fanaticism

Just as veiled women draw on the pro-veiling discourse to defend the wearing of hijab, the unveiled women in this study often justify their abstention from this cultural practice by invoking themes from the antiveiling discourse. Several of these unveiled women argue quite straightforwardly that the veil reinforces gender distinctions that work to Muslim women's collective disadvantage. According to many of the unveiled women, the veil was imposed on Muslim women because of Middle Eastern men's unwillingness to tame their sexual caprice and because of their desire to dominate women. Rabeeya, for example, contends that Muslim women are expected to veil because "Middle Eastern men get caught up in beauty. The veil helps men control themselves." Offering a strikingly similar response, Najwa argues that "men can't control themselves, so they make women veil." Using the same critical terminology— that is, *control*—to make her point, Fozia has an even less sanguine view of the veil's role in Islam. When asked about the significance of the veil in Muslim societies, she states flatly: "The veil is used to control women." In short, many of the unveiled respondents view hijab in much the same way as elite Islamic feminists; that is, as a mechanism of patriarchal control.

Comments such as these suggest points of congruence between the veiled and unveiled respondents' understandings of hijab. Both groups of women seem to agree that hijab is closely related to men's sexuality. Recall that some of the veiled women contrast masculine hypersexuality to a desexualized view of femininity. Such women conclude that the veil is the God-ordained corrective for men's inability to control their own sexual impulses. Likewise, as evidenced in several statements from unveiled women, they link the veil to men's apparent inability (or, better, unwillingness) to contain their sexual desires. However, whereas several of the veiled women see masculine hypersexuality as natural and view the veil as a divine remedy for such sexual differences, many of the unveiled women reject these views. The unveiled respondents seem less willing to accept the notion that categorical gender differences should translate into a cultural practice that (literally and figuratively) falls on the shoulders of women. In a key point of departure from their sisters who wear hijab, the unveiled women in this study trace the origin of the veil not to God but rather to men's difficulties in managing their sexuality (again, "men can't control themselves, so they make women veil"). In men's attempt to manage their sexual impulses, so the account goes, they have foisted the veil on women. Very much in keeping with feminist discourses that take issue with such gendered double standards, the unveiled women conclude that it is unfair to charge women with taming men's sexuality.

Apart from these issues of social control and sexuality, several of the unveiled respondents also invoke themes of religious devotion and ethnic identity when discussing the significance of the veil for Muslims in general and for themselves (as unveiled Islamic women) in particular. Recall that leading Muslims who support veiling often highlight the religious and ethnic distinctiveness of hijab; however, prominent Muslim feminists counter that veiling did not originate with Islam and should not be understood as central to women's religious devoutness or ethnic identities (as non-Westerners). Echoing these Muslim feminist themes, several of the unveiled respondents seek to sever the veil from its religious and ethnic moorings. Fozia says that Muslim "women are made to believe that the veil is religious. In reality, it's all political," while Fatima asserts, "The veil is definitely political. It is used by men as a weapon to differentiate us from Westerners." Yet another respondent, Mah'ha, argues that it is only "fanatical" and "strict" Muslims who use the veil to draw sharp distinctions between Middle Easterners and Westerners. These remarks and others like them are designed to problematize the conflation of religious devotion, ethnic distinctiveness, and hijab evidenced in the proveiling discourse. Whereas the dominant discourse of veiling measures women's devotion to Islamic culture against hijab, many of the unveiled respondents imply—again, via strategic terms such as *political, fanatical,* and *strict*—that religious devotion and ethnic identification are good only in proper measure.

This rhetorical strategy allows these unveiled women to claim more moderate (and modern) convictions over and against those whose devotion to Allah has in their view been transmogrified into political dogmatism, religious extremism, and racial separatism. The unveiled women in our study do not eschew religious commitment altogether, nor are they in any way ashamed of their ethnic heritage. To the contrary, the unveiled respondents champion religious commitment (again, in good measure) and are proud to count themselves among the followers of Muhammad. Yet, they are quick to illustrate that their devotion to Allah and their appreciation of their cultural heritage are manifested through means that do not include the practice of veiling. Amna, for example, says, "Religious education makes me feel like a more pious Muslim. I read the Qur'an weekly and attend Friday prayer sermons," while Rabeeya states, "Being a good Muslim means believing in one God; no idolatry; following the five pillars of Islam; and believing in Muhammad." Concerning the issue of ethnoreligious identity, the basic message articulated by many of the unveiled women can be stated quite succinctly: A Muslim women can be true to her cultural and religious heritage without the veil. Samiya, a 38-year-old unveiled woman, says as much: "Muslim society doesn't exist on the veil. Without the veil, you would still be Muslim." Therefore, many of the unveiled women believe that the veil is of human (actually, male) origin rather than of divine making. And it is this very belief about the veil's this-worldly origins that enables many of the unveiled women to characterize themselves as devout followers of Muhammad who honor their cultural heritage even though they have opted not to veil.

### Standing on Common Ground: Tolerance for the Other among Unveiled Women

Finally, we turn our attention to the subjective contradictions that belie the prima facie critical reactions of our unveiled respondents toward the veil. Interestingly, just as the veiled women are reluctant to judge harshly their unveiled counterparts, these unveiled women who eschew hijab at a personal level nevertheless express understanding and empathy toward their Middle Eastern sisters who veil. At several points during interview encounters, the unveiled respondents escape the polemical hold of the antiveiling discourse by building bridges to their sisters who engage in a cultural practice that they themselves eschew.

First, several respondents imply that it would be wrong to criticize veiled women for wearing hijab when it is men—specifically, male Muslim elites—who are to blame for the existence and pervasiveness of the veil in Islamic culture. Amna, who does not veil, takes on a conciliatory tone toward women who do so by conceding that "the veil helps women in societies where they want to be judged solely on their character and not on their appearances." How is it that such statements, which sound so similar to the justifications for wearing hijab invoked by veiled women, emanate from the unveiled respondents? The strongly antipatriarchal sentiments of the unveiled women (described in the preceding section) seem to exonerate veiled women from charges of gender traitorism. Recall that many of the unveiled respondents, in fact, locate the origin of the veil in *men*'s sexual indiscretion and in *men*'s desire to control women: "Middle Eastern *men* get caught up in beauty. The veil helps *men* control *themselves*" (Rabeeya); "*Men* can't control *themselves*, so *they* make women veil" (Najwa); "The veil is *used to control women*. The women are *made to believe* that the veil is religious" (Fozia) (emphasis added). Ironically, it is the very anti-patriarchal character of these statements that simultaneously enables the unveiled women to express their stinging criticism of the veil itself while proclaiming tolerance and respect for Islamic women who wear the veil. Indeed, since many of the unveiled respondents construe hijab to be a product of *patriarchal* oppression and assorted *masculine* hang-ups (e.g., struggles with sexuality, a preoccupation with domination and control), veiled women cannot legitimately be impugned for wearing hijab.

Second, many of the unveiled respondents are willing to concede that despite their own critical views of the veil, hijab serves an important cultural marker for Islamic women other than themselves. When asked about the role of the veil among Muslim women she knows in the United States, Rabeeya recognizes that many of her veiled Islamic sisters who currently live in America remain "very, very tied to their culture. Or they are trying to be. They [veil because they] want to feel tied to their culture even when they are far away from home." Because she herself is a devout Islamic woman living in a religiously pluralistic and publicly secularized society, Rabeeya is able to empathize with other Muslim women residing in the United States who veil in order to shore up their cultural identity. Similarly, Sonya draws noteworthy distinctions between her personal antipathy toward veiling and veiled women's attraction to hijab: "Some Muslim women need the veil to identify themselves with the Muslim culture. I don't feel that way."

Finally, several of the unveiled women in our study seem to express tolerance and empathy for their sisters in hijab because, at one time or another in the past, they themselves have donned the veil. Two of the unveiled respondents, for example, are native Iranians who are currently living in the United States. When these women return to Iran, they temporarily don the veil. Najwa, one of these women, explains, "As soon as we cross the Iranian border, I go to the bathroom on the airplane and put on the hijab." The experiences of our other native-born Iranian woman, Fatima, speak even more directly to the practical nuances that undergird unveiled women's tolerance for their veiled counterparts. On one hand, Fatima is highly critical of the veil, which has been the legally required dress for women in Iran during the past two decades. Referring to this fact, she impugns the veil as a "political . . . weapon" used by religious elites to reinforce invidious distinctions between Westerners and Middle Easterners. Yet, on the other hand, her personal experiences with hijab lead her to reject the stereotype that women who veil are "backward": "Progress has nothing to do with veiling. Countries without veiling can be very backwards . . . I have nothing against veiling. I feel very modern [in not veiling], but I respect those who veil." Like so many of her unveiled sisters, then, Rabeeya is critical of the veil as a religious icon but is unwilling to look down on Islamic women who wear hijab.

## CONCLUSION AND DISCUSSION

This study has examined how a sample of Muslim women living in Austin, Texas, negotiate their gender identities in light of ongoing Islamic disputes about the propriety of veiling. Interview data with 12 veiled and 12 unveiled women reveal that many of them draw upon the pro-veiling and antiveiling discourses of Muslim elites, respectively, to justify their decisions about the veil. At the same time, the women highlight various subjective contradictions manifested in many of their accounts of veiling. Women who veil are not typically disdainful toward their unveiled Muslim sisters, and unveiled women in our sample seem similarly reluctant to impugn their veiled counterparts. Such findings were unanticipated in light of elite Muslim debates about the propriety of veiling.

What are we to make of the fact that the acrimony manifested between elite Muslim proponents and opponents of veiling is largely absent from these women's accounts of the veil? Several possible answers to this question emerge from our investigation. First, both the veiled and unveiled women in our study clearly exercise agency in crafting their gender identities. Drawing on themes of individualism and tolerance for diversity, the women are able to counterpose their own "choice" to veil or to remain unveiled on one hand with the personal inclinations of their sisters who might choose a path that diverges from their own. In this way, the respondents fashion gender identities that are malleable and inclusive enough to navigate through the controversy surrounding the veil. Second, the social context within which the women are situated seems to provide them with resources that facilitate these gender innovations. As noted above, our sample is composed of middle-class, well-educated Muslim women. We suspect that the progressive, multicultural climate of Austin and the human capital enjoyed by the women foster greater empathy between the veiled respondents and their unveiled counterparts. This degree of tolerance between veiled and unveiled Muslim women evinced in our study may be decidedly different for Islamic women living in other parts of the United States, other Western nations, or particular countries in the Middle East where the veil is a more publicly contested symbol.

Consequently, this study lends further credence to the insight that culture is not simply produced from "above" through the rhetoric of elites to be consumed untransformed by social actors who are little more than judgmental dopes. While the pro-veiling and antiveiling discourses have carved out distinctive positions for veiled Muslim women and their unveiled counterparts within the late twentieth century, the respondents in our study are unique and indispensable contributors to contemporary Islamic culture. It is these women, rather than the often combative elite voices within Islamic circles, who creatively build bridges across the contested cultural terrain of veiling; who forge ties of tolerance with their sisters, veiled and unveiled; and who help foster the sense of community (*ummah*) that is so esteemed by Muslims around the world.

Convictions about Islamic culture and community take on new meaning as they are tested in the crucible of Muslim women's everyday experiences. These findings parallel those that have emerged from other studies of politicized issues in the contemporary United States, including debates about abortion, family decision making, and women's paid labor force participation. These studies have revealed that the contemporary "culture wars" over gender are often waged by a select few—namely, elite ideologists and vanguard activists—whose views do not wholly correspond with the local standpoints of actual women at whom such rhetoric is targeted. * * *

Finally, there are some telling points of convergence between gender relations in contemporary Islam, Orthodox Judaism, and conservative Protestantism. Given the spate of recent studies which suggest that gender is negotiated by conservative Protestants and Orthodox Jews, what parallels might exist between the gendered experiences of Muslim women and their conservative Protestant or Orthodox Jewish counterparts? And, in what ways might the gender practices and the enactment of specific definitions of the religiously "devout woman" (whether Muslim, evangelical, or Orthodox Jew) diverge? No research of which we are aware has compared the processes of identity negotiation among Muslim women with those manifested in other conservative religious contexts. When interpreted in light of the emerging literature on gender negotiation within conservative Protestantism and Orthodox Judaism, our findings suggest that there is much to be gained by drawing more detailed cross-cultural comparisons between the gendered experiences of such women, as well as the culturally specific "patriarchal bargains" (Kandiyoti 1988) with which these groups of women are confronted. In the end, arriving at a richer understanding of gender negotiation in those contexts where we might least expect to find it can shed new light on the transformation of gender relations as we begin the millennium.

## REFERENCES

Al-Swailem, Sheikh Abdullah Ahmed. 1995. Introduction. In *A comparison between veiling and unveiling*, by Halah bint Abdullah. Riyadh, Saudi Arabia: Dar-us-Salam.

Fernea, Elizabeth W. 1993. The veiled revolution. In *Everyday life in the Muslim Middle East*, edited by D. L. Bowen and B. A. Early. Bloomington: Indiana University Press.

Kandiyoti, Deniz. 1988. Bargaining with patriarchy. *Gender & Society* 2:274–90.

Mernissi, Fatima. 1991. *The veil and the male elite: A feminist interpretation of women's rights in Islam*. Translated by Mary Jo Lakeland. New York: Addison-Wesley.

Siddiqi, Muhammad Iqbal. 1983. *Islam forbids free mixing of men and women*. Lahore, Pakistan: Kazi.

# 20

## The Body and Bathing: Help with Personal Care at Home

JULIA TWIGG

*The sociology of the body is a fascinating area of inquiry, whether focused on notions of beauty, fitness, health, or infirmity. The body is a significant object of social meaning and personal identity. In this essay, set in England where bathing is more often preferred to showering, the challenges of being an elderly adult in need of assistance in the bath is explored with considerable sociological imagination. Young, healthy medical professionals can project a sense of superiority when looking upon the infirm elderly. How can an older person, then, maintain a dignified sense of self in such a situation?*

To write about the body is to write about the mundane and the everyday, for that is what the body is: something that is with us always and everywhere—both our constant companion and our essence. Nothing could be more mundane or day to day than the processes of body care. These actions punctuate our daily lives in the forms of dressing, shaving, showering, combing, washing, eating, drinking, excreting, and sleeping, providing us with a rhythm and pattern to the day. The bodily rhythms provide a basic experiential security in daily life. We are, however, mostly acculturated to ignore these patterns, at least at the level of polite speech. The processes of body care are assumed to be both too private and too trivial for comment, certainly too trivial for traditional academic analysis. They belong with those other aspects of bodily life that we are socialized to pass over in silence. Though such bodily processes form the bedrock of daily life, they are bedrocks assumed, rather than reflected on. So long as they are there, functioning correctly, we have no need to comment.

But for many older people this easeful state of bodily ignorance and transcendence is no longer available. Their bodies force themselves into the front of their thoughts, posing a mass of practical problems. The body assumes new prominence by virtue of its inability to do things. Among those things can be the tasks of body care such as washing, showering, and bathing. This chapter explores what happens when older people can no longer cope with these aspects of life but need assistance in doing them. In particular, it focuses on the situation of older people living at home receiving help with personal care, typically washing and bathing.

While a discussion of the everyday activities of washing and bathing is, by definition, concerned with micro-processes, these actions are not outside wider discursive concerns. Bathing is located in a wider set of discourses than the simple discussion of hygiene that tends to permeate accounts in the area. In this chapter, I will explore how far the provision of help does indeed draw on these wider discourses and how far it remains located in a narrower set of pre-occupations. Help with bathing also entails negotiating the management of the body; it involves touch and nakedness and at times verges on the taboo. I will explore how older people feel about this, and who they prefer to help them in these areas. Before doing so, however, I will discuss briefly the paradoxical neglect of the subject of the body in relation to the support of older people.

## THE NEGLECTED BODY OF SOCIAL CARE

Though body care lies at the heart of service provision, this has not been empha-sized in accounts of the sector. There are three primary reasons for this: The first derives from a concern within gerontology to resist the dominant dis-courses of medicine and popular accounts of aging that present it in terms of inevitable bodily decline. The excessive focus on the body is seen as damaging—endorsing ageist stereotypes in which older people are reduced to their aging and sick bodies, which visibly mark them as old. Progressive gerontology by contrast aims to present a more rounded account of age: one that gives due weight to social rather than just bodily elements in the structuring of its expe-riences. The "political economy" approach, in particular, that has dominated social gerontology in Britain and North America since the 1980s, emphasizes the degree to which old age is the product of social structural factors such as retirement age, pension provision, and ageist assumptions (Phillipson and Walker 1986; Estes and Binney 1989; Arber and Ginn 1991). From this perspec-tive, factors like the differential access to resources or social exclusion primar-ily determine the social experience of old age not bodily decline. Close, analytic attention to the body from this perspective is thus regarded as a step backwards.

The second reason for the neglect of the body derives from the way in which the field of community care has traditionally been conceptualized within the debate on aging. "Community care" is the term commonly used in Britain and elsewhere for the support of older and disabled people enabling them to live in the community, typically in their own homes, and it is the principal policy objective in most advanced industrial societies.

Community care is not, however, predominantly conceptualized in terms of the body. Partly this is because the dominant professional group in the field is social work, which concentrates on questions of interpersonal and social func-tioning and whose remit tends to stop short of the body. This territory is tra-ditionally handed over to the care of medicine. As a result, though community care is inherently about the body and its day-to-day problems, this fact is not emphasized in accounts of the sector. The evasion is further compounded by the increasing influence of managerialism in the sector. Managerial discourse, constructed as it is out of the disciplines of economics, business studies, organization, and methods, embodies an abstract and distancing form of theorizing that is far from the messy, dirty realities of bodily life. When community care is discussed, it is done so in a manner that largely dismisses the body, rendering it invisible as a site of concern.

The third reason for neglect comes from work on the body itself. Since the 1980s there has been an explosion of writing in this area (Williams and Bendelow 1998), but its focus has been on younger, sexier, more transgressive bodies. The roots of much of this literature in feminism, queer theory, and cultural studies have not encouraged it to venture into the territory of old age. Indeed, these approaches have displayed a significant degree of ageism in their assumptions about what is interesting and important. More recently, however, new work has begun to address bodily issues in relation to later years (Öberg 1996; Tulle-Winton 2000; Gilleard and Higgs 2000). Some of the best of this work has—belatedly—come out of feminism (Woodward 1991, 1999; Andrews 1999; Furman 1997, 1999). It has been marked by a sense of agency and a desire to emphasize the subjective, meaning-making experiences of people as they engage in the aging process. Often these ideas are linked to concepts of the Third Age.

The Third Age represents a postretirement period of extended middle age in which people who are no longer confined by the labor market and are free from direct responsibility for children can pursue leisure interests, develop aspects of their personalities, and enjoy the fruits of later life. The emergence of this new social space is often linked to theories about identity and selfhood in postmodernity, particularly ones that emphasize self-fashioning. It is open, however, to the familiar critique that such optimistic accounts of the Third Age are only possible by virtue of projecting the negative aspects of aging into a dark Fourth Age, a period of declining health and social loss, sometimes also termed "deep" old age. As Gilliard and Higgs (2000) note, accounts of the Third Age emphasize agency and subjectivity and are described from the perspective of the optimistic self. But accounts of the Fourth Age focus on dependency and are written from the outside. A macro-level perspective dominates this literature. In such accounts, older persons are rarely seen as agents at all but are often presented as the "other."

Physical decline is frequently presented as marking the point of transition between the Third and Fourth Ages, and receiving personal care of a close and intimate kind is a key marker in this transition. In this chapter we focus on just such a personal care situation. In doing so I am thus attempting to extend the analysis in terms of the body to a group who until recently has been excluded from such a perspective. The literature on the body and aging that has emerged of late has tended to focus on the earlier optimistic stage of the Third Age, exploring the ways in which people negotiate issues of bodily aging as they make the transitions from middle to later life. * * *

## PERSONAL CARE AS A SOCIAL MARKER

Why is personal care such a marker of social states? The reason lies in the profound social symbolism that relates to the body and its management. This means that receiving help in these areas erodes the personhood and adult status of the subject. Personal care means being helped with precisely those tasks that as adults we do for ourselves: getting washed and dressed, moving, eating, and excreting. However rich we are, these are things that—at least in the modern West—we do for ourselves, typically alone or in the company of intimates. Body care of this type thus marks the boundary of the truly personal and individual in modern life. Having to be helped in these areas transgresses this boundary and undermines adulthood. Only babies and children are helped in this way, and this underwrites the profoundly infantalizing tendencies of "care."

* * *

Personal care also involves nakedness. Nakedness is not, largely, part of ordinary social interaction. It is a special state reserved for certain situations and relationships, and it is a marker of close, typically sexual, intimacy. To be naked in a social situation, as recipients of personal care are, is therefore to be put in a disjunctive context. It is made all the more so by the fact that the nakedness is asymmetrical: the recipient is naked, while the helper is fully clothed. To be naked in this way is to be exposed and vulnerable, and it inevitably creates a power dynamic in which the helper, usually younger and stronger, is clearly the dominant party.

### Personal Care and Bathing

Personal care has become an increasingly significant issue for social care agencies across the Western world as a result of widespread social and political policies aimed at supporting frail elders living at home. Home care in Britain and elsewhere is no longer primarily a matter of housework and shopping, but of personal care, in which washing and bathing form an important aspect. Historically, in Britain such help was primarily provided by the community nursing service but is now largely provided within a home care system. This same shift in home care can be detected in other Western welfare systems.

The principal driver behind it has been cost reduction, with the desire to move the provision of home care away from the relatively expensive health care sector where staff are trained and where the provision of personal care is often free to the recipient, into the less expensive social care sector where staff are typically untrained and where recipients are often required to fund their care. The shift has, however, also arisen from concerns about the over-medicalization of older people's lives. Home care services are seen as embodying a potentially more sympathetic and caring approach than that of medically directed ones.

This chapter draws on a study of help with washing and bathing provided to older and disabled people living at home in Britain (Twigg 2000a). The study was based on interviews with recipients, caregivers, and managers. In the research, elders received help with bathing from a variety of sources: the local authority home care service; voluntary sector or for profit agencies; or a specialist voluntary sector bathing service (the last is unusual in Britain). Depending on their income, users either received such help free or were expected to meet some or all of the costs.

### The Meanings of Bathing

Within public welfare services, washing and bathing tend to be presented narrowly in terms of a discourse of hygiene and cleanliness. The broader meanings of bathing in terms of luxury, pleasure, and well-being are not emphasized. There are a number of reasons for this: Partly it arises from a narrow concern with health and physical functioning, which is regarded as a particularly legitimate aim for such interventions. Bathing in this context is presented as a concern for hygiene; though in reality, dirtiness has to be extreme before health is genuinely threatened. Partly it comes from long-established political pressures to ensure that the remit of public welfare remains limited in scope and extent; and this is linked to a related puritanism that regards ideas of bodily pleasure in connection with public provision as—at the very least—discordant. * * *

But bathing has much broader meanings. While there is certainly not space here to explore the history of washing and bathing and of the various practices and discourses that have led to its construction (see Twigg 2000a for such a discussion), I will, however, refer briefly here to four recurring strands in that history to suggest some of the ways in which bathing is located in a wider set of discourses than just those of hygiene.

Historically, bathing has long been connected with luxury, pleasure, and to some degree, eroticism. For the Romans, bathing was a social activity associated with relaxation, exercise, conviviality, and pleasure (Yegül 1992). During the Middle Ages it was recurringly presented in connection with images of feasting and courtship (Vigarello 1988). These meanings narrowed by the nineteenth century, when bathing lost its social dimension and became a more private affair, more closely connected with the tasks of getting clean, though the sense of luxury and pleasure that derived from abundant hot water remains (Wilkie 1986; Bushman and Bushman 1988). During the twentieth century, luxurious bathrooms, whether presented in the celebratory imagery of Hollywood or the dreams of real estate promoters, continued to draw on this discourse of pleasure and luxury and only barely suppressed eroticism (Kira 1967).

Bathing is also located in a wider discourse of well-being. Again, this has been so since Roman times, when baths were seen as part of a general regimen of health and well-being. Baths have also been prominent in the alternative medical tradition from hydrotherapy to nature cure, and they remain a central element in the recent revival of spa culture, often in association with diffuse concepts of "Eastern" medicine, which has become a feature of modern Western lifestyles or at least aspirations. Spa treatments are presented as an antidote to stress and other ills of modern living. Through all of this, well-being is the key concept; and the focus is on the experiential body, not the medical body.

The third theme concerns the frequent use of baths and water as markers of social transitions. This is clearest in relation to classic rites of passage, such as Christian baptism, but it also operates in secular contexts like prisons, schools, and hospitals, where people are commonly compelled to have a bath as part of the initiation into the institution, marking their transition from the status of a citizen outside to that of an inmate inside. Individuals also draw on such symbolism in their daily lives, clearly marking out the transitions of the day or week through bodily practices such as bathing and showering. The bedrock of body care punctuates the day, providing a framework of time and of social states in terms of eating and drinking, washing and dressing, and sleeping and rising. No small part of our sense of ontological security is derived from these practices.

Last, bathing also contains darker themes. Baths have been widely used as part of coercive cultures, particularly within institutions. For example, cold plunges, sudden showers, and shockingly cold water have all been used as part of the history of the treatment of the insane. Though the justification for such techniques has often been in terms of shocking the patient back into reason, a clearly coercive, even sadistic, element is also often intensified by the use of machinery or the enforcement of humiliating bodily postures. * * *

## THE ADAPTABILITY OF THE OLD

Before exploring what people feel about receiving help, it is worth reflecting briefly on the adaptability of the old. Accounts of older people often present them as inflexible and unable to cope with change. In fact, the changes imposed on people in their later lives are enormous. No amount of jet travel, adaptation to new information technology systems, or learning to appreciate new music can remotely compare with the changes that older people have to learn to become accustomed to on a day-to-day basis. The aged may lose their lifetime companion; may have to move to a new home, town, or region; and may have to learn to live in an institution among random strangers in a collective way that is wholly at odds with their earlier lives and under the auspices of a staff whose background and worldview may be completely alien to them.

In all of this, bodily experiences can be among the most significant: not being able to move freely, to speak clearly, or to manage your bodily functions present major changes in life. Having to receive help with personal care, in particular, breaches some of the most profound of social expectations, requiring people to cope with new situations and new relationships. As we shall see, some of the respondents expressed dismay at what they had to face, but it is testimony to their adaptability that they did indeed manage to cope. The majority approached old age with stoicism, concentrating on the day and trying to make the best of it. Some developed ingenious and innovative ways to circumvent their physical difficulties.

## WHAT DOES BATHING MEAN IN THIS CONTEXT?

Within the British tradition, the predominant ways of getting clean have been baths, in the sense of bathtubs, and washing at a basin. This is in contrast to Continental and American traditions where showering established itself much earlier as the main alternative to strip washing at a basin. Showering is now common among younger people in Britain, but is still largely unfamiliar or disliked among this older age group. Few people in the study had showers in their homes. In the context of drafty houses and feeble flows of hot water, showers do not warm the body in the way that hot baths do. One or two respondents of Continental origin did prefer showers, sharing the mainland European view that baths are not an adequate way to clean oneself.

People varied in how important baths were to them. Some respondents had never been great bathers and relied instead on a strip wash. For others, a daily bath was a long-established habit and one that they greatly missed. As Mrs. Fitzgerald (all respondents' names have been changed) explained, she loved bathing and continues to see it as a vital part of the day: "All my life, up in a morning, throw open the bed, into the bathroom—that's the way I lived. . . . It's always been terribly important to me. And that's when I got panic-stricken when I thought I wasn't going to be able to have any baths."

The care people actually received from the bathing service was not always in line with their hopes. Some individuals did indeed have a "proper bath," in the sense of being placed directly under the water, with all the warmth and buoyancy that this could bring. But for many, "bathing" really meant sitting on a board over the bath while the caregiver helped them to wash and poured warm water over their bodies. This was enjoyable, but it was not a proper bath, and many regretted this. Mrs. Kennelly, whose severe Parkinson's meant that she could no longer have a bath, remembered the experience with a sense of nostalgia, "I'd love to be able to get in the bath. Just lay there and splash it over . . . wallow in it. Lovely." Mrs. Bridgeman tells of how wonderful it would be to just once receive a proper bath, "I *long* to get my bum in the water. It would be bliss you know."

The problem was that many recipients did not have sufficient flexibility to get down into the tub or the strength to get up, and very few homes had the kind of expensive equipment that would allow for this. Workers were forbidden by Health and Safety legislation from lifting the clients out of the bath (though sometimes they still performed the task). This meant that many had more in the way of an assisted wash than a bath. By and large, recipients were resigned to these limitations and grateful for what assistance they received, but problems did occasionally arise, particularly if clients rebelled and attempted to preempt the situation by sitting down fully in the bath. In these cases, the caregivers were instructed to tell the person that they would not help them up, but would instead ring for an ambulance. The potential humiliation of this was sufficient to keep most clients in line.

## The Experience of Bathing

For some individuals, bathing did remain a pleasurable, even luxurious, experience. Mrs. Fitzgerald, who had most feared the loss, now saw the coming of the bathing service as "the rose of [her] week." Mrs. Napier also relished the experience as something that brings back pleasurable memories of the past, explaining how "we have nice foamy shower gel. . . . It's lovely, like being a baby again." Baths were also a source of pleasure because of the number of aches and pains that many older people suffer from. The warmth and buoyancy of the water restored lightness to limbs that had become heavy, giving back something of the easy, youthful, bodily experience of the past.

Baths also retained their capacity to wash away more than just dirt. For some, they had always been both a source of renewal and a marker of social transitions. As Miss Garfield explained, baths are "part of, sort of washing the day away and all the bothers and troubles, and you're there and it's all very comfortable and nice." But the experience of bathing was inevitably strongly affected by the presence of the caregiver in the room. For most people, bathing is a private affair, a time apart, when individuals can attend to themselves and not worry about others. But the presence of the worker changes that to some degree, disturbing the ease. Their presence in the room inevitably refocuses the event on tasks to be accomplished, rather than a state to be experienced; recipients were no longer free to control the timing of the event as they had been in the past. Workers needed to get the job done, and this sometimes meant that time was now of the essence, not pleasure. This acted to limit the nature of the experience, removing luxury, and centering it instead on cleaning of the client.

Having a worker in the room also removed much of the spontaneity of bathing; it was no longer possible to draw a bath when you simply felt like it. With this also went much of the capacity of baths to act as personal rites of passage or markers of social transitions. Body care still marked out the rhythm of people's days, in the sense of dressing, washing, and eating, but baths now had to be taken at the times they were scheduled; this could mean otherwise "meaningless" times, such as eleven-thirty in the morning, that disrupted rather than underwrote social patterns. For some people this was less disruptive than expected. This was because those who received such bathing assistance were often among the most frail and dependent, people who rarely if ever left the house. For them, the world of conventional timings had become less significant. To quite an extent, they had reordered the pattern of their lives *around* the provision of care. Care-giving had come to operate as a social structure in itself.

## The Gaze of Youth

Much of the recent work in gerontology has emphasized the ways in which we are aged by culture—by the meanings that are ascribed to bodily aging, rather than the aging process itself. Gullette (1997) has described the subtle and omnipresent means by which such meanings are conveyed. We inhale this atmosphere daily, imbuing doses of its toxicity wafting from cartoons, billboards, birthday cards, coffee mugs, newspaper articles, fiction, and poetry: "The system is busy at what ever level of literacy or orality or visual impressionability the acculturated subject is comfortable with." Consumer culture, with its emphasis on youth, is particularly saturated with such messages (Featherstone 1991; Gilleard and Higgs 2000).

The dominant theme in all of this work is that old age is constructed as a negative entity and the bodily process of aging is seen in the same light. Aging represents a form of Otherness, on to which culture projects its fear and denial. As Woodward (1991) argues, our cultural categories here are essentially reducible to two, youth and age, set in a hierarchical arrangement. We are not judged by how old we are, but by how young we are not. Aging is a falling away, a failure to be young. Like disabled people, the old are evaluated as "less than." The bodily realities of aging thus create a version of Erving Goffman's spoilt identity, something that people are, at some level, ashamed of and marked in terms of.

We are accustomed to the idea of the medical gaze in the context of professional power, or the phallic gaze in the context of gender relations, but there is also a gaze of youth. It, too, is an exercise of power in which the "other"—in this case older people—are constituted under its searching eye. Nowhere is the gaze of youth more evident than in relation to bathing care. Here the bodies of older people are directly subject to the gaze of younger workers. From the workers' perspective, this sometimes presents them with a shock. Modern culture, though saturated with visual images of young perfect bodies, rarely permits old imperfect ones to be on display. As a result, the way in which the body looks in old age was something that the younger workers were unprepared for. As one worker explained, seeing old people naked was "weird, and I just had to stop myself staring at people, because I hadn't really seen . . . because you don't really see people naked."

At times this element of gaze was itself part of the professional task. Nurses who do bathing work often comment how the activity is useful in assessing the general state of the older person, in terms not only of illness and physical condition but also in a more extensive way. To be bathed is indeed to be made subject to—very directly subject to—the professional gaze. It is indeed a kind of developed, intimate surveillance.

So how did older people feel about this? It was certainly the case that many respondents appeared to have internalized the wider cultural denigration of the bodies of the old. They constituted their own bodies under the gaze of youth, presenting them as something that it might be unattractive, even distasteful, for people to see or handle. As Mrs. Fitzgerald once remarked of the care-giver, "They're so young and beautiful, it must be awful for them to have to handle old, awkward bodies." At the same time, she added that "they're wonderful people. . . . I must say, I mean they must have something inside them because—it's not the sort of thing—I don't know when I was young whether I would have wanted to have looked after old people." For some, the contrast between their aging bodies and the youthful flesh of the workers was painful to see and experience:

> Mrs. Kennelly: I say to them, "I feel sorry for you, getting up in the morning and this is the kind of job you've got to do." You know, not very nice. . . . This young girl, Amanda it was, came in—twenty-eight, beautiful girl. She's very pretty. And there's the ugly lump. Oh dear!

To be caught within the youthful gaze was disturbing, and many of the elders had turned its corrosive force back on themselves, in turn disciplining their own bodies in the course of assisted practice.

* * *

### Parts of the Body

The body is a landscape onto which meanings are inscribed. These are not, however, evenly distributed over the body, and certain parts come to be more heavily freighted with significance than other bodily parts. In general, there is a familiar privacy gradient whereby certain parts of the body are deemed more personal and private. Access to them by sight or touch is socially circumscribed and varies according to relationship and situation. * * * Areas of the body such as the upper arms and back are relatively neutral and can be touched by a range of people. Knees and thighs are less so. Breasts and genitals are in general off-limits in all but erotic relations. Touch is also a vector of status and authority with the powerful accorded more leeway to touch than the less powerful. There is a gender dimension, with women more likely to receive touch than men. Within a service provision context, women are more likely to interpret touch from a service provider in a positive way, while men are more inclined to see it negatively, interpreting it as a marker of inferiority and dependency. In addition, men are also more likely to see touch as sexual.

These sensitivities affect the experience of bathing. Receiving hands-on help with soaping, rinsing, and washing is more tolerable in relation to some parts of the body than to others. Arms, legs, feet, and hair are all fine. Matters become more sensitive, however, in relation to what is often termed "down below": the genital and anal areas. In practice nearly everyone in the study could manage to wash these parts themselves, at least with some indirect assistance, and a number of respondents expressed relief that they were able to do so. Having to be washed in these areas was seen as humiliating and embarrassing, yet another twist in the spiral of dependency. Maintaining one's independence in relation to these intimate areas was an important part of self-esteem. Caregivers were also reluctant to involve themselves with these parts of the body, which they, too, regarded with a certain amount of ambivalence. In general, bathing was practically managed in such a way as to limit direct contact in relation to more sensitive bodily parts.

\* \* \*

There was one part of the body that was recurringly mentioned in the interviews by both recipients and workers: this was the back. In the context of bathing and the ambivalent intimacies it creates, the back has a special meaning, coming to stand for the body in general, or at least for an acceptable version of the body, one that has a certain neutrality about it. In the interviews, the back was the only part of the body that was spontaneously named by recipients, and they sometimes talked about the process of bathing as if it were confined to the process of washing the back. The back was also the one part of the body where pleasure in touch was openly acknowledged.

A number of recipients described how much they enjoyed having their backs scrubbed. Expressing pleasure in this form of touching was acceptable. Caregivers agreed with this account. One in particular commented that "they do enjoy it, that you know, a lot of people really, 'Oooh,' you know, 'give my back a good rub.'" In general, expressing pleasure in touch was something that recipients were reluctant to do. It seemed to suggest in their eyes something that was not quite right, an ambivalent element that did not belong in this context of relative strangers and of public provision. Presenting bathing in terms of scrubbing the back was one means of deflecting an otherwise disturbing intimacy onto a relatively neutral and public part of the body.

The back is also significant in the bath encounter in that it is the part of the body that is both offered to the gaze of the worker and also used to shelter more private and sensitive parts. It stands in for the public presentation of the body in the context of an otherwise discordant intimacy. The back also offers a safe setting for the expression of affection and closeness. Putting an arm across the back while giving the recipient a hug fits in easily with the way bathing disposes the body, while at the same time providing a relatively neutral form of physical contact. Touch could thus be used to express closeness, but in a manner that does not transgress social codes.

### Bounded Relationships and Access to the Body

Bathing makes for a strange relationship: in one sense intimate and close, involving physical contact, nakedness, and access to the private dimensions of life; yet in another, it is a meeting of strangers in which the worker is paid to do a job and may never have met the recipient before. The intimacy, moreover, occurs in a context that is forced. It arises from disability, not choice. The closeness is imposed, not sought. As a result there is an inherent discordance in the relationship. It is transgressive of normal social codes, and effort is needed on both sides to define the character of the relationship and to put limits on the nature of its intimacy.

How the relationship was experienced was clearly affected by who the helper was. What were people's preferences in this regard? Did they, for example, prefer to be helped by close relatives? An assumption of this sort is often made, resting on the idea that kinship closeness renders the negotiation of bodily closeness easier. While this can certainly sometimes be so, often it is not. We have evidence from other studies (Parker 1993; Daatland 1990) that suggests that while people may like to receive more neutral forms of help from relatives, personal care is different. In these cases many people prefer the formal service system. The reason is that bodily care threatens the nature of a relationship. In particular it erodes the status of the recipient and with that their identity in the relationship.

What older people fear is that the person that they once were—and in their own eyes still are—will be lost, and that person, by and large, is someone with their clothes on, managing their own bodily functions and relating to their families in a sociable way. We should not thus make any easy assumptions about kinship closeness translating unproblematically into bodily closeness.

Even less do people want friends to perform this activity. It is in the nature of friendship that it rests on equality and reciprocity, and few friendships survive marked change in circumstances when these occur on only one side of a valued relationship. Intimate care represents just such a change. Lawler (1991) notes how nurses experience similar unease if cared for by a friend and colleague. Though recipients wanted the care worker to be "friendly," they were quite clear that this was a different and defined sort of relationship. These were not friends in the full sense of the word. As Mrs. Ostrovski said to me, "Friend is a very big word."

Bath work involves a kind of intimacy, though it is of a different nature from that of kinship or friendship. What recipients want is a bounded intimacy, something that is close, but in a specialized and limited way. For these reasons they preferred someone whom they had got to know in these particular circumstances and where the relationship was defined by them. This is not to say that that it was not close, friendly, or based on a kind of trust. In most cases it was all of these, but the relationship was of a special kind, in which bodily closeness played a part but was defined and limited.

At the same time, recipients disliked the experience of having to deal with strangers. Bathing involves both a literal and a psychic unwrapping of the self. Having to participate in this process repeatedly with strangers was exposing and dispiriting. Recipients wanted the ease that comes with familiarity; they did not want constantly to have to readjust to a new person. But agencies could not always be relied on to send the same person, and indeed the constant staff turnover that is characteristic of low-wage sectors in cities like London meant that it was quite difficult for them to do so. Some recipients subverted the problem by refusing to have a bath if an unfamiliar worker was sent, diverting them into other household tasks rather than facing the unwelcome process of self-disclosure. What recipients wanted, therefore, was someone they knew, who was friendly and sensitive and who would offer emotional support, but who understood the limits of the relationship.

\* \* \*

The recipients also made assumptions about gender. This invariably focuses on who was appropriate to do the care work. Responses varied according to whether the person was a man or woman. In general, women-to-women care was regarded as "natural" and unproblematic. Issues arose, however, in relation to cross-gender tending and, to some extent, in relation to same-sex male tending.

What underpinned this asymmetrical pattern were wider assumptions about the meaning and management of the body. Within Western culture, men's and women's bodies have traditionally been treated differently. Women's bodies tend to be regarded with greater circumspection. Access to them, both physical and visual, is more guarded. They are seen as more private, something that is secluded and hidden. Women's bodies are also often presented as more sexual, indeed often coming to represent the principle of sexuality more widely within culture. Women's bodies are also subject to greater control. There is more constraint over what they may do and express. Men's bodies are, by contrast, presented as more public and neutral in character. They tend to embody active principles rather than the passive ones circumscribed on the female body. They desire, rather than are constituted by the desire of others.

These cultural patterns underwrite responses to bathing help. In general women preferred not to have a male worker, and some expressed their feelings very strongly in this regard, "Oh, no. I wouldn't have a man. No thank you!" This was not universal, and some said that they would not mind. But in practice this situation only rarely arose. The majority of workers are female, as are the clients, and this "naturally" delivers a pattern in accord with dominant values. Most agencies also have a policy against men giving personal care to women in their own homes, partly out of respect for client's assumed preferences and partly to avoid accusations of abuse. Running through attitudes toward male care workers was a set of assumptions about the nature of male sexuality as something that is active and potentially predatory. This is in contrast to the assumptions that are made about women. They are presented as passive or asexual in this context, dominated by the values of maternity, not sexuality.

For men, the experience of receiving cross-gender tending was, by its very nature, different. Men are accustomed to being helped by women from child-

hood onwards, and many saw such assistance in old age as a natural extension of that. Such care contained no sense of threat. Indeed, for many men the
idea of being helped by a woman was pleasant. As one manager remarked: "A
lot of the men quite enjoy having a woman. And honestly I think, you know,
specially a nice young girl come to help them have a bath, they like it. You know,
not in any sort of perverted way, just, just in a you know, they like the
attention."

As Mr. Lambert said, provided the women were married—that is where
women were accustomed to seeing men naked—there was no difficulty in cross-
gender tending. Mr. Wagstaff concurred with this sentiment:

> INTERVIEWER: Did you find it embarrassing at first or . . . ?
>
> MR. WAGSTAFFE: Well not really. I thought it might be more embarrassing for
> *them* than for me, but they don't seem to mind a bit.
>
> INTERVIEWER: Why did you think it would be more embarrassing for them?
>
> MR. WAGSTAFFE: Well, the first girl I had she was only about eighteen I think.
> She was a sort of punk, she'd got bright red hair and ear-
> rings in her eyebrows. Sort of girl that a person of my age
> looks at and thinks Gawd Almighty. But she was absolutely
> sweet, she was a lovely girl. It turns out that they nearly all
> live with their boyfriends or something, so I don't bother
> about it now. . . . And young ladies in their early twenties these
> days are rather different from when I was the same age.

For men, therefore, cross-gender tending contains no sense of threat. The issue
is one of managing the encounter in such a way as to avoid embarrassment, in
which they had some remaining sense of responsibility for not disturbing the
innocence of the young. Even in old age, men experience a residual sense of
the power of the phallus.

For men being cared for by men, the assumptions were slightly different.
In many cases this occurred without comment or problems. But for some men
the idea was unwelcome. Men construct other men as sexually predatory in
relation to themselves (Connell 1995). Intimate care by a man raises the possibility of a homosexual encounter, a concern reinforced by ideas that care-
giver was not proper work for a man at all.

* * *

## CONCLUSION

Throughout this chapter, I have argued that bathing and washing exemplify
day-to-day and mundane activities of the old. As a result they have received
little in the way of academic attention, often considered too practical and too
banal to be of interest. But it is in these ordinary and banal patterns that much

of the texture and meaning of life exists. The life of the body is the bedrock on which our existence rests. Tending, caring for, managing our bodies, and using and presenting them in a social life are central to our day-to-day experience, though it is not often brought to the front of our consciousness. Until, that is, some disruption in these taken-for-granted activities forces them and the existential life of the body into conscious consideration. Old age is one such source of disruption. Though we are indeed aged by culture as some theorists suggest, we are also aged by our bodies. The body can impose its own constraints, as we have seen concerning the practical difficulties some people experience in relation to personal care. The ways in which personal care is managed, the meanings it contains, and the discourses that encode it significantly affect how these bodily constraints are experienced.

Among the discourses within which personal care is encoded are those relating to bathing. As we have seen, the official account of service provision presents the activity in a narrow, utilitarian way—as the achievement of adequate standards of hygiene. The discourse of social welfare is a constrained one in which the scope of interventions are limited and in which health and hygiene have a privileged status. But as we have seen, baths and bathing are about more than this. They touch on other matters; their meanings are wider and more diffuse, and the experiences they offer more various. Bathing is part of the experiential life of the body and as such is drawn into a variety of discourses and sets of meanings around pleasure, luxury, eroticism, renewal, initiation, and power. Echoes of these wider meanings reverberate through the experience of bathing in the community. Hearing them enables us to set community care in a broader social and cultural context and thus to rescue it from too narrow a policy context. It also allows us to hear something of the voices of some of the most disabled older people, people whose bodily experiences have received little analytic attention in our overarching focus on the body.

## REFERENCES

Andrews, M. 1999. The Seductiveness of Agelessness. *Ageing and Society* 19: 301–18.

Arber, S., and J. Ginn. 1991. *Gender and Later Life: A Sociological Analysis of Resources and Constraints*. London: Sage Publications.

Bushman, R. L., and C. L. Bushman. 1988. The Early History of Cleanliness in America. *Journal of American History* 74: 1213–38.

Connell, R. W. 1995. *Masculinities*. Cambridge, U.K.: Polity.

Daatland, S. 1990. What are Families For: On Family Solidarity and Preference for Help. *Ageing and Society* 10: 1–15.

Estes, C. L., and E. A Binney. 1989. Biomedicalization of Aging: Dangers and Dilemmas. *The Gerontologist* 29(5): 587–596.

Featherstone, M. 1991. The Body in Consumer Culture. In *The Body: Social Process and Cultural Theory*. Edited by M. Featherstone, M. Hepworth, and B. S. Turner, 170–96. London: Sage.

Furman, F. K. 1997. *Facing the Mirror: Older Women and Beauty Shop Culture.* New York: Routledge.

———. 1999. There Are No Old Venuses: Older Women's Responses to Their Aging Bodies. In *Mother Time: Women, Aging and Ethics.* Edited by M. U. Walker, 7–22. Boulder, Colo.: Rowman & Littlefield.

Gilleard, C, and P. Higgs. 2000. *Culture of Ageing: Self, Citizen and the Body.* London: Prentice Hall.

Gullette, M. M. 1997. *Declining to Decline: Cultural Combat and the Politics of Midlife.* Charlottesville: University Press of Virginia.

Kira, A. 1967. *The Bathroom: Criteria for Design.* New York: Bantam.

Lawler, J. 1991. *Behind the Screens: Nursing, Somology, and the Problems of the Body.* London: Churchill Livingstone.

Lawler, J. (ed.) 1997. Knowing the Body and Embodiment: Methodologies, Discourses and Nursing. In *The Body in Nursing.* Melbourne, Australia: Churchill Livingstone.

Öberg, P. 1996. The Absent Body: A Social Gerontological Paradox. *Ageing and Society* 16: 701–19.

Parker, G. 1993. *With This Body: Caring and Disability in Marriage.* Buckingham, U.K.: Open University Press.

Phillipson, C, and A. Walker. 1986. *Ageing and Social Policy: A Critical Assessment.* Aldershot, U.K.: Gower.

Tulle-Winton, E. 2000. Old Bodies. In *The Body, Culture and Society.* Edited by P. Hancock, B. Hughes, E. Jagger, K. Patterson, R. Russell, E. Tulle-Winton, and M. Tyler. Buckingham, U.K.: Open University Press.

Twigg, J. 2000a. *Bathing: The Body and Community Care.* London: Routledge.

———. 2000b. Carework as a Form of Bodywork. *Ageing and Society* 20: 389–411.

Vigarello, G. 1988. *Concepts of Cleanliness: Changing Attitudes in France Since the Middle Ages.* Cambridge, U.K.: CUP.

Williams, S. J., and G. Bendelow. 1998. *The Lived Body: Sociological Themes, Embodied Issues.* London: Routledge.

Wilkie, J. S. 1986. Submerged Sensuality: Technology and Perceptions of Bathing. *Journal of Social History* 19: 649–54.

Woodward, K. 1991. *Aging and Its Discontents: Freud and Other Fictions.* Bloomington: Indiana University Press.

Woodward, K. (ed.) 1999. *Figuring Age: Women, Bodies, Generations.* Bloomington: Indiana University Press.

Yegül, F. 1992. *Baths and Bathing in Classical Antiquity.* Cambridge: MIT Press.

# 21

## Women without Class: *Chicas, Cholas,* Trash, and the Presence/Absence of Class Identity

### JULIE BETTIE

*This essay predates the author's award-winning book by the same title. It tells the complex story of high school females finding and presenting (performing) identities that express different versions of femininity. The author's participant observation study seeks to make these young women, and their gender, more visible objects of study, with a steady eye on social class as being critical to who they are and wish to become. Add to this the dimension of ethnicity, and you have a quintessential analysis of the major dimensions of social inequality as they play out in contemporary youth culture.*

A cover story in the San Francisco *Examiner Magazine* (Wagner 1996) on the topic of "wiggas" (which, the article explains, is shorthand for "white niggas") reads, "suburban kidz hip-hop across the color line." The story is about white youth who appropriate hip-hop culture and perform "black" identity. The cover picture is a collage of magazine cutouts showing white kids with blue eyes and blond hair (functioning as a code for racial purity) wearing hip-hop fashion and standing in front of a white picket fence behind which sits a charming two-story house and an apple tree. Although there is a girl pictured on the front cover, girls are absent from the story itself.

In a 1993 episode of the TV talk show *Oprah* on the same topic, several groups of boys, white and black, sat on the stage. The audience was confounded by the white boys in hip-hop style who "grew up in 'the 'hood'" and by the young black man who, as one guest explained, "looks like he walked out of Eddie Bauer," as participants debated what it meant to dress black or dress white. During the course of the hour-long program all parties failed to note that, race and ethnicity aside, these were different versions of *masculinity* and that girls were missing again from this story about "youth." The "urban romanticism" and "masculinist overtones" (McRobbie 1991, 20) of subculture studies, where the supposedly gender-neutral term *youth* actually stands for male, are equally often present in popular culture and news media portrayals of youth. In order to envision themselves as class or racial/ethnic subjects in either site, girls must read themselves as boys.

But beyond the invisibility of gender, there is also a failure to "think class" with much clarity. On the *Oprah* show, as with the magazine cover, the same sets of binaries surface repeatedly: white is middle class is suburban; black is lower class is urban. But a slippage occurs where the class references are dropped out and white stands in for middle, where black stands in for lower, or where suburban stands in for white and urban for black. Class and race signifiers are melded together in such a way that "authentic" black, and sometimes brown, identity is imagined as lower class, urban, and often violent and male as well. These are the overly simplified identity categories offered, but they do not reflect the complexity of life. Middle-class youth of color are missing, for example, as are multiracial/multiethnic identity and small-town or rural poverty. The racial/ethnic and class subject positions offered by the "identity formation material" (McRobbie 1994, 192) of popular culture often do not allow for more nuanced social locations.

The observations I make in this article are based on my ethnographic study of working-class white and Mexican-American girls in their senior year of high school in a small town in California's central valley.

* * *

These were girls who knew from experience in their own families of origin that male wages cannot support families alone and that men cannot be counted on to meet their ideals of intimacy and egalitarianism in relationships. These were girls who saw that the men in their working-class community were often unemployed or underemployed and too often dealt with this hardship by abandoning their obligation and responsibilities to the women in their lives and to the children they helped create. These girls were not holding out for princes.

My title, "Women without Class," has multiple meanings. Most simply, it reflects my interest in young women from families of modest means and low educational attainment who therefore have little "cultural capital" (Bourdieu 1984) to enable class mobility. The other meanings of the title speak to the theory debates I engage and to which I already have alluded: a second meaning refers to the fact that class analysis and social theory have, until recently perhaps, remained insufficiently transformed by feminist theory, unable to conceptualize women as class subjects. Ignoring women's experience of class results in a profound androcentric bias such that women are routinely invisible as class subjects. In much leftist analysis women are assumed to be without class, as these theorists often seem unable to see the category "working class" unless it is marked white and male. Such biases promote the invisibility of both white women and women of color as class subjects.

Ironically, some versions of feminism have been complicit in constructing women as without either class or racial/ethnic subjectivity. On a third level, then, my title considers debates *within* feminist theory and refers to feminist accounts that, while working as correctives to androcentric biases and class reduction, tend toward gender reductionism, focusing primarily on the differences between boys and girls or women and men and failing to account for gender differences *within* sex categories. Historically such studies have focused on white middle-class girls or women but have failed to define them as such. Thus, they too were perceived and presented not as class or racial/ethnic subjects but only as gendered.

It was with these theory debates and empirical gaps in mind that I set off to explore if and how young women understand class difference. I intended to foreground, while not privileging, class as I examined how gender, color, and ethnicity intersect with and shape class as a lived culture and a subjective identity. The context of the lives of these young women includes a deindustrializing economy, the growth of service-sector occupations held largely by women and men of color and by white women, the related family revolutions of the twentieth century, the elimination of affirmative action, a rise in anti-immigrant sentiment, and changing cultural representations and iconographies of class, race, and gender meanings. These are social forces that render the term *working class* anachronistic even as many of these girls move toward low-wage, low-prestige jobs in their community.

## NOTES TOWARD CLASS AS "PERFORMANCE" AND "PERFORMATIVE"

My study was done in a small town of approximately forty thousand people. The high school reflects the town demographically, being about 60 percent white and 40 percent Mexican-American, with other people of color composing less than 2 percent each of the population. Located in California's central valley, the town was built on agriculture and the industries that support it. Approximately 16 percent of the Mexican-American students were Mexican-born, while the remainder were second and third generation. The majority of students at the school, both white and Mexican American, were from working-class families, but the children of middle-class professionals were a present minority. Most of the latter were white, but a handful were Mexican American. Working-class students ranged from "hard-living" to "settled-living" (Howell 1973) in experience. The former term describes lives that are chaotic and unpredictable, characterized by low-paying, unstable occupations, lack of health care benefits, and no home ownership. The latter describes lives that are orderly and predictable, characterized by relatively secure, higher-paying jobs, sometimes health benefits, and sometimes ownership of a modest home.

I "hung out" with girls in classrooms and hallways, during lunch hours, at school dances, sports events, Future Homemakers of America meetings, at a Future Farmers of America hay-bucking contest and similar events, at MEChA meetings (Movimiento Estudiantil Chicano de Aztlán; the Chicano student movement organization), in coffee shops, restaurants, the shopping mall, and the school parking lot, near the bleachers behind the school, at birthday parties, and sometimes sitting cross-legged on the floor of a girl's bedroom, "just talkin'." I spent almost every day at the school during the school year, often returning in the evening to attend an extracurricular event and sometimes on weekends to meet and "kick it" with the girls. I came to know more than sixty girls well (approximately half were white and half Mexican American) and many more as acquaintances. I talked with them about such details of their lives as friendships, dating, partying, clothes, makeup, popular culture, school, family, work, and their hopes and expectations for the future.

Over the course of the school year, I came to know the clique structure, or informal peer hierarchy, at the school, as it was the primary way students understood class and racial/ethnic differences among themselves. Labels and descriptions of each group varied, of course, depending on the social location of the student providing the description. Nonetheless, there was a general mapping that almost all students agreed on and provided easily when asked. Although there were exceptions, the groups were largely race/ethnic and class segregated. Among whites they included "preps" (middle class), "skaters/alternatives" (settled-living), "hicks" (settled- and hard-living), and "smokers/rockers /trash" (hard-living); among Mexican-American students there were "Mexican preps" (middle class and settled- and hard-living), "*las chicas*" (settled-living), and "*cholas/os*" or "hard cores" (hard-living).[1]

Group membership was linked to social roles, including curriculum choices (college prep or vocational track) and extracurricular activities (whether a student was involved in what are considered either college-prep or nonprep activities). These courses and activities combined to shape class futures leading some girls to four-year colleges, some to vocational programs at junior colleges, and some to low-wage jobs directly out of high school. While there is a strong correlation between a girl's class of "origin" (by which I mean her parents' socioeconomic status) and her class performance at school (which includes academic achievement, prep or nonprep activities, and membership in friendship groups and their corresponding style), it is an imperfect one, and there are exceptions in which middle-class girls perform working-class identity and vice versa. In other words, some students were engaged in class "passing" as they chose to perform class identities that were not their "own."

Although clique membership was not entirely determined by class, there was certainly "a polarization of attitudes toward class characteristics," and group categories (such as preps, smokers, *cholas*, etc.) were "embodiment[s] of the middle and working-class[es]" (Eckert 1989, 4–5). On the one hand, embracing and publicly performing a particular class culture mattered more than origins in terms of a student's aspirations, her treatment by teachers and other students, and her class future. On the other hand, class origins did matter significantly, of course, as girls' life chances were shaped by the economic and

---

1. *Chola/o* describes a Mexican-American street style that sometimes marks identification with gangs, but it also can mark merely racial/ethnic belonging. Moreover, the degree of commitment to a gang exists on a continuum. Nonetheless, *cholas/os*, like *pachucas/os* before them, are often wrongly assumed to engage in criminal behavior (Vigil 1988).

cultural resources provided at home. Because of the imperfect correlation, I came to define students not only as working or middle class in origin but also as working- or middle-class *performers* (and, synonymously, as prep and non-prep students). Girls who were passing, or metaphorically cross-dressing, had to negotiate their "inherited" identity from home with their "chosen" public identity at school. There was a disparity for them between how their and their friends' families looked and talked at home and their own class performances at school. As I came to understand these negotiations of class as cultural (not political) identities, it became useful to conceptualize class as not only a material location but also a performance.

Consequently, I ask: What are the cultural gestures involved in the performance of class? How is class "authenticity" accomplished? And how is it imbued with racial/ethnic and gender meaning? Little attention has been paid to the ways class subjectivity, as a cultural identity, is experienced in relation to the cultural meanings of race/ethnicity, gender, and sexuality.

## DISSIDENT FEMININITIES

Because I spent my first few days at the school in a college-preparatory class (one that fulfills a requirement for admission to state universities), the first girls I met were college bound. Later I came to know these girls through the eyes of non-college-prep students as "the preps." They were mostly white but included a handful of Mexican-American girls. Some of the white girls were also known as "the 90210s" after the television show *Beverly Hills 90210* about wealthy high schoolers in Beverly Hills. The preps related easily to what they saw as my "school project." They eagerly volunteered to help me out and were ready and willing to talk at length about themselves and others. Displaying both social and academic skills, they were, in short, "teacher's pets" (Luttrell 1993) or "the rich and populars" (Lesko 1988).

The first day I attended Ms. Parker's business skills class was characteristic of my future visits to nonprep classes. On this particular day, there was a substitute teacher taking her place. These girls appeared different from the girls in the college-prep class: they wore more makeup, tight-fitting clothing, and seemed to have little interest in the classroom curriculum. In fact, the class was out of the teacher's hands. The girls, mostly Mexican American, were happy to have me as a distraction, and one, whom I later came to know as Lorena, said loudly (Lorena was always loud), "Oh, we heard you might be coming. What do you want to know? I'll tell you." Completely ignoring the substitute, who had clearly given up on having any control over the class, they invited me to play cards. I hesitated: "What if Mr. D. (the vice principal) comes by?"

LORENA: Oh he never does, besides (flirtatiously) he *likes* me.
  BECKY: He doesn't like me. He's always callin' me into his office for something.
LORENA: He'll just ask me where's the other half of my shirt?

Lorena was referring to her short crop top, fashionable at the moment and against school dress codes because it reveals the midriff. Lorena went on, "That's Mr. H. He's our sub. Don't you think he's attractive? He's from the university too." She called him over to ask a question, and when he arrived, Lorena opened her book and pointed entirely randomly at a paragraph on the page and said coyly, "I don't understand *this*." He tried to respond appropriately by explaining the course material. * * *

The expression of self through one's relationship to and creative use of commodities (both artifacts and the discourses of popular culture) is a central practice in capitalist society. The girls' alternative versions of gender performance were shaped by a nascent knowledge of race and class hierarchies. They were very able to communicate a sense of unfairness, a "structure of feeling" (Williams 1965), where inequalities were felt but not politically articulated. Their struggles were often waged less over explicit political ideologies than over modes of identity expression. In short, among students there existed a symbolic economy of style that was the ground on which class and race relations were played out. A whole array of gender-specific commodities were used as markers of distinction among different groups of girls who performed race/ethnic- and class-specific versions of femininity. Hairstyles, clothes, shoes, and the colors of lip liner, lipstick, and nail polish were key markers used to express group membership as the body became a resource and a site on which difference was inscribed. For example, Lorena and her friends preferred darker colors for lips and nails, in comparison to the preps who either went without or wore clear lip gloss, pastel lip and nail color, or French manicures (the natural look). Each group knew the other's stylistic preferences and was aware that their own style was in opposition. Girls created and maintained symbolic oppositions in which, as Penelope Eckert puts it, "elements of behavior that come to represent one category [are] rejected by the other, and ... may be exploited by the other category through the development of a clearly opposed element" (1989, 50).

The importance of colors as a tool of distinction became evident when *las chicas* explained that the darker lip color they chose and the lighter colors the preps wore were not simply related to skin color. Lorena explained, "it's not that, 'cause some Mexican girls who look kinda white, they wear real dark lip color" so that no one will mistake them as white. When I mentioned that I rarely saw white girls in dark lipstick, Lisa, a white prep, explained, scoffing and rolling her eyes, "oh there are some, but they're girls who are trying to be hard-core," which meant they were white girls who were performing *chola* identity.

Where middle-class performers experienced an extended adolescence by going to college, working-class performers across race began their adult lives earlier. And where middle-class performing girls (both white and Mexican American) chose academic performance and the praise of teachers and parents as signs of achieving adult status, nonprep girls wore different "badges of dignity" (Sennett and Cobb 1972; MacLeod 1995). For them, expressions of sexuality operated as a sign of adult status and served to reject teachers' and parents' methods of keeping them childlike.

It is too simple to treat the meaning of the expression of what appears as a sexualized version of femininity for working-class girls, and girls of color in particular, as a consequence of competitive heterosexuality and gender-subordinate learning. This fails to explain why girls made the choices they did from a variety of gender performances available to them. Rather, girls were negotiating meanings in a race- and class-stratified society, using commodities targeted at them as girls. They performed different versions of femininity that were integrally linked and inseparable from their class and race performances.

*Las chicas*, having "chosen" and/or been tracked into non-college-prep courses, were bored with their vocational schooling and often brought heterosexual romance and girl culture into the classroom as a favorite form of distraction, demonstrated in their repeated attempts to "set me up" with subs (which became almost a hazing ritual). But their gender performance and girl culture were not necessarily designed to culminate in a heterosexual relationship. Despite what appeared to be an obsession with heterosexual romance, a "men are dogs" theme was prevalent among them. Some said they didn't want to marry until their thirties if at all, and they resented their boyfriends' infidelities and attempts to police their sexuality by telling them what they should and should not wear. They knew that men should not be counted on to support them and any children they might have, and they desired economic independence. Their girl culture was less about boys than about sharing rituals of traditional femininity as a kind of friendship bonding among girls. Although the overt concern in girl culture may be with boys and romance, girls often set themselves physically apart from boys (McRobbie 1991). Lorena made this clear one day:

> LORENA: Well, when we go out, to the clubs or someplace. We all get a bunch of clothes and makeup and stuff and go to one person's house to get ready. We do each other's hair and makeup and try on each other's clothes. It takes a long time. It's more fun that way. [Thoughtfully, as if it just occurred to her,] sometimes, I think we have more fun getting ready to go out than we do going out. 'Cause when we go out we just *sit* there.
>
> JULIE BETTIE: So then the clothes and makeup and all aren't for the men, or about getting their attention?
>
> LORENA: Well, we like to see how many we can *meet*. But, well *you* know I don't fall for their lines. We talk to them, but when they start buggin' then we just go.

In short, *las chicas* had no more or less interest in heterosexual romance than did girls who performed prep or school-sanctioned femininity. Nonetheless, teachers and preps often confused the expression of class and race differences in style and activities among working-class girls as evidence of heterosexual interest. They often failed to perceive girls' class and race performances and unknowingly reproduced the commonsense belief that what is most important about girls, working-class performers in particular, is their girlness. *Las chicas'* style was not taken as a marker of race/ethnic and class distinction but was reduced to gender and sexuality.

In spite of the meanings that working-class girls themselves gave to their gender-specific cultural markers, their performances were always overdetermined by broader cultural meanings that code women in heavy makeup and tight clothes as oversexed—in short, cheap. In other words, class differences are often understood as sexual differences, where "the working class is cast as the bearer of an exaggerated sexuality, against which middle-class respectability is defined" (Ortner 1991, 177). Among women, "clothing and cosmetic differences are taken to be indexes of the differences in sexual morals" between classes (178). Indeed, this is what I observed: middle-class performing prep girls (both white and Mexican American) perceived *las chicas*, as well as working-class performing white girls, as overly sexually active.

But Mexican-American nonprep girls were perceived as even more sexually active than their white counterparts because, although there was no evidence that they were more sexually active, they were more likely to keep their babies if they became pregnant, so there was more often a visible indicator of their sexual activity. And while school personnel at times explained working-class Mexican-American girls' gender performances as a consequence of "their" culture—an assumed real ethnic cultural difference in which women are expected to fulfill traditional roles and/or are victims of machismo and a patriarchal culture—the girls' generational status (according to two meanings) was not taken into account. On the one hand, *las chicas* were a generation of girls located in a historical context of dual-wage families, and they did not describe parents who had traditional roles in mind for their daughters. Moreover, they were second-generation Mexican-Americans, young women with no intention of submitting to traditional gender ideologies.

Class was thus a present social force in the versions of femininity that the girls performed, but it was unarticulated and rendered invisible because it was interpreted (by school personnel, by preps, and at times by working-class girls themselves) as primarily about gender and a difference of sexual morality between good girls and bad girls.

## "ACTING WHITE"

Many of the Mexican-American students did have a way to both recognize and displace class simultaneously, at times explaining differences among themselves solely in racial/ethnic terms, such as "acting white" versus acting "the Mexican role." The class coding of these descriptions is revealed when they are pushed only slightly. When I asked Lorena what she meant by "acting white," she gave an animated imitation of a white girl she had met at a Future Business Leaders of America meeting, affecting a stereotypical "valley girl" demeanor and speech pattern: "Ohmigod, like I can't believe I left my cell phone in my car. It was so nice to meet you girls, do keep in touch." Lorena perceived this sentiment as quite disingenuous, since they had just met. Part of working-class girls' interpretation of preps was that they were "fake" and their friendships phony and insincere, always in the interest of social ambition. Lorena went on, "I'm going to play volleyball for Harvard next year." Clearly, "Harvard" was an exaggeration on Lorena's part. But to Lorena any university may as well have been Harvard as it was just as distant a possibility. Erica, a Filipina-American girl who had befriended and been accepted as one of *las chicas*, confided to me, "There's a lot of trashing of white girls really, and Mexican girls who act white." When I asked her what she meant by "acting white," her answer was straightforward: "The preps." "Not the smokers or the hicks?" I asked. "Oh no, never smokers, basically preps."

At some level, the girls knew that they didn't mean white generally but preps specifically (that is, a particular middle-class version of white), but "class" as a way of making distinctions among whites was not easily articulated. The whites most visible to them were those who inflicted the most class injuries, the preps. In fact, working-class whites were often invisible in their talk, unless I asked specifically about them. The most marginalized ones, known as the "smokers," were either unknown to the Mexican-American students or perplexing. As Mariana, a Mexican-American middle-class performer said, almost exasperated, "I mean they're white. They've had the opportunity. What's wrong with them?" Students found it useful or necessary to describe class performances in racial terms such as "acting white" because of the difficulty of coming up with a more apt way to describe class differences in a society in which class discourse as such is absent and because the correlation of race and class (the overrepresentation of people of color among the poor) was a highly visible reality to Mexican-American students.

## MIDDLE-CLASS *CHOLAS*

A handful of the girls were third-generation Mexican Americans from professional middle-class families. They had struggled to find their place in this race-class system. They had grown up in white neighborhoods and gone to elementary school with primarily white kids, where, as Rosa explained, "I knew I was different, because I was brown." In junior high, which was less segregated, some of them became *cholas* and were "jumped in" to a gang. When I asked why, Ana explained that she hated her family:

ANA: My mom wanted this picture-perfect family, you know. And I just hated it.
JULIE: What do you mean by a perfect family?

ANA: You know, we had dinner at night together, and everything was just, okay. She was so *happy*. And I hated that. My life was sad, my friends' lives were sad.

JULIE: Why were they sad?

ANA: One friend's mom was on welfare, the other didn't know who her dad was. Everything was wrong in their families.

As she described class differences between herself and her friends, she struggled for the right words to describe it. And as Lorena sought to describe the difference between herself and her friend Ana, she too searched for words: "Well, in junior high she was way down kinda low, she got in with the bad crowd. But in high school she is higher up kinda. I mean not as high as Patricia is (another middle-class performer) but she's not as low as she used to be." Lorena's perception of Ana as high but low was shaped by Ana's crossover style and the sense that she had "earned" her "low" status by performing *chola* identity and gang-banging. In Ana's attempt to understand her place in a social order where color and poverty correlate more often than not, the salience of color was integral to her identity formation. She felt compelled to perform working-class identity at school as a marker of racial/ethnic belonging. As she explained, "the Mexican Mexicans, they aren't worried about whether they're Mexican or not."

Although Ana, Rosa, and Patricia eventually had accepted the cultural capital their parents had to give them and were now college prep and headed to four-year colleges, they were friendly with *las chicas* and still dressed and performed the kind of race-class femininity that *las chicas* did. In this way, they distanced themselves from preps and countered potential accusations of "acting white." In short, their style confounded the race-class equation and was an intentional strategy. By design, they had middle-class aspirations without assimilation to prep, which for them meant white, style. It went beyond image to a set of race politics as they tried to recruit *las chicas* to be a part of MEChA. In fact, when I went along on a bus ride to tour a nearby business school with *las chicas*, I was surprised to find that Ana, Rosa, and Patricia came along. I asked why they had come along since they had already been accepted to four-year schools. Rosa responded, "Because we're with the girls, you know, we have to be supportive, do these things together."

Mexican-American girls' friendships crossed class performance boundaries more often than white girls' did because of a sense of racial alliance that drew them together in relation to white students at school and because the Mexican-American community brought them together in activities outside school. They were also far more pained about divisions among themselves than white girls ever were (an aspect of whiteness that can seem invisible). They felt the need to present a united front, and this was particularly acute among girls who were politicized about their racial/ethnic identity and participated in MEChA. For white girls, competition among them did not threaten them as a racial/ethnic minority community.

## WHITE TRASH *CHOLA*

Not surprisingly, white students generally did not explain class differences among themselves in racial terms. Rather, class difference was articulated as individual difference (she's "popular" or she's a "loser") and as differences in group membership and corresponding style (hicks, smokers, preps, etc.). But class meaning was at times bound to racial signifiers in the logic of white students, as it was among Mexican-American students. This was apparent in the way the most marginalized white working-class students, who were at times described by other white students as "white trash," worked hard interactionally to clarify that they were not Mexican.[2] In our very first conversation, Tara explained, without any solicitation, "I'm kinda dark, but I'm not Mexican." In our conversation about her boyfriend's middle-class parents, she explained that his mom had "accused me of being Mexican." She explained to me that she was Italian-American, and her color and features did match this self-description.

Similarly, Starr, a white girl who grew up in a Mexican-American neighborhood and went to the largely Mexican-American elementary school in town, also had the sense that some whites, those at the bottom of the heap like herself, were almost brown. We were talking in the lunchroom one day about girls and fights when she told me this story:

> STARR: Well the worst one was back in junior high. All of my friends were Mexican, 'cause I went to London. So I was too.
>
> JULIE: You were what?
>
> STARR: Mexican. Well I acted like it, and they thought I was. I wore my hair up high in front you know. And I had an accent. Was in a gang. I banged [gang-banged] red [gang color affiliation].
>
> JULIE: Were you the only white girl?
>
> STARR: Yeah.
>
> JULIE: What happened? Why aren't you friends with them now?
>
> STARR: We got into a fight. I was in the bowling alley one day with my boyfriend. They came in and called him a piece of white trash. That made me mad and I smacked her. Lucky for her someone called the cops. They came pretty fast.
>
> JULIE: What did she mean by white trash?
>
> STARR: Welfare people. He was a rocker. Had long hair, smoked.

---

2. See Bettie 1995 and Wray and Newitz 1997 for explorations of the race and class meanings of the designation "poor white trash."

This episode ended her *chola* performance, and she was part of the white smoker crowd when I met her. Like most other girls, Starr had told me that girls fight primarily about "guys." But her actual story reveals something different. A boy was central to the story, but the girls were not fighting *over* him. Rather, Starr's *chola* friends were bothered by her association with him, which pointed to her violation of the race-class identity she had been performing as a *chola*. Her friends forced her to make a choice.

Starr's race-class performance was a consequence of the neighborhood in which she grew up, and, like Tara, she had absorbed the commonsense notions that white is middle, that brown is low, and, most interesting, that low may become brown in certain contexts. Not unlike the experience of middle-class *cholas* for whom being middle-class Mexican-American felt too close to being white, Starr's working-class version of whiteness felt too close to being Mexican-American in this geographic context. Girls reported that cross-race friendships were more common in grade school, but in junior high a clear sorting out along racial lines emerged (and along class lines too, although with less awareness). Starr's story is about junior-high girls working to sort out class and color and ethnicity, about the social policing of racial boundaries, and about her move from a brown to a white racial performance (where both remained working class). Not insignificantly, her white performance included a racist discourse by which she distanced herself from Mexican-Americans via derogatory statements about them.

## (MIS)USES OF "CLASS": A CAUTION

Class difference was salient, although not articulated as such, *within* these racial/ethnic groups. But in relationships *across* racial/ethnic groups, race often "trumps" class. One way racial/ethnic alliances across class were manifested was in attitudes toward California's Proposition 209 (misleadingly called the California Civil Rights Initiative), passed in 1996, which eliminated state affirmative-action programs, including admissions policies for the state's university systems. To the pleasure of white conservatives, University of California regent Ward Connerly, a black man, became the leading spokesperson and argued for income instead of race as a fairer admission criterion. In this conservative community, all of the white students I spoke to, without exception, supported Proposition 209. Both working- and middle-class white students were easily swayed by the "class instead of race" logic, which both groups interpreted as white instead of brown, where "class" stands in for white, and "race" stands in for brown (and black).

Working-class performers were less concerned with college admission than with job competition, since the decisive moment of whether a student is going on to college had occurred two to three years earlier, when they began the vocational track. Consequently, by their senior year they lacked the coursework for admission to state universities. Although white working-class students experienced a feeling of unfairness in relation to preps regarding educational achievement and college, they lacked a discourse of class that could explain their own and their parents' "failure" and that would allow them to articulate the class antagonism they felt toward middle-class students. In its absence, a discourse of individualism and meritocracy helped render institutionalized class inequality invisible and consequently left white working-class students feeling like individually flawed "losers." * * * Unfortunately, working-class students were less likely to see themselves as victims of class inequality than as victims of "reverse discrimination."

Somewhat curiously, white middle-class students were also swayed by the color-blind class logic of Proposition 209. Preps' sense of racial competition regarded who was and who was not getting into which college. The students of color most visible to them were the handful who sat next to them in college-prep classes. Preps' own class privilege was unapparent to them, so much so that the mass of working-class whites and working-class Mexican Americans were so "othered" as to be invisible. The only Mexican-American students whom preps could imagine going to college seemed to be very much like them in that they were middle-class performers. At times, these college-prep Mexican-American students were resented as "box checkers" who were perceived to be unfairly benefiting from their "minority" status, as middle-class white students constructed themselves as victims of reverse discrimination. These college-prep Mexican-American students were highly visible, to the disadvantage of their vocational-track peers. Since the large body of working-class vocational students were not in the running for college admission anyway, among college-prep students discussing college admissions, *class* was taken as a code for *white*.

And perhaps rightly so. Class inequality is not adequately addressed by eliminating race as an admission criterion since the vast majority of working-class students of all colors had been tracked out two to three years earlier. When liberal education policy attempts to deal with social inequality by trying to get everyone into college, it fails to address the fundamental fact that the global economy needs uneducated, unskilled workers, and workers need living wages.

## CONCLUSION

Thinking through class as a performance enables us to acknowledge exceptions to the rule that class origin equals class future and to understand that economic and cultural resources often, but not inevitably, determine class futures. It allows us to explore the experience of negotiating inherited and chosen identities, as, for example, when middle-class students of color felt compelled to perform working-class identities as a marker of racial/ethnic belonging. It helps demonstrate, too, how other axes of identity intersect with and inform class identity and consequently shape class futures. Thinking through class as a performance is useful for understanding exceptions, those who are consciously "passing" (whether it be up or down).

But it is also useful to think of class as performative in the sense that class as cultural identity is an *effect* of social structure. Social actors largely perform the cultural capital that is a consequence of the material and cultural resources to which they have had access. Cultural performances most often reflect one's habitus or unconscious learned dispositions, which are not natural or inherent or prior to the social organization of class inequality but are in fact produced by it. Considering class as performative is consistent with regarding it more as a cultural than a political identity and more as a "sense of place" than as class consciousness in a political, marxist sense. It helps explain why class struggle is often waged more over modes of identity expression than over explicit political ideologies.

## REFERENCES

Bettie, Julie. 1995. "Class Dismissed? *Roseanne* and the Changing Face of Working-Class Iconography." *Social Text* 45, vol. 14, no. 4:125–49.

Bourdieu, Pierre. 1984. *Distinction: A Social Critique of the Judgment of Taste.* Cambridge, Mass.: Harvard University Press.

Eckert, Penelope. 1989. *Jocks and Burnouts: Social Categories and Identity in the High School.* New York: Teachers College Press.

Howell, Joseph. 1973. *Hard Living on Clay Street: Portraits of Blue-Collar Families.* Garden City, N.Y.: Anchor.

Lesko, Nancy. 1988. "The Curriculum of the Body: Lessons from a Catholic High School." In *Becoming Feminine: The Politics of Popular Culture*, ed. Leslie G. Roman, Linda K. Christian-Smith, and Elizabeth Ellsworth, 123–42. London: Falmer.

Luttrell, Wendy. 1993. "The Teachers, They All Had Their Pets: Concepts of Gender, Knowledge, and Power." *Signs* 18(3):505–46.

MacLeod, Jay. 1995. *Ain't No Makin' It: Aspirations and Attainment in a Low-Income Neighborhood.* Boulder, Colo.: Westview.

McRobbie, Angela. 1991. *Feminism and Youth Culture.* London: Macmillan.

———. 1994. *Postmodernism and Popular Culture.* London: Routledge.

Ortner, Sherry. 1991. "Preliminary Notes on Class and Culture." In *Recapturing Anthropology: Working in the Present*, ed. Richard G. Fox. Santa Fe, N.M.: School of American Research Press.

Sennett, Richard, and Jonathan Cobb. 1972. *The Hidden Injuries of Class.* New York: Vintage.

Vigil, James Diego. 1988. *Barrio Gangs: Street Life and Identity in Southern California.* Austin: University of Texas Press.

Wagner, Venise. 1996. "Crossover." *San Francisco Examiner Magazine*, November 10, 8–32.

Williams, Raymond. 1965. *Marxism and Literature.* New York: Oxford University Press.

Wray, Matt, and Annalee Newitz, eds. 1997. *White Trash: Race and Class in America.* New York: Routledge.

# 22

## Optional Ethnicities: For Whites Only?

### MARY C. WATERS

*Social status—both positive and negative—is often a matter of choice or accomplish-
ment, what sociologists call achieved status. In other cases status is ascribed, based
on features associated with the group with which we are identified or associated,
like it or not. Sex, age, visible disabilities, and skin color are important ascribed characteristics in American society. Less visible are national origin and ethnicity. Some
people choose to be ethnically identified, usually to benefit from a positive personal
identity or the celebration of a proud tradition. Others do not choose an ethnic identity, nor does it always confer benefits. For them, ethnicity is not optional. This essay
by Mary Waters may help some students understand a little better what others are
saying about the meaning of being Black or Chicano or Asian or American Indian
or another non-optional ethnicity.*

## ETHNIC IDENTITY FOR WHITES IN THE 1990s

What does it mean to talk about ethnicity as an option for an individual? To
argue that an individual has some degree of choice in their ethnic identity
flies in the face of the commonsense notion of ethnicity many of us believe
in—that one's ethnic identity is a fixed characteristic, reflective of blood ties
and given at birth. However, social scientists who study ethnicity have long
concluded that while ethnicity is based in a *belief* in a common ancestry, ethnicity is primarily a *social* phenomenon, not a biological one. The belief that
members of an ethnic group have that they share a common ancestry may not
be a fact. There is a great deal of change in ethnic identities across generations through intermarriage, changing allegiances, and changing social categories. There is also a much larger amount of change in the identities of
individuals over their life than is commonly believed. While most people are
aware of the phenomenon known as "passing"—people raised as one race who
change at some point and claim a different race as their identity—there are
similar life course changes in ethnicity that happen all the time and are not
given the same degree of attention as "racial passing."

White Americans of European ancestry can be described as having a great
deal of choice in terms of their ethnic identities. The two major types of options
White Americans can exercise are (1) the option of whether to claim any specific ancestry, or to just be "White" or American, and (2) the choice of which

of their European ancestries to choose to include in their description of their own identities. In both cases, the option of choosing how to present yourself on surveys and in everyday social interactions exists for Whites because of social changes and societal conditions that have created a great deal of social mobility, immigrant assimilation, and political and economic power for Whites in the United States. Specifically, the option of being able to not claim any ethnic identity exists for Whites of European background in the United States because they are the majority group—in terms of holding political and social power, as well as being a numerical majority. The option of choosing among different ethnicities in their family backgrounds exists because the degree of discrimination and social distance attached to specific European backgrounds has diminished over time.

### The Ethnic Miracle

When European immigration to the United States was sharply curtailed in the late 1920s, a process was set in motion whereby the European ethnic groups already in the United States were for all intents and purposes cut off from any new arrivals. As a result, the composition of the ethnic groups began to age generationally. The proportion of each ethnic group made up of immigrants or the first generation began to gradually decline, and the proportion made up of the children, grandchildren, and eventually greatgrandchildren began to increase. Consequently, by 1990 most European-origin ethnic groups in the United States were composed of a very small number of immigrants, and a very large proportion of people whose link to their ethnic origins in Europe was increasingly remote.

This generational change was accompanied by unprecedented social and economic changes. The very success of the assimilation process these groups experienced makes it difficult to imagine how much the question of the immigrants' eventual assimilation was an open one at the turn of the century. At the peak of immigration from southern and central Europe there was widespread discrimination and hostility against the newcomers by established Americans. Italians, Poles, Greeks, and Jews were called derogatory names, attacked by nativist mobs, and derided in the press. Intermarriage across ethnic lines was very uncommon—castelike in the words of some sociologists (Pagnini and Morgan 1990). The immigrants and their children were residentially segregated, occupationally specialized, and generally poor.

After several generations in the United States, the situation has changed a great deal. The success and social mobility of the grandchildren and great-grandchildren of that massive wave of immigrants from Europe has been called "The Ethnic Miracle" (Greeley 1976). These Whites have moved away from the inner-city ethnic ghettos to White middle-class suburban homes. They are doctors, lawyers, entertainers, academics, governors, and Supreme Court justices. But contrary to what some social science theorists and some politicians predicted or hoped for, these middle-class Americans have not completely given up ethnic identity. Instead, they have maintained some connection with their immigrant ancestors' identities—becoming Irish American doctors, Italian American Supreme Court justices, and Greek American presidential candidates. In the tradition of cultural pluralism, successful middle-class Americans in the late twentieth century maintain some degree of identity with their ethnic backgrounds. They have remained "hyphenated Americans." So while social mobility and declining discrimination have created the option of not identifying with any European ancestry, most White Americans continue to report some ethnic background.

\* \* \*

## Symbolic Ethnicities for White Americans

What do these ethnic identities mean to people and why do they cling to them rather than just abandoning the tie and calling themselves American? My own field research with suburban Whites in California and Pennsylvania found that later-generation descendants of European origin maintain what are called "symbolic ethnicities." Symbolic ethnicity is a term coined by Herbert Gans (1979) to refer to ethnicity that is individualistic in nature and without real social cost for the individual. These symbolic identifications are essentially leisure time activities, rooted in nuclear family traditions and reinforced by the voluntary enjoyable aspects of being ethnic (Waters 1990). Richard Alba (1990) also found later-generation Whites in Albany, New York, who chose to keep a tie with an ethnic identity because of the enjoyable and voluntary aspects to those identities, along with the feelings of specialness they entailed. An example of symbolic ethnicity is individuals who identify as Irish, for example, on occasions such as Saint Patrick's Day, on family holidays, or for vacations. They do not usually belong to Irish American organizations, live in Irish neighborhoods, work in Irish jobs, or marry other Irish people. The symbolic meaning of being Irish American can be constructed by individuals from mass media images, family traditions, or other intermittent social activities. In other words, for later-generation White ethnics, ethnicity is not something that influences their lives unless they want it to. In the world of work and school and neighborhood, individuals do not have to admit to being ethnic unless they choose to. And for an increasing number of European-origin individuals whose parents and grandparents have intermarried, the ethnicity they claim is largely a matter of personal choice as they sort through all of the possible combinations of groups in their genealogies.

\* \* \*

In responding to the ancestry question, the comparative latitude that White respondents have does not mean that Whites pick and choose ethnicities out of thin air. For the most part people choose an identity that corresponds with some element of their family tree. However, there are many anecdotal instances of people adopting ethnicities when they marry or move to a strongly identified neighborhood or community. For instance Micaela di Leonardo (1984) reported instances of non-Italian women who married into Italian American families and "became Italian." Karen Leonard (1992) describes a community of Mexican American women who married Punjabi immigrants in California. Some of the Punjabi immigrants and their descendants were said to have "become Mexican" when they joined their wives' kin group and social worlds. Alternatively she describes the community acknowledging that Mexican women made the best curry, as they adapted to life with Indian-origin men.

But what do these identities mean to individuals? Surely an identity that is optional in a number of ways—not legally defined on a passport or birth certificate, not socially consequential in terms of societal discrimination in terms of housing or job access, and not economically limiting in terms of blocking opportunities for social mobility—cannot be the same as an identity that results from and is nurtured by societal exclusion and rejection. The choice to have a symbolic ethnicity is an attractive and widespread one despite its lack of demonstrable content, because having a symbolic ethnicity combines individuality with feelings of community. People reported to me that they liked having an ethnic identity because it gave them a uniqueness and a feeling of being special. They often contrasted their own specialness by virtue of their ethnic identities with "bland" American-ness. Being ethnic makes people feel unique and special and not just "vanilla," as one of my respondents put it. * * *

* * *

Symbolic ethnicity is the best of all worlds for these respondents. These White ethnics can claim to be unique and special, while simultaneously finding the community and conformity with others that they also crave. But that "community" is of a type that will not interfere with a person's individuality. It is not as if these people belong to ethnic voluntary organizations or gather as a group in churches or neighborhoods or union halls. They work and reside within the mainstream of American middle-class life, yet they retain the interesting benefits—the "specialness"—of ethnic allegiance, without any of its drawbacks.

* * *

## RACE RELATIONS AND SYMBOLIC ETHNICITY

However much symbolic ethnicity is without cost for the individual, there is a cost associated with symbolic ethnicity for the society. That is because symbolic ethnicities of the type described here are confined to White Americans of European origin. Black Americans, Hispanic Americans, Asian Americans, and American Indians do not have the option of a symbolic ethnicity at present in the United States. For all of the ways in which ethnicity does not matter for White Americans, it does matter for non-Whites. Who your ancestors are does affect your choice of spouse, where you live, what job you have, who your friends are, and what your chances are for success in American society, if those ancestors happen not to be from Europe. The reality is that White ethnics have a lot more choice and room for maneuver than they themselves think they do. The situation is very different for members of racial minorities, whose lives are strongly influenced by their race or national origin regardless of how much they may choose not to identify themselves in terms of their ancestries.

When White Americans learn the stories of how their grandparents and great-grandparents triumphed in the United States over adversity, they are usually told in terms of their individual efforts and triumphs. The important role of labor unions and other organized political and economic actors in their social and economic successes are left out of the story in favor of a generational story of individual Americans rising up against communitarian, Old World intolerance and New World resistance. As a result, the "individualized" voluntary, cultural view of ethnicity for Whites is what is remembered.

One important implication of these identities is that they tend to be very individualistic. There is a tendency to view valuing diversity in a pluralist environment as equating all groups. The symbolic ethnic tends to think that all groups are equal; everyone has a background that is their right to celebrate and pass on to their children. This leads to the conclusion that all identities are equal and all identities in some sense are interchangeable—"I'm Italian American, you're Polish American. I'm Irish American, you're African American." The important thing is to treat people as individuals and all equally. However, this assumption ignores the very big difference between an individualistic symbolic ethnic identity and a socially enforced and imposed racial identity.

\* \* \*

When White Americans equate their own symbolic ethnicities with the socially enforced identities of non-White Americans, they obscure the fact that the experiences of Whites and non-Whites have been qualitatively different in the United States and that the current identities of individuals partly reflect that unequal history.

In the next section I describe how relations between Black and White students on college campuses reflect some of these asymmetries in the understanding of what a racial or ethnic identity means. While I focus on Black and White students in the following discussion, you should be aware that the myriad other groups in the United States—Mexican Americans, American Indians, Japanese Americans—all have some degree of social and individual influences on their identities, which reflect the group's social and economic history and present circumstance.

### Relations on College Campuses

Both Black and White students face the task of developing their race and ethnic identities. Sociologists and psychologists note that at the time people leave home and begin to live independently from their parents, often ages eighteen to twenty-two, they report a heightened sense of racial and ethnic identity as they sort through how much of their beliefs and behaviors are idiosyncratic to their families and how much are shared with other people. It is not until one comes in close contact with many people who are different from oneself that individuals realize the ways in which their backgrounds may influence their individual personality. This involves coming into contact with people who are different in terms of their ethnicity, class, religion, region, and race. For White students, the ethnicity they claim is more often than not a symbolic one—with all of the voluntary, enjoyable, and intermittent characteristics I have described above.

Black students at the university are also developing identities through interactions with others who are different from them. Their identity development is more complicated than that of Whites because of the added element of racial discrimination and racism, along with the "ethnic" developments of finding others who share their background. Thus Black students have the positive attraction of being around other Black students who share some cultural elements, as well as the need to band together with other students in a reactive and oppositional way in the face of racist incidents on campus.

Colleges and universities across the country have been increasing diversity among their student bodies in the last few decades. This has led in many cases to strained relations among students from different racial and ethnic backgrounds. The 1980s and 1990s produced a great number of racial incidents and high racial tensions on campuses. While there were a number of racial incidents that were due to bigotry, unlawful behavior, and violent or vicious attacks, much of what happens among students on campuses involves a low level of tension and awkwardness in social interactions.

Many Black students experience racism personally for the first time on campus. The upper-middle-class students from White suburbs were often isolated enough that their presence was not threatening to racists in their high schools. Also, their class background was known by their residence and this may have prevented attacks being directed at them. Often Black students at the university who begin talking with other students and recognizing racial slights will remember incidents that happened to them earlier that they might not have thought were related to race.

\* \* \*

Black students do experience a tension and a feeling of being singled out. It is unfair that this is part of their college experience and not that of White students. Dealing with incidents like this, or the ever-present threat of such incidents, is an ongoing developmental task for Black students that takes energy, attention, and strength of character. It should be clearly understood that this is an asymmetry in the "college experience" for Black and White students. It is one of the unfair aspects of life that results from living in a society with ongoing racial prejudice and discrimination. It is also very understandable that it makes some students angry at the unfairness of it all, even if there is no one to blame specifically. * * *

In some sense then, as Blauner (1992) has argued, you can see Black students coming together on campus as both an "ethnic" pull of wanting to be together to share common experiences and community, and a "racial" push of banding together defensively because of perceived rejection and tension from Whites. In this way the ethnic identities of Black students are in some sense similar to, say, Korean students wanting to be together to share experiences. And it is an ethnicity that is generally much stronger than, say, Italian Americans. But for Koreans who come together there is generally a definition of themselves as "different from" Whites. For Blacks reacting to exclusion, there is a tendency for the coming together to involve both being "different from" but also "opposed to" Whites.

The anthropologist John Ogbu (1990) has documented the tendency of minorities in a variety of societies around the world, who have experienced severe blocked mobility for long periods of time, to develop such oppositional identities. An important component of having such an identity is to describe others of your group who do not join in the group solidarity as devaluing and denying their very core identity. This is why it is not common for successful Asians to be accused by others of "acting White" in the United States, but it is quite common for such a term to be used by Blacks and Latinos. The oppositional component of a Black identity also explains how Black people can question whether others are acting "Black enough." On campus, it explains some of the intense pressures felt by Black students who do not make their racial identity central and who choose to hang out primarily with non-Blacks. This pressure from the group, which is partly defining itself by not being White, is exacerbated by the fact that race is a physical marker in American society. No one immediately notices the Jewish students sitting together in the dining hall, or the one Jewish student sitting surrounded by non-Jews, or the Texan sitting with the Californians, but everyone notices the Black student who is or is not at the "Black table" in the cafeteria.

An example of the kinds of misunderstandings that can arise because of different understandings of the meanings and implications of symbolic versus oppositional identities concerns questions students ask one another in the dorms about personal appearances and customs. A very common type of interaction in the dorm concerns questions Whites ask Blacks about their hair. Because Whites tend to know little about Blacks, and Blacks know a lot about Whites, there is a general asymmetry in the level of curiosity people have about one another. Whites, as the numerical majority, have had little contact with Black culture; Blacks, especially those who are in college, have had to develop bicultural skills—knowledge about the social worlds of both Whites and Blacks. Miscommunication and hurt feelings about White students' questions about Black students' hair illustrate this point. One of the things that happens freshman year is that White students are around Black students as they fix their hair. White students are generally quite curious about Black students' hair—they have basic questions such as how often Blacks wash their hair, how they get it straightened or curled, what products they use on their hair, how they comb it, etc. Whites often wonder to themselves whether they should ask these questions. One thought experiment Whites perform is to ask themselves whether a particular question would upset them. Adopting the "do unto others" rule, they ask themselves, "If a Black person was curious about my hair would I get upset?" The answer usually is "No, I would be happy to tell them." Another example is an Italian American student wondering to herself, "Would I be upset if someone asked me about calamari?" The answer is no, so she asks her Black roommate about collard greens, and the roommate explodes with an angry response such as, "Do you think all Black people eat watermelon too?" Note that if this Italian American knew her friend was Trinidadian American and asked about peas and rice the situation would be more similar and would not necessarily ignite underlying tensions.

* * * Because Blacks tend to have more knowledge about Whites than vice versa, there is not an even exchange going on, the Black freshman is likely to have fewer basic questions about his White roommate than his White roommate has about him. Because of the differences historically in the group experiences of Blacks and Whites there are some connotations to Black hair that don't exist about White hair. (For instance, is straightening your hair a form of assimilation, do some people distinguish between women having "good hair" and "bad hair" in terms of beauty and how is that related to looking "White"?). Finally, even a Black freshman who cheerfully disregards or is unaware that there are these asymmetries will soon slam into another asymmetry if she willingly answers every innocent question asked of her. In a situation where Blacks make up only 10 percent of the student body, if every non-Black needs to be educated about hair, she will have to explain it to nine other students. As one Black student explained to me, after you've been asked a couple of times about something so personal you begin to feel like you are an attraction in a zoo, that you are at the university for the education of the White students.

### Institutional Responses

Our society asks a lot of young people. We ask young people to do something that no one else does as successfully on such a wide scale—that is to live together with people from very different backgrounds, to respect one another, to appreciate one another, and to enjoy and learn from one another. The successes that occur every day in this endeavor are many, and they are too often overlooked. However, the problems and tensions are also real, and they will not vanish on their own. We tend to see pluralism working in the United States in much the same way some people expect capitalism to work. If you put together people with various interests and abilities and resources, the "invisible hand" of capitalism is supposed to make all the parts work together in an economy for the common good.

There is much to be said for such a model—the invisible hand of the market can solve complicated problems of production and distribution better than any "visible hand" of a state plan. However, we have learned that unequal power relations among the actors in the capitalist marketplace, as well as "externalities" that the market cannot account for, such as long-term pollution, or collusion between corporations, or the exploitation of child labor, means that state regulation is often needed. Pluralism and the relations between groups are very similar. There is a lot to be said for the idea that bringing people who belong to different ethnic or racial groups together in institutions with no interference will have good consequences. Students from different backgrounds will make friends if they share a dorm room or corridor, and there is no need for the institution to do any more than provide the locale. But like capitalism, the invisible hand of pluralism does not do well when power relations and externalities are ignored. When you bring together individuals from groups that are differentially valued in the wider society and provide no guidance, there will be problems. In these cases the "invisible hand" of pluralist relations does not work, and tensions and disagreements can arise without any particular individual or group of individuals being "to blame." On college campuses in the 1990s some of the tensions between students are of this sort. They arise from honest misunderstandings, lack of a common background, and very different experiences of what race and ethnicity mean to the individual.

The implications of symbolic ethnicities for thinking about race relations are subtle but consequential. If your understanding of your own ethnicity and its relationship to society and politics is one of individual choice, it becomes harder to understand the need for programs like affirmative action, which recognize the ongoing need for group struggle and group recognition, in order to bring about social change.* It also is hard for a White college student to understand the need that minority students feel to band together against discrimination. It also is easy, on the individual level, to expect everyone else to be able to turn their ethnicity on and off at will, the way you are able to, without understanding that ongoing discrimination and societal attention to minority status makes that impossible for individuals from minority groups to do. The paradox of symbolic ethnicity is that it depends upon the ultimate goal of a pluralist society, and at the same time makes it more difficult to achieve that ultimate goal. It is dependent upon the concept that all ethnicities mean the same thing, that enjoying the traditions of one's heritage is an option available to a

---

*This point is explored further in my essay "Thinking About Affirmative Action" (Massey 2004). [*Editor's note*]

group or an individual, but that such a heritage should not have any social costs associated with it.

* * * [T]here are many societal issues and involuntary ascriptions associated with non-White identities. The developments necessary for this to change are not individual but societal in nature. Social mobility and declining racial and ethnic sensitivity are closely associated. The legacy and the present reality of discrimination on the basis of race or ethnicity must be overcome before the ideal of a pluralist society, where all heritages are treated equally and are equally available for individuals to choose or discard at will, is realized.

## REFERENCES

Alba, Richard D. (1990). *Ethnic Identity: The Transformation of White America.* New Haven: Yale University Press.

Blauner, Robert (1992). "Talking Past Each Other: Black and White Languages of Race." *American Prospect* (summer): 55–64.

di Leonardo, Micaela (1984). *The Varieties of Ethnic Experience: Kinship, Class and Gender Among Italian Americans.* Ithaca, NY: Cornell University Press.

Gans, Herbert (1979). "Symbolic Ethnicity: The Future of Ethnic Groups and Cultures in America." *Ethnic and Racial Studies* 2: 1–20.

Greeley, Andrew H. (1976). "The Ethnic Miracle." *Public Interest* 45 (fall): 20–36.

Leonard, Karen (1992). *Making Ethnic Choices: Califonia's Punjabi Mexican Americans.* Philadelphia: Temple University Press.

Massey, Garth (2004). "Thinking about Affirmative Action: Arguments Supporting Preferential Policies." *Review of Policy Research*, 21 (6): 783–797.

Ogbu, John (1990). "Minority Status and Literacy in Comparative Perspective." *Daedalus* 119: 141–169.

Pagnini, Deanna L., and S. Philip Morgan (1990). "Intermarriage and Social Distance among U.S. Immigrants at the Turn of the Century." *American Journal of Sociology* 96 (2): 405–432.

Waters, Mary C. (1990). *Ethnic Options: Choosing Identities in America.* Berkeley and Los Angeles: University of California Press.

# PART FIVE

# SOCIAL INEQUALITY AND ORGANIZATIONS

# 23

## The Saints and the Roughnecks

### WILLIAM J. CHAMBLISS

*Almost every student can identify the "Saints" and "Roughnecks" in their high school, but it requires an astute observer like William Chambliss to show us the hidden implications of this dichotomy in a class-structured society. Social class matters, just as high school social hierarchies matter, because people are treated according to their position, and not necessarily in terms of who they are or what they actually do.*

Eight promising young men—children of good, stable, white upper-middle-class families, active in school affairs, good pre-college students—were some of the most delinquent boys at Hanibal High School. While community residents knew that these boys occasionally sowed a few wild oats, they were totally unaware that sowing wild oats completely occupied the daily routine of these young men. The Saints were constantly occupied with truancy, drinking, wild driving, petty theft, and vandalism. Yet no one was officially arrested for any misdeed during the two years I observed them.

This record was particularly surprising in light of my observations during the same two years of another gang of Hanibal High School students, six lower-class white boys known as the Roughnecks. The Roughnecks were constantly in trouble with police and community even though their rate of delinquency was about equal with that of the Saints. What was the cause of this disparity? the result? The following consideration of the activities, social class, and community perceptions of both gangs may provide some answers.

## THE SAINTS FROM MONDAY TO FRIDAY

The Saints' principal daily concern was with getting out of school as early as possible. The boys managed to get out of school with minimum danger that they would be accused of playing hookey through an elaborate procedure for obtaining "legitimate" release from class. The most common procedure was for one boy to obtain the release of another by fabricating a meeting of some committee, program, or recognized club. Charles might raise his hand in his 9:00 chemistry class and ask to be excused—a euphemism for going to the bathroom. Charles would go to Ed's math class and inform the teacher that Ed was needed for a 9:30 rehearsal of the drama club play. The math teacher would recognize Ed and Charles as "good students" involved in numerous school activities and would permit Ed to leave at 9:30. Charles would return to his class, and Ed would go to Tom's English class to obtain his release. Tom would engineer Charles's escape. The strategy would continue until as many of the Saints as possible were freed. After a stealthy trip to the car (which had been parked in a strategic spot), the boys were off for a day of fun.

Over the two years I observed the Saints, this pattern was repeated nearly every day. There were variations on the theme, but in one form or another, the boys used this procedure for getting out of class and then off the school grounds. Rarely did all eight of the Saints manage to leave school at the same time. The average number avoiding school on the days I observed them was five.

Having escaped from the concrete corridors the boys usually went either to a pool hall on the other (lower-class) side of town or to a café in the suburbs. Both places were out of the way of people the boys were likely to know (family or school officials), and both provided a source of entertainment. The pool hall entertainment was the generally rough atmosphere, the occasional hustler, the sometimes drunk proprietor and, of course, the game of pool. The café's entertainment was provided by the owner. The boys would "accidentally" knock a glass on the floor or spill cola on the counter—not all the time, but enough to be sporting. They would also bend spoons, put salt in sugar bowls and generally tease whoever was working in the café. The owner had opened the café recently and was dependent on the boys' business which was, in fact, substantial since between the horsing around and the teasing they bought food and drinks.

## THE SAINTS ON WEEKENDS

On weekends the automobile was even more critical than during the week, for on weekends the Saints went to Big Town—a large city with a population of over a million 25 miles from Hanibal. Every Friday and Saturday night most of the Saints would meet between 8:00 and 8:30 and would go into Big Town. Big Town activities included drinking heavily in taverns or nightclubs, driving drunkenly through the streets, and committing acts of vandalism and playing pranks.

By midnight on Fridays and Saturdays the Saints were usually thoroughly high, and one or two of them were often so drunk they had to be carried to the cars. Then the boys drove around town, calling obscenities to women and girls; occasionally trying (unsuccessfully so far as I could tell) to pick girls up; and driving recklessly through red lights and at high speeds with their lights out. Occasionally they played "chicken." One boy would climb out the back window of the car and across the roof to the driver's side of the car while the car was moving at high speed (between 40 and 50 miles an hour); then the driver would move over and the boy who had just crawled across the car roof would take the driver's seat.

Searching for "fair game" for a prank was the boy's principal activity after they left the tavern. The boys would drive alongside a foot patrol-man and ask directions to some street. If the policeman leaned on the car in the course of answering the question, the driver would speed away, causing him to lose his balance. The Saints were careful to play this prank only in an area where they were not going to spend much time and where they could quickly disappear around a corner to avoid having their license plate number taken.

Construction sites and road repair areas were the special province of the Saints' mischief. A soon-to-be-repaired hole in the road inevitably invited the Saints to remove lanterns and wooden barricades and put them in the car, leaving the hole unprotected. The boys would find a safe vantage point and wait for an unsuspecting motorist to drive into the hole. Often, though not always, the boys would go up to the motorist and commiserate with him about the dreadful way the city protected its citizenry.

Leaving the scene of the open hole and the motorist, the boys would then go searching for an appropriate place to erect the stolen barricade. An "appropriate place" was often a spot on a highway near a curve in the road where the barricade would not be seen by an oncoming motorist. The boys would wait to watch an unsuspecting motorist attempt to stop and (usually) crash into the wooden barricade. With saintly bearing the boys might offer help and understanding.

A stolen lantern might well find its way onto the back of a police car or hang from a street lamp. Once a lantern served as a prop for a reenactment of the "midnight ride of Paul Revere" until the "play," which was taking place at 2:00 A.M. in the center of a main street of Big Town, was interrupted by a police car several blocks away. The boys ran, leaving the lanterns on the street, and managed to avoid being apprehended.

Abandoned houses, especially if they were located in out-of-the-way places, were fair game for destruction and spontaneous vandalism. The boys would break windows, remove furniture to the yard and tear it apart, urinate on the walls, and scrawl obscenities inside.

Through all the pranks, drinking, and reckless driving the boys managed miraculously to avoid being stopped by police. Only twice in two years was I aware that they had been stopped by a Big Town policeman. Once was for speeding (which they did every time they drove whether they were drunk or sober), and the driver managed to convince the policeman that it was simply an error. The second time they were stopped they had just left a nightclub and were walking through an alley. Aaron stopped to urinate and the boys began making obscene remarks. A foot patrolman came into the alley, lectured the boys and sent them home. Before the boys got to the car one began talking in a loud voice again. The policeman, who had followed them down the alley, arrested this boy for disturbing the peace and took him to the police station where the other Saints gathered. After paying a $5.00 fine, and with the assurance that there would be no permanent record of the arrest, the boy was released.

The boys had a spirit of frivolity and fun about their escapades. They did not view what they were engaged in as "delinquency," though it surely was by any reasonable definition of that word. They simply viewed themselves as having a little fun and who, they would ask, was really hurt by it? The answer had to be no one, although this fact remains one of the most difficult things to explain about the gang's behavior. Unlikely though it seems, in two years of drinking, driving, carousing, and vandalism no one was seriously injured as a result of the Saints' activities.

## THE SAINTS IN SCHOOL

The Saints were highly successful in school. The average grade for the group was "B," with two of the boys having close to a straight "A" average. Almost all of the boys were popular and many of them held offices in the school. One of the boys was vice president of the student body one year. Six of the boys played on athletic teams.

At the end of their senior year, the student body selected ten seniors for special recognition as the "school wheels"; four of the ten were Saints. Teachers and school officials saw no problem with any of these boys and anticipated that they would all "make something of themselves."

How the boys managed to maintain this impression is surprising in view of their actual behavior in school. Their technique for covering truancy was so successful that teachers did not even realize that the boys were absent from school much of the time. Occasionally, of course, the system would backfire and then the boy was on his own. A boy who was caught would be most contrite, would plead guilty and ask for mercy. He inevitably got the mercy he sought.

Cheating on examinations was rampant, even to the point of orally communicating answers to exams as well as looking at one another's papers. Since none of the group studied, and since they were primarily dependent on one another for help, it is surprising that grades were so high. Teachers contributed to the deception in their admitted inclination to give these boys (and presumably others like them) the benefit of the doubt. When asked how the boys did in school, and when pressed on specific examinations, teachers might admit that they were disappointed in John's performance, but would quickly add that they "knew that he was capable of doing better," so John was given a higher grade than he had actually earned. How often this happened is impossible to know. During the time that I observed the group, I never saw any of the boys take homework home. Teachers may have been "understanding" very regularly.

One exception to the gang's generally good performance was Jerry, who had a "C" average in his junior year, experienced disaster the next year, and failed to graduate. Jerry had always been a little more nonchalant than the others about the liberties he took in school. Rather than wait for someone to come get him from class, he would offer his own excuse and leave. Although he probably did not miss any more class than most of the others in the group, he did not take the requisite pains to cover his absences. Jerry was the only Saint whom I ever heard talk back to a teacher. Although teachers often called him a "cut up" or a "smart kid," they never referred to him as a troublemaker or as a kid headed for trouble. It seems likely, then, that Jerry's failure his senior year and his mediocre performance his junior year were consequences of his not playing the game the proper way (possibly because he was disturbed by his parents' divorce). His teachers regarded him as "immature" and not quite ready to get out of high school.

## THE POLICE AND THE SAINTS

The local police saw the Saints as good boys who were among the leaders of the youth in the community. Rarely, the boys might be stopped in town for speeding or for running a stop sign. When this happened the boys were always polite, contrite and pled for mercy. As in school, they received the mercy they asked for. None ever received a ticket or was taken into the precinct by the local police.

The situation in Big Town, where the boys engaged in most of their delinquency, was only slightly different. The police there did not know the boys at all, although occasionally the boys were stopped by a patrolman. Once they were caught taking a lantern from a construction site. Another time they were stopped for running a stop sign, and on several occasions they were stopped for speeding. Their behavior was as before: contrite, polite and penitent. The urban police, like the local police, accepted their demeanor as sincere. More important, the urban police were convinced that these were good boys just out for a lark.

## THE ROUGHNECKS

Hanibal townspeople never perceived the Saints' high level of delinquency. The Saints were good boys who just went in for an occasional prank. After all, they were well dressed, well mannered and had nice cars. The Roughnecks were a different story. Although the two gangs of boys were the same age, and both groups engaged in an equal amount of wild-oat sowing, everyone agreed that the not-so-well-dressed, not-so-well-mannered, not-so-rich boys were heading for trouble. Townspeople would say, "You can see the gang members at the drugstore, night after night, leaning against the storefront (sometimes drunk) or slouching around inside buying cokes, reading magazines, and probably stealing old Mr. Wall blind. When they are outside and girls walk by, even respectable girls, these boys make suggestive remarks. Sometimes their remarks are downright lewd."

From the community's viewpoint, the real indication that these kids were in trouble was that they were constantly involved with the police. Some of them had been picked up for stealing, mostly small stuff, of course, "but still it's stealing small stuff that leads to big time crimes." "Too bad," people said. "Too bad that these boys couldn't behave like the other kids in town; stay out of trouble, be polite to adults, and look to their future."

The community's impression of the degrees to which this group of six boys (ranging in age from 16 to 19) engaged in delinquency was somewhat distorted. In some ways the gang was more delinquent than the community thought; in other ways they were less.

The fighting activities of the group were fairly readily and accurately perceived by almost everyone. At least once a month, the boys would get into some sort of fight, although most fights were scraps between members of the group or involved only one member of the group and some peripheral hanger-on. Only three times in the period of observation did the group fight together: once against a gang from across town, once against two blacks, and once against a group of boys from another school. For the first two fights the group went out "looking for trouble"—and they found it both times. The third fight followed a football game and began spontaneously with an argument on the football field between one of the Roughnecks and a member of the opposition's football team.

Jack has a particular propensity for fighting and was involved in most of the brawls. He was a prime mover of the escalation of arguments into fights.

More serious than fighting, had the community been aware of it, was theft. Although almost everyone was aware that the boys occasionally stole things, they did not realize the extent of the activity. Petty stealing was a frequent event for the Roughnecks. Sometimes they stole as a group and coordinated their efforts; other things they stole in pairs. Rarely did they steal alone.

The thefts ranged from very small things like paperback books, comics, and ballpoint pens to expensive items like watches. The nature of the thefts varied from time to time. The gang would go through a period of systematically lifting items from automobiles or school lockers. Types of thievery varied with the whim of the gang. Some forms of thievery were more profitable than others, but all thefts were for profit, not just thrills.

Roughnecks siphoned gasoline from cars as often as they had access to an automobile, which was not very often. Unlike the Saints, who owned their own cars, the Roughnecks would have to borrow their parents' cars, an event which occurred only eight or nine times a year. The boys claimed to have stolen cars for joy rides from time to time.

Ron committed the most serious of the group's offenses. With an unidentified associate the boy attempted to burglarize a gasoline station. Although this station had been robbed twice previously in the same month, Ron denied any involvement in either of the other thefts. When Ron and his accomplice approached the station, the owner was hiding in the bushes beside the station. He fired both barrels of a double-barreled shotgun at the boys. Ron was severely injured; the other boy ran away and was never caught. Though he remained in critical condition for several months, Ron finally recovered and served six months of the following year in reform school. Upon release from reform school, Ron was put back a grade in school, and began running around with a different gang of boys. The Roughnecks considered the new gang less delinquent than themselves, and during the following year Ron had no more trouble with the police.

The Roughnecks, then, engaged mainly in three types of delinquency: theft, drinking, and fighting. Although community members perceived that this gang of kids was delinquent, they mistakenly believed that their illegal activities were primarily drinking, fighting, and being a nuisance to passersby. Drinking was limited among the gang members, although it did occur, and theft was much more prevalent than anyone realized.

Drinking would doubtless have been more prevalent had the boys had ready access to liquor. Since they rarely had automobiles at their disposal, they could not travel very far, and the bars in town would not serve them. Most of the boys had little money, and this, too, inhibited their purchase of alcohol. Their major source of liquor was a local drunk who would buy them a fifth if they would give him enough extra to buy himself a pint of whiskey or a bottle of wine.

The community's perception of drinking as prevalent stemmed from the fact that it was the most obvious delinquency the boys engaged in. When one of the boys had been drinking, even a casual observer seeing him on the corner would suspect that he was high.

There was a high level of mutual distrust and dislike between the Roughnecks and the police. The boys felt very strongly that the police were unfair and corrupt. Some evidence existed that the boys were correct in their perception.

The main source of the boys' dislike for the police undoubtedly stemmed from the fact that the police would sporadically harass the group. From the standpoint of the boys, these acts of occasional enforcement of the law were whimsical and uncalled for. It made no sense to them, for example, that the police would come to the corner occasionally and threaten them with arrest for loitering when the night before the boys had been out siphoning gasoline from cars and the police had been nowhere in sight. To the boys, the police were stupid on the one hand, for not being where they should have been and catching the boys in a serious offense, and unfair on the other hand, for trumping up "loitering" charges against them.

From the viewpoint of the police, the situation was quite different. They knew, with all the confidence necessary to be a policeman, that these boys were engaged in criminal activities. They knew this partly from occasionally catching them, mostly from circumstantial evidence ("the boys were around when those tires were slashed"), and partly because the police shared the view of the community in general that this was a bad bunch of boys. The best the police could hope to do was to be sensitive to the fact that these boys were engaged in illegal acts and arrest them whenever there was some evidence that they had been involved. Whether or not the boys had in fact committed a particular act in a particular way was not especially important. The police had a broader view: their job was to stamp out these kids' crimes; the tactics were not as important as the end result.

Over the period that the group was under observation, each member was arrested at least once. Several of the boys were arrested a number of times and spent at least one night in jail. While most were never taken to court, two of the boys were sentenced to six months' incarceration in boys' schools.

## THE ROUGHNECKS IN SCHOOL

The Roughnecks' behavior in school was not particularly disruptive. During school hours they did not all hang around together, but tended instead to spend most of their time with one or two other members of the gang who were their special buddies. Although every member of the gang attempted to avoid school as much as possible, they were not particularly successful and most of them attended school with surprising regularity. They considered school a burden— something to be gotten through with a minimum of conflict. If they were "bugged" by a particular teacher, it could lead to trouble. One of the boys, Al, once threatened to beat up a teacher and, according to the other boys, the teacher hid under a desk to escape him.

Teachers saw the boys the way the general community did, as heading for trouble, as being uninterested in making something of themselves. Some were also seen as being incapable of meeting the academic standards of the school. Most of the teachers expressed concern for this group of boys and were willing to pass them despite poor performance, in the belief that failing them would only aggravate the problem.

The group of boys had a grade point average just slightly above "C." No one in the group failed either grade, and no one had better than a "C" average. They were very consistent in their achievement or, at least, the teachers were consistent in their perception of the boys' achievement.

Two of the boys were good football players. Herb was acknowledged to be the best player in the school and Jack was almost as good. Both boys were criticized for their failure to abide by training rules, for refusing to come to practice as often as they should, and for not playing their best during practice. What they lacked in sportsmanship they made up for in skill, apparently, and played every game no matter how poorly they had performed in practice or how many practice sessions they had missed.

## TWO QUESTIONS

Why did the community, the school, and the police react to the Saints as though they were good, upstanding, nondelinquent youths with bright futures but to the Roughnecks as though they were tough, young criminals who were headed for trouble? Why did the Roughnecks and the Saints in fact have quite different careers after high school—careers which, by and large, lived up to the expectations of the community?

The most obvious explanation for the differences in the community's and law enforcement agencies' reactions to the two gangs is that one group of boys was "more delinquent" than the other. Which group was more delinquent? The answer to this question will determine in part how we explain the differential responses to these groups by the members of the community and, particularly, by law enforcement and school officials.

In sheer number of illegal acts, the Saints were the more delinquent. They were truant from school for at least part of the day almost every day of the week. In addition, their drinking and vandalism occurred with surprising regularity. The Roughnecks, in contrast, engaged sporadically in delinquent episodes. While these episodes were frequent, they certainly did not occur on a daily or even a weekly basis.

The difference in frequency of offenses was probably caused by the Roughnecks' inability to obtain liquor and to manipulate legitimate excuses from school. Since the Roughnecks had less money than the Saints, and teachers carefully supervised their school activities, the Roughnecks' hearts may have been as black as the Saints', but their misdeeds were not nearly as frequent.

There are really no clear-cut criteria by which to measure qualitative differences in antisocial behavior. The most important dimension is generally referred to as the "seriousness" of the offenses.

If seriousness encompasses the relative economic costs of delinquent acts, then some assessment can be made. The Roughnecks probably stole an average of about $5.00 worth of goods a week. Some weeks the figure was considerably higher, but these times must be balanced against long periods when almost nothing was stolen.

The Saints were more continuously engaged in delinquency but their acts were not for the most part costly to property. Only their vandalism and occasional theft of gasoline would so qualify. Perhaps once or twice a month they would siphon a tankful of gas. The other costly items were street signs, construction lanterns, and the like. All of these acts combined probably did not quite average $5.00 a week, partly because much of the stolen equipment was abandoned and presumably could be recovered. The difference in cost of stolen property between the two groups was trivial, but the Roughnecks probably had a slightly more expensive set of activities than did the Saints.

Another meaning of seriousness is the potential threat of physical harm to members of the community and to the boys themselves. The Roughnecks were more prone to physical violence; they not only welcomed an opportunity to fight; they went seeking it. In addition, they fought among themselves frequently. Although the fighting never included deadly weapons, it was still a menace, however minor, to the physical safety of those involved.

The Saints never fought. They avoided physical conflict both inside and outside the group. At the same time, though, the Saints frequently endangered their own and other people's lives. They did so almost every time they drove a car, especially if they had been drinking. Sober, their driving was risky; under the influence of alcohol it was horrendous. In addition, the Saints endangered the lives of others with their pranks. Street excavations left unmarked were a very serious hazard.

Evaluating the relative seriousness of the two gangs' activities is difficult. The community reacted as though the behavior of the Roughnecks was a problem, and they reacted as though the behavior of the Saints was not. But the members of the community were ignorant of the array of delinquent acts that characterized the Saints' behavior. Although concerned citizens were unaware of much of the Roughnecks' behavior as well, they were much better informed about the Roughnecks' involvement in delinquency than they were about the Saints'.

## VISIBILITY

Differential treatment of the two gangs resulted in part because one gang was infinitely more visible than the other. This differential visibility was a direct function of the economic standing of the families. The Saints had access to automobiles and were able to remove themselves from the sight of the community. In as routine a decision as to where to go to have a milkshake after school, the Saints stayed away from the mainstream of community life. Lacking transportation, the Roughnecks could not make it to the edge of town. The center of town was the only practical place for them to meet since their homes were scattered throughout the town and any non-central meeting place put an undue hardship on some members. Through necessity the Roughnecks congregated in a crowded area where everyone in the community passed frequently, including teachers and law enforcement officers. They could easily see the Roughnecks hanging around the drugstore.

The Roughnecks, of course, made themselves even more visible by making remarks to passersby and by occasionally getting into fights on the corner. Meanwhile, just as regularly, the Saints were either at the café on one edge of town or in the pool hall at the other edge of town. Without any particular realization that they were making themselves inconspicuous, the Saints were able to hide their time-wasting. Not only were they removed from the mainstream of traffic, but they were almost always inside a building.

On their escapades the Saints were also relatively invisible, since they left Hanibal and traveled to Big Town. Here, too, they were mobile, roaming the city, rarely going to the same area twice.

## DEMEANOR

To the notion of visibility must be added the difference in the responses of group members to outside intervention with their activities. If one of the Saints was confronted with an accusing policeman, even if he felt he was truly innocent of a wrongdoing, his demeanor was apologetic and penitent. A Roughneck's attitude was almost the polar opposite. When confronted with a threatening adult authority, even one who tried to be pleasant, the Roughneck's hostility and disdain were clearly observable. Sometimes he might attempt to put up a veneer of respect, but it was thin and was not accepted as sincere by the authority.

School was no different from the community at large. The Saints could manipulate the system by feigning compliance with the school norms. The availability of cars at school meant that once free from the immediate sight of the teacher, the boys could disappear rapidly. And this escape was well enough planned that no administrator or teacher was nearby when the boys left. A Roughneck who wished to escape for a few hours was in a bind. If it were possible to get free from class, downtown was still a mile away, and even if he arrived there, he was still very visible. Truancy for the Roughnecks meant almost certain detection, while the Saints enjoyed almost complete immunity from sanctions.

## BIAS

Community members were not aware of the transgressions of the Saints. Even if the Saints had been less discreet, their favorite delinquencies would have been perceived as less serious than those of the Roughnecks.

In the eyes of the police and school officials, a boy who drinks in an alley and stands intoxicated on the street corner is committing a more serious offense than is a boy who drinks to inebriation in a nightclub or a tavern and drives around afterwards in a car. Similarly, a boy who steals a wallet from a store will be viewed as having committed a more serious offense than a boy who steals a lantern from a construction site.

Perceptual bias also operates with respect to the demeanor of the boys in the two groups when they are confronted by adults. It is not simply that adults dislike the posture affected by boys of the Roughneck ilk; more important is the conviction that the posture adopted by the Roughnecks is an indication of their devotion and commitment to deviance as a way of life. The posture becomes a cue, just as the type of the offense is a cue, to the degree to which the known transgressions are indicators of the youths' potential for other problems.

Visibility, demeanor, and bias are surface variables which explain the day-to-day operations of the police. Why do these surface variables operate as they do? Why did the police choose to disregard the Saints' delinquencies while breathing down the backs of the Roughnecks?

The answer lies in the class structure of American society and the control of legal institutions by those at the top of the class structure. Obviously, no representative of the upper class drew up the operational chart for the police which led them to look in the ghettos and on street corners—which led them to see the demeanor of lower-class youth as troublesome and that of upper-middle-class youth as tolerable. Rather, the procedures simply developed from experience—experience with irate and influential upper-middle-class parents insisting that their son's vandalism was simply a prank and his drunkenness only a momentary "sowing of wild oats"—experience with cooperative or indifferent, powerless, lower-class parents who acquiesced to the law's definition of their son's behavior.

## ADULT CAREERS OF THE SAINTS AND THE ROUGHNECKS

The community's confidence in the potential of the Saints and the Roughnecks apparently was justified. If anything, the community members underestimated the degree to which these youngsters would turn out "good" or "bad."

Seven of the eight members of the Saints went on to college immediately after high school. Five of the boys graduated from college in four years. The sixth one finished college after two years in the army, and the seventh spent four years in the air force before returning to college and receiving a B.A. degree. Of these seven college graduates, three went on for advanced degrees. One finished law school and is now active in state politics, one finished medical school and is practicing near Hanibal, and one boy is now working for a Ph.D. The other four college graduates entered submanagerial, managerial, or executive training positions with larger firms.

The only Saint who did not complete college was Jerry. Jerry had failed to graduate from high school with the other Saints. During his second senior year, after the other Saints had gone on to college, Jerry began to hang around with what several teachers described as a "rough crowd"—the gang that was heir apparent to the Roughnecks. At the end of his second senior year, when he did graduate from high school, Jerry took a job as a used-car salesman, got married, and quickly had a child. Although he made several abortive attempts to go to college by attending night school, when I last saw him (ten years after high school) Jerry was unemployed and had been living on unemployment for almost a year. His wife worked as a waitress.

Some of the Roughnecks have lived up to community expectations. A number of them were headed for trouble. A few were not.

Jack and Herb were the athletes among the Roughnecks and their athletic prowess paid off handsomely. Both boys received unsolicited athletic scholarships to college. After Herb received his scholarship (near the end of his senior year), he apparently did an about-face. His demeanor became very similar to that of the Saints. Although he remained a member in good standing of the

Roughnecks, he stopped participating in most activities and did not hang on the corner as often.

Jack did not change. If anything, he became more prone to fighting. He even made excuses for accepting the scholarship. He told the other gang members that the school had guaranteed him a "C" average if he would come to play football—an idea that seems far-fetched, even in this day of highly competitive recruiting.

During the summer after graduation from high school, Jack attempted suicide by jumping from a tall building. The jump would certainly have killed most people trying it, but Jack survived. He entered college in the fall and played four years of football. He and Herb graduated in four years, and both are teaching and coaching in high schools. They are married and have stable families. If anything, Jack appears to have a more prestigious position in the community than does Herb, though both are well respected and secure in their positions.

Two of the boys never finished high school. Tommy left at the end of his junior year and went to another state. That summer he was arrested and placed on probation on a manslaughter charge. Three years later he was arrested for murder; he pleaded guilty to second-degree murder and is serving a 30-year sentence in the state penitentiary.

Al, the other boy who did not finish high school, also left the state in his senior year. He is serving a life sentence in a state penitentiary for first-degree murder.

Wes is a small-time gambler. He finished high school and "bummed around." After several years he made contact with a bookmaker who employed him as a runner. Later he acquired his own area and has been working it ever since. His position among the bookmakers is almost identical to the position he had in the gang; he is always around but no one is really aware of him. He makes no trouble and he does not get into any. Steady, reliable, capable of keeping his mouth closed, he plays the game by the rules, even though the game is an illegal one.

That leaves only Ron. Some of his former friends reported that they had heard he was "driving a truck up north," but no one could provide any concrete information.

## REINFORCEMENT

The community responded to the Roughnecks as boys in trouble, and the boys agreed with that perception. Their pattern of deviancy was reinforced, and breaking away from it became increasingly unlikely. Once the boys acquired an image of themselves as deviants, they selected new friends who affirmed that self-image. As that self-conception became more firmly entrenched, they also became willing to try new and more extreme deviances. With their growing alienation came freer expression of disrespect and hostility for representatives of the legitimate society. This disrespect increased the community's negativism, perpetuating the entire process of commitment to deviance. Lack of a commitment to deviance works the same way. In either case, the process will perpetuate itself unless some event (like a scholarship to college or a sudden failure) external to the established relationship intervenes. For two of the Roughnecks (Herb and Jack), receiving college athletic scholarships created new relations and culminated in a break with the established pattern of deviance. In the case of one of the Saints (Jerry), his parents' divorce and his failing to graduate from high school changed some of his other relations. Being held back in school for a year and losing his place among the Saints had sufficient impact on Jerry to alter his self-image and virtually to assure that he would not go on to college as his peers did. Although the experiments of life can rarely be reversed, it seems likely in view of the behavior of the other boys who did not enjoy this special treatment by the school that Jerry, too, would have "become something" had he graduated as anticipated. For Herb and Jack outside intervention worked to their advantage; for Jerry it was his undoing.

Selective perception and labeling—finding, processing, and punishing some kinds of criminality and not others—means that visible, poor, non-mobile, outspoken, undiplomatic "tough" kids will be noticed, whether their actions are seriously delinquent or not. Other kids, who have established a reputation for being bright (even though underachieving), disciplined, and involved in respectable activities, who are mobile and monied, will be invisible when they deviate from sanctioned activities. They'll sow their wild oats—perhaps even wider and thicker than their lower-class cohorts—but they won't be noticed. When it's time to leave adolescence most will follow the expected path, settling into the ways of the middle class, remembering fondly the delinquent but unnoticed fling of their youth. The Roughnecks and others like them may turn around, too. It is more likely that their noticeable deviance will have been so reinforced by police and community that their lives will be effectively channeled into careers consistent with their adolescent background.

# 24

## Manifesto of the Communist Party

### KARL MARX and FRIEDRICH ENGELS

*Europe in the eighteenth and nineteenth centuries changed dramatically with the onset of industrialization and the phenomenal growth of cities. While some writers saw great promise of abundance and freedom in these changes, the reality for millions of people was increased labor and grinding poverty. Karl Marx (1818–1883) was one of the nineteenth century's most articulate critics of the disparity between possibility and reality. Here he and his collaborator, Friedrich Engels, explain the reasons for this in their pamphlet written for workers.*

## I. BOURGEOIS AND PROLETARIANS[1]

The history of all hitherto existing society[2] is the history of class struggles.

Freeman and slave, patrician and plebeian, lord and serf, guild-master[3] and journeyman, in a word, oppressor and oppressed, stood in constant opposition to one another, carried on an uninterrupted, now hidden, now open fight, a fight that each time ended, either in a revolutionary re-constitution of society at large, or in the common ruin of the contending classes.

In the earlier epochs of history, we find almost everywhere a complicated arrangement of society into various orders, a manifold gradation of social rank. In ancient Rome we have patricians, knights, plebeians, slaves; in the Middle

---

1. By bourgeoisie is meant the class of modern Capitalists, owners of the means of social production and employers of wage-labour. By proletariat, the class of modern wage-labourers who, having no means of production of their own, are reduced to selling their labour-power in order to live. [*Engels, English edition of 1888*]

2. That is, all *written* history. In 1847, the pre-history of society, the social organisation existing previous to recorded history, was all but unknown. Since then, Haxthausen discovered common ownership of land in Russia, Maurer proved it to be the social foundation from which all Teutonic races started in history, and by and by village communities were found to be, or to have been the primitive form of society everywhere from India to Ireland. The inner organisation of this primitive Communistic society was laid bare, in its typical form, by Morgan's crowning discovery of the true nature of the *gens* and its relation to the *tribe*. With the dissolution of these primaeval communities society begins to be differentiated into separate and finally antagonistic classes. I have attempted to retrace this process of dissolution in: "Der Ursprung der Familie, des Privateigenthums und des Staats" [*The Origin of the Family, Private Property and the State*], 2nd edition, Stuttgart 1886. [*Engels, English edition of 1888*]

3. Guild-master, that is, a full member of a guild, a master within, not a head of a guild. [*Engels, English edition of 1888*]

Ages, feudal lords, vassals, guild-masters, journey-men, apprentices, serfs; in almost all of these classes, again, subordinate gradations.

The modern bourgeois society that has sprouted from the ruins of feudal society has not done away with class antagonisms. It has but established new classes, new conditions of oppression, new forms of struggle in place of the old ones.

Our epoch, the epoch of the bourgeoisie, possesses, however, this distinctive feature: it has simplified the class antagonisms: Society as a whole is more and more splitting up into two great hostile camps, into two great classes directly facing each other: Bourgeoisie and Proletariat.

From the serfs of the Middle Ages sprang the chartered burghers of the earliest towns. From these burgesses the first elements of the bourgeoisie were developed.

The discovery of America, the rounding of the Cape, opened up fresh ground for the rising bourgeoisie. The East-Indian and Chinese markets, the colonisation of America, trade with the colonies, the increase in the means of exchange and in commodities generally, gave to commerce, to navigation, to industry, an impulse never before known, and thereby, to the revolutionary element in the tottering feudal society, a rapid development.

The feudal system of industry, under which industrial production was monopolised by closed guilds, now no longer sufficed for the growing wants of the new markets. The manufacturing system took its place. The guild-masters were pushed on one side by the manufacturing middle class; division of labour between the different corporate guilds vanished in the face of division of labour in each single workshop.

Meantime the markets kept ever growing, the demand ever rising. Even manufacture no longer sufficed. Thereupon, steam and machinery revolutionised industrial production. The place of manufacture was taken by the giant, Modern Industry, the place of the industrial middle class, by industrial millionaires, the leaders of whole industrial armies, the modern bourgeois.

Modern industry has established the world-market, for which the discovery of America paved the way. This market has given an immense development to commerce, to navigation, to communication by land. This development has, in its turn, reacted on the extension of industry; and in proportion as industry, commerce, navigation, railways extended, in the same proportion the bourgeoisie developed, increased its capital, and pushed into the background every class handed down from the Middle Ages.

We see, therefore, how the modern bourgeoisie is itself the product of a long course of development, of a series of revolutions in the modes of production and of exchange.

Each step in the development of the bourgeoisie was accompanied by a corresponding political advance of that class. An oppressed class under the sway of the feudal nobility, an armed and self-governing association in the mediaeval commune[4]; here independent urban republic (as in Italy and Germany), there taxable "third estate" of the monarchy (as in France), afterwards, in the period of manufacture proper, serving either the semi-feudal or the absolute monarchy as a counterpoise against the nobility, and, in fact, corner-stone of the great monarchies in general, the bourgeoisie has at last, since the establishment of Modern Industry and of the world-market, conquered for itself, in the modern representative State, exclusive political sway. The executive of the modem State is but a committee for managing the common affairs of the whole bourgeoisie.

The bourgeoisie, historically, has played a most revolutionary part.

The bourgeoisie, wherever it has got the upper hand, has put an end to all feudal, patriarchal, idyllic relations. It has pitilessly torn asunder the motley feudal ties that bound man to his "natural superiors," and has left remaining no other nexus between man and man than naked self-interest, than callous "cash payment." It has drowned the most heavenly ecstasies of religious fervour, of chivalrous enthusiasm, of philistine sentimentalism, in the icy water of egotistical calculation. It has resolved personal worth into exchange value, and in place of the numberless indefeasible chartered freedoms, has set up that single, unconscionable freedom—Free Trade. In one word, for exploitation, veiled by religious and political illusions, it has substituted naked, shameless, direct, brutal exploitation.

The bourgeoisie has stripped of its halo every occupation hitherto honoured and looked up to with reverent awe. It has converted the physician, the lawyer, the priest, the poet, the man of science, into its paid wage-labourers.

The bourgeoisie has torn away from the family its sentimental veil, and has reduced the family relation to a mere money relation.

The bourgeoisie has disclosed how it came to pass that the brutal display of vigour in the Middle Ages, which Reactionists so much admire, found its fitting complement in the most slothful indolence. It has been the first to show what man's activity can bring about. It has accomplished wonders far surpassing Egyptian pyramids, Roman aqueducts, and Gothic cathedrals; it has conducted expeditions that put in the shade all former Exoduses of nations and crusades.

The bourgeoisie cannot exist without constantly revolutionising the instruments of production, and thereby the relations of production, and with them

---

4. "Commune" was the name taken, in France, by the nascent towns even before they had conquered from their feudal lords and masters local self-government and political rights as the "Third Estate." Generally speaking, for the economical development of the bourgeoisie, England is here taken as the typical country; for its political development, France. [*Engels, English edition of 1888*]

This was the name given their urban communities by the townsmen of Italy and France, after they had purchased or wrested their initial rights of self-government from their feudal lords. [*Engels, Gentian edition of 1890*] the whole relations of society. Conservation of the old modes of production in unaltered form, was, on the contrary, the first condition of existence for all earlier industrial classes. Constant revolutionising of production, uninterrupted disturbance of all social conditions, everlasting uncertainty and agitation distinguish the bourgeois epoch from all earlier ones. All fixed, fast-frozen relations, with their train of ancient and venerable prejudices and opinions, are swept away, all new-formed ones become antiquated before they can ossify. All that is solid melts into air, all that is holy is profaned, and man is at last compelled to face with sober senses, his real conditions of life, and his relations with his kind.

The need of a constantly expanding market for its products chases the bourgeoisie over the whole surface of the globe. It must nestle everywhere, settle everywhere, establish connexions everywhere.

The bourgeoisie has through its exploitation of the world-market given a cosmopolitan character to production and consumption in every country. To the great chagrin of Reactionists, it has drawn from under the feet of industry the national ground on which it stood. All old-established national industries have been destroyed or are daily being destroyed. They are dislodged by new industries, whose introduction becomes a life and death question for all civilised nations, by industries that no longer work up indigenous raw material, but raw material drawn from the remotest zones; industries whose products are consumed, not only at home, but in every quarter of the globe. In place of the old wants, satisfied by the productions of the country, we find new wants, requiring for their satisfaction the products of distant lands and climes. In place of the old local and national seclusion and self-sufficiency, we have intercourse in every direction, universal inter-dependence of nations. And as in material, so also in intellectual production. The intellectual creations of individual nations become common property. National one-sidedness and narrow-mindedness become more and more impossible, and from the numerous national and local literatures, there arises a world literature.

The bourgeoisie, by the rapid improvement of all instruments of production, by the immensely facilitated means of communication, draws all, even the most barbarian, nations into civilisation. The cheap prices of its commodities are the heavy artillery with which it batters down all Chinese walls, with which it forces the barbarians' intensely obstinate hatred of foreigners to capitulate. It compels all nations, on pain of extinction, to adopt the bourgeois mode of production; it compels them to introduce what it calls civilisation into their midst, *i.e.*, to become bourgeois themselves. In one word, it creates a world after its own image.

The bourgeoisie has subjected the country to the rule of the towns. It has created enormous cities, has greatly increased the urban population as compared with the rural, and has thus rescued a considerable part of the population from the idiocy of rural life. Just as it has made the country dependent on the towns, so it has made barbarian and semi-barbarian countries dependent on the civilised ones, nations of peasants on nations of bourgeois, the East on the West.

The bourgeoisie keeps more and more doing away with the scattered state of the population, of the means of production, and of property. It has agglomerated population, centralised means of production, and has concentrated property in a few hands. The necessary consequence of this was political centralisation. Independent, or but loosely connected provinces, with separate interests, laws, governments and systems of taxation, became lumped together into one nation, with one government, one code of laws, one national class-interest, one frontier and one customs-tariff.

The bourgeoisie, during its rule of scarce one hundred years, has created more massive and more colossal productive forces than have all preceding generations together. Subjection of Nature's forces to man, machinery, application of chemistry to industry and agriculture, steam-navigation, railways, electric telegraphs, clearing of whole continents for cultivation, canalisation of rivers, whole populations conjured out of the ground—what earlier century had even a presentiment that such productive forces slumbered in the lap of social labour?

We see then: the means of production and of exchange, on whose foundation the bourgeoisie built itself up, were generated in feudal society. At a certain stage in the development of these means of production and of exchange, the conditions under which feudal society produced and exchanged, the feudal organisation of agriculture and manufacturing industry, in one word, the feudal relations of property became no longer compatible with the already developed productive forces; they became so many fetters. They had to be burst asunder; they were burst asunder.

Into their place stepped free competition, accompanied by a social and political constitution adapted to it, and by the economical and political sway of the bourgeois class.

A similar movement is going on before our own eyes. Modern bourgeois society with its relations of production, of exchange and of property, a society that has conjured up such gigantic means of production and of exchange, is like the sorcerer, who is no longer able to control the powers of the nether world whom he has called up by his spells. For many a decade past the history of industry and commerce is but the history of the revolt of modern productive forces against modern conditions of production, against the property relations that are the conditions for the existence of the bourgeoisie and of its rule. It is enough to mention the commercial crises that by their periodical return put on its trial, each time more threateningly, the existence of the entire bourgeois society. In these crises a great part not only of the existing products, but also of the previously created productive forces, are periodically destroyed. In these crises there breaks out an epidemic that, in all earlier epochs, would have seemed an absurdity—the epidemic of over-production. Society suddenly finds itself put back into a state of momentary barbarism; it appears as if a famine, a universal war of devastation had cut off the supply of every means of subsistence; industry and commerce seem to be destroyed; and why? Because there is too much civilisation, too much means of subsistence, too much industry, too much commerce. The productive forces at the disposal of society no longer tend to further the development of the conditions of bourgeois property; on the contrary, they have become too powerful for these conditions, by which they are fettered, and so soon as they overcome these fetters, they bring disorder into the whole of bourgeois society, endanger the existence of bourgeois property. The conditions of bourgeois society are too narrow to comprise the wealth created by them. And how does the bourgeoisie get over these crises? On the one hand by enforced destruction of a mass of productive forces; on the other, by the conquest of new markets, and by the more thorough exploitation of the old ones. That is to say, by paving the way for more extensive and more destructive crises, and by diminishing the means whereby crises are prevented.

The weapons with which the bourgeoisie felled feudalism to the ground are now turned against the bourgeoisie itself.

But not only has the bourgeoisie forged the weapons that bring death to itself; it has also called into existence the men who are to wield those weapons the modern working class—the proletarians.

In proportion as the bourgeoisie, *i.e.*, capital, is developed, in the same proportion is the proletariat, the modern working class, developed—a class of labourers, who live only so long as they find work, and who find work only so long as their labour increases capital. These labourers, who must sell themselves piece-meal, are a commodity, like every other article of commerce, and are consequently exposed to all the vicissitudes of competition, to all the fluctuations of the market.

Owing to the extensive use of machinery and to division of labour, the work of the proletarians has lost all individual character, and consequently, all charm for the workman. He becomes an appendage of the machine, and it is only the most simple, most monotonous, and most easily acquired knack, that is required of him. Hence, the cost of production of a workman is restricted, almost entirely, to the means of subsistence that he requires for his maintenance, and for the propagation of his race. But the price of a commodity, and therefore also of labour,[5] is equal to its cost of production. In proportion, therefore, as the repulsiveness of the work increases, the wage decreases. Nay more, in proportion as the use of machinery and division of labour increases, in the same proportion the burden of toil also increases, whether by prolongation of the working hours, by increase of the work exacted in a given time or by increased speed of the machinery, etc.

Modern industry has converted the little workshop of the patriarchal master into the great factory of the industrial capitalist. Masses of labourers,

---

5. Subsequently Marx pointed out that the worker sells not his labour but his labour power.

crowded into the factory, are organised like soldiers. As privates of the industrial army they are placed under the command of a perfect hierarchy of officers and sergeants. Not only are they slaves of the bourgeois class, and of the bourgeois State; they are daily and hourly enslaved by the machine, by the overlooker, and, above all, by the individual bourgeois manufacturer himself. The more openly this despotism proclaims gain to be its end and aim, the more petty, the more hateful and the more embittering it is.

The less the skill and exertion of strength implied in manual labour, in other words, the more modern industry becomes developed, the more is the labour of men superseded by that of women. Differences of age and sex have no longer any distinctive social validity for the working class. All are instruments of labour, more or less expensive to use, according to their age and sex.

No sooner is the exploitation of the labourer by the manufacturer, so far, at an end, that he receives his wages in cash, than he is set upon by the other portions of the bourgeoisie, the landlord, the shopkeeper, the pawnbroker, etc.

The lower strata of the middle class—the small tradespeople, shopkeepers, and retired tradesmen generally, the handicraftsmen and peasants—all these sink gradually into the proletariat, partly because their diminutive capital does not suffice for the scale on which Modern Industry is carried on, and is swamped in the competition with the large capitalists, partly because their specialised skill is rendered worthless by new methods of production. Thus the proletariat is recruited from all classes of the population.

The proletariat goes through various stages of development. With its birth begins its struggle with the bourgeoisie. At first the contest is carried on by individual labourers, then by the workpeople of a factory, then by the operatives of one trade, in one locality, against the individual bourgeois who directly exploits them. They direct their attacks not against the bourgeois conditions of production, but against the instruments of production themselves; they destroy imported wares that compete with their labour, they smash to pieces machinery, they set factories ablaze, they seek to restore by force the vanished status of the workman of the Middle Ages.

At this stage the labourers still form an incoherent mass scattered over the whole country, and broken up by their mutual competition. If anywhere they unite to form more compact bodies, this is not yet the consequence of their own active union, but of the union of the bourgeoisie, which class, in order to attain its own political ends, is compelled to set the whole proletariat in motion, and is moreover yet, for a time, able to do so. At this stage, therefore, the proletarians do not fight their enemies, but the enemies of their enemies, the remnants of absolute monarchy, the landowners, the non-industrial bourgeois, the petty bourgeoisie. Thus the whole historical movement is concentrated in the hands of the bourgeoisie; every victory so obtained is a victory for the bourgeoisie.

But with the development of industry the proletariat not only increases in number; it becomes concentrated in greater masses, its strength grows, and it feels that strength more. The various interests and conditions of life within the ranks of the proletariat are more and more equalised, in proportion as machinery obliterates all distinctions of labour, and nearly everywhere reduces wages to the same low level. The growing competition among the bourgeois, and the resulting commercial crises, make the wages of the workers ever more fluctuating. The unceasing improvement of machinery, ever more rapidly developing, makes their livelihood more and more precarious; the collisions between individual workmen and individual bourgeois take more and more the character of collisions between two classes. Thereupon the workers begin to form combinations (Trades Unions) against the bourgeois; they club together in order to keep up the rate of wages; they found permanent associations in order to make provision beforehand for these occasional revolts. Here and there the contest breaks out into riots.

Now and then the workers are victorious, but only for a time. The real fruit of their battles lies, not in the immediate result, but in the ever-expanding union of the workers. This union is helped on by the improved means of communication that are created by modern industry and that place the workers of different localities in contact with one another. It was just this contact that was needed to centralise the numerous local struggles, all of the same character, into one national struggle between classes. But every class struggle is a political struggle. And that union, to attain which the burghers of the Middle Ages, with their miserable highways, required centuries, the modern proletarians, thanks to railways, achieve in a few years.

This organisation of the proletarians into a class, and consequently into a political party, is continually being upset again by the competition between the workers themselves. But it ever rises up again, stronger, firmer, mightier. It compels legislative recognition of particular interests of the workers, by taking advantage of the divisions among the bourgeoisie itself. Thus the ten-hours' bill in England was carried.

Altogether collisions between the classes of the old society further, in many ways, the course of development of the proletariat. The bourgeoisie finds itself involved in a constant battle. At first with the aristocracy; later on, with those portions of the bourgeoisie itself, whose interests have become antagonistic to the progress of industry; at all times, with the bourgeoisie of foreign countries. In all these battles it sees itself compelled to appeal to the proletariat, to ask for its help, and thus, to drag it into the political arena. The bourgeoisie itself, therefore, supplies the proletariat with its own elements of political and general education, in other words, it furnishes the proletariat with weapons for fighting the bourgeoisie.

Further, as we have already seen, entire sections of the ruling classes are, by the advance of industry, precipitated into the proletariat, or are at least threatened in their conditions of existence. These also supply the proletariat with fresh elements of enlightenment and progress.

Finally, in times when the class struggle nears the decisive hour, the process of dissolution going on within the ruling class, in fact within the whole range of society, assumes such a violent, glaring character, that a small section of the ruling class cuts itself adrift, and joins the revolutionary class, the class that holds the future in its hands. Just as, therefore, at an earlier period, a section of the nobility went over to the bourgeoisie, so now a portion of the bourgeoisie goes over to the proletariat, and in particular, a portion of the bourgeois ideologists, who have raised themselves to the level of comprehending theoretically the historical movement as a whole.

Of all the classes that stand face to face with the bourgeoisie today, the proletariat alone is a really revolutionary class. The other classes decay and finally disappear in the face of Modern Industry; the proletariat is its special and essential product.

The lower middle class, the small manufacturer, the shopkeeper, the artisan, the peasant, all these fight against the bourgeoisie, to save from extinction their existence as fractions of the middle class. They are therefore not revolutionary, but conservative. Nay more, they are reactionary, for they try to roll back the wheel of history. If by chance they are revolutionary, they are so only in view of their impending transfer into the proletariat, they thus defend not their present, but their future interests, they desert their own standpoint to place themselves at that of the proletariat.

The "dangerous class," the social scum, that passively rotting mass thrown off by the lowest layers of old society, may, here and there, be swept into the movement by a proletarian revolution; its conditions of life, however, prepare it far more for the part of a bribed tool of reactionary intrigue.

In the conditions of the proletariat, those of old society at large are already virtually swamped. The proletarian is without property; his relation to his wife and children has no longer anything in common with the bourgeois family-relations; modern industrial labour, modern subjection to capital, the same in England as in France, in America as in Germany, has stripped him of every trace of national character. Law, morality, religion, are to him so many bourgeois prejudices, behind which lurk in ambush just as many bourgeois interests.

All the preceding classes that got the upper hand, sought to fortify their already acquired status by subjecting society at large to their conditions of appropriation. The proletarians cannot become masters of the productive forces of society, except by abolishing their own previous mode of appropriation, and thereby also every other previous mode of appropriation. They have nothing of their own to secure and to fortify; their mission is to destroy all previous securities for, and insurances of, individual property.

All previous historical movements were movements of minorities, or in the interests of minorities. The proletarian movement is the self-conscious, independent movement of the immense majority, in the interests of the immense majority. The proletariat, the lowest stratum of our present society, cannot stir, cannot raise itself up, without the whole superincumbent strata of official society being sprung into the air.

Though not in substance, yet in form, the struggle of the proletariat with the bourgeoisie is at first a national struggle. The proletariat of each country must, of course, first of all settle matters with its own bourgeoisie.

In depicting the most general phases of the development of the proletariat, we traced the more or less veiled civil war, raging within existing society, up to the point where that war breaks out into open revolution, and where the violent overthrow of the bourgeoisie lays the foundation for the sway of the proletariat.

Hitherto, every form of society has been based, as we have already seen, on the antagonism of oppressing and oppressed classes. But in order to oppress a class, certain conditions must be assured to it under which it can, at least, continue its slavish existence. The serf, in the period of serfdom, raised himself to membership in the commune, just as the petty bourgeois, under the yoke of feudal absolutism, managed to develop into a bourgeois. The modern labourer, on the contrary, instead of rising with the progress of industry, sinks deeper and deeper below the conditions of existence of his own class. He becomes a pauper, and pauperism develops more rapidly than population and wealth. And here it becomes evident, that the bourgeoisie is unfit any longer to be the ruling class in society, and to impose its conditions of existence upon society as an over-riding law. It is unfit to rule because it is incompetent to assure an existence to its slave within his slavery, because it cannot help letting him sink into such a state, that it has to feed him, instead of being fed by him. Society can no longer live under this bourgeoisie, in other words, its existence is no longer compatible with society.

The essential condition for the existence, and for the sway of the bourgeois class, is the formation and augmentation of capital; the condition for capital is wage-labour. Wage-labour rests exclusively on competition between the labourers. The advance of industry, whose involuntary promoter is the bourgeoisie, replaces the isolation of the labourers, due to competition, by their revolutionary combination, due to association. The development of Modern Industry, therefore, cuts from under its feet the very foundation on which the bourgeoisie produces the appropriates products. What the bourgeoisie, therefore, produces, above all, is its own grave-diggers. Its fall and the victory of the proletariat are equally inevitable.

# 25

## The Economic Plight of Inner-City Black Males*

FROM *More than Just Race: Being Black and Poor in the Inner City*

### WILLIAM JULIUS WILSON

*Reading this essay, you are stepping into a minefield. Fortunately, William Julius Wilson, one of our preeminent sociologists for the past thirty years, skillfully leads the way. As a newcomer to sociology you don't know that academic battles have raged, unkind words and accusations have been hurled, character has been impugned, and friends have become enemies over the question Wilson is addressing: Why are so many black males overrepresented among school dropouts, the unemployed, the incarcerated, and the unwed fathers in this country? Fortunately, we no longer have to rely on an explanation that "blames the victim" by castigating their "culture of poverty" and lack of personal responsibility. Nor do we have to blame "the system" and treat those in distress as if they are puppets or robots on a downward-sloping treadmill. Wilson knows what he is talking about when he looks closely at the structural barriers to success and the many ways opportunity is denied millions of black males, including many young black men today. He also knows about the beliefs and attitudes fostered in the inner city and the accepted practices that keep many men from pursuing possibilities that could change their lives. For too long the odds have been against them.*

The economic predicament of low-skilled black men in the inner city has reached catastrophic proportions. Americans may not fully understand the dreadful social and economic circumstances that have moved these black males further and further behind the rest of society, but they often fear black males and perceive that they pose a problem for those who live in the city. Elliot Liebow helped expand our understanding of low-skilled black males when he wrote *Tally's Corner: A Study of Street Corner Men* in the mid-1960s. Since then, researchers have paid more attention to this group.

Although many of Liebow's arguments concerning the work experiences and family lives of black men in a Washington DC ghetto are still applicable to contemporary urban communities, the social and economic predicament of low-skilled black males today, especially their rate of joblessness, has become even more severe. Liebow was perhaps the first scholar to demonstrate that an ongoing lack of success in the labor market (ranging from outright unemployment

---

*Footnotes and references can be found in the original publication of William Julius Wilson's *More than Just Race: Being Black and Poor in the Inner City* (New York: W. W. Norton & Company, 2009). [*Editor's note*]

to being trapped in menial jobs) leads to a lessening of self-confidence and, eventually, to feelings of resignation that frequently result in temporary, or even permanent, abandonment of looking for work.

Even when Liebow's men were successful in finding work, the jobs they occupied paid little and were dirty, physically demanding, and uninteresting. This work did not foster respect, build status, or offer opportunity for advancement. "The most important fact [in becoming discouraged from looking for or keeping a job] is that a man who is able and willing to work cannot earn enough to support himself, his wife, and one or more children," declared Liebow. "A man's chances for working regularly are good only if he is willing to work for less than he can live on, sometimes not even then." Because they held the same ideas about work and reward as other Americans, the street-corner men viewed such jobs disdainfully. "He cannot do otherwise," stated Liebow. "He cannot draw from a job those values which other people do not put into it." Unlike today, menial employment was readily available to these men during the 1960s, and they drifted from one undesirable job to the next.

When I analyzed the data collected from the mid-1980s to the mid-1990s by our research team on poverty and joblessness among black males in inner-city Chicago neighborhoods, I was repeatedly reminded of Liebow's book. Although the job prospects for low-skilled black men were bleak when Liebow conducted his field research in the early 1960s, they were even worse in the last quarter of the twentieth century, when even menial jobs in the service sector were difficult for low-skilled black males to find. That situation persists today.

## THE ROLE OF STRUCTURAL FACTORS

Although African American men continue to confront racial barriers in the labor market, many inner-city black males have also been victimized by other structural factors, such as the decreased relative demand for low-skilled labor. The propagation of new technologies is displacing untrained workers and rewarding those with specialized, technical training, while globalization of the economy is increasingly pitting low-skilled workers in the United States against their counterparts around the world, including laborers in countries such as China, India, and Bangladesh who can be employed for substantially lower wages. This decreasing relative demand in the United States for low-skilled labor means that untrained workers face the growing threat of eroding wages and job displacement.

Over the past several decades, African Americans have experienced sharp job losses in the manufacturing sector. Indeed, as John Schmitt and Ben Zipperer point out, "the share of black workers in manufacturing has actually been falling more rapidly than the overall share of manufacturing employment. From the end of the 1970s through the early 1990s, African Americans were just as likely as workers from other racial and ethnic groups to have manufacturing jobs. Since the early 1990s, however, black workers have lost considerable ground in manufacturing. By 2007, blacks were about 15 percent less likely than other workers to have a job in manufacturing." The dwindling proportion of African American workers in manufacturing is important because manufacturing jobs, especially those in the auto industry, have been a significant source of better-paid employment for black Americans since World War II.

The relative decline of black workers in manufacturing parallels their decreasing involvement in unions. From 1983 to 2007 the proportion of all African American workers who were either in unions or represented by a union at their employment site dropped considerably, from 31.7 to 15.7 percent. In 2007, African American workers were still more likely to be unionized (15.7 percent) than whites (13.5) and Hispanics (10.8). Nonetheless, this reduction (down 16 percentage points) over that time span was greater than that for whites (down 8.9 percentage points) and Hispanics (down 13.4). The lack of union representation renders workers more vulnerable in the workplace, especially to cuts in wages and benefits.

Because they tend to be educated in poorly performing public schools, low-skilled black males often enter the job market lacking some of the basic tools that would help them confront changes in their employment prospects. Such schools have rigid district bureaucracies, poor morale among teachers and school principals, low expectations for students, and negative ideologies that justify poor student performance. Inner-city schools fall well below more advantaged suburban schools in science and math resources, and they lack teachers with appropriate preparation in these subjects. As a result, students from these schools tend to have poor reading and math skills, important tools for competing in the globalized labor market. Few thoughtful observers of public education would disagree with the view that the poor employment prospects of low-skilled black males are in no small measure related to their public-education experiences.

Their lack of education, which contributes to joblessness, is certainly related to their risk of incarceration. As Bruce Western so brilliantly revealed in his important book *Punishment and Inequality in America*, following the collapse of the low-skilled urban labor markets and the creation of jobless ghettos in our nation's inner cities, incarceration grew among those with the highest rates of joblessness. "By the early 2000s," states Western, "the chances of imprisonment were more closely linked to race and school failure than at any time in the previous twenty years." Between 1979 and 1999, the risk of imprisonment for less educated men nearly doubled. Indeed, a significant proportion of black men who have been in prison are high school dropouts. "Among [black] male high school dropouts the risk of imprisonment [has] increased to 60 percent, establishing incarceration as a normal stopping point on the route to midlife."

However, Western's research also revealed that national cultural shifts in values and attitudes contributed to a political context associated with a resurgent Republican Party that focused on punitive "solutions" and worsened the plight of low-skilled black men. This more penal approach to crime was reinforced during Bill Clinton's administration. Indeed, rates of incarceration soared even during periods when the overall crime rate had declined. "The growth in violence among the ghetto poor through the 1960s and 1970s stoked fears of white voters and lurked in the rhetoric of law and order," states Western. "Crime, however, did not drive the rise in imprisonment directly, but formed the background for a new style of politics and punishment. As joblessness and low wages became enduring features of the less skilled inner-city economy, the effects of a punitive criminal justice system concentrated on the most disadvantaged." Western estimates that as many as 30 percent of all civilian young adult black males ages sixteen to thirty-four are ex-offenders. In short, cultural shifts in attitudes toward crime and punishment created structural circumstances—a more punitive criminal justice system—that have had a powerful impact on low-skilled black males.

\* \* \*

For inner-city black male workers, the problems created by these structural factors have been aggravated by employers' negative attitudes toward black men as workers. A representative sample of Chicago-area employers by my research team in the late 1980s clearly reveals employer bias against black males. A substantial majority of employers considered inner-city black males to be uneducated, uncooperative, unstable, or dishonest. For example, a suburban drug store manager made the following comment:

> It's unfortunate but, in my business I think overall [black men] tend to be known to be dishonest. I think that's too bad but that's the image they have. (*Interviewer*: So you think it's an image problem?) *Respondent*: An image problem of being dishonest men and lazy. They're known to be lazy. They are [laughs]. I hate to tell you, but. It's all an image though. Whether they are or not. I don't know, but, it's an image that is perceived. (*Interviewer*: I see. How do you think that image was developed?) *Respondent*: Go look in the jails [laughs].

The president of an inner-city manufacturing firm expressed a different reservation about employing black males from certain ghetto neighborhoods:

> If somebody gave me their address, uh, Cabrini Green I might unavoidably have some concerns. (*Interviewer*: What would your concerns be?) *Respondent*: That the poor guy probably would be frequently unable to get to work and . . . I probably would watch him more carefully even if it wasn't fair, than I would with somebody else. I know what I should do though is recognize that here's a guy that is trying to get out of his situation and probably will work harder than somebody else who's already out of there and he might be the best one around here. But I think I would have to struggle accepting that premise at the beginning.

The prevalence of such attitudes, combined with the physical and social isolation of minorities living in inner-city areas of concentrated poverty, severely limits the access that poor black men have to informal job networks (the casual networks of people or acquaintances who can pass along information about employment prospects). This is a notable problem for black males, especially considering that many low-skilled employees first learn about their jobs through an acquaintance or were recommended by someone associated with the company. Research suggests that only a small percentage of low-skilled employees are hired through advertised job openings or cold calls. The importance of knowing someone who knows the boss can be seen by another employer's comments to our interviewer:

> All of a sudden, they take a look at a guy, and unless he's got an in, the reason why I hired this black kid the last time is cause my neighbor said to me, yeah I used him for a few [days], he's good, and I said, you know what, I'm going to take a chance. But it was a recommendation. But other than that, I've got a walk-in, and, who knows? And I think that for the most part, a guy sees a black man, he's a bit hesitant.

These attitudes are classic examples of what social scientists call statistical discrimination: employers make generalizations about inner-city, black male workers and reach decisions based on those assumptions without reviewing the qualifications of an individual applicant. The net effect is that many inner-city, black male applicants are never given the opportunity to prove themselves. Although some of these men scorn entry-level jobs because of the poor working conditions and low wages, many others would readily accept such employment. And although statistical discrimination contains some elements of class bias against poor, inner-city workers, it is clearly a racially motivated practice. It is a frustrating and disturbing fact that inner-city black males are effectively screened out of employment far more often than their Hispanic or white peers who apply for the same jobs. A number of other studies have documented employer bias against black males. For example, research by Devah Pager revealed that a white applicant with a felony conviction was more likely to receive a callback or job offer than was a black applicant with a clean record.

\* \* \*

Forced to turn to the low-wage service sector for employment, inner-city black males—including a significant number of ex-offenders—have to compete, often unsuccessfully, with a growing number of female and immigrant workers. If these men complain or otherwise manifest their dissatisfaction, they seem even more unattractive to employers and therefore encounter even greater discrimination when they search for employment. Because the feelings that many inner-city black males express about their jobs and job prospects reflect their plummeting position in a changing economy, it is important to link these attitudes and other cultural traits with the opportunity structure—that is, the spectrum of life chances available to them in society at large.

Many people would agree that both the structural factors and the national cultural factors discussed earlier have had a very large impact on the experiences of low-skilled black males. But no such consensus exists with respect to the role of cultural factors that have emerged in inner-city ghetto neighborhoods in shaping and directing the lives of young black men.

## THE ROLE OF CULTURAL FACTORS

Throughout this discussion I have suggested that cultural factors must be brought to bear if we are to explain economic and social outcomes for racial groups. The exploration of the cultural dimension must do three things: (1) provide a compelling reason for including cultural factors in a comprehensive discussion of race and poverty, (2) show the relationship between cultural analysis and structural analysis, and (3) determine the extent to which cultural factors operate independently to contribute to or reinforce poverty and racial inequality. However, the evidence for the influence of cultural factors on the social and economic circumstances of low-skilled black males is far less compelling than structural arguments, in part because of a dearth of research in this area.

According to Orlando Patterson of Harvard University, since the mid-1960s a strong bias against cultural explanations for human behavior has led social scientists and policy analysts to ignore different groups' distinctive cultural attributes in favor of an emphasis on structural factors to account for the behavior and social outcomes of its members. So instead of looking at attitudes, norms, values, habits, and worldviews (all indications of cultural orientations), we focus on joblessness, low socioeconomic status, and under-performing public schools—in short, structural factors.

Patterson revisited the role of culture and raised several questions that might be better addressed when cultural elements are considered in conjunction with structural and historical explanations. Patterson asks, "Why do so many young unemployed black men have children—several of them—which they have no resources or intention to support? And why . . . do they murder each other at nine times the rate of white youths?" And, he adds, why do young black males turn their backs on low-wage jobs that immigrants are happy to fill? Referring to research conducted by UCLA sociologist Roger Waldinger, Patterson states that such jobs enable the chronically unemployed to enter the labor market and obtain basic work skills that they can later use in securing better jobs. But he also notes that those who accepted the low-paying jobs in Waldinger's study were mostly immigrants.

To help answer his own questions about the behavior of young black men in the ghetto, Patterson refers to anecdotal evidence collected several years ago by one of his former students. He states that the student visited her former high school to discover why "almost all the black girls graduated and went to college whereas nearly all the black boys either failed to graduate or did not go on to college." Her distressing finding was that all of the black boys were fully aware of the consequences of failing to graduate from high school and go on to college. (They indignantly exclaimed, "We're not stupid!") So, Patterson wonders, why were they flunking out? The candid answer that these young men gave to his former student was their preference for what some call the "cool-pose culture" of young black men, which they found too fulfilling to give up. "For these young men, it was almost like a drug, hanging out on the street after school, shopping and dressing sharply, sexual conquests, party drugs, hip-hop music and culture."

Patterson maintains that cool-pose culture blatantly promotes the most anomalous models of behavior in urban, lower-class neighborhoods, featuring gangsta rap, predatory sexuality, and irresponsible fathering. "It is reasonable to conclude," he states, "that among a large number of urban, Afro-American lower-class young men, these models are now fully normative and that men act in accordance with them whenever they can." For example, Patterson argues that black male pride has become increasingly defined in terms of the impregnation of women. However, this trend is not unique to the current generation of young black males, he notes. Several decades ago the sociologist Lee Rainwater uncovered a similar pattern. Not only did a majority of the inner-city, young black male respondents he interviewed state that they were indifferent to the fact that their girlfriends were pregnant, but some even expressed the proud belief that getting a girl pregnant proves you're a man. The fact that Elijah Anderson and others discovered identical models decades later suggests the possibility of a pattern of cultural transmission—that is, the attitudes and behaviors valorizing a kind of "footloose fatherhood" have been passed down to younger generations. A counterargument—one that does not assume cultural transmission—could also be posed: young black men in roughly similar structural positions in different generations developed similar cultural responses.

Patterson argues that a thoughtful cultural explanation of the self-defeating behavior of poor, young black men could not only speak to the immediate relationship of their attitudes, behavior, and undesirable outcomes, but also examine their brutalized past, perhaps over generations, to investigate the origins and changing nature of these views and practices. Patterson maintains that we cannot understand the behavior of young black men without deeply examining their collective past.

I believe that Patterson tends to downplay the importance of immediate socioeconomic factors: if there is indeed a cool-pose culture, it is reasonable to assume that it is partly related to employment failures and disillusionment with the poorly performing public schools and possibly has its roots in the special social circumstances fostered by pre-1960s legal segregation. But I fully concur with Patterson's view that cultural explanations that include historical context should be part of our attempt to fully account for behavior that is so contradictory to mainstream ideas of how work and family should fit into a man's life.

In her ethnographic research—that is, work using evidence gathered through field observation and through extended, often repeated, interviews—Katherine Newman reveals that young, low-wage workers in New York City's Harlem neighborhood not only adhere to mainstream values regarding work, but also tend to accept low-skilled, low-wage, often dead-end jobs. In his impressive study of how young, inner-city black men perceive opportunity and mobility in the United States, Alford Young found that although some men associated social mobility with the economic opportunity structure, including race- and class-based discrimination, all of his respondents shared the view that individuals are largely accountable for their failure to advance in society.

The research conducted by my team in Chicago provides only mixed evidence for a subculture of defeatism. Consistent with Liebow's findings in *Tally's Corner,* the ethnographic research in our study revealed that many young black males had experienced repeated failures in their job search, had given up hope, and therefore no longer bothered to look for work. * * * [O]ur research pointed to negative employer attitudes and actions toward low-skilled black males as powerful influences in this cycle. Our ethnographic research suggested that repeated failure results in resignation and the development of cultural attitudes that discourage the pursuit of steady employment in the formal labor market.

On the other hand, data from our large, random survey of black residents in the inner city revealed that despite the overwhelming joblessness and poverty around them, black residents in ghetto neighborhoods, consistent with the findings of Alford Young, spoke unambiguously in support of basic American values concerning individual initiative. For example, nearly all of the black people we questioned felt that plain hard work is either very important or somewhat important for getting ahead. In addition, in a series of open-ended interviews conducted by members of our research team, participants overwhelmingly endorsed the dominant American belief system concerning poverty. The views of some of these individuals—who lived in some of the most destitute neighborhoods in America—were particularly revealing. A substantial majority agreed that America is a land of opportunity where anybody can get ahead, and that individuals get pretty much what they deserve.

The response of a thirty-four-year-old black male, a resident in a ghetto area of the South Side of Chicago where 29 percent of the population was destitute (i.e., with incomes 75 percent below the poverty line) was typical: "Everybody get pretty much what they deserve because if everybody wants to do better they got to go out there and try. If they don't try, they won't make it." Another black male who was residing in an equally impoverished South Side neighborhood stated, "For some it's a land of opportunity, but you can't just let opportunity come knock on your door, you just got to go ahead and work for it. You got to go out and get it for yourself." Although their support of this abstract American ideal was not always consistent with their perceptions and descriptions of the social barriers that impeded the social progress of their neighbors and friends, these endorsements stand in strong contrast to the subculture of defeatism. Nonetheless, I should note that there is frequently a gap between what people state in the abstract and what they perceive to be possible for themselves given their own situations. In other words, it should not be surprising if some residents support the abstract American ideal of individual initiative and still feel that they cannot get ahead, because of factors beyond their control.

The inconsistency between what people say in the abstract and what they believe applies to them maybe seen in other ways. Jennifer Hochschild's analysis of national survey data reveals that poor blacks tend to acknowledge the importance of discrimination when they respond to national surveys, but they are not likely to feel that it affects them personally. Often, discrimination is the least mentioned factor among other important forces that black people select when asked what determines their chances in life. Thus, among poor blacks, structural factors such as discrimination and declining job opportunities "do not register as major impediments to achieving their goals. Deficient motivation and individual effort do." The emphasis that poor blacks place on the importance of personal attributes over structural factors for success in America should not come as a surprise. As Hochschild astutely points out, "poor African Americans are usually badly educated and not widely traveled, so they are unlikely to see structural patterns underlying individual actions and situations. Thus even if (or because) the American dream fails as a description of American society, it is a highly seductive prescription for succeeding in that society to those who cannot see the underlying flaw." To repeat, the evidence for a subculture of defeatism is mixed. Nonetheless, until more compelling studies are produced, it remains an important hypothesis for research.

\* \* \*

Sandra Smith provides a compelling and nuanced cultural analysis of other factors that contribute to the complex and often difficult world of work inhabited by low-skilled blacks. Smith conducted in-depth interviews with 105 black men and women in Michigan between the ages of twenty and forty who had no more than a high school education so that she could examine the informal personal networks of low-skilled black job holders and job seekers.

Smith's data provide new information to help explain why informal job networks among blacks were less useful in helping job seekers find employment in the formal economy. She found that distrust on the part of black job holders and the defensive individualism typical of black job seekers profoundly affected the use of job referrals in the search for employment. She points out that the neighborhoods of the black poor are "characterized by chronic poverty and a history of exploitation" and tend to feed the inclination to distrust, "inhibiting the development of mutually beneficial cooperative relationships such as those that facilitate the job-matching process." The cooperation between job seekers and job holders is thwarted by a lack of mutual trust. Thus, low-skilled black job seekers are frequently unable to use their friendships, acquaintances, and family ties—their informal network—to gain employment. Black job holders were reluctant to refer their relatives and friends for jobs because they feared that their own reputations with employers could be jeopardized if the work of the people they recommended was substandard.

\* \* \*

## CONCLUSION

The disproportionate number of low-skilled black males in this country is one of the legacies of historical segregation and discrimination. However, aside from the effects of current segregation and discrimination, including those caused by employer bias, I highlighted a number of impersonal economic forces that have contributed to the incredibly high jobless rate of low-skilled black males and their correspondingly low incomes. These forces include the decreased relative demand for low-skilled labor caused by the computer revolution, the globalization of economic activity, the declining manufacturing sector, and the growth of service industries in which most of the new jobs for workers with limited skills and education are concentrated.

I noted that the shift to service industries has created a new set of problems for low-skilled black males because those industries feature jobs that require workers to serve and relate to consumers. Why are such requirements a problem for black men? Simply because employers believe that women and recent immigrants of both genders are better suited than black males, especially those with prison records, for such jobs. This image has been created partly by cultural shifts in national attitudes that reflected concerns about the growth of violence in the ghettos through the 1960s and '70s. In the eyes of many Americans, black males symbolized this violence. Cries for "law and order" resulted in a more punitive criminal justice system and a dramatic increase in black male incarceration.

Cultural arguments have been advanced to explain the social and economic woes of low-skilled black males, but the evidence is mixed. For example, a number of studies have associated black joblessness with high reservation wages, the lowest wages that a worker is willing to accept. Nonetheless, one of the more compelling studies found no significant relationship between the reservation wages of black men and the duration of joblessness. The findings in an important recent study, however, clearly suggest that chronic poverty and exploitation in poor black neighborhoods tend to feed inclinations to distrust. These cultural traits undermine the development of cooperative relationships that are so vital in informal job networks. Black workers in the inner city tend to be less willing to recommend friends and relatives for jobs that become available. Thus, the structural problem of employer job discrimination and the cultural inclination to distrust combine to severely handicap low-skilled, black male workers, especially those with prison records.

# 26

## Employing Parents Who Can't Make a Living*

FROM *The Moral Underground: How Ordinary Americans*
*Subvert an Unfair Economy*

### LISA DODSON

*The author's years of ethnographic fieldwork inform her examination of one of the dilemmas of the low-wage economy. It reveals the "human agency" we all have in broaching the rules and practices of large organizations in order to be true to our moral values. Worker resistance is one way to see what is happening here, as the ranks of the working poor grow and the wealth of the 1 percent swells. What does this mean for managers who feel pressure from above but an obligation to those below them? More broadly, how do we hold a society together—with the moral fabric early sociologists like Émile Durkheim thought was essential—in the face of such problematic rents in the social fabric?*

> Do we have any responsibility for what happens to them?
> —Ellen, a manager in a company that employed many low-wage workers, 2002

Ellen raised this question during a community conversation with other employers from a variety of businesses in the Milwaukee area. They had been talking about common problems they faced with "entry-level" employees. Together they came up with a list of inconveniences and disruptions that come with people "who are disorganized" and bring that disarray to the workplace. They are absent too much, come to work late, get calls that distract them, or leave early, and they are often just "not focused on the job." They said that there always seems to be some problem going on that complicates getting work done; their lives "just aren't organized" or "they don't have that work ethic."

Most of the employers at this meeting supervised workers who were mothers, and they spoke at length about "family problems." Eventually, their description of these troubles turned into a discussion about how inconvenient it was that these workers *had families at all*, because raising children is so time demanding. With some honesty, members of this group acknowledged that if you make $18,000—even $30,000—a year and have kids, "family life is going to create a problem" for those who employ you. Frequently, employers who discussed such issues were raising families themselves and had intimate knowledge of

---

*References and footnotes can be found in the original publication of Lisa Dodson's *The Moral Underground: How Ordinary Americans Subvert an Unfair Economy* (New York: The New Press, 2009). [*Editor's note*]

how much time—or in lieu of time, money—it takes to keep kids on a schedule; manage all their schooling, extracurricular, and emotional needs; and just keep a stable family routine. If you can't be home to make sure all this is taken care of and you can't buy substitute care, well, "it's just a mess," said one young manager, herself a mother of two.

On this day, the five men and two women started examining an idea that reemerged in employer conversations over the years that followed. They raised the notion that if you pay people wages that guarantee they can't really "keep things organized at home" and then, because of that, the flow of work is disrupted, well, is that only the employee's problem? Or is it just built into this labor market? And if it is wired into America's jobs, as Ellen, a middle-aged white woman, asked the others, "do we have any responsibility for what happens to them?" Over the course of hundreds of interviews and discussions this question was often at the center.

## INEQUALITY AT WORK

During the 1990s and into the first part of the first decade of the millennium, the United States saw a surge in wealth among the richest Americans. But that decade of economic gain was largely limited to those at the very top. Today, one in four U.S. workers earns less than $9 an hour—about $19,000 per year; 39 percent of the nation's children live in low-income households. The Economic Policy Institute reported that in 2005, minimum-wage workers earned only 32 percent of the average hourly wage. And African American and Latino families are much more likely to be poor or low-income and are less likely to have assets or home equity to offset low wages. Furthermore, the living standards for households in the middle relative to the previous decade have seen a decline, particularly "working-age households," those headed by at least one adult of working age. Thus the nation increasingly became divided into acutely different ways of life: millions of working families—the economic bottom third—that cannot make a living, millions in the middle clinging to their standard of living, and the very top economic tier of ever-greater wealth.

*This* America is not lost on ordinary people. As a Midwestern father of two who drives a "big rig" across states for a living said, "*That* money [gained by the richest people] came from somewhere, didn't it? It came out of my pocket and my kids' mouths." While most busy working people don't sit down to study the macro economy, many understand the rippling effects that shake their world.

At the university where I teach about poverty issues, I always ask students if they think that it *matters* if wealth increases for a few while others lose ground. For example, does it matter if that dad, driving his truck eighteen hours a day and seldom seeing his family, is able to buy less now than he could five years ago, when his days were shorter? Yes, of course it matters to him, his spouse, and his children. But does it matter beyond their private world? And always students point out that "maybe he's not driving as well" after eighteen hours. Thus, certainly with many jobs, there is a danger effect of low wages and overwork, causing damage that can spread. But a fair number of other students ponder harm beyond self-interest and even our public interest in avoiding a forty-ton truck slamming down the highway with a sleepy driver. Do losses to a family, probably an extended family, maybe even a community eroded by mounting poverty-induced problems—does all that matter in a larger way? Even assuming that we can avoid all those trucks, is *America* harmed when our workers and their families are ground down by an economy that has been funneling wealth to only a few?

There is always a range of responses to this challenge to the way the economy distributes its resources. Many young people particularly believe that we can do better, and they are ready to get on board. In every class that I have ever taught some students speak of wanting the chance to devote real time—years, not just term breaks—to working for another kind of democracy. They are part of a deep, still untapped well of commitment to an economically just society—not the only source by any means, but a very valuable one. As young people have pointed out, this is the world they will take on and they should make it a more equitable one.

Alongside that sentiment, some young people point out that there is also a sound business management argument that doing better by our lower-wage workers means that we all gain, because both the society *and* businesses do better. This "high road" argument counsels investing in better wages, decent schedules, and benefits for low-wage workers because, ultimately, this pays off for companies and the nation. Others also point out that investing in lower-income families will mean that millions of children are better prepared for school, are healthier, and have more stable families, all of which build the nation. Essentially, this is the argument that other nations use to invest public funding in families raising children and guarantee a minimum family income. So there is a defensible set of arguments—albeit not a winning one in the United States, but a compelling one—that we ought to pay people a decent income because it takes care of our people, serves productivity, and upholds the nation as a whole.

Yet, talking with employers, students, and many others, I found another public impulse largely left outside most economic debate. Sometimes middle-class people talked about a sense of obligation—a social obligation—at the core of their individual identity and their understanding of being part of this country. And many talked about their jobs—the work they do each day—as key to fulfilling the sense of being part of something bigger.

This idea of work was almost always explained to me personally, not as a philosophical stand. Middle-income people would describe relationships with others at work whose earnings were so low that *if* you decided to think about it, you knew there was no way they could support a family. Managers, business owners, and other professionals told me about getting to know certain people who seemed to be doing everything they possibly could, but that wasn't enough. And so all kinds of personal and family troubles would mount up, spill over, and eventually turn up at work. I heard about how when you hire, supervise, or even just work next to working-poor people—and, like it or not, get close to them—the harms they live with can start leaking into your world too.

A question would be raised: do we have some responsibility for people to whom we are connected through our jobs and economic role in their daily lives, and indirectly, the families that count on them? Do we have some obligation to others—not just our family, but those who are co-workers, neighbors, part of our society, and who are being diminished? I found nothing near a consensus. But a wide array of people diverse in background, religion, profession, race, ethnicity, and geography spoke of this reflection as part of their workaday lives, where they are connected to those who are working hard but living poor.

As a young mother who was a sales clerk in Denver in 2001 put it, "This took everything . . . just to keep this job. You know, you're a single mother, you're not born with a silver spoon in your mouth. . . . My child keeps calling me [while the child is home alone] and begging me to quit. . . . This is my responsibility."

## "I COULDN'T HELP FEELING LIKE I WAS ALMOST TO BLAME"

Bea was a fortyish white woman in a flowery blouse and pink slacks; she wore a square plastic badge that read BEA, FLOOR MANAGER. In 2004 she agreed to talk to me over a cup of coffee near the store where she was a manager of "about thirty-five" employees. It was a well-known low-end retail chain, a "big box." She had worked there for five years. She described the workforce as largely local people, and that meant "almost all white, mostly women, and with maybe high school diplomas, for the most part." Bea herself had lived in that general area of Maine all her life.

After many interviews, my questions had been honed for gathering information about how it is to manage a workforce and what if any conflicts arise. Bea quickly focused on the dilemma of "knowing too much" about the personal lives of the people who worked for her and how that contrasted poorly with what she understood as the model of how a professional manager behaves.

"Some of what they teach you in this business is to learn to think of them as part of the job . . . the way to try to get the job done. That means being friendly [to the workers], learning everybody's name; that's very important. But you keep people . . . it's important to keep a distance. You do that to keep it professional. But I think . . . it is also how to keep it clean."

"What does that mean?"

"It can get messy quickly if you start encouraging people to tell you what is going on, because they all have these problems. They have child care problems, problems with someone is sick . . . there's domestic abuse. They have a lot of crises. It's better not to ask because it opens the door to all that and then you have to tell them they have to stay late or you have to cut hours or someone wants a raise . . . all of that other comes up in your mind."

"And that makes it hard to . . . ?"

"That makes it hard to flip back into the business mode. I have to keep in mind my job is to serve the business, which is serving the public. We serve the public." This phrase, often repeated among the managers I met, seemed like a mooring, something to grab on to when human matters started to rock the boat.

"And . . . these people . . . aren't really . . . the public?"

"No, in business the public is the people who pay. . . . It isn't the public, really, it is the customer, the paying public."

"So . . . how does this work, for you?"

Bea's capitulation was immediate.

"Not very well really. I actually break my rules all the time. I know a lot more about a lot of people than I should. I get involved more than I should. I am that kind of person; my husband is always telling me that. Not that he really blames me; he does the same thing at [a local lumber business]. But, like before . . . when we were talking about what they pay . . . ?" Bea and I had discussed the company wages of $6–8 an hour. "I know that when someone asks for a raise, *they really need it*." At that point Bea started reciting the needs of many of these workers. Clearly she had annihilated her dictate to "keep it clean."

Here is just one of the stories that she told.

" 'Nancy' has two kids, her husband's on disability, and she couldn't buy her daughter a prom dress. This kid has worked very, very hard to graduate." Apparently Nancy's daughter had been employed throughout most of her high school years to help the family. "I'm like, 'How is it fair that this family can't buy her a prom dress?' "

Bea looked away, out the window. She disconnected from me for a few seconds as though recalling and applying manager rules. But it didn't work. When she looked back at me, she was teary. And she seemed a little angry too.

"I remember how much my prom meant to me. I don't know about where you live, but around here, it's a big deal. The girls . . . we all hope for a big wedding someday but your high school graduation, that's something you have earned. You want to look glamorous—not just good, but runway good. No way was Edy going to have the dress, the hair, the manicure. And I couldn't help but feeling that I was almost to blame, or partly. Nancy doesn't make what she deserves. . . . I am not saying they all work that hard, but . . . really, many do."

Bea was quiet for a while, and I began to think that was the end of the story. I tried to think of how to draw out what was being said, to hear more about this balance of roles and rules and Bea's conflict. She had started with her manager badge. But then she moved along a spectrum of moral thinking that I was to hear about many times. Bea put it simply. "Actually we sell prom dresses in this store. . . . Did you see them?" I had not.

Again Bea was silent and she looked at my tape recorder. I asked, "You want me to turn it off?"

Bea said, "No, that's okay . . . Well, let's just say . . . we made some mistakes with our prom dress orders last year. Too many were ordered, some went back. It got pretty confusing."

When Bea looked me in the eye this time, there were no tears and no apology.

I thought I knew my line. "So . . . Edy looked good at her prom?" Bea laughed, with a touch of gratitude I thought. "She knocked them dead," she said.

Over this and another conversation, Bea talked about how she could not make up for even a small part of what the workforce was lacking, because their wages meant they could not make their bills, never mind buy prom dresses, a fan for hot days, a child's plastic pool. So she found small ways to help out, to subsidize poor wages and try to make jobs move workers an inch closer to a decent life.

I thought a lot about Bea's story as I reread other employer interviews over the years that followed. In the short time I spent with her, she had quickly traveled the length of a moral domain I was trying to map out. I sat down with a woman who struck me as cautious and proud of her success as a manager, and who would offer me the straight and narrow supervisor line. She set it out and then trespassed all over it, trampled on the idea of "keeping her distance."

But more came out. She had been engaging in subtle acts of resistance from inside her small corner of the economy by subsidizing its extremely low wages. Bea told me that she wouldn't pass along cash to augment low wages. But she took advantage of everyday moments of abundant commerce—mixed-up orders, unsold goods, end-of-season returns, layaways that sometimes lay away forever. Bea was making her own little market adjustments to keep from feeling complicit with what she saw as unfair compensation. Sometimes, as she said, "you just have to level the playing field a little."

But what does that make Bea?

I didn't ask her if she was a thief. I would have loved to hear her words on that question, but it didn't feel right to ask. I knew that other people would say that her actions made her one. And they have when I have presented Bea's story in public talks. But I am glad to say others in the audiences have countered that idea, calling that pretense of moral simplicity "a sham." In community discussions, people have argued that all taking is not equal. It's one thing to steal for yourself when you don't need it; *that* most people view as morally illegitimate and corrupt. But most say it's something else to steal when your children are in real need, for example. Just about everyone I've ever talked with over the years—working- or middle-class—says that when it comes to a hungry child, there is no such thing as stealing.

Yet breaking the rules as Bea did, for someone who has a hungry child or hungers for a moment of triumph after years of work, like a prom dress for their daughter—this is a morally complicated place. Rule breaking in these cases was not seen merely as an act of survival. Rather, these transgressions were discussed as acts of conscience and finally acts of solidarity. And they mark what is usually kept invisible, how people will step out of a culture of utter self-interest, the market culture, and then intentionally turn against it.

## RESIGNING CONSCIENCE TO THOSE IN POWER

The tension between obedience to the rule of law and obedience to deeply held beliefs about justice and fairness is as old as America. Long before tea was dumped in Boston Harbor, people were weighing the necessity of disobedience in the face of tyranny. Long before an active underground railroad gave passage out of hell, Americans were reflecting on their moral identity in a nation in which slavery was legal, whether or not they were slave owners. In 1849, in his essay on civil disobedience, Henry David Thoreau asks, "Must the citizen ever for a moment, or in the least degree, resign his conscience to the legislator? Why has every man a conscience then?"

Why do we possess our own moral response to circumstances if we should remain unquestionably bound by the current rules and rulers? I heard Bea answer Thoreau's challenge. But Bea wasn't focused on the local or even larger legislative bodies; rather, Bea's act of conscience was directed at the center of power in American society today, corporate power.

The massive shift of the nation's wealth and power to an inestimably wealthy few *is* the American social landscape. But Bea thinks it's ugly. She sees the economy down in the small cracks of social life amid long hours and tiny paychecks and children left to languish, in the sense that they are not worth a dress or a chance. And she has rejected the idea that business should be free to treat workers as disposable and their families as collateral damage. More, she refused to resign her conscience to others' rules no matter how powerful they are. Rule by market interest, others like Bea have told me, requires that matters of conscience are supposed to be "left at the door" of the company, of the market system, regardless of the human harm you see. But I have heard it said, "I need to be able to sleep at night" or "I have to look at myself in the mirror." When the apparatus of business and voices of institutions are silent, sometimes looking into the face of a rule breaker lets you sleep at night.

Bea was one of the first of a wide spectrum of middle-income people who explained to me that being asked to collude with rules that are immoral and treat people unfairly eventually will lead to acts of disobedience.

Others agreed.

Andrew, the manager of the Midwestern fast food restaurant quoted in the introduction, had given more detail: "I don't think [the workers] are paid enough. They don't make enough to live. Yeah, so I do try to do what I can."

With a little nudging he continued. "Okay, I'll tell you that I add to their paychecks. I actually put them in for more hours, or what I can do more easily is put them in as working overtime and they get paid a higher rate. And sometimes I just pad them; that's all there is to it. I pad their paychecks because you can't live on what they make. I punch them out after they have left for a doctor's appointment or to take care [of a family member]. And I give them food to take home . . . I actually order extra and send some home with them." Andy referred to himself as a "Robin Hood" with a chuckle, but he meant it.

Margaret, a business owner in the Midwest, said, "I would like to share a story, where I decided it was a turning point in my life, being involved in management with single parents. . . . You can't go on about this being business as usual. I have changed how I supervise people."

Margaret described being geared up to confront a young mother who was absent from work, again, as she had been several times in recent weeks. But when she looked at the young woman who came into the store carrying two sick children despite the bitter cold, Margaret suddenly imagined what that young mother had to do each day just to come to work. She called it a turning point in her life.

Joaquin, a food company manager in the West, confessed, "I basically try to feed them most of the time. I let them make meals for after their shifts. And the truth is that some of the women, some of them are single moms, and when their kids come in after school, I feed them . . . pretty regularly, really. I don't think they can feed their families on what they make here. . . . I think part of my issue is that, how would I feel if my kids weren't getting enough to eat? I can't imagine that idea that I can't afford to feed them, so you know, here are these people and they don't make enough money to really feed their kids."

Joaquin seemed a little embarrassed because his voice got tight when he spoke of the idea of being unable to feed children. To Joaquin, watching parents working hard and going home without enough money to buy food for their kids is far worse than breaking the rules, funneling some food their way, and risking the consequences.

Judy, a health care business manager in the East, said quietly, "I have to say that most of these parents are doing everything . . . to be there [for their children] and at the same time do this job. They are doing everything, but, honestly, I don't see how they are supposed to. . . . I couldn't. So sometimes I just look the other way . . . when, you know, there's an issue about . . . something." She did not want to elaborate but repeated, "Sometimes you just look the other way."

If these four people found themselves sitting in a room together, they might have assumed that they had little in common. While they were all middle-class, their earnings ranged widely from the median to a high income. They were racially, culturally, and geographically diverse; one was in his early twenties while another was in her late fifties. I didn't ask about their religious or political views but heard opinions that suggested a wide range. They would seem truly different by any ordinary opinion poll measures. But I found that they have something profound in common. They all think that working people should earn a livelihood and be able to keep their families safe. That's the kind of society they want to live in. While they did not go into an elaborate discussion about fairness, each acted upon the idea of economic justice, even at some personal risk. And though these gestures are small, they are also disruptive; they send tiny shivers through a market system that relies on obedience to the rule of self-interest regardless of harm to others.

# 27

## Hanging Tongues: A Sociological Encounter with the Assembly Line

### WILLIAM E. THOMPSON

*This story may sound familiar to many of you: what looks like a well-paying job and an avenue to the good life turns out to be a mirage, a treadmill, and a trap. By the time we recognize the mirage for what it is, the alternative paths have become blocked by consumer debt and family commitments, creating obstacles that can prove nearly insurmountable.*

This qualitative sociological study analyzes the experience of working on a modern assembly line in a large beef plant. It explores and examines a special type of assembly line work which involves the slaughtering and processing of cattle into a variety of products intended for human consumption and other uses.

Working in the beef plant is "dirty work," not only in the literal sense of being drenched with perspiration and beef blood, but also in the figurative sense of performing a low-status, routine, and demeaning job. Although the work is honest and necessary in a society which consumes beef, slaughtering and butchering cattle is generally viewed as an undesirable and repugnant job. In that sense, workers at the beef plant share some of the same experiences as other workers in similarly regarded occupations (for example, ditch-diggers, garbage collectors, and other types of assembly line workers).

\* \* \*

### THE SETTING

The setting for the field work was a major beef processing plant in the Midwest. At the time of the study, the plant was the third largest branch of a corporation which operated ten such plants in the United States.

\* \* \*

The beef plant was organizationally separated into two divisions: Slaughter and Processing. This study focused on the Slaughter division in the area of the plant known as the *kill floor*. A dominant feature of the kill floor was the machinery of the assembly line itself. The line was composed of an overhead stainless steel rail which began at the slaughter chute and curved its way around every work station in the plant. Every work station contained specialized machinery for the job performed at that place on the line. Dangling from the rail were hundreds of stainless steel hooks pulled by a motorized chain. Virtually every part of the line and all of the implements (tubs, racks, knives, etc.) were made of stainless steel. The walls were covered with a ceramic tile and the floor was made of sealed cement. There were floor drains located at every work station, so that at the end of each work segment (at breaks, lunch, and shift's end) the entire kill floor could be hosed down and cleaned for the next work period.

Another dominant feature of the kill floor was the smell. Extremely difficult to describe, yet impossible to forget, this smell combined the smells of live cattle, manure, fresh beef blood, and internal organs and their contents. This smell not only permeated the interior of the plant, but was combined on the outside with the smell of smoke from various waste products being burned and could be smelled throughout much of the community. This smell contributed greatly to the general negative feelings about work at the beef plant, as it served as the most distinguishable symbol of the beef plant to the rest of the community. The single most often asked question of me during the research by those outside the beef plant was, "How do you stand the smell?" In typical line workers' fashion, I always responded, "What smell? All I smell at the beef plant is money."

\* \* \*

## METHOD

The method of this study was nine weeks of full-time participant observation as outlined by Schatzman and Strauss (1973) and Spradley (1979; 1980). To enter the setting, the researcher went through the standard application process for a summer job. No mention of the research intent was made, though it was made clear that I was a university sociology professor. After initial screening, a thorough physical examination, and a helpful reference from a former student and part-time employee of the plant, the author was hired to work on the *Offal* crew in the Slaughter division of the plant.

\* \* \*

## THE WORK

\* \* \* The line speed on the kill floor was 187. That means that 187 head of cattle were slaughtered per hour. At any particular work station, each worker was required to work at that speed. Thus, at my work station, in the period of one hour, 187 beef tongues were mechanically pulled from their hooks; dropped into a large tub filled with water; had to be taken from the tub and hung on a large stainless steel rack full of hooks; branded with a "hot brand" indicating they had been inspected by a USDA inspector; and then covered with a small plastic bag. The rack was taken to the cooler, replaced with an empty one, and the process began again.

It would be logical to assume that if a person worked at a steady, continuous pace of handling 187 tongues per hour, everything would go smoothly; not so. In addition to hanging, branding, and bagging tongues, the worker at that particular station also cleaned the racks and cleaned out a variety of empty stainless steel tubs used to hold hearts, kidneys, and other beef organs. Thus, in order to be free to clean the tubs when necessary, the "tongue-hanger" had to work at a slightly faster pace than the line moved. Then, upon returning from cleaning the tubs, the worker would be behind the line (*in a hole*) and had to work much faster to catch up with the line. Further, one fifteen-minute break and a thirty-minute lunch break were scheduled for an eight-hour shift. Before the "tongue-hanger" could leave his post for one of these, all tongues were required to be properly disposed of, all tubs washed and stored, and the work area cleaned.

My first two nights on the job, I discovered the consequences of working at the line speed (hanging, branding, and bagging each tongue as it feel in the tub). At the end of the work period when everybody else was leaving the work floor for break or lunch, I was furiously trying to wash all the tubs and clean the work area. Consequently, I missed the entire fifteen-minute break and had only about ten minutes for lunch. By observing other workers, I soon caught on to the system. Rather than attempting to work at a steady pace consistent with the line speed, the norm was to work sporadically at a very frenzied pace, actually running ahead of the line and plucking tongues from the hooks before they got to the station. With practice, I learned to hang two or three tongues at a time, perform all the required tasks, and then take an unscheduled two or three minute break until the line caught up with me. Near break and lunch everybody worked at a frantic pace, got ahead of the line, cleaned the work areas, and even managed to add a couple of minutes to the scheduled break or lunch.

Working ahead of the line seems to have served as more than merely a way of gaining a few minutes of extra break time. It also seemed to take on a symbolic meaning. The company controlled the speed of the line. Seemingly, that took all element of control over the work process away from the workers. * * * However, when the workers refused to work at line speed and actually worked faster than the line, they not only added a few minutes of relaxation from the work while the line caught up, but they symbolically regained an element of control over the pace of their own work.

* * *

## COPING

One of the difficulties of work at the beef plant was coping with three aspects of the work: monotony, danger, and dehumanization. While individual workers undoubtedly coped in a variety of ways, some distinguishable patterns emerged.

### Monotony

The monotony of the line was almost unbearable. At my work station, a worker would hang, brand, and bag between 1,350 and 1,500 beef tongues in an eight-hour shift. With the exception of the scheduled fifteen-minute break and a thirty-minute lunch period (and sporadic brief gaps in the line), the work was mundane, routine, and continuous. As in most assembly line work, one inevitably drifted into daydreams (e.g., Garson, 1975; King, 1978; Linhart, 1981). It was not unusual to look up or down the line and see workers at various stations singing to themselves, tapping their feet to imaginary music, or carrying on conversations with themselves. I found that I could work with virtually no attention paid to the job, with my hands and arms almost automatically performing their tasks. In the meantime, my mind was free to wander over a variety of topics, including taking mental notes. In visiting with other workers, I found that daydreaming was the norm. Some would think about their families, while others fantasized about sexual escapades, fishing, or anything unrelated to the job. One individual who was rebuilding an antique car at home in his spare time would meticulously mentally rehearse the procedures he was going to perform on the car the next day.

Daydreaming was not inconsequential, however. During these periods, items were most likely to be dropped, jobs improperly performed, and accidents incurred. Inattention to detail around moving equipment, stainless steel hooks, and sharp knives invariably leads to dangerous consequences. Although I heard rumors of drug use to help fight the monotony, I never saw any workers take any drugs nor saw any drugs in any workers' possession. It is certainly conceivable that some workers might have taken something to help them escape the reality of the line, but the nature of the work demanded enough attention that such a practice could be ominous.

### Danger

The danger of working in the beef plant was well known. Safety was top priority (at least in theory) and management took pride in the fact that only three employee on-the-job deaths had occurred in twelve years. Although deaths were uncommon, serious injuries were not. The beef plant employed over 1,800 people. Approximately three-fourths of those employed had jobs which demanded the use of a knife honed to razor-sharpness. Despite the use of wire-mesh aprons and gloves, serious cuts were almost a daily occurrence. Since workers constantly handled beef blood, danger of infection was ever present. As one walked along the assembly line, a wide assortment of bandages on fingers, hands, arms, necks, and faces could always be seen.

In addition to the problem of cuts, workers who cut meat continuously sometimes suffered muscle and ligament damage to their fingers and hands. In one severe case, I was told of a woman who worked in processing for several years who had to wear splints on her fingers while away from the job to hold them straight. Otherwise, the muscles in her hand would constrict her fingers into the grip position, as if holding a knife.

\* \* \*

When I spoke with fellow workers about the dangers of working in the plant, I noticed interesting defense mechanisms. \* \* \* After a serious accident, or when telling about an accident or death which occurred in years past, the workers would almost immediately dissociate themselves from the event and its victim. Workers tended to view those who suffered major accidents or death on the job in much the same way that nonvictims of crime often view crime victims as either partially responsible for the event, or at least as very different from themselves (Barlow, 1981). "Only a part-timer," "stupid," "careless" or something similar was used, seemingly to reassure the worker describing the accident that it could not happen to him. The reality of the situation was that virtually all the jobs on the kill floor were dangerous, and any worker could have experienced a serious injury at any time.

\* \* \*

### Dehumanization

Perhaps the most devastating aspect of working at the beef plant (worse than the monotony and the danger) was the dehumanizing and demeaning elements of the job. In a sense, the assembly line worker became a part of the assembly line. The assembly line is not a tool used by the worker, but a machine which controls him/her. A tool can only be productive in the hands of somebody skilled in its use, and hence becomes an extension of the person using it. A machine, on the other hand, performs specific tasks, thus its operator becomes an extension of it in the production process. \* \* \* When workers are viewed as mere extensions of the machines with which they work, their human needs become secondary in importance to the smooth mechanical functioning of the production process. In a bureaucratic structure, when "human needs collide with systems needs the individual suffers" (Hummel, 1977: 65).

Workers on the assembly line are seen as interchangeable as the parts of the product on the line itself. An example of one worker's perception of this phenomenon at the beef plant was demonstrated the day after a fatal accident occurred. I asked the men in our crew what the company did in the case of an employee death (I wondered if there was a fund for flowers, or if the shift was given time off to go to the funeral, etc.). One worker's response was: "They drag off the body, take the hard hat and boots and check 'em out to some other poor sucker, and throw him in the guy's place." While employee death on the job was not viewed quite that coldly by the company, the statement fairly accurately summarized the overall result of a fatal accident, and importance of any individual worker to the overall operation of the production process. If accurately summarized the workers' perceptions about management's attitudes toward them.

\* \* \*

### Sabotage

It is fairly common knowledge that assemblyline work situations often led to employee sabotage or destruction of the product or equipment used in the production process (Garson, 1975; Balzer, 1976; Shostak, 1980). This is the classic experience of alienation as described by Marx (1964a, b). \* \* \* At the beef plant I quickly learned that there was an art to effective sabotage. Subtlety appeared to be the key. "The art lies in sabotaging in a way that is not immediately discovered," as a Ford worker put it (King, 1978:202). This seemed to hold true at the beef plant as well.

\* \* \*

The greatest factor influencing the handling of beef plant products was its status as a food product intended for human consumption. \* \* \* Though not an explicitly altruistic group, the workers realized that the product would be consumed by people (even family, relatives, and friends), so consequently, they rarely did anything to actually contaminate the product.

Despite formal norms against sabotage, some did occur. It was not uncommon for workers to deliberately cut chunks out of pieces of meat for no reason (or for throwing at other employees). While regulations required that anything that touched the floor had to be put in tubs marked "inedible," the informal procedural norms were otherwise. When something was dropped, one usually looked around to see if an inspector or foreman noticed. If not, the item was quickly picked up and put back on the line.

Several explanations might be offered for this type of occurrence. First, since the company utilized a profit-sharing plan, when workers damaged the product, or had to throw edible pieces into inedible tubs (which sold for pet food at much lower prices), profits were decreased. A decrease in profits to the company ultimately led to decreased dividend checks to employees. Consequently, workers were fairly careful not to actually ruin anything. Second, when something was dropped or mishandled and had to be rerouted to "inedible," it was more time-consuming than if the product had been handled properly and kept on the regular line. In other words, if no inspector noticed, it was easier to let it go through on the line. There was a third, and seemingly more meaningful, explanation for this behavior, however. It was against the rules to do it, it was a challenge to do it, and thus it was fun to do it.

The workers practically made a game out of doing forbidden things simply to see if they could get away with it. * * * New workers were routinely socialized into the subtle art of rulebreaking as approved by the line workers. At my particular work station, it was a fairly common practice for other workers who were covered with beef blood to come over to the tub of swirling water designed to clean the tongues, and as soon as the inspector looked away, wash their hands, arms, and knives in the tub. This procedure was strictly forbidden by the rules. If witnessed by a foreman or inspector, the tub had to be emptied, cleaned, and refilled, and all the tongues in the tub at the time had to be put in the "inedible" tub. All of that would be a time-consuming and costly procedure, yet the workers seemed to absolutely delight in successfully pulling off the act. As Balzer (1976:90) indicates:

> Since a worker often feels that much if not all of what he does is done in places designated by the company, under company control, finding ways to express personal freedom from this institutional regimentation is important.

Thus, artful sabotage served as a symbolic way in which the workers could express a sense of individuality, and hence, self-worth.

## THE FINANCIAL TRAP

Given the preceding description and analysis for work at the beef plant, why did people work at such jobs? Obviously, there are a multitude of plausible answers to that question. Without doubt, however, the key is money. The current economic situation, the lack of steady employment opportunities (especially for the untrained and poorly educated), combined with the fact that the beef plant's starting wage exceeded the minimum wage by approximately $5.50 per hour emerge as the most important reasons people went to work there.

Despite the high hourly wage and fringe benefits, however, the monotony, danger, and hard physical work drove many workers away in less than a week. During my study, I observed much worker turnover. Those who stayed displayed an interesting pattern which helps explain why they did not leave. Every member of my work crew answered similarly my questions about why they stayed at the beef plant. Each of them took the job directly after high school, because it was the highest-paying job available. Each of them had intended to work through the summer and then look for a better job in the fall. During that first summer on the job they fell victim to what I label the "financial trap."

The "financial trap" was a spending pattern which demanded the constant weekly income provided by the beef plant job. This scenario was first told to me by an employee who had worked at the plant for over nine years. He began the week after his high school graduation, intending only to work that summer in order to earn enough money to attend college in the fall. After about four weeks' work he purchased a new car. He figured he could pay off the car that summer and still save enough money for tuition. Shortly after the car purchase, he added a new stereo sound system to his debt; next came a motorcycle; then the decision to postpone school for one year in order to continue working at the beef plant and pay off his debts. A few months later he married; within a year purchased a house; had a child; and bought another new car. Nine years later, he was still working at the beef plant, hated every minute of it, but in his own words "could not afford to quit." His case was not unique. Over and over again, I heard stories about the same process of falling into the "financial trap." The youngest and newest of our crew had just graduated high school and took the job for the summer in order to earn enough money to attend welding school the following fall. During my brief tenure at the beef plant, he purchased a new motorcycle, a new stereo, and a house trailer. When I left, he told me he had decided to postpone welding school for one year in order "to get everything paid for." I saw the financial trap closing in on him fast; he did too.

\* \* \*

## SUMMARY AND CONCLUSIONS

There are at least three interwoven phenomena in this study which deserve further comment and research.

First is the subtle sense of unity which existed among the line workers. \* \* \* The line both symbolically and literally linked every job, and consequently every worker, to each other. \* \* \* A system of "uncooperative teamwork" seemed to combine simultaneously a feeling of "one-for-all, all-for-one, and every man for himself." Once a line worker made it past the first three or four days on the job which "weeded out" many new workers, his status as a *beefer* was assured and the sense of unity was felt as much by the worker of nine weeks as it was by the veteran of nine years. Because the workers maintained largely secondary relationships, this feeling of unification is not the same as the unity typically found on athletic teams, in fraternities, or among various primary groups. Yet it was a significant social force which bound the workers together and provided a sense of meaning and worth. Although their occupation might not be highly respected by outsiders, they derived mutual self-respect from their sense of belonging.

A second important phenomenon was the various coping methods \* \* \* the beef plant line workers developed and practiced \* \* \* for retaining their humanness. Daydreaming, horseplay and occasional sabotage protected their sense of self. Further, the prevailing attitude among workers that it was "us" against "them" served as a reminder that, while the nature of the job might demand subjugation to bosses, machines, and even beef parts, they were still human beings.

* * *

A third significant finding was that consumer spending patterns among the beefers seemed to "seal their fate" and make leaving the beef plant almost impossible. A reasonable interpretation of the spending patterns of the beefers is that having a high-income/low-status job encourages a person to consume conspicuously. The prevailing attitude seemed to be "I may not have a nice job, but I have a nice home, a nice car, etc." This conspicuous consumption enabled workers to take indirect pride in their occupations. One of the ways of overcoming drudgery and humiliation on the job was to surround oneself with as many desirable material things as possible off the job. These items (cars, boats, motorcycles, etc.) became tangible rewards for the sacrifices endured at work.

The problem, of course, is that the possession of these expensive items required the continual income of a substantial paycheck which most of these men could only obtain by staying at the beef plant. These spending patterns were further complicated by the fact that they were seemingly "contagious." Workers talked to each other on breaks about recent purchases, thus reinforcing the norm of immediate gratification. A common activity of a group of workers on break or lunch was to run to the parking lot to see a fellow worker's new truck, van, car or motorcycle. Even the seemingly more financially conservative were usually caught up in this activity and often could not wait to display their own latest acquisitions. Ironically, as the workers cursed their jobs, these expensive possessions virtually destroyed any chance of leaving them.

Working at the beef plant was indeed "dirty work." It was monotonous, difficult, dangerous, and demeaning. Despite this, the workers at the beef plant worked hard to fulfill employer expectations in order to obtain financial rewards. Through a variety of symbolic techniques, they managed to overcome the many negative aspects of their work and maintain a sense of self-respect about how they earned their living.

## REFERENCES

Balzer, Richard (1976). *Clockwork: Life In and Outside an American Factory.* Garden City, NY: Doubleday.

Barlow, Hugh (1981). *Introduction to Criminology.* 2d ed. Boston: Little, Brown.

Garson, Barbara (1975). *All the Livelong Day: The Meaning and Demeaning of Routine Work.* Garden City, NY: Doubleday.

Hummel, Ralph P. (1977). *The Bureaucratic Experience.* New York: St. Martin's Press.

King, Rick (1978). "In the sanding booth at Ford." Pp. 199–205 in John and Erna Perry (eds.), *Social Problems in Today's World.* Boston: Little, Brown.

Linhart, Robert (translated by Margaret Crosland) (1981). *The Assembly Line*. Amherst: University of Massachusetts Press.

Marx, Karl (1964a). *Economic and Philosophical Manuscripts of 1844*. New York: International Publishing (1844).

_____. (1964b). *The Communist Manifesto*. New York: Washington Square Press (1848).

Schatzman, Leonard, and Anselm L. Strauss (1973). *Field Research*. Englewood Cliffs, NJ: Prentice-Hall.

Shostak, Arthur (1980). *Blue Collar Stress*. Reading, MA: Addison-Wesley.

Spradley, James P. (1979). *The Ethnographic Interview*. New York: Holt, Rinehart & Winston.

_____. (1980). *Participant Observation*. New York: Holt, Rinehart & Winston.

# 28

## "Getting" and "Making" a Tip

FROM *Dishing It Out: Power and Resistance among*
*Waitresses in a New Jersey Restaurant*

### GRETA FOFF PAULES

*Waitresses, like many people who provide a service, are highly vulnerable to the*
*whims of the customers who, by their tips, decide their daily earnings. Waitresses*
*structure their encounters with more care than most of us realize. The reason for*
*this is the need to have some power over their work and their livelihood. For those of*
*you who have never been a waiter or waitress, this participant observation study*
*may forever change the way you think about being served and treat those who serve*
*you.*

> The waitress can't help feeling a sense of personal failure and public censure
> when she is "stiffed."
>
> *—William F. Whyte,* "When Workers and Customers Meet"

> They're rude, they're ignorant, they're obnoxious, they're inconsiderate.... Half
> these people don't deserve to come out and eat, let alone try and tip a waitress.
>
> *—Route [Restaurant] waitress*

The financial and emotional hazards inherent in the tipping system have
drawn attention from sociologists, and more recently anthropologists, concerned with the study of work. In general these researchers have concluded
that workers who receive gratuities exercise little control over the material outcome of tipping and less over its symbolic implications.

\* \* \*

## MAKING A TIP AT ROUTE [RESTAURANT]

A common feature of past research is that the worker's control over the tipping system is evaluated in terms of her efforts to con, coerce, compel, or otherwise manipulate a customer into relinquishing a bigger tip. Because these
efforts have for the most part proven futile, the worker has been seen as having little defense against the financial vicissitudes of the tipping system. What
these studies have overlooked is that an employee can increase her tip income
by controlling the number as well as the size of tips she receives. This over-
sight has arisen from the tendency of researchers to concentrate narrowly on

the relationship between server and served, while failing to take into account the broader organizational context in which this relationship takes place.

Like service workers observed in earlier studies, waitresses at Route strive to boost the amount of individual gratuities by rendering special services and being especially friendly. As one waitress put it, "I'll sell you the world if you're in my station." In general though, waitresses at Route Restaurant seek to boost their tip income, not by increasing the amount of individual gratuities, but by increasing the number of customers they serve. They accomplish this (a) by securing the largest or busiest stations and working the most lucrative shifts; (b) by "turning" their tables quickly; and (c) by controlling the flow of customers within the restaurant.

Technically, stations at Route are assigned on a rotating basis so that all waitresses, including rookies, work fast and slow stations equally. Station assignments are listed on the work schedule that is posted in the office window where it can be examined by all workers on all shifts, precluding the possibility of blatant favoritism or discrimination. Yet a number of methods exist whereby experienced waitresses are able to circumvent the formal rotation system and secure the more lucrative stations for themselves. A waitress can trade assignments with a rookie who is uncertain of her ability to handle a fast station; she can volunteer to take over a large station when a *call-out* necessitates reorganization of station assignments; or she can establish herself as the only waitress capable of handling a particularly large or chaotic station. Changes in station assignments tend not to be formally recorded, so inconsistencies in the rotation system often do not show up on the schedule. Waitresses on the same shift may notice of course that a co-worker has managed to avoid an especially slow station for many days, or has somehow ended up in the busiest station two weekends in a row, but the waitresses' code of noninterference * * * inhibits them from openly objecting to such irregularities.

A waitress can also increase her tip income by working the more lucrative shifts. Because day is the busiest and therefore most profitable shift at Route, it attracts experienced, professional waitresses who are most concerned and best able to maximize their tip earnings. There are exceptions; some competent, senior-ranking waitresses are unable to work during the day due to time constraints of family or second jobs. Others choose not to work during the day despite the potential monetary rewards, because they are unwilling to endure the intensely competitive atmosphere for which day shift is infamous.

The acutely competitive environment that characterizes day shift arises from the aggregate striving of each waitress to maximize her tip income by serving the greatest possible number of customers. Two strategies are enlisted to this end. First, each waitress attempts to *turn* her tables as quickly as possible. Briefly stated, this means she takes the order, delivers the food, clears and resets a table, and begins serving the next party as rapidly as customer lingering and the speed of the kitchen allow. A seven-year veteran of Route describes the strategy and its rewards:

> What I do is I prebus my tables. When the people get up and go all I got is glasses
> and cups, pull off, wipe, set, and I do the table turnover. But see that's from day
> shift. See the girls on graveyard . . . don't understand the more times you turn
> that table the more money you make. You could have three tables and still make
> a hundred dollars. If you turn them tables.

As the waitress indicates, a large part of turning tables involves getting the table cleared and set for the next customer. During a rush, swing and grave waitresses tend to leave dirty tables standing, partly because they are less experienced and therefore less efficient, partly to avoid being given parties, or *sat,* when they are already behind. In contrast, day waitresses assign high priority to keeping their tables cleared and ready for customers. The difference in method reflects increased skill and growing awareness of and concern with money-making strategies.

A waitress can further increase her customer count by controlling the flow of customers within the restaurant. Ideally the hostess or manager running the front house rotates customers among stations, just as stations are rotated among waitresses. Each waitress is given, or *sat,* one party at a time in turn so that all waitresses have comparable customer counts at the close of a shift. When no hostess is on duty, or both she and the manager are detained and customers are waiting to be seated, waitresses will typically seat incoming parties.

Whether or not a formal hostess is on duty, day waitresses are notorious for bypassing the rotation system by racing to the door and directing incoming customers to their own tables. A sense of the urgency with which this strategy is pursued is conveyed in the comment of one five-year veteran, "They'll run you down to get that person at the door, to seat them in their station." The competition for customers is so intense during the day that some waitresses claim they cannot afford to leave the floor (even to use the restroom) lest they return to find a co-worker's station filled at their expense. "In the daytime, honey," remarks an eight-year Route waitress, "in the daytime it's like pulling teeth. You got to stay on the floor to survive. To survive." It is in part because they do not want to lose customers and tips to their co-workers that waitresses do not take formal breaks. Instead, they rest and eat between waiting tables or during lulls in business, returning to the floor intermittently to check on parties in progress and seat customers in their stations.

The fast pace and chaotic nature of restaurant work provide a cover for the waitress's aggressive pursuit of customers, since it is difficult for other servers to monitor closely the allocation of parties in the bustle and confusion of a rush. Still, it is not uncommon for waitresses to grumble to management and co-workers if they notice an obvious imbalance in customer distribution. Here again, the waitress refrains from directly criticizing her fellow servers, voicing her displeasure by commenting on the paucity of customers in her own station, rather than the overabundance of customers in the stations of certain co-waitresses. In response to these grumblings, other waitresses may moderate somewhat their efforts to appropriate new parties, and management may make a special effort to seat the disgruntled server favorably.

A waitress can also exert pressure on the manager or hostess to keep her station filled. She may, for instance, threaten to leave if she is not seated enough customers.

> I said, "Innes [a manager], I'm in [station] one and two. If one and two is not filled at all times from now until three, I'm getting my coat, my pocketbook, and I'm leaving." And one and two was filled, and I made ninety-five dollars.

Alternatively, she can make it more convenient for the manager or hostess to seat her rather than her co-workers, either by keeping her tables open (as described), or by taking extra tables. If customers are waiting to be seated, a waitress may offer to pick up parties in a station that is closed or, occasionally, to pick up parties in another waitress's station. In attempting either strategy, but especially the latter, the waitress must be adept not only at waiting tables, but in interpersonal restaurant politics. Autonomy and possession are of central concern to waitresses, and a waitress who offers to pick up tables outside her station must select her words carefully if she is to avoid being accused of invading her co-workers' territory. Accordingly, she may choose to present her bid for extra parties as an offer to help—the manager, another waitress, the restaurant, customers—rather than as a request.

The waitress who seeks to increase her tip income by maximizing the number of customers she serves may endeavor to cut her losses by refusing to serve parties that have stiffed her in the past. If she is a low-ranking waitress, her refusal is likely to be overturned by the manager. If she is an experienced and valuable waitress, the manager may ask someone else to take the party, assure the waitress he will take care of her (that is, pad the bill and give her the difference), or even pick up the party himself. Though the practice is far from common, a waitress may go so far as to demand a tip from a customer who has been known to stiff in the past.

> This party of two guys come in and they order thirty to forty dollars worth of food . . . and they stiff us. Every time. So Kaddie told them, "If you don't tip us, we're not going to wait on you." They said, "We'll tip you." So Kaddie waited on them, and they tipped her. The next night they came in, I waited on them and they didn't tip me. The third time they came in [the manager] put them in my station and I told [the manager] straight up, "I'm not waiting on them . . ." So he made Hailey pick them up. And they stiffed Hailey. So when they came in the next night . . . [they] said, "Are you going to give us a table?" I said, "You going to tip me? I'm not going to wait on you. You got all that money, you sell all that crack on the streets and you come here and you can't even leave me a couple bucks?" . . . So they left me a dollar. So when they come in Tuesday night, I'm telling them a dollar ain't enough.

The tactics employed by waitresses, and particularly day-shift waitresses, to increase their customer count and thereby boost their tip earnings have earned them a resounding notoriety among their less competitive co-workers. Day (and some swing) waitresses are described as "money hungry," "sneaky little bitches," "self-centered," "aggressive," "backstabbing bitches," and "cutthroats over tables." The following remarks of two Route waitresses, however, indicate that those who employ these tactics see them as defensive, not aggressive measures. A sense of the waitress's preoccupation with autonomy and with protecting what is hers also emerges from these comments.

> You have to be like that. Because if you don't be like that, people step on you. You know, like as far as getting customers. I mean, you know, I'm sorry everybody says I'm greedy. I guess that's why I've survived this long at Route. Cause I am greedy. . . . *I want what's mine,* and if it comes down to me cleaning your table or my table, I'm going to clean my table. Because see I went through all that stage where I would do your table. To be fair. And you would walk home with seventy dollars, and I'd have twenty-five, cause I was being fair all night. (emphasis added)
>
> If the customer comes in the door and I'm there getting that door, don't expect me to cover your backside while you in the back smoking a cigarette and I'm here working for myself. You not out there working for me. . . . When I go to the door and get the customers, when I keep my tables clean and your tables are dirty, and you wonder why you only got one person . . . then that's just tough shit. . . . You're damn right my station is filled. *I'm not here for you.* (emphasis added)

Whether the waitress who keeps her station filled with customers is acting aggressively or defensively, her tactics are effective. It is commonly accepted that determined day waitresses make better money than less competitive co-workers even when working swing or grave. Moreover Nera, the waitress most infamous for her relentless use of "money-hungry" tactics, is at the same time most famous for her consistently high daily takes. While other waitresses jingle change in their aprons, Nera is forced to store wads of bills in her shoes and in paper bags to prevent tips from overflowing her pockets. She claims to make a minimum of five hundred dollars a week in tip earnings; her record for one day's work exceeds two hundred dollars and is undoubtedly the record for the restaurant.

## INVERTING THE SYMBOLISM OF TIPPING

It may already be apparent that the waitress views the customer—not as a master to pamper and appease—but as substance to be processed as quickly and in as large a quantity as possible. The difference in perspective is expressed in the objectifying terminology of waitresses: a customer or party is referred to as a *table,* or by table number, as *table five* or simply *five;* serving successive parties at a table is referred to as *turning the table;* taking an order is also known as *picking up a table;* and to serve water, coffee, or other beverages is to *water, coffee*, or *beverage* a table, number, or customer. Even personal acquaintances assume the status of inanimate matter, or tip-bearing plants, in the language of the server:

> I got my fifth-grade teacher [as a customer] one time. . . . I kept her coffeed. I kept her boyfriend coked all night. Sodaed. . . . And I kept them filled up.

If the customer is perceived as material that is processed, the goal of this processing is the production or extraction of a finished product: the tip. This image too is conveyed in the language of the floor. A waitress may comment that she "got a good tip" or "gets good tips," but she is more likely to say that she "made" or "makes good tips." She may also say that she "got five bucks out of" a customer, or complain that some customers "don't want to give up on" their money. She may accuse a waitress who stays over into her shift of "tapping on" her money, or warn an aspiring waitress against family restaurants on the grounds that "there's no money in there." In all these comments (and all are actual), the waitress might as easily be talking about mining for coal or drilling for oil as serving customers.

Predictably, the waitress's view of the customer as substance to be processed influences her perception of the meaning of tips, and especially substandard tips. At Route, low tips and stiffs are not interpreted as a negative reflection on the waitress's personal qualities or social status. Rather, they are felt to reveal the refractory nature or poor quality of the raw material from which the tip is extracted, produced, or fashioned. In less metaphorical terms, a low tip or stiff is thought to reflect the negative qualities and low status of the customer who is too cheap, too poor, too ignorant, or too coarse to leave an appropriate gratuity. In this context, it is interesting to note that *stiff,* the term used in restaurants to refer to incidents of nontipping or to someone who does not tip, has also been used to refer to a wastrel or penniless man, * * * a hobo, tramp, vagabond, deadbeat, and a moocher.

* * *

Evidence that waitresses assign blame for poor tips to the tipper is found in their reaction to being undertipped or stiffed. Rather than breaking down in tears and lamenting her "personal failure," the Route waitress responds to a stiff by announcing the event to her co-workers and managers in a tone of angry disbelief. Co-workers and managers echo the waitress's indignation and typically ask her to identify the party (by table number and physical description), or if she has already done so, to be more specific. This identification is crucial for it allows sympathizers to join the waitress in analyzing the cause of the stiff, which is assumed a priori to arise from some shortcoming of the party, not the waitress. The waitress and her co-workers may conclude that the customers in question were rude, troublemakers, or bums, or they may explain their behavior by identifying them as members of a particular category of customers. It might be revealed for instance, that the offending party was a church group: church groups are invariably tightfisted. It might be resolved that the offenders were senior citizens, Southerners, or business people: all well-known cheapskates. If the customers were European, the stiff will be attributed to ignorance of the American tipping system; if they were young, to immaturity; if they had children, to lack of funds.

These classifications and their attendant explanations are neither fixed nor trustworthy. New categories are invented to explain otherwise puzzling incidents, and all categories are subject to exception. Though undependable as predictive devices, customer typologies serve a crucial function: they divert blame for stiffs and low tips from the waitress to the characteristics of the customer. It is for this reason that it is "important" for workers to distinguish between different categories of customers, despite the fact that such distinctions are based on "unreliable verbal and appearance clues." In fact, it is precisely the unreliability, or more appropriately the flexibility, or customer typologies that makes them valuable to waitresses. When categories can be constructed and dissolved on demand, there is no danger that an incident will fall outside the existing system of classification and hence be inexplicable.

While waitresses view the customer as something to be processed and the tip as the product of this processing, they are aware that the public does not share their understanding of the waitress-diner-tip relationship. Waitresses at Route recognize that many customers perceive them as needy creatures willing to commit great feats of service and absorb high doses of abuse in their anxiety to secure a favorable gratuity or protect their jobs. They are also aware that some customers leave small tips with the intent to insult the server and that others undertip on the assumption that for a Route waitress even fifty cents will be appreciated. One waitress indicated that prior to being employed in a restaurant, she herself subscribed to the stereotype of the down-and-out waitress "because you see stuff on television, you see these wives or single ladies who waitress and they live in slummy apartments or slummy houses and they dress in rags." It is these images of neediness and desperation, which run so strongly against the waitress's perception of herself and her position, that she attacks when strained relations erupt into open conflict.

> Five rowdy black guys walked in the door and they went to seat themselves at table seven. I said, "Excuse me. You all got to wait to be seated." "We ain't got to do *shit*. We here to eat. . . ." So they went and sat down. And I turned around and just looked at them. And they said, "Well, I hope you ain't our waitress, cause you blew your tip. Cause you ain't getting nothing from us." And I turned around and I said, "You need it more than I do, baby."

This waitress's desire to confront the customer's assumption of her destitution is widely shared among service workers whose status as tipped employees marks them as needy in the eyes of their customers. [One study] reports that among cabdrivers "a forever repeated story is of the annoyed driver, who, after a grueling trip with a Lady Shopper, hands the coin back, telling her, 'Lady, keep your lousy dime. You need it more than I do.'" [Another study reports] a hotel waitress's claim that "if she had served a large family with children for one or two weeks, and then was given a 10p[ence] piece, she would give the money back, saying, 'It's all right, thank you, I've got enough change for my bus fare home.'" In an incident I observed (not at Route), a waitress followed two male customers out of a restaurant calling, "Excuse me! You forgot this!" and holding up the coins they had left as a tip. The customers appeared embarrassed, motioned for her to keep the money, and continued down the sidewalk. The waitress, now standing in the outdoor seating area of the restaurant and observed by curious diners, threw the money after the retreating men and returned to her work. Episodes such as these allow the worker to repudiate openly the evaluation of her financial status that is implied in an offensively small gratuity, and permit her to articulate her own understanding of what a small tip says and about whom. If customers can only afford to leave a dime, or feel a 10p piece is adequate compensation for two weeks' service, they must be very hard up or very ignorant indeed.

In the following incident the waitress interjects a denial of her neediness into an altercation that is not related to tipping, demonstrating that the customer's perception of her financial status is a prominent and persistent concern for her.

> She [a customer] wanted a California Burger with mayonnaise. And when I got the mayonnaise, the mayonnaise had a little brown on it. . . . So this girl said to me, she said, "What the fuck is this you giving me?" And I turned around, I thought, "Maybe she's talking to somebody else in the booth with her." And I turned around and I said, "Excuse me?" She said, "You hear what I said, I said, 'What the fuck are you giving me?'" And I turned around, I said, "I don't know if you're referring your information to *me*," I said, "but if you're referring your information to *me*," I said, "I don't *need* your bullshit." I said, "I'm not going to even take it. . . . Furthermore, I could care less if you eat or *don't* eat. . . . And you see this?" And I took her check and I ripped it apart. . . . And I took the California Burger and I says, "You don't have a problem anymore now, right?" She went up to the manager. And she says, "That black waitress"—I says, "Oh. By the way, what is my name? I don't have a name, [using the words] 'that black waitress.' . . . My name happens to be Nera. . . . That's N-E-R-A. . . . And I don't need your bullshit, sweetheart. . . . People like you I can walk on, because you don't know how to talk to human beings." And I said, "I don't need you. I don't need your quarters. I don't need your nickels. I don't need your dimes. So if you want service, be my guest. Don't you *ever* sit in my station, cause I won't wait on you." The manager said, "Nera, please. Would you wait in the back?" I said, "No. I don't take back seats no more for nobody."

In each of these cases, the waitress challenges the customer's definition of the relationship in which tipping occurs. By speaking out, by confronting the customer, she demonstrates that she is not subservient or in fear of losing her job; that she is not compelled by financial need or a sense of social hierarchy to accept abuse from customers; that she does not, in Nera's words, "take back seats no more for nobody." At the same time, she reverses the symbolic force of the low tip, converting a statement on her social status or work skills into a statement on the tipper's cheapness or lack of savoir faire.

# 29

## Upward Mobility through Sport?

### D. STANLEY EITZEN

*You can trace the history of twentieth-century immigration in the United States by reading the list of boxers who held the title of Champion of the World. The names of Irish, Jewish, Italian, African American, and Latino boxers record the stirrings of upward mobility for those who shared the boxers' ethnicity or nationality. But the lives of the boxers themselves were often far less successful than a championship title would indicate. And what of sports more generally? In true sociological fashion, Stanley Eitzen shows us that sports may do far less in advancing the life chances of young people than is often assumed.*

Typically, Americans believe that sport is a path to upward social mobility. This belief is based on the obvious examples we see as poor boys and men (rarely girls and women) from rural and urban areas, whether white or black, sometimes skyrocket to fame and fortune through success in sports. Sometimes the financial reward has been astounding, such as the high pay that some African American athletes received in recent years. In 1997 Tracy McGrady, an NBA-bound high school star, bypassed college, signed a $12 million deal over 6 years with Adidas. Golfer Tiger Woods in his first year as a professional made $6.82 million in winnings (U.S. and worldwide) and appearance fees plus signed a series of five-year deals with Nike, Titleist, American Express, and Rolex worth $95.2 million. In 1998 Wood's earnings from endorsements totaled $28 million. Boxer Mike Tyson made $75 million in 1996. It is estimated that Michael Jordan made over $100 million in 1998, including salary, endorsements, and income from merchandise and videos. The recent deals for baseball stars, some exceeding $15 million a year for multiyear contracts, further underscores the incredible money given to some individuals for their athletic talents.

But while the possibility of staggering wealth and status through sport is possible, the reality is that dramatic upward mobility through sport is highly improbable. A number of myths, however, combine to lead us to believe that sport is a social mobility escalator.

### MYTH: SPORT PROVIDES A FREE EDUCATION

Good high school athletes get college scholarships. These athletic scholarships are especially helpful to poor youth who otherwise would not be able to attend college because of the high costs. The problem with this assumption is that while true for some, very few high school athletes actually receive full scholarships. Football provides the easiest route to a college scholarship because Division I-A colleges have 85 football scholarships, but even this avenue is exceedingly narrow. In Colorado there were 3,481 male high school seniors who played football during the 1994 season. Of these, 31 received full scholarships at Division I-A schools (0.0089 percent).

Second, of all the male varsity athletes at all college levels only about 15 percent to 20 percent have full scholarships. Another 15 percent to 25 percent have partial scholarships, leaving 55 percent to 70 percent of all intercollegiate athletes without any sport related financial assistance. Third, as low as the chances are for men, women athletes have even less chance to receive an athletic scholarship. While women comprise about 52 percent of all college students, they make up only 35 percent of intercollegiate athletes with a similar disproportionate distribution of scholarships. Another reality is that if you are a male athlete in a so-called minor sport (swimming, tennis, golf, gymnastics, cross-country, wrestling), the chances of a full scholarship are virtually nil. The best hope is a partial scholarship, if that, since these sports are underfunded and in danger of elimination at many schools.

## MYTH: SPORT LEADS TO A COLLEGE DEGREE

College graduates exceed high school graduates by hundreds of thousands of dollars in lifetime earnings. Since most high school and college athletes will never play at the professional level, the attainment of a college degree is a crucial determinant of upward mobility through sport. The problem is that relatively few male athletes in the big time revenue producing sports, compared to their non-athletic peers, actually receive college degrees. This is especially the case for African American men who are over represented in the revenue producing sports. In 1996, for example, looking at the athletes who entered Division I schools in 1990, only 45 percent of African American football players and 39 percent of African American basketball players had graduated (compared to 56 percent of the general student body).

There are a number of barriers to graduation for male athletes. The demands on their time and energy are enormous even in the off-season. Many athletes, because of these pressures, take easy courses to maintain eligibility but do not lead to graduation. The result is either to delay graduation or to make graduation an unrealistic goal.

Another barrier is that they are recruited for athletic prowess rather than academic ability. Recent data show that football players in big time programs are, on average, more than 200 points behind their non-athletic classmates on SAT test scores. Poorly prepared students are the most likely to take easy courses, cheat on exams, hire surrogate test takers, and otherwise do the minimum.

A third barrier to graduation for male college athletes is themselves, as they may not take advantage of their scholarships to obtain a quality education. This is especially the case for those who perceive their college experience only as preparation for their professional careers in sport. Study for them is necessary only to maintain their eligibility. The goal of a professional career is unrealistic for all but the superstars. The superstars who do make it at the professional level, more likely than not, will have not graduated from college; nor will they go back to finish their degrees when their professional careers are over. This is also because even a successful professional athletic career is limited to a few years, and not many professional athletes are able to translate their success in the pros to success in their post-athletic careers. Such a problem is especially true for African Americans, who often face employment discrimination in the wider society.

## MYTH: A SPORTS CAREER IS PROBABLE

A recent survey by the Center for the Study of Sport in Society found that two-thirds of African American males between the ages of 13 and 18 believe that they can earn a living playing professional sports (more than double the proportion of young white males who hold such beliefs). Moreover, African American parents were four times more likely than white parents to believe that their sons are destined for careers as professional athletes.

If these young athletes could play as professionals, the economic rewards are excellent, especially in basketball and baseball. In 1998 the average annual salary for professional basketball was $2.24 million. In baseball the average salary was $1.37 million with 280 of the 774 players on opening day rosters making $1 million or more (of them, 197 exceeded $2 million or more, while 32 of them made $6 million or more). The average salaries for the National Hockey League and National Football League were $892,000 and $795,000, respectively. In football, for example, 19 percent of the players (333 of 1,765) exceeded $1 million in salary. These numbers are inflated by the use of averages, which are skewed by the salaries of the superstars. Use of the median (in which half the players make more and half make less), reveals that the median salary in basketball was $1.4 million; baseball—$500,000; football—$400,000; and hockey—$500,000. Regardless of the measure, the financial allure of a professional sports career is great.

A career in professional sports is nearly impossible to attain because of the fierce competition for so few openings. In an average year there are approximately 1,900,000 American boys playing high school football, basketball, and baseball. Another 68,000 men are playing those sports in college, and 2,490 are participating at the major professional level. In short, one in 27 high school players in these sports will play at the college level, and only one in 736 high school players will play at the major professional level (0.14 percent). In baseball, each year about 120,000 players are eligible for the draft (high school seniors, college seniors, collegians over 21, junior college players, and foreign players). Only about 1,200 (1 percent) are actually drafted, and most of them will never make it to the major leagues. Indeed, only one in ten of those players who sign a professional baseball contract ever play in the major leagues for at least one day.

The same rigorous condensation process occurs in football. About 15,000 players are eligible for the NFL draft each year. Three hundred thirty-six are drafted and about 160 actually make the final roster. Similarly, in basketball and hockey, only about 40 new players are added to the rosters in the NBA and 60 rookies make the NHL each year. In tennis only about 100 men and 100 women make enough money to cover expenses. In golf, of the 165 men eligible for the PGA tour in 1997, their official winnings ranged from $2,066,833 (Tiger Woods) to $10,653 (Chip Beck). The competition among these golfers is fierce. On average, the top 100 golfers on the tour play within 2 strokes of each other for every 18 holes, yet Tiger Woods, the tops in winnings won over $2 million, and the 100th finisher won only $250,000. Below the PGA tour is the Nike Tour where the next best 125 golfers compete. Their winnings were a top of $225,201 to a low of $9,944.

## MYTH: SPORT IS A WAY OUT OF POVERTY

Sport appears to be a major way for African Americans to escape the ghetto. African Americans dominate the major professional sports numerically. While only 12 percent of the population, African Americans comprise about 80 percent of the players in professional basketball, about 67 percent of professional football players, and 18 percent of professional baseball players (Latinos also comprise about 17 percent of professional baseball players). Moreover, African Americans dominate the list of the highest moneymakers in sport (salaries, commercial sponsorships). These facts, while true, are illusory.

While African Americans dominate professional basketball, football, and to a lesser extent baseball, they are rarely found in certain sports such as hockey, automobile racing, tennis, golf, bowling, and skiing. Moreover, African Americans are severely under-represented in positions of authority in sport—as head coaches, referees, athletic directors, scouts, general managers, and owners. In the NFL in 1997, for example, where more than two-thirds of the players were African American, only three head coaches and five offensive or defensive coordinators were African American. In that year there were 11 head coaching vacancies filled none by African Americans. The reason for this racial imbalance in hiring, according to white sports columnist for the *Rocky Mountain News* Bob Kravitz is that: "something here stinks, and it stinks a lot like racism."

Second, while the odds of African American males making it as professional athletes are more favorable than is the case for whites (about 1 in 3,500 African American male high school athletes, compared to 1 in 10,000 white male high school athletes) these odds remain slim. Of the 40,000 or so African Americans boys who play high school basketball, only 35 will make the NBA and only 7 will be starters. Referring to the low odds for young African Americans, Harry Edwards, an African American sociologist specializing in the sociology of sport, said with a bit of hyperbole: "Statistically, you have a better chance of getting hit by a meteorite in the next ten years than getting work as an athlete."

Despite these discouraging facts, the myth is alive for poor youth. As noted earlier, two-thirds of African American boys believe they can be professional athletes. Their parents, too, accept this belief (African American parents are four times more likely than white parents to believe that their children will be professional athletes). The film *Hoop Dreams* and Darcey Frey's book *The Last Shot: City Street, Basketball Dreams* document the emphasis that young African American men place on sports as a way up and their ultimate disappointments from sport. For many of them, sport represents their only hope of escape from a life of crime, poverty, and despair. They latch on to the dream of athletic success partly because of the few opportunities for middle-class success. They spend many hours per day developing their speed, strength, jumping height, or "moves" to the virtual exclusion of those abilities that have a greater likelihood of paying off in upward mobility such as reading comprehension, mathematical reasoning, communication skills, and computer literacy.

Sociologist Jay Coakley puts it this way: "My best guess is that less than 3,500 African Americans . . . are making their livings as professional athletes. At the same time (in 1996), there are about 30,015 black physicians and about 30,800 black lawyers currently employed in the U.S. Therefore, there are 20 times more blacks working in these two professions than playing top level professional sports. And physicians and lawyers usually have lifetime earnings far in excess of the earnings of professional athletes, whose playing careers, on average, last less than five years."

Harry Edwards posits that by spending their energies and talents on athletic skills, young African Americans are not pursuing occupations that would help them meet their political and material needs. Thus, because of belief in the "sports as a way up" myth, they remain dependent on whites and white institutions. Salim Muwakkil, an African American political analyst, argues that "If African Americans are to exploit the socio-economic options opened by varied civil rights struggles more fully, blacks must reduce the disproportionate allure of sports in their communities. Black leadership must contextualize athletic success by promoting other avenues to social status, intensifying the struggle for access to those avenues and better educating youth about those pot-holes on the road to the stadium."

John Hoberman in his book *Darwin's Athletes* also challenges the assumption that sport has progressive consequences. The success of African Americans in the highly visible sports gives white Americans a false sense of black progress and interracial harmony. But the social progress of African Americans in general has little relationship to the apparent integration that they have achieved on the playing fields.

Hoberman also contends that the numerical superiority of African Americans in sport, coupled with their disproportionate under-representation in other professions, reinforces the racist ideology that African Americans, while physically superior to whites, are inferior to them intellectually.

I do not mean to say that African Americans should not seek a career in professional sport. What is harmful is that the odds of success are so slim, making the extraordinary efforts over many years futile and misguided for the vast majority.

## MYTH: WOMEN HAVE SPORT AS A VEHICLE

Since the passage of Title IX in 1972 that required schools receiving federal funds to provide equal opportunities for women and men, sports participation by women in high school and college has increased dramatically. In 1973, for example, when 50,000 men received some form of college scholarship for their athletic abilities, women received only 50. Now, women receive about 35 percent of the money allotted for college athletic scholarships (while a dramatic improvement, this should not be equated with gender equality as many would have us believe). This allows many women athletes to attend college who otherwise could not afford it, thus receiving an indirect upward mobility boost.

Upward mobility as a result of being a professional athlete is another matter for women. Women have fewer opportunities than men in professional team sports. Beach volley-ball is a possibility for a few but the rewards are minimal. Two professional women's basketball leagues began in 1997, but the pay was very low compared to men and the leagues were on shaky financial ground (the average salary in the American Basketball League was $80,000). The other option for women is to play in professional leagues in Europe, Australia, and Asia but the pay is relatively low.

Women have more opportunities as professionals in individual sports such as tennis, golf, ice-skating, skiing, bowling, cycling, and track. Ironically, the sports with the greatest monetary rewards for women are those of the middle and upper classes (tennis, golf, and ice skating). These sports are expensive and require considerable individual coaching and access to private facilities.

Ironically, with the passage of Title IX, which increased the participation rates of women so dramatically, there has been a decline in the number and proportion of women as coaches and athletic administrators. In addition to the glaring pay gap between what the coaches of men's teams receive compared to the coaches of women's teams, men who coach women's teams tend to have higher salaries than women coaching women's teams. Women also have fewer opportunities than men as athletic trainers, officials, sports journalists, and other adjunct positions.

## MYTH: SPORT PROVIDES LIFELONG SECURITY

Even when a professional sport career is attained, the probabilities of fame and fortune are limited. Of course, some athletes make incomes from salaries and endorsements that if invested wisely, provide financial security for life. Many professional athletes make relatively low salaries. During the 1996 season, for example, 17 percent of major league baseball players made the minimum salary of $247,500 for veterans and $220,000 for rookies. This is a lot of money, but for these marginal players their careers may not last very long. Indeed, the average length of a professional career in a team sport is about five years. A marginal athlete in individual sports such as golf, tennis, boxing, and bowling, struggle financially. They must cover their travel expenses, health insurance, equipment, and the like with no guaranteed paycheck. The brief career diverts them during their youth from developing other career skills and experiences that would benefit them.

Ex-professional athletes leave sport, on average, when they are in their late 20s or early 30s, at a time when their non-athletic peers have begun to establish themselves in occupations leading toward retirement in 40 years or so. What are the ex-professional athletes to do with their remaining productive years?

Exiting a sports career can be relatively smooth or difficult. Some athletes have planned ahead, preparing for other careers either in sport (coaching, scouting, administering) or some non-sport occupation. Others have not prepared for this abrupt change. They did not graduate from college. They did not spend the off seasons apprenticing non-sport jobs. Exiting the athlete role is difficult for many because they lose: (1) What has been the focus of their being for most of their lives; (2) the primary source of their identities; (3) their physical prowess; (4) the adulation bordering on worship from others; (5) the money and the perquisites of fame; (6) the camaraderie with teammates; (7) the intense "highs" of competition; and (8) for most ex-athletes retirement means a loss of status. As a result of these "losses," many ex-professional athletes have trouble adjusting to life after sport. A study by the NFL Players Association found, that emotional difficulties, divorce, and financial strain were common problems for ex-professional football players. A majority had "permanent injuries" from football.

The allure of sport, however, remains strong and this has at least two negative consequences. First, ghetto youngsters who devote their lives to the pursuit of athletic stardom are, except for the fortunate few, doomed to failure in sport and in the real world where sports skills are essentially irrelevant to occupational placement and advancement. The second negative consequence is more subtle but very important. Sport contributes to the ideology that legitimizes social inequalities and promotes the myth that all it takes is extraordinary effort to succeed. Sport sociologist George H. Sage makes this point forcefully: "Because sport is by nature meritocratic—that is, superior performance brings status and rewards—it provides convincing symbolic support for hegemonic [the dominant] ideology—that ambitious, dedicated, hard working individuals, regardless of social origin, can achieve success and ascend in the social hierarchy, obtaining high status and material rewards, while those who don't move upward simply didn't work hard enough. Because the rags-to-riches athletes are so visible, the social mobility theme is maintained. This reflects the opportunity structure of society in general—the success of a few reproduces the belief in social mobility among the many."

# 30

## Uses of the Underclass in America

### HERBERT J. GANS

*This essay is vintage sociology, taking what everyone thinks they know and turning it on its head. Gans shows how the lives and work of the so-called "undeserving poor" benefit the nonpoor in ways most Americans seldom recognize. "Poverty is good for you," is another way to express Gans's message, "as long as you are not among the poor." This essay also shows how functional analysis, often accused of being conservative, can be a critical perspective.*

## I. INTRODUCTION

Poverty, like any other social phenomenon, can be analyzed in terms of the *causes* which initiate and perpetuate it, but once it exists, it can also be studied in terms of the consequences or *functions* which follow. These functions can be both *positive* and *negative*, adaptive and destructive, depending on their nature and the people and interests affected.

Poverty has many negative functions (or dysfunctions), most for the poor themselves, but also for the nonpoor. Among those of most concern to both populations, perhaps the major one is that a small but visible proportion of poor people is involved in activities which threaten their physical safety, for example street crime, or which deviate from important norms claimed to be "mainstream," such as failing to work, bearing children in adolescence and out of wedlock, and being "dependent" on welfare. In times of high unemployment, illegal and even legal immigrants are added to this list for endangering the job opportunities of native-born Americans.

Furthermore, many better-off Americans believe that the number of poor people who behave in these ways is far larger than it actually is. More important, many think that poor people act as they do because of moral shortcomings that express themselves in lawlessness or in the rejection of mainstream norms. Like many other sociologists, however, I argue that the behavior patterns which concern the more fortunate classes are *poverty-related*, because they are, and have historically been, associated with poverty. * * * They are in fact caused by poverty, although a variety of other causes must also be at work since most poor people are not involved in any of these activities.

\* \* \*

Because their criminal or disapproved behavior is ascribed to moral short-comings, the poor people who resort to it are often classified as unworthy or *undeserving*. For example, even though the failure of poor young men (or women) to work may be the effect of a lack of jobs, they are frequently accused of laziness, and then judged undeserving. Likewise, even though poor young mothers may decide not to marry the fathers of their children, because they, being jobless, cannot support them, the women are still accused of violating conventional familial norms, and also judged undeserving. Moreover, once judged to be undeserving, poor people are then no longer thought to be deserving of public aid that is financially sufficient and secure enough to help them escape poverty.

Judgments of the poor as undeserving are not based on evidence, but derive from a stereotype, even if, like most others, it is a stereotype with a "kernel of truth" (e.g., the monopolization of street crime by the poor). Furthermore, it is a very old stereotype; Cicero already described the needy of Rome as criminals. By the middle of the sixteenth century, complicated laws to distinguish between the deserving and undeserving were in existence. However, the term undeserving poor was first used regularly in England in the 1830s, at the time of the institution of the Poor Law.[1]

In America, a series of other, more specific, terms were borrowed or invented, with new ones replacing old ones as conditions and fashions changed. Such terms have included *beggar, pauper*, the *dangerous class, rabble, vagabond* and *vagrant*, and so on, which the United States borrowed from Europe. America also invented its own terms, including *shiftless, tramp*, and *feeble-minded*, and in the late twentieth century, terms like *hard-core, drifter, culturally deprived*—and most recently, *underclass*.[2] Nonetheless, in terms of its popular uses and the people to whom it is applied, the term underclass differs little from its predecessors.[3]

---

1. However, the *Oxford English Dictionary*, compiled by J. A. Simpson and E. S. Weiner (New York: Oxford University Press, 1989), 19: 996, already has a 1647 reference to beggars as undeserving, and the adjective itself was earlier used to refer to nonpoor people, for example, by Shakespeare.

2. These terms were often, but not exclusively, applied to the poor "races" who arrived in the nineteenth and early twentieth century from Ireland, Germany, and later, Eastern and Southern Europe. They have also been applied, during and after slavery, to Blacks. Nonetheless, the functions to be discussed in this article are consequences of poverty, not of race, even though a disproportionate rate of those "selected" to be poor have always been darker-skinned than the more fortunate classes.

3. The popular definition of underclass must be distinguished from Gunnar Myrdal's initial scholarly one, which viewed the underclass as a stratum driven to the margins or out of the labor force by what are today called the postindustrial and global economies. Gunnar Myrdal, *Challenge to Affluence* (New York: Pantheon Books, 1963), 10 and passim. Myrdal's definition viewed the underclass as victims of economic change, and said nothing about its moral state.

It is not difficult to understand why people, poor and more fortunate, are fearful of street crime committed by poor people, and even why the jobless poor and welfare recipients, like paupers before them, may be perceived as economic threats for not working and drawing on public funds, at least in bad economic times. Also, one can understand why other forms of poverty-related behavior, such as the early sexual activity of poor youngsters and the dramatic number of poor single-parent families are viewed as moral threats, since they violate norms thought to uphold the two-parent nuclear family and related normative bases of the social order. However, there would seem to be no inherent reason for exaggerating these threats, for example, in the case of welfare recipients who obtain only a tiny proportion of governmental expenditures, or more generally, by stereotyping poor people as undeserving without evidence of what they have and have not done, and why.

One reason, if not the only one, for the exaggeration and the stereotyping, and for the continued attractiveness of the concept of the undeserving poor itself, is that undeservingness has a number of *positive* functions for the better-off population. Some of these functions, or uses, are positive for everyone who is not poor, but most are positive only for some people, interest groups, and institutions, ranging from moderate income to wealthy ones. Needless to say, that undeservingness has uses for some people does not justify it; the existence of functions just helps to explain why it persists.

My notion of function, or empirically observable adaptive consequence, is adapted from the classic conceptual scheme of Robert K. Merton. My analysis will concentrate on those positive functions which Merton conceptualized as *latent*, which are unrecognized and/or unintended, but with the proviso that the functions which are identified as latent would probably not be abolished once they were widely recognized. Positive functions are, after all, also benefits, and people are not necessarily ready to give up benefits, including unintended ones, even if they become aware of them.

\* \* \*

## II. FUNCTIONS OF THE UNDESERVING POOR[4]

I will discuss five sets of positive functions: microsocial, economic, normative-cultural, political, and macrosocial, which I divide into 13 specific functions, although the sets are arbitrarily chosen and interrelated, and I could add many more functions. The functions are not listed in order of importance, for such a listing is not possible without empirical research on the various beneficiaries of undeservingness.

---

4. For brevity's sake, I will hereafter refer to the undeserving poor instead of the poor-labeled undeserving, but I always mean the latter.

### Two Microsocial Functions

1. *Risk reduction.* Perhaps the primary use of the idea of the undeserving poor, primary because it takes place at the microsocial scale of everyday life, is that it distances the labeled from those who label them. By stigmatizing people as undeserving, labelers protect themselves from the responsibility of having to associate with them, or even to treat them like moral equals, which reduces the risk of being hurt or angered by them. Risk reduction is a way of dealing with actual or imagined threats to physical safety, for example from people who might be muggers, or cultural threats attributed to poor youngsters or normative ones imagined to come from welfare recipients. All pejorative labels and stereotypes serve this function, which may help to explain why there are so many such labels.

2. *Scapegoating and displacement.* By being thought undeserving, the stigmatized poor can be blamed for virtually any shortcoming of everyday life which can be credibly ascribed to them—violations of the laws of logic or social causation notwithstanding. Faulting the undeserving poor can also support the desire for revenge and punishment. In a society in which punishment is reserved for legislative, judicial, and penal institutions, *feelings* of revenge and punitiveness toward the undeserving poor supply at least some emotional satisfaction.

Since labeling poor people undeserving opens the door for nearly unlimited scapegoating, the labeled are also available to serve what I call the displacement function. Being too weak to object, the stigmatized poor can be accused of having caused social problems which they did not actually cause and can serve as cathartic objects on which better-off people can unload their own problems, as well as those of the economy, the polity, or of any other institutions, for the shortcomings of which the poor can be blamed.

Whether societywide changes in the work ethic are displaced on to "shiftlessness," or economic stagnation on to "welfare dependency," the poor can be declared undeserving for what ails the more affluent. This may also help to explain why the national concern with poor Black unmarried mothers, although usually ascribed to the data presented in the 1965 Moynihan Report, did not gather steam until the beginning of the decline of the economy in the mid-1970s. Similarly, the furor about poor "babies having babies" waited for the awareness of rising adolescent sexual activity among the better-off classes in the 1980s—at which point rates of adolescent pregnancy among the poor had already declined. But when the country became ambivalent about the desirability of abortions, the issue was displaced on the poor by making it almost impossible for them to obtain abortions.

Many years ago, James Baldwin, writing in *The Fire Next Time*, illustrated the displacement function in racial terms, arguing that, as Andrew Hacker put it, Whites "need the 'nigger' because it is the 'nigger' within themselves that they cannot tolerate. Whatever it is that Whites feel 'nigger' signifies about Blacks—lust and laziness, stupidity or squalor, in fact exists within themselves. * * * By creating such a creature, Whites are able to say that because only members of the Black race can carry that taint, it follows that none of its attributes will be found in White people.[5]

### Three Economic Functions

3. *Economic banishment and the reserve army of labor.* People who have successfully been labeled as undeserving can be banished from the formal labor market. If young people are designated "school dropouts," for example; they can also be thought to lack the needed work habits, such as proper adherence to the work ethic, and may not be offered jobs to begin with. Often, they are effectively banished from the labor market before entering it because employers imagine them to be poor workers simply because they are young, male, and Black. Many ex-convicts are declared unemployable in similar fashion, and some become recidivists because they have no other choice but to go back to their criminal occupations.

Banishing the undeserving also makes room for immigrant workers, who may work for lower wages, are more deferential, and are more easily exploitable by being threatened with deportation. In addition, banishment helps to reduce the official jobless rate, a sometimes useful political function, especially if the banished drop so completely out of the labor force that they are not even available to be counted as "discouraged workers."

The economic banishment function is in many ways a replacement for the old reserve army of labor function, which played itself out when the undeserving poor could be hired as strikebreakers, as defense workers in the case of sudden wartime economic mobilization, as "hypothetical workers," who by their very presence could be used to depress the wages of other workers, or to put pressure on the unions not to make wage and other demands. Today, however, with a plentiful supply of immigrants, as well as of a constantly growing number of banished workers who are becoming surplus labor, a reserve army is less rarely needed—and when needed, can be recruited from sources other than the undeserving poor.

\* \* \*

4. *Supplying illegal goods.* The undeserving poor who are banished from other jobs remain eligible for work in the manufacture and sale of illegal goods, including drugs. Although it is estimated that 80 percent of all illegal drugs are sold to Whites who are not poor, the sellers are often people banished from the formal labor market. Other suppliers of illegal goods include the illegal immigrants, considered undeserving in many American communities, who work for garment industry sweatshops manufacturing clothing under illegal conditions.

---

5. Hacker is paraphrasing Baldwin. Andrew Hacker, *Two Nations: Black and White, Separate, Hostile, Unequal* (New York: Scribner, 1992), 61.

5. *Job creation.* Perhaps the most important economic function of the undeserving poor today is that their mere presence creates jobs for the better-off population, including professional ones. Since the undeserving poor are thought to be dangerous or improperly socialized, their behavior either has to be modified so that they act in socially approved ways, or they have to be isolated from the deserving sectors of society. The larger the number of people who are declared undeserving, the larger also the number of people needed to modify and isolate as well as control, guard, and care for them. Among these are the social workers, teachers, trainers, mentors, psychiatrists, doctors and their support staffs in juvenile training centers, "special" schools, drug treatment centers, and penal behavior modification institutions, as well as the police, prosecutors, defense attorneys, judges, court officers, probation personnel and others who constitute the criminal courts, and the guards and others who run the prisons.

Jobs created by the presence of undeserving poor also include the massive bureaucracy of professionals, investigators, and clerks who administer welfare. Other jobs go to the officials who seek out poor fathers for child support monies they may or may not have, as well as the welfare office personnel needed to take recipients in violation of welfare rules off the rolls, and those needed to put them back on the rolls when they reapply. In fact, one can argue that some of the rules for supervising, controlling, and punishing the undeserving poor are more effective at performing the latent function of creating clerical and professional jobs for the better-off population than the manifest function of achieving their official goals.

More jobs are created in the social sciences and in journalism for conducting research about the undeserving poor and producing popular books, articles, and TV documentaries for the more fortunate who want to learn about them. The "job chain" should also be extended to the teachers and others who train those who serve, control, and study the undeserving poor.

In addition, the undeserving poor make jobs for what I call the salvation industries, religious, civil, or medical, which also try to modify the behavior of those stigmatized as undeserving. Not all such jobs are paid, for the undeserving poor also provide occasional targets for charity and thus offer volunteer jobs for those providing it—and paid jobs for the professional fundraisers who obtain most of the charitable funds these days. Among the most visible volunteers are the members of "café" and "high" society who organize and contribute to these benefits.

### Three Normative Functions

6. *Moral legitimation.* Undeservingness justifies the category of deservingness and thus supplies moral and political legitimacy, almost by definition, to the institutions and social structures that include the deserving and exclude the undeserving. Of these structures, the most important is undoubtedly the class hierarchy, for the existence of an undeserving class or stratum legitimates

the deserving classes, if not necessarily all of their class-related behavior. The alleged immorality of the undeserving also gives a moral flavor to, and justification for, the class hierarchy, which may help to explain why upward mobility itself is so praiseworthy.

7. *Norm reinforcement.* By violating, or being imagined as violating, a number of mainstream behavioral patterns and values, the undeserving poor help to reaffirm and reinforce the virtues of these patterns—and to do so visibly, since the violations by the undeserving are highly publicized. As Emile Durkheim pointed out nearly a century ago, norm violations and their punishments also provide an opportunity for preserving and reaffirming the norms. This is not insignificant, for norms sometimes disparaged as "motherhood" values gain new moral power when they are violated, and their violators are stigmatized.

If the undeserving poor can be imagined to be lazy, they help to reaffirm the Protestant work ethic; if poor single-parent families are publicly condemned, the two-parent family is once more legitimated as ideal. In the 1960s, middle-class morality was sometimes criticized as culturally parochial and therefore inappropriate for the poor, but since the 1980s, mainstream values have once more been regarded as vital sources of behavioral guidance for them.

Enforcing the norms also contributes further to preserving them in another way, for one of the standard punishments of the undeserving poor for misbehaving—as well as standard obligation in exchange for help—is practicing the mainstream norms, including those that the members of the mainstream may only be preaching, and that might die out if the poor were not required to incorporate them in their behavior. Old work rules that can no longer be enforced in the rest of the economy can be maintained in the regulations for workfare; old-fashioned austerity and thrift are built into the consumption patterns expected of welfare recipients. Economists like to argue that if the poor want to be deserving, they should take any kind of job, regardless of its low pay or demeaning character, reflecting a work ethic which economists themselves have never practiced.

Similarly, welfare recipients may be removed from the rolls if they are found to be living with a man—but the social worker who removes them has every right to cohabit and not lose his or her job. In most states, welfare recipients must observe rules of housecleaning and child care that middle-class people are free to ignore without being punished. While there are many norms and laws governing child care, only the poor are monitored to see if they obey these. Should they use more physical punishment on their children than social workers consider desirable, they can be charged with child neglect or abuse and can lose their children to foster care.[6]

---

6. Poor immigrants who still practice old-country discipline norms are particularly vulnerable to being accused of child abuse.

The fact is that the defenders of such widely preached norms as hard work, thrift, monogamy, and moderation need people who can be accused, accurately or not, of being lazy, spendthrift, promiscuous, and immoderate. One reason that welfare recipients are a ready target for punitive legislation is that politicians, and most likely some of their constituents, imagine them to be enjoying leisure and an active sex life at public expense. Whether or not very many poor people actually behave in the ways that are judged undeserving is irrelevant if they can be imagined as doing so. Once imagining and stereotyping are allowed to take over, then judgments of undeservingness can be made without much concern for empirical accuracy. For example, in the 1990s, the idea that young men from poor single-parent families were highly likely to commit street crimes became so universal that the news media no longer needed to quote experts to affirm the accuracy of the charge.

Actually, most of the time most of the poor are as law abiding and observant of mainstream norms as are other Americans. Sometimes they are even more observant; thus the proportion of welfare recipients who cheat is always far below the percentage of taxpayers who do so. Moreover, survey after survey has shown that the poor, including many street criminals and drug sellers, want to hold respectable jobs like everyone else, hope someday to live in the suburbs, and generally aspire to the same American dream as most moderate and middle-income Americans.[7]

8. *Supplying popular culture villains.* The undeserving poor have played a long-term role in supplying American popular culture with villains, allowing the producers of the culture both to reinforce further mainstream norms and to satisfy audience demands for revenge, notably by showing that crime and other norm violations do not pay. Street criminals are shown dead or alive in the hands of the police on local television news virtually every day, and more dramatically so in the crime and action movies and television series.

For many years before and after World War II, the criminal characters in Hollywood movies were often poor immigrants, frequently of Sicilian origin. Then they were complemented for some decades by communist spies and other Cold War enemies who were not poor, but even before the end of the Cold War, they were being replaced by Black and Hispanic drug dealers and gang leaders.

At the same time, however, the popular culture industry has also supplied music and other materials offering marketable cultural and political protest which does not reinforce mainstream norms, or at least not directly. Some of the creators and performers come from poor neighborhoods, however, and it may be that some rap music becomes commercially successful by displacing on ghetto musicians the cultural and political protest of record buyers from more affluent classes.

---

7. See Mark R. Rank, *Living on the Edge: The Realities of Welfare in America* (New York: Columbia University Press, 1994), 93.

## Three Political Functions

9. *Institutional scapegoating.* The scapegoating of the undeserving poor mentioned in Function 2 above also extends to institutions which mistreat them. As a result, some of the responsibility for the existence of poverty, slum unemployment, poor schools, and the like is taken off the shoulders of elected and appointed officials who are supposed to deal with these problems. For example, to the extent that educational experts decide that the children of the poor are learning disabled or that they are culturally or genetically inferior in intelligence, attempts to improve the schools can be put off or watered down.

To put it another way, the availability of institutional scapegoats both personalizes and exonerates social systems. The alleged laziness of the jobless and the anger aimed at beggars take the heat off the failure of the economy and the imagined derelictions of slum dwellers and the homeless, off the housing industry. In effect, the undeserving poor are blamed both for their poverty and also for the absence of "political will" among the citizenry to do anything about it.

10. *Conservative power shifting.* Once poor people are declared undeserving they also lose their political legitimacy and whatever little political influence they had before they were stigmatized. Some cannot vote, and many do not choose to vote or mobilize because they know politicians do not listen to their demands. Elected officials might ignore them even if they voted or mobilized because these officials and the larger polity cannot easily satisfy their demands for economic and other kinds of justice.[8] As a result, the political system is able to pay additional attention to the demands of more affluent constituents. It can therefore shift to the "right."

The same shift to the right also takes place ideologically. Although injustices of poverty help justify the existence of liberals and the more radical left the undeserving poor themselves provide justification and opportunities for conservatives to attack their ideological enemies on their left. When liberals can be accused of favoring criminals over victims, their accusers can launch and legitimate incursions on the civil liberties and rights of the undeserving poor, and concurrently on the liberties and rights of defenders of the poor. Moreover, the undeservingness of the poor can be used to justify attacks on the welfare state. Charles Murray understood the essence of this ideological function when he argued that welfare and other welfare state legislation for the poor only increased the number of poor people.[9]

---

8. In addition, the undeserving poor make a dangerous constituency. Politicians who say kind words about them or who act to represent their interests are likely to be attacked for their words and actions. Jesse Jackson was hardly the first national politician to be criticized for being too favorable to the poor.

9. Charles Murray, *Losing Ground: American Social Policy, 1950–1980* (New York: Basic Books, 1984).

11. *Spatial purification.* Stigmatized populations are often used, deliberately or not, to stigmatize the areas in which they live, making such areas eligible for various kinds of purification. As a result, "underclass areas" can be torn down and their inhabitants moved to make room for more affluent residents or higher taxpayers.

However, such areas can also be used to isolate stigmatized poor people and facilities by selecting them as locations for homeless shelters, halfway houses for the mentally ill or for ex-convicts, drug treatment facilities, and even garbage dumps, which have been forced out of middle- and working-class areas following NIMBY (not in my backyard) protests. Drug dealers and other sellers of illegal goods also find a haven in areas stigmatized as underclass areas, partly because these supply some customers, but also because police protection in such areas is usually minimal enough to allow illegal activities without significant interference from the law. In fact, municipalities would face major economic and political obstacles to their operations without stigmatized areas in which stigmatized people and activities can be located.

### Two Macrosocial Functions

12. *Reproduction of stigma and the stigmatized.* For centuries now, undeservingness has given rise to policies and agencies which are manifestly set up to help the poor economically and otherwise to become deserving, but which actually prevent the undeserving poor from being freed of their stigma, and which also manage, unwittingly, to see to it that their children face the same obstacles. In some instances, this process works so speedily that the children of the stigmatized face "anticipatory stigmatization," among them the children of welfare recipients who are frequently predicted to be unable to learn, to work, and to remain on the right side of the law even before they have been weaned.

If this outcome were planned deliberately, one could argue that politically and culturally dominant groups are reluctant to give up an easily accessible and always available scapegoat. In actuality, however, the reproduction function results unwittingly from other intended and seemingly popular practices. For example, the so-called War on Drugs, which has unsuccessfully sought to keep hard drugs out of the United States, but has meanwhile done little to provide drug treatment to addicts who want it, thereby aids the continuation of addiction, street crime, and a guaranteed prison population, not to mention the various disasters that visit the families of addicts and help to keep them poor.

The other major source of reproducing stigma and the stigmatized is the routine activities of the organizations which service welfare recipients, the homeless, and other stigmatized poor, and end up mistreating them. For one thing, such agencies, whether they exist to supply employment to the poor or to help the homeless, are almost certain to be underfunded because of the powerlessness of their clientele. No organization has ever had the funds or power to buy, build, or rehabilitate housing for the homeless in sufficient number. Typically, they have been able to fund or carry out small demonstration projects.

In addition, organizations which serve stigmatized people often attract less well-trained and qualified staff than those with high-status clients, and if the clients are deemed undeserving, competence may become even less important in choosing staff. Then too, helping organizations generally reflect the societal stratification hierarchy, which means that organizations with poor, low-status clients frequently treat them as undeserving. If they also fear some of their clients, they may not only withhold help, but attack the clients on a pre-emptive strike basis. Last but not least, the agencies that serve the undeserving poor are bureaucracies which operate by rules and regulations that routinize the work, encourage the stability and growth of the organizations, and serve the needs of their staffs before those of their clients.

When these factors are combined, as they often are, and become cumulative, as they often do, it should not be surprising that the organizations cut off escape routes from poverty not only for the clients, but in doing so, also make sure that some of their children remain poor as well.

13. *Extermination of the surplus.* In earlier times, when the living standards of all poor people were at or below subsistence, many died at an earlier age than the better off, thus performing the set of functions for the latter forever associated with Thomas Malthus. Standards of living, even for the very poor, have risen considerably in the last century, but even today, morbidity and mortality rates remain much higher among the poor than among moderate-income people. To put it another way, various social forces combine to do away with some of the people who have become surplus labor and are no longer needed by the economy.

Several of the killing illnesses and pathologies of the poor change over time; currently, they include AIDS, tuberculosis, hypertension, heart attacks, and cancer, as well as psychosis, substance abuse, street crime, injury and death during participation in the drug trade and other underworld activities, and intraclass homicide resulting from neighborhood conflicts over turf and "respect." Whether the poor people whose only problem is being unfairly stereotyped and stigmatized as undeserving die earlier than other poor people is not known.

Moreover, these rates can be expected to remain high or even to rise as rates of unemployment—and of banishment from the labor force—rise, especially for the least skilled. Even the better-off jobless created by the downsizing of the 1990s blame themselves for their unemployment if they cannot eventually find new jobs, become depressed, and in some instances begin the same process of being extruded permanently from the labor market experienced by the least skilled of the jobless.

\* \* \*

The early departure of poor people from an economy and society which do not need them is useful for those who remain. Since the more fortunate classes have already developed a purposive blindness to the structural causes of unemployment and to the poverty-related causes of pathology and crime that follow, those who benefit from the current job erosion and the possible extermination of the surplus labor may not admit it consciously either. Nonetheless, those left over to compete for scarce jobs and other resources will have a somewhat easier time in the competition, thus assigning undeservingness a final positive function for the more fortunate members of society.

## III. CONCLUSION

I have described thirteen of the more important functions of the undeserving poor, enough to support my argument that both the idea of the undeserving poor and the stigmas with which some poor people are thus labeled may persist in part because they are useful in a variety of ways to the people who are not poor.

This analysis does not imply that undeservingness will or should persist. Whether it *will* persist is going to be determined by what happens to poverty in America. If it declines, poverty-related crime should also decline, and then fewer poor people will probably be described as undeserving. If poverty worsens, so will poverty-related crime, as well as the stereotyping and stigmatization of the poor, and any worsening of the country's economy is likely to add to the kinds and numbers of undeserving poor, if only because they make convenient and powerless scapegoats.

The functions that the undeserving poor play cannot, by themselves, perpetuate either poverty or undeservingness, for as I noted earlier, functions are not causes. For example, if huge numbers of additional unskilled workers should be needed, as they were for the World War II war effort, the undeserving poor will be welcomed back into the labor force, at least temporarily. Of course, institutions often try to survive once they have lost both their reasons for existence and their functions. Since the end of the Cold War, parts of the military-industrial establishment both in the United States and Russia have been campaigning for the maintenance of some Cold War forces and weapons to guarantee their own futures, but these establishments also supply jobs to their national economies, and in the United States, for the constituents of elected officials. Likewise, some of the institutions and interest groups that benefit from the existence of undeservingness, or from controlling the undeserving poor, may try to maintain undeservingness and its stigma. They may not even need to, for if Émile Durkheim was right, the decline of undeservingness would lead to the criminalization, or at least stigmatization, of new behavior patterns.

Whether applying the label of undeservingness to the poor *should* persist is a normative question which ought to be answered in the negative. Although people have a right to judge each other, that right does not extend to judging large numbers of people as a single group, with one common moral fault, or to stereotyping them without evidence either about their behavior or their values.

Even if a case could be made for judging large cohorts of people as undeserving, these judgments should be distributed up and down the socioeconomic hierarchy, requiring Americans also to consider whether and how people in the working, middle, and upper classes are undeserving.

The same equality should extend to the punishment of crimes. Today, many Americans and courts still treat white-collar and upper-class criminals more leniently than poor ones. The public excuse given is that the street crime of the undeserving poor involves violence and thus injury or death, but as many students of white-collar and corporate crime have pointed out, these also hurt and kill people, and often in larger numbers, even if they do so less directly and perhaps less violently.

Changes also need to be made in the American conception of deviance, which like that of other countries, conflates people whose behavior is *different* with those whose behavior is socially *harmful*. Bearing children without marriage is a long-standing tradition among the poor. Born of necessity rather than preference, it is a poverty-related practice, but it is not, by itself, harmful, or at least not until it can be shown that either the children—or the moral sensibilities of the people who oppose illegitimacy—are significantly hurt. Poor single-parent families are hardly desirable, but as the lack of condemnation of more affluent single-parent families should suggest, the major problem of such families is not the number of parents, actual or surrogate, in the family, but its poverty.

Finally, because many of the poor are stereotyped unjustly as undeserving, scholars, writers, journalists, and others should launch a systematic and public effort to deconstruct and delegitimate the notion of the undeserving poor. This effort, which is necessary to help make effective antipoverty programs politically acceptable again, should place the following five ideas on the public agenda and encourage discussion as well as dissemination of available research.

The five ideas, all discussed earlier in this article, are that (1) the criminal and deviant behavior among the poor is largely poverty related rather than the product of free choice based on distinctive values; (2) the undeservingness of the poor is an ancient stereotype, and like all stereotypes, it vastly exaggerates the actual dangers that stem from the poor; (3) poverty-related deviance is not necessarily harmful just because it does not accord with mainstream norms; (4) the notion of undeservingness survives in part because of the positive functions it has for the better-off population; and (5) the only certain way to eliminate both this notion and the functions is to eliminate poverty.[10]

---

10. A fuller discussion of policy proposals * * * appear[s] in my * * * book, *Ending the War against the Poor.*

# PART SIX

# SOCIAL CONTROL AND ORGANIZATIONAL POWER

# 31

## Panopticism

FROM *Discipline and Punish: The Birth of the Prison*

MICHEL FOUCAULT

*Michel Foucault, a social historian and social theorist, is one of the most important sociologists of the last half century. As you read what appears to be a discussion of something long ago, you should realize he's also talking about society right now. Not only can we be watched wherever we are, but our comings and goings are now recorded with hidden cameras and microphones, iPhones, and webcams. Corporations are mining your every Internet search and web post. The National Security Agency (NSA) is collecting and storing every call you've made and every e-mail you've sent or received. This is the perfect panopticon, with an incredible capability to discipline and punish.*

\* \* \*

Bentham's\* *Panopticon* is the architectural figure of this composition. We know the principle on which it was based: at the periphery, an annular building; at the centre, a tower; this tower is pierced with wide windows that open onto the inner side of the ring; the peripheric building is divided into cells, each of which extends the whole width of the building; they have two windows, one on the inside, corresponding to the windows of the tower; the other, on the outside, allows the light to cross the cell from one end to the other. All that is needed, then, is to place a supervisor in a central tower and to shut up in each cell a madman, a patient, a condemned man, a worker or a schoolboy. By the effect of backlighting, one can observe from the tower, standing out precisely against the light, the small captive shadows in the cells of the periphery. They are like so many cages, so many small theatres, in which each actor is alone, perfectly individualized and constantly visible. The panoptic mechanism arranges spatial unities that make it possible to see constantly and to recognize immediately. In short, it reverses the principle of the dungeon; or rather of its three functions—to enclose, to deprive of light and to hide—it preserves only the first and eliminates the other two. Full

---

\*Jeremy Bentham (1748–1832), an English political theorist, was one of the founders of utilitarianism, an ethical philosophy that argued what is right and best is what provides the greatest happiness to the most people, identifying happiness with pleasure. [*Editor's note*]

lighting and the eye of a supervisor capture better than darkness, which ultimately protected. Visibility is a trap.

To begin with, this made it possible—as a negative effect—to avoid those
compact, swarming, howling masses that were to be found in places of con-
finement, those painted by Goya or described by [the English prison reformer
John] Howard. Each individual, in his place, is securely confined to a cell from
which he is seen from the front by the supervisor; but the side walls prevent
him from coming into contact with his companions. He is seen, but he does
not see; he is the object of information, never a subject in communication. The
arrangement of his room, opposite the central tower, imposes on him an axial
visibility; but the divisions of the ring, those separated cells, imply a lateral
invisibility. And this invisibility is a guarantee of order. If the inmates are con-
victs, there is no danger of a plot, an attempt at collective escape, the planning
of new crimes for the future, bad reciprocal influences; if they are patients,
there is no danger of contagion; if they are madmen there is no risk of their
committing violence upon one another; if they are schoolchildren, there is no
copying, no noise, no chatter, no waste of time; if they are workers, there are
no disorders, no theft, no coalitions, none of those distractions that slow down
the rate of work, make it less perfect or cause accidents. The crowd, a compact mass, a locus of multiple exchanges, individualities merging together, a
collective effect, is abolished and replaced by a collection of separated individualities. From the point of view of the guardian, it is replaced by a multi-
plicity that can be numbered and supervised; from the point of view of the
inmates, by a sequestered and observed solitude (Bentham, 60–64).

Hence the major effect of the Panopticon: to induce in the inmate a state of
conscious and permanent visibility that assures the automatic functioning of
power. So to arrange things that the surveillance is permanent in its effects,
even if it is discontinuous in its action; that the perfection of power should tend
to render its actual exercise unnecessary; that this architectural apparatus
should be a machine for creating and sustaining a power relation independent
of the person who exercises it; in short, that the inmates should be caught up
in a power situation of which they are themselves the bearers. To achieve this,
it is at once too much and too little that the prisoner should be constantly
observed by an inspector: too little, for what matters is that he knows himself
to be observed; too much, because he has no need in fact of being so. In view
of this, Bentham laid down the principle that power should be visible and unverifiable. Visible: the inmate will constantly have before his eyes the tall outline
of the central tower from which he is spied upon. Unverifiable: the inmate must
never know whether he is being looked at at any one moment; but he must be
sure that he may always be so.

\* \* \*

A real subjection is born mechanically from a fictitious relation. So it is not
necessary to use force to constrain the convict to good behaviour, the mad-

man to calm, the worker to work, the schoolboy to application, the patient to the observation of the regulations. Bentham was surprised that panoptic institutions could be so light: there were no more bars, no more chains, no more heavy locks; all that was needed was that the separations should be clear and the openings well arranged. The heaviness of the old "houses of security," with their fortress-like architecture, could be replaced by the simple, economic geometry of a "house of certainty." The efficiency of power, its constraining force have, in a sense, passed over to the other side—to the side of its surface of application. He who is subjected to a field of visibility, and who knows it, assumes responsibility for the constraints of power; he makes them play spontaneously upon himself; he inscribes in himself the power relation in which he simultaneously plays both roles; he becomes the principle of his own subjection. By this very fact, the external power may throw off its physical weight; it tends to the non-corporal; and, the more it approaches this limit, the more constant, profound and permanent are its effects: it is a perpetual victory that avoids any physical confrontation and which is always decided in advance.

\* \* \*

The Panopticon is a privileged place for experiments on men, and for analysing with complete certainty the transformations that may be obtained from them. The Panopticon may even provide an apparatus for supervising its own mechanisms. In this central tower, the director may spy on all the employees that he has under his orders: nurses, doctors, foremen, teachers, warders; he will be able to judge them continuously, alter their behaviour, impose upon them the methods he thinks best; and it will even be possible to observe the director himself. An inspector arriving unexpectedly at the centre of the Panopticon will be able to judge at a glance, without anything being concealed from him, how the entire establishment is functioning. And, in any case, enclosed as he is in the middle of this architectural mechanism, is not the director's own fate entirely bound up with it? The incompetent physician who has allowed contagion to spread, the incompetent prison governor or workshop manager will be the first victims of an epidemic or a revolt. "By every tie I could devise," said the master of the Panopticon, "my own fate had been bound up by me with theirs." The Panopticon functions as a kind of laboratory of power.

\* \* \*

The celebrated, transparent, circular cage, with its high tower, powerful and knowing, may have been for Bentham a project of a perfect disciplinary institution; but he also set out to show how one may "unlock" the disciplines and get them to function in a diffused, multiple, polyvalent way throughout the whole social body. These disciplines, which the classical age had elaborated in specific, relatively enclosed places—barracks, schools, workshops—and whose total implementation had been imagined only at the limited and temporary scale of a plague-stricken town, Bentham dreamt of transforming into a network of mechanisms that would be everywhere and always alert, running through society without interruption in space or in time. The panoptic arrangement provides the formula for this generalization. It programmes, at the level of an elementary and easily transferable mechanism, the basic functioning of a society penetrated through and through with disciplinary mechanisms.

# 32

## From the Panopticon* to Disney World:
## The Development of Discipline

### CLIFFORD D. SHEARING and PHILLIP C. STENNING

*To live in a modern society is to know and live within a vast array of invisible struc-
tures designed to ensure orderly behavior. Other structures are quite visible but not
recognized: actual physical barriers, corridors, and messages directing us to come,
go, turn, stop, be silent, not smoke, wear a shirt and shoes, and so forth. We conform
to control systems with our own consent or what Shearing and Stenning call "structured compliance." Disney World is not the only place where this occurs, but it offers
a good illustration for your own investigations.*

One of the most distinctive features of that quintessentially American playground known as Disney World is the way it seeks to combine a sense of
comfortable—even nostalgic—familiarity with an air of innovative technological advance. Mingled with the fantasies of one's childhood are the dreams of
a better future. Next to the Magic Kingdom is the Epcot Center. As well as
providing for a great escape, Disney World claims also to be a design for better living. And what impresses most about this place is that it seems to run
like clockwork.

Yet the Disney order is no accidental by-product. Rather, it is a designed-in
feature that provides—to the eye that is looking for it, but not to the casual
visitor—an exemplar of modern private corporate policing. Along with the rest
of the scenery of which it forms a discreet part, it too is recognizable as a design
for the future.

We invite you to come with us on a guided tour of this modern police facility in which discipline and control are, like many of the characters one sees
about, in costume.

The fun begins the moment the visitor enters Disney World. As one arrives
by car one is greeted by a series of smiling young people who, with the aid of
clearly visible road markings, direct one to one's parking spot, remind one to
lock one's car and to remember its location and then direct one to await the
rubber-wheeled train that will convey visitors away from the parking lot. At
the boarding location one is directed to stand safely behind guard rails and to
board the train in an orderly fashion. While climbing on board one is reminded

---

*Jeremy Bentham (1748–1832) coined this term to describe a perfect prison where nothing
could be done outside the view of the custodial staff. [*Editor's note*]

to remember the name of the parking area and the row number in which one is parked (for instance, "Donald Duck, 1"). Once on the train one is encouraged to protect oneself from injury by keeping one's body within the bounds of the carriage and to do the same for children in one's care. Before disembarking one is told how to get from the train back to the monorail platform and where to wait for the train to the parking lot on one's return. At each transition from one stage of one's journey to the next, one is wished a happy day and a "good time" at Disney World (this begins as one drives in and is directed by road signs to tune one's car radio to the Disney radio network).

As one moves towards the monorail platform the directions one has just received are reinforced by physical barriers (that make it difficult to take a wrong turn), pavement markings, signs and more cheerful Disney employees who, like their counterparts in other locations, convey the message that Disney World is a "fun place" designed for one's comfort and pleasure. On approaching the monorail platform one is met by enthusiastic attendants who quickly and efficiently organize the mass of people moving onto it into corrals designed to accommodate enough people to fill one compartment on the monorail. In assigning people to these corrals the attendants ensure that groups visiting Disney World together remain together. Access to the edge of the platform is prevented by a gate which is opened once the monorail has arrived and disembarked the arriving passengers on the other side of the platform. If there is a delay of more than a minute or two in waiting for the next monorail one is kept informed of the reason for the delay and the progress the expected train is making towards the station.

Once aboard and the automatic doors of the monorail have closed, one is welcomed aboard, told to remain seated and "for one's own safety" to stay away from open windows. The monorail takes a circuitous route to one of the two Disney locations (the Epcot Center or the Magic Kingdom) during which time a friendly disembodied voice introduces one briefly to the pleasure of the world one is about to enter and the methods of transport available between its various locations. As the monorail slows towards its destination one is told how to disembark once the automatic doors open and how to move from the station to the entrance gates, and reminded to take one's possessions with one and to take care of oneself, and children in one's care, on disembarking. Once again these instructions are reinforced, in a variety of ways, as one moves towards the gates.

It will be apparent from the above that Disney Productions is able to handle large crowds of visitors in a most orderly fashion. Potential trouble is anticipated and prevented. Opportunities for disorder are minimized by constant instruction, by physical barriers which severely limit the choice of action available and by the surveillance of omnipresent employees who detect and rectify the slightest deviation.

The vehicles that carry people between locations are an important component of the system of physical barriers. Throughout Disney World vehicles are used as barriers. This is particularly apparent in the Epcot Center, ... where many exhibits are accessible only via special vehicles which automatically secure one once they begin moving.

Control strategies are embedded in both environmental features and structural relations. In both cases control structures and activities have other functions which are highlighted so that the control function is overshadowed. Nonetheless, control is pervasive. For example, virtually every pool, fountain, and flower garden serves both as an aesthetic object and to direct visitors away from, or towards, particular locations. Similarly, every Disney Productions employee, while visibly and primarily engaged in other functions, is also engaged in the maintenance of order. This integration of functions is real and not simply an appearance: beauty *is* created, safety *is* protected, employees *are* helpful. The effect is, however, to embed the control function into the "woodwork" where its presence is unnoticed but its effects are ever present.

A critical consequence of this process of embedding control in other structures is that control becomes consensual. It is effected with the willing cooperation of those being controlled so that the controlled become, as Foucault (1977) has observed, the source of their own control. Thus, for example, the batching that keeps families together provides for family unity while at the same time ensuring that parents will be available to control their children. By seeking a definition of order within Disney World that can convincingly be presented as being in the interest of visitors, order maintenance is established as a voluntary activity which allows coercion to be reduced to a minimum. Thus, adult visitors willingly submit to a variety of devices that increase the flow of consumers through Disney World, such as being corralled on the monorail platform, so as to ensure the safety of their children. Furthermore, while doing so they gratefully acknowledge the concern Disney Productions has for their family, thereby legitimating its authority, not only in the particular situation in question, but in others as well. Thus, while profit ultimately underlies the order Disney Productions seeks to maintain, it is pursued in conjunction with other objectives that will encourage the willing compliance of visitors in maintaining Disney profits. This approach to profit making, which seeks a coincidence of corporate and individual interests (employee and consumer alike), extends beyond the control function and reflects a business philosophy to be applied to all corporate operations (Peters and Waterman, 1982).

The coercive edge of Disney's control system is seldom far from the surface, however, and becomes visible the moment the Disney-visitor consensus breaks down, that is, when a visitor attempts to exercise a choice that is incompatible with the Disney order. It is apparent in the physical barriers that forcefully prevent certain activities as well as in the action of employees who detect breaches of order. This can be illustrated by an incident that occurred during a visit to Disney World by Shearing and his daughter, during the course of which she developed a blister on her heel. To avoid further irritation she removed her shoes and proceeded to walk barefooted. They had not progressed ten yards before they were approached by a very personable security guard dressed as a Bahamian police officer, with white pith helmet and white gloves that perfectly suited the theme of the area they were moving through (so that he, at first, appeared more like a scenic prop than a security person), who informed them that walking barefoot was, "for the safety of visitors," not permitted. When informed that, given the blister, the safety of this visitor was likely to be better secured by remaining barefooted, at least on the walkways, they were informed that their safety and how best to protect it was a matter for Disney Productions to determine while they were on Disney property and that unless they complied he would be compelled to escort them out of Disney World. Shearing's daughter, on learning that failure to comply with the security guard's instruction would deprive her of the pleasures of Disney World, quickly decided that she would prefer to further injure her heel and remain on Disney property. As this example illustrates, the source of Disney Productions' power rests both in the physical coercion it can bring to bear and in its capacity to induce cooperation by depriving visitors of a resource that they value.

The effectiveness of the power that control of a "fun place" has is vividly illustrated by the incredible queues of visitors who patiently wait, sometimes for hours, for admission to exhibits. These queues not only call into question the common knowledge that queueing is a quintessentially English pastime (if Disney World is any indication Americans are at least as good, if not better, at it), but provide evidence of the considerable inconvenience that people can be persuaded to tolerate so long as they believe that their best interests require it. While the source of this perception is the image of Disney World that the visitor brings to it, it is, interestingly, reinforced through the queueing process itself. In many exhibits queues are structured so that one is brought close to the entrance at several points, thus periodically giving one a glimpse of the fun to come while at the same time encouraging one that the wait will soon be over.

Visitor participation in the production of order within Disney World goes beyond the more obvious control examples we have noted so far. An important aspect of the order Disney Productions attempts to maintain is a particular image of Disney World and the American industrialists who sponsor its exhibits (General Electric, Kodak, Kraft Foods, etc.). Considerable care is taken to ensure that every feature of Disney World reflects a positive view of the American Way, especially its use of, and reliance on, technology. Visitors are, for example, exposed to an almost constant stream of directions by employees, robots in human form and disembodied recorded voices (the use of recorded messages and robots permits precise control over the content and tone of the directions given) that convey the desired message. Disney World acts as a giant magnet attracting millions of Americans and visitors from other lands who pay to learn of the wonders of American capitalism.

Visitors are encouraged to participate in the production of the Disney image while they are in Disney World and to take it home with them so that they can reproduce it for their families and friends. One way this is done is through the "Picture Spots," marked with signposts, to be found throughout Disney World, that provide direction with respect to the images to capture on film (with cameras that one can borrow free of charge) for the slide shows and photo albums to be prepared "back home." Each spot provides views which exclude anything unsightly (such as garbage containers) so as to ensure that the visual images visitors take away of Disney World will properly capture Disney's order. A related technique is the Disney characters who wander through the complex to provide "photo opportunities" for young children. These characters apparently never talk to visitors, and the reason for this is presumably so that their media-based images will not be spoiled.

As we have hinted throughout this discussion, training is a pervasive feature of the control system of Disney Productions. It is not, however, the redemptive soul-training of the carceral project but an ever-present flow of directions for, and definitions of, order directed at every visitor. Unlike carceral training, these messages do not require detailed knowledge of the individual. They are, on the contrary, for anyone and everyone. Messages are, nonetheless, often conveyed to single individuals or small groups of friends and relatives. For example, in some of the newer exhibits, the vehicles that take one through swivel and turn so that one's gaze can be precisely directed. Similarly, each seat is fitted with individual sets of speakers that talk directly to one, thus permitting a seductive sense of intimacy while simultaneously imparting a uniform message.

In summary, within Disney World control is embedded, preventative, subtle, cooperative and apparently non-coercive and consensual. It focuses on categories, requires no knowledge of the individual and employs pervasive surveillance. Thus, although disciplinary, it is distinctively non-carceral. Its order is instrumental and determined by the interests of Disney Productions rather than moral and absolute. As anyone who has visited Disney World knows, it is extraordinarily effective.

While this new instrumental discipline is rapidly becoming a dominant force in social control it is as different from the Orwellian totalitarian nightmare as it is from the carceral regime. Surveillance is pervasive but it is the antithesis of the blatant control of the Orwellian State: its source is not government and its vehicle is not Big Brother. The order of instrumental discipline is not the unitary order of a central State but diffuse and separate orders defined by private authorities responsible for the feudal-like domains of Disney World, condominium estates, commercial complexes and the like. Within contemporary discipline, control is as fine-grained as Orwell imagined but its features are very different. It is thus, paradoxically, not to Orwell's socialist-inspired Utopia that we must look for a picture of contemporary control but to the capitalist-inspired disciplinary model conceived of by Huxley, who, in his *Brave New World*, painted a picture of consensually based control that bears a striking resemblance to the disciplinary control of Disney World and other corporate control systems. Within Huxley's imaginary world people are seduced into conformity by the pleasures offered by the drug "soma" rather than coerced into compliance by threat of Big Brother, just as people are today seduced to conform by the pleasures of consuming the goods that corporate power has to offer.

The contrasts between morally based justice and instrumental control, carceral punishment and corporate control, the Panopticon and Disney World and Orwell's and Huxley's visions is succinctly captured by the novelist Beryl Bainbridge's (1984) observations about a recent journey she made retracing J. B. Priestley's (1933) celebrated trip around Britain. She notes how during his travels in 1933 the center of the cities and towns he visited were defined by either a church or a center of government (depicting the coalition between Church and State in the production of order that characterizes morally based regimes).

During her more recent trip one of the changes that struck her most forcibly was the transformation that had taken place in the center of cities and towns. These were now identified not by churches or town halls, but by shopping centers, often vaulted glass-roofed structures that she found reminiscent of the cathedrals they had replaced both in their awe-inspiring architecture and in the hush that she found they sometimes created. What was worshipped in these contemporary cathedrals, she noted, was not an absolute moral order but something much more mundane: people were "worshipping shopping" and through it, we would add, the private authorities, the order and corporate power their worship makes possible.

## REFERENCES

Bainbridge, B. (1984). Television interview with Robert Fulford on "Realities." Global Television, Toronto, October.

Foucault, M. (1977). *Discipline and Punish: The Birth of the Prison.* New York: Vintage.

Peters, T. J. and Waterman, R. H. (1982). *In Search of Excellence.* New York: Warner Books.

Priestley, J. B. (1934). *English Journey: Being a Rambling but Truthful Account of What One Man Saw and Heard and Felt and Thought during a Journey through England Autumn of the Year 1933.* London: Heinemann and Gollancz.

# 33

## The McDonald's System

FROM *The McDonaldization of Society*

### GEORGE RITZER

*McDonald's has become a buzzword not only for fast food but for a way of organizing activities, calculated to maximize efficiency by minimizing opportunities for error. For some this is wonderful, but for others this is lifeless and without joy, despite the images that appear in McDonald's commercials. Ultimately, it may not be as efficient as it seems.*

## THE DIMENSIONS OF MCDONALDIZATION: FROM DRIVE-THROUGHS TO UNCOMFORTABLE SEATS

Even if some domains are able to resist McDonaldization, this book intends to demonstrate that many other aspects of society are being, or will be, McDonaldized. This raises the issue of why the McDonald's model has proven so irresistible. Four basic and alluring dimensions lie at the heart of the success of the McDonald's model and, more generally, of the process of McDonaldization.

First, McDonald's offers *efficiency*. That is, the McDonald's system offers us the optimum method for getting from one point to another. Most generally, this means that McDonald's proffers the best available means of getting us from a state of being hungry to a state of being full. * * * Other institutions, fashioned on the McDonald's model, offer us similar efficiency in losing weight, lubricating our cars, filling eyeglass prescriptions, or completing income tax forms. In a fast-paced society in which both parents are likely to work, or where there may be only a single parent, efficiently satisfying the hunger and many other needs of people is very attractive. In a highly mobile society in which people are rushing, usually by car, from one spot to another, the efficiency of a fast-food meal, perhaps without leaving one's car while passing by the drive-through window, often proves impossible to resist. The fast-food model offers us, or at least appears to offer us, an efficient method for satisfying many of our needs.

Second, McDonald's offers us food and service that can be easily *quantified* and *calculated*. In effect, McDonald's seems to offer us "more bang for the buck." (One of its recent innovations, in response to the growth of other fast-food franchises, is to proffer "value meals" at discounted prices.) We often feel that we are getting a *lot* of food for a modest amount of money. Quantity has become equivalent to quality; a lot of something means it must be good. As two observers of contemporary American culture put it, "As a culture, we tend to believe—deeply—that in general 'bigger is better.'" Thus, we order the *Quarter Pounder*, the *Big* Mac, the *large* fries. We can quantify all of these things and feel that we are getting a lot of food, and, in return, we appear to be shelling out only a nominal sum of money. This calculus, of course, ignores an important point: the mushrooming of fast-food outlets, and the spread of the model to many other businesses, indicates that our calculation is illusory and it is the owners who are getting the best of the deal.

There is another kind of calculation involved in the success of McDonald's—a calculation involving time. People often, at least implicitly, calculate how much time it will take them to drive to McDonald's, eat their food, and return home and then compare that interval to the amount of time required to prepare the food at home. They often conclude, rightly or wrongly, that it will take less time to go and eat at the fast-food restaurant than to eat at home. This time calculation is a key factor in the success of Domino's and other home-delivery franchises, because to patronize them people do not even need to leave their homes. To take another notable example, Lens Crafters promises us "Glasses fast, glasses in one hour." Some McDonaldized institutions have come to combine the emphases on time and money. Domino's promises pizza delivery in one-half hour, *or* the pizza is free. Pizza Hut will serve us a personal pan pizza in five minutes, or it, too, will be free.

Third, McDonald's offers us *predictability*. We know that the Egg McMuffin we eat in New York will be, for all intents and purposes, identical to those we have eaten in Chicago and Los Angeles. We also know that the one we order next week or next year will be identical to the one we eat today. There is great comfort in knowing that McDonald's offers no surprises, that the food we eat at one time or in one place will be identical to the food we eat at another time or in another place. We know that the next Egg McMuffin we eat will not be awful, but we also know that it will not be exceptionally delicious. The success of the McDonald's model indicates that many people have come to prefer a world in which there are no surprises.

Fourth and finally, *control*, especially through the *substitution of non-human for human technology*, is exerted over the human beings who enter the world of McDonald's. The humans who work in fast-food restaurants are trained to do a very limited number of things in precisely the way they are told to do them. Managers and inspectors make sure that workers toe the line. The human beings who eat in fast-food restaurants are also controlled, albeit (usually) more subtly and indirectly. Lines, limited menus, few options, and uncomfortable seats all lead diners to do what the management wishes them to do—eat quickly and leave. Further, the drive-through (and in some cases walk-through) window leads diners to first leave and then eat rapidly. This attribute has most recently been extended by the Domino's model, according to which customers are expected to *never* come, yet still eat speedily.

McDonald's also controls people by using nonhuman technology to replace human workers. Human workers, no matter how well they are programmed and controlled, can foul up the operation of the system. A slow or indolent worker can make the preparation and delivery of a Big Mac inefficient. A worker who refuses to follow the rules can leave the pickles or special sauce off a hamburger, thereby making for unpredictability. And a distracted worker can put too few fries in the box, making an order of large fries seem awfully skimpy. For these and other reasons, McDonald's is compelled to steadily replace human beings with nonhuman technologies, such as the soft-drink dispenser that shuts itself off when the glass is full, the french-fry machine that rings when the fries are crisp, the preprogrammed cash register that eliminates the need for the cashier to calculate prices and amounts, and, perhaps at some future time, the robot capable of making hamburgers. (Experimental robots of this type already exist.) All of these technologies permit greater control over the human beings involved in the fast-food restaurant. The result is that McDonald's is able to reassure customers about the nature of the employee to be encountered and the nature of the service to be obtained.

In sum, McDonald's (and the McDonald's model) has succeeded because it offers the consumer efficiency and predictability, and because it seems to offer the diner a lot of food for little money and a slight expenditure of effort. It has also flourished because it has been able to exert greater control through non-human technologies over both employees and customers, leading them to behave the way the organization wishes them to. The substitution of non-human for human technologies has also allowed the fast-food restaurant to deliver its fare increasingly more efficiently and predictably. Thus, there are good, solid reasons why McDonald's has succeeded so phenomenally and why the process of McDonaldization continues unabated.

## A CRITIQUE OF MCDONALDIZATION: THE IRRATIONALITY OF RATIONALITY

There is a downside to all of this. We can think of efficiency, predictability, calculability, and control through nonhuman technology as the basic components of a *rational* system. However, as we shall see in later chapters, rational systems often spawn irrationalities. The downside of McDonaldization will be dealt with most systematically under the heading of the *irrationality of rationality*. Another way of saying this is that rational systems serve to deny human reason; rational systems can be unreasonable.

For example, the fast-food restaurant is often a dehumanizing setting in which to eat or work. People lining up for a burger, or waiting in the drive-through line, often feel as if they are dining on an assembly line, and those who prepare the burgers often appear to be working on a burger assembly line. Assembly lines are hardly human settings in which to eat, and they have been shown to be inhuman settings in which to work. As we will see, dehumanization is only one of many ways in which the highly rationalized fast-food restaurant is extremely irrational.

Of course, the criticisms of the irrationality of the fast-food restaurant will be extended to all facets of our McDonaldizing world. This extension has recently been underscored and legitimated at the opening of Euro Disneyland outside Paris. A French socialist politician acknowledged the link between Disney and McDonald's as well as their common negative effects when he said that Euro Disney will "bombard France with uprooted creations that are to culture what fast food is to gastronomy."

Such critiques lead to a question: Is the headlong rush toward McDonaldization around the world advantageous or not? There are great gains to be made from McDonaldization, some of which will be discussed below. But there are also great costs and enormous risks, which this book will focus on. Ultimately, we must ask whether the creation of these rationalized systems creates an even greater number of irrationalities. At the minimum, we need to be aware of the costs associated with McDonaldization. McDonald's and other purveyors of the fast-food model spend billions of dollars each year outlining the benefits to be derived from their system. However, the critics of the system have few outlets for their ideas. There are no commercials on Saturday morning between cartoons warning children of the dangers associated with fast-food restaurants. Although few children are likely to read this book, it is aimed, at least in part, at their parents (or parents-to-be) in the hope that it will serve as a caution that might be passed on to their children.

A legitimate question may be raised about this analysis: Is this critique of McDonaldization animated by a romanticization of the past and an impossible desire to return to a world that no longer exists? For some critics, this is certainly the case. They remember the time when life was slower, less efficient, had more surprises, when people were freer, and when one was more likely to deal with a human being than a robot or a computer. Although they have a point, these critics have undoubtedly exaggerated the positive aspects of a world before McDonalds, and they have certainly tended to forget the liabilities associated with such a world. More importantly, they do not seem to realize that we are *not* returning to such a world. The increase in the number of people, the acceleration in technological change, the increasing pace of life—all this and more make it impossible to go back to a nonrationalized world, if it ever existed, of home-cooked meals, traditional restaurant dinners, high-quality foods, meals loaded with surprises, and restaurants populated only by workers free to fully express their creativity.

While one basis for a critique of McDonaldization is the past, another is the future. The future in this sense is what people have the potential to be if they are unfettered by the constraints of rational systems. This critique holds that people have the potential to be far more thoughtful, skillful, creative, and well-rounded than they now are, yet they are unable to express this potential because of the constraints of a rationalized world. If the world were less rationalized, or even derationalized, people would be better able to live up to their human potential. This critique is based not on what people were like in the past, but on what they could be like in the future, if only the constraints of McDonaldized systems were eliminated, or at least eased substantially. The criticisms to be put forth in this book are animated by the latter, future-oriented perspective rather than by a romanticization of the past and a desire to return to it.

## THE ADVANTAGES OF MCDONALDIZATION: FROM THE CAJUN BAYOU TO SUBURBIA

Much of this book will focus on the negative side of McDonald's and McDonaldization. At this point it is important, however, to balance this view by mentioning some of the benefits of these systems and processes. The economic columnist, Robert Samuelson, for example, is a strong supporter of McDonald's and confesses to "openly worship McDonald's." He thinks of it as "the greatest restaurant chain in history." (However, Samuelson does recognize that there are those who "can't stand the food and regard McDonald's as the embodiment of all that is vulgar in American mass culture.")

Let me enumerate some of the advantages of the fast-food restaurant as well as other elements of our McDonaldized society:

- The fast-food restaurant has expanded the alternatives available to consumers. For example, more people now have ready access to Italian, Mexican, Chinese, and Cajun foods. A McDonaldized society is, in this sense, more egalitarian.
- The salad bar, which many fast-food restaurants and supermarkets now offer, enables people to make salads the way they want them.
- Microwave ovens and microwavable foods enable us to have dinner in minutes or even seconds.
- For those with a wide range of shopping needs, supermarkets and shopping malls are very efficient sites. Home shopping networks allow us to shop even more efficiently without ever leaving home.
- Today's high-tech, for-profit hospitals are likely to provide higher-quality medical care than their predecessors.
- We can receive almost instantaneous medical attention at our local, drive-in "McDoctors."
- Computerized phone systems (and "voice mail") allow people to do things that were impossible before, such as obtain a bank balance in the middle of the night or hear a report on what went on in their child's class during the day and what homework assignments were made. Similarly, automated bank teller machines allow people to obtain money any time of the day or night.
- Package tours permit large numbers of people to visit countries that they would otherwise not visit.

- Diet centers like Nutri/System allow people to lose weight in a carefully regulated and controlled system.
- The 24-second clock in professional basketball has enabled outstanding athletes such as Michael Jordan to more fully demonstrate their extraordinary talents.
- Recreational vehicles let the modern camper avoid excessive heat, rain, insects, and the like.
- Suburban tract houses have permitted large numbers of people to afford single-family homes.

## CONCLUSION

The previous list gives the reader a sense not only of the advantages of McDonaldization but also of the range of phenomena that will be discussed under that heading throughout this book. In fact, such a wide range of phenomena will be discussed under the heading of McDonaldization that one is led to wonder: What isn't McDonaldized? Is McDonaldization the equivalent of modernity? Is everything contemporary McDonaldized?

While much of the world has been McDonaldized, it is possible to identify at least three aspects of contemporary society that have largely escaped McDonaldization. First, there are phenomena traceable to an earlier, "premodern" age that continue to exist within the modern world. A good example is the Mom and Pop grocery store. Second, there are recent creations that have come into existence, at least in part, as a reaction against McDonaldization. A good example is the boom in bed and breakfasts (B&Bs), which offer rooms in private homes with personalized attention and a homemade breakfast from the proprietor. People who are fed up with McDonaldized motel rooms in Holiday Inn or Motel 6 can instead stay in so-called B&Bs. Finally, some analysts believe that we have moved into a new, "postmodern" society and that aspects of that society are less rational than their predecessors. Thus, for example, in a postmodern society we witness the destruction of "modern" high-rise housing projects and their replacement with smaller, more livable communities. Thus, although it is ubiquitous, McDonaldization is *not* simply another term for contemporary society. There *is* more to the contemporary world than McDonaldization.

In discussing McDonaldization, we are *not* dealing with an all-or-nothing process. Things are not either McDonaldized or not McDonaldized. There are degrees of McDonaldization; it is a continuum. Some phenomena have been heavily McDonaldized, others moderately McDonaldized, and some only slightly McDonaldized. There are some phenomena that may have escaped McDonaldization completely. Fast-food restaurants, for example, have been heavily McDonaldized, universities moderately McDonaldized, and the Mom and Pop grocers mentioned earlier only slightly McDonaldized. It is difficult to think of social phenomena that have escaped McDonaldization totally, but I suppose there is local enterprise in Fiji that has been untouched by this process. In this context, McDonaldization thus represents a process—a process by which more and more social phenomena are being McDonaldized to an increasing degree.

Overall, the central thesis is that McDonald's represents a monumentally important development and the process that it has helped spawn, McDonaldization, is engulfing more and more sectors of society and areas of the world. It has yielded a number of benefits to society, but it also entails a considerable number of costs and risks.

Although the focus is on McDonald's and McDonaldization, it is important to realize that this system has important precursors in our recent history. * * * That is, McDonaldization is not something completely new, but rather its success has been based on its ability to bring together a series of earlier innovations. Among the most important precursors to McDonaldization are bureaucracy, scientific management, the assembly line, and the original McDonald brothers' hamburger stand.

# 34

## Inequality in the Toy Store*

### CHRISTINE L. WILLIAMS

*Who would think a comparison of two toy stores could tell so much about race, class, and gender? This article summarizes the author's* Inside Toyland, *one of the best organizational ethnographies to appear in the past decade. She recounts working in an upscale store (Diamond Toys) and a low-brow store (Toy Warehouse), stores not so different from ones where you may have worked. Gender segregation, racial stereotyping, social class, and "interpellation" (the integration of job expectations into one's identity) are only some of the sociological concepts that help make sense of how, in the face of organizational rules and practices, people in the low-wage economy seek and find—often through resistance—what Randy Hodson calls dignity at work.*

This article presents a workplace ethnography of two toy stores, which I call Toy Warehouse and Diamond Toys. Toy Warehouse is a big-box superstore in a low-income redevelopment zone offering a vast array of low-cost popular toys, while Diamond Toys is a downtown high-end chain store selling a more limited range of reputedly high-quality toys. I spent three months, a total of over 300 hours, working as a clerk at these two stores. My goal in undertaking this study was to investigate the social conditions of retail work. I am interested in how inequalities based on gender, race, and class are reproduced, or possibly challenged, in the retail industry.

\* \* \*

### STRATIFICATION IN RETAIL STORES

The growth of retail employment is part of the general deindustrialization of the U.S. economy. Service jobs gradually replaced manufacturing jobs during the 1980s and 1990s. This economic restructuring resulted in boom times for wealthy American consumers while eroding conditions for workers in the bottom half of the labor market. Like other jobs in the service sector, jobs in retail became more "flexible," temporary, and part time as employers increased their

---

*References and footnotes can be found in the original publication of Christine L. Williams's article, "Inequality in the Toy Store."

power to fire employees at will. Workers in these jobs experienced a loss of job security, a diminishment in the power of unions, and a lessening of the value of the minimum wage. The power of ordinary workers was reduced while the giant corporations they worked for enjoyed unprecedented prosperity and political clout.

George Ritzer (2002) aptly uses the term "McJobs" to describe the working conditions found in a variety of service industries today. The word is a pun on McDonald's, the fast food giant often credited with inventing this system of labor control and management. McJobs are not careers; they are designed to discourage long-term commitment. They have short promotion ladders, they provide few opportunities for advancement or increased earnings, and the technical skills they require are not transferable outside of the immediate work environment. They target sectors of the labor force that presumably don't "need" money in order to support themselves or their families: young people looking for "fun jobs" before college; mothers seeking part-time opportunities to fit around their family responsibilities; older, retired people looking for the chance to get out of the house and to socialize. However, this image does not resonate with the increasing numbers of workers in these jobs who are struggling to support themselves and their families (Ehrenreich 2001; Talwar 2002). The marketing of McJobs on television commercials for Wal-Mart and fast-food restaurants obscures the harsh working conditions and low pay that contribute to the impoverished state of the working poor.

In addition to exacerbating economic inequality, jobs in the retail industry are structured in ways that enhance inequality by gender and race. Although all retail workers are low paid, white men employed in this industry earn more money than any other group. Overall, about as many men as women work in retail trades, but they are concentrated in different kinds of stores. For example, men make up more than three-quarters of workers in retail jobs selling motor vehicles, lumber, and home and auto supplies, while women predominate in apparel, gift, and needlework stores.

In both stores where I worked the gender ratio was about 60:40, with women outnumbering men. I was surprised that so many men worked in these toy stores—in my admittedly limited experience, I associated women with the job of selling toys. But I learned that because of the way jobs are divided and organized, customers usually don't see the substantial numbers of men who work in toy stores.

Retail work is also organized by race and ethnicity. Eleven percent of all employees in the retail trade industry are African American, and 13 percent are of Hispanic origin, slightly less then their overall representation in the U.S. population. But again, whites, African Americans, and Latinos are likely to work in different types of stores. For example, African Americans are underrepresented (less than 5 percent) in stores that sell hardware, gardening equipment, and needlework supplies, and overrepresented (more than

15 percent) in department stores, variety stores, and shoe stores. Similarly, Latinas/os are underrepresented (less than 6 percent) in book stores and gas stations, and overrepresented (more than 16 percent) in retail bakeries and clothing stores.

The two stores where I worked had radically different racial compositions. Sixty percent of the workers at Toy Warehouse were African American, and sixty percent of those at Diamond Toys were white. Only three African Americans, all women, worked at Diamond Toys; no black men worked there. In contrast, there were only four white women (including me) who worked at Toy Warehouse.

As in other large retail establishments, the more than seventy workers at Toy Warehouse and Diamond Toys are organized in elaborate hierarchies. Each store is governed by a regional office, which in turn is overseen by the national corporate headquarters. There is no local autonomy in the layout or the merchandise sold in the stores. Within each store, directors are at the top, followed by managers, supervisors, and associates. Directors and managers are salaried, while everyone else is paid hourly. Most directors and managers have a college degree. Candidates for these jobs apply to the regional headquarters and, once hired, they are assigned to specific stores. These may not be the closest stores to where they live. Olive, my manager at Toy Warehouse, had a two-hour commute each way, even though there was a Toy Warehouse within five miles of her home.

The hierarchy of jobs and authority within the stores is marked by race and gender. In both stores, the directors and assistant directors were white men. Immediately below were managers, who were a more diverse group and included men and women, whites and Latinos, and, at Toy Warehouse, an African American woman (Olive). There were far more managers at Diamond Toys than at Toy Warehouse; I met at least ten managers during my time there, and only two at Toy Warehouse.

The next layer of the hierarchy was supervisors, who were drawn from the ranks of associates. They were among those who had the most seniority and thus were most knowledgeable about store procedures, and they had limited authority to do things such as voiding register transactions. All of the supervisors at Diamond Toys were white, and most were men, while those at Toy Warehouse were more racially diverse, and most were women. It took me a long time to figure out who the supervisors were at Toy Warehouse. Many of those I presumed to be supervisors were actually regular employees. They had many of the same responsibilities as supervisors but, as I came to find out, they were competing with each other for promotion to this position. When I asked why they were acting like supervisors, it was explained that Toy Warehouse wouldn't promote anyone before they were proficient at the higher-level job. This policy justifies giving workers more responsibilities without more pay. At Diamond Toys, in contrast, job descriptions were clearer and they were enforced.

Associates (sometimes referred to as the staff) comprised the largest group of workers at the stores. They included men and women of all races and ethnic groups and of different ages, except at Diamond Toys, where I noted that there were no black men. Despite the apparent diversity among the staff, the tasks they were assigned were substantially segregated by race and gender. Employees of large toy stores are divided between back- and front-of-house workers. The back-of-house employees and managers work in the storage areas, on the loading docks, and in the assembly rooms. In both stores, the back-of-house workers were virtually all men. The front-of-house workers, who interact with customers, included both men and women. But there, too, was job segregation by gender and race although, as I will discuss, it was harder to discern and, on occasion, broke down.

There are two other jobs in the toy store: security guards and janitors, both of whom are subcontracted workers. Both Toy Warehouse and Diamond Toys employed plainclothes security guards who watched surveillance monitors in their back offices and roamed the aisles looking for shoplifters. At Toy Warehouse, the individuals who filled those jobs were mostly African American men and women, while Diamond Toys hired only white men and women. Finally, all of the cleaners at the two stores were Latinas, recent immigrants who didn't speak English.

What accounts for the race and gender segregation of jobs in the toy store? For years, economists have argued that job segregation is the product of differences in human capital attainment. According to this view, the marketplace sorts workers into jobs by their qualifications. Because men and women of different racial/ethnic groups possess different skills, aptitudes, and work experiences, they will be (and indeed should be) hired into different jobs. Economists see this process as benign, if not beneficial, in a society founded on meritocracy, individual liberty, and freedom of choice.

Instead of freedom, sociologists look at job segregation and see discrimination. Obtaining the right qualifications for a high-paying job is easier for some groups than others. Differential access to college education is an obvious example: Society blocks opportunities for poor people to acquire this human capital asset while smoothing the path for the well-to-do. But the sociological critique of job segregation goes deeper than this. The definition of who is qualified and what it means to be qualified for a job are linked to stereotypes about race and gender. Joan Acker (1990) argues that jobs are "gendered," meaning that qualities culturally associated with men (leadership, physical strength, aggression, goal orientation) are built into the job descriptions of the higher status and higher paid occupations in our economy. Qualities associated with women (dexterity, passivity, nurturing) tend to be favored in lower paying jobs. In addition to being gendered, jobs are also racialized. Black women have been subjected to a different set of gendered stereotypes than have white women. Far from being seen as delicate and passive, they have been perceived as dominant, insubordinate, and aggressive.

Those who make hiring decisions draw upon these kinds of racialized stereotypes of masculinity and femininity when appointing workers to specific jobs.

Leslie Salzinger (2003) has examined how this job placement works in manufacturing plants along the U.S.-Mexico border. She uses the concept of "interpellation" to describe how managers imagine a specific, embodied worker in each job, and how workers come to see themselves in these imaginings. Workers, in other words, typically consent to and embrace the stereotypes because their opportunities depend on their conformity to them. She shows that in order to get a job on the assembly line, young women workers have to represent themselves as docile, dexterous, and unencumbered by family responsibilities. They really have no choice: To get a job they must become the embodiment of their bosses' stereotypes. Eventually, she argues, the line between the stereotype and the authentic self blurs.

Similarly, at the toy stores where I worked, managers imagined different kinds of people in each job, who came to see themselves in terms of these stereotypical expectations. Because these jobs involved interacting with customers, managers also considered the public's expectations when making job assignments, which was not an issue in the factories studied by Salzinger. Furthermore, I observed far more worker resistance than Salzinger found in her study, especially at Toy Warehouse. Ultimately, I maintain, job segregation in retail work reflects the dynamic outcome of conflicts among workers' desires, managers' interests, and customer expectations.

\* \* \*

Talwar (2002) notes in her study of fast-food restaurants that African American men are sometimes preferred as cashiers during the nighttime shifts, especially in dangerous neighborhoods, presumably to offer some protection in case of attempted robbery. Here again we see how the image of "cashier" is linked to managers' race and gender stereotypes regarding the qualifications for the job. These images are not created in a vacuum, but are based on managers' beliefs of what the public wants and expects in service workers. At Toy Warehouse, African American men were not routinely assigned to the register at any time of day or night, but were used to perform a security function in the evening. When the store closed at the end of the day, Olive would make an announcement over the public intercom instructing two black men to "clear the store" and "check the bathrooms." This was often said in a menacing way to scare the remaining stragglers into leaving, especially if it had to be repeated more than once. This task assignment drew upon and bolstered stereotypes about the strength and inherent aggressiveness of African American men.

Cashiers did perform some security tasks at Toy Warehouse. In addition to being responsible for requesting pulls, we were expected to check the customers' bags and receipts whenever the alarm sounded at the front door. The alarm was set off when people left the store with merchandise affixed with security tags that had not been properly de-activated. This happened approximately every ten minutes. Half of the people who set off the alarm turned around immediately to offer proof that they were not guilty, and the other half just continued walking out the door. We tended to ignore both groups. We were usually too busy with other customers to stop and check those who came back into the store, so we just waved them out. We certainly were not going to run after those customers who just continued walking out, and expose ourselves to the potential danger of a physical confrontation. I thought this should have been the job of a uniformed security force, but Olive told me that a uniformed guard would damage the store's image as a welcoming and happy place.

A few men were regularly assigned to work as cashiers at Toy Warehouse, but this happened only in the electronics department. The electronics department was cordoned off from the rest of the store by a metal detector gate intended to curtail theft. In another example of interpellation, all of the men with this regular assignment were Asian American. They had sought out this assignment because they were interested in computers and gaming equipment. Working a register in that section may have been more acceptable to them in part because the section was separated from the main registers, and in part because Asian masculinity—as opposed to black or white masculinity—is often defined through technical expertise. My sense is that the stereotypical association of Asian American men with computers made these assignments desirable from management's perspective as well.

Occasionally men were assigned to work the registers outside of the electronics department, but this happened only when there were staffing shortages or scheduling problems. Once I came to work to find Deshay, a 25-year-old African American man, and Shuresh, a 21-year-old second generation Indian American, both stationed at the main registers. I flew to the back of the store to clock in so I could take my station next to them, eager to observe them negotiating the demands of "women's work." But the minute I took my station they were relieved of cashiering, and told to cash out their registers and return to their regular tasks. When a woman was available, the men didn't have to do the job.

On a previous occasion, I had observed Deshay skillfully evade the assignment to work the register. Deshay is normally a merchandiser, and he also works in the storeroom unloading boxes from the delivery trucks. I noticed when he was called to the register because I had never seen an African American man work there. Olive had called Deshay to her office over the walkietalkie (without telling him why—if he had known why, he later told me, he wouldn't have responded to the page). I then saw him with a register drawer, and he was told to start counting out the cash, in preparation for cashiering. He took the till over to the service desk; I turned around for a moment and he was gone! Eventually I caught up with him in the break room and asked him what happened. I said, "That was some disappearing act!" He told me, with mounting exasperation and anger, that he did not want to work register, he was not hired to work register, and he had too many other jobs to do, and that if they forced him to work register he would file a lawsuit against them. He didn't say outright that cashiering was a lousy job, I assumed because that was my job.

This is another example of interpellation: Deshay had come to see himself in managerial stereotypes about the appropriate roles for black men. But I think another reason that Deshay didn't want to cashier was that he felt his masculinity was at stake. For many men, work functions as outward proof of their masculine identity. Their poise, sense of strength, and even their heterosexuality is challenged when they do "women's work." Even though there is nothing inherently feminine about working a cash register, management had defined the job as "women's work," and Deshay was eager to distance himself from any job considered "feminine."

\* \* \*

The stores exploit young men's insecurity in their masculinity by assigning them to jobs requiring a great deal of heavy lifting. They move freight and deliver large items (like baby car seats, play sets, and bikes) to the front of the store and occasionally to the customer's car. Several men told me that the physical aspect of their work wore them out, causing their jobs in retail to be temporary. At the same time they took a great deal of pride in these tasks—because these jobs were defined as masculine, they experienced a personal boost of recognition for accomplishing them.

Women also crossed over into the men's jobs, but far less frequently. Management never assigned a woman to work in the back areas to make up for temporary staff shortages. At each store, only one woman worked back-of-house, and both were African American. Darlene, who worked at Toy Warehouse, was once described to me by a co-worker as "very masculine" (but also "really great"). Darlene worked in a contracting business on the side and took a lot of pride in her physical strength and stamina. She was lesbian, which made her the butt of mean-spirited, surreptitious joking, but also probably made this assignment less dissonant in the eyes of management (women in nontraditional jobs are often stereotyped as lesbian). At Diamond Toys, 18-year-old Chandrika worked back-of-house. She had started working there but asked for and received a transfer to the gift wrap department. Chandrika, who was one of only three African Americans who worked at Diamond Toys, said she hated working in the storeroom because the men were racist and "very misogynistic," telling sexist jokes and challenging her competence at the job.

Men and women experience crossing over differently. When a job is identified as masculine, men often will erect barriers against women, making them feel out of place and unwanted, which is what happened to Chandrika. In contrast, I never observed women trying to exclude men or marginalize men in "their" jobs. On the contrary, men tried to exclude themselves from "women's work." Job segregation by gender is in large part a product of men's efforts to establish all-male preserves, which helps them prove and maintain their masculinity.

Management colludes in this insofar as they share similar stereotypes of appropriate task assignments for men and women, or if they perceive the public to embrace such stereotypes. But they also insist on employee "flexibility," the widespread euphemism for their fundamental right to hire, fire, and assign employees at will. At Toy Warehouse, employees were often threatened that their hours would be cut if they were not "flexible" in their available hours and willingness to perform any job. But in general, managers shared men's preference to avoid register duty unless no one else was available.

How and why a specific job comes to be "gendered" and "racialized," or considered appropriate only for women or for men, or for whites or nonwhites, is largely determined by the local context. Thus, in contrast to Toy Warehouse, both men and women were employed as cashiers at Diamond Toys, only two of whom—both women—were African American. At Toy Warehouse, most of the registers were lined up in the front of the store. Diamond Toys was organized like a department store, with cash registers scattered throughout the different sections. The preference for white workers seemed consistent with the marketing of the store's workers as "the ultimate toy experts." In retail work, professional expertise is typically associated with whiteness, similar to domestic service.

Although both men and women worked the registers at Diamond Toys, there was gender segregation by type of toy sold. Only women were assigned to work in the doll and stuffed animal sections, for example, and only men worked in sporting goods and electronics. Only women worked in gift wrap. Some sections, like the book department, were gender neutral, but most were as gender marked as the toys we sold.

This gender segregation occasionally would break down at Diamond Toys, and men would be assigned to work in the women's sections when enough women weren't available. Carl, a 30-year-old white man, once had to work backup with me in the doll department. He performed the role in a completely campy style, swishing around the floor and answering the phone "Barbie speaking!" Carl, who normally didn't act this way, was parodying the assumed homosexuality of any man interested in dolls (and, indeed, many of the high-end Barbie customers were gay). Turning the role into a joke made his temporary assignment seem more palatable and less inconsistent with his masculinity.

\* \* \*

## HOURS, BENEFITS, AND PAY

When I started this project I thought I had the perfect career to combine with a part-time job in retail. As a college professor, I teach two courses per semester that meet for six hours each week. I thought I could schedule twenty hours a week that accommodated those teaching commitments—wrong. To get a job in retail, a worker must be available to work any hours and be willing to change her schedule from one week to another to meet the staffing needs of the store. This is the meaning of the word "flexible" in retail. It is exactly the kind of schedule that is incompatible with doing anything else.

Retail is often marketed as a great part-time work opportunity because of the "flexible" schedules. Mothers seeking to combine work with their primary family responsibilities are drawn to these jobs. I met a mother of three preschool children with this goal in mind at a job fair. She and I met in a seminar room along with four others who were applying for a job at a children's warehouse store. Before the formal presentation started, we talked about why we were there. She told me that she preferred not to work, that she valued her role as full-time wife and mother, and that she would never put her kids in day care, but she decided to get a job because of an argument she had with her husband. She had recently asked him to buy her a cell phone. He told her that if she really wanted a cell phone, she should get a job. So she decided to look for a retail job for the hours five to ten o'clock in the evening, when her husband would be home from work and available to look after the children. She noted, with a devious smile, that he'd also have to feed them and put them to bed.

I did not get that job, and I suspect that she didn't either. We wanted flexible jobs, but the store wanted flexible workers. I learned from my experience to never limit the hours I would work on job applications. Giant retailers do not cater to the needs of employees; their goal is to hire a constant stream of entry-level, malleable, and replaceable workers. This organizational preference for high turnover keeps labor costs down (Talwar 2002).

Workers with seniority can gain some control over their schedules, but it takes years of "flexibility" to attain to this status. Moreover, in my experience, this control was guaranteed at Diamond Toys only thanks to the union. Senior associates who had worked there more than a year had the same weekly schedule. This did not apply to the supervisors, however. They had to be willing to fill in as needed because a supervisor was required to be on the floor at all times. Occasionally they even had to forgo breaks.

* * *

Those who didn't live in the city faced long and often grueling commutes. When I first met Mario, a 25-year-old Latino, he was trying to take a nap on one of the ratty couches in the break room. It was almost 9:00 a.m., the start of my shift, and I asked him when he was on. He told me that his shift didn't start until noon, but he had to come in early to get a ride with his sister, Angie, who worked nine-to-five. They lived in a suburb about thirty-five miles away, and since it took about two and a half hours to get to work by public transportation, he figured he came out ahead (and saved some money) by coming in three hours early. When he was hired at Diamond Toys he lived in the city, but he moved out to the suburbs about a year ago, where there were no jobs as good as this one. He said he had just found out that he had to have dental work done, probably a root canal, and that it was going to cost $2,000 but would all be paid for, thanks to the union benefits. So the job—with the long commute— was worth it to him.

\* \* \*

Interestingly, no one at Diamond Toys appeared to have any children. I asked Dennis about this and he verified that no one he could think of had children, a fact he attributed to their youth and their college attendance. Several gay men worked at the store (at the managerial level), another possible reason for the childlessness. I did meet one young associate who had a 6-year-old daughter, but I later learned that the daughter lived with her father in another state. The complete absence of parents suggests a systematic bias in the hiring and/or retention of workers. Perhaps those with child care responsibilities are less able to conform to the "flexible" requirements of the job.

This was a huge contrast to my experience at Toy Warehouse, where most of my women co-workers were single mothers. I met only three other women besides me who didn't have children. (Interestingly, those three were full-time employees at the supervisory level.) Most of the men also had children. Here, the systematic hiring bias favored parents. This was in part a consequence of the fact that Toy Warehouse participated in the "workfare" program, whereby businesses hiring former welfare recipients received reimbursement for part of their wages. Since welfare was designed to provide aid to families with dependent children, all recipients had children. All new hires (including me) were given a form certifying their employment for the welfare office. These forms were also used by the store to obtain a federal reimbursement under the "work opportunity tax credit." This tax credit, part of the welfare reform of 1996, reimburses businesses for 35 percent of wages for the first year and 50 percent the second to a maximum of $8,500 per new hire (qualified wages are capped at $10,000 per year). Participating in the program helped Toy Warehouse significantly reduce its labor costs.

The unpredictability of scheduling presented a nightmare for many single mothers at Toy Warehouse. Schedules for the following week, beginning on Sunday, were posted on Friday. This two-day notice made it especially difficult to arrange for child care. (In contrast, schedules came out on Tuesday for the following week at Diamond Toys, another union benefit.) Even worse, while I was working at Toy Warehouse, management reduced everyone's hours, purportedly to make up for revenue shortfalls. We were all asked to fill in a form indicating our "availability" to work, from six a.m. until ten p.m. This form, which was attached to our paychecks, warned that "associates with the flexible availability will get more hours than those who are limited." Part-timers who limited their availability were hit hard when schedules came out the following week, causing a great deal of anger and bad feelings. Angela, an experienced associate, was scheduled for only four hours, and she was so mad that no one could even talk to her. Some said that they were going to apply for unemployment. Deshay offered to get me the phone number for the county unemployment office because I was given only 13.5 hours, well below the 20 that he told me was the maximum one could work in order to qualify for unemployment benefits.

One of the reasons management gave for cutting our hours was that the store had been experiencing major problems with "shrink," the retailer term for theft. It was insinuated that the workers were stealing, but I could never figure out how that could happen. In both stores, there were very elaborate surveillance systems set up to monitor employees. Hidden cameras recorded activity throughout the store, including the areas around the emergency exits. Our bags, pockets, and purses were checked every time we left the store. Cashiers were monitored continuously via a backroom computer hooked up to every register. As I noted, the contents of the till have to match exactly with the register report. Being even slightly under is enough to cause a major panic.

\* \* \*

To reward us for good customer service, the Toy Warehouse management would occasionally give us "toy bucks," script-like coupons redeemable for a Coke or ice cream bar. The coupons are given for a variety of reasons, including "never letting a guest leave our store dissatisfied" and "thanking guests and inviting them to return." Once, after an especially busy day, the entire closing staff got a toy buck, prompting one of my co-workers to cynically remark, "How many of these does it take to get a TV?"

Toy bucks were miserly rewards, but they did improve the morale of some workers who, after all, were making very miserly incomes. Toy Warehouse paid employees less than Diamond Toys. I earned $7.50 an hour, which I later found out was a relatively high starting salary. Pak Chew, who was hired at the same time as me, made only $7.10,† but this was his first job ever. Later Pak Chew was offered a full-time job at UPS for $11 an hour, and to his, and everyone's, amazement Mark offered him $9 to stay (he didn't).

Although there were no rules against discussing wages at Toy Warehouse, it was a topic most workers avoided. It was an embarrassing subject, especially if it were revealed that some people (especially the new hires) earned more than the longer-term employees. I learned that some of my co-workers who had been at the store much longer than me made the same wage I did. Vern, a 50-year-old black man who had worked in bike assembly for two years, was distressed to learn that Paul, a new hire, was making as much as him, even though Vern had just received a 25-cent raise. Paul, a 22-year-old heavily tattooed white man, was hired at $8 an hour, as he informed me when I first met him in the break room. He was complaining about his low wage and announced that in one month

---

†Williams's fieldwork was done prior to federal legislation in July 2009 that raised the minimum wage to $7.25. [*Editor's note*]

he would demand a raise to $9. He explained that his father was a good friend of Jack's, the supervisor of the bike department. That was how he got the job, along with the promise that he soon would be making more money.

Paul was one exception to the norm about not talking about wages, and it didn't make him any friends. Most thought he was a braggart and avoided him. Another exception was Michelle, a 33-year-old African American woman. Michelle talked about wages and working conditions at every opportunity, but she was enormously popular and well-liked. One day before my shift I was in the break room when Michelle arrived. She was furious because her paycheck didn't reflect the overtime she was forced to work the previous Saturday when the staff was required to come to an unscheduled meeting. (The issue of unpaid overtime is the subject of recent class action lawsuits brought against Wal-Mart.) Other employees said they would make a point of noticing whether they were also shorted. Then Michelle started ad libbing wonderful rap songs about our lousy jobs and the whole break room erupted with laughter and shouting.

One of the issues that Michelle raised is that the new hires (including me) were taking the established workers' hours. None of the new workers are African American (we are white, Asian American, and Latina), which forms an unspoken backdrop to her complaint. Michelle had tried to start a petition drive to complain about the diminishing hours, but no one would sign her petition. She was very frustrated. People told her, "I don't want to lose my job; I need this job." Well, so did she, but who will fight for their rights, she wanted to know. She did not involve the new workers in the organizing, but she complained to me later that the others were not brave enough to fight for their rights. They talk a good deal in the break room, she said, but when push comes to shove they are not there to support her and her campaign for better working conditions.

Michelle is one of several workers who have two jobs. Nationally, about 6 percent of all workers hold two jobs, but nearly every associate I met at Toy Warehouse also worked someplace else to supplement their income. Michelle worked for the school district as a janitor, making about $11 an hour. She started at Toy Warehouse at Christmas time, when school was out, and Olive asked her to stay on. When she explained about her other job Olive promised to work around it, but as it turned out that didn't happen. She complained that sometimes she was asked to be at work at noon, but her other job required her to be there until 1:30, so how could she make it on time? Subsequently she would be written up for tardiness, which seemed totally unfair to her. She had two demerits against her that she had been called into the main office to sign, and she had declined, saying she didn't agree that she was in the wrong. She was told the demerits would go in her file anyway; she responded, then what is the point of signing?

Michelle is also upset because her perceived insubordination resulted in her being demoted to cashier. She had been working at the service desk, a position with more authority and more varied responsibilities, but not more pay. The service desk worker can clear voided transactions and open registers to make change and pull out large amounts of cash to put into the safe. A person in this position wears register keys around her neck, a symbolic marker of her higher authority and status (only women were ever assigned this job). Michelle is furious to be assigned to a register, a situation made worse by the fact that the person assigned to the service desk is new at the job and has to ask Michelle how to perform most of her tasks.

Michelle was so frustrated that she eventually decided to resign. She composed her letter of resignation at the register next to mine, so we talked about it while she was working on it. The letter was addressed to Mark, the store director, who replaced the director who had been in charge when Michelle was hired. She told me (in the break room with the others) that when she was hired she had been promised $10 an hour, which she thought was acceptable combined with her other job which paid her $11. She subsequently discovered she was getting only $9.25, which she thought insulting granted her prior experience at Kmart. (One of the others backed her up, saying that anything promised by the previous director was probably not honored, since he often lied to employees.) When she confronted the managers about this they said this was standard, but that after three months there would be a 25-to-50-cent raise. After three months she was given 25 cents, which set her off. In fact, the first time I met Michelle she was carrying on in the break room, shouting that she was going to tell the manager to shove that 25 cents up her ass.

## TAKE THIS JOB AND SHOVE IT—OR NOT

Over the course of working at the two stores, I witnessed a great deal of employee turnover. I outlasted the two who were hired with me at Toy Warehouse, and by the time I left Diamond Toys, I was third in seniority among the ten associates who worked in my section. On one of my last days there I was given the walkie-talkie, the direct line of communication to the storeroom and the managers' office, which indicated that I was at that time the most senior staff member in the section.

For most employees, retail work is a revolving door.[1] Employers know this, expect this, and even cultivate it (Talwar 2002). Most new hires are not expected to last through the three-month probation period. One of my co-workers at Toy Warehouse told me he rarely talked to the new people since they generally did not last long. Kevin, a 26-year-old African American supervisor, predicted I wouldn't stay very long because I didn't have the right personality for retail work. I asked him, "What kind of people stay at the store?" He answered, people who are quiet, who don't stress out easily (my major flaw), and, he whispered, people who can kiss up to management. I asked him if he did that and he said yes, but in a different kind of way, not too obviously.

---

1. According to the National Retail Federation the employee turnover rate is between 100 percent and 160 percent for part-time workers, and 80 percent to 120 percent for full-time workers. Data published on the BLS website shows that the monthly turnover rate in retail is about 5–6 percent, or 60–72 percent per year, higher than any other industry (www.bls.gov).

When I asked how, he explained that he didn't tell people what he "really" thought if he thought he was being screwed over.

Kevin was one of a handful of hourly workers who saw their job at Toy Warehouse as their lifelong work. He said he "grew up" at Toy Warehouse, and he could never imagine leaving. There were also a half-dozen or so associates at Diamond Toys who had worked at the store long term (which I arbitrarily define as more than a year). It is much more understandable why workers might choose to stay there, granted the union benefits. An extra incentive is the possibility of moving into management. At least a third of the managers at Diamond Toys started working as regular associates. When they become managers they leave the union and earn salaries that start at about $35,000. In contrast, no associate ever moved into management at Toy Warehouse, although one of my young co-workers maintained that it could happen. Vannie, a 21-year-old first generation immigrant from the Philippines, told me that she met someone at another store in the chain (which had since closed) who knew someone who had worked his way up from janitor to store director. I told her I thought this seemed unlikely; janitorial services are subcontracted, and director and management positions require a college degree and involve a completely separate application process through the regional office in a different state. The story sounded like a Horatio Alger myth to me. But Vannie said that this man was a great inspiration to her, and I believed her.

Although acquiring a management position at Diamond Toys wasn't unprecedented, few of the long-term associates seemed interested in pursuing it. Some seemed resigned to their position with its guaranteed hours, schedule, and benefits. Alyss, for example, had worked two years in the doll department, and had a set schedule from 8:00 to 4:30, five days a week. She told me she couldn't believe she had worked at the store that long, but at this point, she considered the job pretty easy. The only drawbacks were her dealings with Dorothy (the irritable section manager) and the occasional neurotic high-end Barbie collector. She had no interest in pursuing a supervisory position because that would mean losing her schedule and taking on more work.

Alyss and the other long-timers didn't exactly like their job, but they had become experts in the work, no small feat. Barbara Ehrenreich (2001) writes that there is no such thing as an unskilled job, an observation I confirmed during my first two weeks at each of the two toy stores. The first days on the job are a nightmare. Very little training is given, not surprising given the high turnover, which can make a new worker feel like a complete buffoon. Doing the simplest things, such as locating the proper place to reshelve a toy, can take ages to accomplish, not unlike placing one piece in a jigsaw puzzle. I once spent twenty minutes trying to find out where to put a 50-cent pack of cotton balls (I eventually gave up). Customers are always asking where they can find particular toys. Where is Gumby? When will the Harry Potter merchandise arrive? Do you have any electric trains that make hooting noises? Where can I find the chess sets that were advertised for $1.99? Customers are impatient and assume you are stupid if you don't know and have to ask. And then there are the myriad tasks associated with selling merchandise, such as finding the correct price for the last item remaining when the tag is missing, finding the original shipping carton for the $750 Barbie, figuring out mailing charges, or dialing in credit card authorizations when the computers crash.

After two weeks, this knowledge becomes second nature, but those two weeks are very hard to endure. Every question or task has to be deferred; new workers depend on those more experienced for the answers. This just adds more work for them, another request in the queue; it is not uncommon for them to feel harassed by new workers. Experienced workers sometimes avoid the newcomers—"Let them figure it out for themselves like I had to"—adding to the overall frustration. Sometimes the new worker is reduced to begging for help, because the problem does not go away until the answer is found (or the shift is over). I once almost cried because no one would answer my page at Toy Warehouse, and the customers in line were getting impatient and surly. This is a powerful incentive to stay on the job. No one wants to start over. The cultural capital needed to work retail simply doesn't transfer from one store to another, even in the same chain. Everyone who is new starts at the bottom (Talwar 2002).

Another reason it is hard to leave once expertise is acquired is that, ironically, workers come to feel needed. Although we all knew we were replaceable, there is a strong feeling that people depend on you to do your job. To promote this feeling the schedule is organized in waves: No one can take a break or have lunch until the person currently on break returns. Since breaks are very precious to workers who are on their feet all day, we monitored each other carefully to ensure that we could go on break as scheduled. Mutual dependence is also evident when someone doesn't show up to work, which immediately increases the stress level for everyone else, who have that many more transactions to complete. Quitting is hard, too, because who is going to answer all those questions if you're not there? Solving problems and dealing with difficult situations all day builds a sense of authority and a feeling of occupying a critical role in the overall division of labor. I agonized over quitting my jobs for this reason—I didn't want to let my co-workers down.

Every job enmeshes workers in social relationships so it is not surprising that many come to feel as attached and committed to their jobs as I did. The importance of these ties is especially apparent in the case of long-term workers. I jokingly referred to Dennis, one of my supervisors at Diamond Toys, as a "misanshop" because he constantly complained about the incivility of shoppers and the hopelessness of a retail career. Knowing how much he hated his job—which he had worked for seven years—I was shocked the first time I saw him in the break room on his day off. He was waiting for a co-worker to take his lunch break so they could go out together, and he had brought in his laptop computer to show others his new computer games. It was clear that his social life revolved around the store.

Many long-time workers developed quasi-familial bonds at the stores, referring to each other as brother and sister, mother and grandmother. This happened at both stores. There were also real kin networks, most evident at Toy Warehouse. Some of the older employees brought their children or grandchildren with them to the store during their shift. These kids hung out in the break room or played with the demonstration toys including the video games that were set up in the electronics department. All the employees helped to keep an eye on them. Those with older children sometimes got them jobs in the store.

I was very clearly an outsider to these family and friendship networks, but I was often very touched by the mutual support and caring I witnessed among my co-workers, especially at Toy Warehouse. For the long-time workers, the store was an extension of their family networks and responsibilities. They used their employee discount cards (10 percent at Toy Warehouse; 30 percent at Diamond Toys) to buy toys for their kin and quasi-kin. But more important was the social and emotional support they experienced there.

I was struck by this once when I was in the break room at Toy Warehouse and my co-workers Dwain and Lamonica walked in on a day they were not scheduled to work. They are an African American couple in their early twenties who had been dating for a short time. They had come in to pick up their paychecks and to talk to Selma, an African American woman in her forties who had worked at the store for six years. Dwain was upset with his mother, who was giving him a very hard time by telling him he's worthless and criticizing him for being too dependent. During the discussion Lamonica was sitting on a stack of chairs behind Dwain, sucking on her Jamba Juice. She smiled during the conversation, or rolled her eyes as if to say, "What are you going to do?" But she didn't really participate. Selma, on the other hand, gave him reassurance, sympathy, and moral support. I asked her if she knew Dwain's mother and she said no, just what Dwain had told her. I realized that Selma was a mentor for Dwain; he clearly cherished her advice and encouragement.

This is definitely the backstage of the store that most shoppers don't see, but is critical for understanding why people stay in crummy jobs with low pay, a conundrum that Barbara Ehrenreich (2001) considers in her study of low-wage work. She wonders why workers don't leave when other, higher paying opportunities arise. At Toy Warehouse, most workers stayed no longer than three months. Those who stayed long term did so because that is where their family was.

\* \* \*

## CONCLUSION

Most sociological research on retail stores considers them sites of consumption. But stores are also workplaces. Retail work makes up an increasing proportion of the jobs in our economy. Yet these are "bad" jobs. In this article, I have argued that the social organization of work in large toy stores reflects and contributes to class, gender, and race inequalities. As I have indicated, a union does make a difference for workers, but unions are not a panacea for these structural problems. The unionized job where I worked offered better pay and benefits than the nonunionized job—but still not a "living wage"—and it was characterized by racial exclusion and gender segregation.

Debating the relative strengths and weaknesses of unionized jobs may be moot, however. Union membership is at an all-time low, hovering at around 9 percent of the private work force. Regrettably, early in 2003 it was announced that the Diamond Toys store where I had worked was closing, unable to compete with the low prices of the nonunion discount chains. Retail giants have been extremely successful at preventing the formation of unions among their workers. High job turnover and "right to work" laws make it easy for employers to fire anyone who attempts to organize in the workplace. In the few instances where organizing efforts have been successful, national retailers (including Kmart and Wal-Mart) have shown that they would rather shut down franchises rather than recognize a union.

Nevertheless, conditions seemed favorable for mobilizing workers at Toy Warehouse. Several of my co-workers expressed interest in employee organizing and spoke often of the importance of defending their rights. In fact, on my first day of work at Toy Warehouse I was lectured by a 21-year-old security guard for not protecting my rights. Clearly, as Michelle's experience suggests, not everyone at the store would support collective action. But there seemed to be critical mass, especially among my African American co-workers at Toy Warehouse, that would support organizing efforts.

Because of the difficulty of unionizing low-wage retail workers, a more effective strategy for enhancing these jobs may be through organizing "living wage" campaigns. These campaigns demand not minimum wages but "living" wages for all employees, defined as "enough so that a full-time, year round worker can support a family at the poverty line" (Clawson 2003, p. 164). The basic goal is to transform all low-level jobs, including retail work in toy stores, into "good jobs," paying above-poverty wages and providing health care benefits, sick leave, and vacation pay. This is in contrast to current public policy, which guarantees only a minimum wage (which does not raise a worker's income to the family poverty level) and encourages workers in these "bad" jobs who want to enhance their living standard to seek retraining for "better" jobs. This latter approach leaves "bad" jobs intact. In my view, upgrading existing jobs is the only way to insure that all workers can become self-sufficient.

Consumers have an interest in pressing for living wages because they in effect subsidize the poverty wages currently paid by retail establishments. Tax dollars paid part of the workers' wages at Toy Warehouse, through reimbursements to the toy store for hiring welfare recipients. Taxpayers' contributions are sometimes more indirect: By refusing to pay living wages and health care benefits, giant retailers like Wal-Mart and Toy Warehouse pass these costs onto the American public. A television expose of Wal-Mart disclosed that the store teaches workers how to apply for welfare benefits. Shoppers at these stores may save money by paying less for their toys, but they have to spend more in higher taxes to support the social welfare infrastructure (social security, TANF, food stamps, Medicare) that many toy store workers are compelled to use.[2]

\* \* \*

Restructuring jobs in toy stores is also necessary to alter their gender and race dynamics. As I have argued, the hierarchical and functional placement of workers according to managerial stereotypes results in advantages for white men and (to a lesser extent) white women, and disadvantages for racial/ethnic minority men and women. These stereotypes are perhaps more deeply entrenched than low wages, based as they are on perceptions of customer preferences. Consumers therefore have a role in pressing for changes in these job assignments. But in my view, the struggle for equal access to "bad jobs" is hardly worth an organized effort. There is little point of demanding equal access to jobs that don't support a family. Similarly, career ladders have to be created before equal opportunities for advancement can be demanded. The fight against racism and sexism, then, should be folded into efforts to economically upgrade these jobs. The goal of restructuring jobs in toy stores, and in retail work in general, should be self-sufficiency—and hope—for all workers, regardless of race or gender.

## REFERENCES

Acker, J. (1990). Hierarchies, jobs, bodies: A theory of gendered organizations. *Gender & Society, 4,* 139–158.

Clawson, D. (2002). *The next upsurge: Labor and the new social movements.* Ithaca: ILR Press.

Ehrenreich, B. (2001). *Nickel and dimed.* New York: Metropolitan Books.

Ritzer, G. (2002). *McDonaldization: The reader.* Thousand Oaks, CA: Pine Forge Press.

Salzinger, L. (2003). *Genders in production: Making workers in Mexico's global factories.* Berkeley: University of California Press.

Talwar, J. P. (2002). *Fast food, fast track: Immigrants, big business, and the American Dream.* Boulder: Westview Press.

Zabin, C., Dube, A., & Jacobs, K. (2004). *The hidden public costs of low-wage jobs in California.* UC Berkeley Center for Labor Research and Education, white paper. Retrived June 7, 2004 from http://laborcenter.berkeley.edu/livingwage/working-poor.pdf

---

2. The television expose was on Bill Moyer's *NOW,* aired on public broadcasting stations in the summer of 2003. A study by the UC Berkeley Center for Labor Research and Education finds that, in California, nearly half of public assistance money goes to families with at least one member in the labor force. This is a form of public subsidy for low-wage employers. The retail industry was cited as the worst offender in this regard: Workers in this industry collected about $2 billion in public assistance, over twice that of any other sector (see Zabin, Dube and Jacobs 2004).

# 35

## The Rise and Fall of Mass Rail Transit

FROM *Building American Cities: The Urban Real Estate Game*

JOE R. FEAGIN and ROBERT PARKER

*There are more automobiles than people in Los Angeles. Is this a consequence of the preferences and choices of individual consumers, a reflection of the so-called American love affair with the automobile, or is it the result of structured choices? The authors show that farsighted corporations found common cause in organizing transportation to suit their interests, and the romance of Americans and their cars began a new chapter.*

Most U.S. cities have become *multinucleated*, with major commercial, industrial, and residential areas no longer closely linked to or dependent upon the downtown center. Decentralization has become characteristic of our cities from coast to coast. Essential to decentralization has been the development and regular extension of an automobile-dominated transportation system serving businesses and the general citizenry, but mostly paid for by rank-and-file taxpayers. With and without citizen consent, corporate capitalists, industrialists and developers, and allied political officials have made key decisions fundamentally shaping the type of transportation system upon which all Americans now depend.

### THE AUTO-OIL-RUBBER INDUSTRIAL COMPLEX

The auto-oil-rubber industrial complex has long been central to both the general economy and the urban transportation system in the United States. Automobile and auto-related industries provide a large proportion, sometimes estimated at one-sixth, of all jobs, although this proportion may be decreasing with the decline and stagnation in the auto industry over the last two decades. An estimated one-quarter to one-half of the land in central cities is used for the movement, storage, selling, and parking of automobiles, trucks, and buses. The expanding production of automobiles and trucks has been coordinated with the expansion of highways and freeways and has facilitated the bulging suburbanization around today's cities.

Because of the dominance of autos and trucks in the U.S. transportation system, the traditional social scientists * * * have typically viewed that transportation system as preordained by the American "love" for the automobile. For example, in a recent book on Los Angeles, historian Scott Bottles argues that

"America's present urban transportation system largely reflects choices made by the public itself"; the public freely chose the automobile as a "liberating and democratic technology." Conventional explanations for auto-centered patterns focus on the response of a market system to these consumers. Auto-linked technologies are discussed as though they force human decisions: Thus "the city dweller, especially in recent times, has been a victim of the technological changes that have been wrought in transportation systems." * * * [T]raditional ecologists and other social scientists view the complexity and shape of cities as largely determined by technological developments in transportation—a reasonable view—but these technologies are not carefully examined in terms of their economic contexts, histories, and possible technological alternatives. For example, unlike the United States, numerous capitalist countries in Europe, including prosperous West Germany, have a mixed rail transit/automobile transport system. There interurban and intraurban rail transit remains very important. For this reason, the U.S. system cannot be assumed to be simply the result of "free" consumer choices in a market context. The capitalistic history and decision-making contexts that resulted in the positioning of automobiles at the heart of the U.S. transportation system must be examined.

## EARLY MASS RAIL TRANSIT

Rural and urban Americans have not always been so dependent on automobiles for interurban and intraurban transport. In the years between the 1880s and the 1940s many cities had significant mass transit systems. By 1890 electric trolleys were in general use. Indeed, electric trolley routes, elevated railroads, and subways facilitated the first urban expansion and decentralization. Some investor-owned rail transit companies extended their trolley lines beyond existing urbanized areas out into the countryside in an attempt to profit from the land speculation along the rail lines. Glenn Yago has documented how transit owners and real estate speculators worked together to ensure the spatial and economic development of cities by private enterprise. Transit companies were a significant force in urban sprawl. The suburban spread of Los Angeles, for example, got its initial push from the expansion of trolley rail lines. Not initially laid out as an automobile city, this sprawling metropolis developed along streetcar tracks; only later was the streetcar network displaced by automobiles.

The reorganization and disruption of mass rail transit that took place in the early 1900s did not result just from the challenge of improved automobile technology. Rather, capitalist entrepreneurs and private corporations seeking profits reorganized and consolidated existing rail transit systems. Electrification of horse-drawn streetcars increased investment costs and stimulated concentration of ownership in larger "transit trusts" of landowning, finance, and utility entrepreneurs. Mergers of old transit firms and the assembly of new companies were commonplace, and there was much speculation in transit company stock. Yago has provided evidence on the corrupt accounting practices, over-extension of lines for real estate speculation, and overcapitalization which led to the bankruptcy of more than one-third of the private urban transit companies during the period 1916–1923. Sometimes the capitalists involved in the transit companies were too eager for profits. "These actions in turn," Charles Cheape notes, "drained funds, discouraged additional investment, and contributed significantly to the collapse and reorganization of many transit systems shortly after World War I and again in the 1930s."

Ironically, one consequence of the so-called "progressive" political reform movement in cities in the first decades of the twentieth century was that supervision of rail transit systems was often placed in the hands of business-dominated regulatory commissions, many of whose members were committed to the interests of corporate America (for example, transit stock manipulation for profit), rather than to the welfare of the general public. In numerous cases the extraordinary profits made by rail transit entrepreneurs, together with their ties to corrupt politicians, created a negative public image—which in turn made the public less enthusiastic about new tax-supported subsidies and fare hikes for the troubled rail transit systems. Moreover, as the profits of many of the private transit firms declined, public authorities in some cities, including Boston and New York, were forced to take over the transit lines from the poorly managed private companies in response to citizen pressure for mass transportation. This fact suggests that there has long been popular *demand* for publicly owned rail transit that is reliable, convenient, and inexpensive. Indeed, during the period 1910–1930 a *majority* of Americans either could not afford, because of modest incomes, or could not use, because of age or handicap, an automobile.

## A CORPORATE PLAN TO KILL MASS TRANSIT?

By the late 1910s and 1920s the ascension of the U.S. auto-oil-rubber industrial complex brought new corporate strategies to expand automobile markets and secure government subsidies for road infrastructure. Mass rail transit hindered the profit-oriented interests of this car-centered industrial complex, whose executives became involved not only in pressuring governments to subsidize roads but also in the buying up of mass transit lines. For example, in the early 1920s, Los Angeles had the largest and most effective trolley car system in the United States. Utilizing more than a thousand miles of track, the system transported millions of people yearly. During World War II, the streetcars ran 2,800 scheduled runs a day. But by the end of that war, the trolleys were disappearing. And their demise had little to do with consumer choice. As news analyst Harry Reasoner has observed, it "was largely a result of a criminal conspiracy":

> The way it worked was that General Motors, Firestone Tire and Standard Oil of California and some other companies, depending on the location of the target, would arrange financing for an outfit called National City Lines, which cozied

up to city councils and county commissioners and bought up transit systems like L.A.'s. Then they would junk or sell the electric cars and pry up the rails for scrap and beautiful, modern buses would be substituted, buses made by General Motors and running on Firestone Tires and burning Standard's gas.

Within a month after the trolley system in Los Angeles was purchased, 237 new buses arrived. It is important to realize that, for all the financial and management problems created by the private owners of the rail transit firms, the old transit systems were still popular. In the year prior to the takeover, the Los Angeles electric lines made $1.5 million in profits and carried more than 200 million passengers. The logic behind the corporate takeover plan was clear. The auto-related firms acted because a trolley car can carry the passengers of several dozen automobiles.

During the 1930s GM created a holding company through which it and other auto-related companies channeled money to buy up electric transit systems in 45 cities from New York to Los Angeles. As researcher Bradford Snell has outlined it, the process had three stages. First, General Motors (GM) helped the Greyhound corporation displace long-distance passenger transportation from railroads to buses. Then GM and other auto-related companies bought up and dismantled numerous local electric transit systems, replacing them with the GM-built buses. Moreover, in the late 1940s, GM was convicted in a Chicago federal court of having conspired to destroy electric transit and to convert trolley systems to diesel buses, whose production GM monopolized. William Dixon, the man who put together the criminal conspiracy case for the federal government, argued that individual corporate executives should be sent to jail. Instead, each received a trivial $1 fine. The corporations were assessed a modest $5,000 penalty, the maximum under the law. In spite of this conviction, GM continued to play a role in converting electric transit systems to diesel buses. And these diesel buses provided more expensive mass transit: "The diesel bus, as engineered by GM, has a shorter life expectancy, higher operating costs, and lower overall productivity than electric buses. GM has thus made the bus economically noncompetitive with the car also." One source of public discontent with mass transit was this inferiority of the new diesel buses compared to the rail transit cars that had been displaced without any consultation with consumers. Not surprisingly, between 1936 and 1955 the number of operating trolley cars in the United States dropped from about 40,000 to 5,000.

In a lengthy report GM officials have argued that electric transit systems were already in trouble when GM began intervening. As noted above, some poorly managed transit systems were declining already, and some had begun to convert partially to buses before GM's vigorous action. So from GM's viewpoint, the corporations direct intervention only accelerated the process. This point has been accented by Bottles, who shows that GM did not single-handedly destroy the streetcar systems in Los Angeles. These privately controlled systems were providing a lesser quality of service before GM became involved.

The profit milking and corruption of the private streetcar firms in Los Angeles were not idiosyncratic but were common for privately owned mass transport in numerous cities.

Also important in destroying mass transit was the new and aggressive multimillion-dollar marketing of automobiles and trucks by General Motors and other automobile companies across the United States. And the automobile companies and their advertisers were not the only powerful actors involved in killing off numerous mass transit systems. Bankers and public officials also played a role. Yago notes that "after World War II, banks sold bankrupt and obsolete transit systems throughout the country at prices that bore no relation to the systems' real values." Often favoring the auto interests, local banks and other financial institutions tried to limit government bond issues that could be used to finance new equipment and refurbish the remaining rail transit systems.

Because of successful lobbying by executives from the auto-oil-rubber complex, and their own acceptance of a motorization perspective, most government officials increasingly backed street and highway construction. They cooperated with the auto industry in eliminating many mass transit systems. Increased governmental support for auto and truck transportation systems has meant systematic disinvestment in mass transit systems. Over the several decades since World War II, governmental mass transit subsidies have been small compared with highway subsidies. This decline has hurt low-and moderate-income people the most. Less public transit since World War II has meant increased commuting time in large cities where people are dependent on the automobile, which is especially troublesome for moderate-income workers who may not be able to afford a reliable car; less mass transit has also meant increased consumer expenditures for automobiles and gasoline. Auto expansion has frustrated the development of much mass transit because growing street congestion slows down buses and trolleys, further reducing their ridership. As a result, governmental funding for public rail transit has been cut, again chasing away riders who dislike poorly maintained equipment. And fares have been increased. Riders who can use automobiles do so. And the downward spiral has continued to the point of extinction of most public rail transit systems.

Mass transit was allowed to decline by the business-oriented government officials in most cities. Consumer desires were only partly responsible for this. Consumers did discover the freedom of movement of autos, and even in cities with excellent rail transit systems many prefer the auto for at least some types of travel. But consumers make their choices *from the alternatives available*. With no real rail transportation alternative to the automobile in most urban areas, consumers turned to it as a necessity. Ironically, as the auto and truck congestion of the cities has mounted between the 1950s and the 1980s, more and more citizens, and not a few business leaders, have called for new mass transit systems for their cities.

\* \* \*

## MASS TRANSIT IN OTHER CAPITALISTIC COUNTRIES

Comparative research on U.S. and German transportation systems by Yago has demonstrated the importance of looking at corporate power and economic structure. Mass rail transport developed in Germany before 1900. In the 1870s and 1880s the German national and local governments became interested in mass transit; at that time the coal, steel, iron, chemical, and electrical manufacturing companies were dominant in German capitalism. Interestingly, corporate executives in these industries supported the development of rail transportation; by 1900 the national and local governments had subsidized and institutionalized intraurban and interurban rail transport systems, which served the transport needs not only of the citizenry but also of the dominant coal, steel, chemical, and electrical industries. These industries also supplied equipment and supplies for the rail networks. In contrast, in the United States early transport companies were involved in manipulation and land speculation; transit service was rarely the central goal of the early rail transit firms. In contrast to Germany, dominance of U.S. industry by a major economic concentration did not come to the United States until after 1900, and when it did come, the auto-oil-rubber industrial complex was dominant. There was no other integrated industrial complex to contest this dominance of the auto-related firms, and governmental intervention was directed at support of motorization and the automobile. In Germany governmental intervention for mass rail transit had preceded this dominance of the motorization lobby. This suggests that the *timing* of the implementation of technological innovations in relation to corporate development is critical to their dominance, or lack of dominance, in cities and societies.

Interestingly, it was the Nazi interest in motorization and militarization in the 1930s that sharply increased the role of auto and truck transport in Germany. Adolf Hitler worked hard to motorize the military and the society. After World War II, the German auto lobby increased in power, and an auto transport system was placed alongside the rail transport system. However, the West German government and people have maintained a strong commitment to both systems; and the OPEC-generated oil crises of the 1970s brought an unparalleled revival of mass transit in Germany, whereas in the United States there was a more modest revival. The reason for the dramatic contrast between the two countries was that Germany had retained a rail passenger transport system, one that is still viable and energy conserving to the present day.

# 36

## Size Does Count, at Least for French Fries:
## Minnesota's Straight River

FROM *Water Follies: Groundwater Pumping and
the Fate of America's Fresh Waters*

### ROBERT GLENNON

*When most of us make a decision, we usually think about how the decision will affect
us. But the sociological perspective urges us to look beyond ourselves to what are
called the manifest and latent functions and the dysfunctions of social actions. That
is, as sociologists we seek to anticipate and recognize unintended consequences. With
growing awareness of human threats to the natural environment, one branch of sociology traces the chain of human activities to realms normally examined by the physical and biological sciences, and in so doing has expanded the sociological perspective
to include global ecology. In this chapter from the author's book,* Water Follies, *a
seemingly benign decision by McDonald's to make its French fries "consumer friendly"
sets off a chain reaction of social and environmental change far beyond whatever
discussions might have been held in the boardroom of the corporation.*

> I wish to make it clear to you, there is not sufficient water to irrigate all the lands
> which could be irrigated.
>
> —John Wesley Powell (1893)

Ray Kroc, the founder of McDonald's, revolutionized the french fry in the
1950s. It was not mere marketing prowess that allowed him to do so. It was
science. He discovered that potatoes vary widely in their water content. A
potato that contains too much water will become soggy when fried. Kroc actually sent employees armed with hydrometers into the potato fields of his suppliers to ensure that the potatoes contained the optimum percentage of water.
A freshly harvested potato typically consists of 80 percent water. The french
frying process essentially removes most of that water and replaces it with fat.
The high fat content makes french fries unhealthy, but it also makes them delicious. The typical American consumes thirty pounds of french fries a year, a
700 percent increase since the 1950s, when Ray Kroc began to mass-produce
french fries. According to Eric Schlosser, author of *Fast Food Nation*, "French
fries have become the most widely sold foodservice item in the United States."
Frozen french fries have also nudged aside fresh potatoes, called "table stock"
by the food industry, in the at-home diets of many Americans. Potato manufacturers have thoughtfully nurtured our enjoyment of convenience foods by
packaging french fries to suit our every whim for a fry of a certain size, shape,
or flavoring. The freezer section of a Safeway supermarket is likely to carry

some twelve different types of Ore-Ida french fries: shoestring, crinkles, twirls, crispers, fajita-seasoned, zesties, country style, tater tots, hash browns (country and southern style), potatoes O'Brien, and, of course, plain old french fries.

Any baking potato will suffice to make french fries, though the fast-food industry prefers Burbank russet potatoes, a variety that is mealy or starchy, not waxy. When ready for processing, the potatoes are washed, steam-peeled, sliced, and blanched, all of which ensures that the inside will have a fluffy texture. After quick drying, the potatoes are deep-fried for thirty seconds to produce a crisp shell. These steps usually occur at a processing plant located close to the potato fields to save on transportation costs. The fries are then frozen and shipped to a warehouse, which delivers them to retail outlets as needed. The fries remain frozen until the moment of service. At this point, they are deep-fried again for approximately three minutes.

Some potato species that we cultivate today were gathered and cultivated in the Peruvian and Bolivian Andes of South America for thousands of years before the first European explorations. Potatoes first reached North America from England in the early 1600s. The Irish potato blight in the 1840s taught the lesson that cross-fertilization and new cultivars ward off insects and fungi that attack potatoes. In the United States, the intense cultivation of Burbank russets has required growers to use large quantities of insecticides, pesticides, and herbicides to protect the single cultivar. One recent study found that babies in the Red River Valley in North Dakota, a major potato farming region, had low birth weights and a high incidence of birth defects, conditions blamed on the local use of herbicides and other agricultural chemicals.

The potato industry has recently fallen on hard times. To break even, a potato farmer must receive about $5 per hundred pounds. In 1996–97, potato prices fell to $1.50 per hundredweight. By 2001, the prices had declined to $1 per hundred pounds. Most small producers have left the business, and the process of consolidation has resulted in a small number of corporate farms, each growing thousands of acres of potatoes. As large as these farms are, the farmers are still beholden to the processors, who, in turn, must answer to the fast-food chains. In the business of potato farming, a very small number of buyers wield extraordinary power over a large number of sellers.

The advent of the fast-food industry and the converging technologies that made it possible have created American consumers who expect the same uniformity in their food products that they find in their vehicles, shoes, or notebook paper. In the past, fast-food french fries came in small waxed paper bags. The small bags would not stand up, so they often tipped over and spilled the fries, making a bit of a mess. For marketing reasons, in 1988, McDonald's began to offer consumers "super-sized" meals with larger portions of fries now served in rectangular boxes with flat bottoms. They were a huge hit.

French fries are a tremendously competitive component of the fast-food industry. The hook that keeps customers coming back to a particular franchise is not only the taste of the french fries but also their appearance. According to Dean John Gardner of the University of Missouri Agricultural Extension program, the fast-food industry decided that the french fry, to appeal aesthetically to consumers, had to be a certain length. It needed to jut out of the supersize box by just the right amount, so that the consumer can grasp the potato between index finger and thumb and dip it in ketchup.

Ron Offutt grew up on his family's 240-acre farm in Moorhead, Minnesota. After graduation from college in 1964, he began to expand his family's potato growing operation. He recognized that the sandy soil of central Minnesota would provide an ideal medium for growing potatoes if the lands were irrigated. The R. D. Offutt Company now farms 200,000 acres of land in eleven states, with 66,000 acres in potatoes, making Ron the country's largest potato grower. His farms annually produce 2.9 billion pounds of potatoes.

As Ron's farming operation expanded, he needed a lot of tractors, so he acquired a John Deere franchise. Soon, RDO Equipment Co. became the nation's largest John Deere agricultural retailer *and* its largest construction equipment dealer, with forty-six stores in ten states. Ron also realized, in the 1970s, that it would be useful to own a french fry processing plant. So he bought one. In 1980, he completed construction of another processing plant in Park Rapids, Minnesota. He has since added two more processing facilities. Today, R. D. Offutt Company serves as the umbrella for a vast, vertically integrated agribusiness enterprise. Dean Gardner describes R. D. Offutt Company as "a classic, commercial success story for the production of an industrial potato for french fries." Industrial, he suggests, because the length and size of the potato is a critical part of the marketing. A uniform-length fry requires a uniform potato, which requires irrigation.

Until rather recently, many farms in the United States were "dryland farmed," meaning that the farmers had no system of irrigation. Their fortunes varied with the precipitation that Mother Nature provided, from flood to drought, in any given growing season. Many farmers, especially in the Midwest and the East, have come to realize that an occasional supplemental irrigation produces greater yields per acre and larger crops. Irrigation also enables farmers to apply fertilizers or pesticides to their fields through water-soluble solutions.

Americans' love affair with processed foods caused potato farmers to shift from dryland to irrigation farming. The problem with dryland potatoes is that their size, shape, and texture depend heavily on seasonal weather patterns. During the growing season, potatoes need constant moisture or they will have knobs and odd shapes. A misshapen or knobby potato is perfectly edible, but it is not an acceptable potato for the fast-food industry, at least in the United States. According to a potato processing executive, "American consumers were spoiled by the McDonald's of the world. They haven't made that mistake in Japan, where the specifications for potatoes are more reasonable. More of the potato gets used there than here." In Minnesota, potato farmers irrigate their fields because the two big suppliers for fast-food restaurants—Frito-Lay and Simplot—will contract only with potato growers who irrigate their fields in order to obtain potatoes with a uniform length, appearance, and color.

The R. D. Offutt Company farm near Park Rapids, Minnesota, in the Straight River basin, grows about 7,500 acres of Burbank russet potatoes, mostly for french fries, though also for tater tots, hash browns, and potato wedges. During the four-week harvesting season, potatoes are sent to the Lamb Weston/RDO Frozen processing plant in Park Rapids, which is a joint venture between Lamb-Weston Foods Corp. (a major supplier to McDonald's) and R. D. Offutt Company. The plant immediately processes some potatoes but stores the rest for up to eleven months. Storing potatoes creates two problems for processors. Most American consumers understand the first problem: they occasionally purchase a bag of potatoes, which they store under the sink and promptly forget. When finally discovered, the potatoes have become soft and flabby through dehydration and are suitable only for a child's science project. Once harvested, a potato begins to lose moisture to the air. To combat this problem, growers and processors store potatoes in a 95 percent humidity environment to prevent the loss of weight, which can be as much as 30 percent, or nearly one-third of the cash value.

Minnesota potato growers and processors face an additional problem. Most of us have enjoyed a summertime glass of iced tea with moisture on the outside of the glass. As we may remember from our own science classes, the cold glass chills the air immediately around it, and because the chilled air cannot hold the same amount of moisture as warmer air elsewhere in the room, water vapor condenses on the outside of the glass. The differential in temperature that produces condensation poses a problem for potato storage. The moisture in the high-humidity storage facility eventually condenses, which usually occurs on the facility's inside walls in a place with winters as cold as Minnesota. As moisture forms on the walls and ceiling of the plant, it begins to drip onto the potatoes, which, if wet, will eventually rot.

The humidity and temperature of stored potatoes are not important to the typical consumer who buys a large bag of potatoes, stores them in the garage or attic during the wintertime, and eats them over a six- or eight-month period. But humidity and temperature *are* critical for the fast-food industry. When a potato is stored at a cool temperature, its carbohydrates naturally turn to sugars. When baked, the potato will be somewhat sweeter from the sugars that caramelize during baking. If this potato is used for french fries, the caramelized sugar produces a brown color that is aesthetically unacceptable. As Larry Monico, director of operations for the R. D. Offutt farm in Park Rapids has explained, "We as Americans, or somebody, has decided that french fries should be white in color and not brown. If you made french fries out of potatoes that have been stored at a cold temperature, they would be brown in color like shoe leather. Not that they would taste bad, or anything else, but they are undesirable to us as consumers." Consequently, processors must use water to store potatoes at a precise temperature and humidity.

The Lamb Weston/RDO Frozen storage facility in Park Rapids, Minnesota, has a capacity of 26.5 million pounds of potatoes. They must store the entire crop so that there is not more than a one degree Fahrenheit difference between any two potatoes in the entire building. Otherwise, when fried, they might be slightly different colors. According to Larry Monico, "McDonald's won't accept french fries that aren't all white, and so, therefore, we have to keep the temperature constant so that they will all fry to the same color." To achieve the required uniform humidity and temperature, the inside walls are entirely separated from the exterior walls by an air space or cavity that creates an envelope separating the potato storage area from the exterior walls. A separate furnace heats the cavity to a certain temperature and prevents the outside air from affecting the temperature and the humidity at which the potatoes are stored. A computer-controlled system regulates the temperature and humidity in the storage area.

The Straight River in north-central Minnesota, about 180 miles northwest of the Twin Cities, is quite deep and meanders, contrary to its name, in a series of S turns. Typical of rivers and streams in the upper Midwest, the Straight River flows through glacial outwash. As a consequence of the sandy soil, the surface and groundwater are very closely connected hydrologically. At the end of Minnesota's legendary winters, snowmelt rapidly recharges substantial quantities of water to shallow aquifers that, in turn, quickly transmit the water to the river.

In the past, local farmers eked out a living by dryland farming corn and small grains such as wheat, barley, and oats. The sandy soil made farming a marginal economic enterprise. The genius of Ron Offutt was to realize the region's potential for growing potatoes, if the lands were irrigated. The uniform texture of the sandy soils, aided by the application of water, provided an ideal medium for producing the uniform potatoes demanded by the fast-food industry. The threat to the Straight River comes from this shift from dryland to irrigated farming and from changes in the technology of irrigation.

Airplane passengers regularly query flight attendants about conspicuous green circles that dot the landscape of the Great Plains from North Dakota to Texas and that contrast dramatically with the arid land surrounding them. The circles are produced by center-pivot irrigation systems. In a center-pivot system, a well drilled in the center of a quarter-section (160 acres) attaches by a swivel to aluminum pipes suspended six or eight feet off the ground, which are supported by A-frame towers with tandem wheels on the base. A hydraulic drive or a diesel or electric motor supplies power that slowly pivots the pipes and towers in a circle around the well. The resulting irrigation-water pattern produces a perfect circle easily seen from 35,000 feet. Unlike older forms of row irrigation, center-pivot systems allow farmers to tailor precisely the frequency and amount of water applied in order to achieve better yields. Modern center-point systems reduce evaporation loss by using low pressure with specially designed nozzles that produce larger droplets aimed toward the ground and that can achieve an efficiency of 90 percent. Older systems relied on high pressure to spray fine mists of water into the air. Much of the water evaporated before it ever reached the ground.

Center-pivot irrigation has transformed the Straight River basin; in the 1940s, there were only five irrigation wells in the area. By 1998, farmers had drilled seventy center-pivot irrigation systems within two miles of the river, and they now pump almost 3 billion gallons of groundwater each growing season. Groundwater adjacent to the Straight River irrigates the potatoes and provides water for processing.

Beneath and immediately adjacent to the Straight River, the glacial out-wash constitutes a shallow, quite permeable aquifer. Below this aquifer lies a confining layer of glacial till, a mixture of clay and other relatively impermeable sediments, and below that lies a deeper aquifer from deposits during earlier glacial periods. The confining layer retards but does not completely block water moving between the shallow and deep aquifers. Pumping from the deep aquifer will increase recharge from the shallow aquifer to the deep aquifer and, depending on the location of the well, may also reduce discharge from the shallow aquifer to the Straight River. One thing is certain: groundwater pumping from the *shallow* aquifer reduces discharge from the aquifer to the Straight River.

Hydrologists are confident about this conclusion for a quite surprising reason. All water bodies contain radioactive isotopes, the product of either natural geologic processes or atomic fallout from nuclear bomb tests that stopped in the 1950s. Because isotopes have differing half-lives, the law of radioactive decay allows hydrologists to calculate the length of time that it takes for precipitation to infiltrate the ground and to discharge to a stream. It turns out that 95 percent of the water in the Straight River comes from discharge from the shallow aquifer. As of 1988, about half the irrigation wells pumped water from the shallow aquifer and the other half from the deeper aquifer.

One of Minnesota's most productive trout fishing streams, the Straight River contains brown trout that can weigh up to nine pounds. Although brown trout are not as sensitive to water temperatures as other trout species, they still require cold, clear water. Reduced flow in the Straight River produces higher ambient water temperatures that threaten the brown trout. A 1994 U.S. Geological Survey (USGS) report identified three factors that degrade the Straight River's trout habitat: (1) a decrease in stream flow from groundwater withdrawals for irrigation that reduces discharge from the aquifer to the stream; (2) higher-temperature irrigation water that percolates into the groundwater system and then discharges to the river; and (3) the introduction of agricultural chemicals to the river when irrigation water percolates into the ground and then discharges into the river. According to the USGS, the river's flow typically decreased during the summer, "possibly as a result of groundwater withdrawal for irrigation." Compared to farms in the West, Minnesota farmers use only a small amount of groundwater—approximately twelve inches per acre per year. Even this modest amount of pumping has the potential, according to the USGS, to reduce the Straight River's flow by as much as 34 percent during the irrigation season. This reduction in flow would increase the water temperature and might adversely affect the brown trout.

The USGS also found an increase in nitrate concentrations in the shallow aquifer along the Straight River. Farmers typically apply 235 pounds per acre of nitrogen fertilizer to grow Burbank russets. Biochemical processes convert organic nitrogen into inorganic nitrate that dissolves in water and leaches into the aquifer. Although the number of documented cases of human illness caused by nitrate-contaminated groundwater is small, the potential health hazards pose a significant environmental concern. A 1994 USGS study found that 6 percent of 600 groundwater samples from shallow wells in the Midwest had nitrate levels that exceeded the U.S. Environmental Protection Agency drinking water limit.

In the mid-1990s, Lamb Weston/RDO Frozen proposed a $60 million expansion of the potato processing plant at Park Rapids. The Minnesota chapter of Trout Unlimited, the Minnesota Center for Environmental Advocacy, and the Headwaters Chapter of the Audubon Society filed a lawsuit to prevent the state of Minnesota from issuing the necessary permits for the plant. The environmental groups feared that the plant's increased groundwater pumping would reduce Straight River flows and that the plant's effluent would adversely affect water quality. The lawsuit ultimately was settled when Lamb Weston/RDO Frozen agreed to change its operations in significant ways. First, it funded monitoring and other data collection efforts. Lamb Weston/RDO Frozen donated in excess of $300,000 to the Minnesota Department of Natural Resources (DNR) to help fund a comprehensive watershed study and a hydrologic model that could predict changes in river flow from groundwater pumping. Between 1996 and 1998, DNR placed a moratorium on issuing new water appropriation permits in order to conduct its study, but the resulting model was not precise enough to provide sufficiently accurate data to predict the impact of specific wells on the river. Lamb Weston/RDO Frozen also capped wells located at the processing plant and drilled two new ones, at a cost of $100,000, about a mile north of the plant in an area that hydrologists determined would not affect the Straight River. The company made these changes solely for the possible benefit of the Straight River. To get the water from the new wells to the processing plant, it built an $80,000 pipeline. Lamb Weston/RDO Frozen also upgraded the wastewater treatment facilities, at a cost of $14 million, and uses the effluent from the treatment plant to irrigate nearby crops.

After DNR lifted its moratorium, Lamb Weston/RDO Frozen ultimately obtained the necessary permits and expanded the plant, which is an enormous operation. Each day, seventy-five semitrailer truckloads of potatoes arrive for processing. Each year, the plant receives almost one billion pounds of potatoes and produces approximately 540 million pounds of french fries. It takes two pounds of potatoes to make one pound of french fries that are acceptable to the plant's largest customer—McDonald's. The plant uses 600 million gallons per year of groundwater in its washing, peeling, and storing operations. It's a lot of water, but R. D. Offutt Company's potato farming and processing businesses employ approximately 600 people and generate $11 million in annual payroll, which has a huge impact in rural Minnesota.

For the moment, the Straight River trout population is in no danger. However, a tall stack of groundwater permit applications waits to be processed by DNR. A large increase in irrigation for potatoes, with new wells being drilled in the deeper aquifer, would change the equilibrium. A 1999 Minnesota DNR study concluded: "Potential expansion in potato farming and irrigation could put the Straight River trout population at further risk of thermal impact and eventually raise water temperatures beyond their threshold of survival." Increased pumping from the deeper aquifer would increase recharge from the shallow aquifer, thus reducing discharge from the shallow aquifer to the river. Lower flows would mean higher ambient water temperatures and less dilution of nitrates that contaminate the river. One long-term answer, of course, is for us, as American consumers, to accept french fries that have slightly different colors, or minor discolorations, or even ones that are not long enough to stick out from a super-size carton.

# 37

## Scott's Law of Anarchist Calisthenics

FROM *Two Cheers for Anarchism: Six Easy Pieces on Autonomy,
Dignity, and Meaningful Work and Play*

### JAMES C. SCOTT

*Sociologists are fascinated by the way people follow social norms, usually with
little awareness of their conformity. Thinking for ourselves can feel like a major
undertaking; it can even be life changing. In what begins like a primer for any students who plan to study abroad, the author finds reason to challenge a practice of
his host. It's not easy, but an awareness of the pressure to conform is the first step in
sociological understanding. In the second part of the essay, the author offers an exciting possibility for changing many aspects of life to enhance "human agency" and the
ability to work together.*

I invented this law in Neubrandenburg, Germany, in the late summer of 1990.

In an effort to improve my barely existing German-language skills before
spending a year in Berlin as a guest of the Wissenschaftskolleg, I hit on the
idea of finding work on a farm rather than attending daily classes with pimply
teenagers at a Goethe Institut center. Since the Wall had come down only a
year earlier, I wondered whether I might be able to find a six-week summer
job on a collective farm (landwirtschaftliche Produktionsgenossenschaft, or
LPG), recently styled "cooperative," in eastern Germany. A friend at the Wissenschaftskolleg had, it turned out, a close relative whose brother-in-law was
the head of a collective farm in the tiny village of Pletz. Though wary, the
brother-in-law was willing to provide room and board in return for work and
a handsome weekly rent.

As a plan for improving my German by the sink-or-swim method, it was perfect; as a plan for a pleasant and edifying farm visit, it was a nightmare. The
villagers and, above all, my host were suspicious of my aims. Was I aiming to
pore over the accounts of the collective farm and uncover "irregularities"? Was
I an advance party for Dutch farmers, who were scouting the area for land to
rent in the aftermath of the socialist bloc's collapse?

The collective farm at Pletz was a spectacular example of that collapse. Its
specialization was growing "starch potatoes." They were no good for pommes
frites, though pigs might eat them in a pinch; their intended use, when refined,
was to provide the starch base for Eastern European cosmetics. Never had a
market flatlined as quickly as the market for socialist bloc cosmetics the day
after the Wall was breached. Mountain after mountain of starch potatoes lay
rotting beside the rail sidings in the summer sun.

Besides wondering whether utter penury lay ahead for them and what role I might have in it, for my hosts there was the more immediate question of my frail comprehension of German and the danger it posed for their small farm. Would I let the pigs out the wrong gate and into a neighbor's field? Would I give the geese the feed intended for the bulls? Would I remember *always* to lock the door when I was working in the barn in case the Gypsies came? I had, it is true, given them more than ample cause for alarm in the first week, and they had taken to shouting at me in the vain hope we all seem to have that yelling will somehow overcome any language barrier. They managed to maintain a veneer of politeness, but the glances they exchanged at supper told me their patience was wearing thin. The aura of suspicion under which I labored, not to mention my manifest incompetence and incomprehension, was in turn getting on my nerves.

I decided, for my sanity as well as for theirs, to spend one day a week in the nearby town of Neubrandenburg. Getting there was not simple. The train didn't stop at Pletz unless you put up a flag along the tracks to indicate that a passenger was waiting and, on the way back, told the conductor that you wanted to get off at Pletz, in which case he would stop specially in the middle of the fields to let you out. Once in the town I wandered the streets, frequented cafes and bars, pretended to read German newspapers (surreptitiously consulting my little dictionary), and tried not to stick out.

The once-a-day train back from Neubrandenburg that could be made to stop at Pletz left at around ten at night. Lest I miss it and have to spend the night as a vagrant in this strange city, I made sure I was at the station at least half an hour early. Every week for six or seven weeks the same intriguing scene was played out in front of the railroad station, giving me ample time to ponder it both as observer and as participant. The idea of "anarchist calisthenics" was conceived in the course of what an anthropologist would call my participant observation.

Outside the station was a major, for Neubrandenburg at any rate, intersection. During the day there was a fairly brisk traffic of pedestrians, cars, and trucks, and a set of traffic lights to regulate it. Later in the evening, however, the vehicle traffic virtually ceased while the pedestrian traffic, if anything, swelled to take advantage of the cooler evening breeze. Regularly between 9:00 and 10:00 p.m. there would be fifty or sixty pedestrians, not a few of them tipsy, who would cross the intersection. The lights were timed, I suppose, for vehicle traffic at midday and not adjusted for the heavy evening foot traffic. Again and again, fifty or sixty people waited patiently at the corner for the light to change in their favor: four minutes, five minutes, perhaps longer. It seemed an eternity. The landscape of Neubrandenburg, on the Mecklenburg Plain, is flat as a pancake. Peering in each direction from the intersection, then, one could see a mile of so of roadway, with, typically, no traffic at all. Very occasionally a single, small Trabant made its slow, smoky way to the intersection.

Twice, perhaps, in the course of roughly five hours of my observing this scene did a pedestrian cross against the light, and then always to a chorus of scolding tongues and fingers wagging in disapproval. I too became part of the scene. If I had mangled my last exchange in German, sapping my confidence, I stood there with the rest for as long as it took for the light to change, afraid to brave the glares that awaited me if I crossed. If, more rarely, my last exchange in German had gone well and my confidence was high, I would cross against the light, thinking, to buck up my courage, that it was stupid to obey a minor law that, in this case, was so contrary to reason.

It surprised me how much I had to screw up my courage merely to cross a street against general disapproval. How little my rational convictions seemed to weigh against the pressure of their scolding. Striding out boldly into the intersection with apparent conviction made a more striking impression, perhaps, but it required more courage than I could normally muster.

As a way of justifying my conduct to myself, I began to rehearse a little discourse that I imagined delivering in perfect German. It went something like this. "You know, you and especially your grandparents could have used more of a spirit of lawbreaking. One day you will be called on to break a big law in the name of justice and rationality. Everything will depend on it. You have to be ready. How are you going to prepare for that day when it really matters? You have to stay 'in shape' so that when the big day comes you will be ready. What you need is 'anarchist calisthenics.' Every day or so break some trivial law that makes no sense, even if it's only jaywalking. Use your own head to judge whether a law is just or reasonable. That way, you'll keep trim; and when the big day comes, you'll be ready."

Judging when it makes sense to break a law requires careful thought, even in the relatively innocuous case of jaywalking. I was reminded of this when I visited a retired Dutch scholar whose work I had long admired. When I went to see him, he was an avowed Maoist and defender of the Cultural Revolution, and something of an incendiary in Dutch academic politics. He invited me to lunch at a Chinese restaurant near his apartment in the small town of Wageningen. We came to an intersection, and the light was against us. Now, Wageningen, like Neubrandenburg, is perfectly flat, and one can see for miles in all directions. There was absolutely nothing coming. Without thinking, I stepped into the street, and as I did so, Dr. Wertheim said, "James, you must wait." I protested weakly while regaining the curb, "But Dr. Wertheim, nothing is coming." "James," he replied instantly, "It would be a bad example for the children." I was both chastened and instructed. Here was a Maoist incendiary with, nevertheless, a fine-tuned, dare I say Dutch, sense of civic responsibility, while I was the Yankee cowboy heedless of the effects of my act on my fellow citizens. Now when I jaywalk I look around to see that there are no children who might be endangered by my bad example.

\* \* \*

## A MODEST, COUNTERINTUITIVE EXAMPLE:
## RED LIGHT REMOVAL

The regulation of daily life is so ubiquitous and so embedded in our routines and expectations as to pass virtually unnoticed. Take the example of traffic lights at intersections. Invented in the United States after World War I, the traffic light substituted the judgment of the traffic engineer for the mutual give-and-take that had prevailed historically between pedestrians, carts, motor vehicles, and bicycles. Its purpose was to prevent accidents by imposing an engineered scheme of coordination. More than occasionally, the result has been the scene in Neubrandenburg with which I opened the book: scores of people waiting patiently for the light to change when it was perfectly apparent there was no traffic whatever. They were suspending their independent judgment out of habit, or perhaps out of a civic fear of the ultimate consequences of exercising it against the prevailing electronic legal order.

What would happen if there were no electronic order at the intersection, and motorists and pedestrians had to exercise their independent judgment? Since 1999, beginning in the city of Drachten, the Netherlands, this supposition has been put to the test with stunning results, leading to a wave of "red light removal" schemes across Europe and in the United States. Both the reasoning behind this small policy initiative and its results are, I believe, diagnostic for other, more far-reaching efforts to craft institutions that enlarge the scope for independent judgment and expand capacities.

Hans Moderman, the counterintuitive traffic engineer who first suggested the removal of a red light in Drachten in 2003, went on to promote the concept of "shared space," which took hold quickly in Europe. He began with the observation that, when an electrical failure incapacitated traffic lights, the result was improved flow rather than congestion. As an experiment, he replaced the busiest traffic-light intersection in Drachten, handling 22,000 cars a day, with a traffic circle, an extended cycle path, and a pedestrian area. In the two years following the removal of the traffic light, the number of accidents plummeted to only two, compared with thirty-six crashes in the four years prior. Traffic moves more briskly through the intersection when all drivers know they must be alert and use their common sense, while backups and the road rage associated with them have virtually disappeared. Monderman likened it to skaters in a crowded ice rink who manage successfully to tailor their movements to those of the other skaters. He also believed that an excess of signage led drivers to take their eyes off the road, and actually contributed to making junctions less safe.

Red light removal can, I believe, be seen as a modest training exercise in responsible driving and civic courtesy. Monderman was not against traffic lights in principle, he simply did not find any in Drachten that were truly useful in terms of safety, improving traffic flow, and lessening pollution. The traffic circle seems dangerous: and that is the point. He argued that when "motorists are made more wary about how they drive, they behave more carefully," and the statistics on "post–traffic light" accidents bear him out. Having to share the road with other users, and having no imperative coordination imposed by traffic lights, the context virtually requires alertness—an alertness abetted by the law, which, in the case of an accident where blame is hard to determine, presumptively blames the "strongest" (i.e., blames the car driver rather than the bicyclist, and the bicyclist rather than the pedestrian.)

The shared space concept of traffic management relies on the intelligence, good sense, and attentive observation of drivers, bicyclists, and pedestrians. At the same time, it arguably, in its small way, actually expands the skills and capacity of drivers, cyclists, and pedestrians to negotiate traffic without being treated like automata by thickets of imperative signs (Germany alone has 648 valid traffic symbols, which accumulate as one approaches a town) and signals. Monderman believed that the more numerous the prescriptions, the more it impelled drivers to seek the maximum advantage within the rules: speeding up between signals, beating the light, avoiding all unprescribed courtesies. Drivers had learned to run the maze of prescriptions to their maximum advantage. Without going overboard about its world-shaking significance, Moderman's innovation does make a palpable contribution to the gross human product.

The effect of what was a paradigm shift in traffic management was euphoria. Small towns in the Netherlands put up one sign boasting that they were "Free of Traffic Signs" (*Verkeersbordvrij*), and a conference discussing the new philosophy proclaimed "Unsafe is safe."

# PART SEVEN

# SOCIAL INSTITUTIONS

# 38

## Love, Arranged Marriage, and the Indian Social Structure
### GIRI RAJ GUPTA

*For most of you, the idea of marrying someone you do not love borders on the absurd or abusive. In many societies, however, arranged marriages are common and result in lasting and satisfying bonds between husband and wife. Marital success is dependent not only on how partners feel toward one another. The social supports for their partnership and family are critical. In India's Hindu and Muslim societies, the family not only plays a major role in arranging a marriage but in making the marriage a success.*

Marriage is an immemorial institution which, in some form, is found everywhere. Mating patterns are closely associated with marriage, more so with the social structure. It's not the institution of marriage itself, but the institutionalization of mating patterns which determine the nature of family relationships in a society. Primitive societies present a wide array of practices ranging from marriage by capture to mutual love and elopement. Yet, the people who marry through customary practice are those who are eligible, who consciously followed the established norms, and who did the kind of things they were supposed to do. The main purpose of marriage is to establish a family, to produce children, and to further the family's economic and social position. Perhaps, there are some transcendental goals too. Generally, women hope for kind and vigorous providers and protectors and men for faithful mothers and good housekeepers; both undoubtedly hope for mutual devotion and affection too. Irrespective of the various ways of instituting marriage, most marriages seem to have these common goals.

There are few works commenting on mating patterns in India. Though some monographs on tribal and rural India have treated the subject, nevertheless, serious sociological attention has only infrequently been given. The present paper attempts to explain the variables as a part of the cultural system which help in promotion and sustenance of the arranged marriage, particularly in the Hindu society in India. In addition, the paper also critically analyzes the present-day mating patterns which relate to precautionary controls working against the potentially disintegrative forces of change; especially those endangering family unity, religious structure, and the stratification system.

## ROMANTIC LOVE VERSUS CONJUGAL LOVE

One is intrigued by the cultural pattern in India where the family is characterized by arranged marriage. Infatuation as well as romantic love, though, is reported quite in abundance in the literature, sacred books, and scriptures, yet is not thought to be an element in prospective marital alliance (see Meyer 1953: 322–39).

Sanskrit or Hindi terms like *sneh* (affection) and *prem* or *muhbbat* carry two different meanings. *Sneh* is nonsensual love, while *prem* is a generic term connoting love with god, people, nation, family, [neighbor], and, of course, lover or beloved. In fact, there is a hierarchy of relationships. In Urdu literature, concepts like *ishque ruharti* (love with the spirit), *ishque majazi* (love with the supreme being), and *ishque haqiqi* (love with the lover or beloved) are commonly referred to love relationships. Interestingly, the humans supposedly reach the highest goal of being in love with god through the love they cherish among humans. Great love stories in mythology and history illustrate the emotion, as opposed to reason, which characterize the thoughts and acts of persons in love. The quality of the emotions may be characterized best by the altruistic expressions of a person for the person in love. Most people in India do not go around singing of their love as one might imagine after watching Indian movies and dramatic performances. Even the proximity, intimacy, freedom, and permissiveness characterized in such media are rarely commonplace in the reality of the day-to-day life. In general, to verbalize and manifest romantic expressions of love is looked upon as a product of poets' or novelists' fantasies. Yet, at least theoretically, to be in love with someone is a highly cherished ideal.

In one of the most ancient scriptures, Rgveda, it was wished that a person's life be of a hundred-year duration. The Hindu sages in their theory of *pu-rusharthas* suggested four aims of life: *dharma*, righteousness, which provides a link between animal and god in man; *artha*, acquisitive instinct in man, enjoyment of wealth and its manifestations; *kama*, instinctive and emotional life of man and the satisfaction of sex drives and aesthetic urges; and *moksha*, the end of life and the realization of an inner spirituality in man (see Kapadia 1966: 25).

The Hindu scriptures written during 200 B.C. to A.D. 900 mention eight modes of acquiring a wife known as Brahma, Daiva, Arsha, Prajapatya, Asura, Gandharva, Rakshasa, and Paisacha. Only the first four are known as *dharmya*, that is, according to religion. An exchange of gifts between the subjects' families marks the wedding ceremony, but no dowry is paid. In the Asura form payment of the bride price is the main element, while Rakshasa and Paisacha, respectively, pertain to the abduction and seduction of a girl when she is unconscious. The Gandharva marriage refers to a marriage by mutual choice. The Hindu lawgivers differ in their opinions and interpretations of this kind of marriage; some called it the best mode of marriage, while others viewed it stigmatic on religious and moral grounds. However, there is no reliable data to support or justify the popularity of any one of these modes of marriage. The first four kinds pertain to arranged marriages in which the parental couple ritually gives away the daughter to a suitable person, and this ideal continues to be maintained in the Hindu society. Opposed to these are four others, three of which were objected to by the scriptwriters in the past and viewed as illegal today, though nevertheless, they happen. The Gandharva mode, though opposed to the accepted norm, is nearest to what may be variously termed as "free-choice," "romantic," or "love" marriage. Yet through the ages Hindu revivalism and other socioreligious and economic factors discredited the importance of Gandharva marriage.

Diversified sects of Muslims and Christians view marriage as a civil contract as opposed to a sacrament. However, marriages are arranged most often with the consent of the subjects. The Muslims, at least theoretically, permit polygamy according to Islamic law; however, they prefer monogamy. As opposed to Hindu and Christian communities it is customary that the boy's party initiates a marriage proposal (see Kapadia 1966: 209–14; Kurian 1974: 357–58, 1975).

Most Indian marriages are arranged, although sometimes opinions of the partners are consulted, and in cases of adults, their opinions are seriously considered. Another aspect of this pattern is that individuals come to believe that their life mate is predestined, their fate is preordained, they are "right for each other," they are helpless as far as choice is concerned and therefore must succumb to the celestial forces of the universe. That the entire syndrome, typical for the society, represents a complex set of forces working around and upon the individual to get married to a person whom one is destined to love. It is also believed to be good and desirable that critical issues like the choosing of a life partner should be handled by responsible persons of family and kin group. However, it is generally possible that persons in love could marry if related prohibitions have been effectively observed.

Generally, love is considered a weak basis for marriage because its presence may overshadow suitable qualities in spouses. Therefore, arranged marriages result from more or less intense care given to the selection of suitable partners so that the family ideals, companionship, and co-parenthood can grow, leading to love. Ernest Van Den Haag writes about the United States:

> A hundred years ago, there was every reason to marry young—though middle-class people seldom did. The unmarried state had heavy disadvantages for both sexes. Custom did not permit girls to be educated, to work, or to have social, let alone sexual, freedom. . . . And, though less restricted than girls shackled to their families, single men often led a grim and uncomfortable life. A wife was nearly indispensable, if only to darn socks, sew, cook, clean, take care of her man. (1973: 181)

Goode views romantic love paradoxically, and calls it the antithesis of "conjugal love," because marriage is not based upon it, actually a couple strives to seek it within the marital bond (1959: 40). The latter, presumably, protect the couple against the harmful effects of individualism, freedom, and untoward personality growth. It may be worthwhile here to analyze the structural conditions under which mating relationships occur and to see how they relate to various values and goals in Indian society.

A study conducted in 1968, on 240 families in Kerala, a state which has the highest literacy rate in India, reveals that practical consideration in the selection of mates rather than free-choice or romantic love becomes the basis of marriage. In order of importance, the study reports that the major qualities among the girls considered important are: good character, obedience, ability to manage home, good cook, should take active part in social and political affairs, educated, religious, depending entirely on husband for major decisions, fair complexion, good companion with similar intellectual interests, and beauty (Kurian 1974: 335). Among the boy's qualities, his appearance, charm, and romantic manifestation do not count much, while the social and economic status of his family, education, and earning potential overshadow his personal qualities (Kurian 1974: 355; see also Ross 1961: 259).

The Kerala study further illustrates some interesting trends, such as: that only 59 percent of the respondents thought that meeting the prospective wife before marriage contributes to marital happiness. The parental preferences about the nature of choice of spouse of their children showed that 5.8 percent wanted to arrange the marriage without consulting sons and daughters, while 75.6 percent wanted to arrange the marriage with the consent of sons and daughters, 17.3 percent were willing to allow free choice to their children with their approval, and only 1.3 percent will allow freedom of choice without parental interference (Kurian 1974: 358). In fact, what Srinivas observed over three decades ago in Mysore was that "romantic love as a basis of marriage is still not very deep or widely spread in the family mores of India today," has not yet changed much (see Srinivas 1942: 60).

The dilemma of a boy who had fallen in love with a girl from a lower caste is reported from a study of Bangalore, a city of about a million people:

> My love affair has caused me great trouble, for my intense love of the girl and the devotion to my parents cannot be reconciled. My parents don't like our engagement, and I cannot displease them, but on the other hand I cannot give up my girl who has done so much for me. She is responsible for progress and the bright future which everyone says is ahead of me. The problem is my greatest headache at the present time. (Ross 1961: 269)

During my own fieldwork during 1963–67, in Awan, a community of about three thousand people in Rajasthan state, having extensive and frequent urban contacts, it took me no time to figure out that a question inquiring about "romantic" or "love" marriage would be futile, because people simply laughed it away. Parental opinion was reinforced by several other considerations. One man, a community elite, remarked:

> Young people do not know what love is; they are, if at all, infatuated which is very transitory and does not entail considerations of good marital life. If my son marries, I wish to see that the girl is well-raised, obedient, preserves the family traditions, ready to bear the hardships with us, and to nurse us in our old age.

Love, a premarital manifestation, is thus thought to be a disruptive element in upsetting the firmly established close ties in the family, a transference of loyalty from the family of orientation to a person, and a loss of allegiance of a person, leaving the family and kin group in disdain for personal goals.

Continued loyalty of the individual to the family of orientation and kin group is the most cherished ideal in the Indian family system. To preserve this ideal, certainly the simplest recourse is child marriage or adolescent marriage. The child is betrothed, married, and most often placed in a job and generally provides the deference demanded by the elders. Though this pattern does not give much opportunity to the individual to act freely in matrimonial affairs, it maintains a close link of the couple with the father's household which requires much physical, social, and emotional care throughout the family cycle and particularly in old age. The relationships in the extended joint family are all-important.

The Hindu scriptural texts prescribe that a person should go through *grahstaslirama* (a stage of householder's life) which includes procreation of children. The status system gives high prestige to the parents of large families. Kinship and religious values stress the need for a male heir. Large families provide security, both in economic and social terms, for the old and the destitute and the ill in a country where old-age pensions, disability, sickness benefits, and unemployment as well as medical insurance are either nonexistent or inadequate. When a family has several children, their marriages have to be spaced for economic as well as social reasons, which in turn necessitates early marriages.

Similar to other indigenous civilizations, a high value is placed upon chastity, especially female virginity in its ideal form. Love as play or premarital activity is not encouraged. Rather, elders consider it as their most important duty to supervise nubile girls. Marriage is an ideal, a duty, and a social responsibility usually preceded by highly ritualized ceremonial and festive events illustrating gradual involvement, especially of the female preparatory to the initiation of her marital role. Interestingly, all these ritual activities are role oriented (such as contributing to the long and prosperous life of the prospective husband) rather than person oriented (such as taking vows for the success of a person who is in love). This is one of those most pertinent factors which infuses longevity to the marital bond. The upper caste ideal that a girl could be ritually married only once in her lifetime and destined to marry the same person in lives to come continues to determine explicit and categorical aversion among girls to premarital interactions with strangers. Paradoxically, though, there is an implicit assumption that a person's marriage to a person of the opposite sex is governed by supreme celestial forces; in actual practice, mundane realities usually settle a marriage.

The early marriage of the person does not permit much personal independence and is further linked with another structural pattern in which the kinship rules define a class (caste, subcaste, regional group) of eligible future spouses. In other words, in the interest of homogamy and sanctity of the kin group, marriage should occur early. Thus, this would eliminate the chances of an unmarried adult to disregard a link with his or her kin group and caste. Problems arise at times when a person goes across the narrow limits of a group, often losing his chances of obtaining the usual support from the family, the kin group, and the caste. However, transgressions of basic family norms by an individual which may cause loss of identity, rejection, and an aggravated departure from the value system are rare. Often it is circumventing rather than contradicting the system which provides clues to change. Under such a pattern, elders negotiate and arrange marriages of their children and dependents with a likelihood of minimum generational conflict reinforcing greater chances of family unity. Adolescent physical and social segregation is marked by a greater emphasis on the learning of discrete sex roles idealizing, at least theoretically, parental roles.

As found in Western cultures, the youth culture frees the individual from family attachments thus permitting the individual to fall in love; and love becomes a substitute for the interlocking of kinship roles. The structural isolation of the Western family also frees the married partners' affective inclinations, that they are able to love one another (Parsons 1949: 187–89). Such a pattern is absent in the Indian family system.

Contrary to this, in India, marriage of a boy indirectly strengthens his bonds with the family of orientation. It is one of the major crises which marks his adulthood and defines his responsibilities towards his parents and the kin group. His faith and sentimental involvement in the family of orientation is an acknowledgment of the usual obligations incurred in his raising and training. A pervasive philosophy of individualism appears to be spreading and suggests a trend toward free mate choices, equality for women, equal divorce rights, and taking up of traditionally known ritually inferior but lucrative occupations; this militantly asserts the importance of the welfare of the person over any considerations of the continuity of the group. The trend toward conjugal family systems, widespread as it is, is generally confined to the urbanized regions (Gore 1958; Kapur 1970). Moreover, these changes where they appear on one hand, are viewed as social problems and as symptoms of the breakdown of time-honored ways; on the other, they are looked at as indicators of personal achievement, individual fulfilment, and family prestige.

## SOCIALIZATION

The cultural pattern demands that a child in India cannot isolate himself from his parents, siblings, and other members of the extended family.

The maturation process is rarely fraught with problems or turmoil associated with parent and adolescent children as they all learn to play new roles and feel new feelings. A child's expanding world gradually gives a mature sense of responsibilities to share in most of the important decisions in his life cycle. Covert parent-child conflict is shadowed by affection and sentimental ties helping the adolescents to achieve desirable balance between rebellion and conformity, individual wishes and feelings of the parents. Occasionally, this causes some problems. Since parents make decisions about most significant aspects of the family, including the marriage of their children, passive, indifferent, and sometimes negative feelings develop in the children as they seek to be dependent on other members of the family.

The family in India is known for its cohesive function, especially providing for the emotional needs of its members. Most often, this function is effectively performed by the extended kin group which, in fact, is a segment of the caste or subcaste. Adults, as well as children, must have love and security in order to maintain emotional stability under the stresses of life and in order to meet the emotional demands made upon them by the crises. In addition to providing the positive emotional needs of its members by personal sacrifices done by the members on a regular basis throughout the life cycle of the family, it also provides a safe outlet for negative feelings. Conflicts arising from interpersonal relations are generally handled by the older members, and care is taken by them to ensure that roles and responsibilities are clearly defined. Conflicts are resolved and mitigated by a general concern in the group favoring the emotional satisfaction of the individual. A person throughout his adolescence is never isolated from the family. Thus, not only generations, but extended and local units of kin groups are forced into a more intensive relationship. The affectional ties are solidified by mutual care, help in crisis situations, and assistance provided. This often destroys negative feelings. Several rituals, rites, and ceremonial occasions reinforce the unity of the family (Dube 1955: 131–58; Gupta 1974: 104–16). In general, a person substantially invests his emotions and feelings in his family and kin group, denial of which may be hazardous to his psyche. Such a deep involvement of the individual causes his emotional dependence on the family and acceptance to its wishes in most of the crucial decisions and events in his life, including marriage.

## PREMARITAL INTERACTION AND MATE SELECTION

India is perhaps the only subcontinent which provides a wide variety of mate selection processes from an open to a very closed system, from marriage by capture in the primitives to the arranged marriage among Hindus and Muslims.

Moreover, rules prohibiting certain classes of persons from marrying one another also vary, such as three to four clan avoidance rules in central and northern parts to preferential cross-cousin or maternal uncle and niece marriages in the south. In other words, rules regarding the definition of incest or areas of potential mates vary substantially. Most people in the Northern states, for example, prohibit marriage between persons of similarly named clans and extend this rule to several other related clans, such as of mothers clan, mother's mother clan, and father's mother clan. The people bearing these clan names may be living several hundred miles away * * * but are usually thought to be related. From this point of view, then, the ideal mate for any person could also be a stranger, an outsider, but an individual related to him in distant terms. * * * A person living across a state belonging to one's caste has a greater chance of being an eligible for a prospective mate than a person belonging to some other caste living next door. Caste is thus an extended kin group and, at least theoretically, membership in which is related through various kinds of kinship ties. Marriage alliances within the *jati* (caste or subcaste) reinforce kinship and family ties and cause a sort of evolution of the class system. Class generally determines future marital alliances within the caste. The resources assessed by a family in seeking a marital alliance from another family play a crucial role in determining the decision about the alliance. The voices of the significant members of the family are crucial in making a marriage since newlywed couples are barely into adulthood and have neither the material nor psychological resources to start a household of their own. Later in their married life when they have resources, they may still consider the opinions of the significant members because the disadvantages of not adhering to such opinions are greater than the annoyances of living together.

## A SOCIOLOGICAL PARADIGM OF ARRANGED MARRIAGES

Recent research on the changing aspects of the family in India (Collver 1963; Conklin 1974; Desai 1964; Gore 1965; Gould 1968; Gupta 1974; Hooja 1968; Kapur 1970; Kurian 1961, 1974; Orenstein 1959, 1961, 1966; Ross 1961; Shah 1974; Singer 1968) suggests that there has been little change in the joint family system in India, which is a vanguard of the arranged marriage.

The above discussion gives us to understand that what is needed in our approach to arranged marriage is a frame of reference which is more fully on the sociological level. As a step toward this goal, a general theoretical approach to the arranged marriage or "conjugal love" relationship has been formulated which, it is believed, takes account of the historical, cultural, and psychological levels, and brings into central focus the sociological level. The following tentative theoretical formulation is proposed only as a first attempt to outline what sociological factors are generally responsible to the growth of "conjugal love" as opposed to "romantic love." By any conservative estimate, love marriages occur in only less than 1 percent of the population.

1. It is important to note that arranged marriages are closely associated with "closed systems" wherein the hierarchies are very intricate and more than one factor such as historical origins, ritual positions, occupational affiliations, and social distance determinants play significant roles in defining the in-group and the out-group, particularly in marital alliances. In such systems, group identity is marked by strong senses of esoteric values, and such values are preserved and reinforced by attributes which distinguish a group in rank and its interaction with others. That is, most proximate ties of the individuals ought to be within their own group.

2. Continuity and unity of the extended family is well-preserved since all the significant members of the family share the mate-selection decision make-up which involves several persons who are supposedly known to have experience and qualifications to find a better choice as against the free choice of the subject. Obviously, this leads to lower age at marriage and, in turn, strengthens the predominance of the family over the individual choice.

3. Any possible problems emerging from a couple's functioning in marital life become problems for the whole family. Advice and counseling from the members of the extended family to improve the couple's relationship, weathering life's storms, or even sharing in crises are reinforced by the shared responsibilities. This is also partly responsible for denouncing the idea of divorce and forces working against it. This is not to say that this, in fact, resolves all the conflicts in marriage.

4. As long as the social system is unable to develop a value system to promote individualism, economic security outside the family system, and a value system which advances the ideals of nuclear family, the individuals in such a system continue to demand support from the family which, in turn, would lead to reemphasizing the importance of arranged marriage. Forces of modernization supporting the "romantic ideal" would continue to find partial support in such a system as long as the sources of moral and material support for the individual are based in the extended/joint family system.

5. It is difficult to assume that arranged marriage is related to the low status of a woman since man is also a party to it. If the concept of "free choice" is applicable to either sex, perhaps it will not support the ideal of arranged marriage. Apparently, an individual who opts for free choice or a "love marriage" is likely to dissociate from his/her family, kin group, caste, and possibly community, which he/she cannot afford unless he/she has been ensured tremendous support from sources other than these conventional institutions.

6. Arranged marriages, in general, irrespective of caste or class categories, help in maintaining closer ties with several generations.

Families in such a system are an insurance for the old and the orthodox, a recluse for the devout and the defiant, a haven for the invalid
and the insipid.
7. The demographic situation in India, as in most developing societies,
is also a contributing factor, among others, to the early arranged marriages. After independence, India has made many advancements in
science, technology, and medicine. * * * life expectancy, which was
29 years in 1947, is now 54 years. However, the vicious circle of early
child marriage, early pregnancy, high mortality rate, and replacement of the population are closely interwoven to ensure society from
extinction. While the value system notoriously maintains this chain-
work, the declining mortality rate further accentuates early marriages to shelve off the economic burden of the family by spacing
weddings. The family protects and insulates from ruining itself by
arranging marriages as early as possible and for using its resources
for status aggrandizement.

Since the changes in Indian society often present a welter of traditional and
modern, conventional as well as prestige and [glamor]-oriented marital role
models with significant changes in the value system, it is quite probable that
in the long run, "romantic ideal" will pervade the system. Whether such changes
will be a part of a continuum, that is, revitalization of the mythological past or
acceptance of the ideals of the modern West, preserving tenacity and positive
elements of its own against the swaggering forces of change, has yet to be seen.

## REFERENCES

Chekki, D. A. (1968). Mate selection, age at marriage and propinquity among the Lin-
gayats of India. *Journal of Marriage and the Family,* 30 (November): 707–11.
Collver, A. (1963). The family cycle in India and the United States. *American Sociolog-
ical Review,* 28: 86–96.
Conklin, G. H. (1974). The extended family as an independent factor in social change:
A case from India. *Journal of Marriage and Family,* 36 (November): 798–804.
Cormack, M. (1953). *The Hindu woman.* New York: Bureau of Publications, Columbia
University.
Desai, I. P. (1964). *Some aspects of family in Mahuva.* Bombay: Asia Publishing House.
Dube, S. C. (1955). *Indian village.* New York: Cornell University Press.
Goode, W. J. (1959). The theoretical importance of love. *American Sociological Review,*
24: 38–47.
_____. (1963). *World revolution and family patterns.* New York: Free Press.
Gore, M. S. (1968). *Urbanization and family change.* Bombay: Popular Prakashan.
Gould, H. A. (1968). Time dimension and structural change in an Indian kinship sys-
tem: A problem of conceptual refinement. In Milton Singer and Bernard S. Cohn,
Eds., *Structure and change in Indian society.* New York: Wenner-Gren Foundation
for Anthropological Research.

Gupta, G. R. (1974). *Marriage, religion and society: Pattern of change in an Indian village.* New York: Halsted Press.

Hate, C. A. (1970). Raising the age at marriage. *The Indian Journal of Social Work*, 30: 303–09.

Hooja, S. (1968). Dowry system among the Hindus in North India: A case study. *The Indian Journal of Social Work*, 38: 411–26.

Kapadia, K. M. (1966). *Marriage and family in India,* 3rd ed. London: Oxford University Press.

Kapur, P. (1970). *Marriage and the working woman in India*, Delhi: Vikas Publications.

Karve, I. (1965). *Kinship organization in India.* Bombay: Asia Publishing House.

Klass, M. (1966). Marriage rules in Bengal. *American Anthropologist,* 68: 951–70.

Kurian, G. (1961). *The Indian family in transition.* The Hague: Mouton.

———. (1974). Modern trends in mate selection and marriage with special reference to Kerala. In G. Kurian, Ed., *The Family in India—A Regional View* (pp. 351-67). The Hague: Mouton.

———. (1975). Structural changes in the family in Kerala, India. In T. R. Williams, ed., *Psychological Anthropology.* The Hague: Mouton.

Madan, T. N. (1965). *Family and kinship: A study of the Pandits of rural Kashmir.* New York: Asia Publishing House.

Mandelbaum, D. G. (1970). *Society in India,* vol. I & II. Berkeley: University of California Press.

Meyer, J. J. (1953). *Sexual life in ancient India.* New York: Barnes & Noble.

Orenstein, H. (1959). The recent history of the extended family in India. *Social Problems,* 8: 341–50.

———. (1961). The recent history of family in India. *Social Problems*, 8 (Spring): 341–50.

———. (1966). The Hindu joint family: The norms and the numbers. *Pacific Affairs,* 39 (Fall-Winter): 314–25.

Parsons, T. (1949). *Essays in sociological theory.* Glencoe, Illinois: Free Press.

Ross, A. D. (1961). *The Hindu family in its urban setting.* Toronto: University of Toronto Press.

Shah, A. M. (1974). *The household dimension of family in India.* Berkeley: University of California Press.

Singer, M. (1968). The Indian joint family in modern industry. In M. Singer & B. S. Cohn, Eds., *Structure and change in Indian society.* Chicago: Aldine Publishing Co.

Srinivas, M. N. (1942). *Marriage and family in Mysore.* Bombay: New Book Co.

Van Den Haag, E. (1973). Love or marriage. In M. E. Lasswell & Thomas E. Lasswell, Eds., *Love, marriage and family: A developmental approach* (pp. 181–86). Glenview, Illinois: Scott, Foresman and Co.

Vatuk, S. (1972). *Kinship and urbanization.* Berkeley: University of California Press.

# 39

## The Radical Idea of Marrying for Love*

FROM *Marriage, a History*

### STEPHANIE COONTZ

*As Peter Berger discussed in reading 1, what everyone knows is often not actually the case. Social historian Stephante Coontz, in the best sociological fashion, explains with insight and humor how marital bonding and long-term partnerships have only recently been the responsibility of "so strong yet transient an emotion" as love. Author of the very popular* The Way We Never Were *and other books, Coontz's historical and anthropological evidence provides some welcome understanding of marital patterns that may seem inappropriate, unnatural, or even immoral to those of us raised to believe there is one person with whom we can forever be happy. Record numbers of young people today are delaying marriage, and many who will never marry will be parents and have long-term monogamous relationships. Perhaps the Western version of love and marriage is changing, and those who embrace it can find guidance with Coontz's sociological insights.*

George Bernard Shaw described marriage as an institution that brings together two people "under the influence of the most violent, most insane, most delusive, and most transient of passions. They are required to swear that they will remain in that excited, abnormal, and exhausting condition continuously until death do them part."

Shaw's comment was amusing when he wrote it at the beginning of the twentieth century, and it still makes us smile today, because it pokes fun at the unrealistic expectations that spring from a dearly held cultural ideal—that marriage should be based on intense, profound love and a couple should maintain their ardor until death do them part. But for thousands of years the joke would have fallen flat.

For most of history it was inconceivable that people would choose their mates on the basis of something as fragile and irrational as love and then focus all their sexual, intimate, and altruistic desires on the resulting marriage. In fact, many historians, sociologists, and anthropologists used to think romantic love was a recent Western invention. This is not true. People have always fallen in love, and throughout the ages many couples have loved each other deeply.

---

*Footnotes and references can be found in the original publication of Stephanie Coontz's *Marriage, a History*. [*Editor's note*]

But only rarely in history has love been seen as the main reason for getting married. When someone did advocate such a strange belief, it was no laughing matter. Instead, it was considered a serious threat to social order.

In some cultures and times, true love was actually thought to be incompatible with marriage. Plato believed love was a wonderful emotion that led men to behave honorably. But the Greek philosopher was referring not to the love of women, "such as the meaner men feel," but to the love of one man for another.

Other societies considered it good if love developed after marriage or thought love should be factored in along with the more serious considerations involved in choosing a mate. But even when past societies did welcome or encourage married love, they kept it on a short leash. Couples were not to put their feelings for each other above more important commitments, such as their ties to parents, siblings, cousins, neighbors, or God.

In ancient India, falling in love before marriage was seen as a disruptive, almost antisocial act. The Greeks thought lovesickness was a type of insanity, a view that was adopted by medieval commentators in Europe. In the Middle Ages the French defined love as a "derangement of the mind" that could be cured by sexual intercourse, either with the loved one or with a different partner. This cure assumed, as Oscar Wilde once put it, that the quickest way to conquer yearning and temptation was to yield immediately and move on to more important matters.

In China, excessive love between husband and wife was seen as a threat to the solidarity of the extended family. Parents could force a son to divorce his wife if her behavior or work habits didn't please them, whether or not he loved her. They could also require him to take a concubine if his wife did not produce a son. If a son's romantic attachment to his wife rivaled his parents' claims on the couple's time and labor, the parents might even send her back to her parents. In the Chinese language the term *love* did not traditionally apply to feelings between husband and wife. It was used to describe an illicit, socially disapproved relationship. In the 1920s a group of intellectuals invented a new word for love between spouses because they thought such a radical new idea required its own special label.

In Europe, during the twelfth and thirteenth centuries, adultery became idealized as the highest form of love among the aristocracy. According to the Countess of Champagne, it was impossible for true love to "exert its powers between two people who are married to each other."

In twelfth-century France, Andreas Capellanus, chaplain to Countess Marie of Troyes, wrote a treatise on the principles of courtly love. The first rule was that "marriage is no real excuse for not loving." But he meant loving someone outside the marriage. As late as the eighteenth century the French essayist Montaigne wrote that any man who was in love with his wife was a man so dull that no one else could love him.

Courtly love probably loomed larger in literature than in real life. But for centuries, noblemen and kings fell in love with courtesans rather than the wives they married for political reasons. Queens and noblewomen had to be more discreet than their husbands, but they too looked beyond marriage for love and intimacy.

This sharp distinction between love and marriage was common among the lower and middle classes as well. Many of the songs and stories popular among peasants in medieval Europe mocked married love.

The most famous love affair of the Middle Ages was that of Peter Abelard, a well-known theologian in France, and Héloïse, the brilliant niece of a fellow churchman at Notre Dame. The two eloped without marrying, and she bore him a child. In an attempt to save his career but still placate Héloïse's furious uncle, Abelard proposed they marry in secret. This would mean that Héloïse would not be living in sin, while Abelard could still pursue his church ambitions. But Heloise resisted the idea, arguing that marriage would not only harm his career but also undermine their love.

## LOVE, IN AND OUT OF MARRIAGE

### "Nothing Is More Impure than to Love One's Wife as if She Were a Mistress"

Even in societies that esteemed married love, couples were expected to keep it under strict control. In many cultures, public displays of love between husband and wife were considered unseemly. A Roman was expelled from the Senate because he had kissed his wife in front of his daughter. Plutarch conceded that the punishment was somewhat extreme but pointed out that everyone knew that it was "disgraceful" to kiss one's wife in front of others.

Some Greek and Roman philosophers even said that a man who loved his wife with "excessive" ardor was "an adulterer." Many centuries later Catholic and Protestant theologians argued that husbands and wives who loved each other too much were committing the sin of idolatry. Theologians chided wives who used endearing nicknames for their husbands, because such familiarity on a wife's part undermined the husband's authority and the awe that his wife should feel for him. Although medieval Muslim thinkers were more approving of sexual passion between husband and wife than were Christian theologians, they also insisted that too much intimacy between husband and wife weakened a believer's devotion to God. And, like their European counterparts, secular writers in the Islamic world believed that love thrived best outside marriage.

Many cultures still frown on placing love at the center of marriage. In Africa, the Fulbe people of northern Cameroon do not see love as a legitimate emotion, especially within marriage. One observer reports that in conversations with their neighbors, Fulbe women "vehemently deny emotional attachment to a husband." In many peasant and working-class communities, too much love between husband and wife is seen as disruptive because it encourages the couple to withdraw from the wider web of dependence that makes the society work.

As a result, men and women often relate to each other in public, even after marriage, through the conventions of a war between the sexes, disguising the fondness they may really feel. They describe their marital behavior, no matter how exemplary it may actually be, in terms of convenience, compulsion, or self-interest rather than love or sentiment. In Cockney rhyming slang, the term for *wife* is *trouble and strife.*

Whether it is valued or not, love is rarely seen as the main ingredient for marital success. Among the Taita of Kenya, recognition and approval of married love are widespread. An eighty-year-old man recalled that his fourth wife "was the wife of my heart. . . . I could look at her and no words would pass, just a smile." In this society, where men often take several wives, women speak wistfully about how wonderful it is to be a "love wife." But only a small percentage of Taita women experience this luxury, because a Taita man normally marries a love wife only after he has accumulated a few more practical wives.

In many cultures, love has been seen as a desirable outcome of marriage but not as a good reason for getting married in the first place. The Hindu tradition celebrates love and sexuality in marriage, but love and sexual attraction are not considered valid reasons for marriage. "First we marry, then we'll fall in love" is the formula. As recently as 1975, a survey of college students in the Indian state of Karnataka found that only 18 percent "strongly" approved of marriages made on the basis of love, while 32 percent completely disapproved.

Similarly, in early modern Europe most people believed that love developed after marriage. Moralists of the sixteenth and seventeenth centuries argued that if a husband and wife each had a good character, they would probably come to love each other. But they insisted that youths be guided by their families in choosing spouses who were worth learning to love. It was up to parents and other relatives to make sure that the woman had a dowry or the man had a good yearly income. Such capital, it was thought, would certainly help love flower.

### "[I]t Made Me Really Sick, Just as I Have Formerly Been When in Love with My Wife"

I don't believe that people of the past had more control over their hearts than we do today or that they were incapable of the deep love so many individuals now hope to achieve in marriage. But love in marriage was seen as a bonus, not as a necessity. The great Roman statesman Cicero exchanged many loving letters with his wife, Terentia, during their thirty-year marriage. But that didn't stop him from divorcing her when she was no longer able to support him in the style to which he had become accustomed.

Sometimes people didn't have to make such hard choices. In seventeenth-century America, Anne Bradstreet was the favorite child of an indulgent father who gave her the kind of education usually reserved for elite boys. He later arranged her marriage to a cherished childhood friend who eventually became the governor of Massachusetts. Combining love, duty, material security, and marriage was not the strain for her that it was for many men and women of that era. Anne wrote love poems to her husband that completely ignored the injunction of Puritan ministers not to place one's spouse too high in one's affections. "If ever two were one," she wrote him, "then surely we; if ever man were loved by wife, then thee. . . . I prize thy love more than whole mines of gold, or all the riches that the East doth hold; my love is such that rivers cannot quench, nor ought but love from thee, give recompense."

The famous seventeenth-century English diarist Samuel Pepys chose to marry for love rather than profit. But he was not as lucky as Anne. After hearing a particularly stirring piece of music, Pepys recorded that it "did wrap up my soul so that it made me really sick, just as I have formerly been when in love with my wife." Pepys would later disinherit a nephew for marrying under the influence of so strong yet transient an emotion.

There were always youngsters who resisted the pressures of parents, kin, and neighbors to marry for practical reasons rather than love, but most accepted or even welcomed the interference of parents and others in arranging their marriages. A common saying in early modern Europe was "He who marries for love has good nights and bad days." Nowadays a bitter wife or husband might ask, "Whatever possessed me to think I loved you enough to marry you?" Through most of the past, he or she was more likely to have asked, "Whatever possessed me to marry you just because I loved you?"

### "Happily Ever After"

Through most of the past, individuals hoped to find love, or at least "tranquil affection," in marriage. But nowhere did they have the same recipe for marital happiness that prevails in most contemporary Western countries. Today there is general agreement on what it takes for a couple to live "happily ever after." First, they must love each other deeply and choose each other unswayed by outside pressure. From then on, each must make the partner the top priority in life, putting that relationship above any and all competing ties. A husband and wife, we believe, owe their highest obligations and deepest loyalties to each other and the children they raise. Parents and in-laws should not be allowed to interfere in the marriage. Married couples should be best friends, sharing their most intimate feelings and secrets. They should express affection openly but also talk candidly about problems. And of course they should be sexually faithful to each other.

This package of expectations about love, marriage, and sex, however, is extremely rare. When we look at the historical record around the world, the customs of modern America and Western Europe appear exotic and exceptional.

Leo Tolstoy once remarked that all happy families are alike, while every unhappy family is unhappy in its own way. But the more I study the history of marriage, the more I think the opposite is true. Most unhappy marriages in history share common patterns, leaving their tear-stained—and sometimes bloodstained—records across the ages. But each happy, successful marriage seems to be happy in its own way. And for most of human history, successful marriages have not been happy in *our* way.

A woman in ancient China might bring one or more of her sisters to her husband's home as backup wives. Eskimo couples often had cospousal arrangements, in which each partner had sexual relations with the other's spouse. In Tibet and parts of India, Kashmir, and Nepal, a woman may be married to two or more brothers, all of whom share sexual access to her.

In modern America, such practices are the stuff of trash TV: "I caught my sister in bed with my husband"; "My parents brought their lovers into our home"; "My wife slept with my brother"; "It broke my heart to share my husband with another woman." In other cultures, individuals often find such practices normal and comforting. The children of Eskimo cospouses felt that they shared a special bond, and society viewed them as siblings. Among Tibetan brothers who share the same wife, sexual jealousy is rare.

In some cultures, cowives see one another as allies rather than rivals. In Botswana women add an interesting wrinkle to the old European saying "Woman's work is never done." There they say: "Without cowives, a woman's work is never done." A researcher who worked with the Cheyenne Indians of the United States in the 1930s and 1940s told of a chief who tried to get rid of two of his three wives. All three women defied him, saying that if he sent two of them away, he would have to give away the third as well.

Even when societies celebrated the love between husband and wife as a pleasant by-product of marriage, people rarely had a high regard for marital intimacy. Chinese commentators on marriage discouraged a wife from confiding in her husband or telling him about her day. A good wife did not bother her husband with news of her own activities and feelings but treated him "like a guest," no matter how long they had been married. A husband who demonstrated open affection for his wife, even at home, was seen as having a weak character.

In the early eighteenth century, American lovers often said they looked for "candor" in each other. But they were not talking about the soul-baring intimacy idealized by modern Americans, and they certainly did not believe that couples should talk frankly about their grievances. Instead candor meant fairness, kindliness, and good temper. People wanted a spouse who did *not* pry too deeply. The ideal mate, wrote U.S. President John Adams in his diary, was willing "to palliate faults and Mistakes, to put the best Construction upon Words and Action, and to forgive Injuries."

Modern marital advice books invariably tell husbands and wives to put each other first. But in many societies, marriage ranks very low in the hierarchy of meaningful relationships. People's strongest loyalties and emotional connections may be reserved for members of their birth families. On the North American plains in the 1930s, a Kiowa Indian woman commented to a researcher that "a woman can always get another husband, but she has only one brother." In China it was said that "you have only one family, but you can always get another wife." In Christian texts prior to the seventeenth century, the word *love* usually referred to feelings toward God or neighbors rather than toward a spouse.

In Confucian philosophy, the two strongest relationships in family life are between father and son and between elder brother and younger brother, not between husband and wife. In thirteenth-century China the bond between father and son was so much stronger than the bond between husband and wife that legal commentators insisted a couple do nothing if the patriarch of the household raped his son's wife. In one case, although the judge was sure that a woman's rape accusation against her father-in-law was true, he ordered the young man to give up his sentimental desire "to grow old together" with his wife. Loyalty to parents was paramount, and therefore the son should send his wife back to her own father, who could then marry her to someone else. Sons were sometimes ordered beaten for siding with their wives against their father. No wonder that for 1,700 years women in one Chinese province guarded a secret language that they used to commiserate with each other about the griefs of marriage.

In many societies of the past, sexual loyalty was not a high priority. The expectation of mutual fidelity is a rather recent invention. Numerous cultures have allowed husbands to seek sexual gratification outside marriage. Less frequently, but often enough to challenge common preconceptions, wives have also been allowed to do this without threatening the marriage. In a study of 109 societies, anthropologists found that only 48 forbade extramarital sex to both husbands and wives.

When a woman has sex with someone other than her husband and he doesn't object, anthropologists have traditionally called it wife loaning. When a man does it, they call it male privilege. But in some societies the choice to switch partners rests with the woman. Among the Dogon of West Africa, young married women publicly pursued extramarital relationships with the encouragement of their mothers. Among the Rukuba of Nigeria, a wife can take a lover at the time of her first marriage. This relationship is so embedded in accepted custom that the lover has the right, later in life, to ask his former mistress to marry her daughter to his son.

Among the Eskimo of northern Alaska, as I noted earlier, husbands and wives, with mutual consent, established comarriages with other couples. Some anthropologists believe cospouse relationships were a more socially acceptable outlet for sexual attraction than was marriage itself. Expressing open jealousy about the sexual relationships involved was considered boorish.

Such different notions of marital rights and obligations made divorce and remarriage less emotionally volatile for the Eskimo than it is for most modern Americans. In fact, the Eskimo believed that a remarried person's partner had an obligation to allow the former spouse, as well as any children of that union, the right to fish, hunt, and gather in the new spouse's territory.

Several small-scale societies in South America have sexual and marital norms that are especially startling for Europeans and North Americans. In these groups, people believe that any man who has sex with a woman during her pregnancy contributes part of his biological substance to the child. The husband is recognized as the primary father, but the woman's lover or lovers also have paternal responsibilities, including the obligation to share food with the woman and her child in the future. During the 1990s researchers taking life histories of elderly Bari women in Venezuela found that most had taken lovers during at least one of their pregnancies. Their husbands were usually aware and did not object. When a woman gave birth, she would name all the men she had slept with since learning she was pregnant, and a woman attending the birth would tell each of these men: "You have a child."

In Europe and the United States today such an arrangement would be a sure-fire recipe for jealousy, bitter breakups, and very mixed-up kids. But among the Bari people this practice was in the best interests of the child. The secondary fathers were expected to provide the child with fish and game, with the result that a child with a secondary father was twice as likely to live to the age of fifteen as a brother or sister without such a father.

Few other societies have incorporated extramarital relationships so successfully into marriage and child rearing. But all these examples of differing marital and sexual norms make it difficult to claim there is some universal model for the success or happiness of a marriage.

About two centuries ago Western Europe and North America developed a whole set of new values about the way to organize marriage and sexuality, and many of these values are now spreading across the globe. In this Western model, people expect marriage to satisfy more of their psychological and social needs than ever before. Marriage is supposed to be free of the coercion, violence, and gender inequalities that were tolerated in the past. Individuals want marriage to meet most of their needs for intimacy and affection and all their needs for sex.

Never before in history had societies thought that such a set of high expectations about marriage was either realistic or desirable. Although many Europeans and Americans found tremendous joy in building their relationships around these values, the adoption of these unprecedented goals for marriage had unanticipated and revolutionary consequences that have since come to threaten the stability of the entire institution.

# 40

## Domestic Networks

FROM *All Our Kin: Strategies for Survival in a Black Community*

### CAROL B. STACK

*How far do family ties and responsibilities extend? For many African American fam-
ilies they extend beyond parents and children to cousins, aunts, uncles, and even fic-
tive kin. Decades of discrimination and institutional racism have left many people
with few resources of their own to draw on in times of need, and so helping relationships have remained a critical feature of the extended family. Linking ethnicity, class,
and gender, Carol Stack reminds us of the strength and resilience of the human
community.*

In The Flats the responsibility for providing food, care, clothing, and shelter
and for socializing children within domestic networks may be spread over several households. Which household a given individual belongs to is not a particularly meaningful question, as we have seen that daily domestic organization
depends on several things: where people sleep, where they eat, and where they
offer their time and money. Although those who eat together and contribute
toward the rent are generally considered by Flats residents to form minimal
domestic units, household changes rarely affect the exchanges and daily depen-
dencies of those who take part in common activity.

The residence patterns and cooperative organization of people linked in
domestic networks demonstrate the stability and collective power of family life
in The Flats. Michael Lee grew up in The Flats and now has a job in Chicago.
On a visit to The Flats, Michael described the residence and domestic organization of his kin. "Most of my kin in The Flats lived right here on Cricket Street,
numbers sixteen, eighteen, and twenty-two, in these three apartment buildings joined together. My mama decided it would be best for me and my three
brothers and sister to be on Cricket Street too. My daddy's mother had a small
apartment in this building, her sister had one in the basement, and another
brother and his family took a larger apartment upstairs. My uncle was really
good to us. He got us things we wanted and he controlled us. All the women
kept the younger kids together during the day. They cooked together too. It
was good living."

Yvonne Diamond, a forty-year-old Chicago woman, moved to The Flats from
Chicago with her four children. Soon afterwards they were evicted. "The landlord said he was going to build a parking lot there, but he never did. The old
place is still standing and has folks in it today. My husband's mother and father

took me and the kids in and watched over them while I had my baby. We stayed on after my husband's mother died, and my husband joined us when he got a job in The Flats."

When families or individuals in The Flats are evicted, other kinsmen usually take them in. Households in The Flats expand or contract with the loss of a job, a death in the family, the beginning or end of a sexual partnership, or the end of a friendship. Welfare workers, researchers, and landlords have long known that the poor must move frequently. What is much less understood is the relationship between residence and domestic organization in the black community.

The spectrum of economic and legal pressures that act upon ghetto residents, requiring them to move—unemployment, welfare requirements, housing shortages, high rents, eviction—are clear-cut examples of external pressures affecting the daily lives of the poor. Flats residents are evicted from their dwellings by landlords who want to raise rents, tear the building down, or rid themselves of tenants who complain about rats, roaches, and the plumbing. Houses get condemned by the city on landlords' requests so that they can force tenants to move. After an eviction, a landlord can rent to a family in such great need of housing that they will not complain for a while.

Poor housing conditions and unenforced housing standards coupled with overcrowding, unemployment, and poverty produce hazardous living conditions and residence changes. "Our whole family had to move when the gas lines sprung a leak in our apartment and my son set the place on fire by accident," Sam Summer told me. "The place belonged to my sister-in-law's grandfather. We had been living there with my mother, my brother's eight children, and our eight children. My father lived in the basement apartment 'cause he and my mother were separated. After the fire burned the whole place down, we all moved to two places down the street near my cousin's house."

When people are unable to pay their rent because they have been temporarily "cut off aid," because the welfare office is suspicious of their eligibility, because they gave their rent money to a kinsman to help him through a crisis or illness, or because they were laid off from their job, they receive eviction notices almost immediately. Lydia Watson describes a chain of events starting with the welfare office stopping her sister's welfare checks, leading to an eviction, co-residence, overcrowding, and eventually murder. Lydia sadly related the story to me. "My oldest sister was cut off aid the day her husband got out of jail. She and her husband and their three children were evicted from their apartment and they came to live with us. We were in crowded conditions already. I had my son, my other sister was there with her two kids, and my mother was about going crazy. My mother put my sister's husband out 'cause she found out he was a dope addict. He came back one night soon after that and murdered my sister. After my sister's death my mother couldn't face living in Chicago any longer. One of my other sisters who had been adopted and raised by my mother's paternal grandmother visited us and persuaded us to move to The Flats, where she was staying. All of us moved there—my mother, my two sisters and their children, my two baby sisters, and my dead sister's children. My sister who had been staying in The Flats found us a house across the street from her own."

Overcrowded dwellings and the impossibility of finding adequate housing in The Flats have many long-term consequences regarding where and with whom children live. Terence Platt described where and with whom his kin lived when he was a child. "My brother stayed with my aunt, my mother's sister, and her husband until he was ten, 'cause he was the oldest in our family and we didn't have enough room—but he stayed with us most every weekend. Finally my aunt moved into the house behind ours with her husband, her brother, and my brother; my sisters and brothers and I lived up front with my mother and her old man."

## KIN-STRUCTURED LOCAL NETWORKS

The material and cultural support needed to absorb, sustain, and socialize community members in The Flats is provided by networks of cooperating kinsmen. Local coalitions formed from these networks of kin and friends are mobilized within domestic networks; domestic organization is diffused over many kin-based households which themselves have elastic boundaries.

People in The Flats are immersed in a domestic web of a large number of kin and friends whom they can count on. From a social viewpoint, relationships within the community are "organized on the model of kin relationships." * * * Kin-constructs such as the perception of parenthood, the culturally determined criteria which affect the shape of personal kindreds, and the idiom of kinship, prescribe kin who can be recruited into domestic networks.

There are similarities in function between domestic networks and domestic groups which [one scholar] characterizes as "workshops of social reproduction." Both domains include three generations of members linked collaterally or otherwise. Kinship, jural and affectional bonds, and economic factors affect the composition of both domains and residential alignments within them. There are two striking differences between domestic networks and domestic groups. Domestic networks are not visible groups, because they do not have an obvious nucleus or defined boundary. But since a primary focus of domestic networks is child-care arrangements, the cooperation of a cluster of adult females is apparent. Participants in domestic networks are recruited from personal kindreds and friendships, but the personnel changes with fluctuating economic needs, changing life styles, and vacillating personal relationships.

In some loosely and complexly structured cognatic systems, kin-structured local networks (not groups) emerge. Localized coalitions of persons drawn from personal kindreds can be organized as networks of kinsmen. Good enough * * * correctly points out that anthropologists frequently describe "localized kin groups," but rarely describe kin-structured local groups. * * * The localized, kin-based, cooperative coalitions of people described in this chapter are organized as kin-structured domestic networks. For brevity, I refer to them as domestic networks.

\* \* \*

## GENEROSITY AND POVERTY

The combination of arbitrary and repressive economic forces and social behavior, modified by successive generations of poverty, make it almost impossible for people to break out of poverty. There is no way for those families poor enough to receive welfare to acquire any surplus cash which can be saved for emergencies or for acquiring adequate appliances or a home or a car. In contrast to the middle class, who are pressured to spend and save, the poor are not even permitted to establish an equity.

The following examples from Magnolia and Calvin Waters' life illustrates the ways in which the poor are prohibited from acquiring any surplus which might enable them to change their economic condition or life style.

In 1971 Magnolia's uncle died in Mississippi and left an unexpected inheritance of $1,500 to Magnolia and Calvin Waters. The cash came from a small run-down farm which Magnolia's uncle sold shortly before he died. It was the first time in their lives that Magnolia or Calvin ever had a cash reserve. Their first hope was to buy a home and use the money as a down payment.

Calvin had retired from his job as a seasonal laborer the year before and the family was on welfare. AFDC alloted the family $100 per month for rent. The housing that the family had been able to obtain over the years for their nine children at $100 or less was always small, roach infested, with poor plumbing and heating. The family was frequently evicted. Landlords complained about the noise and often observed an average of ten to fifteen children playing in the household. Magnolia and Calvin never even anticipated that they would be able to buy a home.

Three days after they received the check, news of its arrival spread throughout their domestic network. One niece borrowed $25 from Magnolia so that her phone would not be turned off. Within a week the welfare office knew about the money. Magnolia's children were immediately cut off welfare, including medical coverage and food stamps. Magnolia was told that she would not receive a welfare grant for her children until the money was used up, and she was given a minimum of four months in which to spend the money. The first surplus the family ever acquired was effectively taken from them.

During the weeks following the arrival of the money, Magnolia and Calvin's obligations to the needs of kin remained the same, but their ability to meet these needs had temporarily increased. When another uncle became very ill in the South, Magnolia and her older sister, Augusta, were called to sit by his side. Magnolia bought round-trip train tickets for both of them and for her three youngest children. When the uncle died, Magnolia bought round-trip train tickets so that she and Augusta could attend the funeral. Soon after his death, Augusta's first "old man" died in The Flats and he had no kin to pay for the burial. Augusta asked Magnolia to help pay for digging the grave. Magnolia was unable to refuse. Another sister's rent was two months overdue and Magnolia feared that she would get evicted. This sister was seriously ill and had no source of income. Magnolia paid her rent.

Winter was cold and Magnolia's children and grandchildren began staying home from school because they did not have warm winter coats and adequate shoes or boots. Magnolia and Calvin decided to buy coats, hats, and shoes for all of the children (at least fifteen). Magnolia also bought a winter coat for herself and Calvin bought himself a pair of sturdy shoes.

Within a month and a half, all of the money was gone. The money was channeled into the hands of the same individuals who ordinarily participate in daily domestic exchanges, but the premiums were temporarily higher. All of the money was quickly spent for necessary, compelling reasons.

Thus random fluctuations in the meager flow of available cash and goods tend to be of considerable importance to the poor. A late welfare check, sudden sickness, robbery, and other unexpected losses cannot be overcome with a cash reserve like more well-to-do families hold for emergencies. Increases in cash are either taken quickly from the poor by the welfare agencies or dissipated through the kin network.

Those living in poverty have little or no chance to escape from the economic situation into which they were born. Nor do they have the power to control the expansion or contraction of welfare benefits * * * or of employment opportunities, both of which have a momentous effect on their daily lives. In times of need, the only predictable resources that can be drawn upon are their own children and parents, and the fund of kin and friends obligated to them.

# 41

## African Americans and the Birth of the Modern Marriage*

FROM *Families as They Really Are*

### DONNA L. FRANKLIN

*Quite often the examination of black families emphasizes social problems associated with a history of discrimination and exclusion. Donna Franklin's social history of African American couples offers something different. In the period of first-wave feminism, black women were active in a wide range of civic organizations, with considerable support from their husbands. Not so for white women. Black women worked outside the home in much greater numbers than did white women, again with their husbands' support. In the past half century, African American and white women's marital and educational fortunes have continued to diverge. Why?*

We can trace the roots of dual-career marriages in the black professional community to the late nineteenth and early twentieth centuries. In an era when very few married white women worked outside the home, married black females were combining care for their families with employment responsibilities.

But as industrial capitalism developed, with its low wages, obstacles to upward mobility, and poor working conditions, marriage became an attractive alternative to working for many white women. And hand in hand with that, in the culture as a whole a new ideal took hold—the image of women as fragile, delicate, and economically dependent, needing to be sheltered and supported.

The different conventions regarding work and marriage in the white and black communities were reflected in a letter that the leading women's suffragist, Susan B. Anthony, wrote to her black friend and fellow activist, Ida B. Wells-Barnett, in 1890. Anthony had never married and doubted that women could combine marriage with a career. She lamented that Wells-Barnett's activism was suffering since she married and began having children:

> Women like you who have a special call for work should never marry. I know of no one in all this country better fitted to do the work you had in hand. Since you've gotten married, agitation practically seems to have ceased. Besides, you're trying to help in the formation of this league and your baby needs your attention at

---

*References and footnotes can be found in the original publication of this article, pages 63–74 of *Families as They Really Are*. [*Editor's note*] home. You're distracted over the thought that he's not being looked after as he would be if you were there, and that makes for divided duty.

When Ida B. Wells moved to Chicago and married Ferdinand Barnett she was thirty-two and her antilynching campaign was in full swing. Their marriage was a union of two black professionals. He was a prominent Chicago attorney and founder and publisher of the *Conservator*, Chicago's first black newspaper.

Barnett never expected Wells to stay home and be a housewife after their marriage. He employed household help, and he personally did most of the cooking for the family. Their temperaments complemented each other. Their daughter, Alfreda Duster, remembered that her "father was a very mild mannered man; he was not aggressive . . . or outspoken like my mother." With the support of her husband, Ida B. Wells-Barnett remained a force to be reckoned with both inside and outside the home.

But even with such a supportive husband, Wells struggled with the conflicting demands of activism and her maternal role. She had her first child during an election year and was asked to campaign throughout Illinois for the Women's State Central Committee, a Republican political organization. She agreed on the condition that a nurse be provided to help with her six-month-old son. Wells-Barnett recalled, "I honestly believe that I am the only woman in the United States who ever traveled throughout the country with a nursing baby to make political speeches."

A year later she was pregnant again. By then her husband had been appointed assistant state's attorney. She resigned from the presidency of the Ida B. Wells Club and announced that she was retiring from public life to devote more time to her family. The "retirement" lasted five months.

Black women seemed to have an easier time juggling the role of activist with the role of mother and wife. This was reflected in the dramatic differences in the marital status of white and black women activists at the end of the nineteenth century. Historian Linda Gordon found that 85 percent of black women activists were married, compared to only 34 percent of white women activists.

\* \* \*

In general, black female activists were viewed more favorably within their own community than were their white counterparts because they were seen as fighting for the greater good of all black people and did not pose a threat to the political objectives of black men. Slavery, having rendered black men and women equally powerless, had leveled the gender "playing field" within the black community. In contrast, much of white women's activism, such as the fight for female suffrage, posed a direct challenge to the privileges of white men and patriarchy.

When historian Stephanie J. Shaw examined the lives of professional black women from the 1870s through the 1950s, she found that 74 percent were married at least once in their lifetime. In addition to being more likely than their white activist counterparts to be married, 51 percent of them had professional husbands. Among the more affluent black women who emerged as leaders, marriage to prominent black men often gave them a distinct advantage in that it gave them greater access to the network of powerful black men. Shaw notes that many of the women in her study had been socialized in such a way that "the model of womanhood held before [them] was one of achievement in *both* the public and private spheres. Parents cast domesticity as a complement rather than a contradiction to the public arenas."

\* \* \*

## FREE AT LAST

The defeat of the Confederacy in the Civil War and the abolition of slavery brought profound changes to black family life, altering the economic, social, and legal arrangements within which the former slaves lived. Freed slaves began creating communities, establishing networks of institutions, churches, schools, and mutual aid societies. When they were slaves, blacks had established secret churches and families, and after emancipation these institutions provided an important sense of community. With their newfound freedom, black men and women shared a common dream of living as free people.

The freed slaves particularly welcomed the opportunity to marry, a right that had been denied to them. In 1850, escaped slave Henry Bibb had written that "there are no class of people in the United States who so highly appreciate the legality of marriage as those persons who have been held and treated as property." When laws were passed requiring marriages among former slaves to be registered, some whites were "astonished by the eagerness with which former slaves legalized their marriage bonds."

\* \* \*

## A BLACK WOMAN'S ERA

Although black women faced many challenges, the emergence of black female leaders and the conscious efforts to improve the education of black women bore significant fruit around the turn of the century. Novelist Francis Harper, whose writings focused on the political struggles of African American people, characterized this period as a "woman's era." Chicago activist Fannie Barrier Williams declared that although "the colored man and the colored woman started even, the achievements of black women during this period eclipsed black men."

From 1890 to 1910, the number of professional black women increased by 219 percent, compared to a 51 percent rise for black men. In 1890, about 25 percent of all black professionals were women. By 1910, that number had risen to 43 percent. The growing achievement of women was reflected in the fact that in 1910 female graduates outnumbered male graduates by two to one at Dunbar High School, the leading black high school in Washington, D.C.

In her study of black women's education, Jeanne Noble argued that black women had higher levels of educational achievement than men because the

> social system of the Negro rewarded the enterprising, clever, ambitious woman. Later, when attitudes that challenged the women's right to college education emerged, missionaries and earlier college founders were able to overcome these attitudes partly because of the need for teachers to educate the masses of ignorant Negroes.

\* \* \*

Two additional factors encouraged black women's academic achievements. The first was the high probability that even married black women would need to find employment outside the home. In addition, many black women sought to avoid the degradation of domestic service, seen as a continuation of the oppression they had experienced during slavery.

The growth in black women's quest for education during this period can be seen in the enrollment trends at the thirteen schools of higher education run by the Baptist Home Mission. In 1880, male enrollment in these schools was twice as high as female enrollment. But by 1892, female students outnumbered males nearly three to two, and 120 of the 202 teachers were women. Most of the female students specialized in teacher training.

\* \* \*

## THE COMMITMENT TO MARRIAGE

Studying black middle- and upper-income women in Illinois at the turn of the century historian Shirley Carlson found that:

> The black community did not regard intelligence and femininity as conflicting values, as the larger society did. That society often expressed the fear that intelligent women would develop masculine characteristics. . . . Blacks seemed to have no such trepidations, or at least they were willing to have their women take these risks.

\* \* \*

In that era, prominent black women tended to have experienced greater upward mobility than their white counterparts. About 90 percent of the black women who were classified as middle to upper class had been born into working-class families, compared to 35 percent of white women. The difference owed in part to the fact that blacks had been emancipated for only a relatively short time and higher education was the vehicle for social mobility for African Americans. Surveys conducted during that period found that black women were going to college for two primary reasons: to train for a vocation and to prepare for marriage and family life.

Many educated black males were also enthusiastic about marriage and family life with an educated woman. Lugenia Burns and John Hope were both University of Chicago graduate students during their courtship. John, eager to marry and start a family, proposed after Lugenia received her degree. But she had been looking forward to a life of service and declined John's first proposal. Lugenia had four other men also vying for her hand in marriage. But John had an advantage over her other suitors because of his commitment to marital equality. He wrote her a letter saying that when they marry "neither of us [is] to be the servant, yet both of us gladly serve each other in love and patience."

In writing about these marriages, Dr. Marion Cuthbert described them as a "deference of comradeship" by the men to their wives. Anna Julia Cooper described the wives as having a "partnership with husbands on a plane of intellectual equality."

## CHANGES IN AFRICAN AMERICAN MARRIAGE

The strong tradition of black women's education and professional employment that began during the club women's movement continued through the twentieth century. Jessie Bernard documented the higher levels of professional achievement found among black women, noting that in 1960 black women constituted 60.8 percent of black professionals, while white women constituted only 37.2 percent of the white professional class.

One reason for the lower professional involvement of white women was the persistence of the nineteenth-century ethos that a woman's place was in the home. When Adlai Stevenson addressed the graduating class of Smith College (ironically the alma mater of both Gloria Steinem and Betty Friedan) in 1955, he told the students that their role in life was to "restore valid, meaningful purpose to life in your home."

Three decades after Jessie Bernard's study of black and white females in the professions, Andrew Hacker found that black women made up 65.1 percent of black professionals, a rise of less than 5 percent, while white women had increased 15 points to 52.6 percent of white professionals. The women's movement had been a catalyst for white women to move into the professional arena. An analysis conducted since Hacker's has found that despite gains in educational attainment and occupational status between 1975 and 2000, the median earnings of white women grew by 32 percent while the median earnings of black women grew by only 22 percent. In addition, although the proportion of black women with college degrees increased, a racial gap in education has endured. In 2007, 19 percent of black women 25 and older had college degrees compared with over 30 percent of white and non-Hispanic women. This gap is even wider between white and black men.

In the three decades between the Bernard and Hacker studies, the black community has undergone what demographers describe as a "marriage squeeze," where a decrease in the availability of eligible partners leads to lower marriage rates, especially among women.

Using the College and Beyond (C&B) database, which contains the records of more than 80,000 undergraduate students who matriculated at twenty-eight academically selective colleges and universities in 1951, 1976, and 1989, we can compare the marriage and divorce patterns of black and white college-educated men and women. The "marriage squeeze" is reflected in the marriage rates of black graduates of these academically selective institutions roughly twenty years after they entered these schools. Blacks in the database were less likely to be married and more likely to be divorced or separated than their white counterparts. Whereas 77 percent of white women were married, 51 percent of black women were. For male graduates, these figures were 79 percent and 61 percent respectively. Some 14 percent of the black women were divorced or separated, compared to 6 percent of the white female graduates. For males, the differences in divorce and separation rates were miniscule, 6 percent for black men and 5 percent for white men. Of the four groups, black women had by far the highest rates of marital breakups.

Although the marriage squeeze and/or the mate availability perspectives were first used to explain trends among blacks in lower economic strata, it also affects higher educated black women in that there are fewer black men with equivalent education who are available for them to marry. Social scientists and policy analysts have not paid enough attention to the challenges faced by professional black women in this regard.

For African American women, the marriage squeeze has been exacerbated by the marriage of some of the most eligible black men to either white or Hispanic women. The C&B database didn't indicate the race of a graduate's spouse, but there is reason to believe that many of the black male graduates are not married to black women. In the three decades since the *Loving v. Virginia* decision was declared unconstitutional, ending all race-based legal restrictions on marriage, mixed couples tripled from 2 percent to 6 percent of all marriages. Black/white interracial married couples have increased from 51,000 in 1960 to 363,000 in 2000, a sevenfold increase. The majority of these marriages were of professional black men to white or Hispanic women. In view of this, it is not surprising that well-educated black women have fewer marriage options than their black male counterparts.

Black women are also more likely to be married to men who earn less money than they do. Data from the C&B studies show that white married women's *household* incomes were higher than those of black married female graduates, even though the *personal* incomes of the black women were 6 percent higher. This is because the husbands of white women graduates made substantially more money than the husbands of the black women. In fact, black women graduates also earned considerably *more* money than their husbands—exactly the opposite of the pattern for the white women graduates. This was because many of the black women graduates were married to men with less education than they had.

* * *

The late C. Wright Mills, in *The Sociological Imagination*, distinguished between an individual's personal troubles, such as being unable to find a job or being involved in a divorce, and public issues, such as patterns of widespread joblessness or high rates of marital disruption. Mills argued that the "sociological imagination" allows us to see the interconnection between an individual's troubles and broader patterns in society.

Marriage in the African American community is a case in point. The historical analysis of black marriage over the past 100 years demonstrates that African Americans were in the vanguard of creating the modern egalitarian marriage. Marriage has both public and private domains, and the evolution of the institution is determined both by the individual emotions, cultural ideals, practices that couples bring to their unions, and by the values and constraints of any given historical moment. African Americans have helped shape modern marriage, and now they must adapt to economic circumstances where wives are not only equal partners, but often out-earn their husbands. The complex reality that couples must pave new paths but also feel pressure to adapt to current conditions must be addressed as we create public policy to support marriage as an institution.

# 42

## The Emotional Geography of Work and Family Life

FROM *The Time Bind: When Work Becomes Home and Home Becomes Work*

### ARLIE RUSSELL HOCHSCHILD

*In the past three decades Americans employed full-time are working more and more hours, despite their support for "family values" and a belief that parents need to spend more time with their children. The apparent contradiction is addressed by Arlie Hochschild in this essay that preceded her book* The Time Bind. *On the basis of fieldwork with many working parents, she provides an analysis of how people manage both their time and emotions. This leads to some interesting insights about the possible future of work and family.*

Over the last two decades, American workers have increasingly divided into a majority who work too many hours and a minority with no work at all. This split hurts families at both extremes, but I focus here on the growing scarcity of time among the long-hours majority. For many of them, a speed-up at the office and factory has marginalized life at home, so that the very term "work-family balance" seems to them a bland slogan with little bearing on real life. In this chapter, I describe the speed-up and review a range of cultural responses to it, including "family-friendly reforms" such as flextime, job sharing, part time work and parental leave. Why, I ask, do people not resist the speed-up more than they do? When offered these reforms, why don't more take advantage of them? Drawing upon my ongoing research in an American Fortune 500 company, I argue that a company's "family-friendly" policy goes only as deep as the "emotional geography" of the workplace and home, the drawn and redrawn boundaries between the sacred and the profane. I show how ways of talking about time (for example, separating "quality" from "quantity" time) become code words to describe that emotional geography. * * *

### A WORK-FAMILY SPEED-UP

Three factors are creating the current speedup in work and family life in the United States. (By the term "family," I refer to committed unmarried couples, same-sex couples, single mothers, two-job couples and wage-earner-housewife couples. My focus is on all families who raise children.) First of all, increasing numbers of mothers now work outside the home. In 1950, 22 per cent of American mothers of children eighteen and under worked for pay; in 1991, 67 per cent did. Half of the mothers of children age one year and younger work for pay.

Second, they work in jobs which generally lack flexibility. The very model of "a job" and "career" has been based, for the most part, on the model of a traditional man whose wife cared for the children at home. Third, over the last 20 years, both women and men have increased their hours of work. In her book *The Overworked American*, the economist Juliet Schor argues that over the last two decades American workers have added an extra 164 hours to their year's work—an extra month of work a year. Compared to 20 years ago, workers take fewer unpaid absences, and even fewer *paid* ones. Over the last decade, vacations have shortened by 14 per cent. The number of families eating evening meals together has dropped by 10 per cent. Counting overtime and commuting time, a 1992 national sample of men averaged 48.8 hours of work, and women, 41.7. Among young parents, close to half now work more than 8 hours a day. Compared to the 1970s, mothers take less time off for the birth of a child and are more likely to work through the summer. They are more likely to work continuously until they retire at age 65. Thus, whether they have children or not, women increasingly fit the profile of year-round, lifelong paid workers, a profile that has long characterized men. Meanwhile, male workers have not reduced their hours but, instead, expanded them.

Not all working parents with more free time will spend it at home tending children or elderly relatives. Nor, needless to say, if parents do spend time at home, will all their children find them kind, helpful and fun. But without a chance for more time at home, the issue of using it well does not arise at all.

## COOL MODERN, TRADITIONAL, WARM MODERN STANCES TOWARD THE SPEED-UP

Do the speed-up people think the speed-up is a problem? Does anybody else? If so, what cultural stances toward gender equity, family life and capitalism underlie the practical solutions they favor? If we explore recent writing on the hurried life of a working parent, we can discern three stances toward it.

One is a *cool modern* stance, according to which the speed-up has become "normal," even fashionable. Decline in time at home does not "marginalize" family life, proponents say, it makes it different, even better. Like many other popular self-help books addressed to the busy working mother, *The Superwoman Syndrome*, by Marjorie Schaevitz, offers busy mothers tips on how to fend off appeals for help from neighbors, relatives, friends, and how to stop feeling guilty about their mothering. It instructs the mother how to frugally measure out minutes of "quality time" for her children and abandons as hopeless the project of getting men more involved at home. Such books call for no changes in the workplace, no changes in the culture and no change in men. The solution to rationalization at work is rationalization at home. Tacitly such books accept the corrosive effects of global capitalism on family life and on the very notion of what people need to be happy and fulfilled.

A second stance toward the work-family speed-up is traditional in that it calls for women's return to the home, or quasi-traditional in that it acquiesces to a secondary role, a lower rank "mommy track," for women at work. Those who take this sort of stance acknowledge the speed-up as a problem but deny the fact that most women now have to work, want to work, and embrace the concept of gender equity. They essentialize different male and female "natures," and notions of time, for men and women—"industrial" time for men, and "family" time for women.

A third warm modern stance is both humane (the speed-up is a problem) and egalitarian (equity at home and work is a goal). Those who take this approach question the terms of employment—both through a nationwide program of worksharing, (as in Germany), a shorter working week, and through company-based family friendly reforms. What are these family-friendly reforms?

- flextime; a workday with flexible starting and quitting times, but usually 40 hours of work and the opportunity to "bank" hours at one time and reclaim them later;
- flexplace; home-based work, such as telecommuting;
- regular or permanent part-time; less than full-time work with full- or pro-rated benefits and promotional opportunities in proportion to one's skill and contribution;
- job sharing; two people voluntarily sharing one job with benefits and salary pro-rated;
- compressed working week; four 10-hour days with 3 days off, or three 12-hour days with 4 days off;
- paid parental leave;
- family obligations as a consideration in the allocation of shift work and required overtime.

Together, worksharing and this range of family-friendly reforms could spread work, increase worker control over hours, and create a "warm modern" world for women to be equal within. As political goals in America over the last 50 years, worksharing and a shorter working week have "died and gone to heaven" where they live on as Utopian ideals. In the 1990s, family-friendly reforms are the lesser offering on the capitalist bargaining table. But are companies in fact offering these reforms? Are working parents pressing for them?

The news is good and bad. Recent nationwide studies suggest that more and more American companies offer their workers family-friendly alternative work schedules. According to one recent study, 88 per cent of 188 companies surveyed offer part-time work, 77 per cent offer flextime of some sort, 48 per cent offer job-sharing, 35 per cent offer some form of flexplace, and 20 per cent offer a compressed working week. (But in most companies, the interested worker must seek and receive the approval of a supervisor or department head. Moreover, most policies do not apply to lower-level workers whose conditions of work are covered by union contracts.)

But even if offered, regardless of need, few workers actually take advantage of the reforms. One study of 384 companies noted that only nine companies reported even one father who took an official unpaid leave at the birth of his child. Few are on temporary or permanent part-time. Still fewer share a job.

* * *

## INSIDE A FORTUNE 500 COMPANY

Why, when the opportunity presents itself, do so few working parents take it? To find out, I set about interviewing managers, and clerical and factory workers in a large manufacturing company in the northeastern United States—which I shall call, simply, the Company. I chose to study this Company because of its reputation as an especially progressive company. Over the last 15 years, for example, the Company devoted millions of dollars to informing workers of its family-friendly policies, hiring staff to train managers to implement them, making showcase promotions of workers who take extended maternity leaves or who work part-time. If change is to occur anywhere, I reasoned, it was likely to be within this Company.

But the first thing I discovered was that even in this enlightened Company, few young parents or workers tending elderly relatives took advantage of the chance to work more flexible or shorter hours. Among the 26,000 employees, the average working week ranged from 45 to 55 hours. Managers and factory workers often worked 50 or 60 hours a week while clerical workers tended to work a more normal, 40-hour, week. Everyone agreed the Company was a "pretty workaholic place." Moreover, for the last 5 years, hours of work had increased.

## EXPLANATIONS THAT DON'T WORK

Perhaps workers shy away from applying for leaves or shortening their hours because they can't afford to earn less. This certainly explains why many young parents continue to work long hours. But it doesn't explain why the wealthiest workers, the managers and professionals, are among the least interested in additional time off. Even among the Company's factory workers, who in 1993 averaged between eleven and twelve dollars an hour, and who routinely competed for optional overtime, two 40-hour-a-week paychecks with no overtime work were quite enough to support the family. A substantial number said they could get by on one paycheck if they sold one of their cars, put in a vegetable garden and cut down on "extras." Yet, the overwhelming majority did not want to.

Perhaps, then, employees shied away from using flexible or shorter hour schedules because they were afraid of having their names higher on the list of workers who might be laid off in a period of economic downturn. Through the 1980s, a third of America's largest companies experienced some layoffs, though this did not happen to managers or clerical workers at this company.

By union contract, production workers were assured that layoffs, should they occur, would be made according to seniority and not according to any other criteria—such as how many hours an employee had worked. Yet, the workaholism went on. Employees in the most profitable sectors of the Company showed no greater tendency to ask for shorter or more flexible hours for family reasons than employees in the least profitable sectors.

Is it, then, that workers who could afford shorter hours didn't *know* about the Company's family-friendly policies? No. All of the 130 working parents I spoke with had heard about alternative schedules and knew where they could find out more.

Perhaps the explanation lies not with the workers but with their managers. Managers responsible for implementing family-friendly policies may be openly or covertly undermining them. Even though Company policy allowed flexibility, the head of a division could, for reasons of production, openly refuse a worker permission to go part-time or to job-share, which some did. For example, when asked about his views on flextime, the head of the engineering division of the Company replied flatly, "My policy on flextime is that there is no flextime." Other apparently permissive division heads had supervisors who were tough on this issue "for them." Thus, there seemed to be some truth to this explanation for why so few workers stepped forward.

But even managers known to be cooperative had few employees asking for alternative schedules. Perhaps, then, workers ask for time off, but do so "off the books." To some extent, this "off the books" hypothesis did hold, especially for new fathers who may take a few days to a week of sick leave for the birth of a baby instead of filing for "parental leave," which they feared would mark them as unserious workers.

Even counting informal leaves, most women managers returned to full-time 40- to 55-hour work schedules fairly soon after their 6 weeks of paid maternity leave. Across ranks, most women secretaries returned after 6 months; most women production workers returned after 6 weeks. Most new fathers took a few days off at most. Thus, even "off the books," working parents used very little of the opportunity to spend more time at home.

Far more important than all these factors seemed to be a company "speed-up" in response to global competition. In the early years of the 1990s, workers each year spoke of working longer hours than they had the year before, a trend seen nationwide. When asked why, they explained that the Company was trying to "reduce costs," in part by asking employees to do more than they were doing before.

But the sheer existence of a company speed-up doesn't explain why employees weren't trying to actively resist it, why there wasn't much back-talk. Parents were eager to tell me how their families came first, how they were clear about that. (National polls show that next to a belief in God, Americans most strongly believe in "the family.") But, practices that might express this belief—such as sharing breakfast and dinner—were shifting in the opposite direction. In the minds of many parents of young children, warm modern intentions seemed curiously, casually, fused with cool modern ideas and practices. In some ways, those within the work-family speed-up don't seem to want to slow down. . . .

## WORK AND FAMILY AS EMOTIONAL CULTURES

Through its family-friendly reforms, the Company had earned a national reputation as a desirable family-friendly employer. But at the same time, it wasn't inconvenienced by having to arrange alternate schedules for very many employees. One can understand how this might benefit a company. But how about the working parents?

For the answer, we may need a better grasp of the emotional cultures, and the relative "draw" of work and family. Instead of thinking of the workplace or the family as unyielding thing-like structures, Anthony Giddens suggests that we see structures as fluid and changeable. "Structuration," Giddens, [author of *New Rules of Sociological Method*] tells us, is the "dynamic process whereby structures come into being." For structures to change, there must be changes in what people do. But in doing what they do, people unconsciously draw on resources, and depend on larger conditions to develop the skills they use to change what they do.

With this starting point, then, let us note that structures come with—and also "are"—emotional cultures. A change in structure requires a change in emotional culture. What we lack, so far, is a vocabulary for describing this culture, and what follows is a crude attempt to create one. An emotional culture is a set of rituals, beliefs about feelings and rules governing feeling which induce emotional focus, and even a sense of the "sacred." This sense of the sacred selects and favors some social bonds over others. It selects and reselects relationships into a core or periphery of family life.

Thus, families have a more or less *sacred core* of private rituals and shared meanings. In some families what is most sacred is sexuality and marital communication (back rubs, pillow talk, sex), and in other families the "sacred" is reserved for parental bonds (bedtime cuddles with children, bathtime, meals, parental talk about children). In addition, families have secondary zones of less important daily, weekly, seasonal rituals which back up the core rituals. They also have a profane outer layer, in which members might describe themselves as "doing nothing in particular"—doing chores, watching television, sleeping. The character and boundaries of the sacred and profane aspects of family life are in the eye of the beholder. "Strong families" with "thick ties" can base their sense of the sacred on very different animating ideas and practices. Families also differ widely on how much one member's sense of the sacred matches another's and on how much it is the occasion for expressing harmony or conflict. Furthermore, families creatively adapt to new circumstances by ritualizing new activities—for example, couples in commuter marriages may "ritualize" the phone call or the daily e-mail exchange. Couples with "too much time together" may de-ritualize meals, sex, or family events. Furthermore, families have different structures of sacredness. Some have thick actual cores and thin peripheries, others have a porous core and extensive peripheral time in which people just "hang out." But in each case, emotional culture shapes the experience of family life.

Emotional cultures stand back-to-back with ideas about time. In the context of the work—family speed-up, many people speak of actively "managing time, finding time, making time, guarding time, or fighting for time." Less do they speak of simply "having" or "not having" time. In their attempt to take a more active grip on their schedules, many working parents turn a telephone answering machine on at dinner, turn down work assignments and social engagements, and actively fight to defend "family time."

One's talk about time is itself a verbal practice that does or doesn't reaffirm the ritual core of family life. In the core of family life, we may speak more of living in the moment. Because a sacred activity is an end in itself, and not a means to an end, the topic of time is less likely to arise. If it does, one speaks of "enjoying time," or "devoting time." With the work-family speed-up, the term "quality time" has arisen, as in "I need more quality time with my daughter," a term referring to freedom from distraction, time spent in an attitude of intense focus. In general, we try to "make" time for core family life because we feel it matters more.

In the intermediate and peripheral zones of family life, we may speak of "having time on our hands, wasting or killing time." In the new lexicon, we speak of "quantity time." In general, we feel we can give up peripheral time, because it matters less. More hotly contested is the time to participate in a child's school events, help at the school auction, buy a birthday gift for a babysitter, or call an elderly neighbor.

With a decline in this periphery, the threads of reciprocity in the community and neighborhood grow weaker. By forcing families to cut out what is "least important," the speed-up thins out and weakens ties that bind it to society. Thus, under the press of the "speed-up," families are forced to give up their periphery ties with neighbors, distant relatives, bonds sustained by "extra time." The speed-up privatizes the family. The "neighborhood goes to work," where it serves the emotional interests of the workplace. Where are one's friends? At work.

Although the family in modern society is separated from the workplace, its emotional culture is ecologically linked to and drawn from it. Both the family and workplace are also linked to supportive realms. For the family, this often includes the neighborhood, the church, the school. For the workplace, this includes the pub, the golf club, the commuter van friendship network. A loss of supportive structure around the family may result in a gain for the workplace, and vice versa. Insofar as the "periphery" of family life protected its ritual core, to a certain degree for working parents these ties are not so peripheral at all.

A gender pattern is clear. Because most women now must and for the most part want to work outside the home, they are performing family rituals less. At the same time, men are not doing them very much more. Together, these two facts result in a net loss in ritual life at home.

At the same time, at some workplaces, an alternative cultural magnet is drawing on the human need for a center, a ritual core. As family life becomes deritualized, in certain sectors of the economy, the engineers of corporate cultures are re-ritualizing the workplace. Thus, the contraction of emotional culture at home is linked to a socially engineered expansion of emotional culture at work.

## WORK LIKE A FAMILY, AND FAMILY, FOR SOME, LIKE WORK

At a certain point, change in enough personal stories can be described as a change in culture, and I believe many families at the Company are coming to this turning point now. Pulled toward work by one set of forces and propelled from the family by another set of forces, a growing number of workers are unwittingly altering the twin cultures of work and family. As the cultural shield surrounding work has grown stronger, the supportive cultural shield surrounding the family has weakened. Fewer neighborhood "consultants" talk to one when trouble arises at home, and for some, they are more to help out with problems at work.

* * *

## THE MODEL OF FAMILY AS A HAVEN IN A HEARTLESS WORLD*

When I entered the field, I assumed that working parents would *want* more time at home. I imagined that they experienced home as a place where they could relax, feel emotionally sheltered and appreciated for who they "really are."

---

*This refers to Christopher Lasch's examination of the American family in his book *Haven in a Heartless World*. [*Editor's note*]

I imagined home to feel to the weary worker like the place where he or she could take off a uniform, put on a bathrobe, have a beer, exhale—a picture summed up in the image of the worker coming in the door saying, "Hi honey, I'm home!." To be sure, home life has its emergencies and strains but I imagined that home was the place people thought about when they thought about rest, safety and appreciation. Given this, they would want to maximize time at home, especially time with their children. I also assumed that these working parents would not feel particularly relaxed, safe or appreciated at work, at least not more so than at home, and especially not factory workers.

When I interviewed workers at the Company, however, a picture emerged which partly belied this model of family life. For example, one 30-year-old factory shift supervisor, a remarried mother of two, described her return home after work in this way:

> I walk in the door and the minute I turn the key in the lock my oldest daughter is there. Granted she needs somebody to talk to about her day. The baby is still up . . . she should have been in bed two hours ago and that upsets me. The oldest comes right up to the door and complains about anything her father said or did during the evening. She talks about her job. My husband is in the other room hollering to my daughter, "Tracy, I don't ever get no time to talk to your mother because you're always monopolizing her time first before I even get a chance!" They all come at me at once.

The unarbitrated quarrels, the dirty dishes, and the urgency of other people's demands she finds at home contrast with her account of going to work:

> I usually come to work early just to get away from the house. I go to be there at a quarter after the hour and people are there waiting. We sit. We talk. We joke. I let them know what is going on, who has to be where, what changes I have made for the shift that day. We sit there and chitchat for five or ten minutes. There is laughing. There is joking. There is fun. They aren't putting me down for any reason. Everything is done in humour and fun from beginning to end. It can get stressful, though, when a machine malfunctions and you can't get the production out.

Another 38-year-old working mother of two, also a factory worker, had this to say:

> My husband is a great help (with caring for their son). But as far as doing housework, or even taking the baby when I'm at home, no. When I'm home, our son becomes my job. He figures he works five days a week, he's not going to come home and clean. But he doesn't stop to think that I work seven days a week. . . . Why should I have to come home and do the housework without help from anybody else? My husband and I have been through this over and over again. Even

> if he would pack up the kitchen table and stack the dishes for me when I'm at work, that would make a big difference. He does nothing. On his weekends off, I have to provide a sitter for the baby so he can go fishing. When I have my day off, I have the baby all day long. He'll help out if I'm not here . . . the minute I'm here he lets me do the work.

To this working mother, her family was not a haven, a zone of relief and relaxation. It was a workplace. More than that, she could only get relief from this domestic workplace by going to the factory. As she continued:

> I take a lot of overtime. The more I get out of the house, the better I am. It's a terrible thing to say, but that's the way I feel!

I assumed that work would feel to workers like a place in which one could be fired at the whim of a profit-hungry employer, while in the family, for all its hassles, one was safe. Based as it is on the impersonal mechanism of supply and demand, profit and loss, work would feel insecure, like being in "a jungle." In fact, many workers I interviewed had worked for the Company for 20 years or more. But they were on their second or third marriages. To these employed, *work* was their rock, their major source of security, while they were receiving their "pink slips" at home.

To be sure, most workers *wanted* to base their sense of stability at home, and many did. But I was also struck by the loyalty many felt toward the Company and a loyalty *they felt* coming from it, despite what might seem like evidence to the contrary—the speed-up, the restructuring. When problems arose at work, many workers felt they could go to their supervisors or to a human resources worker and resolve it. If one division of the Company was doing poorly, the Company might "de-hire" workers within that division and rehire in a more prosperous division. This happened to one female engineer, very much upsetting her, but her response to it was telling:

> I have done very well in the Company for twelve years, and I thought my boss thought very highly of me. He'd said as much. So when our division went down and several of us were de-hired, we were told to look for another position within the Company *or* outside. I thought, "Oh my God, *outside!*" I was stunned! Later, in the new division it was like a remarriage. . . . I wondered if I could love again.

Work was not always "there for you," but increasingly "home," as they had known it, wasn't either. As one woman recounted, "One day my husband came home and told me, 'I've fallen in love with a woman at work. . . . I want a divorce.'"

Finally, the model of family-as-haven led me to assume that the individual would feel most known and appreciated at home and least so at work. Work might be where they felt unappreciated, "a cog in the machine"—an image brought to mind by the Charlie Chaplin classic film on factory life, *Modern Times*. But the factory is no longer the archetypical workplace and, sadly, many workers felt more appreciated for what they were doing at work than for what they were doing at home. For example, when I asked one 40-year-old technician whether he felt more appreciated at home or at work, he said:

> I love my family. I put my family first . . . but I'm not sure I feel more appreciated by them (laughs). My 14-year-old son doesn't talk too much to anyone when he gets home from school. He's a brooder. I don't know-how good I've been as a father . . . we fix cars together on Saturday. My wife works opposite shifts to what I work, so we don't see each other except on weekends. We need more time together—need to get out to the lake more. I don't know. . . .

This worker seemed to feel better about his skill repairing machines in the factory than his way of relating to his son. This is not as unusual as it might seem. In a large-scale study, Arthur Emlen found that 59 per cent of employees rated their family performance "good or unusually good" while 86 per cent gave a similar rating to their performance on the job.

This overall cultural shift may account for why many workers are going along with the work-family speed-up and not joining the resistance against it. A 1993 nationally representative study of 3400 workers conducted by the Families and Work Institute reflects two quite contradictory findings. On one hand, the study reports that 80 per cent of workers feel their jobs require "working very hard" and 42 per cent "often feel used up by the end of the work day." On the other hand, when workers are asked to compare how much time and energy they *actually* devoted to their family, their job or career and themselves, with how much time they would *like* to devote to each, there was little difference. Workers estimate that they actually spend 43 per cent of their time and energy on family and friends, 37 per cent on job or career, and 20 per cent on themselves. But they *want* to spend just about what they *are* spending—47 per cent on family and friends, 30 per cent on the job, and 23 per cent on themselves. Thus, the workers I spoke to who were "giving" in to the work-family speed-up may be typical of a wider trend.

## CAUSAL MECHANISMS

Three sets of factors may exacerbate this reversal of family and work cultures; trends in the family, trends at work, and a cultural consumerism which reinforces trends in the family and work.

First, half of marriages in America end in divorce—the highest divorce rate in the world. Because of the greater complexity of family life, the emotional skills of parenting, woefully underestimated to begin with, are more important than ever before. Many workers spoke with feeling about strained relationships with stepchildren and ex-wives or husbands. New in scope, too, are the numbers of working wives who work "two shifts," one at home and one at work, and face their husband's resistance to helping fully with the load at home—a strain that often leaves both spouses feeling unappreciated.

Second, another set of factors apply at work. Many corporations have emotionally engineered for top and upper middle managers a world of friendly ritual and positive reinforcement. New corporate cultures call for "valuing the individual" and honoring the "internal customer" (so that requests made by employees within the Company are honored as highly as those by customers outside the Company). Human relations employees give seminars on human problems at work. High-performance teams, based on co-operation between relative equals who "manage themselves," tend to foster intense relations at work. The Company frequently gives out awards for outstanding work at award ceremonies. Compliments run freely. The halls are hung with new plaques praising one or another worker on recent accomplishments. Recognition luncheons, department gatherings and informal birthday remembrances are common. Career planning sessions with one's supervisor, team meetings to talk over "modeling, work relations, and mentoring" with co-workers all verge on, even as they borrow from, psychotherapy. For all its aggravation and tensions, the workplace is where quite a few workers feel appreciated, honored, and where they have real friends. By contrast, at home there are fewer "award ceremonies" and little helpful feedback about mistakes.

In addition, courtship and mate selection, earlier more or less confined to the home-based community, may be moving into the sphere of work. The later age for marriage, the higher proportion of unmarried people, and the high divorce rate all create an ever-replenishing courtship pool at work. The gender desegregation of the workplace, and the lengthened working day also provide opportunity for people to meet and develop romantic or quasi-romantic ties. At the factory, romance may develop in the lunchroom, pub, or parking lot; and for upper management levels, at conferences, in "fantasy settings" in hotels and dimly lit restaurants.

In a previous era, an undetermined number of men escaped the house for the pub, the fishing hole, and often the office. A common pattern, to quote from the title of an article by Jean Duncombe and Dennis Marsden, was that of "workaholic men" and "whining women." Now that women compose 45 percent of the American labor force and come home to a "second shift" of work at home, some women are escaping into work too—and as they do so, altering the cultures of work and home.

Forces pulling workers out of family life and into the workplace are set into perpetual motion by consumerism. Consumerism acts as a mechanism which maintains the emotional reversal of work and family. Exposed to advertisements, workers expand their material "needs." To buy what they now "need," they need money. To earn money, they work longer hours. Being away from home so many hours, they make up for their absence at home with gifts which cost money. They "materialize" love. And so the cycle continues.

Once work begins to become a more compelling arena of appreciation than home, a self-fulfilling prophecy takes hold. For, if workers flee into work from the tensions at home, tensions at home often grow worse. The worse the tensions at home, the firmer the grip of the workplace on the worker's human needs, and hence the escalation of the entire syndrome.

If more workers conceive of work as a haven, it is overwhelmingly in some sense *against their wishes*. Most workers in this and other studies say they value family life above all. Work is what they do. Family is why they live. So, I believe the logic I have described proceeds despite, not because of, the powerful intentions and deepest wishes of those in its grip.

## MODELS OF FAMILY AND WORK IN THE FLIGHT PLAN OF CAPITALISM

To sum up, for some people work may be becoming more like family, and family life more like work. Instead of the model of the *family* as haven from work, more of us fit the model of *work* as haven from home. In this model, the tired parent leaves a world of unresolved quarrels, unwashed laundry and dirty dishes for the atmosphere of engineered cheer, appreciation and harmony at work. It is at work that one drops the job of *working* on relating to a brooding adolescent, an obstreperous toddler, rivaling siblings or a retreating spouse. At last, beyond the emotional shield of work, one says not, "Hi honey, I'm home," but "Hi fellas, I'm here!" For those who fit this model, the ritual core of family life is not simply smaller, it is less of a ritual core.

How extensive is this trend? I suspect it is a slight tendency in the lives of many working parents, and the basic reality for a small but growing minority. This trend holds for some people more than others and in some parts of society more than in others. Certain trends—such as the growth of the contingency labor force†—may increase the importance of the family, and tend toward reinstalling the model of family as haven, and work as "heartless world." A growing rate of unemployment might be associated with yet a third "double-negative" model according to which neither home nor work are emotional bases, but rather the gang at the pub, or on the street.

But the sense of sacred that we presume to be reliably attached to home may be more vulnerable than we might wish.

Most working parents more deeply want, or want to want, a fourth, "double-positive" model of work-family balance. In the end, these four patterns are unevenly spread over the class structure—the "haven in a heartless world" more at the top, the "double-negative" more at the bottom, the "reverse-haven" emerging in the middle.

---

†The contingency labor force refers to those employees who work on a short-term contractual basis or are hired as temporary workers. [*Editor's note*]

Each pattern of work and family life is to be seen somewhere in the flight plan of late capitalism. For, capitalist competition is not simply a matter of market expansion around the globe, but of local geographies of emotion at home. The challenge, as I see it, is to understand the close links between economic trends, emotional geographies, and pockets of cultural resistance. For it is in those pockets that we can look for "warm modern" answers.

# 43

## From *The Protestant Ethic and the Spirit of Capitalism*

### MAX WEBER

*Why did capitalism (and industrialization) emerge in Western Europe rather than in ancient China, Egypt, or India? All had sufficient knowledge and resources. What made the difference? In this classic study, Max Weber (1864–1920) presents his famous thesis about the connection between early Protestant beliefs and the emergence of industrial capitalism. His view of the fate of the Protestant ethic is, to many people, prophetic for the twentieth and twenty-first centuries. A contemporary of Émile Durkheim, Weber began writing soon after the death of Karl Marx. Weber is one of sociology's founders.*

In the title of this study is used the somewhat pretentious phrase, the *spirit* of capitalism. What is to be understood by it? The attempt to give anything like a definition of it brings out certain difficulties which are in the very nature of this type of investigation.

If any object can be found to which this term can be applied with any understandable meaning, it can only be an historical individual, i.e. a complex of elements associated in historical reality which we unite into a conceptual whole from the standpoint of their cultural significance.*

\* \* \*

"Remember, that *time* is money. He that can earn ten shillings a day by his labour, and goes abroad, or sits idle, one half of that day, though he spends but sixpence during his diversion or idleness, ought not to reckon *that* the only expense; he has really spent, or rather thrown away, five shillings besides.

\* \* \*

"Remember, that money is of the prolific, generating nature. Money can beget money, and its offspring can beget more, and so on. Five shillings turned is six, turned again it is seven and threepence, and so on, till it becomes a hundred pounds. The more there is of it, the more it produces every turning, so that the profits rise quicker and quicker. He that kills a breedingsow, destroys

---

*This is what Weber calls an "ideal type" concept, which has become a commonly used feature of sociology. [*Editor's note*]

all her offspring to the thousandth generation. He that murders a crown, destroys all that it might have produced, even scores of pounds.

\* \* \*

"For six pounds a year you may have the use of one hundred pounds, provided you are a man of known prudence and honesty.

"He that spends a groat a day idly, spends idly above six pounds a year, which is the price for the use of one hundred pounds.

"He that wastes idly a groat's worth of his time per day, one day with another, wastes the privilege of using one hundred pounds each day.

"He that idly loses five shillings' worth of time, loses five shillings, and might as prudently throw five shillings into the sea.

"He that loses five shillings, not only loses that sum, but all the advantage that might be made by turning it in dealing, which by the time that a young man becomes old, will amount to a considerable sum of money."

It is Benjamin Franklin who preaches to us in these [preceding paragraphs].

\* \* \*

That it is the spirit of capitalism which here speaks in characteristic fashion, no one will doubt, however little we may wish to claim that everything which could be understood as pertaining to that spirit is contained in it. Let us pause a moment to consider this passage, the philosophy of which Kürnberger sums up in the words, "They make tallow out of cattle and money out of men." The peculiarity of this philosophy of avarice appears to be the ideal of the honest man of recognized credit, and above all the idea of a duty of the individual toward the increase of his capital, which is assumed as an end in itself. Truly what is here preached is not simply a means of making one's way in the world, but a peculiar ethic. The infraction of its rules is treated not as foolishness but as forgetfulness of duty. That is the essence of the matter. It is not mere business astuteness, that sort of thing is common enough, it is an ethos: *This* is the quality which interests us.

\* \* \*

And in truth this peculiar idea, so familiar to us to-day, but in reality so little a matter of course, of one's duty in a calling, is what is most characteristic of the social ethic of capitalistic culture, and is in a sense the fundamental basis of it. It is an obligation which the individual is supposed to feel and does feel towards the content of his professional activity, no matter in what it consists, in particular no matter whether it appears on the surface as a utilization of his personal powers, or only of his material possessions (as capital).

\* \* \*

Thus the capitalism of today, which has come to dominate economic life, educates and selects the economic subjects which it needs through a process of economic survival of the fittest. But here one can easily see the limits of the concept of selection as a means of historical explanation. In order that a manner of life so well adapted to the peculiarities of capitalism could be selected at all, i.e. should come to dominate others, it had to originate somewhere, and not in isolated individuals alone, but as a way of life common to whole groups of men. This origin is what really needs explanation. Concerning the doctrine of the more naïve historical materialism,† that such ideas originate as a reflection or superstructure of economic situations. * * * At this point it will suffice for our purpose to call attention to the fact that without doubt, in the country of Benjamin Franklin's birth (Massachusetts), the spirit of capitalism (in the sense we have attached to it) was present before the capitalistic order. There were complaints of a peculiarly calculating sort of profit-seeking in New England, as distinguished from other parts of America, as early as 1632. It is further undoubted that capitalism remained far less developed in some of the neighbouring colonies, the later Southern States of the United States of America, in spite of the fact that these latter were founded by large capitalists for business motives.

* * *

To be sure the capitalistic form of an enterprise and the spirit in which it is run generally stand in some sort of adequate relationship to each other, but not in one of necessary interdependence. Nevertheless, we provisionally use the expression spirit of (modern) capitalism to describe that attitude which seeks profit rationally and systematically in the manner which we have illustrated by the example of Benjamin Franklin. This, however, is justified by the historical fact that that attitude of mind has on the one hand found its most suitable expression in capitalistic enterprise, while on the other the enterprise has derived its most suitable motive force from the spirit of capitalism.

* * *

It will be our task to find out whose intellectual child the particular concrete form of rational thought was, from which the idea of a calling and the devotion to labour in the calling has grown, which is, as we have seen, so irrational from the standpoint of pure * * * self-interest, but which has been and still is one of the most characteristic elements of our capitalistic culture. We are here particularly interested in the origin of precisely the irrational element which lies in this, as in every conception of a calling.

---

†Weber is critiquing Marx's idea of historical materialism. [*Editor's note*]

## LUTHER'S CONCEPTION OF THE CALLING

\* \* \*

Now it is unmistakable that even in the German word *Beruf,* and perhaps still more clearly in the English *calling,* a religious conception, that of a task set by God, is at least suggested. \* \* \* And if we trace the history of the word through the civilized languages, it appears that neither the predominantly Catholic peoples nor those of classical antiquity have possessed any expression of similar connotation for what we know as a calling (in the sense of a life-task, a definite field in which to work), while one has existed for all predominantly Protestant peoples.

\* \* \*

Like the meaning of the word, the idea is new, a product of the Reformation. \* \* \* It is true that certain suggestions of the positive valuation of routine activity in the world, which is contained in this conception of the calling, had already existed in the Middle Ages, and even in late Hellenistic antiquity. We shall speak of that later. But at least one thing was unquestionably new: the valuation of the fulfilment of duty in worldly affairs as the highest form which the moral activity of the individual could assume. This it was which inevitably gave every-day worldly activity a religious significance, and which first created the conception of a calling in this sense. The conception of the calling thus brings out that central dogma of all Protestant denominations. \* \* \* The only way of living acceptably to God was not to surpass worldly morality in monastic asceticism, but solely through the fulfilment of the obligations imposed upon the individual by his position in the world. That was his calling.

Luther developed the conception in the course of the first decade of his activity as a reformer.

\* \* \*

[L]abour in a calling appears to him as the outward expression of brotherly love. This he proves by the observation that the division of labour forces every individual to work for others. \* \* \* [T]he fulfilment of worldly duties is under all circumstances the only way to live acceptably to God. It and it alone is the will of God, and hence every legitimate calling has exactly the same worth in the sight of God.

\* \* \*

## ASCETICISM AND THE SPIRIT OF CAPITALISM

[I]f that God, whose hand the Puritan sees in all the occurrences of life, shows one of His elect a chance of profit, he must do it with a purpose. Hence the faithful Christian must follow the call by taking advantage of the opportunity. "If God show you a way in which you may lawfully get more than in another way (without wrong to your soul or to any other), if you refuse this, and choose the less gainful way, you cross one of the ends of your calling, and you refuse to be God's steward, and to accept His gifts and use them for Him when He requireth it: you may labour to be rich for God, though not for the flesh and sin."‡

\* \* \*

Wealth is thus bad ethically only in so far as it is a temptation to idleness and sinful enjoyment of life, and its acquisition is bad only when it is with the purpose of later living merrily and without care. But as a performance of duty in a calling it is not only morally permissible, but actually enjoined. The parable of the servant who was rejected because he did not increase the talent which was entrusted to him seemed to say so directly. To wish to be poor was, it was often argued, the same as wishing to be unhealthy; it is objectionable as a glorification of works and derogatory to the glory of God. Especially begging, on the part of one able to work, is not only the sin of slothfulness, but a violation of the duty of brotherly love according to the Apostle's own word.

The emphasis on the ascetic importance of a fixed calling provided an ethical justification of the modern specialized division of labour. In a similar way the providential interpretation of profit-making justified the activities of the business man. \* \* \* But, on the other hand, it has the highest ethical appreciation of the sober, middle-class, self-made man. "God blesseth His trade" is a stock remark about those good men who had successfully followed the divine hints.

\* \* \*

Let us now try to clarify the points in which the Puritan idea of the calling and the premium it placed upon ascetic conduct was bound directly to influence the development of a capitalistic way of life. As we have seen, this asceticism turned with all its force against one thing: the spontaneous enjoyment of life and all it had to offer.

\* \* \*

As against this the Puritans upheld their decisive characteristic, the principle of ascetic conduct. For otherwise the Puritan aversion to sport, even for the Quakers, was by no means simply one of principle. Sport was accepted if it served a rational purpose, that of recreation necessary for physical efficiency. But as a means for the spontaneous expression of undisciplined impulses, it was under suspicion; and in so far as it became purely a means of enjoyment, or awakened pride, raw instincts or the irrational gambling instinct, it was of

---

‡Richard Baxter, Nonconformist (Puritan) scholar, 1615–1691. [*Editor's note*]

course strictly condemned. Impulsive enjoyment of life, which leads away both from work in a calling and from religion, was as such the enemy.

\* \* \*

Man is only a trustee of the goods which have come to him through God's grace. He must, like the servant in the parable, give an account of every penny entrusted to him, and it is at least hazardous to spend any of it for a purpose which does not serve the glory of God but only one's own enjoyment. What person, who keeps his eyes open, has not met representatives of this viewpoint even in the present? The idea of a man's duty to his possessions, to which he subordinates himself as an obedient steward, or even as an acquisitive machine, bears with chilling weight on his life. The greater the possessions the heavier, if the ascetic attitude toward life stands the test, the feeling of responsibility for them, for holding them undiminished for the glory of God and increasing them by restless effort. The origin of this type of life also extends in certain roots, like so many aspects of the spirit of capitalism, back into the Middle Ages. But it was in the ethic of ascetic Protestantism that it first found a consistent ethical foundation. Its significance for the development of capitalism is obvious.

This worldly Protestant asceticism, as we may recapitulate up to this point, acted powerfully against the spontaneous enjoyment of possessions; it restricted consumption, especially of luxuries. On the other hand, it had the psychological effect of freeing the acquisition of goods from the inhibitions of traditionalistic ethics. It broke the bonds of the impulse of acquisition in that it not only legalized it, but (in the sense discussed) looked upon it as directly willed by God. The campaign against the temptations of the flesh, and the dependence on external things, was, as besides the Puritans the great Quaker apologist Barclay expressly says, not a struggle against the rational acquisition, but against the irrational use of wealth.

\* \* \*

On the side of the production of private wealth, asceticism condemned both dishonesty and impulsive avarice. What was condemned as covetousness, Mammonism, etc., was the pursuit of riches for their own sake. For wealth in itself was a temptation. But here asceticism was the power "which ever seeks the good but ever creates evil"; what was evil in its sense was possession and its temptations. For, in conformity with the Old Testament and in analogy to the ethical valuation of good works, asceticism looked upon the pursuit of wealth as an end in itself as highly reprehensible; but the attainment of it as a fruit of labour in a calling was a sign of God's blessing. And even more important: the religious valuation of restless, continuous, systematic work in a worldly calling, as the highest means to asceticism, and at the same time the surest and most evident proof of rebirth and genuine faith, must have been the most powerful conceivable lever for the expansion of that attitude toward life which we have here called the spirit of capitalism.

When the limitation of consumption is combined with this release of acquisitive activity, the inevitable practical result is obvious: accumulation of capital through ascetic compulsion to save. The restraints which were imposed upon the consumption of wealth naturally served to increase it by making possible the productive investment of capital.

\* \* \*

As far as the influence of the Puritan outlook extended, under all circumstances—and this is, of course, much more important than the mere encouragement of capital accumulation—it favoured the development of a rational bourgeois economic life; it was the most important, and above all the only consistent influence in the development of that life. It stood at the cradle of the modern economic man.

\* \* \*

## THE SPIRIT OF CAPITALISM TODAY

At present under our individualistic political, legal, and economic institutions, with the forms of organization and general structure which are peculiar to our economic order, this spirit of capitalism might be understandable, as has been said, purely as a result of adaptation. The capitalistic system so needs this devotion to the calling of making money, it is an attitude toward material goods which is so well suited to that system, so intimately bound up with the conditions of survival in the economic struggle for existence, that there can today no longer be any question of a necessary connection of that acquisitive manner of life with any single *Weltanschauung*. In fact, it no longer needs the support of any religious forces, and feels the attempts of religion to influence economic life, in so far as they can still be felt at all, to be as much an unjustified interference as its regulation by the State. In such circumstances men's commercial and social interests do tend to determine their opinions and attitudes. Whoever does not adapt his manner of life to the conditions of capitalistic success must go under, or at least cannot rise. But these are phenomena of a time in which modern capitalism has become dominant and has become emancipated from its old supports.

The Puritan wanted to work in a calling; we are forced to do so. For when asceticism was carried out of monastic cells into everyday life, and began to dominate worldly morality, it did its part in building the tremendous cosmos of the modern economic order. This order is now bound to the technical and economic conditions of machine production which to-day determine the lives of all the individuals who are born into this mechanism, not only those directly concerned with economic acquisition, with irresistible force. Perhaps it will so determine them until the last ton of fossilized coal is burnt. In Baxter's view the care for external goods should only lie on the shoulders of the "saint like a light cloak, which can be thrown aside at any moment." But fate decreed that the cloak should become an iron cage.

Since asceticism undertook to remodel the world and to work out its ideals in the world, material goods have gained an increasing and finally an inexorable power over the lives of men as at no previous period in history. To-day the spirit of religious asceticism—whether finally, who knows?—has escaped from the cage. But victorious capitalism, since it rests on mechanical foundations, needs its [asceticism's] support no longer. The rosy blush of its laughing heir, the Enlightenment, seems also to be irretrievably fading, and the idea of duty in one's calling prowls about in our lives like the ghost of dead religious beliefs. Where the fulfilment of the calling cannot directly be related to the highest spiritual and cultural values, or when, on the other hand, it need not be felt simply as economic compulsion, the individual generally abandons the attempt to justify it at all. In the field of its highest development, in the United States, the pursuit of wealth, stripped of its religious and ethical meaning, tends to become associated with purely mundane passions, which often actually give it the character of sport.

No one knows who will live in this cage in the future, or whether at the end of this tremendous development entirely new prophets will arise, or there will be a great rebirth of old ideas and ideals, or, if neither, mechanized petrification, embellished with a sort of convulsive self-importance. For of the last stage of this cultural development, it might well be truly said: "Specialists without spirit, sensualists without heart; this nullity imagines that it has attained a level of civilization never before achieved."

# 44

## From *Amish Society*

### JOHN A. HOSTETLER

*One of the most basic sociological truths is that people seek to organize their lives, families, and communities in order to become the kind of people they most admire. This is especially true for the Amish, who see their own beliefs as tied to the mainte-nance of their communities. In this study you can see how beliefs dictate a way of living, while at the same time a pattern of social structure upholds and reinforces the beliefs that dominate the society.*

Small communities, with their distinctive character—where life is stable and intensely human—are disappearing. Some have vanished from the face of the earth, others are dying slowly, but all have undergone change as they have come into contact with an expanding machine civilization. The merging of diverse peoples into a common mass has produced tension among members of the minorities and the majority alike.

The Old Order Amish, who arrived on American shores in colonial times, have survived in the modern world in distinctive, viable, small communities. They have resisted the homogenization process more successfully than others. In planting and harvest time one can see their bearded men working the fields with horses and their women hanging out the laundry in neat rows to dry. Many American people have seen Amish families, with the men wearing broad-brimmed black hats and the women in bonnets and long dresses, in rail-way depots or bus terminals. Although the Amish have lived with industrial-ized America for over two and a half centuries, they have moderated its influence on their personal lives, their families, communities, and their values.

The Amish are often perceived by other Americans to be relics of the past who live an austere, inflexible life dedicated to inconvenient and archaic cus-toms. They are seen as renouncing both modern conveniences and the Amer-ican dream of success and progress. But most people have no quarrel with the Amish for doing things the old-fashioned way. Their conscientious objection was tolerated in wartime, for after all, they are meticulous farmers who prac-tice the virtues of work and thrift.

In recent years the status of the Amish in the minds of most Americans has shifted toward a more favorable position. This change can scarcely be attrib-uted to anything the Amish have done; rather, it is the result of changes in the way Americans perceive their minority groups. A century ago, hardly anyone knew the Amish existed. A half-century ago they were viewed as an obscure sect living by ridiculous customs, as stubborn people who resisted education and exploited the labor of their children. Today the Amish are the unwilling objects of a thriving tourist industry on the eastern seaboard. They are revered as hard-working, thrifty people with enormous agrarian stamina, and by some, as islands of sanity in a culture gripped by commercialism and technology run wild.

In the academic community several models have been advanced for understanding Amish society. Social scientists, like other Americans, have been influenced by the upward push of an advancing civilization and changes in the social discourse between the dominant society and its minorities. University teachers have traditionally taught their students to think of the Amish people as one of many old-world cultural islands left over in the modern world.

\* \* \*

The Amish are a church, a community, a spiritual union, a conservative branch of Christianity, a religion, a community whose members practice simple and austere living, a familistic entrepreneuring system, and an adaptive human community. In this chapter several models will be discussed in terms of their usefulness and limitations as avenues for understanding Amish society as a whole. By models I mean structured concepts currently used by anthropologists to characterize whole societies. The serious reader will want to transcend the scientific orientation and ask, What is the meaning of the Amish system? What, if anything, is it trying to say to us?

## A COMMONWEALTH

The Amish are in some ways a little commonwealth, for their members claim to be ruled by the law of love and redemption. The bonds that unite them are many. Their beliefs, however, do not permit them solely to occupy and defend a particular territory. They are highly sensitive in caring for their own. They will move to other lands when circumstances force them to do so.

Commonwealth implies a place, a province, which means any part of a national domain that geographically and socially is sufficiently unified to have a true consciousness of its unity. Its inhabitants feel comfortable with their own ideas and customs, and the "place" possesses a sense of distinction from other parts of the country. Members of a commonwealth are not footloose. They have a sense of productivity and accountability in a province where "the general welfare" is accepted as a day-to-day reality. Commonwealth has come to have an archaic meaning in today's world, because when groups and institutions become too large, the sense of commonwealth or the common good is lost. Thus it is little wonder that the most recent dictionaries of the American English language render the meaning of commonwealth as "obsolescent." In reality, the Amish are in part a commonwealth. There is, however, no provision for outcasts.

It may be argued that the Amish have retained elements of wholesome provincialism, a saving power to which the world in the future will need more and more to appeal. Provincialism need not turn to ancient narrowness and ignorance, confines from which many have sought to escape. A sense of province or commonwealth, with its cherished love of people and self-conscious dignity, is a necessary basis for relating to the wider world community. Respect for locality, place, custom, and local idealism can go a long way toward checking the monstrous growth of consolidation in the nation and thus help to save human freedom and individual dignity.

## A SECTARIAN SOCIETY

Sociologists tend to classify the Amish as a sectarian society. Several European scholars have compared the social structure of "sect" and "church" types of religious institutions. The established church was viewed as hierarchic and conservative. It appealed to the ruling classes, administered grace to all people in a territorial domain, and served as an agency of social control. The sect was egalitarian. Essentially a voluntary religious protest movement, its members separated themselves from others on the basis of beliefs, practices, and institutions. The sects rejected the authority of the established religious organizations and their leaders. The strains between sect and church were viewed as a dialectic principle at work within Christianity. The use of an ideal type helped to clarify particular characteristics of the sectarian groups. The Anabaptists, for example, were described as small, voluntary groupings attempting to model their lives after the spirit of the Sermon on the Mount (Matt. 5, 6, 7) while also exercising the power to exclude and discipline members. Absolute separation from all other religious loyalties was required. All members were considered equal, and none were to take oaths, participate in war, or take part in worldly government.

Sects have employed various techniques of isolation for maintaining separateness. Today the extreme mobility of modern life brings people together in multiple contexts. The spatial metaphors of separation (i.e., valley, region, sector, etc.) are fast becoming obsolete. Nevertheless, modern sectarians turn to psychic insularity and contexts that protect them from mainstream values and competing systems. Members of the sect remain segregated in various degrees, chiefly by finding a group whose philosophy of history contradicts the existing values so drastically that the group sustains itself for a generation or more. To the onlooker, sectarianism, like monasticism, may appear to serve as a shelter from the complications of an overly complex society. For its participants, it provides authentic ways of realizing new forms of service and humility as well as protection from mainstream culture.

Sectarians, it is claimed, put their faith first by ordering their lives in keeping with it. The established churches compromise their faith with other interests and with the demands of the surrounding environment. Sectarians are pervasively religious in that they practice their beliefs in everyday life. Sects are often considered marginal or odd groups of alienated people with fanatic ideas. Yet the sects have had an immense influence in shaping the course of history. The British sociologist Bryan Wilson has observed that sects are "self-conscious attempts by men to construct their own societies, not merely as political entities with constitutions, but as groups with a firm set of values and mores, of which they are conscious." The growth of religious toleration in America has resulted in the development of religious pluralism in a manner that has not been realized in Europe. Wilson, who has characterized modern Christian sects into several types, classes the Amish as *introversionist* rather than *conversionist* or *reformist*. "Salvation is to be found in the community of those who withdraw from involvement in the affairs of mankind." The Amish recognize the evil circumstance of man, attempt to moderate its influence upon them, and retreat into a community to experience, cultivate, and preserve the attributes of God in ethical relationships.

The sectarian model lends itself to a historical, religious context. As a model, it offers some insight into the proliferation of groups with a negative orientation during a specific time period. Today there are many types of movements that did not exist in the early stages of industrialization. Sects may lose their spontaneity in a variety of ways. While the model may teach us something of how sects originate and grow from a protest movement to a separate religious entity, it does not provide us with a knowledge of the dynamics of the group. The Amish, for example, are not sectarians in the sense that they demand that others conform to their practices. Nor do they claim to base all actions on holy writ. They are not in conflict with the dominant culture in the same way, or with the same intensity, as are a number of sects such as the "apocalyptic" or "manipulationist" types.

Many sectarian societies, including the Amish, make little or no attempt to communicate their message. They recognize instinctively that authentic communication would mean greater literacy, education, and sophistication, and this would mean the beginning of the end. "The contribution of the sect to the larger society is," according to Martin Marty, "made best through the sympathetic observer who carries with him a picture of the advantages or particularity and assertiveness back to the world of dialogical complexity." In the Amish case, the message of the sectarian society is exemplary. A way of living is more important than communicating it in words. The ultimate message is the life. An Amish person will have no doubt about his basic convictions, his view of the meaning and purpose of life, but he cannot explain it except through the conduct of his life.

## A FOLK SOCIETY

Anthropologists, who have compared societies all over the world, have tended to call semi-isolated peoples "folk societies," "primitives," or merely "simple societies." These societies constitute an altogether different type in contrast to the industrialized, or so-called civilized, societies. The "folk society," as conceptualized by Robert Redfield, is a small, isolated, traditional, simple, homogeneous society in which oral communication and conventionalized ways are important factors in integrating the whole of life. In such an ideal-type society, shared practical knowledge is more important than science, custom is valued more than critical knowledge, and associations are personal and emotional rather than abstract and categoric.

Folk societies are uncomfortable with the idea of change. Young people do what the old people did when they were young. Members communicate intimately with one another, not only by word of mouth but also through custom and symbols that reflect a strong sense of belonging to one another. A folk society is *Gemeinschaft*-like,[1] there is a strong sense of "we-ness." Leadership is personal rather than institutionalized. There are no gross economic inequalities. Mutual aid is characteristic of the society's members. The goals of life are never stated as matters of doctrine, but neither are they questioned. They are implied by the acts that constitute living in a small society. Custom tends to become sacred. Behavior is strongly patterned, and acts as well as cultural objects are given symbolic meaning that is often pervasively religious. Religion is diffuse and all-pervasive. In the typical folk society, planting and harvesting are as sacred in their own ways as singing and praying.

The significance of the Amish as an intimate, face-to-face primary group has long been recognized. Charles P. Loomis was the first to conceptualize the character of the Amish. In his construction of a scale he contrasted the Amish as a familistic *Gemeinschaf*-type system with highly rational social systems of the *Gesellschaft*-type in contemporary civilization.

The folk model lends itself well to understanding the tradition-directed character of Amish society. The heavy weight of tradition can scarcely be explained in any other way. The Amish, for example, have retained many of the customs and small-scale technologies that were common in rural society in the nineteenth century. Through a process of syncretism, Amish religious values have been fused with an earlier period of simple country living when everyone farmed with horses and on a scale where family members could work together. The Amish exist as a folk or "little" community in a rural subculture within the modern state, as distinguished from the primitive or peasant types described in anthropological literature. Several aspects of Redfield's folk-society model and features of the Töennies-Loomis *Gemeinscliaft* aid us in understanding the parameters of Amish society. They are *distinctiveness, smallness of scale, homogeneous culture patterns*, and the *strain toward self-sufficiency*.

*Distinctiveness.* The Amish people are highly visible. The outsider who drives through an Amish settlement cannot help but recognize them by their clothing, farm homes, furnishings, fields, and other material traits of culture. Although

---

1. The German term *Gemeinschaft* is often translated as "community." Ferdinand Tönnies's classic work, *Gemeinschaft und Gesellschaft* provided sociology with this concept which is contrasted to urban, modern and industrialized society (*Gesellschaft*).

they speak perfect English with outsiders, they speak a dialect of German among themselves.

Amish life is distinctive in that religion and custom blend into a way of life. The two are inseparable. The core values of the community are religious beliefs. Not only do the members worship a deity they understand through the revelation of Jesus Christ and the Bible, but their patterned behavior has a religious dimension. A distinctive way of life permeates daily life, agriculture, and the application of energy to economic ends. Their beliefs determine their conceptions of the self, the universe, and man's place in it. The Amish world view recognizes a certain spiritual worth and dignity in the universe in its natural form. Religious considerations determine hours of work and the daily, weekly, seasonal, and yearly rituals associated with life experience. Occupation, the means and destinations of travel, and choice of friends and mate are determined by religious considerations. Religious and work attitudes are not far distant from each other. The universe includes the divine, and Amish society itself is considered divine insofar as the Amish recognize themselves as "a chosen people of God." The Amish do not seek to master nature or to work against the elements, but try to work with them. The affinity between Amish society and nature in the form of land, terrain, and vegetation is expressed in various degrees of intensity.

Religion is highly patterned, so one may properly speak of the Amish as a tradition-directed group. Though allusions to the Bible play an important role in determining their outlook on the world, and on life after death, these beliefs have been fused with several centuries of struggling to survive in community. Out of intense religious experience, societal conflict, and intimate agrarian experience, a mentality has developed that prefers the old rather than the new. While the principle seems to apply especially to religion, it has also become a charter for social behavior. "The old is the best, and the new is of the devil," has become a prevalent mode of thought. By living in closed communities where custom and a strong sense of togetherness prevail, the Amish have formed an integrated way of life and a folklike culture. Continuity of conformity and custom is assured and the needs of the individual from birth to death are met within an integrated and shared system of meanings. Oral tradition, custom, and conventionality play an important part in maintaining the group as a functioning whole. To the participant, religion and custom are inseparable. Commitment and culture are combined to produce a stable human existence.

These are some of the qualities of the little Amish community that make it distinctive. "Where the community begins and where it ends is apparent. The distinctiveness is apparent to the outside observer and is expressed in the group consciousness of the people of the community." The Amish community is in some aspects a functional part of modern society but is a distinctive subculture within it.

# 45

## Politicized Evangelicalism and Secular Elites: Creating a Moral Other*

FROM *Evangelicals and Democracy in America; Volume II: Religion and Politics*

### RHYS H. WILLIAMS

*Among the most important ways social movements succeed is by creating effective "frames" that identify a problem and motivate movement participants to work toward a solution. Political sociology guides us through this process. Religious sentiments have, and continue to, inform and guide many successful social movements. In the United States today, none is more effective in pressing its political agenda than evangelical Christianity. Its bête noir is secular humanism and non-believing "elites." Their demonization provides an effective framing device for adherents of a more religiously infused politics.*

In the discourse of much contemporary conservative Protestant evangelicalism, particularly that concerned with the place of religion in politics and the public sphere, one group stands out—portrayed as perhaps a singular threat to evangelical religion specifically, religion in general, and America's social and moral well-being. Under a variety of names, much of politicized evangelicalism has constructed "secular elites" as its primary political opponent, and even more expansively, as the primary threat to our societal health. This chapter examines the construction of secular elites as a moral "other," and the ways in which that construction works as a resource for political mobilization and resonates within evangelical culture. In particular, I argue that a construction labeled secular elites has become the primary foil and moral other for organized political evangelicalism.

\* \* \*

## POLITICAL CULTURE AND THE RHETORIC OF MOBILIZATION

A truism in sociology is that people's definition of a situation plays a large role in shaping social reality. A definition may begin as a subjective perception, but if it is acted upon, or is picked up and shared by others and regarded as an accurate understanding of the world, the consequences are decidedly

---

*References and footnotes can be found in the original publication of this article in Brint and Schroedel (eds.) *Evangelicals and Democracy in America; Volume II: Religion and Politics*. [*Editor's note*]

real—the definition of the situation moves from subjective understanding to objectively understood social reality. Shared definitions can in essence create their own reality.

The sociology of social movements has gained great understanding of collective action by studying how advocacy groups collectively define their situations, their opponents, and themselves. Social movements develop and promote *frames*—bundles of rhetorical claims and symbols that together represent a movement's attempt to communicate to its members and to others. Scholars have spent considerable energy examining the social movement frames that define issues, as well as studying framing processes through which collective actors develop these definitions. Effective movement frames are definitions of social situations and social identities that accomplish two tasks: they mobilize those who agree with the frames to take action—that is, they mobilize "internally" the movement's supporters; and they become generally and publicly accepted as the proper understandings of the issue among broader publics, such as news media or neutral bystanders—that is, they have "external" resonance in public discourse. Any given movement's frames are almost always countered by opponents who sponsor alternative frames. Thus, a significant aspect of public politics is the struggle over whose definition of the situation will dominate.

Effective social movement rhetoric, and the frames that comprise it, have several key components. First, movement frames must present a persuasive diagnosis of the social conditions the movement seeks to rectify—"here is the problem and here is why it is a problem." This diagnosis must identify the problem as an injustice, adding a moral valence to the situation, and assign responsibility for it—that is, who is to blame for the problem. Thus, movement frames are inherently moral claims—there is an injustice and a villain identified.

Second, effective frames must offer a prescription for solving the diagnosed problem. The seeds of the solution are often implied in the elements that go into the definition of the problem, but the diagnosis does not always determine the prescription. For example, Joseph Gusfield noted that solving the problem of alcohol-related traffic accidents could have resulted in a push for more mass transit; however, when the diagnostic frame became "drunk drivers," with an attendant moral condemnation, the prescription more easily became a legal crackdown and moral suasion aimed at individuals.

In addition to prescribing the solution, a movement's framing must be clear that a solution is possible—that is, provide activists a sense of agency by arguing that the problem is not so big as to be inevitable. This stands in a bit of tension with the diagnostic needs for emphasizing the seriousness and urgency of a problem. If a problem becomes constructed as too big, too entrenched, or inevitable, that framing undercuts the sense of agency that empowers people to feel that collective action can make a difference.

Finally, a good framing must motivate people to take action with regard to the cause. Partly this comes from a sense of agency—the conviction that things can change. But importantly, it makes those who are listening responsible for action and solving the problem. Just as responsibility for causing the problem is assigned, so must the responsibility for participating in the solution be accepted and borne willingly. One dimension of this motivation is constructing the basis for a collective identity, a sense of we that is connected to the issue at hand, and is clearly differentiated from those responsible for the problem. A collective identity is a distinction, and for movements it separates *them* as villains of the problem from *us* as the solution. A movement's collective identity can be an existing social category, but more often emerges during mobilization and is a cornerstone for the solidarity and commitment necessary for collective action.

Such definitional work is most effective when the boundaries between us and them are drawn clearly, but neither the we nor the they is defined too clearly. Specifying too clearly who constitutes the us may discourage some sympathetic constituents from joining, thinking they are not welcome, or else preclude forming alliances with other groups in the future. For example, one-time Christian Coalition director Ralph Reed consistently referred to the coalition's constituency as "people of faith." By not making explicit sectarian references, Reed implicitly expanded the forces of good to those with faith—without specifying which faith—while making those without faith the primary enemy. Similarly, one wants some flexibility in defining one's opponents in order to be able to adapt to circumstances.

Thus, social movement framings produce boundary-drawing distinctions between us and them. They are responsible for the problems identified, and those problems pose a threat and an injustice. But the problem can be solved and we are the ones with the moral responsibility for solving it. They are the problem, we are the solution, and there is a moral boundary dividing us. This distinction is seldom pregiven and unchanging; rather the differences emerge as a collective product of attempts at defining the situation.

One way of accomplishing this identity distinction is to create *demons*—identify another social group as the moral other against which one's own group stands as a bulwark. Thus political demonizing is a common outcome of the symbolic discourse of politics.

## CREATING THE MORAL OTHER

The dynamic of creating an other is a broader phenomenon, however, and need not be confined to explicit attempts at a movement mobilization. One way to understand the discourse that shapes, and is shaped by, the evangelical worldview, as with any worldview, is to view it as a collection of symbolic boundaries that serve to distinguish those within the group or subculture from those outside it. Social groups create and maintain their collective identity at least in part by comparing and contrasting themselves to other groups. In that sense, collective identity is largely relational—its particular content may be centered in specific ideas, rituals, or ascribed characteristics, but those features are socially meaningful only because they serve comparatively to make one group distinct from others. As social creatures, we know who we are—in particular, who fits within the category of we—because we can determine who we are not based on certain socially significant features. Making these distinctions through comparison and contrast are key features of any group's ability to define itself. Thus it is not surprising that in political and social conflict, competing groups often mobilize themselves around a definition of their enemy—and rivals demonize each other with remarkably similar terms. Collective identity, particularly among people who do not share obvious social background characteristics, emerges and is defined in relation to others.

There is an important corollary to this relational logic when it concerns the world of politics. As Pierre Bourdieu persuasively argued, distinctions do not just order the social world horizontally—that is, by helping group members distinguish one group (us) from others (them), in the social landscape. Distinctions also have a vertical dimension in that this sorting has clear implications for social and institutional hierarchies. Bourdieu understood the cultural realm, the definition and enforcement of distinctions, as a key way in which inequalities are reinforced. Those with the ability to define standards apply them to others, leaving the others wanting, and in turn, reaffirming the worthiness of those in control. They create the "normal." Social movement culture similarly creates moral metrics that allocate worthiness and condemnation, and movements use these in the quest for change.

It seems as though it should be possible to make identity distinctions without implying normative differences between better and worse, privileged and despised. With some distinctions, that may be the case. However, when the markers of distinction—the things about which groups are judged differently—are loaded with normative meaning (such as who is moral, or who represents the one true religion, or who is responsible for a social threat), identity distinctions help create, reinforce, and challenge hierarchy and inequality. In the case I examine here, for reasons that I argue are integral to the American evangelical worldview, the distinctions being created—implicitly or explicitly—are marked as religious differences. These differences are theologized, and divide the social world not just into separate groups, but as well into the religious and the secular, the moral and the immoral—or in stark terms, good and evil. A binary classification scheme, which is commonly found in fundamentalist religious thought, though not only there, totalizes the world and infuses it with religious significance. The boundaries creating these distinctions pull together in powerful and easily comprehended terms the injustice frames needed for movement rhetoric, assign moral responsibility for public politics and social problems, and align moral identity with hierarchy and legitimacy

If boundaries become identified as sacred, their importance and need for protection is that much greater. Impermissible boundary crossing becomes a violation, and can be seen as pollution. For exclusivist religions—those that claim all divine truth for themselves—rival faiths can form just that sort of polluting menace. If one has the whole truth, other systems of belief can only be unwelcome and threatening. This often translates into a suspicion of religious pluralism in society, because most religious faiths have clear ideas about organizing human relationships and social institutions. Similarly, the secular world and its pleasures can also hold a polluting danger. And yet, in contemporary societies, religious people must live in that world and are often surrounded by other faiths, as well as those who are not religious. This condition helps explain the proliferation of what might be called "defensive fundamentalisms"—groups that are primarily interested in keeping the secular world out. For these groups, there is an easily identified and comprehended threat because secular modernity seems so ubiquitous. But whether the threats are rival religions or the secular world, totalizing groups must constantly be guarding their social boundaries and their worldviews.

However, many religions have as one of their missions changing this world to be in more accord with Divine Will, and they may have to interact with religious others or the secular to achieve that. This presents a paradox—the threat of pollution means that boundaries must be sharp and distinct, but many boundaries need to be potentially permeable to allow the faithful to reach out, organize, and convert the world. In practice, this dilemma can heighten, rather than lower, the need for clear marks of distinction.

This makes it clear why, for evangelical Protestants, the boundaries separating themselves from others are both important and potentially problematic. If one pursues an evangelical and universalistic faith, one is committed to the idea that others can be, potentially, converts. Christianity has an inherent universalism in its message, with the idea that the non-Christian can and should be brought into the fold. The conversion event is a key part of the evangelical identity. Further, there is a deep religious duty to help create a godly society, even if that goal is ultimately not achievable through human striving. But the risk of pollution is always present. Thus the boundaries between the godly and the secular are always tenuous and often fluid. The godly have certain responsibilities for reaching across boundaries to the other, but must be careful not to fall themselves. Given this ambiguity and the accompanying need for clear boundaries to mark the path of righteousness, it is small wonder that issues of subversion or infiltration are seen as such a threat. Those who might be a threat, but are disguised or hidden, make boundary issues all the more of a concern.

In sum, who gets constructed as other, especially religiously other in a deeply religious country whose moral tradition is constructed around differences between them and us, has implications for national identity, claims to public legitimacy, and political authority.

\* \* \*

## THE EMERGENCE OF A NEW OTHER: THE SECULAR ELITE

Anyone reading the books, advocacy literature, activist interviews, letters to the editor, or weblogs from contemporary evangelicals in the last decade or so cannot help but notice how seldom the descriptions of their current opponents, or the descriptions of those who threaten America's moral health, are named as Catholics, Jews, or communists. Certainly suspicion of religious others has not disappeared, but it is not difficult to claim that the demonizing of other religions within the Judeo-Christian tradition has diminished, particularly as a dimension of public political culture. Justin Watson summarized this transition in the primary other:

> [The Christian Coalition wants] a return to the de facto or quasi-establishment of evangelical Protestantism of the nineteenth century. The anti-Catholic nativism and anti-Semitism of that era would be dismissed by [Pat] Robertson and [Ralph] Reed because they define their enemies in terms of *hostility to religion* rather than by different religious beliefs. Catholics and Jews with a conservative or traditionalist orientation are seen as cobelligerents against secularism.

Rather than demonize rival faiths, much of the current rhetoric of outrage generated by politicized evangelicalism, the mobilizing frames calling American Christians to active political engagement, is directed at liberals, Hollywood, the media, the American Civil Liberties Union, and often, academics. These enemies are not associated with a competing religious faith or its people; instead, they are identified with secular professions or political ideologies that advocate secularizing public and political life. The opponents are said to be elites, and are regularly accused of being antireligious; sometimes they are called secularists. Thus, even though the term "secular elites" is only occasionally used as invective, I use it here because it encapsulates the fears of evangelical activists, and pulls together the two basic critiques of their opponents—that they are hostile to religion and they are antipopulist. Both qualities show them to be fundamentally un-American.

* * *

Tim LaHaye, whose 1980 book *The Battle for the Mind* is often credited with bringing the term *secular humanism* into the discourse of conservative Protestantism, is equally expansive. At some point in the book, humanism entails atheism, communism, liberalism, socialism, Freudianism, higher criticism, feminism, sexual liberation, art, self-determination, rock music, tolerance, evolution, rationalism, empiricism, situational ethics, and Unitarianism.

It is tempting to dismiss these loose and shotgun definitions, except that such ambiguity is neither trivial nor inconsequential. To the contrary, lack of precision is a strength of social movement rhetoric. There is an "artful ambiguity" that must be maintained for a mobilizing discourse to make the most of its potential audience. Too much specificity can open rhetorical claims up to debunking or ridicule. For example, Tim LaHaye once made the claim that just 275,000 dedicated humanists hold the media, the schools, and nearly the entire country under their control—a claim that could not possibly be substantiated and even supporters found exaggerated. Too much precision and specificity thus increases the potential for disconfirmation.

Those interested in mobilizing groups tend to avoid specificity and nuance in movement claims for two other reasons. First, well-defined frames may lead some sympathizers to conclude that they do not full agree with activists' calls to action. Leaving the framing symbols open enough for some individualized interpretation maximizes the number of potential supporters. Second, one power of symbols is to help produce unity; a symbol's emotive power can reach across cognitive differences in meanings and blur those differences until agreement seems to exist. In that way, an effective symbol can help create its own unity as it keeps people centered in a moral and affective core, rather than focusing on the cognitive differentiation that specificity entails. It is not in these activists' interest to generate tomes on exactly who forms their elite opposition—they want to generate activism and it is enough to know that they are secular and elites and we are Christians, believers, and Americans. It provides the necessary social and religious distinctions for collective identity and effective movement frames. And academic analysts who find it maddeningly vague simply demonstrate that their elite culture is out of touch with our emotive, populist sensibilities.

\* \* \*

Academics and liberals in other culture industries have spearheaded or applauded many of the changes that de-Protestantized and secularized the public sphere. Groups such as the American Civil Liberties Union (ACLU), often representing secular plaintiffs, have challenged many dimensions of public religiosity since the 1960s. Evangelical Protestant values and attitudes have not disappeared, but there is more room for secular lifestyles and expressions in public and political culture. Further, as Robert Wuthnow and others have noted, the main political cleavages dividing American religion have shifted from denominational affiliations to ideological and cultural coalitions that cut across religious affiliation groups.

The expansion of higher education and the cultural conflicts of the 1960s divided liberal and conservatives within many religious groups.

Thus, politicized evangelicalism is not wholly inaccurate in identifying secular elites as their political rivals. Highly educated, upper-middle-class people with looser ties to religious communities, and with deep suspicions of conservative Protestantism, have worked to make the American public square more secular and more diverse. Whereas those who value public religious expressions now see the public square as "naked," more secular people find it more diverse, more accommodating, and less oppressive. There are different visions of the proper role of religion in American public life, and the visions of politicized evangelicals and politically progressive secular people conflict. The opponents are real, even if the rhetorical constructions of them as all-powerful and ubiquitous are exaggerated and fuzzily defined.

\* \* \*

## WHY OTHERING SECULAR ELITES WORKS

Constructing a secular elite as their primary political and cultural opponent has a number of advantages for politicized evangelicalism. As part of a social movement mobilizing frame, secular elites as other works just as sociologists argue such frames should. Christian Right advocacy groups find the nation beset by a number of social problems, many of them connected to changes in sex, gender, family relations, and raising children. They identify the retreat of evangelical Protestantism from the public square and a general secularization of society (in that major institutions such as schools do not reinforce what they consider a correct moral code) as the cause. That claim aligns convincingly with elements of evangelical culture, particularly the notion of a covenanted relationship between God and nation—if the nation neglects God's will, the Almighty removes his protection and the nation's favored status.

These diagnostic frames identify the social problems as well as those responsible for the situation. Demonizing secular elites—and naming the secular dimension as the salient qualifying adjective—clearly identifies that group, however vaguely defined, as responsible for these significant changes in American society, and thus the creators of the social problems that evangelical advocacy groups care about. Along with positing an identifiable agent responsible for causing the problem, the causal story about the secular elite establishes, through oppositional relation, evangelical Christians as responsible for the solution. Evangelicals become the hero of the frame in two ways—both as solving critical social problems caused by others, and, with their religious identity reaffirmed, proving their status as the quintessential American Christians.

\* \* \*

Thus, the elitism charge, and the idea that the elites are conspiring against us in the hidden recesses of institutional power, resonates. Elite and conspiracy theories appeal because they assign blame to a definable group, cannot be falsified, and are parsimonious in that they explain many things with very few causal factors. But for evangelical Protestants, tales of conspiracies by elites align with many millennial religious accounts of evil being directed by a hidden, shadowy force, and the belief in an active evil in the world—as Satan disguises himself, often using ordinary people to infiltrate society and undermine God's kingdom.

Important to the resonance is the areas in which these elites are thought to operate. Three institutions in particular—Hollywood, the media, and higher educations—are major sites of knowledge and symbol production in our society. These institutions value education, cosmopolitan attitudes, and international perspectives, and the people in them are part of a new class that seems less connected to traditional communities. Further, they seem, to many evangelicals, to exude arrogance combined with a hedonistic disregard for the cultural proscriptions of Victorian bourgeois culture. This helps explain why the 1960s and their excesses remain so vivid to many on the Christian Right.

Moreover, Hollywood, the mainstream news media, and elite higher education are located on the coasts, the sources of liberalism and home to urbanism and immigrants, and are often portrayed as antithetical to the "real America" that exists in the Heartland (the historically Protestant-heavy Midwest and South).

\* \* \*

## CONCLUSION: EVANGELICAL PROTESTANTS AND SECULAR CULTURE

\* \* \*

A number of indicators suggest that many evangelical Protestants find those with no religion particularly threatening. Secularism or secular humanism is often portrayed as a specific ideological threat that is oppressive to evangelicals and a threat to their children. Secular media and those that control cultural industries are often portrayed as enemies of American culture and a nefarious force in the nation's politics. It may be that evangelicals feel constrained to not level public attacks against members of rival religious groups: anti-Catholic and anti-Jewish prejudice is not as acceptable or normative in public discourse as it once was, and most evangelical political leaders avoid it. But such a taboo does not seem to apply to seculars, and for at least some sector of the evangelical population the appetite for books that criticize secularists as America's most dangerous enemy is seemingly insatiable. This suggests that evangelical culture finds its particular *bête noir* in the ranks of seculars, agnostics, and atheists. They have been constructed as political demons in ways that make that imagery a powerful mobilizing rhetoric and an idea that aligns closely with some long-standing elements of evangelical religious culture.

This rhetoric has potentially deleterious consequences for political life in a religiously pluralistic society, but the dynamics of the construction of this moral other has been a significant political resource for political mobilization, capturing attention in the public sphere and reaffirming evangelical identity.

# PART EIGHT

# SOCIAL CHANGE

# 46

## Job on the Line

### WILLIAM M. ADLER

*Two women share the same job. For decades Molly James performs the work in Paterson, New Jersey; then Balbina Duque Granados does it in Matamoros, Mexico. Molly James is laid off; Balbina Duque Granados struggles to make ends meet. The global transformation of work benefits consumers with lower prices and a wider range of products. It brings industry to formerly agrarian countries and changes them forever. But the unrecorded costs are considerable. In this highly personal account we are able to see many of the negative features of globalization. The challenge of globalization in the years ahead will be to address these often-hidden costs.*

At 3 o'clock on a warm June afternoon, the second of two wash-up bells rings for the final time. Mollie James stands hunched over the sink as she rinses her hands with industrial soap alongside her co-workers. She first came to work here, on the assembly line at Universal Manufacturing Company in Paterson, New Jersey, a few years after the factory opened in 1951. She was the first woman at the factory to run a stamping machine, the first to laminate steel. She was among the first female union stewards and among the first African American stewards; hers was a self-assured presence any grievant would want on their side. And now, after 34 years on the line—nearly two-thirds of her life—she is the last to go.

At the end of every other shift for more than three decades, Mollie and her fellow employees beat a quick path to the plant parking lot. On this day there is less sense of hurry. There are still children to feed, clothes to wash, bills to pay, errands to run, other jobs to race to. But as she and the others leave the washroom, no one seems pressed to leave. All about the plant entrance, and out in the lot, people stand in small clusters, like mourners at their own wake, talking, laughing, hugging, crying. Almost always Mollie James is outgoing and outspoken, her voice loud and assertive, her smile nicely lighted. At 59 she is a strong woman, her strength forged from a life of hard work and sacrifice, and faith in God. She is not one to betray her emotions, but this day is different. Her bearing has turned to reserve, her normally quick eyes dull and watery. Her working life is over, and that is the only life she has ever known.

Universal had always turned a tidy profit. Its signature product, ballasts that regulate the current in fluorescent lights, attracted attention only when the ballast failed—causing the light fixture to hum or flicker. In the mid-1980s, however, the locally owned company was twice swept up in the gale winds of Wall Streets merger mania. Twice within eight months Universal was sold, both times to firms headed by disciples of Michael Milken, the Street's reigning evil genius. Not long after the second sale, to a Los Angeles-based electrical components conglomerate called MagneTek, Inc., movers began pulling up the plant's massive machinery, much of which had been bolted to the floor when the factory opened.

Mollie had sensed what was happening in January 1989, the morning she came to work and noticed the hole in the floor. It wasn't a hole, really, in the sense of an opening; it was more of a void: a great yawning space of discolored concrete where just the afternoon before had sat a steel-stamping machine, a hulking piece of American industrial might. Before long, more holes appeared, each tracing the outline of the base of another machine, like chalk around a sidewalk corpse.

Now, on the last day, when there is no one left to say goodbye to, Mollie slumps behind the wheel of her rusting 1977 Dodge Charger and follows the procession out of the lot. It is not far, three miles or so, from the plant in Paterson's industrial Bunker Hill neighborhood to the three-story, three-family house she owns on the near East Side. Upon pulling into her customary space in the driveway, Mollie sits in the car a good long while, letting the heat of the summer afternoon settle her. By the time she fits the key into the back-door lock and begins climbing the three flights of stairs to her bedroom, she has stopped crying.

The machine that Mollie used to stamp steel for three decades makes its way south, past factories that Universal opened in Mississippi and Arkansas during the 1960s and 1970s to take advantage of cheaper labor and taxes, before arriving in Matamoros, Mexico, a booming border city just across the Rio Grande from Brownsville, Texas. On a blindingly blue morning, MagneTek executives from "corporate" in L.A. arrive for the gala ribbon cutting of the first MagneTek plant here. Plant manager Chuck Peeples, an affable Arkansas expatriate, leads the officials on a tour of the gleaming factory. Outfitted in natty going-native panama hats emblazoned with the company's royal-blue capital-M "power" logo, the MagneTek honchos parade past equipment ripped from the shopworn floor in Paterson, machinery now operated by a young, almost entirely female workforce. These women, primarily in their teens and 20s, have come north to Matamoros in search of work and a better future than the bleakness promised in the jobless farming towns of the interior.

Balbina Duque Granados found a job at MagneTek in 1993, after leaving her family's home in a picturesque but poor mountain village of central Mexico. Just out of her teens, she has an easy, dimpled smile and long black hair worn in a ponytail. With its comparatively low wages, endless supply of labor, lack of regulation, and proximity to the United States, Matamoros is a magnet for *maquiladoras*, the foreign-owned assembly plants that wed First World engineering with Third World working conditions. Balbina's probationary pay is slightly less than $26 a week, or about 65 cents an hour. It is difficult work, winding coils, repetitive and tiring and mind numbing, but it is a job she is thrilled to have—her "answered prayer." And although Balbina doesn't know it, it is not just any job. It is Mollie's job.

The job in which Mollie James once took great pride, the job that both fostered and repaid her loyalty by enabling her to rise above humble beginnings and provide for her family—that job does not now pay Balbina Duque a wage sufficient to live on. Embedded in that central fact, and in the intersecting lives and fates of the two women who held that single job, is a broader story about the fundamental changes currently remaking the economy—the ways in which "free trade" harms democracy, undermines stable businesses and communities, and exploits workers on both sides of the border, both ends of the global assembly line.

At a few minutes before 2 o'clock on a cold, pitch-black morning in November 1950, Mollie and her father, Lorenzo Brown, waited anxiously on the platform of the ornate World War I-era train station in Richmond, Virginia. The Browns were from Cartersville, 45 miles west, in the rolling farmland of central Virginia. Mollie was headed to Penn Station in Newark, New Jersey, to meet her fiancé, Sam James, who would take her home, to Paterson, to her new life. She was dressed in her finest: a new navy-blue suit, new shoes, new hairdo. She carried nearly everything she owned in a half-dozen sky-blue suitcases her father had given her for the trip.

Mollie was traveling alone, but the "colored" train cars of the Silver Meteor, and indeed those of the other great northbound coaches—the Champion, the Florida Sunbeam, the Silver Comet—were full of Mollie Browns: black southerners crossing the Mason-Dixon Line, heading for the promised land. Mollie's intended was waiting at the station in his new, yellow, two-door Ford to take her to Paterson, a city of 140,000 residents some 15 miles west of New York City. Sam drove her home to the one-room apartment he rented for $20 a week above the flat where his sister and brother-in-law lived. Although the accommodations were far from luxurious—Mollie and Sam shared a kitchen and bath with other upstairs tenants—her new life seemed as bright as Sam's shiny car.

Paterson at precisely the middle of the 20th century was absolutely humming, filled with vibrant neighborhoods, a bustling downtown retail and cultural district, and above all, factories small and large, producing everything from textiles to machine tools to electrical components. "There were so many places to work, I could have five jobs in the same day," Mollie recalled years later. "And if I didn't like one, I could leave and get another, sure."

Mollie's new hometown was born of entrepreneurial dreamers and schemers. The city had been founded on the 16th anniversary of the Declaration of Independence, July 4, 1792, not as a municipality but as a business: the home of the country's first industrial corporation, the Society for Useful Manufactures. The grand plans of the society and its guiding light, Alexander Hamilton, ultimately failed, but Paterson established itself as a cradle of American industry. The city became renowned for its textile mills—silk, especially—and later for the union-busting tactics of its mill owners. During the 19th century, textile manufacturers in Paterson were responsible for what were probably the nation's first runaway shops, opening "annexes" in rural Pennsylvania to take advantage of workers who could be subjected to longer hours for half the wages paid in New Jersey. In 1913, the Industrial Workers of the World mobilized Paterson's 25,000 employees to walk away from their looms, effectively nailing shut the nation's silk-manufacturing center. Able to rely on their nonunion factories, mill owners refused to negotiate; starved into submission, the strikers were forced to return to work with neither gains in wages nor improved working conditions.

By the time the 19-year-old Mollie Brown arrived in Paterson, the economy was booming. Unemployment was low, wages high. In her first few years in town, Mollie ran through several jobs. "You'd just catch the bus and go from factory to factory and see who was hiring." Among her stops was a low-slung cement building in northeast Paterson. The sign out front said Universal Manufacturing Co. The owner himself, a gregarious man named Archie Sergy, showed her through the plant, explaining that the company made a part for fluorescent lights called a ballast. "They showed me how it was made, the whole assembly line. I learned there's a lot to it, a *very* lot." The starting salary was 90 cents an hour, but the company was about to implement a second shift, from 3 p.m. to midnight, that would pay an extra dime an hour. Those hours were ideal for Mollie. She and Sam had three children under the age of five and another on the way, and if she were to work nights and he days, the couple could care for the children without hiring a sitter. She accepted the job. "I hope you'll be here a long time," Sergy told her. "I hope we'll all be here a long time!"

By the early 1960s, Universal employed a workforce of some 1,200. Archie Sergy and his top managers continued to demonstrate a sincere interest in the welfare of their employees. "They never treated you as inferior, regardless of whether you cleaned the toilets or whatever your job was," Mollie says. "They'd walk up and down the line and talk to us, joke with us, sometimes have their sandwiches with us right there on the line. * * * If you needed a home loan, they'd give it to you, and you could make arrangements to pay it back."

Sergy saw the world as an industrialist, not a financier, and he maintained a steely-eyed focus on quality and customer service to the degree that it probably hurt profit margins. But his company was no social service agency; it venerated the bottom line as much as any self-respecting capitalist enterprise. Mollie and her co-workers enjoyed good wages and job security in large part because they belonged to Teamsters Local 945, which bargained for higher pay and better benefits. In 1963, determined to insulate Universal from threats of work stoppage, Sergy followed the tradition established by the early Paterson silk makers: He opened an annex, a Universal factory in the Deep South. The new plant was located in rural Mississippi, providing Sergy with a low-wage workforce as well as an ever-present threat of plant closing to quiet employees in Paterson.

That same year, strapped for operating capital and lacking a successor, Sergy also succumbed to the lure of Wall Street: He sold Universal to a New York–based conglomerate. Sergy remained as titular head of Universal, but outsiders controlled the economic destiny of the women and men who toiled there. This was most evidently revealed when Sergy announced to the employees in April 1968, seven months before his death, that the parent company itself had been swallowed whole by *another* conglomerate. "We're all working for a company out of Chicago," he said. "Who they are I have no idea."

Whether those who held the purse strings were faceless financiers from New York or Chicago or Los Angeles didn't matter much to Mollie James. Owners came and went, and the principal visible sign of each transition was a new company name on the payroll checks. So when word spread in early 1986 that an outfit called MagneTek was the new owner, Mollie took the news calmly. Surely some things would change—managers in, managers out, maybe—but she had no reason to question her job security. Although the company had added a second Southern plant, in Arkansas, Paterson was still the flagship. Mollie came to work for Universal—and stayed—because of the peace of mind that came from a secure job: a job she could raise a family on, buy a house, a car, borrow money against, count on for the future.

But right away Mollie could tell the future was darkening. Like the earlier owners, MagneTek was a faraway, far-flung holding company, but the previous management's hands-off, don't fix-it-if-it-ain't-broke page was missing from its corporate manual. "It started the day our name disappeared from the building," she says. "Poof, no more Universal."

By the end of 1988, not only had Universal's name vanished from the plant; its machines, too, were disappearing, torn from the floor like trees from their roots. "The movers came at night, like thieves, sometimes just taking one piece at a time," Mollie recalls. "We'd come in in the mornings and there'd be another hole in the floor."

The machinery had been used to make a large specialty ballast known as the HID, or High Intensity Discharge, the kind used in thousand-watt fixtures installed in outdoor stadiums. Paterson was the lone Universal plant manufacturing the HID; making its precision-wound coils required different training and equipment than the garden-variety 40-watt fluorescent ballast the two Southern plants pumped out by the tens of thousands daily.

If Paterson's workers were more sophisticated, they were also more costly. Mollie earned $7.91 an hour, 75 cents more than she would have earned in Mississippi and almost a dollar more than in Arkansas. But if the wages down South were low, they were not low enough. They were not the cheapest possible wages. They weren't as low as workers earned in Mexico, where the prevailing pay at the maquiladoras was less than $8 a day. And so, in the early months of 1988, the machines began disappearing, bound ultimately for Matamoros. "All we kept hearing was how good a job we were doing," Mollie says, "that we had nothing to worry about, that we'd always have work in Paterson."

The nightly bus to Matamoros would not roll through the depot nearest Balbina Duque's village until 9:15. It was only mid-morning, just a couple of hours since she'd said her goodbyes to the family, since she'd pressed her lips for the last time to her baby son's cheek and handed him to her mother. It was only mid-morning, and already Balbina could feel the tropical sun on her face, could feel her funds dwindling fast. She had started with 200 pesos, the equivalent of about $65, and now that she'd paid a man nearly $20 to taxi her the hour from Monte Bello, her mountain village—a place of clean and clear air, brilliant high-desert flowers, and almost surrealistically bright light—to the bus station in town, and now that she'd bought a couple of tamales from a sidewalk vendor and a one-way ticket to the border for $30, Balbina was down to less than $15.

Balbina had turned 20 only weeks earlier. She was leaving for Matamoros, 400 miles north, to look for work in the maquiladoras. She was torn about going, especially about having to leave behind her 18-month-old son, Iban. "If there were work here," Balbina said in Spanish during a visit home some years later, "everyone would stay."

There was nothing to keep them at home. Balbina's village comprised maybe 1,000 people living in a couple of hundred pastel-colored homes with thatched roofs. There was neither running water nor electricity. Much of Balbina's day was spent filling and refilling a water bucket from a central well down a hill and carrying it back on her head to use for bathing, laundry, washing dishes, cooking, and drinking. A typical day might require 24 trips to the well, a chore that claimed three to four hours beginning at first light.

The interminable, grueling days were not for Balbina. Monte Bello felt like a sentence from which she needed to escape. It was a place for "people too old to work or too young to work," she said. "For me there was nothing. If you do not work in the fields there is nothing else to do." She decided she would celebrate her 20th birthday with her family, and then, as soon as she had saved enough for the bus fare, would take off for the border, where the maquiladoras favor young women for their nimble fingers and compliant minds, and where a job in a *maquila* trumps any other employment options.

It was dark when Balbina finally boarded the bus. Heading north, through a vast valley of corn, Highway 85 was flat as a tortilla. With two seats to herself, Balbina was able to curl into a comfortable enough position, and sleep came at once. When the bus pulled into Matamoros at dawn, she had to rouse herself from a dream about her son. Meeting her at the central station on Canales Avenue was a distant aunt, who escorted her to a small dwelling in the liltingly named *Colonia Vista Hermosa*—Beautiful View. But there was little beauty in the *colonia*; it was wedged between a pungent, milky-white irrigation canal and the Finsa park, the massive industrial park where MagneTek and other foreign-owned maquiladoras employed most of the working-age residents of Vista Hermosa.

One morning, the second Friday of 1993, Balbina and her younger sister, Elsa, caught a ride downtown to the headquarters of the big maquiladora workers' union, the SJOI—the Spanish acronym for the Union of Industrial Workers and Day Laborers. Four times weekly, waves of several thousand applicants washed up at dawn at the SJOI offices, the de facto employment agency for the maquilas. All nonsalaried workers applied through its central hiring hall, women on Mondays and Fridays, men on Tuesdays and Thursdays.

It was not yet 7 o'clock, and Balbina and Elsa had already been in line for an hour, a line that snaked through the three-story building, past the armed guard at the door, and stretched outside for more than a block. By eight, they had squeezed and elbowed and prodded their way inside the assembly hall, a room roughly the size and ambience of a drafty old high-school gymnasium. Mounted fans whirred overhead, efficiently distributing the rank air and grime into all corners.

At 8:30, with no conspicuous signal that the cattle call was on the verge of starting, there was a near stampede toward the makeshift elevated stage at the front quadrant of the room. The entire room seemed like an aquarium, one rear corner of which had suddenly been tipped, causing its entire contents to flow into its diagonal. For the next few hours, Balbina, Elsa, and 1,600 other hopefuls would be crammed nose to shoulder, as close to the stage as possible, like groupies at a rock concert.

At 8:40, three union officials emerged from the anteroom beside the stage. Through a two-way mirror, they had been keeping an eye on the surging crowd while their clerks matched the day's maquila employment needs with the application forms on file. All morning long, the fax machines and phones in the union headquarters had been ringing with the day's specifications from the companies. One maquila, for instance, asked for 91 applicants, all of whom should be 16 (the legal minimum age) or older, with a secondary-school education and without "scheduling problems"—code for childless. All the maquilas favor youth, and some, MagneTek for one, insist on it. *"No mayores de 27 años"*—None older than 27—the company's director of industrial relations instructed in a faxed letter to the union. Women in their late teens and early 20s are considered in the prime of their working lives; a 31-year-old is unlikely to be hired, and a 35-year-old is considered a relic.

When the tally of the day's employment needs was deemed complete, the officials stepped onto the stage, and into the bedlam. Between them and the spirited throng were three steps cordoned by a thin chain, a flimsy plywood railing, and a bouncer the size of an offensive lineman, whose sartorial taste ran to late Elvis: a white shirt unbuttoned nearly the length of his heroic torso, a gold medallion dangling to his midsection, and a formidable, gleaming pompadour crowning a Frigidaire face and muttonchop sideburns.

Following a call to order on a tinny public-address system, a woman unceremoniously announced the day's available jobs. "We're calling workers for Deltronicos," she said, referring to the GM car-radio subsidiary, and then read a list of 50 names. The "lucky ones," as one disappointed applicant called them, made their way through a pair of swinging doors, where a fleet of old Loadstar school buses waited to transport them to the Finsa park for a job interview and medical screening with their prospective employer. If their luck held, they would then be hired for a 30-day probationary period at lower, "training" wages before attaining full-employee status.

The drill was repeated for each maquila until the day's hiring needs were met. Neither Balbina nor Elsa were among the lucky ones, but they knew that few are chosen on the first go-round; some they met had endured several months of twice-weekly trips to the hall. Each Monday and Friday over the next few weeks the Duques returned faithfully. In March, Balbina's prayers were finally answered. She was assigned to a third-shift coil-winding job at MagneTek. All she knew about the job was that her sister-in-law once worked in the same plant, a low-lying white building no more than 75 yards from her tiny house. What she did not know was that Mollie James once held that very job.

Balbina started work at MagneTek the same year President Clinton signed the North American Free Trade Agreement, designed in large part to hasten the spread of maquiladoras. The trade deal enables companies to take advantage of 700,000 workers at 1,800 plants all along the border in ways that would not be tolerated in the United States. When MagneTek first set up shop in Matamoros, employees worked six-day weeks in a stifling, poorly ventilated plant; speaking on the line or going to the bathroom was grounds for suspension.

Although the company has improved working conditions in the last few years, sexual harassment and discrimination remain a constant of factory life. Many female employees at MagneTek have firsthand stories to tell about sexism on the job. "When new girls come in," says a 31-year-old MagneTek retiree who asked not to be identified, "a supervisor gives them the eye and asks them to go for a walk." Balbina says she received similar propositions when she started work at Plant 1. "My supervisor asked if I wanted to work more overtime. I told him I did, but that I wouldn't go to a hotel with him to get it."

The other constant of factory life is low wages. Even when she works an eight-hour overtime shift, as she usually does two or three times a week, Balbina finds it impossible to make ends meet on a MagneTek salary. "*No alcance*," she says. It doesn't reach. For years she surmounted her weekly shortfall by pooling her income and expenses with Elsa. The sisters lived, like nearly all of their co-workers, "*en montón*"—in a heap: two adults and five children in two small rooms, the kitchen in front, the bedroom in the rear. Their shared three-family flat was a cement structure 45 feet by 15 feet by 10 feet high. Its corrugated metal roof doubled as the ceiling. Their were cinder-block walls between the three units that stopped about a foot short of the ceiling, making for a pungent stew of sound and aroma when all three families were home.

The shadeless yard—of mud or dust, depending on the season—was fenced by chicken wire and a rickety gate, and served as an extension of the kitchen. The residents shared a clothesline, an outhouse, and a single spigot—the lone source of water. Balbina believes the water flowed from an open canal running near plants in the industrial park that manufacture pesticides or use toxic solvents. The water had to be boiled, of course; sometimes there was propane to do so, sometimes not.

The neighborhood, Vista Hermosa, exists in a commercial and municipal twilight zone. It sprang up to serve the maquiladoras, not the residents. There are several high-priced convenience stores in the colonia, but no full-fledged grocers, no place to buy meat. Nor is there a pharmacy or medical clinic. There is no police presence, and vandalism and petty theft are rampant. There is one school, an overcrowded kindergarten. Older students catch the same bus to school that drops off first-shift workers at the industrial park. "You have to adapt to the maquilas' routine," says a neighbor with school-age children, "because they're not going to adapt to ours."

The city mostly shuns residents because of the high cost and low return of providing them with services. "They have no money," says Andres Cuellar, the city historian of Matamoros, "so no city official accepts responsibility." But a former mayor offers a different explanation: Federal policy prevents the city from taxing the maquilas to improve the colonias. "We insisted before the federal government that we don't have the financial means to support the maquilas' growth," says Fernando Montemayor Lozano, mayor from 1987 until 1989. "Besides the salaries paid to Mexican workers, the maquiladora contribution is practically zero here." It was not until 1991 that running water was piped into the neighborhood (but not as yet into houses), and only in 1993 were the first houses wired for electricity. The roads remain unpaved and deeply rutted. Nor does the city provide trash pickup; Balbina and her neighbors burn their garbage in a nearby ditch.

Vista Hermosa breeds disease like it does mosquitoes. The lack of septic and sewage lines, potable water, and sanitation services puts the neighborhood at great risk for all manner of illnesses, from intestinal parasites to tuberculosis. But the gravest, most frightening threat comes not from the neighborhood, but from beyond the chain-link fence around the Finsa park. The fence, less than a football field away from Balbina's house, may divide the First and Third worlds, but it also unites them under a single toxic cloud. When the maquilas illegally dump toxic waste into irrigation canals, when a hot north wind blows the acrid smell of *chapapote*—pitch—from the Magne-Tek plant over its workers' homes, when runoff from a pesticide plant spills into a ditch, when chemical spills or leaks or explosions or fires erupt in the air, it doesn't take a Sierra Club member to understand the environmental wasteland the maquilas have created.

Nor does it take an epidemiologist to question the cause of an outbreak of anencephaly—babies born with either incomplete or missing brains and skulls. In one 36-hour period in the spring of 1991, three babies were born without brains at a single hospital across the river in Brownsville. Doctors soon learned of dozens of other anencephalic births in Brownsville and Matamoros. From 1989 to 1991, the rate of such defects for Brownsville was 10 times the U.S. average, or about 30 anencephalic births per 10,000 births. During the same years, there were 68 cases in Matamoros and 81 in Reynosa, a maquila site upriver.

Many who have studied the outbreak suspect it was due to industrial pollution unchecked by regulatory agencies in both countries. "These were atrocities committed by two uncaring governments," says Dr. Margaret Diaz, the occupational health specialist in Brownsville who detected the anencephaly cluster. "They are the product of years of neglect."

In a lawsuit filed in 1993, families of 28 children born with anencephaly or spina bifida—an incomplete closure of the spinal cord—blamed the outbreak on contamination from the Matamoros maquilas. The families sued 40 maquilas, including MagneTek, charging that the companies negligently handled "toxic compounds" and that the birth defects occurred after "exposure to toxins present in the local environment." The companies steadfastly denied wrongdoing, but internal memoranda documented that some plants released toxic emissions into the air in quantities impermissible in the United States. And trash sifted from the Matamoros city dump established that the maquilas were burning their industrial waste there, rather than disposing of it in the United States, as required by law. One videotape made by an investigator for the families portrays the charred but clearly visible remains of a MagneTek rapid-start ballast. The companies eventually paid a total of $17 million to the stricken families and cleaned up their worst excesses.

Although MagneTek and other companies insist they are improving conditions both inside and outside their plants, wages remain at poverty levels. Rolando Gonzalez Barron, a maquila owner and former president of the Matamoros Maquila Association, points to an advertising supplement in the *Brownsville Herald* lauding companies for their financial contributions to Matamoros schools. "Take 'Adopt-a-School,'" he says. "We put sewerage and bathrooms in schools where little girls had to do their necessities outside."

What about paying a living wage so that the parents of those little girls could afford indoor plumbing themselves? "Yes," Gonzalez replies, "housing needs to be developed, but our main goal is to create value for our customers."

What about your employees? What is your obligation to them? "If a worker is not eating," Gonzalez says, sounding every bit the farmer discussing a plow horse, "he's not going to work for you. We need to meet at least the basic needs."

But the basic needs—"eating, housing, clothing," as Gonzalez puts it—are unmet, and the evidence is as obvious and irrefutable as the colonia in MagneTek's backyard, where Balbina and her neighbors wrestle every single day with ferociously difficult decisions: Should I work overtime or huddle with my children to keep them warm? Buy meat or medicine? Pay the light bill or the gas bill? She makes those decisions based on a daily salary of 58 pesos, the equivalent of $7.43. That's an hourly wage of 92 cents—roughly the same starting wage Mollie James earned nearly half a century before. And Balbina often makes those decisions after working a grueling double shift—from 3:30 in the afternoon until six the following morning, after which she arrives home in time to fix breakfast for her children, accompany her oldest to school, and squeeze in a few hours of sleep before heading back to the plant in the afternoon.

*No alcance.* It doesn't reach. Over and over one hears this. *No alcance,* but we make it reach. They make it reach by taking odd jobs, or by scavenging for recyclables at the Matamoros city dump—an otherworldly metropolis of its own covering 50 acres—or peddling wares in the plant during breaks and shift changes. "It's prohibited," Balbina says, "but the company looks the other way and almost everybody does it." There are the ubiquitous Avon ladies, as well as sellers of homemade candy, tamales and gorditas, clothes, marijuana. And some sell their bodies, living *la doble vida*—the double life of coil-winder by day and prostitute by night.

Balbina has yet to resort to a second job. Instead, she works overtime as often as possible and recently moved into a government-subsized house; it is more comfortable than the one she shared with her sister, but it is hers only as long as she keeps her job. She is 29, an advanced age for a maquiladora worker. She lives with her boyfriend, a fellow MagneTek employee, and they stagger their shifts so that one provides child care while the other is working. Still, even the small necessities remain out of reach. "I need a lock for the door," Balbina says one afternoon. "I don't need it now, but soon I will."

Why not now?

"There is nothing worth locking now," she replies.

Mollie James never again found full-time work. She received a severance payment, after taxes, of $3,171.66—about $93 for each of the 34 years she worked. She collected unemployment benefits for six months and then enrolled in a computer-repair school, receiving a certificate of completion and numerous don't-call-us responses to job inquiries. Late last year, at the age of 68, she took a part-time job as an attendant at a nursing home. For the remainder of her income, she depends on Social Security and the rent she collects from the three-family house she owns, as well as a monthly pension of $71.23 from her Teamsters local. "That's nothing," she says. "That doesn't even pay your telephone bill. It's gone before you know it."

Although Paterson is a tenacious city, it seems defined by what is gone. Its last heyday was during and after World War II, when entrepreneurs like Archie Sergy and migrants like Mollie James helped sustain the city as a proud symbol of industrial might. But the old factory district near the Great Falls has been in ruins for decades, and although a number of the ancient brick mills have been splendidly restored—as a museum, a hospital clinic, and housing for artists—Paterson today is thought of as one of those discarded American places, a city so squalid, so defeated, that few people who do not live or work in Paterson venture there.

Mollie James has spent a half-century in Paterson. She married and divorced there, raised four children, bought a house. She sank deep roots, and would like nothing better than to see the seeds of renewal take sprout, but she is fed up with high taxes, crime, the unstable economy. Like many "up-South" blacks of retirement age, she thinks often about going home, to rural central Virginia, to the land she left as a teenager. She still owns her childhood home amid three wooded acres.

During a trip back home not long ago, Mollie visited the cemetery where her parents are buried. It is where she wishes to be buried as well. "They better not put me in no dirt up there in New Jersey," she says. "Bring me back home, brother."

Balbina, too, dreams of returning to her ancestral home, to the quiet and clear air of Monte Bello, where she could raise her children in a calm, safe place. But there is no work around Monte Bello for her, no future there for her children. She is more concerned with the immediate future of her job. In the last couple of years, MagneTek closed the two old Universal plants in Arkansas and Mississippi and transferred the bulk of those operations not to Malamoros, but 60 miles upriver to Reynosa, where the union is even weaker, the wages lower still. Now the talk in Matamoros is that the company will once again use the threat of a move, as it did first in Paterson and then in the Southern plants, as a lever for lower wages.

Balbina scoffs at the notion of transferring to Reynosa if the company relocates her job there. "What if they were to move again?" she asks. "Maybe to Juárez or Tijuana? What then? Do I chase my job all over the world?"

# 47

## Grassroots Activism: Mothers of East Los Angeles

### MARY PARDO

*This retrospective on community activism in East Los Angeles shows how places and individuals are changed when people make their voices heard. Mary Pardo's life-history approach allows us to hear the voices of the women who worked on behalf of their families and communities. Despite obstacles of gender, class, ethnicity, and personal inexperience, they organized and confronted the powerful forces of the city and state. This is democracy in action.*

## THE COMMUNITY CONTEXT: EAST LOS ANGELES RESISTING SIEGE

In 1984, the state of California commissioned a public relations firm to assess the political difficulties facing the construction of energy-producing waste incinerators. The report provided a "personality profile" of those residents most likely to organize effective opposition to projects:

> middle and upper socioeconomic strata possess better resources to effectuate their opposition. Middle and higher socioeconomic strata neighborhoods should not fall within the one-mile and five-mile radii of the proposed site. Conversely, older people, people with a high school education or less are least likely to oppose a facility.[1]

The state accordingly placed the [toxic waste incinerator] plant in Commerce, a predominantly Mexican American, low-income community. This pattern holds throughout the state and the country: three out of five Afro-Americans and Latinos live near toxic waste sites, and three of the five largest hazardous waste landfills are in communities with at least 80 percent minority populations.

Similarly, in March 1985, when the state sought a site for the first state prison in Los Angeles County, Governor Deukmejian resolved to place the 1,700-inmate institution in East Los Angeles, within a mile of the long-established Boyle

---

1. Cerrell Associates, Inc., "Political Difficulties Facing Waste-to-Energy Conversion Plant Siting," Report Prepared for California Waste Management Board, Slate of California (Los Angeles, 1984): 43.

Heights neighborhood and within two miles of thirty-four schools. Furthermore, violating convention, the state bid on the expensive parcel of industrially zoned land without compiling an environmental impact report or providing a public community hearing. * * *

In spring 1986, after much pressure from the 56th assembly district office and the community, the Department of Corrections agreed to hold a public information meeting, which was attended by over 700 Boyle Heights residents. From this moment on, Vigil observed, "the tables turned, the community mobilized, and the residents began calling the political representatives and requesting their presence at hearings and meetings."[2] By summer 1986, the community was well aware of the prison site proposal. Over two thousand people, carrying placards proclaiming "No Prison in ELA," marched from Resurrection Church in Boyle Heights to the 3rd Street bridge linking East Los Angeles with the rapidly expanding downtown Los Angeles. This march marked the beginning of one of the largest grassroots coalitions to emerge from the Latino community in the last decade.

Prominent among the coalition's groups is "Mothers of East Los Angeles," a loosely knit group of over 400 Mexican American women. MELA initially coalesced to oppose the state prison construction but has since organized opposition to several other projects detrimental to the quality of life in the central city. Its second large target is a toxic waste incinerator proposed for Vernon, a small city adjacent to East Los Angeles. This incinerator would worsen the already debilitating air quality of the entire county and set a precedent dangerous for other communities throughout California. When MELA took up the fight against the toxic waste incinerator, it became more than a single-issue group and began working with environmental groups around the state. As a result of the community struggle, AB58 (Roybal-Allard), which provides all Californians with the minimum protection of an environmental impact report before the construction of hazardous waste incinerators, was signed into law. But the law's effectiveness relies on a watchful community network. Since its emergence, "Mothers of East Los Angeles" has become centrally important to just such a network of grassroots activists including a select number of Catholic priests and two Mexican American political representatives. Furthermore, the group's very formation, and its continued spirit and activism, fly in the face of the conventional political science beliefs regarding political participation.

Predictions by the "experts" attribute the low formal political participation (i.e., voting) of Mexican American people in the U.S. to a set of cultural "retardants" including primary kinship systems, fatalism, religious traditionalism traditional cultural values, and mother country attachment. The core activ-

---

2. James Vigil, Jr., field representative for Assemblywoman Gloria Molina, 1984–1986, Personal Interview, Whittier, Calif., 27 September 1989.

ists in MELA may appear to fit this description, as well as the state-commissioned profile of residents least likely to oppose toxic waste incinerator projects. All the women live in a low-income community. Furthermore, they identify themselves as active and committed participants in the Catholic Church; they claim an ethnic identity—Mexican American; their ages range from forty to sixty; and they have attained at most high school educations. However, these women fail to conform to the predicted political apathy. Instead, they have transformed social identity—ethnic identity, class identity, and gender identity—into an impetus as well [as] a basis for activism. And, in transforming their existing social networks into grassroots political networks, they have also transformed themselves.

## TRANSFORMATION AS A DOMINANT THEME

From the life histories of the group's core activists and from my own field notes, I have selected excerpts that tell two representative stories. One is a narrative of the events that led to community mobilization in East Los Angeles. The other is a story of transformation, the process of creating new and better relationships that empower people to unite and achieve common goals.

First, women have transformed organizing experiences and social networks arising from gender-related responsibilities into political resources. When I asked the women about the first community, not necessarily "political," involvement they could recall, they discussed experiences that predated the formation of MELA. Juana Gutiérrez explained:

> Well, it didn't start with the prison, you know. It started when my kids went to school. I started by joining the Parents Club and we worked on different problems here in the area. Like the people who come to the parks to sell drugs to the kids. I got the neighbors to have meetings. I would go knock at the doors, house to house. And I told them that we should stick together with the Neighborhood Watch for the community and for the kids.

Erlinda Robles similarly recalled:

> I wanted my kids to go to Catholic school and from the time my oldest one went there, I was there every day. I used to take my two little ones with me and I helped one way or another. I used to question things they did. And the other mothers would just watch me. Later, they would ask me, "Why do you do that? They are going to take it out on your kids." I'd say, "They better not." And before you knew it, we had a big group of mothers that were very involved.

Part of a mother's "traditional" responsibility includes overseeing her child's progress in school, interacting with school staff, and supporting school activities. In these processes, women meet other mothers and begin developing a network of acquaintanceships and friendships based on mutual concern for the welfare of their children.

Although the women in MELA carried the greatest burden of participating in school activities, Erlinda Robles also spoke of strategies they used to draw men into the enterprise and into the networks:

> At the beginning, the priests used to say who the president of the mothers guild would be; they used to pick 'em. But, we wanted elections, so we got elections. Then we wanted the fathers to be involved, and the nuns suggested that a father should be president and a mother would be secretary or be involved there [at the school site].

Of course, this comment piqued my curiosity, so I asked how the mothers agreed on the nuns' suggestion. The answer was simple and instructive:

> At the time we thought it was a "natural" way to get the fathers involved because they weren't involved; it was just the mothers. Everybody [the women] agreed on them [the fathers] being president because they worked all day and they couldn't be involved in a lot of daily activities like food sales and whatever. During the week, a steering committee of mothers planned the group's activities. But now that I think about it, a woman could have done the job just as well!

So women got men into the group by giving them a position they could manage. The men may have held the title of "president," but they were not making day-to-day decisions about work, nor were they dictating the direction of the group. Erlinda Robles laughed as she recalled an occasion when the president insisted, against the wishes of the women, on scheduling a parents' group fundraiser—a breakfast—on Mother's Day. On that morning, only the president and his wife were present to prepare breakfast. This should alert researchers against measuring power and influence by looking solely at who holds titles.

Each of the cofounders had a history of working with groups arising out of the responsibilities usually assumed by "mothers"—the education of children and the safety of the surrounding community. From these groups, they gained valuable experiences and networks that facilitated the formation of "Mothers of East Los Angeles." Juana Gutiérrez explained how preexisting networks progressively expanded community support:

> You know nobody knew about the plan to build a prison in this community until Assemblywoman Gloria Molina told me. Martha Molina called me and said, "You know what is happening in your area? The governor wants to put a prison in Boyle Heights!" So, I called a Neighborhood Watch meeting at my house and we got fifteen people together. Then, Father John started informing his people at

the Church and that is when the group of two to three hundred started showing up for every march on the bridge.

MELA effectively linked up preexisting networks into a viable grassroots coalition.

Second, the process of activism also transformed previously "invisible" women, making them not only visible but the center of public attention. From a conventional perspective, political activism assumes a kind of gender neutrality. This means that anyone can participate, but men are the expected key actors. In accordance with this pattern, in winter 1986 an informal group of concerned businessmen in the community began lobbying and testifying against the prison at hearings in Sacramento. Working in conjunction with Assemblywoman Molina, they made many trips to Sacramento at their own expense. Residents who did not have the income to travel were unable to join them. Finally, Molina, commonly recognized as a forceful advocate for Latinas and the community, asked Frank Villalobos, an urban planner in the group, why there were no women coming up to speak in Sacramento against the prison. As he phrased it, "I was getting some heat from her because no women were going up there."

In response to this comment, Veronica Gutiérrez, a law student who lived in the community, agreed to accompany him on the next trip to Sacramento. He also mentioned the comment to Father John Moretta at Resurrection Catholic Parish. Meanwhile, representatives of the business sector of the community and of the 56th assembly district office were continuing to compile arguments and supportive data against the East Los Angeles prison site. Frank Villalobos stated one of the pressing problems:

> We felt that the Senators whom we prepared all this for didn't even acknowledge that we existed. They kept calling it the "downtown" site, and they argued that there was no opposition in the community. So, I told Father Moretta, what we have to do is demonstrate that there is a link (proximity) between the Boyle Heights community and the prison.

The next juncture illustrates how perceptions of gender-specific behavior set in motion a sequence of events that brought women into the political limelight. Father Moretta decided to ask all the women to meet after mass. He told them about the prison site and called for their support. When I asked him about his rationale for selecting the women, he replied:

> I felt so strongly about the issue, and I knew in my heart what a terrible offense this was to the people. So, I was afraid that once we got into a demonstration situation we had to be very careful. I thought the women would be cooler and calmer than the men. The bottom line is that the men came anyway. The first

times out the majority were women. Then they began to invite their husbands and their children, but originally it was just women.

Father Moretta also named the group. Quite moved by a film, *The Official Story*, about the courageous Argentine women who demonstrated for the return of their children who disappeared during a repressive right-wing military dictatorship, he transformed the name "Las Madres de la Plaza de Mayo" into "Mothers of East Los Angeles."

However, Aurora Castillo, one of the cofounders of the group, modified my emphasis on the predominance of women:

> Of course the fathers work. We also have many, many grandmothers. And all this IS with the support of the fathers. They make the placards and the posters; they do the security and carry the signs; and they come to the marches when they can.

Although women played a key role in the mobilization, they emphasized the group's broad base of active supporters as well as the other organizations in the "Coalition Against the Prison." Their intent was to counter any notion that MELA was composed exclusively of women or mothers and to stress the "inclusiveness" of the group. All the women who assumed lead roles in the group had long histories of volunteer work in the Boyle Heights community; but formation of the group brought them out of the "private" margins and into "public" light.

Third, the women in "Mothers of East L.A." have transformed the definition of "mother" to include militant political opposition to state-proposed projects they see as adverse to the quality of life in the community. Explaining how she discovered the issue, Aurora Castillo said,

> You know if one of your children's safety is jeopardized, the mother turns into a lioness. That's why Father John got the mothers. We have to have a well-organized, strong group of mothers to protect the community and oppose things that are detrimental to us. You know the governor is in the wrong and the mothers are in the right. After all, the mothers have to be right. Mothers are for the children's interest, not for self-interest; the governor is for his own political interest.

The women also have expanded the boundaries of "motherhood" to include social and political community activism and redefined the word to include women who are not biological "mothers." At one meeting a young Latina expressed her solidarity with the group and, almost apologetically, qualified herself as a "resident," not a "mother," of East Los Angeles. Erlinda Robles replied:

When you are fighting for a better life for children and "doing" for them, isn't that what mothers do? So we're all mothers. You don't have to have children to be a "mother."

\* \* \*

Fourth, the story of MELA also shows the transformation of class and ethnic identity. Aurora Castillo told of an incident that illustrated her growing knowledge of the relationship of East Los Angeles to other communities and the basis necessary for coalition building:

And do you know we have been approached by other groups? [She lowers her voice in emphasis.] You know that Pacific Palisades group asked for our backing. But what they did, they sent their powerful lobbyist that they pay thousands of dollars to get our support against the drilling in Pacific Palisades. So what we did was tell them to send their grassroots people, not their lobbyist. We're suspicious. We don't want to talk to a high-salaried lobbyist; we are humble people. We did our own lobbying. In one week we went to Sacramento twice.

The contrast between the often tedious and labor-intensive work of mobilizing people at the "grassroots" level and the paid work of a "high salaried lobbyist" represents a point of pride and integrity, not a deficiency or a source of shame. If the two groups were to construct a coalition, they must communicate on equal terms.

The women of MELA combine a willingness to assert opposition with a critical assessment of their own weaknesses. At one community meeting, for example, representatives of several oil companies attempted to gain support for placement of an oil pipeline through the center of East Los Angeles. The exchange between the women in the audience and the oil representative was heated, as women alternated asking questions about the chosen route for the pipeline:

"Is it going through Cielito Lindo [Reagan's ranch]?" The oil representative answered, "No." Another woman stood up and asked, "Why not place it along the coastline?" Without thinking of the implications, the representative responded, "Oh, no! If it burst, it would endanger the marine life." The woman retorted, "You value the marine life more than human beings?" His face reddened with anger and the hearing disintegrated into angry chanting.

The proposal was quickly defeated. But Aurora Castillo acknowledged that it was not solely their opposition that brought about the defeat:

We won because the westside was opposed to it, so we united with them. You know there are a lot of attorneys who live there and they also questioned the representative. Believe me, no way is justice blind. . . . We just don't want all this garbage thrown at us because we are low-income and Mexican American. We are lucky now that we have good representatives, which we didn't have before.

Throughout their life histories, the women refer to the disruptive effects of land use decisions made in the 1950s. As longtime residents, all but one share the experience of losing a home and relocating to make way for a freeway.

* * *

The freeways that cut through communities and disrupted neighborhoods are now a concrete reminder of shared injustice, of the vulnerability of the community in the 1950s. The community's social and political history thus informs perceptions of its current predicament; however, today's activists emphasize not the powerlessness of the community but the change in status and progression toward political empowerment.

Fifth, the core activists typically tell stories illustrating personal change and a new sense of entitlement to speak for the community. They have transformed the unspoken sentiments of individuals into a collective community voice. Lucy Ramos related her initial apprehensions:

> I was afraid to get involved. I didn't know what was going to come out of this and I hesitated at first. Right after we started, Father John came up to me and told me, "I want you to be a spokesperson." I said, "Oh no, I don't know what I am going to say." I was nervous. I am surprised I didn't have a nervous breakdown then. Every time we used to get in front of the TV cameras and even interviews like this, I used to sit there and I could feel myself shaking. But as time went on, I started getting used to it.
>
> And this is what I have noticed with a lot of them. They were afraid to speak up and say anything. Now, with this prison issue, a lot of them have come out and come forward and given their opinions. Everybody used to be real "quietlike."

She also related a situation that brought all her fears to a climax, which she confronted and resolved as follows:

> When I first started working with the coalition, Channel 13 called me up and said they wanted to interview me and I said OK. Then I started getting nervous. So I called Father John and told him, "You better get over here right away." He said, "Don't worry, don't worry, you can handle it by yourself." Then Channel 13 called me back and said they were going to interview another person, someone I had never heard of, and asked if it was OK if he came to my house. And I said OK again. Then I began thinking, what if this guy is for the prison? What am I going to do? And I was so nervous and I thought, I know what I am going to do!

Since the meeting was taking place in her home, she reasoned that she was entitled to order any troublemakers out of her domain:

> If this man tells me anything, I am just going to chase him out of my house. That is what I am going to do! All these thoughts were going through my head. Then Channel 13 walk into my house followed by six men I had never met. And I thought, Oh, my God, what did I get myself into? I kept saying to myself, if they get smart with me I am throwing them ALL out.

At this point her tone expressed a sense of resolve. In fact, the situation turned out to be neither confrontational nor threatening, as the "other men" were also members of the coalition. This woman confronted an anxiety-laden situation by relying on her sense of control within her home and family—a quite "traditional" source of authority for women—and transforming that control into the courage to express a political position before a potential audience all over one of the largest metropolitan areas in the nation.

People living in Third World countries as well as in minority communities in the United States face an increasingly degraded environment. Recognizing the threat to the well-being of their families, residents have mobilized at the neighborhood level to fight for "quality of life" issues. The common notion that environmental well-being is of concern solely to white middle-class and upper-class residents ignores the specific way working-class neighborhoods suffer from the fallout of the city "growth machine" geared for profit.

In Los Angeles, the culmination of postwar urban renewal policies, the growing Pacific Rim trade surplus and investment, and low-wage international labor migration from Third World countries are creating potentially volatile conditions. Literally palatial financial buildings swallow up the space previously occupied by modest, low-cost housing. Increasing density and development not matched by investment in social programs, services, and infrastructure erode the quality of life, beginning in the core of the city. Latinos, the majority of whom live close to the center of the city, must confront the distilled social consequences of development focused solely on profit. The Mexican American community in East Los Angeles, much like other minority working-class communities, has been a repository for prisons instead of new schools, hazardous industries instead of safe work sites, and one of the largest concentrations of freeway interchanges in the country, which transports much wealth past the community. And the concerns of residents in East Los Angeles may provide lessons for other minority as well as middle-class communities. Increasing environmental pollution resulting from inadequate waste disposal plans and an out-of-control "need" for penal institutions to contain the casualties created by the growing bipolar distribution of wages may not be limited to the Southwest. These conditions set the stage for new conflicts and new opportunities, to transform old relationships into coalitions that can challenge state agendas and create new community visions.

Mexican American women living east of downtown Los Angeles exemplify the tendency of women to enter into environmental struggles in defense of their community. Women have a rich historical legacy of community activism, partly reconstructed over the last two decades in social histories of women who contested other "quality of life issues," from the price of bread to "Demon Rum" (often representing domestic violence).

But something new is also happening. The issues "traditionally" addressed by women—health, housing, sanitation, and the urban environment—have moved to center stage as capitalist urbanization progresses. Environmental issues now fuel the fires of many political campaigns and drive citizens beyond the rather restricted, perfunctory political act of voting. Instances of political mobilization at the grassroots level, where women often play a central role, allow us to "see" abstract concepts like participatory democracy and social change as dynamic processes.

\* \* \*

The work "Mothers of East Los Angeles" do to mobilize the community demonstrates that people's political involvement cannot be predicted by their cultural characteristics. These women have defied stereotypes of apathy and used ethnic, gender, and class identity as an impetus, a strength, a vehicle for political activism. They have expanded their—and our—understanding of the complexities of a political system, and they have reaffirmed the possibility of "doing something."

They also generously share the lessons they have learned. One of the women in "Mothers of East Los Angeles" told me, as I hesitated to set up an interview with another woman I hadn't yet met in person,

> You know, nothing ventured nothing lost. You should have seen how timid we were the first time we went to a public hearing. Now, forget it, I walk right up and make myself heard and that's what you have to do.

# 48

## Occupy's Predicament: The Moment and the Prospects for the Movement

### TODO GITLIN

*For at least the last two decades, young people have been viewed by their elders as self-absorbed, distracted by technology, indecisive, and unwilling to commit. They have been unfavorably compared to (and often by) the baby boomers who protested and demonstrated for civil rights and women's and gay rights, in opposition to the Vietnam War, and to protect the environment. That view changed with the encampment of Zuccotti Park in 2011. The Occupy Movement sprang up in dozens of towns and cities. But was it a social movement? Its leaders' reluctance to organize in conventional fashion seemed to condemn it to a moment in time, while movements around the world continue to topple governments and forge paths for social change. Or maybe something else was going on.*

## THE INNER MOVEMENT AND ITS STRUCTURE OF FEELING

One Occupy organizer in New York, Shen Tong, began his political life in Beijing in 1989, as a leader of the students who occupied Tiananmen Square until they were dispersed by troops, tanks, rifles, and a bloodbath. He was one of the leaders able to flee to the USA, where he earned advanced degrees, and in the storybook way of immigrant successes started a software company with an office near Wall Street, where (in a departure from the storybook) he observed a new social fact right down the street and felt the stirrings of a new "structure of feeling" (as Raymond Williams would have put it) and proceeded to devote himself for the better part of a year to Occupy Wall Street. "There are two crises for a movement", he told me. "One is to be massacred. The other is to succeed." The "massacre" part is easy to understand. What did he mean by "succeed"? Why does it make sense to speak of the Occupy movement as a qualified success?

Last September, Occupy Wall Street was one of those upheavals that burst out of nowhere, like the volcano that famously erupted from a farmer's cornfield in Mexico in 1943 and suddenly transformed the landscape. Except that in this case, the volcano triggered hundreds more around the country. After it arrived, the eruption seemed inevitable, for the ground had been rumbling for weeks. There were, as some of us say, structural preconditions—those grand social features so conspicuous in retrospect, so indecipherable in prospect. (The molten undermass was there for years, but where was the eruption?) Before the ground trembled, no one—not the participants who camped out in Zuccotti Park, not the pundits or politicians or the rest of the political class—saw the eruption coming. When it arrived, a host of journalists and pundits, whether or not they approved of the politics of plutocracy, pronounced it peculiar, incomprehensible, dangerous, evanescent, and ineffectual, if not revolting.

What erupted in Zuccotti Park and spilled across the USA in 2011 was, in truth, a movement's beginning, or "the beginning of the beginning," as one placard put it, acknowledging, or wishing, that a campaign to reverse the accretion of plutocratic power in recent decades must endure a matter of years. It was spontaneous, but there were rumblings during the preceding months. It was organized, but not in any obvious way, and the organizers had tried to ignite previous incarnations, and failed.

Many if not most of the prime movers in Occupy—the inner movement— were anarchists and democratic radicals, desirous of reorganizing social decisions around directly democratic, "horizontal" assemblies. But the flame caught, and burned, not only because of the spunk and audacity of the young insurgents but because there was ample tinder: indignation over the consequential but obscured fact that America's leading institutions had, for more than three decades—since the end of cheap oil in the early 1970s, growing competition from abroad and the beginning of wholesale deregulation in the late 1970s— for more than three decades the concentrated energies of American capital had safeguarded themselves while heightening a "Great Divergence" of wealth and leaving the living conditions of the great majority of the population to stagnate or worse, thus breaking the implied contract that had been wrestled out of the convulsions and reforms of the previous four decades, namely, that a collective bargain among capital, labour, and the state would not only produce growth but keep inequality in check. (In fact, it was generally assumed that growth was tethered to incrementally growing equality.) It was easily established that the proverbial "99%," most of whom consider themselves "middle class," did not benefit from the economic growth of these decades.

The share of total wealth in the hands of the wealthiest 1 per cent grew to two-fifths. However famously optimistic they used to be, Americans were, in the main, persuaded that the world was not going their way, and some were ready to understand the situation as more than a regrettable economic condition but as a moral crisis.

A moral crisis with a conspicuous nemesis—a savage capitalism that brought the global economy to its knees by building castles in the air with counterfeit paper. This movement could not have erupted and grown were there not passionate indignation everywhere at the moral default of society's chief institutions. The inner and outer movement alike could agree that the political class was largely in hock to the wealthy (partly in the case of the Democrats, almost wholly in the case of the Republicans), with Robert Rubin and Alan Greenspan elevated into the power couple of bipartisan, deregulatory Washington.

(Culture did not lag behind, if you recall Reagan-era *Dallas* and *Dynasty*, and *Lifestyles of the Rich and Famous.*) As bankers lavished conspicuously inscribed gift buildings and sanctuaries upon the universities, hospitals, museums, and worshipful palaces of their choice, and were primped, flattered, solicited for benison and lionized, there was an ideological and moral vacuum to be filled. The universities and colleges held their palms up, contributing their own measure to the exaltation of wealth, for the main note struck in business schools and economics departments was that markets were self-regulating. * * * The churches were inert, speaking of Jesus but quietly; the line about the rich man and the eye of the needle was written in invisible ink. So there arrived an Occupy movement that in its soul wished to amount to a new Awakening to join the line of religious and moral Awakenings that have shaped American history since the seventeenth century.

* * *

The larger movement's hostility to electoral politics and big hierarchical organizations did not accord with the weakened unions' idea of how to invest their energies during a presidential campaign year. The inner core of the movement was phobic about the risk of being co-opted. It didn't want different policies; it wanted a different way of life; or better, it wanted to be, in its daily functioning, its direct democracy and provision of services, that way of life.

At the core of Occupy was an identity, however absurd it appeared to the outside. It prided itself on a famously horizontal style, a will toward a cooperative commonwealth, a repertory of rituals and repertories of playful, sometimes confrontational, action. What floated this style was that Occupy was, believe it or not, the first American social movement to begin with the benefit of majority support for its main thrust. The industrial union surge of the 1930s did not; neither did the civil rights movement—nor the movement against the Vietnam War, nor the women's nor gay movements. But recently, and consistently, American supermajorities consistently agree that the power of money in politics needs to be curbed, that taxes should be more progressive, that the too-big-to-fail banks were a pyramid of negligence and self-dealing if not criminality, acting irresponsibly and with impunity to plunge the world into financial crisis, and that the government has, by and large, been their handmaiden. The public did not like all Occupy's tactics or its ragamuffin image; and indeed, levels of support for the movement plunged after the fall of 2011, as they did earlier for the Tea Party. But the Occupy movement's terminology ("1%," "99%") entered into popular lore so readily because it summed up, albeit crudely, the sense that the wielders of power are at once arrogant, self-dealing, incompetent, and incapable of remedying the damage they have wrought; and that their dominance constitutes a moral crisis that can only be addressed by a moral awakening. As one Occupy slogan had it: *The system's not broken, it's fixed.*

Occupy Wall Street was jump-started by a radical core, roughly anarchist, veterans of left-wing campaigns running back to the anti-globalization movement of 1999, or even earlier, whose master stroke was to devise a form of action, occupation, that parlayed electronic networks into the forming of face-to-face community in public places, as (earlier in the year) in Cairo's Tahrir Square and Madrid's Puerta del Sol. The core created an inner movement which had a definable thrust—stop plutocracy—within an intense existential affirmation of its communal self; an insistence that what it "stood for" was the virtue of encampment itself, assembly as a way of life, a form of being. The political edge, while not articulated in the form of specific demands, was plain in slogans like "We are the 99%" and "Banks got bailed out, we got sold out." These resonated with a larger public that was severely disillusioned with political-economic establishments widely seen as having superintended the economic breakdown of 2008 and then having thrived with impunity. Restive young people rebelling against political stagnation had in fact made an appearance three years earlier in the Obama campaign of 2008, but with Obama in the White House, they had gone into early retirement, what with Obama's own lack of interest in sustaining it coupled with their general disinclination to remain publicly clamorous and engaged.

Now, with the country awash in debt and unemployment, Wall Street had become an enemy both symbolic and concrete—a system and a moral abomination. The emotional tenor of OWS, a structure of feeling with roots in the antiglobalization movement a decade earlier—combining hope, earnestness, spunk, and playful nonviolence—struck chords in a much larger public. Rapidly, and with the at least implicit support of institutions, including unions and elements of the Democratic Party, OWS and its spin-offs moved political culture at the popular level.

They did so by infusing eighteenth-century constitutional principles, enshrining the value of public assembly with twenty-first century methods (social media, text messages and the like) for summoning such assembly. Around kitchen tables and on late-night comedy shows, the Occupy movement gained currency. This was something apparently new under the sun. Whatever it was, it was a story, and it floated to the top of the detritus of newsworthy sensations borne along on the torrential gush of media. It outlasted the media's misrecognitions, the framing of its diffuseness and deviance front and center as a failed organization, a failed platform, or a poor excuse for a political party—anything but that unruly social fact, a social movement. It had to thank its own theatrical vigor along with no small assistance from brutal and clumsy police response straight out of Central Casting's villain rolls, playing Bull Connor to Martin Luther King, who knew exactly what he was doing when he chose the thuggish police chief of Birmingham, Alabama, as conspicuous antagonist. Some of Occupy's antagonists were cast in that role, like the police who arrested 700 protesters who were half-courting arrest on the Brooklyn Bridge on October 1, 2012. When the police went for overkill—pepper spray, mass arrests—pictures of official abuse flew around the world through the movement's own media and then via the mainstream. Support for the movement mushroomed.

So Occupy poured forth as a social amalgam, a sort of polyform, polychromatic organism that floated on a wave of public opinion, having captured—for the moment—that indispensable commodity of contemporary culture: attention. As a focus of the collective imagination it quickly caught up with the Tea Party, which had erupted in 2009, in local uprisings fueled by right-wing media and money and Washington-based organization, converging on the conviction that "the government" was the root of all evil. Occupy, on the contrary, defined the financial sector of plutocratic power, symbolized by Wall Street, as the adversary, with government as a too-willing accomplice. In its first two months, producing clever theatrical events, it garnered popular sympathy. Camping out cheek-by-jowl with Wall Street, using online networks to build up face-to-face communities—spaces to meet, argue, eat, take shelter, care for each other, argue some more, shout, rant, drum, sleep, read, consult, drift by, dig deeper, learn, refuse to learn—it won points by confronting corrupt adversaries in whimsical and inventive ways. It brought hardcore activists—anarchists, revolutionaries, drifters, homeless people, foreclosed and indebted people, desperate people, reformers of many stripes—together with myriad allies. These were people who wanted community, a new start, a society in secession or a society somehow of their own. Caught off-guard, city administrations dithered for a time, then responded with toleration, brutality, and eventually, dispersal.

\* \* \*

## THE OUTER MOVEMENT AND ITS STRUCTURE OF FEELING

The movement's activist core numbered—still numbers—a few tens of thousands of activists nationwide. By inspection, they are largely young and largely—by circumstance or choice—disconnected from social institutions. This number is very likely commensurate with the civil rights activist community that devoted itself to civil disobedience, mobilized larger networks and circles, and suffered murders and beatings during the peak civil rights years of 1955–65. After Occupy's sites were disbanded in November–December 2011, the core struggled with mixed results to contain their divergences. They quarreled, on the one hand, over whether to be more explicit than before about their non-violence or whether, on the other hand, to affirm that a "diversity of tactics" is legitimate. They fought over their majority whiteness, and over the place of women and transgendered people. Although all factions paid, and pay, lip service, at least, to the idea of "organizing in the community," there are not so many enduring networks of such organizers, and they are largely untrained— though the OWS core did perform yeoman relief work in flood-battered districts of New York after Hurricane Sandy. The activists know they need a wider base, but do not know how to find or activate one. In many working groups, entropy prevails. As some new recruits pile in, older ones burn out. The core movement devotes proportionately more energy tending to its own— bailing them out, defending them in court, sustaining their morale, feeding them. The care and feeding of infrastructure outweighs the building of exo- structure—a sustaining network of organizers.

The Occupy movement loomed much larger in numbers and influence because on special occasions it was able to gather hundreds of thousands of people, possibly low millions, nationally, in grand mobilizations. Another way of putting it, adopted by some activists, was that Occupy was the core of a larger (or perhaps a different) movement, a "99% movement" (an overstate- ment, of course, with symbolic pizzazz), whose political expectations were more concrete and more contained than revolution in behalf of an anarcho- syndicalist vision of a society governed by directly democratic assemblies.

The movement was famously unwilling to make specific demands, to agree on a simple charter, to speak of the British precedent of a previous century. But its thrust, if its whole amalgam of longings and fears could be translated— was overall clear. I mentioned "Banks got bailed out, we got sold out." The other main chant was, "We are the 99%." Beneath surface appearances, you didn't have to be a cryptographer to discern what the movement was "about." It wanted all sorts of things, but there was an intersection, a crosshatch area: a redress of the gross imbalance of wealth. As I said, to the movement, flagrant inequality—which might be characterized as the collapse of the middle class, and of upward mobility—expressed not just an economic fact and a cause of financial misery and inefficiency but a palpable indecency—a grotesque squan- dering of wealth and a warping of values.

The Occupy camps were also revolutionary—in an American sense. They restated primordial revolutionary impulses. When I say primordial I mean that they descended from the eighteenth-century Enlightenment impulse which ele- vated public assembly to a high place, which is why in the USA we have a First Amendment that doesn't just address freedom of religion, and speech, and the press, but explicitly specifies "the right of the people peaceably to assemble, to petition the government for redress of grievances." This is why an even more explicit terminology justifying assembly appears in so many state constitutions, beginning with Pennsylvania's from 1776, which will remind you of the third segment of the First Amendment:

Congress shall make no law respecting an establishment of religion, or prohib- iting the free exercise thereof; or abridging the freedom of speech, or of the press; or the right of the people peaceably to assemble, and to petition the government for a redress of grievances.

—First Amendment to the United States Constitution

which is the part commonly neglected both in jurisprudence and in scholarship. "Assembly," in the language of the time, conveyed something substantially more than a lot of speech. It spoke to a collective right, an affirmation of republication procedure. The same point is made in many state constitutions:

> The citizens have a right in a peaceable manner to assemble together for their common good, and to apply to those invested with the powers of government for redress of grievances or other proper purposes by petition, address or remonstrance.
>
> —Constitution of the Commonwealth of Pennsylvania (1776)

But in the minds of the political class that ordered the clearing of the Occupy camps, the idea of "consulting upon the common good," has become radical—as in a way, it is, going to the heart of the democratic idea that government of, by, and for the people requires that the people speak to each other—in their fashion, which might be utopian (indulging in fantasies of a moneyless society, for example), might be dithering, meandering, highly disruptive, and by an efficiency measure, grossly inefficient and off-putting, suitable strictly for the hard-core 24/7 activists.

As you will have noticed, not so many Americans are anarchists, radicals, professional drummers or street puppeteers. There are not so many here-and-now revolutionaries. Let me underscore that the much greater numbers of people who marched with Occupy on its days of maximum pageantry (up to 30,000 or more in New York City) were middle-class people, union members, progressives of various stripes—not so photogenic, not outré, though far more numerous.

It was the combination of the verve of the inner movement and the outer movement numbers showing up on special occasions that remade the political landscape—even as the core of the movement heatedly and anomalously objected to electoral politics during an election year. But most progressives turned, however grumpily, toward election campaign work.

As long as the encampments lasted and their epiphany moments could multiply, the outer movement was willing to live with the inner movement's participatory disorder and radicalism of style. It would turn out when invited and play its part. But when the central rallying places were dispersed, the respectable citizens peeled away from the Occupy core. Then centrifugal motion prevailed. All the fissures of politics and style deepened. Wounds festered. Some activists got into a go-for-broke mood, with no small assistance from intransigent authorities. It became routine for demonstrators to be penned up in remote "free speech areas" as the police became specialists in intimidation, deployed noxious chemicals and rolled out tanks. Such shows of force fueled disruptive tactics. Some riots started. In the popular mind, it didn't matter who threw the first stone or smashed the first window. Collisions tended to play as the fault of the protest. A police attack would be framed as "a violent demonstration." The encampments did not always demonstrate that (to use their slogan) "another world is possible," except a more unsettling world, a world less congenial and more dangerous.

The outer movement was repelled by the drugs, the boisterousness, the "black bloc" provocations, the unruly rejections of any authority, even the movement's own. After the American Autumn, there would be two more large mobilizations—on May 1 and the anniversary date of September 17. But in public estimate, the movement crashed.

\* \* \*

Beginnings, however joyous, don't sustain the momentum that movements need if they are to leave big imprints. In other words, OWS changed the political landscape, but it can't build a home there. Thus its predicament. What it built, in a burst of social entrepreneurship, was camps—useful for a time, inspired, inspiring, and self-limited. The camps animated just about all the anarchists and full-time radicals in America, and inserted the movement into the public topography. This was a substantial achievement, but not nearly enough to transform the country and address the moral crisis.

\* \* \*

The moral upheaval that Occupy invoked is still more notional than actual. It cannot be the exclusive property of a tiny movement—a subculture—that hungers for the politics of the streets. There are not enough saints. None of the great movements of the last half-century—not civil rights, not anti-Vietnam war, not feminist, not LGTB—were movements of saints alone. Once again, a sustained majority-backed movement is possible, one that feels, thinks, plans, judges, tries things, assesses results, sizes up who might join and what adversaries are up to—a community that in manifold ways "consults upon the common good" and "keeps its eyes on the prize," in the words of a civil rights anthem, but has the acumen, stamina, and luck not to fall on its face.

# 49

## The Cuba Diet

BILL McKIBBEN

*Invention born of necessity might explain what is happening throughout the United States. There is an emerging social movement around food: what is grown, how it is grown, and by whom it is grown, processed, transported, and marketed. Michael Pollan (reading 13) gives voice to this, as do many others who promote food co-ops, farmers markets, organic farms, and locally produced food. With the continuing U.S. embargo, coupled with the disappearance of support by the Soviet Union following its collapse, Cuba's people faced many crises, not the least of which was the provision of food. Their response, definitely born of necessity, looks very much like the social movement about food now growing in the United States.*

The pictures hanging in Havana's Museum of the Revolution document the rise (or, depending on your perspective, the fall) of Cuba in the years after Castro's revolt, in 1959. On my visit there last summer, I walked through gallery after gallery, gazing upon the stock images of socialist glory: "anti-imperialist volunteers" fighting in Angola, Cuban boxers winning Olympic medals, five patients at a time undergoing eye surgery using a "method created by Soviet academician Fyodorov." Mostly, though, I saw pictures of farm equipment. "Manual operation is replaced by mechanized processes," read the caption under a picture of some heavy Marxist metal cruising a vast field. Another caption boasted that by 1990, seven bulk sugar terminals had been built, each with a shipping capacity of 75,000 tons a day. In true Soviet style, the Cubans were demonstrating a deeply held (and to our eyes now almost kitschy) socialist belief that salvation lay in the size of harvests, in the number of tractors, and in the glorious heroic machinery that would straighten the tired backs of an oppressed peasantry—and so I learned that day that within thirty years of the people's uprising, the sugarcane industry alone employed 2,850 sugarcane lifting machines, 12,278 tractors, 29,857 carts, and 4,277 combines.

Such was communism. But then I turned a corner and the pictures changed. The sharply focused shots of combines and Olympians now were muddied, as if Cubans had forgotten how to print photos or, as was more likely the case, had run short of darkroom chemicals. I had reached the gallery of the "Special Period." That is to say, I had reached the point in Cuban history where everything came undone. With the sudden collapse of the Soviet Union, Cuba fell off a cliff of its own. All those carts and combines had been the products of an insane "economics" underwritten by the Eastern bloc for ideological purposes. Castro spent three decades growing sugar and shipping it to Russia and East Germany, both of which paid a price well above the world level, and both of which sent the ships back to Havana filled with wheat, rice, and more tractors. When all that disappeared, literally almost overnight, Cuba had nowhere to turn. The United States, Cuba's closest neighbor, enforced a strict trade embargo (which it strengthened in 1992, and again in 1996) and Cuba had next to no foreign exchange with anyone else—certainly the new Russia no longer wanted to pay a premium on Cuban sugar for the simple glory of supporting a tropical version of its Leninist past.

In other words, Cuba became an island. Not just a real island, surrounded by water, but something much rarer: an island outside the international economic system, a moon base whose supply ships had suddenly stopped coming. There were other deeply isolated places on the planet—North Korea, say, or Burma—but not many. And so most observers waited impatiently for the country to collapse. No island is an island, after all, not in a global world. The *New York Times* ran a story in its Sunday magazine titled "The Last Days of Castro's Cuba"; in its editorial column, the paper opined that "the Cuban dictator has painted himself into his own corner. Fidel Castro's reign deserves to end in homegrown failure." Without oil, even public transportation shut down—for many, going to work meant a two-hour bike trip. Television shut off early in the evening to save electricity; movie theaters went dark. People tried to improvise their ways around shortages. "For drinking glasses we'd get beer bottles and cut the necks off with wire," one professor told me. "We didn't have razor blades, till someone in the city came up with a way to resharpen old ones."

But it's hard to improvise food. So much of what Cubans had eaten had come straight from Eastern Europe, and most of the rest was grown industrial-style on big state farms. All those combines needed fuel and spare parts, and all those big rows of grain and vegetables needed pesticides and fertilizer—none of which were available. In 1989, according to the United Nations Food and Agriculture Organization, the average Cuban was eating 3,000 calories per day. Four years later that figure had fallen to 1,900. It was as if they suddenly had to skip one meal a day, every day, week after month after year. The host of one cooking show on the shortened TV schedule urged Cubans to fry up "steaks" made from grapefruit peels covered in bread crumbs. "I lost twenty pounds myself," said Fernando Funes, a government agronomist.

Now, just by looking across the table, I saw that Fernando Funes had since gained the twenty pounds back. In fact, he had a little paunch, as do many Cuban men of a certain age. What happened was simple, if unexpected. Cuba had learned to stop exporting sugar and instead started growing its own food again, growing it on small private farms and thousands of pocket-sized urban market gardens—and, lacking chemicals and fertilizers, much of that food became de facto organic. Somehow, the combination worked. Cubans have as much food as they did before the Soviet Union collapsed. They're still short of meat, and the milk supply remains a real problem, but their caloric intake has returned to normal—they've gotten that meal back.

In so doing they have created what may be the world's largest working model of a semi-sustainable agriculture, one that doesn't rely nearly as heavily as the rest of the world does on oil, on chemicals, on shipping vast quantities of food back and forth. They import some of their food from abroad—a certain amount of rice from Vietnam, even some apples and beef and such from the United States. But mostly they grow their own, and with less ecological disruption than in most places. In recent years organic farmers have visited the island in increasing numbers and celebrated its accomplishment. As early as 1999 the Swedish parliament awarded the Organic Farming Group its Right Livelihood Award, often styled the "alternative Nobel," and Peter Rosset, the former executive director of the American advocacy group Food First, heralded the "potentially enormous implications" of Cuba's new agricultural system.

The island's success may not carry any larger lesson. Cuban agriculture isn't economically competitive with the industrial farming exemplified by a massive food producer across the Caribbean, mostly because it is highly labor-intensive. Moreover, Cuba is a one-party police state filled with political prisons, which may have some slight effect on its ability to mobilize its people—in any case, hardly an "advantage" one would want to emulate elsewhere.

There's always at least the possibility, however, that larger sections of the world might be in for "Special Periods" of their own. Climate change, or the end of cheap oil, or the depletion, of irrigation water, or the chaos of really widespread terrorism, or some other malign force might begin to make us pay more attention to the absolute bottom-line question of how we get our dinner (a question that only a very few people, for a very short period of time, have ever been able to ignore). No one's predicting a collapse like the one Cuba endured—probably no modern economy has ever undergone such a shock. But if things got gradually harder? After all, our planet is an island, too. It's somehow useful to know that someone has already run the experiment.

Villa Alamar was a planned community built outside Havana at the height of the Soviet glory days; its crumbling, precast-concrete apartments would look at home (though less mildewed) in Ljubljana or Omsk. Even the names there speak of the past: a central square, for instance, is called Parque Hanoi. But right next to the Parque Hanoi is the Vivero Organopónico Alamar.

*Organopónico* is the Cuban term for any urban garden. (It seems that before the special period began, the country had a few demonstration hydroponic gardens, much bragged about in official propaganda and quickly abandoned when the crisis hit. The high-tech-sounding name stuck, however, recycled to reflect the new, humbler reality.) There are thousands of *organopónicos* in Cuba, more than 200 in the Havana area alone, but the Vivero Organopónico Alamar is especially beautiful: a few acres of vegetables attached to a shady yard packed with potted plants for sale, birds in wicker cages, a cafeteria, and a small market where a steady line of local people come to buy tomatoes, lettuce, oregano, potatoes—twenty-five crops were listed on the blackboard the day I visited—for their supper. Sixty-four people farm this tiny spread. Their chief is Miguel Salcines López, a tall, middle-aged, intense, and quite delightful man.

"This land was slated for a hospital and sports complex," he said, leading me quickly through his tiny empire. "But when the food crisis came, the government decided this was more important," and they let Salcines begin his cooperative. "I was an agronomic engineer before that," he said. "I was fat, a functionary. I was a bureaucrat." Now he is not. Most of his farm is what we would call organic—indeed, Salcines showed off a pyramidal mini-greenhouse in which he raises seedlings, in the belief that its shape "focuses energy." Magnets on his irrigation lines, he believes, help "reduce the surface tension" of the water—give him a ponytail and he'd fit right in at the Marin farmers' market. Taking a more "traditional" organic approach, Salcines has also planted basil and marigolds at the row ends to attract beneficial insects, and he rotates sweet potato through the rows every few plantings to cleanse the soil; he's even got neem trees to supply natural pesticides. But Salcines is not obsessive even about organicity. Like gardeners everywhere, he has trouble with potato bugs, and he doesn't hesitate to use man-made pesticide to fight them. He doesn't use artificial fertilizer, both because it is expensive and because he doesn't need it—indeed, the garden makes money selling its own compost, produced with the help of millions of worms ("California Reds") in a long series of shaded trenches.

While we ate rice and beans and salad and a little chicken, Salcines laid out the finances of his cooperative farm. For the last six months, he said, the government demanded that the *organopónico* produce 835,000 pesos' worth of food. They actually produced more than a million pesos' worth. Writing quickly on a piece of scrap paper, Salcines predicted that the profit for the whole year would be 393,000 pesos. Half of that he would reinvest in enlarging the farm; the rest would go into a profit-sharing plan. It's not an immense sum when divided among sixty-four workers—about $150—but for Cuban workers this is considered a good job indeed. A blackboard above the lunch line reminded employees what their monthly share of the profit would be: depending on how long they'd been at the farm, and how well they produced, they would get 291 pesos this month, almost doubling their base salary. The people worked hard, and if they didn't their colleagues didn't tolerate them.

What is happening at the Vivero Organopónico Alamar certainly isn't unfettered capitalism, but it's not exactly collective farming either. Mostly it's incredibly productive—sixty-four people earn a reasonable living on this small site, and the surrounding neighbors get an awful lot of their diet from its carefully tended rows. You see the same kind of production all over the city—every formerly vacant lot in Havana seems to be a small farm. The city grew 300,000 tons of food last year, nearly its entire vegetable supply and more than a token amount of its rice and meat, said Egidio Páez Medina, who oversees the *organopónicos* from a small office on a highway at the edge of town. "Tens of thousands of people are employed. And they get good money, as much as a thousand pesos a month. When I'm done with this job I'm going to start farming myself—my pay will double." On average, Páez said, each square meter of urban farm produces five kilograms of food a year. That's a lot. (And it's not just cabbage and spinach; each farm also seems to have at least one row of spearmint, an essential ingredient for the mojito.)

So Cuba—happy healthy miracle. Of course, Human Rights Watch, in its most recent report, notes that the government "restricts nearly all avenues of political dissent," "severely curtails basic rights to free expression," and that "the government's intolerance of dissenting voices intensified considerably in 2003." It's as if you went to Whole Foods and noticed a guy over by the soy-milk with a truncheon. Cuba is a weird political system all its own, one that's been headed by the same guy for forty-five years. And the nature of that system, and that guy, had something to do with the way the country responded to its crisis.

For one thing, Castro's Cuba was so rigidly (and unproductively) socialist that simply by slightly loosening the screws on free enterprise it was able to liberate all kinds of pent-up energy. Philip Peters, a Cuba analyst at the conservative Lexington Institute, has documented how the country redistributed as much as two thirds of state lands to cooperatives and individual farmers and, as with the *organopónico* in Alamar, let them sell their surplus above a certain quota. There's no obvious name for this system. It's a lot like share-cropping, and it shares certain key features with, say, serfdom, not to mention high feudalism. It is not free in any of the ways we use the word—who the hell wants to say thank you to the government for "allowing" you to sell your "surplus"? But it's also different from monolithic state communism.

In 1995, as the program geared up, the markets were selling 390 million pounds of produce; sales volume tripled in the next three years. Now the markets bustle, stacked deep with shiny heaps of bananas and dried beans, mangos and tomatoes. But the prices, though they've dropped over the years, are still beyond the reach of the poorest Cubans. And the government, which still sells every citizen a basic monthly food ration for just a few pesos, has also tried to reregulate some of the trade at the farmers' markets, fearing they were creating a two-tier system. "It's not reform like you've seen in China, where they're devolving a lot of economic decision making out to the private sector," Peters said. "They made a decision to graft some market mechanisms onto what remains a fairly statist model. It could work better. But it has worked."

Fidel Castro, as even his fiercest opponents would admit, has almost from the day he took power spent lavishly on the country's educational system.

Cuba's ratio of teachers to students is akin to Sweden's; people who want to go to college go to college. Which turns out to be important, because farming, especially organic farming, especially when you're not used to doing it, is no simple task. You don't just tear down the fence around the vacant lot and hand someone a hoe, quoting him some Maoist couplet about the inevitable victory of the worker. The soil's no good at first, the bugs can't wait to attack. You need information to make a go of it. To a very large extent, the rise of Cuba's semi-organic agriculture is almost as much an invention of science and technology as the high-input tractor farming it replaced, which is another thing that makes this story so odd.

\* \* \*

One afternoon, near an *organopónico* in central Havana, I knocked on the door of a small two-room office, the local Center for Reproduction of Entomophages and Entomopathogens. There are 280 such offices spread around the country, each manned by one or two agronomists. Here, Jorge Padrón, a heavyset and earnest fellow, was working with an ancient Soviet refrigerator and autoclave (the writing on the gauges was in Cyrillic) and perhaps three hundred glass beakers with cotton gauze stoppers. Farmers and backyard gardeners from around the district would bring him sick plants, and he'd look at them under the microscope and tell them what to do. Perhaps he'd hand them a test tube full of a *trichoderma* fungus, which he'd grown on a medium of residue from sugarcane processing, and tell them to germinate the seed in a dilute solution; maybe he'd pull a vial of some natural bacteria—*verticillium lecanii* or *beauveria bassiana*—from a rusty coffee can. "It is easier to use chemicals. You see some trouble in your tomatoes, and chemicals take care of it right away," he said. Over the long run, though, thinking about the whole system yields real benefits. "Our work is really about preparing the fields so plants will be stronger. But it works." It is the reverse, that is, of the Green Revolution that spread across the globe in the 1960s, an industrialization of the food system that relied on irrigation, oil (both for shipping and fertilization), and the massive application of chemicals to counter every problem.

The localized application of research practiced in Cuba has fallen by the wayside in countries where corporate agriculture holds sway. I remember visiting a man in New Hampshire who was raising organic apples for his cider mill. Apples are host to a wide variety of pests and blights, and if you want advice about what chemical to spray on them, the local agricultural extension agent has one pamphlet after another with the answers, at least in part, because pesticide companies like Monsanto fund huge amounts of the research that goes on at the land-grant universities. But no one could tell my poor orchardist anything about how to organically control the pests on his apples, even though there must have been a huge body of such knowledge once upon a time, and he ended up relying on a beautifully illustrated volume published in the 1890s. In Cuba, however, all the equivalents of Texas A&M or the University of Nebraska are filled with students looking at antagonist fungi, lion-ant production for sweet potato weevil control, how to intercrop tomatoes and sesame to control the tobacco whitefly, how much yield grows when you mix green beans and cassava in the same rows (60 percent), what happens to plantain production when you cut back on the fertilizer and substitute a natural bacterium called *A. chroococcum* (it stays the same), how much you can reduce fertilizer on potatoes if you grow a rotation of jack beans to fix nitrogen (75 percent), and on and on and on. "At first we had all kinds of problems," said a Japanese-Cuban organoponicist named Olga Oye Gómez, who grows two acres of specialty crops that Cubans are only now starting to eat: broccoli, cauliflower, and the like. "We lost lots of harvests. But the engineers came and showed us the right biopesticides. Every year we get a little better."

Not every problem requires a Ph.D. I visited Olga's farm in midsummer, when her rows were under siege from slugs, a problem for which the Cuban solution is the same as in my own New England tomato patch: a saucer full of beer. In fact, since the pressure is always on to reduce the use of expensive techniques, there's a premium on old-fashioned answers. Consider the question of how you plow a field when the tractor that you used to use requires oil you can't afford and spare parts you can't obtain. Cuba—which in the 1980s had more tractors per hectare than California, according to Nilda Pérez—suddenly found itself relying on the very oxen it once had scorned as emblems of its peasant past. There were perhaps 50,000 teams of the animals left in Cuba in 1990, and maybe that many farmers who still knew how to use them. "None of the large state farms or even the mechanized cooperatives had the necessary infrastructure to incorporate animal traction," wrote Arcadio Ríos, of the Agricultural Mechanization Research Institute, in a volume titled *Sustainable Agriculture and Resistance*. "Pasture and feed production did not exist on site; and at first there were problems of feed transportation." Veterinarians were not up on their oxen therapy.

But that changed. Rios's institute developed a new multi-plow for plowing, barrowing, riding, and tilling, specially designed not "to invert the top-soil layer" and decrease fertility. Harness shops were set up to start producing reins and yokes, and the number of blacksmith shops quintupled. The ministry of agriculture stopped slaughtering oxen for food, and "essentially all the bulls in good physical condition were selected and delivered to cooperative and state farms." Oxen demonstrations were held across the country. (The socialist love of exact statistics has not waned, so it can be said that in 1997 alone, 2,344 oxen events took place, drawing 64,279 participants.) By the millennium there were 400,000 oxen teams plying the country's fields. And one big result, according to a score of Ph.D. theses, is a dramatic reduction in soil compaction, as hooves replaced tires. "Across the country we see dry soils turning healthier, loamier," Professor Pérez said. Soon an ambitious young Cuban will be able to get a master's degree in oxen management.

One question is: How resilient is the new Cuban agriculture? Despite ever tougher restrictions on U.S. travel and remittances from relatives, the country has managed to patch together a pretty robust tourist industry in recent years: Havana's private restaurants fill nightly with Canadians and Germans. The government's investment in the pharmaceutical industry appears to be paying off, too, and now people who are fed by ox teams are producing genetically engineered medicines at some of the world's more advanced labs. Foreign exchange is beginning to flow once more; already many of the bicycles in the streets have been replaced by buses and motorbikes and Renaults. Cuba is still the most unconsumer place I've ever been—there's even less to buy than in the old Soviet Union—but sooner or later Castro will die. What then?

Most of the farmers and agronomists I interviewed professed conviction that the agricultural changes ran so deep they would never be eroded. Pérez, however, did allow that there were a lot of younger oxen drivers who yearned to return to the cockpits of big tractors, and according to news reports some of the country's genetic engineers are trying to clone White Udder herself from leftover tissue. If Cuba simply opens to the world economy—if Castro gets his professed wish and the U.S. embargo simply disappears, replaced by a free-trade regime—it's very hard to see how the sustainable farming would survive for long. We use pesticides and fertilizers because they make for incredibly cheap food. None of that dipping the seedling roots in some *bacillus* solution, or creeping along the tomato rows looking for aphids, or taking the oxen off to be shoed. Our industrial agriculture—at least as heavily subsidized by Washington as Cuba's farming once was subsidized by Moscow—simply overwhelms its neighbors.

\* \* \*

You can also ask the question in reverse, though: Does the Cuban experiment mean anything for the rest of the world? An agronomist would call the country's farming "low-input," the reverse of the Green Revolution model, with its reliance on irrigation, oil, and chemistry. If we're running out of water in lots of places (the water table beneath China and India's grain-growing plains is reportedly dropping by meters every year), and if the oil and natural gas used to make fertilizer and run our megafarms are changing the climate (or running out), and if the pesticides are poisoning farmers and killing other organisms, and if everything at the Stop & Shop has traveled across a continent to get there and tastes pretty much like crap, might there be some real future for low-input farming for the rest of us? Or are its yields simply too low? Would we all starve without the supermarket and the corporate farm?

\* \* \*

[S]trict organic agriculture isn't what the Cubans practice (remember those pesticides for the potato bugs). "If you're going to grow irrigated rice, you'll almost always need some fertilizer," said Jules Pretty, a professor at the University of Essex's Department of Biological Sciences, who has looked at sustainable agriculture in fields around the world. "The problem is being judicious and careful." It's very clear, he added, "that Cuba is not an anomaly. All around the world small-scale successes are being scaled up to regional level." Farmers in northeast Thailand, for instance, suffered when their rice markets disappeared in the Asian financial crisis of the late 1990s. "They'd borrowed money to invest in 'modern agriculture,' but they couldn't get the price they needed. A movement emerged, farmers saying, 'Maybe we should just concentrate on local markets, and not grow for Bangkok, not for other countries.' They've started using a wide range of sustainability approaches—polyculture, tree crops and agroforestry, fish ponds. One hundred and fifty thousand farmers have made the shift in the last three years."

Almost certainly, he said, such schemes are as productive as the monocultures they replaced. "Rice production goes down, but the production of all sorts of other things, like leafy vegetables, goes up." And simply cutting way down on the costs of pesticides turns many bankrupt peasants solvent. "The farmer field schools began in Indonesia, with rice growers showing one another how to manage their paddies to look after beneficial insects," just the kinds of predators the Cubans were growing in their low-tech labs. "There's been a huge decrease in costs and not much of a change in yields."

And what about the heartlands of industrial agriculture, the U.S. plains, for instance? "So much depends on how you measure efficiency," Pretty said. "You don't get something for nothing." Cheap fertilizer and pesticide displace more expensive labor and knowledge—that's why 219 American farms have gone under every day for the last fifty years and yet we're producing ever more grain and a loaf of bread might as well be free. On the other hand, there are those bereft Midwest counties. And the plumes of pesticide poison spreading through groundwater. And the dead zone in the Gulf of Mexico into which the tide of nitrogen washes each planting season. And the cloud of carbon dioxide that puffs out from the top of the fertilizer factories. If you took those things seriously, you might decide that having one percent of your population farming was not such a wondrous feat after all.

The American model of agriculture is pretty much what people mean when they talk about the Green Revolution: high-yielding crop varieties, planted in large monocultures, bathed in the nurturing flow of petrochemicals, often supported by government subsidy, designed to offer low-priced food in sufficient quantity to feed billions. Despite its friendly moniker, many environmentalists and development activists around the planet have grown to despair about everything the Green Revolution stands for. Like Pretty, they propose a lowercase greener counterrevolution: endlessly diverse, employing the insights of ecology instead of the brute force of chemistry, designed to feed people but also keep them on the land. And they have some allies even in the rich countries—that's who fills the stalls at the farmers' markets blooming across North America.

But those farmers' markets are still a minuscule leaf on the giant stalk of corporate agribusiness, and it's not clear that, for all the paeans to the savor of a local tomato, they'll ever amount to much more. Such efforts are easily co-opted—when organic produce started to take off, for instance, industrial growers soon took over much of the business, planting endless monoculture rows of organic lettuce that in every respect, save the lack of pesticides, mirrored all the flaws of conventional agriculture. (By some calculations, the average bite of organic food at your supermarket has traveled even farther than the 1,500-mile journey taken by the average bite of conventional produce.) That is to say, in a world where we're eager for the lowest possible price, it's extremely difficult to do anything unconventional on a scale large enough to matter.

And it might be just as hard in Cuba were Cuba free. I mean, would Salcines be able to pay sixty-four people to man his farm or would he have to replace most of them with chemicals? If he didn't, would his customers pay higher prices for his produce or would they prefer lower-cost lettuce arriving from California's Imperial Valley? Would he be able to hold on to his land or would there be some more profitable use for it? For that matter, would many people want to work on his farm if they had a real range of options? In a free political system, would the power of, say, pesticide suppliers endanger the government subsidy for producing predatory insects in local labs? Would Cuba not, in a matter of several growing seasons, look a lot like the rest of the world? Does an *organopónico* depend on a fixed ballot?

There's clearly something inherently destructive about an authoritarian society—it's soul-destroying, if nothing else. Although many of the Cubans I met were in some sense proud of having stood up to the Yanquis for four decades, Cuba was not an overwhelmingly happy place. Weary, I'd say. Waiting for a more normal place in the world. And poor, much too poor. Is it also possible, though, that there's something inherently destructive about a globalized free-market society—that the eternal race for efficiency, when raised to a planetary scale, damages the environment, and perhaps the community, and perhaps even the taste of a carrot? Is it possible that markets, at least for food, may work better when they're smaller and more isolated? The next few decades may be about answering that question. It's already been engaged in Europe, where people are really debating subsidies for small farmers, and whether or not they want the next, genetically modified, stage of the Green Revolution, and how much it's worth paying for Slow Food. It's been engaged in parts of the Third World, where in India peasants threw out the country's most aggressive free-marketeers in the last election, sensing that the shape of their lives was under assault. Not everyone is happy with the set of possibilities that the multinational corporate world provides. People are beginning to feel around for other choices. The world isn't going to look like Cuba—Cuba won't look like Cuba once Cubans have some say in the matter. But it may not necessarily look like Nebraska either.

\* \* \*

# 50

## The Arab Counterrevolution

### HUSSEIN AGHA and ROBERT MALLEY

*In the spring of 2011, massive street protests sparked political upheaval in the Arab world, bringing down dictatorships in Egypt, Yemen, Tunisia, and Libya. What began as a wave of democracy, however, has led to civil wars throughout the Middle East and renewed oppression in many countries. Things have not gone according to plan. As the authors of this prophetic essay, two veterans of the International Crisis Group, explain, "Revolutions devour their children." They explain why victory—here and throughout time—more often goes not to the youthful idealists but to those who understand power.*

> When the music's over, turn out the lights.
>
> —Jim Morrison

The Arab uprising that started in Tunisia and Egypt reached its climax on February 11, 2011, the day President Hosni Mubarak was forced to step down. It was peaceful, homegrown, spontaneous, and seemingly unified. Lenin's theory was turned on its head. The Russian leader postulated that a victorious revolution required a structured and disciplined political party, robust leadership, and a clear program. The Egyptian rebellion, like its Tunisian precursor and unlike the Iranian Revolution of 1979, possessed neither organization nor identifiable leaders nor an unambiguous agenda.

Since Mubarak's ouster, everything that has happened in the region has offered a striking contrast with what came before. Protests turned violent in Yemen, Bahrain, Libya, and Syria. Foreign nations got involved in each of these conflicts. Ethnic, tribal, and sectarian divisions have come to the fore. Old parties and organizations as well as political and economic elites contend for power, leaving many protesters with the feeling that the history they were making not long ago is now passing them by.

Amid rising insecurity and uncertainty there is fear and a sense of foreboding. In many places there are blood, threats, and doubts. People once thrilled by the potential benefits of change are dumbfounded by its actual and obvious costs. As anxiety about the future grows, earlier episodes cease to be viewed as pristine or untouchable. Accounts of the uprisings as transparent, innocent affairs are challenged. In Egypt and Tunisia, plots and conspiracies are imagined and invented; the military and other remnants of the old regime, which continue to hold much power, are suspected of having engineered preemptive coups. In Bahrain, protesters are accused of being Iranian agents; in Syria, they are portrayed as foreign-backed Islamist radicals. Little evidence is offered. It doesn't seem to matter.

February 11 was the culmination of the Arab revolution. On February 12, the counterrevolution began.

# 1

The Arab upheaval of 2011 is often heralded as an unparalleled occurrence in the region's history. Ghosts of the European revolutions of 1848 and the popular protests that brought down the Soviet bloc in 1989 are summoned. There is no need to look so far back or so far away. The current Arab awakening displays unique features, but in the feelings first unleashed and the political and emotional arc subsequently followed, it resembles events that swept the Arab world in the 1950s and 1960s.

In the days well before social media and 24/7 television, Gamal Abdel Nasser, a young Egyptian army officer, captivated the imagination of millions of Arabs, prompting displays of popular exhilaration that would withstand comparison with anything witnessed today. The Baath Party took power in Syria and Iraq, promising the restoration of dignity and championing freedom and modernity; a triumphant national liberation movement marched to victory in Algeria; a socialist republic was established in South Yemen; and the odd blend that was Muammar Qaddafi came to power in Libya.

At the time, many people were moved by the illegitimacy and inefficacy of state institutions; rampant corruption and inequitable distribution of wealth; the concentration of power in the hands of parasitic elites; revulsion with subservience to former and current colonial masters; and humiliation, epitomized above all by the Palestinian catastrophe and the inability to redress it. Slogans from that era celebrated independence, Arab unity, freedom, dignity, and socialism.

Although the military was the vanguard then, the rebellions of 2011 arose from similar emotions and were inspired by similar aspirations. The misfortunes of Arab unity have rendered the concept suspect. Socialism too has been tainted. But substitute local and domestic unity within each country (*Wihda Wataniyah*) for Pan-Arab unity (*Wihda Arabiyah*) and social justice, as well as attacks against crony capitalism for socialism, and it is hard not to hear clear echoes of the past in today's calls for change.

The fate of that earlier Arab rejuvenation offers a useful precedent but, more than that, a cautionary tale. Amid the turmoil and excitement, numerous political currents competed. Several espoused a blend of secular nationalism and pan-Arabism, others variants of Marxism, still others more Western-oriented liberalism. In the end, leftists and Communists were suppressed, most violently in Iraq and Sudan; elsewhere, they were co-opted or defeated. Liberal activists never established an authentic foothold; suspected of links to foreign powers, they were marginalized. After briefly flirting with Islamists, regimes quickly came to view them as a threat and, with varying degrees of bloodletting, drove them underground in Egypt, North Africa, and the Levant.

What emerged were ruling coalitions of the army and various secular nationalist movements. These yielded authoritarian, militaristic republics whose professed ideologies of modernism, pan-Arabism, and socialism were more make-believe than real. They exercised power through extensive internal security organizations—the much-dreaded *Mukhabarat*; the suppression of dissent; and enlistment of diverse social groups in support of the regime— merchants, peasants, industrialists, and state bureaucrats. Politics was the exclusive province of rulers. For others, it became a criminal activity.

The experiment ended in unmitigated failure. Wealth was concentrated in the hands of the few; corruption was endemic. Segments of society that had most enthusiastically greeted their new leaders, from the rural underclass to the urban declassed, were discarded or ignored. Where Arab regimes promised most they arguably accomplished least. They had vowed to reassert genuine national independence. Yet on the regional and international scenes the voice of the Arab world eventually went silent. On crucial issues such as the fate of Palestine, Iraq, and Sudan, regimes made noise of the most grandiloquent sort, but with no discernible impact. As the new millennium set in, even the clatter that by then had become a joke began to fade.

The legacy of this era goes further than material privation, or dysfunctional governance, or internal repression. Regimes born in the heyday of Nasser and Pan-Arabism lost the asset that would have allowed much to be forgiven and without which nothing else will suffice: a sense of authenticity and national dignity. Arab states were viewed as counterfeit. Citizens were put off by how their rulers took over public goods as private possessions and made national decisions under foreign influence. When that happens, the regimes' very existence— the merciless domination they impose on their people and the debasing subservience they concede to outsiders—becomes a constant, unbearable provocation.

## 2

The Arab uprising of 2011 was a popular rebuke to this waste. By pouring onto the streets, many thousands of people rejected what they perceived as alien and aggressive transplants. Although initial slogans alluded to reform, the actual agenda was regime change. In Tunisia and Egypt, they won round one in spectacular fashion. Elsewhere, things got messier, as regimes had time to adapt and shape their response. Violence spread, civil war threatened, foreign powers joined the melee, and centrifugal powers—sectarian, ethnic, tribal, or geographic—asserted themselves.

The Arab awakening is a tale of three battles rolled into one: people against regimes; people against people; and regimes against other regimes. The first involves the tug-of-war between regimes and spontaneous protesters. The demonstrators, most of them political only in the broadest sense of the term, are stirred by visceral, nebulous emotions—paramount among them the basic feeling of being fed up. Many don't know what they want or who they support but are confident of what they refuse—daily indignities, privations, and the stifling of basic freedoms—and who they reject, which makes them formidable adversaries. Neither of the instruments used by rulers to maintain control, repression and co-optation, can easily succeed: repression because it further solidifies the image of the state as hostile; co-optation because there are no clearly empowered leaders to win over and attempts to seduce convey a message of weakness, which further emboldens the demonstrators.

The second struggle involves a focused fight among more organized political groups. Some are associated with the old order; they include the military, social and economic elites, local chieftains, as well as a coterie of ersatz traditional parties. Others are the outlawed or semitolerated opposition, including exiled personalities, parties, and, most importantly, Islamists. In Libya and Syria, armed groups with various leanings and motivations have emerged. Little of the enthusiasm or innocence of the protest movements survives here; this is the province of unsentimental dealings and raw power politics.

Relations between young protesters and more traditional opposition parties can be tenuous and it is not always clear how representative either are. In Egypt, where the street battle against the regime was quickly won and Mubarak rapidly resigned, organized opposition groups—from the Muslim Brotherhood to long-established parties—subsequently stepped in and sought to muscle the disorganized protesters out. In Yemen, street demonstrators coexist uneasily with organized opposition parties and defectors from the regime. In Libya, rivalry among strands of the opposition has led to bloodshed and could portend a chaotic future. Some of the local popular committees that spontaneously emerged in Syria warily eye and distrust the exiled opposition.

The third struggle is a regional and international competition for influence. It has become an important part of the picture and assumes an increasingly prominent role. The region's strategic balance is at stake: whether Syria will remain in alliance with Iran; whether Bahrain will drift from Saudi Arabia's influence; whether Turkey will emerge bolstered or battered; whether stability in Iraq will suffer. One suspects more than faithfulness to reforms and infatuation with democratic principles when Saudi Arabia and Bahrain, which both ruthlessly suppress dissent at home, urge Syria to allow peaceful protesters; when Iran, which backs the regime in Damascus, castigates the oppression in Bahrain; and when Ankara hedges its bets between the Syrian regime and its foes.

\* \* \*

The U.S. has not been the last to get involved, but it has done so without a clear sense of purpose, wishing to side with the protesters but unsure it can live with the consequences. The least visible, curiously yet wisely, has been Israel. It knows how much its interests are in the balance but also how little it can do to protect them. Silence has been the more judicious choice.

# 3

Any number of outcomes could emerge from this complex brew. Regional equilibriums could be profoundly unsettled, with Iran losing its Syrian ally; the U.S. its Egyptian partner; Saudi Arabia, stability in the Gulf; Turkey, its newly acquired prestige; Iraq, its budding but fragile democracy. A wider Middle Eastern conflict could ensue. At the domestic level, some uprisings could result in a mere reshuffling of cards as new configurations of old elites keep control. There could be prolonged chaos, instability, and the targeting of minority groups.

The uprisings, partly motivated by economic hardship, ironically make those hardships still more severe. Where elections take place, they likely will prompt confusion, as groups with uncertain political experience compete. As with all upheavals, there will be a messy chapter before clarity sets in and the actual balance of power becomes evident. Increasing numbers could well question whether emerging regimes are improvements. Nostalgia for the past cannot lag far behind.

Some states might fragment because of ethnic, sectarian, or tribal divides. Civil war, a variant of which has broken out in Yemen and is deeply feared in Syria, may emerge.*

\* \* \*

For all this uncertainty, there seems little doubt—as protesters tire and as the general public tires of them—in what direction the balance will tilt. After the dictator falls, incessant political upheaval carries inordinate economic and security costs and most people long for order and safety. The young street demonstrators challenge the status quo, ignite a revolutionary spirit, and point the

---

*Written in 2011, this essay's prediction about civil war in Syria proved all too accurate. In more than three years of war at least 150,000 people have lost their lives and a third of the country's population is displaced, either within Syria or as international refugees. [*Editor's note*]

way for a redistribution of power. But what they possess in enthusiasm they lack in organization and political experience. What gives them strength during the uprising—their amorphous character and impulsiveness—leads to their subsequent undoing. Their domain is the more visible and publicized. The real action, much to their chagrin, takes place elsewhere.

The outcome of the Arab awakening will not be determined by those who launched it. The popular uprisings were broadly welcomed, but they do not neatly fit the social and political makeup of traditional communities often organized along tribal and kinship ties, where religion has a central part and foreign meddling is the norm. The result will be decided by other, more calculating and hard-nosed forces.

Nationalists and leftists will make a bid, but their reputation has been sullied for having stood for a promise already once betrayed. Liberal, secular parties carry scant potential; the appeal they enjoy in the West is inversely proportional to the support they possess at home. Fragments of the old regime retain significant assets: the experience of power; ties to the security services; economic leverage; and local networks of clients. They will be hard to dislodge, but much of the protesters' ire is directed at them and they form easy targets. They can survive and thrive, but will need new patrons and protectors.

That leaves two relatively untarnished and powerful forces. One is the military, whose positions, as much as anything, have molded the course of events. In Libya and Yemen, they split between regime and opposition supporters, which contributed to a stalemate of sorts. In Syria, they so far have sided with the regime; should that change, much will change with it. In Egypt, although closely identified with the former regime, they dissociated themselves in time, sided with the protesters, and emerged as central power brokers. They are in control, a position at once advantageous and uncomfortable. Their preference is to rule without the appearance of ruling, in order to maintain their privileges while avoiding the limelight and accountability. To that end, they have tried to reach understandings with various political groups. If they do not succeed, a de facto military takeover cannot be ruled out.†

\* \* \*

---

†Indeed, the military deposed Egypt's first freely elected president, Mohamed Morsi, arrested him and thousands of members of the Islamic Brotherhood, killed more than a thousand protesters in the weeks following the coup, and firmly established themselves and elites from the former authoritarian regime as the government. After exchanging his uniform for a suit, the general who led the coup, Abdel Fattah el-Sisi, was elected president in May 2014. [*Editor's note*]

# 4

Of all the features of the initial Arab uprisings, the more notable relate to what they were not. They were not spearheaded by the military, engineered from outside, backed by a powerful organization, or equipped with a clear vision and leadership. Nor, remarkably, were they violent. The excitement generated by these early revolutionary moments owed as much to what they lacked as to what they possessed. The absence of those attributes is what allowed so many, especially in the West, to believe that the spontaneous celebrations they were witnessing would translate into open, liberal, democratic societies.

Revolutions devour their children. The spoils go to the resolute, the patient, who know what they are pursuing and how to achieve it. Revolutions almost invariably are short-lived affairs, bursts of energy that destroy much on their pathway, including the people and ideas that inspired them. So it is with the Arab uprising. It will bring about radical changes. It will empower new forces and marginalize others. But the young activists who first rush onto the streets tend to lose out in the skirmishes that follow. Members of the general public might be grateful for what they have done. They often admire them and hold them in high esteem. But they do not feel they are part of them. The usual condition of a revolutionary is to be tossed aside.

The Arab world's immediate future will very likely unfold in a complex tussle between the army, remnants of old regimes, and the Islamists, all of them with roots, resources, as well as the ability and willpower to shape events. Regional parties will have influence and international powers will not refrain from involvement. There are many possible outcomes—from restoration of the old order to military takeover, from unruly fragmentation and civil war to creeping Islamization. But the result that many outsiders had hoped for—a victory by the original protesters—is almost certainly foreclosed.

# 51

## Change the World

### GEORGE PACKER

*Silicon Valley and the tech industry worldwide have brought forth the means to change the world, or at least how we communicate within the technological matrix of our work lives and leisure pursuits. To the millionaires and billionaires who have profited by our thirst for new information technologies, the way we now communicate and the social organizations that brought this about offer a model for solving many of today's social and economic problems. But can social change come, not—as Mao Zedong once thought, "from the barrel of a gun"—but from the wallets of the fabulously rich and innovative?*

In 1978, the year that I graduated from high school, in Palo Alto, the name Silicon Valley was not in use beyond a small group of tech *cognoscenti*. Apple Computer had incorporated the previous year, releasing the first popular personal computer, the Apple II. The major technology companies made electronics hardware, and on the way to school I rode my bike through the Stanford Industrial Park, past the offices of Hewlett-Packard, Varian, and Xerox PARC. The neighborhoods of the Santa Clara Valley were dotted with cheap, modern, one-story houses—called Eichlers, after the builder Joseph Eichler—with glass walls, open floor plans, and flat-roofed carports. (Steve Jobs grew up in an imitation Eichler, called a Likeler.) The average house in Palo Alto cost about a hundred and twenty-five thousand dollars. Along the main downtown street, University Avenue—the future address of PayPal, Facebook, and Google—were sports shops, discount variety stores, and several art-house cinemas, together with the shuttered, X-rated Paris Theatre. Across El Camino Real, the Stanford Shopping Center was anchored by Macy's and Woolworth's, with one boutique store—a Victoria's Secret had opened in 1977—and a parking lot full of Datsuns and Chevy Novas. High-end dining was virtually unknown in Palo Alto, as was the adjective "high-end." The public schools in the area were excellent and almost universally attended; the few kids I knew who went to private school had somehow messed up. The Valley was thoroughly middle class, egalitarian, pleasant, and a little boring.

Thirty-five years later, the average house in Palo Alto sells for more than two million dollars. The Stanford Shopping Center's parking lot is a sea of Lexuses and Audis, and their owners are shopping at Burberry and Louis Vuitton. There are fifty or so billionaires and tens of thousands of millionaires in

Silicon Valley; last year's Facebook public stock offering alone created half a dozen more of the former and more than a thousand of the latter. There are also record numbers of poor people, and the past two years have seen a twenty percent rise in homelessness, largely because of the soaring cost of housing. After decades in which the country has become less and less equal, Silicon Valley is one of the most unequal places in America.

Private-school attendance has surged, while public schools in poor communities—such as East Palo Alto, which is mostly cut off from the city by Highway 101—have fallen into disrepair and lack basic supplies. In wealthy districts, the public schools have essentially been privatized; they insulate themselves from shortfalls in state funding with money raised by foundations they have set up for themselves. In 1983, parents at Woodside Elementary School, which is surrounded by some of the Valley's wealthiest tech families, started a foundation in order to offset budget cuts resulting from the enactment of Proposition 13, in 1978, which drastically limited California property taxes. The Woodside School Foundation now brings in about two million dollars a year for a school with fewer than five hundred children, and every spring it hosts a gala with a live auction. I attended it two years ago, when the theme was Rock-Star, and one of Google's first employees sat at my table after performing in a pickup band called Parental Indiscretion. School benefactors, dressed up as Tina Turner or Jimmy Page, and consuming Jump'n Jack Flash hanger steaks, bid thirteen thousand dollars for Pimp My Hog! ("Ride through town in your very own customized 1996 Harley Davidson XLH1200C Sportster") and twenty thousand for a tour of the Japanese gardens on the estate of Larry Ellison, the founder of Oracle and the country's highest-paid chief executive. The climax arrived when a *Mad Men* Supper Club dinner for sixteen guests—which promised to transport couples back to a time when local residents lived in two-thousand-square-foot houses—sold for forty-three thousand dollars.

The technology industry's newest wealth is swallowing up the San Francisco Peninsula. If Silicon Valley remains the center of engineering breakthroughs, San Francisco has become a magnet for hundreds of software start-ups, many of them in the South of Market area, where Twitter has its headquarters. (Half the start-ups seem to have been founded by Facebook alumni.) A lot of younger employees of Silicon Valley companies live in the city and commute to work in white, Wi-Fi-equipped company buses, which collect passengers at fifteen or so stops around San Francisco. The buses—whose schedules are withheld from the public—have become a vivid emblem of the tech boom's stratifying effect in the Bay Area. Rebecca Solnit, who has lived in San Francisco for thirty years, recently wrote in *The London Review of Books*, "Sometimes the Google Bus just seems like one face of Janus-headed capitalism; it contains the people too valuable even to use public transport or drive themselves. Right by the Google bus stop on Cesar Chavez Street immigrant men from Latin America stand waiting for employers in the building trade to scoop them up, or to be arrested and deported by the government." Some of the city's hottest restaurants are popping up in the neighborhoods with shuttle stops. Rents there are rising even faster than elsewhere in San Francisco, and in some cases they have doubled in the past year.

The buses carry their wired cargo south to the "campuses" of Google, Facebook, Apple, and other companies, which are designed to be fully functioning communities, not just places for working. Google's grounds, in Mountain View—a working-class town when I was growing up—are modelled on the casual, Frisbee-throwing feel of Stanford University, the incubator of Silicon Valley, where the company's founders met, in grad school. A polychrome Google bike can be picked up anywhere on campus, and left anywhere, so that another employee can use it. Electric cars, kept at a charging station, allow employees to run errands. Facebook's buildings, in Menlo Park, between 101 and the salt marshes along the Bay, surround a simulated town square whose concrete surface is decorated with the word "HACK," in letters so large that they can be seen from the air.

At Facebook, employees can eat sushi or burritos, lift weights, get a haircut, have their clothes dry-cleaned, and see a dentist, all without leaving work. Apple, meanwhile, plans to spend nearly five billion dollars to build a giant, impenetrable ringed headquarters in the middle of a park that is technically part of Cupertino. These inward-looking places keep tech workers from having even accidental contact with the surrounding community. The design critic Alexandra Lange, in her recent e-book, *The Dot-Com City: Silicon Valley Urbanism*, writes, "The more Silicon Valley tech companies embrace an urban model, the harder it becomes for them to explain why they need to remain aloof. People who don't have badges aren't just a security risk."

The industry's splendid isolation inspires cognitive dissonance, for it's an article of faith in Silicon Valley that the technology industry represents something more utopian, and democratic, than mere special-interest groups. The information revolution (the phrase itself conveys a sense of business exceptionalism) emerged from the Bay Area counterculture of the sixties and seventies, influenced by the hobbyists who formed the Homebrew Computer Club and by idealistic engineers like Douglas Engelbart, who helped develop the concept of hypertext and argued that digital networks could boost our "collective I.Q." From the days of Apple's inception, the personal computer was seen as a tool for personal liberation; with the arrival of social media on the Internet, digital technology announced itself as a force for global betterment. The phrase "change the world" is tossed around Silicon Valley conversations and business plans as freely as talk of "early-stage investing" and "beta tests."

When financiers say that they're doing God's work by providing cheap credit, and oilmen claim to be patriots who are making the country energy-independent, no one takes them too seriously—it's a given that their motivation is profit. But when technology entrepreneurs describe their lofty goals there's no smirk or wink. "Many see their social responsibility fulfilled by their businesses, not by social or political action," one young entrepreneur said of his colleagues. "It's remarkably convenient that they can achieve all their goals just by doing their start-up." He added, "They actually think that Facebook is going to be the panacea for many of the world's problems. It isn't cynicism—it's arrogance and ignorance."

A few years ago, when Barack Obama visited one Silicon Valley campus, an employee of the company told a colleague that he wasn't going to take time from his work to go hear the President's remarks, explaining, "I'm making more of a difference than anybody in government could possibly make." In 2006, Google started its philanthropic arm, Google.org, but other tech giants did not follow its lead. At places like Facebook, it was felt that making the world a more open and connected place could do far more good than working on any charitable cause. Two of the key words in industry jargon are "impactful" and "scalable"—rapid growth and human progress are seen as virtually indistinguishable. One of the mottoes posted on the walls at Facebook is "Move fast and break things." Government is considered slow, staffed by mediocrities, ridden with obsolete rules and inefficiencies.

Reid Hoffman, the co-founder of the professional network LinkedIn and an investor in dozens of Silicon Valley firms, told me, "In investing, you want to have milestones that go between three and twelve months, to know you're making progress. The government *purchasing process* is a year plus!" Joshua Cohen, a Stanford political philosopher who also edits *Boston Review*, described a conversation he had with John Hennessy, the president of Stanford, who has extensive financial and professional ties to Silicon Valley. "He was talking about the incompetent people who are in government," Cohen recalled. "I said, 'If you think they're so incompetent, why don't you include in a speech you're making some urging of Stanford students to go into government?' He thought this was a ridiculous idea."

In a 2008 interview, Mark Zuckerberg recounted how young Lebanese Muslims who might have been tempted by extremism broadened their views after going on Facebook and friending people "who have gone to Europe." He suggested that the social network could help solve the problem of terrorism. "It's not out of a deep hatred of anyone," Zuckerberg offered. "It comes from a lack of connectedness, a lack of communication, a lack of empathy, and a lack of understanding." Successive U.S. Administrations had failed to resolve the Israeli-Palestinian conflict; perhaps the answer was to get as many people as possible on Facebook.

The conflicting pressures of Silicon Valley—its work ethic, status consciousness, idealism, and greed—were summed up in an ad for the University of San Francisco that I spotted on a public bus shelter south of Market Street: "Become wildly successful without becoming a jerk no one likes. Change the world from here."

The technology industry, by sequestering itself from the community it inhabits, has transformed the Bay Area without being changed by it—in a sense, without getting its hands dirty. Throughout most of Silicon Valley's history, its executives have displayed a libertarian instinct to stay as far from politics and government as possible. Reid Hoffman described the attitude this way: "Look what I can do as an individual myself—everyone else should be able to do that, too. I can make a multibillion-dollar company with a little bit of investment. Why can't the whole world do that?" But the imperative to change the world has recently led some Silicon Valley leaders to imagine that the values and concepts behind their success can be uploaded to the public sphere.

When Zuckerberg created Facebook, in 2004, he was a sophomore at Harvard. Most of his roommates joined the effort, but Joe Green did not. Zuckerberg and Green, who were members of Harvard's Jewish fraternity, had collaborated on Facemash, a site where Harvard students could rate the hotness of their classmates. This brought them both before the university's disciplinary board, and Green's father, a U.C.L.A. math professor, was not pleased. In any case, Green didn't really consider himself a tech persons—he was a political guy. At Santa Monica High School, he had won the student seat on the local school board and organized a living-wage campaign. At Harvard, he studied under Marshall Ganz, the theorist of community activism, and for his senior thesis he interviewed working-class men in Louisville about their ideas of economic opportunity and the American Dream. (In general, they believed that people were fundamentally equal and that income distribution should reflect that.) In the summer of 2003, between his sophomore and junior years, Green volunteered for John Kerry's Presidential campaign in New Hampshire, where he realized that the job of a political organizer would be much easier if everyone were on Friendster—an early, and doomed, social network that he had joined. He returned to Harvard, and urged Zuckerberg to use his programming talent to build a political social network. But Zuckerberg was more interested in starting a business. He had an idea for a college social network.

"No more Zuckerberg projects," Green's father warned him. And so Green chose not to drop out and move to Silicon Valley with Zuckerberg and the other roommates. That summer, while Facebook was being created, he went to work as a Kerry field organizer in Arizona and Nevada. For years afterward, Zuckerberg teased him: Instead of getting billions of dollars, he'd lost two states for Kerry.

In another era, Green might have gone on to an internship at *The Nation* or a job on Capitol Hill. Instead, he headed West after graduating and, with no programming skills, started two technology companies. In 2007, he and Sean Parker, the Silicon Valley entrepreneur, launched Causes, a Facebook application that helps grass-roots organizations and nonprofits raise money. * * * All the while, he continued to try to interest his ex-roommate in politics, but for a long time Zuckerberg was interested only in his own company.

"People in tech, when they talk about why they started their company, they tend to talk about changing the world," Green said. "I think it's actually genuine. On the other hand, people are just completely disconnected from politics. Partly because the operating principles of politics and the operating principles of tech are completely different." Whereas politics is transactional and opaque, based on hierarchies and handshakes, Green argued, technology is empirical and often transparent, driven by data.

In 2010, just ahead of the première of the film *The Social Network*, which portrayed the origins of Facebook in an unflattering light, Zuckerberg announced that he would pledge up to a hundred million dollars to the Newark public-school system—his first visible foray into philanthropy. The money was intended to encourage certain reforms in the education bureaucracy, including merit pay for teachers. Green pointed out that Zuckerberg was spending a lot of money just to change the rules in one mid-sized urban school district. He could spend that money in politics and potentially be more effective.

I recently met with Marc Andreessen, a general partner in one of Silicon Valley's most powerful venture-capital firms, Andreessen Horowitz. His office, in an idyllic ghetto of similar companies on Sand Hill Road, in Menlo Park, was clearly inspired by the décor of *Mad Men*: paintings by Robert Rauschenberg and other American artists of the sixties, a sideboard displaying bottles of expensive whiskey. On his desk sat the record player that adorned the office of Pete Campbell in the show's first three seasons. Andreessen is a big, bullet-headed man from Wisconsin, with a blunt, fast-talking manner. He supported Obama in 2008 but switched to Mitt Romney last year, because, he told me, Romney was a superb chief executive.

Andreessen described to me the stages of the industry's attitude toward political engagement. The first, prevailing in the seventies and eighties, was "Just leave us alone. Let us do our thing." T. J. Rodgers, the founder of Cypress Semiconductor, said that anyone who got involved in politics was making a big mistake, warning, "If you talk to these people, they'll just get in your ass." The Valley's libertarianism—which ignores the federal government's crucial role in providing research money—is less doctrinal than instinctive. Andreessen said, "It's very possible for somebody to show up here—a twenty-four-year-old engineer who's completely state of the art in building companies and products—and have had absolutely no exposure at all to politics, social issues, history. When the government shows up, it's bad news. They go, 'Oh, my God, government is evil, I didn't understand how bad it was. We must fight it.'"

Andreessen himself once fit this type. In 1993, when he was just twenty-one, he helped develop Mosaic, the first popular Web browser. After the company he co-founded, Netscape, launched its Navigator browser, the government insisted that its encryption—which was so strong that U.S. intelligence couldn't break it—be weakened for foreign sales, so that terrorists and other criminals couldn't use Netscape's cryptography. This demand required the company to create a different product for export. Ben Horowitz, Andreessen's partner, who ran Netscape's product division, said, "It's hard to describe what a royal pain in the ass this was. We were totally flabbergasted." Later, after other technology leaders were given classified briefings on how terrorists operated, he and Andreessen realized that the Feds had a point. "Maybe they didn't totally understand all the implications of everything," Horowitz said. "But we didn't understand their job, either." Eventually, industry arguments prevailed and the government, which didn't want foreign competitors to gain an advantage over U.S. businesses, withdrew its request.

Horowitz—who is the son of David Horowitz, the radical-turned-conservative polemicist—attributed Silicon Valley's strain of libertarianism to the mentality of engineers. "Libertarianism is, theoretically, a relatively elegant solution," he said. "People here have a great affinity for that kind of thing—they want elegance. Most people here are relatively apolitical and not that knowledgeable about how these large complicated systems of societies work. Libertarianism has got a lot of the false positives that Communism had, in that it's a very simple solution that solves everything." The intellectual model is not the dour Ayn Rand but Bay Area philosophers and gurus who imagine that limitless progress can be achieved through technology. Stewart Brand, now seventy-four, popularized the term "personal computer" and made "hacker" the tech equivalent of freedom fighter. His *Whole Earth Catalog*—a compendium of hippie products, generated by users, that is now considered an analog precursor of the Web—can still be found on desks at Facebook.

In the past fifteen years or so, Andreessen explained, Silicon Valley's hands-off attitude has changed, as the industry has grown larger and its activities keep colliding with regulations. Technology leaders began to realize that Washington could sometimes be useful to them. "A small number of very high-end Valley people have got involved in politics, but in a way that a lot of us think is relentlessly self-interested," Andreessen said. The issues that first animated these technology executives were stock options, subsidies, and tax breaks. "They started giving the Valley a bad name in Washington—that the Valley was just another special-interest group."

In early 2011, Zuckerberg, Steve Jobs, and other Silicon Valley moguls attended a dinner with President Obama in Woodside, at the home of John Doerr, a venture capitalist with ties to the Democratic Party. Instead of having a wide-ranging discussion, the tech leaders focussed narrowly on pet issues. John Chambers, of Cisco, kept pushing for a tax holiday on overseas profits that are reinvested in the United States. According to Walter Isaacson's biography of Jobs, while Chambers was lobbying Obama, over cod and lentil salad, Zuckerberg turned to Valerie Jarrett, the President's adviser, and whispered, "We should be talking about what's important to the country. Why is he just talking about what's good for him?" When it was Jobs's turn, he asked for more H-1B visas for foreign students who earn engineering degrees in the U.S.—a longtime Silicon Valley desire. Obama told him that the issue could be addressed only in the context of broader immigration reforms, such as allowing children who had arrived here illegally with their parents to gain legal status.

Zuckerberg came away from the gathering impressed with Obama but sorely disappointed in his own industry. The most dynamic sector of the American economy had no larger agenda.

Zuckerberg spoke about his concerns with Green, who said that the country's biggest challenge was to equip more Americans to benefit from the Information Age. With so many jobs lost to automation, and more wealth concentrated in fewer hands, that prospect was slipping farther away. Silicon Valley was racing into the future, but the kinds of people Green had interviewed in Louisville were becoming increasingly marginal. Fixing this dynamic would require the expertise, the time, and the money of technology leaders. "How do we move America into the knowledge economy?" Green asked me. "And how do we create a voice for the knowledge community that is about the future and not selfish? If we organize this community, it could be one of the most powerful voices in politics." He dropped the idea of selflessness. "I think our selfish interest actually aligns with the broader interest of creating jobs and growing the economy."*

Earlier this year, Zuckerberg began teaching a class on entrepreneurship, one afternoon a week, to middle-school students in a poor community near Facebook's headquarters. He decided to ask his students about their college plans. One young man said that he might not be able to attend college, because he and his parents had illegally entered the country, from Mexico, when he was a baby. The story stuck with Zuckerberg. After the Republican losses in the 2012 elections, comprehensive immigration reform—including more H-1B visas—suddenly seemed possible in Washington. It also looked like the most promising issue for technology leaders to organize around—a case of self-interest aligning with the broader interest.

Zuckerberg and Green began talking to Silicon Valley leaders about starting a political-advocacy group: Andreessen; Horowitz; Reid Hoffman; Marissa Mayer, of Yahoo; Eric Schmidt, of Google; and at least three dozen others. The interest was strong, as if they had all been waiting for something like this. Though Andreessen and Horowitz didn't join the project, Andreessen thought it represented "the maturation of the industry" and a greater level of engagement in politics—"deeper, longer-term, with, frankly, more money."

Hoffman, who believes that immigration reform would right a wrong and also create new jobs at every level, from software engineers to dry cleaners, told Zuckerberg, "The normal Silicon Valley thing is to focus on high-end visas and say, 'The rest of it's not my problem.'"

"Yes," Zuckerberg said. "But there's this huge moral component. We might as well go after all of it."

"O.K., good," Hoffman said. "I'm in."

Earlier this year, Green wrote up a fifteen-page plan—subsequently leaked to Politico—which had more to do with tapping Silicon Valley's potential as a political force than with the issue of immigration. One section of the text listed several reasons that "people in tech" could be organized into "one of the most

---

*What would Garrett Harden, author of "The Tragedy of the Commons" (reading 3), say about this? [*Editor's note*]

powerful political forces," including, "Our voice carries a lot of weight because we are broadly popular with Americans." This spring, the founders held a dinner, and pledged money from their personal fortunes; reportedly, the collective goal was fifty million dollars. A staff was hired in San Francisco, and political consultants from both parties were engaged in Washington. One afternoon last month, Green sat on the sunny rooftop terrace of a friend's town house in Pacific Heights, just south of the Presidio, with views of the Golden Gate Bridge and the Marin hills. He was barefoot, in jeans and a red T-shirt, with his left leg propped on a decorative rock bowl and immobilized in a brace. (He had broken it skiing.) A young assistant named Manny brought water and walnuts. Green's frizzy hair fluttered in the wind blowing off the ocean as he worked his phone and his MacBook Air, which was decorated with a sticker that said, "The Dream Is Now." An op-ed by Zuckerberg was going to run in the *Washington Post* the next morning, announcing the formation of a new group in Silicon Valley, called FWD. us. "I'm the president of the organization," Green said. "There will be an actual office." He was returning to his first passion, political organizing. His wide, stubbly face broke into a smile: he had spent ten years trying to convince Zuckerberg that politics matters, and he had finally done it.

\* \* \*

Technology can be an answer to incompetence and inefficiency. But it has little to say about larger issues of justice and fairness, unless you think that political problems are bugs that can be fixed by engineering rather than fundamental conflicts of interest and value. Evgeny Morozov, in his new book *To Save Everything, Click Here*, calls this belief "solutionism." Morozov, who is twenty-nine and grew up in a mining town in Belarus, is the fiercest critic of technological optimism in America, tirelessly dismantling the language of its followers. "They want to be 'open,' they want to be 'disruptive,' they want to 'innovate,'" Morozov told me. "The open agenda is, in many ways, the opposite of equality and justice. They think anything that helps you to bypass institutions is, by default, empowering or liberating. You might not be able to pay for health care or your insurance, but if you have an app on your phone that alerts you to the fact that you need to exercise more, or you aren't eating healthily enough, they think they are solving the problem."

\* \* \*

A favorite word in tech circles is "frictionless." It captures the pleasures of an app so beautifully designed that using it is intuitive, and it evokes a fantasy in which all inefficiencies, annoyances, and grievances have been smoothed out of existence—that is, an apolitical world. Dave Morin, who worked at Apple and Facebook, is the founder of a company called Path—a social network limited to one's fifty closest friends. In his office, which has a panoramic view of south San Francisco, he said that one of his company's goals is to make technology increasingly seamless with real life. He described San Francisco as a place where people already live in the future. They can hang out with their friends even when they're alone. They inhabit a "sharing economy": they can book a weeklong stay in a cool apartment through Airbnb, which has disrupted the hotel industry, or hire a luxury car anywhere in the city through the mobile app Uber, which has disrupted the taxi industry. "San Francisco is a place where we can go downstairs and get in an Uber and go to dinner at a place that I got a restaurant reservation for halfway there," Morin said. "And, if not, we could go to my place, and on the way there I could order takeout food from my favorite restaurant on Postmates, and a bike messenger will go and pick it up for me. We'll watch it happen on the phone. These things are crazy ideas."

It suddenly occurred to me that the hottest tech start-ups are solving all the problems of being twenty years old, with cash on hand, because that's who thinks them up.

In the real San Francisco, as elsewhere, Morin added, things don't always work very well: "There are all kinds of infrastructure problems that are, like, really, guys? This is San Francisco. The fact that some of the buses still run on diesel is crazy, or that the bus stop doesn't talk to your iPhone." [Former mayor of San Francisco Gavin] Newsom, in his book, describes an innovation in which hackers created an iPad app that allowed municipal transport workers to keep track of the status of trains and buses without standing on the street with clipboards and watching them go by. "What I'd like to see is 'Hackers 10,000, City 0,'" Newsom writes. "This is the perfect example of how the government can do best by simply getting out of the way." (Unfortunately, as Newsom notes, San Francisco's "budget crunch means the city hasn't yet bought the iPads needed to fully implement the app.") If innovation put the public-transportation system in San Francisco out of business, Newsom said, "I'm not inherently offended by that notion." Page and Brin, of Google, have led him to think that the company's emerging fleet of driverless cars might make long-term spending on high-speed rail in California irrelevant.

Near the Caltrain station south of Market Street, a twenty-nine-year-old entrepreneur named Logan Green is trying to realize something like this vision. Green grew up in Southern California and attended the University of California at Santa Barbara, where he decided to get by without a car, so that the inconvenience would force him to find creative solutions to transit and environmental problems. He joined the county transportation board, and found that the bus routes made no sense but couldn't be fixed, because of budget shortfalls and pressure from constituents.

"I learned that it's an incredibly broken and unscalable system," Green said. "I came out thinking, God, government's really not the right place to experiment with anything new. Government's really not the right place to look to solve these problems and to create innovative solutions and scalable solutions in transportation. This really belongs more in the private sector, where you're not burdened with all these impossible restrictions."

Last year, Green co-founded Lyft, a "rideshare" company with services in San Francisco and other cities. Its motto is "Your friend with a car." Through a mobile app, customers can call a car driven by an ordinary citizen who has been approved by Lyft, and who is available to give rides while going about his regular business. The cars have a telltale fuzzy pink mustache fastened to the front grille. "You get in the front seat, and the driver gives you a fist bump," Green explained. "It's a peer-to-peer relationship, not a service relationship." The customer pays a suggested donation, twenty per cent of which goes to Green's company. So far, Lyft has registered several hundred drivers, and Green hopes that a crowdsourced transportation system like Lyft will ultimately replace the existing public one, perhaps with a fleet of Google's driverless cars. That, however, would mean no fist bump.

San Francisco is becoming a city without a middle class. Pockets of intense poverty, in districts like the Fillmore and the Tenderloin, are increasingly isolated within the general rise of exorbitantly priced housing. The black population has dwindled from more than ten per cent of the electorate, in 1970, to less than four per cent today—that's not enough people to fill the forty thousand seats at A.T.&T. Park, where the Giants play. The number of Latinos is increasing much more slowly than elsewhere in California. Rent control and other features of the city's traditional liberalism still hold in check a mass exodus of all San Franciscans who don't work in tech, but it's common to hear stories of working families pushed south, into Bayview or Daly City, or across the bridge, into the East Bay.

Christina Olague, a former member of the city's Board of Supervisors, took me on a tour of several blocks in the Mission District, where she works at a nonprofit that prepares low-income people for whatever jobs might be available. The Mission, once a Latino neighborhood, has become extremely popular with technology workers. We met at a café on Valencia Street, called Four Barrel Coffee, which offers single-origin, hand-roasted craft coffee. Olague, who is in her fifties, is the daughter of Mexican farmworkers, and was once active in a local group called the Mission Anti-Displacement Coalition. "This is the kind of place I used to protest," she told me, looking around at the young Apple users. "And now here I am, hanging out, waiting for half an hour to get a cup of coffee." She was having trouble connecting with the newcomers. "People seem more self-absorbed, maybe more individualistic in a way, less empathetic," she went on. "They're really addicted to their iPads or phones. They communicate more, but there's less communication with the people they're actually around." Her larger complaint, though, was about the techies' indifference to the pain that their industry's triumph is inflicting on many people who have been a part of the fabric of San Francisco for decades. "Everyone's kind of wary, I think. A lot of people in the tech industry, sadly, feel judged—because they are."

Out on Valencia Street, Olague took me past an eyeglass boutique that had replaced a bookstore and, in the twin bays of a vanished auto-body shop, two artisanal establishments: one made pastries, the other chocolate. On the wall of the pastry shop, there were quotes that appealed to the customers' idea of their jobs as inspirational callings, including one from Saint-Exupéry: "If you want to build a ship don't gather people together to collect wood and don't assign them tasks and work but rather teach them to long for the endless immensity of the sea." In all the new restaurants, the menus highlighted locally sourced food. "But where are the local people?" Olague said. A few unmarked doors led up to S.R.O. hotels, protected by the city's affordable-housing ordinances, where immigrant families squeezed into one room. But no one on the sidewalk was speaking Spanish.

In the past few years, San Francisco's political leaders have grown close to the technology companies. Corey Cook, a political scientist at the University of San Francisco, who focuses on local politics, said, "The dominant narrative of the city is 'What's good for the tech industry is good for San Francisco.'" Historically, he said, what was good for General Motors wasn't always good for the country: there was conflict between business and labor, which was resolved by insuring that factories offered middle-class jobs. He added, "Now there's no conflict, but there are no middle-class jobs."

In 2011, Twitter, whose San Francisco headquarters employs a thousand people but draws tourists from around the world—the company turns them away—threatened to move out of the city. Liberal candidates in the mayoral election lined up to offer the company tax breaks, and called existing taxes "job killers." Cook said, sardonically, "It's Twitter! Twitter *has* to be in San Francisco." There was far less concern at City Hall when, in 2006, the 49ers announced their intention to move to Santa Clara.

\* \* \*

Cook predicted that if, with the tech industry's money and competence, schools improved and buses ran on time then San Franciscans would put up with the soaring cost of living. He added, "But if that doesn't happen, and it's just seen as an agglomeration of wealth, then it won't be win-win-win, and there could be a backlash."

One question for technology boosters—maybe the crucial one—is why, during the decades of the personal computer and the Internet, the American economy has grown so slowly, average wages have stagnated, the middle class has been hollowed out, and inequality has surged. Why has a revolution that is supposed to be as historically important as the industrial revolution coincided with a period of broader economic decline? I posed the question in one form or another to everyone I talked to in the Bay Area. The answers became a measure of how people in the technology industry think about the world beyond it.

Few of them had given the topic much consideration. One young techie wondered if it was really true; another said that the problem was a shortage of trained software engineers; a third noted that the focus of the tech industry was shifting from engineering to design, and suggested that this would open up new job opportunities. Sam Lessin, who leads Facebook's "identity product group," which is in charge of the social network's Timeline feature, posited that traditional measures of wealth might not be applicable in the era of social media. He said, "I think as communication technology gets less expensive, and people can entertain each other and interact with each other and do things for each other much more efficiently, what's actually going to happen is that the percentage of the economy that's in cash is going to decline. Some people will choose to build social capital rather than financial capital. Given the opportunity to spend an extra hour or an extra dollar, they will choose to spend time with friends. It might be that the GDP, in the broader sense, is actually growing quite quickly—it's just that we're not measuring it properly."

We were talking in a Facebook conference room. Posters on nearby walls bore the messages "Keep Shipping" and "What Would You Do If You Weren't Afraid?" Lessin, wearing a green T-shirt and jeans, with a baseball cap that had "/lessin" on the front, spoke very quickly while drawing a graph—first on a napkin, then on a whiteboard—that plotted the vectors of technology, social capital, and cash, with tech rising fastest, social not far behind, and cash starting to lag. Lessin was a classmate of Zuckerberg's at Harvard. His late father was a prominent investment banker, and Lessin grew up in a New Jersey suburb where he understood the adult world through the filter of *Seinfeld*. This led him to formulate the Kramer Principle: nearly all the annoyances that gave the show its jokes—the time wasted trying to track down a friend, the inefficiencies that lead to ridiculous misunderstandings—had been "kind of erased." He said, "Most of those problems are now gone because of smartphones, GPS, traffic maps, texting, messaging. That's a huge deal. That's moving the ball forward—making people more efficient with their time and able to effectively live longer lives therefore, you know, and making them happier." Lessin found it impossible to believe that people's lives had not improved since the days of *Seinfeld*, because of technology.

Not everyone in Silicon Valley is so sanguine. Joshua Cohen, the Stanford political philosopher, founded Stanford's Program on Global Justice, where he has done research on how the supply chains of corporate products can be improved in the areas of fair compensation, working conditions, and the right of workers to organize. Since 2011, Cohen has also been a half-time professor at Apple University, down the street from Apple's headquarters, which offers courses to its executives on company culture and related topics. According to *Inside Apple*, by Adam Lashinsky, one course focused on "the fallen grocery store chain A&P as an example of what happened to a company that once dominated its field." The classrooms—sleek and white, like the company's devices, with huge black screens at the front—bear names that span the social sciences and the literature of hipness: "Margaret Mead," "Tocqueville," "Kerouac," "Pirsig."

In his office, Cohen freely criticized the tech industry for its casual optimism in assuming that its products can change the world. He said, "There is this complete horseshit attitude, this ridiculous attitude out here, that if it's new and different it must be really good, and there must be some new way of solving problems that avoids the old limitations, the roadblocks. And with a soupçon of 'We're smarter than everybody else.' It's total nonsense."

But, when it came to Apple, he insisted that anything he said about the company had to be off the record, including the titles and the content of the courses he teaches. When I asked how he viewed the relation between the information revolution and inequality, he hesitated. He started to answer, then hesitated again: "Um. I don't have any deep thoughts about it. I wish I did." This seemed surprising, since Cohen, an expert on democracy and justice, co-edited a book called *The New Inequality*, in the late nineties, before it was a hot topic, and has devoted many pages of *Boston Review* to the subject. I had imagined that his perch at Apple University would give him the perfect vantage point to think about just this problem. Later, I wondered if the question had put Cohen on the defensive. It was Steve Jobs, after all, who told President Obama that Apple's manufacturing jobs would not be coming back from China. Apple's position on issues like inequality was expressed last year by an executive who said, "We don't have an obligation to solve America's problems. Our only obligation is making the best product possible."

One obstacle in Silicon Valley to thinking about conditions in the rest of the country is the tech world's belief in itself as a meritocracy. "Not an aspirational meritocracy but an actual one," Mitch Kapor, who founded the software company Lotus, in the early eighties, told me. In this view, he explained, "it's the best and the brightest who have succeeded here." Kapor and his wife, Freada, now run a foundation, in Oakland, that seeks to make the benefits of technology more equally available. Kapor said that asking questions about the lack of racial and gender diversity in tech companies leaves people in Silicon Valley intensely uncomfortable. For example, only eight per cent of venture-backed tech start-ups are owned by women, and, in a region where Hispanics make up nearly a quarter of the working-age population, they constitute less than five per cent of employees in large tech companies; the representation of both Hispanics and blacks is actually declining. People in Silicon Valley may be the only Americans who don't like to advertise the fact if they come from humble backgrounds. According to Kapor, they would then have to admit that someone helped them along the way, which goes against the Valley's self-image.

The young start-up entrepreneur insisted that a person's race, gender, or class "just doesn't matter here. It's not a positive or a negative. What's cool here is having a lot of money—everybody knows you have a lot of money, but you don't show it off. Money is the metric by which people view and judge success, but, unlike in Hollywood or New York, you have to be very careful about how you spend that money." The way to convey status in Silicon Valley is by wearing jeans, driving a Tesla, and casually mentioning that you were hired at Facebook in 2005 and invested in Twitter in 2008. But, as the wealth reaches spectacular levels, these self-conscious restraints are breaking down amid displays of hedge fund–level decadence. Last June, David Sacks, a former PayPal executive who founded Yammer, a social network for businesses, threw himself a fortieth birthday party, in a Los Angeles château, that was rumored to have cost $1.4 million; the theme was "Let Him Eat Cake," with attendees dressed in Louis XVI costumes, and entertainment by Snoop Dogg. (Sacks, forgetting what kind of world he and his friends have created, ordered his several hundred guests not to share any of this on social media. The first picture from the party was tweeted by Snoop.) Soon after his birthday bash, Sacks sold Yammer to Microsoft, then bought a twenty-million-dollar fixer-upper in Pacific Heights. When I interviewed him, two years ago, Sacks said, "Part of believing in capitalism is you don't have to feel guilty about wanting to make money."

The ideal of a frictionless world, in which technology is a force for progress as well as a source of wealth, leaves out the fact that politics inevitably means clashing interests, with winners and losers. Silicon Valley tends to ignore even its own version of conflict: beneath its much popularized stories of aspiration and success is a netherworld of ruthless struggle that punishes more people than it rewards. "This is one of the things nobody talks about in the Valley," Andreessen told me. Trying to get a start-up off the ground is "absolutely terrifying. Everything is against you." Many young people wilt under the pressure. As a venture capitalist, he hears pitches from three thousand people a year and funds just twenty of them. "Our day job is saying no to entrepreneurs and crushing their dreams," he said. Meanwhile, "every entrepreneur has to pretend in every interaction that everything is going great. Every party you go to, every recruiter, every press interview—'Oh, everything's fantastic!'— and, inside, your soul is just being chewed apart, right? It's sort of like everybody's fake happy all the time."

One day, I dropped by the offices of a start-up company called Delphi, just down the road from Google, in Mountain View. Delphi makes software that allows cities to put large amounts of financial data online for public use. Two of its founders are Nate Levine, who is twenty-two, and Zac Bookman, who is thirty-three. They had just ordered pizza for lunch, and they seemed to be all but sleeping at the company. In a spare room, there was an austere metal bunk bed.

\* \* \*

Young people drawn to Silicon Valley can be more insular than those in other industries—they tend to come from educated families and top universities, and achieve success at a very early age. "They're ignorant, because many of them don't feel the need to educate themselves outside their little world, and they're not rewarded for doing so," the young start-up entrepreneur said. "If you're an engineer in Silicon Valley, you have no incentive to read *The Economist*. It's not brought up at parties, your friends aren't going to talk about it, your employers don't care." He found that college friends who came out to the Valley to seek their fortune subsequently lost interest in the wider world. "People with whom I used to talk about politics or policy or the arts, they're just not as into it anymore. They don't read the *Wall Street Journal* or the *New York Times*. They read *TechCrunch* and *VentureBeat*, and maybe they happen to see something from the *Times* on somebody's Facebook news feed." He went on, "The divide among people in my generation is not as much between traditional liberals and libertarians. It's a divide between people who are inward-facing and outward-facing."

The more successful and wealthy entrepreneurs become, the more they can afford to face outward. Reid Hoffman, of LinkedIn, who published a book last year called *The Start-Up of You*, is regarded as one of the Valley's leading public voices, although, until recently, his political engagement had been limited to campaign contributions. Hoffman described Silicon Valley's intellectual culture as underdeveloped. Part of the problem, he said, is the competitiveness, which requires an unyielding focus on one's company, and "part of it is because of that libertarian strain—we're just all out building stuff, and everything else is kind of extraneous." Hoffman says that when he was a Stanford undergraduate, in the late eighties, his only concern was "how do I strengthen public intellectual culture in the U.S.: who are we as individuals and a society, and who should we be?" But he decided that the academic life would have too small a platform, and he became an Internet billionaire instead. When LinkedIn was in its early stages, a decade ago, Hoffman went a few years without reading a single book. Now in his mid-forties, he wants to make Silicon Valley a more reflective place, and increase its influence around the country and the world. He has started a monthly salon, flying in authors of new books on public affairs to talk with small groups of tech people, over dinner at a top-rated French restaurant in Palo Alto.

\* \* \*

Mark Zuckerberg, in his op-ed announcing FWD.us, wrote, "In a knowledge economy, the most important resources are the talented people we educate and attract to our country. A knowledge economy can scale further, create better jobs, and provide a higher quality of living for everyone in our nation." Zuckerberg described himself as the great-grandson of immigrants, and the beneficiary of national policies that have created equal opportunity and upward mobility across generations.

"Everyone in FWD.us hopes it will go beyond immigration, over time," Reid Hoffman said. Other possible issues include education reform and spending on scientific research. "But, as with an entrepreneurial start-up, if we can't demonstrate that we can do something good about this problem, then what use are we to the other ones?"

Like industries that preceded it, Silicon Valley is not a philosophy, a revolution, or a cause. It's a group of powerful corporations and wealthy individuals with their own well-guarded interests. Sometimes those interests can be aligned with the public's, sometimes not. Though tech companies promote an open and connected world, they are extremely secretive, preventing outsiders from learning the most basic facts about their internal workings. Marc Andreessen predicted that conflicts over issues like privacy, intellectual property, and monopolies will bring a period of increased tension between the Valley and other sectors of society, along with new government intervention. Brian Goldsmith, who has known Green since college, and who now runs an online investment start-up called PubVest, said, "If this new generation of smart, wealthy, successful tech leaders want to make a difference in terms of policy, it's the right idea to leave their cool headquarters and gorgeous campuses and actually engage. They have a lot to bring to the table, and they may also learn the limits of their power and influence. I think it's healthy that they've decided to branch out and actually get involved in the political process the way that other industries and corporations do."

FWD.us has got off to a rough start—rougher than Facebook did. Rather than bringing fresh ideas to the project of organizing Americans and their elected leaders behind immigration reform, the group has hired veteran Washington operatives from both parties, who, following their standard practice, are spending Silicon Valley money on harsh and cynical political ads. The campaign attempts to bolster politicians who support immigration reform even though they represent states where the idea is unpopular. One ad, intended to cover Senator Lindsey Graham's right flank, in South Carolina, attacks Obama's health-care law; another, on behalf of Mark Begich, the Alaska senator, endorses oil drilling and a natural-gas pipeline there.

\* \* \*

The South Carolina ad began airing in late April. It was made by a FWD.us shell organization called Americans for a Conservative Direction. Crude graphics are combined with footage of Graham attacking Obama. "'Change you can believe in,' after this health-care-bill debacle, has now become an empty slogan," he says. "And it's really been replaced by seedy Chicago politics, when you think about it." The ad doesn't embody the spirit of "innovation" or of "disruption." But if Silicon Valley's idea of itself as a force for irresistible progress is running up against the unlovely reality of current American politics, that isn't necessarily a bad thing. It might mean that the industry is growing up.

# CREDITS

**William M. Adler:** "Job on the Line" from *Mother Jones*, March/April 2000, pp. 41–47, 86–87. Copyright © 2000, Foundation for National Progress. Reprinted by permission.

**Hussein Agha and Robert Malley:** "The Arab Counterrevolution" from *The New York Review of Books*, September 29, 2011. Copyright © 2011 by Hussein Agha and Robert Malley. Reprinted by permission of The New York Review of Books.

**Elijah Anderson:** "The Code of the Streets" by Elijah Anderson. From *The Atlantic Monthly*, May 1994, pp. 81–94. Reprinted by permission of the author.

**Peter L. Berger:** Excerpt(s) from *Invitation to Sociology: A Humanistic Perspective* by Peter L. Berger, copyright © 1963 by Peter L. Berger. Copyright © renewed 1991 by Peter L. Berger. Used by permission of Doubleday, an imprint of the Knopf Doubleday Publishing Group, a division of Random House LLC. All rights reserved.

**Joel Best:** Excerpts from *Damned Lies and Statistics: Untangling Numbers from the Media, Politicians, and Activists* by Joel Best. Copyright © 2001 by the Regents of the University of California. Reprinted by permission of the University of California Press.

**Julie Bettie:** From "Women without Class: Chicas, Cholas, Trash, and the Presence/Absence of Class Identity" by Julie Bettie from *Signs*, Vol. 26, No. 1. Copyright © 2000 by the University of Chicago Press. Reprinted by permission.

**Allan M. Brandt:** "Racism and Research: The Case of the Tuskegee Syphilis Study" from *The Hastings Center Report*, December 1978, pp. 21–29. Reprinted by permission of the publisher.

**Michael Burawoy:** "Public Sociologies: Contradiction, Dilemmas and Possibilities" by Michael Burawoy. From *Social Forces*, Vol. 82, No. 4, pp. 1603–1618. Copyright © 2004 by the University of North Carolina Press. Used by permission of Oxford University Press.

**William J. Chambliss:** "The Saints and the Roughnecks" by William J. Chambliss. *Society*, Vol. 11, No. 1 (1973), pp. 24–31. Copyright © 1973 by Springer. Reprinted with kind permission from Springer Science and Business Media.